ENVIRONMENTAL LOSS AND DAMAGE IN A COMPARATIVE LAW PERSPECTIVE

Edited by
Barbara Pozzo
Valentina Jacometti

INTERSENTIA

Cambridge – Antwerp – Chicago

Intersentia Ltd
8 Wellington Mews
Wellington Street | Cambridge
CB1 1HW | United Kingdom
Tel: +44 1223 736 170
Email: mail@intersentia.co.uk
www.intersentia.com | www.intersentia.co.uk

Distribution for the UK and
Rest of the World (incl. Eastern Europe)
NBN International
1 Deltic Avenue, Rooksley
Milton Keynes MK13 8LD
United Kingdom
Tel: +44 1752 202 301 | Fax: +44 1752 202 331
Email: orders@nbninternational.com

Distribution for Europe
Lefebvre Sarrut Belgium NV
Hoogstraat 139/6
1000 Brussels
Belgium
Tel: +32 (0)800 39 067
Email: mail@intersentia.be

Distribution for the USA and Canada
Independent Publishers Group
Order Department
814 North Franklin Street
Chicago, IL 60610
USA
Tel: +1 800 888 4741 (toll free) | Fax: +1 312 337 5985
Email: orders@ipgbook.com

Environmental Loss and Damage in a Comparative Law Perspective
© The editors and contributors severally 2021

Image on cover: Jenny Bailey / Alamy Stock Photo

ISBN 978-1-83970-026-2
D/2021/7849/25
NUR 823

British Library Cataloguing in Publication Data. A catalogue record for this book is available from the British Library.

ENVIRONMENTAL LOSS AND DAMAGE IN
A COMPARATIVE LAW PERSPECTIVE

PREFACE

1. THE CONFERENCE IN COMO

The sixth EELF Annual Conference was held at the University of Insubria in Como in September 2018. Attendance at the conference was high, as there were more the 140 participants and around 90 speakers and chairpersons.

The conference took a slightly different pattern from the previous European Environmental Law Forum conferences, which were devoted to more general topics, focusing on a more specific but at the same time crosscutting issue: environmental loss and damage.

As announced in the original call for papers, the book that we present here is a collection of peer-reviewed contributions of the speakers at the conference. The book reflects the structure of the conference and has the aim of analysing and comparing the regulation of environmental loss and damage in a comparative, interdisciplinary and both public- and private-law perspective. It delves into conceptual and specific legal issues related to liability, compensation and restoration of damage in different sectors and jurisdictions, also taking into account the contributions of economic analysis in this field of regulation. Specific attention has been devoted to the role that liability and insurance may play in terms of mitigation and adaptation to climate change, as well as the prevention of damage from natural hazards. The scope of analysis encompasses national as well as supranational and international regimes, also in view of possible legal transplants and "cross-fertilisation".[1] The book includes 30 contributions that are subdivided into eight parts: (i) liability for environmental harm in the EU; (ii) private and corporate environmental liability; (iii) the role of criminal liability; (iv) legal transplants in the environmental field: the case of environmental liability; (v) state and international environmental liability; (vi) climate change liability; (vii) liability, climate change and natural hazards: the role of insurance; and (viii) real compensation and offset regimes: the strategy of "no net loss".

---

[1] On this point, the bibliography is now boundless. To underline the relevance of the theme, the International Academy of Comparative Law dedicated a whole session to the theme of "Legal Cultures and Legal Transplants", published in the Isaidat Law Review (2011) Volume 1 – Special Issue 1.

2. THE DIALECTIC BETWEEN GLOBAL LAW AND LOCAL LAW

One of the aspects that the conference aimed at underlining was the different keys to understanding the current dialectic between global and local law in the environmental field.

In recent decades, in fact, we have been witnessing the development of a body of rules that tends towards a progressive approach to the development of common operational choices in addressing environmental problems. This global environmental law has emerged because of several factors. First, the environmental problem, in addition to having affected all legal systems in an almost contemporary way, is suitable to involve by its very nature multiple countries at the same time.[2] Secondly, legal problems in the environmental field are closely intertwined with aspects of the natural sciences, which present themselves as universal, and with economic problems that appear to be common in the globalised world,[3] whereas the link to a particular cultural, social or legal background seems to fade away.

As a consequence, in the field of environmental law, the fact that the problems to be addressed are – in more than one respect – intimately linked to scientific knowledge and cover, for this reason, a certain degree of technicality will lead, in a greater number of cases, to new phenomena of legal transplants. On the other hand, legal transplants of environmental protection models have been strongly characterised and – consequently – influenced by the globalised perception of the environmental phenomenon, and by that of its protection.[4] In particular, with the Rio Conference of 1992,[5] a new era of international environmental law began:[6] international cooperation no longer refers only to the prevention of

---

[2]   *P.H. Sand*, The evolution of international environmental law, in D. Bodansky, J. Brunnée & E. Hey (eds.), The Oxford Handbook of International Environmental Law, Oxford University Press, 2007; *B. Pozzo*, Tutela dell'ambiente (diritto internazionale), Enciclopedia del Diritto, Annali, III, p. 1156, 1161 et seq.

[3]   *J.B. Wiener*, Something Borrowed for Something Blue: Legal Transplants and the Evolution of Global Environmental Law, Ecology L.Q. 2001 (27), pp. 1295 et seq.

[4]   *T. Yang & R.V. Percival*, The Emergence of Global Environmental Law, Ecology L.Q. 2009 (36), pp. 615 et seq.; *R.V. Percival*, Fifteenth Annual: Lloyd K. Garrison Lectures on Environmental Law: The Globalization of Environmental Law, Pace Envtl. L. Rev. 2009 (26), pp. 451 et seq.; *R.V. Percival*, Environmental Law in the Twenty-First Century, Va. Envtl. L.J. 2007 (25), pp. 1 et seq.; *R.V. Percival*, Global Law and the Environment, Wash. L. Rev. 2011 (86), pp. 579 et seq.; *Wiener, supra*, note 3.

[5]   *M. Pallemaerts*, International environmental law from Stockholm to Rio: back to the future?, Review of European Community & International Environmental Law 1992 (1), pp. 254–266, *E. Brown Weiss*, International Environmental Law: Contemporary Issues and the Emergence of a New World Order, Geo. L.J. 1992 (81), pp. 675 et seq.

[6]   *P. Birnie*, The Development of International Environmental Law, British Journal of International Studies 1977 (3), pp. 169–190.

transboundary pollution issues, but concerns global issues that can jeopardise natural balances essential for the maintenance of the conditions of life on earth.[7]

3. LEGAL TRANSPLANTS IN THE ENVIRONMENTAL FIELD AND THE NEED FOR A COMPARATIVE LAW APPROACH

A special session of the conference was devoted to legal transplants, taking advantage of the various and different backgrounds and origins of the participants and the speakers. The study of this phenomenon seems in fact very promising for all those scholars who are interested in the dynamic of environmental law evolution.

Today the reasons that drive the circulation of models can be very heterogeneous, traditional concepts of "prestige" and "imposition" as drivers of legal transplants need to be re-interpreted in the light of current circumstances, and new methods of analysing the phenomenon have been suggested.[8]

With the drafting of large international conventions, homogeneous rules and standards are developed. It is not therefore difficult to find a rule formulated in a similar way in the European Union, the United States, Russia or China. This cannot come as a surprise: to similar and common problems, not included in the casts of the different legal traditions, the different legal systems have developed similar answers.

In addition, an important role is played today by international cooperation, which in recent decades has affected many aspects of the legislation of emerging economies.[9] As the European experience can teach us, environmental cooperation has become one of the leading instruments in inducing legal transplants, as "environmental integration clauses are included in most EU agreement of a general nature".[10] A vast literature points out how Europe has become in this sector a *normative power*, able to impose its own perspective and regulation on

---

[7]   G. *Palmer*, New ways to make international environmental law, American Journal of International Law 1992, pp. 259–283.

[8]   M. *Graziadei*, Comparative Law as the Study of Transplants and Receptions, in M. Reimann & R. Zimmermann (eds.), The Oxford Handbook of Comparative Law, Oxford University Press, 2007, pp. 441–475.

[9]   J. *Delisle*, Lex Americana? United States Legal Assistance, American Legal Models and Legal Change in Post-Communist World and Beyond, U. Pa. J. Int'l Econ. L. 1999 (20), pp. 179 et seq.; N. *Wheeler*, The role of American NGOs in China's modernization, invited influence, Routledge, 2013.

[10]   G. *Marín Durán & E. Morgera*, Environmental Integration in the EU's External Relations, Beyond Multilateral Dimensions, Hart Publishing, 2012, p. 57.

how environmental protection should be taken into consideration,[11] becoming a global producer of norms in this as in other important fields.[12] On the other hand, we can also observe the willingness, by countries that have undergone a rapid process of democratisation, to refer to authoritative models, mostly arising from Western or international models, in the field of the protection of human rights and of the environment. In addition, even the practices of large multinational companies can have an impact on facilitating the circulation of Western models in emerging economies by private contracting.[13]

With regard to the EU, other factors that might drive legal transplants in the environmental field can also be linked to the formation of regulations at the regional supranational level. In this case, legal transplants might be induced by the imposition of harmonised supranational legislation, which finds its roots in one or more advanced legal systems and aims at creating common conditions in all Member States.[14]

Given the complexity of the questions at stake, however, even if today environmental law can be considered at least partially a global law where it is possible to identify common trends, one should not overlook the fact that environmental law has uneven application around the world, partly because environmental law is quite new and growing rapidly and partly because its application is *local* and depends on the differentiated conditions of each legal system.

In fact, the globalisation process that we are witnessing should not lead us into the temptation to believe that global environmental rules will lead everywhere to the same results. Indeed, rules and institutions borrowed in the environmental field will also have to deal with the particular *legal process* of the target system and with a particular *path dependence* that will vary from context to context, as well as with factors that will surely affect the efficacy of

---

[11] I. *Manners*, Normative power Europe: a contradiction in terms?, JCMS: Journal of Common Market Studies 2002 (40), pp. 235–258; S. *Lightfoot & J. Burchell*, The European Union and the World Summit on Sustainable Development: Normative Power Europe in Action?, JCMS: Journal of Common Market Studies 2005 (43), pp. 75–95; M. *Braun*, EU Climate Norms in East-Central Europe, JCMS: Journal of Common Market Studies 2014 (52), pp. 445–460.

[12] M. *De Morpurgo*, The European Union as a Global Producer of Transnational Law of Risk Regulation: A Case Study on Chemical Regulation, European Law Journal 2013 (19), pp. 779–798.

[13] *Li-Wen Lin*, Legal Transplants through Private Contracting: Codes of Vendor Conduct in Global Supply Chains as an Example, Am. J. Comp. L. 2009 (57), pp. 711–744.

[14] The environmental competences enter the Treaty of Rome with the Single European Act of 1987, which inserts a new Title VII, dedicated to the "Environment", consisting of three articles: 130R, 130S and 130T. The Single European Act states that action by the Community relating to the environment shall be based on the principles that preventive action should be taken that environmental damage should as priority be rectified at source and that the polluter should pay. It further provides that environmental protection requirements shall be component of the Community's other policies.

the transplanted rule or instrument. In this perspective, not only the letter of the law counts, but also and above all the existence of tools to make it effective, and therefore the legal system as a whole in which it will be imbedded.

It is therefore necessary to promote a comparative law approach in the study of the spreading of environmental rules, which will help us in understanding the profound reasons for legal transplants and the true effectiveness of the available remedies.

As the judges of the Indian Supreme Court have masterfully reminded us: "If the mere enactment of laws relating to the protection of environment was to ensure a clean and pollution-free environment, then India would, perhaps, be the least polluted country in the world. But this is not so. There are stated to be over 200 Central and State statutes which have at least some concern with environment protection, either directly or indirectly. The plethora of such enactments has, unfortunately, not resulted in preventing environmental degradation which, on the contrary, has increased over the years".[15]

Barbara Pozzo and Valentina Jacometti
Como, August 2020

---

[15]   Supreme Court of India, Indian Council for Enviro-Legal Action v. Union of India 1996 (5) SCC 281, 293.

CONTENTS

PART V. STATE AND INTERNATIONAL ENVIRONMENTAL LIABILITY

The Myth of Plurality of Regimes in the Law of State Responsibility

The Right to a Healthy Environment and its Consequences
for Other Human Rights: A Challenging Approach

PART VII. LIABILITY, CLIMATE CHANGE AND NATURAL HAZARDS: THE ROLE OF INSURANCE

Insurance Instruments for Adapting to Climate Change: A Comparative Perspective

Multi-Country Pooling Schemes for the Financing and Transfer of Climate-Related Disaster Risk: A Comparative Overview

Environmental Liability, Catastrophic Risk Mitigation and Sustainability:
The Role of Insurers Beyond the Insurance Coverage

PART VIII. REAL COMPENSATION AND OFFSET REGIMES:
THE STRATEGY OF "NO NET LOSS"

No Net Loss in Recovery: The Overall End-of-Waste Impact Assessment

No Net Loss and Forest Offsets in the Flemish Region: A Cautionary
Tale of How Not to Reconcile Science-Based Conservation Policies
with Economic Interests and Vested Rights?

LIST OF AUTHORS

Mariusz Baran
Assistant Professor, Department of Environmental Law, Faculty of Law and
Administration, Jagiellonian University, Krakow, Poland

Letizia Casertano
Researcher and Adjunct Professor of Private Law, University of Insubria, Italy

Marta Cenini
Associate Professor of Private Law, University of Insubria, Italy

Yu Cheng
Law School, Beijing Normal University; Institute of Green Development
Strategies, China University of Political Science and Law, China

Nadia Coggiola
Associate Professor, Department of Management, University of Turin, Italy

Merve Demir
Doctoral Candidate in Environmental Law, Department of Life &
Environmental Sciences, and Researcher in Environment & Threats Strategic
Research Group, Bournemouth University, United Kingdom

Robert Esser
Professor of Law, Research Centre for Human Rights in Criminal Proceedings
(HRCP), University of Passau, Germany

Stefano Fanetti
Postdoctoral Research Fellow in Comparative Private Law, University of
Insubria, Italy

Joris Gazendam
Doctoral Candidate, Groningen Centre of Energy Law and Sustainability,
University of Groningen, the Netherlands

Carlo Vittorio Giabardo
"Juan de la Cierva" Postdoctoral Research Fellow in Law, Department of
Law, Càtedra de Cultura Juridica, University of Girona, Spain; Research
Associate at Global Law Initiatives for Sustainable Development (gLAWcal),
United Kingdom

Tilak Ginige
Senior Academic in Environmental Law and Management, Department of Life & Environmental Sciences, and Convener in Environment & Threats Strategic Research Group, Bournemouth University, United Kingdom

Carola Glinski
Associate Professor, Centre of Private Governance, Faculty of Law, University of Copenhagen, Denmark

Iain Green
Senior Academic in Biological Sciences, Department of Life & Environmental Sciences, and Convener in Environment & Threats Strategic Research Group, Bournemouth University, United Kingdom

Theodoros Iliopoulos
Doctoral Candidate in Environmental and Energy Law, Hasselt University, Belgium

Valentina Jacometti
Associate Professor of Comparative Private Law, University of Insubria, Italy

Nikolay Kichigin
Acting Head of the Department of Environmental and Agricultural Legislation, Institute of Legislation and Comparative Law under the Government of the Russian Federation, Russia

Alena Kodolova
Senior Research Fellow, Saint Petersburg Scientific Research Center for Environmental Safety, Russian Academy of Science, Russia

Ludwig Krämer
Environmental Law Consultant, Derecho y Medio Ambiente, Madrid, Spain

Emanuele La Rosa
Assistant Professor of Criminal Law, Department of Law, Economics and Human Sciences, "Mediterranea" University of Reggio Calabria, Italy

Francesco Martines
Assistant Professor of Administrative Law, University of Messina, Italy

Carlo Masieri
Postdoctoral Research Fellow, University of Milan, Italy

Khazar Masoumi
University Lecturer, Anhembi Morumbi University, São Paulo, Brazil; Associate Researcher, SAGE Laboratory (UMR 7363), University of Strasbourg, France

Anna Teresa Memola
PhD in Comparative Law, University of Milan, Italy

Alberto Monti
Full Professor of Comparative Law, University School for Advanced Studies IUSS Pavia, Italy

Susanna Paleari
Researcher, Research Institute on Sustainable Economic Growth – National Research Council, Italy

Chiara Perini
Associate Professor of Criminal Law, University of Insubria, Italy

Barbara Pozzo
Full Professor of Comparative Private Law, University of Insubria, Italy

Bartosz Rakoczy
Professor of Environmental Protection Law and Head of the Chair of Environmental Protection Law and Public Business Law, Nicolaus Copernicus University, Poland

Wenhong Ren
Doctoral Candidate in Environmental Law, Beihang University, Beijing, China

Miriam Ruiz Arias
PhD in Criminal Law from the University of Salamanca, Spain; occasional Lecturer at the Antioquia Institute of Technology, Colombia

Hendrik Schoukens
Postdoctoral Researcher, Department of European, Public and International Law, Ghent University, Belgium

Laura Stănilă
Senior Lecturer at the Faculty of Law, West University Timişoara, Romania

Sergiu Stănilă
Senior Lecturer at the Faculty of Law, West University Timişoara, Romania

Topi Turunen
Postdoctoral Researcher, University of Eastern Finland Law School, Finland

Patrick Van Calster
Senior Academic in Criminology, Department of Social Sciences & Social Work, and Convener in Environment & Threats Strategic Research Group, Bournemouth University, United Kingdom

Anna Vanhellemont
Doctoral Candidate in Environmental Law, Hasselt University, Belgium

Geert Van Hoorick
Professor, Department of European, Public and International Law, Ghent University, Belgium

Congwen Yao
Research Institute of Environmental Law, Wuhan University, China

PART I

LIABILITY FOR ENVIRONMENTAL HARM IN THE EU

THE EU AND THE SYSTEM
OF ENVIRONMENTAL LOSS AND DAMAGE

Liability, Restoration and Compensation

Ludwig KRÄMER

1. SPECIFICITY OF ENVIRONMENTAL LOSS AND DAMAGE

There are two aspects which are specific to the discussion of environmental loss and damage: the environment is victimless and the environment is sick.

Let us start by considering the first aspect: *the environment is victimless*. Who can claim that he/she is affected in his or her rights or interests by the disappearance of elephants or tigers, by ocean pollution or even by climate change? Obviously, all humans are affected and this is different from normal cases concerning loss and damage: in such normal cases, there is a wrongdoer and a person who is affected in his or her individual rights of life, health, property, etc. The wish to protect individual interests and rights against harm allowed claims and actions against the wrongdoer and, since the arrival of large-scale administrations, against public authorities. Law developed sophisticated provisions concerning the burden of proof, causation, repair, compensation for pain and suffering, prescription and other mechanisms to balance the interests of the wrongdoer and the victim, in administrative law instruments such as the separation of powers ("the king can do no wrong"), the shielding of individual officials, presumptions in favour of the administration and other mechanisms.

Most of these instruments and mechanisms do not work in environmental law. Trees have no standing and cannot address a court, nor can tigers, elephants or eagles claim damages. Furthermore, environmental conflicts with neighbours only play a minimal role in the overall impairment of the environment. Since in all industrialised countries – and beyond – the protection of the "environment" as a general interest has been put into the hands of public authorities, which at the same time permit and monitor economic or infrastructural activities that are harmful to the environment, the defence of the environmental interests often has to turn against public authorities when these either authorised or tolerated damaging activities or remained passive when damaging activities were deployed by economic operators.

This description touches on the second aspect of relevance: *the environment is sick*. The law on damages of industrialised countries is based on the assumption that there is a damaging act or activity and a victim whose rights or interests are impaired and who thus looks for compensation. In environmental law, such a scenario is only part of the truth. For example, all cars which run on public roads are licensed, certified to be in compliance with legal requirements and regularly checked. Yet their "legal" emissions might cause serious air pollution or excessive noise, and the infrastructure needed for cars destroys landscapes and affects flora and fauna. The environment can most probably survive accidents such as the Fukushima or Chernobyl nuclear accidents, the Aznalcollar mine accident, etc.; sooner or later – in fact more likely later – nature will recover. What is more problematic is the slow but progressive degradation of the environment, the contamination of the air, soil and oceans, the disappearance of species, increases in greenhouse gas emissions, etc. For an individual person, it is much easier to prove that his or her health was damaged by an accident than by continued exposure to harmful pollutants or excessive noise – as evidenced by the different characteristics of accident and sickness insurance. Similar problems exist in environment-related damage, with the difference that no environmental health insurance system exists.

An assessment of EU law on damage and losses, as well as the questions of liability, restoration and compensation must begin by drawing attention to the fact that, as the EU is not a state, responsibility for the protection of the environment is shared between the EU and its Member States. The principles on conferral, subsidiarity and proportionality, laid down in Article 5 of the Treaty on European Union (TEU),[1] limit EU action. It will be shown in detail below how this repartition of tasks influenced EU environmental law.

2. THE EU ENVIRONMENTAL LIABILITY PROVISIONS

The history of EU law-making is good evidence of the development of environmental liability. When the EU started to consider legislative initiatives

---

[1]   Article 5 TEU: "… Under the principle of conferral, the Union shall act only within the limits of the competences conferred upon it by the Member States … Under the principle of subsidiarity … the Union shall act only if and in so far as the objectives of the proposed action cannot be sufficiently achieved by the Member States … but can rather, by means of the scale or effects of the proposed action, be better achieved at Union level … Under the principle of proportionality, the content and form of Union action shall not exceed what is necessary to achieve the objectives of the Treaties".

on environmental liability, its legislative proposal had the classic situation in mind of a polluter who caused injury to the environment.[2] A plaintiff would be entitled to ask that the incriminated activity be stopped or prohibited, and to ask for reimbursement of the costs of preventive measures he had taken, for reimbursement of expenses to compensate for damage to property, and for the payment of costs to restore the environment.[3] Action would be allowed by natural persons and public authorities and by common interest groups to the extent that this was allowed under the law of Member States. However, the proposal was never adopted by the EU legislature.

Discussions at EU level quickly abandoned a civil law approach. The activity of public authorities came more into focus, also under the influence of the environmental liability law of the United States. In the US, the Environment Protection Agency had the power – and the necessary financial resources – to initiate clean-up actions with regard to contaminated land, and when it discovered the private company responsible for that contamination, it could take action to recover the money which it had spent. The EU took up the model that public authorities should take the initiative to restore the damaged environment. However, the EU legislation which was finally adopted[4] took care to exclude any civil law compensation for damage to humans or the environment and limited itself to providing for the restoration of the impaired environment. Furthermore, it did not provide for any institution or body, similar to the US EPA, to actively promote environmental restoration, but left any initiative in this regard to the Member States. As no financial resources were made available for the restoration activity either, the incentive for Member States to become active was limited. Finally, it was made clear in the EU legislation, contrary to the situation in US law, that public authorities had no obligation to provide for environmental restoration, when the person who had caused the damage could not be identified or had a defence under Directive 2004/35 which excluded his liability.[5]

---

[2]   See Commission Proposal for a Directive on civil liability for damage caused by waste, OJ 1989, C 251/3, Article 3: "The producer of waste shall be liable under civil law for the damage and injury to the environment caused by the waste, irrespective of fault on his part".

[3]   Id., Article 4.

[4]   Directive 2004/35 on environmental liability with regard to prevention and remedying of environmental damage, OJ 2004, L 143/56.

[5]   Id., Article 6(3): "The competent authority shall require that the remedial measures are taken by the operator. If the operator … cannot be identified or is not required to bear the costs under this Directive, the competent authority *may* take these measures itself, as a means of last resort" (emphasis added).

This deliberately very limited approach to liability for environmental damage has considerable practical consequences, as may be illustrated with some examples.

2.1. AIR POLLUTION

In numerous urban agglomerations of the EU, air pollution is a serious problem. It is caused by the emission of dangerous pollutants – sulphur dioxide, nitrogen oxides, particulate matters, etc. – into the air. These pollutants stem from economic (industry, transport) or non-economic (heating) activities. While the individual specific activity might be perfectly legal, the overall result on air pollution is such that the European Environment Agency and the European Commission estimate that there are between 400,000 and 480,000 premature deaths per year in the EU, and economic damage of more than €20 billion per year;[6] the damage to the environment is not really included in this figure.

No natural or legal person is held liable for this damage, which is taken as an act of God (*force majeure*) by the public authorities. While civil law has developed the principle of joint and several liability, this is not applied to air pollution damage. Such damage is even specifically excluded from the field of application of Directive 2004/35.[7]

This state of affairs is based on a deliberate choice. It would be possible to fix much more stringent emission limits for cars than those currently in force.[8] It would be possible to restrict or prohibit, with appropriate transition periods, domestic heating with peat, lignite, coal or petrol. It would be possible to annually check a car's compliance with existing emission limits in the same way as its roadworthiness or the functioning of its brakes is checked.[9] It would be possible to abandon the policy of adapting cities to the needs of motor vehicles, etc.

---

[6] EU Commission, Clean Air Package, COM(2013) 918; European Environment Agency, Air quality in Europe, 2017 report, Copenhagen, 2018, p. 55.

[7] Directive 2004/35, Recital 4: "Environmental damage also includes damage caused by airborne elements as far as these cause damage to water, land or protected species or natural habitats".

[8] Some drastic ways would be to provide that cars must be constructed to run not quicker than 100km/h, a speed that is anyway normally not reached in modern transport; it would be possible to determine that cars do not consume more than three litres of fuel per 100km – which would lead to the construction of smaller and lighter cars. In the same way as lead in petrol was phased out some years ago, it would be possible to impose the reduction of NO_x from cars. It would be possible to change the tax system for cars so that larger cars with higher consumption of fuels (and higher emissions) are taxed higher, etc.

[9] At present, there is only a regular control of the carbon monoxide emissions required, see Directive 2014/45 on periodic roadworthiness tests for motor vehicles and their trailers, OJ 2014, L 127/51.

Another problem is that of the victim: who can sue in cases of air pollution? The individual victim could at best make a claim to have his/her damage compensated, but would not, in most national legislation of EU Member States and certainly not under EU law, have standing to ask the court to pronounce an end to air pollution or the payment of damages. In additional, the victim would have to prove that his/her respiratory illness was caused by the pollution caused by a specific operator – which is generally impossible. And should the local administration be sued if it did not properly ensure compliance with existing air quality standards? Or the EU institutions that adopted insufficient legal provisions or did not call Member States to order where air pollution was in breach of existing EU rules? EU law is very restrictive in this regard: a natural or legal person must be directly and individually concerned by a measure of an EU institution in order to have access to an EU court;[10] this condition largely excludes court actions against legislative acts. Actions in the general interest of the environment are not foreseen. And any action must be begun within two months of the adoption of the relevant measure.

2.2. DIESELGATE

Closely related to the problem of air pollution is the issue of Dieselgate: since the beginning of the 21st century, a considerable number of European and Japanese car manufacturers had manipulated their cars with so-called defeat devices which had the effect that the cars emitted many more nitrogen oxide pollutants into the air than was legally permitted. Volkswagen alone admitted the manipulation of some 11 million cars worldwide.

The individual car owner may, in Europe, ask for the defeat device to be removed from his car. He/she will not normally obtain compensation for the loss of value of his/her car. And he/she certainly cannot claim compensation for all the nitrogen oxides that were released into the air in breach of existing provisions and that impaired the environment for everyone. This damage to the environment is neither restored nor compensated.

Moreover, the question of whom to sue is crucial. The EU Commission did not properly check compliance with the ban on defeat devices. National authorities did not even request all the documentation from the manufacturers which would have allowed the fraud to be discovered. And car manufacturers argue that they are not in a contractual relationship with car owners.

At the end of the day, car manufacturers might have to pay some compensation to car users. But this has nothing to do with the damage to the environment which was caused and which remains unresolved.

---

[10]   See Article 263(4) TFEU.

2.3. CLIMATE CHANGE

The warming up of the planet, due to the excessive emissions of greenhouse gases into the atmosphere, causes at present and will cause in future extreme weather conditions, rising sea levels, droughts and higher levels of precipitation, which will have a significant impact on humans. Who can claim damages for liability to the environment in such cases? Any action would be in the general interest to protect the environment. As our legal systems in Europe, based on statutes, have their roots in the 19th century, they allow claims in the personal, individual interest, but normally not in the *general* interest; and administrations and judges tend to be middle-class conservatives with limited ambition to align the existing rules to a changing reality.[11]

2.4. OCEAN POLLUTION

For centuries, rivers, coastal waters and oceans were used as sewers for liquid and solid wastes. This habit has not yet come to an end, and ocean pollution by hydrocarbons or waste remains a continuing problem. Another problem that is increasing in the era of plastics is the pollution by plastic materials. The annual input of plastics into the oceans is estimated to be six to eight million tons. They come from ships, land-based activities, discharge of waste and other sources. More and more plastic parts are found in animals and plants, included in dead whales, dolphins, turtles and birds.

The question of liability for such pollution sounds almost absurd: the pollution is known, but not the polluter. An individual polluter cannot be held liable for all ocean pollution. This does not mean, though, that measures to reduce the generation and use of plastics and plastic waste, reduce their ending up the sea, prevent discharges, and increase reuse and recycling of plastic could not be improved.

EU legislation is relatively limited and ineffective. As at the end of 2019, as regards plastics there is only one provision that provides for a target of separate collection of 50 per cent of plastic packaging waste materials by 2025.[12] Most, though not all, ships that use EU ports are obliged to pay a fee for discharging ship-generated waste on land; the fee may also be charged even when the land installation is not used.[13] This vague provision creates differences in the

---

[11] In this regard, Anglo-Saxon common law certainly offers greater flexibility.
[12] Directive 94/62 on packaging and packaging waste, OJ 1994, L 365/10, as amended by Directive 2018/852, OJ 2018, L 150/141, Article 11.
[13] Directive 2000/59 on port reception facilities for ship-generated waste and cargo residues, OJ 2000, L 332/81; see also Proposal for an amendment of that directive, COM(2018) 33.

application of the Directive. Moreover, studies have shown that the fees are not sufficiently high to act as a deterrent.[14] Proposals for reducing the generation of one-way plastic products are being discussed, but would affect only modest quantities of such products.

3. RESTORATION OF THE IMPAIRED ENVIRONMENT

Restoration of the impaired environment by the responsible person should be a priority for any rational environmental policy, since only when a polluter has to bear the costs of restoration can there a preventive, deterrent effect on him and on other potential polluters. One should have not too many illusions, though: in the same way as a lost arm or leg cannot be restored, therefore limiting "restoration" to either an artificial limb and/or to financial compensation, it will normally not be possible to completely restore the impaired environment.

In the water sector, Directive 2000/60 provided that surface and groundwater bodies shall normally be restored to good water status.[15] This status was to be achieved by 2015, but there was scope to extend this deadline, without much effort, to 2027.[16] Member States were allowed to reach fewer environmental objectives when it was "infeasible or disproportionally expensive" to achieve good water status, and when some other conditions were complied with.[17] However, it was the Member States that decided whether all such conditions were met, and the EU Commission – which would have had the burden of proof – did not take up one single case with any of the Member States to check whether reaching a good status was really infeasible or too expensive. Court actions by individual persons or environmental organisations to insist on full restoration were not foreseen by Directive 2000/60 and were, under national law, either not possible or not initiated in practice.

The European Environment Agency reported in 2018 that about 40 per cent of EU surface waters had a good chemical and quantitative status; for groundwater,

---

[14] The Commission estimated in 2018 that between 60,000 and 300,000 tons of waste per year generated by ships in the waters adjacent to the EU territory are not delivered at EU ports, nor are, furthermore, some 31,000m^3 of oily waste and some 136,000m^3 of sewage: Commission, SWD(2018) 21, p. 5.

[15] Directive 2000/60 establishing a framework for Community action in the field of water policy, OJ 2000, L 327/1.

[16] Id., Article 4(4): "The deadlines established under paragraph 1 [15 years after the entry into force of the Directive] may be extended … Extensions shall be limited to a maximum of two further updates of the river basin management plans [six years] except in cases, where the natural conditions are such that the objectives cannot be achieved within this period". The Commission would have to prove that by 2027 a restoration could have been achieved.

[17] Id., Article 4(5).

this figure was 80/86 per cent.[18] The Agency was prudent enough not to talk about the restoration of surface waters, but reported that the pressure on water from point sources and diffuse sources remained high in the EU.

In the waste sector, the Framework Directive 2008/98 makes no mention of soil restoration. A Commission proposal for a directive on the protection of soil[19] did not find a sufficient majority in the Council and was not pursued.

A small contribution to soil restoration came from the Court of Justice. On several applications from the Commission, it decided that the unauthorised disposal of waste within or outside of landfills was not in compliance with EU waste law. Later, it specified that such unauthorised landfills had to be closed and the waste that had been disposed of there had to be removed, as it continued to present an environmental risk.[20] Though the Commission or Member States themselves are far from enforcing this obligation systematically, it nevertheless constitutes a welcome improvement to see the soil partially restored.

Until now, the EU has not taken systematic action to progressively clean up all contaminated sites, which include – apart from waste disposal sites – abandoned industrial sites, military grounds and sites with war residuals (ammunition). The European Environment Agency estimated the number of contaminated sites within the EU at some 2.5 million.[21] Each Member State decides for itself whether and to what extent it intends to restore its contaminated sites.

No coordinated or common EU activities exist, neither with regard to soil erosion nor desertification.

As regards the conservation of nature, the EU does not have a general instrument to protect biodiversity or the landscape in general. The main instrument adopted by the EU is the Habitats Directive, which established the Natura 2000 network.[22] This network groups habitats of EU-wide importance. Within an identified habitat, projects, plans or programmes that are likely to have a significant effect on the habitat are in principle prohibited. Member States may for imperative reasons of overriding public interest grant derogations. They must then take measures to ensure that the general coherence of the Natura 2000

---

[18] European Environment Agency, European waters. Assessment of status and pressures, Technical Report 7/2018, Copenhagen, 2018.

[19] Commission, COM(2006) 232.

[20] Beginning with Court of Justice, case C-365/97, Commission v. Italy, ECLI:EU:C:1999:544; see also cases C-37/07, Commission v. Portugal, ECLI:EU:C:2010:331 and C-196/13, Commission v. Italy, ECLI:EU:C:2014:2407. In case C-387/97, Commission v. Greece, ECLI:EU:C:2000:356, the Commission had satisfied itself with the fencing in of an illegal landfill by Greece and had stopped the financial sanction, see L. Krämer, European Environmental Law, Sweet & Maxwell, 8th ed., 2015, p. 451.

[21] European Environment Agency, The European Environment. State and outlook, Copenhagen, 2005, p. 17.

[22] Directive 92/43 on the conservation of natural habitats and of wild fauna and flora, OJ 1992, L 206/7.

network is not affected and adopt compensatory measures. However, that these compensatory measures are effectively executed is almost not monitored.

Often, buildings or other constructions are built in breach of EU nature conservation provisions. An example is the Waldschlösschen Bridge in Dresden (Germany),[23] which was built in an area designated as a "world heritage site" by UNESCO and destroyed the overall scenery. Restoration – which would mean the destruction of the bridge – was mentioned by the CJEU as one of the possible options, but was not seriously considered by the German authorities. In Spain, the construction of some 300 villas, two hotels, a marina and more within a Natura 2000 site was authorised by the competent regional government, but later declared to be illegal by the Spanish Supreme Court.[24] The Court also ordered the destruction of the buildings and the restoration of the site; this requirement is even found in the Spanish Constitution.[25] However, the regional government refused to restore the site, arguing that it was too expensive. Another judgment of the Supreme Court, from 2016,[26] which declared the construction of a hotel in the Cabo de Gata nature reserve illegal, has also yet to be executed.[27] A recent judgment of the Supreme Court,[28] ordering the destruction of two skyscrapers, which had been built in Valencia in breach of the coastal protection legislation, and the restoration of the impaired environment, might cost the responsible authorities some €200 million and is again likely not to be executed. In France, the construction of a bridge linking the isle of Ré with the mainland was declared illegal by the French Conseil d'Etat,[29] without any further consequences. Similar examples may be found in most other Member States.

The conclusion is that restoration of the impaired environment is, to put it mildly, not a priority within the Member States. And the liability of officials, polluters or other persons who are responsible for the impairment is not seriously considered. Directive 2004/35 suggests that natural or legal persons could ask the public authorities to actively restore the impaired environment. If their request is sufficiently documented and the public authorities nevertheless do not act, the natural or legal person may ask a court to decide whether a restoration is required. However, there is no incentive for persons or NGOs to follow this procedure. Their message to the public authorities may be delayed,

---

[23] Court of Justice, case C-399/14, Grüne Liga Sachsen, ECLI:EU:C:2016:10.

[24] Tribunal Supremo (Spain), judgment of 29 January 2014 in cases 2414/2011 and 2940/2011 Valdecanas.

[25] Constitution of Spain, Article 118: "*Es obligado cumplir las sentencias y demas resoluciones de los Jueces y Tribunales*" (it is mandatory to execute the judgments and other resolutions of the judges and of the courts (translated by the author)).

[26] Tribunal Supremo, Contencioso 172/2016 sentencia del 10-2-2016.

[27] Construction of the hotel in 2003; estimated demolition costs of more than €7 million.

[28] Tribunal Supremo, Sala de lo Contencioso-Administrativo, prudencia del 22-11-2018, 3419/2018, TorresGemelos 28 (Benidorm).

[29] Conseil d'Etat 10/5 SSR of 8-3-1989, 90453, île de Ré.

considered to be insufficiently documented or rejected for other reasons. They bear the cost risk of any court procedure. Why should a natural or legal person venture to follow this path?

In the United States, the Netherlands and some other countries, a person may ask the public authorities to take action against environmental impairment. If the authorities do not comply with that request within a specific time span, the person has the right to go to court him/herself. Apparently, giving such a right – even a conditional right – of access to the courts was considered unacceptable to the EU legislature. Therefore, it is no surprise that Directive 2004/35 only led to a small number of court actions in the EU.[30] Overall, the Directive does not offer effective means to protect the environment against illegal activities and hold the wrongdoer liable.[31]

4. ENVIRONMENTAL PROTECTION THROUGH CRIMINAL LAW

For a long time it was disputed whether the EU was competent at all to adopt provisions concerning criminal law, in particular in order to protect the environment. The Member States preferred, in this area, forms of intergovernmental cooperation, but were opposed to binding EU-wide measures. Following long preparatory work by the Council of Europe, in 2003 the EU Council adopted a framework decision on criminal sanctions in environmental law, which provided for intergovernmental cooperation, recognising, however, that criminal law measures were necessary to protect the environment.[32] The Commission then presented a proposal for an EU directive[33] and tackled at the same time the Council act before the Court of Justice.

The Court of Justice argued that, as the need to protect the environment through criminal law provisions was recognised by the Council, there was no reason why the EU should not adopt common, EU-wide binding provisions in this area.[34] Following this judgment, the EU adopted a directive to protect

---

[30] The Commission reported that as of 2013, there had been 132 cases where the public authorities had been asked to take action, of which 93 in Italy alone. In 60 cases, judicial action was taken, of which 44 cases were from Poland. See Commission, COM(2016) 204, p.5. See also more generally, COM(2010) 581 and the evaluation report on the Directive, Commission, SWD(2016) 121.

[31] Commission, COM(2016) 204, p. 8: "The implementation of the ELD has improved the prevention and remediation of environmental damage to a limited extent". See also the considerably stronger criticism of the Directive in Commission, SWD(2016) 121.

[32] Decision 2003/80, OJ 2003, L 29/35.

[33] Commission, OJ 2001, C 180E/238.

[34] Court of Justice, case C-176/03, Commission v. Council, ECLI:EU:C:2005:442.

the environment through criminal law.[35] And as the Court of Justice stipulated in a later decision that the type and level of criminal environmental sanctions continued to be the competence of Member States,[36] the Lisbon Treaties of 2009 provided that for particularly severe criminal acts, the EU could adopt provisions concerning the type and level of sanctions. The list of particularly severe crimes was laid down in Article 83(1) TFEU;[37] environmental crimes were not included, though the list could be extended by a unanimous decision of the European Parliament and the Council.

Though in theory the environment is thus also protected by EU criminal law provisions, the practical effects of these developments are limited, for several reasons. First, there are some illegal actions classified as environmental crimes, but this list is not complete. In particular, provisions are lacking to cover cases of illegal logging, hunting and fishing, and animal welfare.

Second, most of the cases which are under EU law considered to be environmental crimes are so classified only when there is a risk to human health or life, as some examples might demonstrate. The Commission had proposed[38] to consider as an environmental crime "the illegal discharge of hydrocarbons, waste oils or sewage sludge"; Directive 2008/99 provided that the illegal discharge of a quantity of materials which caused or was likely to cause death or serious injury to humans or substantial damage to the environment should constitute a crime. The Commission had also proposed that the illegal operation of a landfill should constitute a crime; according to Directive 2008/99, the illegal disposal of waste which causes or is likely to cause death or serious injury to any person or substantive damage to the quality of the air, the quality of soil or the quality of water, or to animals or plants constitutes a crime. And finally, the Commission had proposed to consider the illegal operation of a plant where a dangerous activity was carried out to be a crime; Directive 2008/99 considered this to be a crime where the activity caused or was likely to cause risks to humans or to the environment outside the plant. The addition of the risk of damage to humans practically takes away the criminalisation of *environmental* impairment. Moreover, the term "substantive damage" is vague and leaves a considerable discretion to police or prosecutors. It is similar to the term "significant damage"

---

[35]   Directive 2008/99 on the protection of the environment through criminal law, OJ 2008, L 328/28.

[36]   Court of Justice, case C-440/05, Commission v. European Parliament and Council, ECLI:EU:C:2007:625.

[37]   The list includes terrorism, trafficking of human beings and sexual exploitation of women and children, illicit drug trafficking, illicit arms trafficking, money laundering, corruption, counterfeiting measures of payment, computer crime and organised crime.

[38]   Commission, *supra*, note 33.

in Directive 2004/35 on environmental liability. With regard to this last term, the Commission had rightly complained that it led to a rather varied application of the Directive in Member States.[39]

Third, there is no clarification on the relationship between criminal law sanctions and administrative sanctions. Indeed, in most legal systems of the EU, public authorities have the competence to pronounce administrative sanctions against polluters or other wrongdoers, and even give *de iure* or *de facto* priority to administrative sanctions over criminal law sanctions: when an administrative sanction is pronounced, the criminal prosecution of an act is normally no longer possible. As administrative sanctions in environmental matters are not codified and no public discussion and decision on such cases takes place, this practice invites arrangements between public authorities and environmental wrongdoers. The environment has no voice and most administrative decisions in environmental matters are not even published and thus remain unknown to the public.

This aspect is linked to the fourth problem: sanctions, under EU law, have to be effective, proportionate and dissuasive,[40] and this formula applies to administrative as well as to criminal sanctions. However, the European Commission never examined national criminal environmental sanctions in terms of their compliance with the formula nor undertook steps to make the sanctions more effective, proportionate and dissuasive. It normally does not even insist on knowing precisely what kind of sanctions are available within the different Member States and what sanctions are applied in practice, nor has it ever examined whether the administrative sanctions are effective and dissuasive.

Furthermore, the application of criminal law is a specific problem: in the above-mentioned case of Valdecanas,[41] the permit to build the holiday village was granted by the regional government of Extremadura, in clear breach of existing legal provisions. However, no criminal law investigation was ever started against the regional prime minister or the person(s) responsible for granting the permit. Society is gradually becoming accustomed to seeing government representatives or officials sued in court for corruption, etc., but not yet for damaging the environment.

The air pollution in many urban agglomerations of the European Union is another, similar issue: the binding quality requirements of the EU have been in existence since at least 2008 and have, in numerous cases, been continuously

---

[39] Commission, COM(2006) 204.
[40] This formula goes back to Court of Justice, case C-68/88, Commission v. Greece, ECLI:EU:C:1989:339.
[41] See text to note 24, *supra*.

exceeded in some agglomerations.[42] Despite the premature deaths of some 400,000 persons per year due to air pollution, as mentioned above,[43] there has never been any criminal prosecution against the mayor or other officials of any municipality which had tolerated air pollution limits being exceeded for several years.

Birdlife International, a recognised environmental protection organisation, estimates that annually there are millions of birds killed or captured in the EU in breach of existing environmental law.[44] The number of criminal cases to stop this practice is extremely small, the sanctions all too often ridiculous.

The situation of the ortolan bird (*Emberiza hortulana*) in France is another good example of the administrative inertia of the French authorities to take action against these practices (and then of the EU Commission for not bringing France before the CJEU). The bird has been protected under EU law since 1979 and may not be hunted.[45] It is estimated, though, that every year about 30,000–50,000 ortolans are captured in France, have their eyes put out in order to make them eat more, then drowned in alcohol (armagnac) and sold to restaurants for a price of up to €150 per bird. France has promised several times to stop this practice. When in 2010 the Commission lost patience and started formal proceedings against France under Article 258 TFEU, it received a new promise that this practice would end – and satisfied with this promise, stopped all its proceedings (though the practice of hunting ortolan still continues).

In Portugal, there were in 2017 more than 20,000 wild fires, which led to 117 fatalities and some 540,000 hectares of land burnt. EFFIS, the international forest fire association, concluded that 32.7 per cent of those fires were laid intentionally and 49.7 per cent came about by negligence.[46] The number of criminal prosecutions in this case is again very small, demonstrating once more how EU law on environmental crime is not enforced in Member States.

Overall, EU criminal law, as well as environmental liability provisions, are relatively imperfect instruments to protect the environment, because of their

---

[42]　In case C-488/14, the Court of Justice found that the quality objectives of Directive 2008/50 on ambient air pollution, OJ 2008, L 152/1, had been exceeded in Bulgaria since 2008, thus for about 10 years. In case C-336/16, Commission v. Poland, ECLI:EU:C:2018:94, cases of non-compliance were found to have existed since 2007. See also text to note 61, *infra*.

[43]　See text to note 6, *supra*.

[44]　A.L. Brochet et al., Preliminary assessment of the scope and scale of illegal killing and taking of birds in the Mediterranean, Bird Conservation International 2016 (26), p. 1. The 10 Member States with the highest numbers of killed and taken birds are (estimations): Italy (3.4–7.8 million birds per year), Cyprus (1.3–5.2 million), Greece (485,000–922,000), France (149,000–895,000), Croatia (166,000–855, 000), Spain (103,000–405,000), Romania (22,300–177,000), Germany (53,000–146,000), Malta (5,800–211,000) and Belgium (12,800–107,000).

[45]　Directive 2009/147 on the conservation of wild birds, OJ 2010, L 20/7.

[46]　European Commission, Joint Research Center, European Forest Fire Information System (EFFIS): Forest Fires in Europe, Middle East and North Africa 2017, Brussels, 2018, p. 59.

poor and vague drafting as well as the failure to apply it. The victim – the environment – cannot complain. It dies away in silence. This contrasts with the general observation that the big environmental problems – climate change, loss of biodiversity, bad resource management, insufficient measures to react to demographic developments – are increasing.

5. BETTER IMPLEMENTATION

Civil law, administrative law and criminal law liability in the environmental sector have in common that their main objective is to prevent future environmental impairment; sanctioning the impairment committed is the second objective, as normally the environment cannot be restored. This approach corresponds to good European tradition,[47] though the words of Seneca should be read with caution: he is not against sanctions nor is against the protection of the society by the punishment of wrongdoers. This next section seeks to demonstrate that in the environmental area, EU law does not take the threat and application of sanctions seriously.

Article 191 TFEU stipulated that environmental policy shall be based on the principle that "the polluter should pay". Even the drafting of this provision shows the legislature's uncertainty as to what this principle meant: while the English version declares that the polluter "should" pay, the Italian and Danish version state that the polluter "shall" pay.[48] The French version mentions the "polluter-payer principle" (*principe du pollueur-payeur*) and the German version of Article 191 TFEU refers to the "principle of causation" (*Verursacherprinzip*).

The Court of Justice declared that a court action could not be based on the "polluter pays" principle of Article 191 TFEU alone, because legal consequences only flowed from acts that were adopted on the basis of Article 192 TFEU.[49] However, the same Court of Justice declared that the principle that environmental impairment should be combated at source, which also was laid down in Article 191 TFEU, had far-reaching implications on the management of waste, and allowed regional import bans from other EU Member States and obliging Member States to organise their waste management in a specific way.[50]

There is a consensus that the "polluter pays" principle could be made operational in secondary EU law and be applied. However, EU environmental

---

[47] Seneca: "*nemo prudens punit, quia peccatur, sed ne peccetur*" (No wise man punishes, because of a crime that was committed, but in order to prevent future crimes).

[48] Italian: "*chi inquina paga*"; Danish: "*forureneren betaler*".

[49] Court of Justice, case C-534/13, Fipa Group, ECLI:EU:C:2015:253.

[50] Court of Justice, case C-2/90, Commission v. Belgium, ECLI:EU:C:1992:310.

law is far from such a solution, as the following examples might demonstrate. There is a difference in the taxation of diesel and petrol fuels, without any environmental justification.[51] The environmental impairment caused by cars, such as air pollution, congestion, noise, needs of infrastructure (roads), waste, etc., is not priced into the price of a car or of the fuel. Rather, such costs are imposed on society, contrary to the "polluter pays" principle. The example of contaminated sites was already mentioned above.[52] Water pollution from agricultural sources, regulated by legislation since 1991,[53] has not led to a significant reduction of livestock (as per the stipulations of Directive 91/676 as concerns water pollution) where the nitrate levels in water exceeded the fixed thresholds, but rather to date to more than 28 derogations for Member States granted by the EU Commission. Residues from lindane, a persistent organic pollutant which was used as a pesticide, exist in some 40 places in the EU, but in most cases the polluter is not charged with their elimination; rather, when a clean-up is undertaken at all, it is the taxpayer who bears the cost of the decontamination. It may thus be concluded that the "polluter pays" principle is a valuable principle, but its establishment in secondary EU environmental law and in particular its application in practice is completely ineffective.

Another aspect of improving individual and collective responsibility for environmental impairment is the task of fact-finding. Article 17 TEU assigns to the EU Commission the task of ensuring the application of EU law, including EU environmental law, throughout the whole territory of the EU. The main instrument at the Commission's disposal to become informed of what happens in the Member States are the Member States' implementation reports, which provide information on the transposition and application of EU environmental legislative acts. Most environmental directives and regulations provide that Member States shall, at regular intervals, report on the implementation and application of the respective legislative act, and that the Commission shall regularly publish an EU-wide implementation report.

The Member States' reports are, with greater or lesser regularity, sent to the Commission, though frequently not made public. The Commission neither insists on obtaining the national reports nor itself regularly publishes the EU-wide reports on implementation.

---

[51]   Directive 2003/96 restructuring the Community framework for the taxation of energy products and electricity, OJ 2003, L 283/51. The reason for this differentiation is probably the hidden subvention which the transport and agricultural sectors obtain through the cheaper diesel price.

[52]   See text to note 21, *supra*.

[53]   Directive 91/676 concerning the protection of waters against pollution caused by nitrates from agricultural sources, OJ 1991, L 375/20.

The content of the reports is weighted more seriously. Member States have the tendency to report, at best, on the measures taken – in particular legislation introduced – but not on the results. They present their national situation in the best possible light and omit to describe omissions, failures or negative examples. The Commission reports, in general, do not name and shame Member States that transpose or apply EU environmental law incorrectly, meaning that the public has little opportunity to take up matters and pursue cases of non-compliance at national level.

The EU does not have environmental inspectors. Timid and half-hearted attempts by the Commission some 20 years ago[54] were unsuccessful, and though the enlargement of the EU in the 21st century has accentuated the problem of non-application of EU environmental law,[55] no change has occurred.

The introduction of inspectors would not be a legal problem. Such inspectors exist in competition law, veterinary law, customs law, agricultural and fisheries law, etc. By way of example, two sectors may be mentioned in more detail. In the competition sector, the inspection powers of the Commission are laid down in Articles 17 to 22 of Regulation1/2003.[56] According to these rules, the Commission may carry out all necessary inspections of undertakings and associations of undertakings, enter premises, land and means of transport, examine the books and other records, take copies and ask for information. The undertakings are obliged to cooperate; otherwise, they face penalties.

As regards food and feed law, the EU Commission has obtained very large monitoring and inspection competences. According to Regulation 2017/625,[57] it may execute inspections and audits in Member States, make on-the-spot verifications, verify the functioning of the national monitoring systems and investigate enforcement practices.

It is to be noted that both Regulations are secondary law provisions. This proves that the question of giving inspection and other monitoring rights to the Commission in environmental law would not be a question of transferring new

---

[54]   Recommendation 2001/331, OJ 2001, L 118/41 recommends that Member States provide for inspectors in environmental matters. A corresponding recommendation for EU inspectors does not exist.

[55]   In an admittedly simplified way, one can argue that the Member States that have joined the EU since 2004 were ready to adopt any (environmental) provision, in order to obtain their entrance ticket to the EU. The practical application of EU (environmental) law was and is, though, another matter.

[56]   Regulation 1/2003 the implementation of the rules on competition laid down in Articles 81 and 82 of the Treaty, OJ 2003, L 1/1; see also Commission Regulation 773/2004 relating to the conduct of the proceedings by the Commission pursuant to Articles 81 and 82 of the EC Treaty, OJ 2004, L 123/18.

[57]   Regulation 2017/625 on official controls and other official activities performed to ensure the application of food and feed law, rules on animal health and welfare, plant health and plant protection products, OJ 2017, L 95/1, Article 116.

competences to the EU level, but would be a normal consequence of Article 17 TEU and the establishment of common, generally applicable protection provisions all over the EU. Compliance with existing protection rules is the biggest problem EU environmental law faces, and the different degrees of compliance is a permanent source of jealousy, populist arguments and political dispute.

6.   HOLDING MEMBER STATES LIABLE

The Commission shall, as mentioned, ensure the application of EU law by the Member States. Article 258 TFEU instructs it, in principle, to act as soon as it discovers a case of non-compliance by a Member State.[58] However, the Court of Justice has not discussed the issue that the word "may" is only used in the second sentence of Article 258 TFEU, whereas in the first sentence the word "shall" is used;[59] it declared in settled case law that the Commission had a margin of discretion as to whether or not to start formal proceedings under Article 258 TFEU. It held that this discretion could not be controlled by the Court of Justice, and that neither Article 265 TFEU nor Article 340 TFEU enabled natural or legal persons to enforce the initiation of formal proceedings by the Commission.

This jurisprudence is not limited to environmental law, but applies to all areas of EU law. However, in the case of the environment, which has no voice and no powerful vested interest group behind it to defend its interests,[60] it is of particular importance. The Commission is restrictive in initiating or pursuing environmental procedures under Article 258 TFEU. In the last two decades, it has become even more hesitant to initiate court actions against Member States, as the following table of cases brought by the Commission and decided by the Court of Justice under Articles 258, 260 and 279 TFEU shows:[61]

---

[58]   Article 258 TFEU: "If the Commission considers that a Member State has filed to fulfil an obligation under the Treaties, it shall deliver a reasoned opinion on the matter after giving the State concerned the opportunity to submit its observations. If the State concerned does not comply with the opinion within the period laid down by the Commission, the latter may bring the matter before the Court of Justice of the European Union".

[59]   The first judgment in this area is apparently case 48/65, Lütticke v. Commission, ECLI:EU:C:1966:8, where the Court declared: "No measure taken by the Commission during this stage [the prejudicial stage of the present Article 258 TFEU] has any binding force. Consequently, an application for the annulment of the measure by which the Commission arrived at a decision on the application is inadmissible". This reasoning is unconvincing.

[60]   Such as farmers for agricultural law, fishermen for fisheries law, competitors for competition law, transporters for transport law, etc.

[61]   See also L. Krämer, On the effectiveness of monitoring the application of EU environmental law, in A. García-Ureta (ed.), Nuevas perspectivas del derecho ambiental en el siglo XXI, 2018, p. 259.

Table 1. Court judgments in environmental matters initiated by the Commission

Year	Absence of transposition	Incomplete/incorrect transposition	Bad application	Total
2002	16	16	6	38
2003	16	17	8	41
2004	11	23	14	48
2005	7	17	12	36
2006	14	12	6	32
2007	8	14	17	39
2008	8	13	4	25
2009	8	17	6	31
2010	7	8	5	20
2011	1	8	9	18
2012	0	9	10	19
2013	0	5	5	10
2014	0	6	6	12
2015	0	4	3	7
2016	0	1	9	10
2017	0	1	9	10
2018	0	11	4	15

Source: Author.

The table clearly shows that the sanction of a pecuniary penalty, introduced in Article 260(3) TFEU in 2009, has had the effect that since then Member States have transposed EU environmental legislation into their national legal order within the time limit for transposition. However, the overall number of cases brought by the Commission and decided by the Court of Justice has fallen by about 65–75 per cent.

One reason for this development is that the Commission has concentrated its action on cases of non-transposition and lack of complete and correct transposition of EU law. As it does not have inspectors or other means of monitoring at its disposal, it depends to a very large extent on complaints and other information that civil society – private persons or environmental organisations – submits. How else can it know, for example, what happens in Extremadura, on Crete or in Brandenburg? However, the Commission makes considerable efforts to deter environmental complaints. It never has codified the complaint procedure in any form, such that complainants could align themselves. It has not granted any rights to complainants, for example the right to be heard, the right to participate in meetings with the concerned Member State's officials or the polluter, or the right to learn details about a Member State's arguments in defence.[62] Only at the very end of the complaint procedure – which may easily take a year or more – is the complainant asked to comment on the Commission's preliminary conclusion of a case.

Even when the Commission learns of cases of non-compliance, it is reluctant to open formal proceedings against a Member State. The cases regarding the ortolan in France or Valdecanas in Spain, already mentioned, are examples of cases where the Commission remained passive. Some other cases might be mentioned to illustrate the problem: the European turtle dove (*Streptopylia turtur*) is a migrating bird which has been hunted in France during its migration period for more than 30 years without any action by the Commission. Under Regulation 715/2007,[63] which prohibits defeat devices in cars to deceive assessors regarding cars' emissions, Member States were requested to adopt efficient, proportionate and dissuasive sanctions and inform the Commission of their measures. The Commission did not receive this information, but took no action. In the German *Land* of Brandenburg, the media have identified 168 illegal landfills, and the environmental minister is reported to have said that he could use public money in a better way than complying with the law and eliminating that waste. In November 2018, the Commission applied to the Court of Justice, arguing that Germany, France, Hungary, Romania, Italy and the United Kingdom were not complying with the air pollution requirements of Directive 2008/50.[64] The applications make clear that the quality standards had not been respected since 2005 (Hungary), 2007 (Romania), 2008 (Italy) and 2010 (Germany, France, United Kingdom).[65] In the Natura 2000 area of Donana (Spain), one of the most important nature protection sites of the EU, there are some 800 illegal wells, where water is taken in particular for agricultural purposes, seriously impairing the Donana habitat.[66]

---

[62]   Compare to this Regulation 773/2004, where it is stated that: "[c]omplaints are an essential source of information for detecting infringements of competition rules" (Recital 5) and "[n]atural or legal persons having chosen to lodge a complaint should be given the possibility to be associated closely with the proceedings initiated by the Commission with a view to finding an infringement" (Recital 8). When oral hearings take place, a complainant may be given the right to put questions (Article 14), etc.

[63]   Regulation 715/2007 on type approval of motor vehicles with regard to emissions from light passenger and commercial vehicles (Euro 5 and Euro 6) and on access to vehicle repair and maintenance information OJ 2007, L 171/1.

[64]   Court of Justice, cases pending against Germany (C-635/18), France (C-636/18), Hungary (C-637/18), Romania (C-638/18), Italy (C-644/18) and the United Kingdom (C-646/19).

[65]   As regards air pollution and the application of Directive 2008/50, tribute is to be paid to the environmental organisation ClientEarth which initiated court proceedings before British courts in 2011, gradually succeeding in making this topic a priority issue in numerous EU Member States and at EU level, and leading to numerous air pollution cases before national courts; see Court of Justice, case C-404/13, ClientEarth, ECLI:EU:C:2014:2382.

[66]   See also World Heritage Committee (UNESCO) Decision 41 COM 7B.9 adopted at its 41st session, 2017, on the Donana National Park.

Similar examples could be quoted for every sector of environmental law and with regard to most EU Member States. One should be aware that there is a systemic deficiency in the EU's system of ensuring the application of EU environmental law. The request to allow citizens to bring such cases before the European or the national courts appears all the more justified when the EU Commission or national public authorities do not take judicial action within a specific time span.

7. WHAT CAN BE DONE TO IMPROVE THE PRESENT SITUATION?

A more general look at the EU system of environmental loss and damage reveals that the present system set up by the EU leaves significant room for improvement. Some of the possible improvements that could be adopted at EU level have already been mentioned. They are taken up here in a more systematic manner.

7.1. IMPROVING TRANSPARENCY

As the environment has no voice, it is most important to ensure that environmental impairment can be discussed in an open, transparent manner. Therefore, the Commission should systematically make accessible – through publication or via the internet – all national legislation that Member States adopt in order to transpose EU environmental legislation into their national legal order and that they send to the Commission anyway. The Commission should furthermore make accessible all implementation reports that Member States are obliged to send to it at regular intervals. And the Commission should insist that these reports are delivered on time and that they also cover the application of the law and not only the measures which were taken; after all, according to Article 288 TFEU, a directive first of all aims at achieving *results*.

The Commission should take seriously its own obligation to establish EU-wide reports on the application of environmental directives and regulations and get away from general observations without naming (and shaming) deficient Member States. The reader of some national or Commission reports sometimes has the impression of reading a publicity pamphlet and not a critical – though constructive – assessment of successes and failures of the respective environmental legislative act.

The Commission should no longer largely ignore information on the practical application of EU environmental law from civil society, citizens, environmental organisations or even media. Often enough, the impression is given that the

Commission does not even wish to know how environmental law is (not) applied, though nothing undermines the credibility of public authorities more than rules that are not applied. It is a shame that competition complaints are welcomed by the EU, whereas environmental complaints are, if possible, largely ignored.

Numerous environmental directives contain possibilities for derogating, under certain conditions, from their provisions. The Commission should ensure that it is systematically informed of derogations and should systematically publish any decision which it takes to accept a derogation and all derogations that Member States are granted. At the same time, the Commission should ensure that the (too) frequent granting of derogations does not turn the exception (the derogation) into the rule. One example of this kind is the above-mentioned Directive on water pollution by nitrates from agricultural sources, where the Commission granted, as of 31 May 2020, 30 derogations, covering the whole territory of some Member States for decades.

This author does not see any serious argument against the publication of letters of formal notice and reasoned opinions which the Commission issues under Article 258 TFEU. Why should citizens not be informed of arguments about deficiencies that exist or might exist in national legislation? The argument that the discussions between the Commission and the Member States should take place in an atmosphere of "mutual confidence", which is invoked to justify confidentiality, is completely unconvincing and democratically unacceptable. Citizens must also have confidence that the EU institutions ensure the application of EU law and do not bargain "in confidence" on issues of non-compliance. It would be democratically beneficial and useful if there were a public discussion, in the Member State concerned and elsewhere, whether this or that national legislation completely and correctly transposes EU environmental law; at present, this kind of discussion is largely paralysed by the confidential treatment of actions under Article 258 TFEU. The sad part of this story is that where economic interests are concerned – such as in the area of pharmaceutical products, chemicals, pesticides, industrial products or installations, but also in transport, energy law or trade law, etc. – the Commission's letters of formal notice and reasoned opinions are made public through informal channels in the Member States, and perhaps also at EU level. This leads to open and frank discussions in the media at national and EU level, to the benefit of all sides. The confidentiality in environmental matters thus *de facto* creates a double standard.

Article 1 TEU states that EU decisions shall be taken as openly as possible and as closely as possible to the citizen. Article 4 of Regulation 1367/2006 asks EU institutions and bodies to actively and systematically disseminate environmental information to the public, and to regularly update it. At regular intervals, "not exceeding four years", a report on the state of the EU environment shall be published.[67] The day-to-day practice of the EU is some way away from these requirements. Not only does the Commission abstain from systematically disseminating environmental information wherever it can – such as information on air, water and soil pollution, infrastructure projects without environmental impact assessments, problems with fisheries and the environment, logging and environmental protection, compliance with Directive 2010/75 on industrial emissions,[68] etc. – but the EU agencies also do not comply with this requirement. For example, the European Environment Agency publishes its report on the state of the environment every *five* years, in clear infringement of Article 4(4) of Regulation 1367/2006.[69] Numerous other agencies do not disseminate active and systematic environmental information.[70]

7.2. INVESTIGATION POWERS

It is obvious from the above that the present system of control and investigation powers of the European Commission is discriminating against the environment. Why should the Commission be allowed to carry out investigations and control visits, etc., or take copies or other means of evidence, when it has the suspicion that two undertakings infringed competition rules, when it has no such powers if it has the suspicion that these undertakings discharged pollutants into the air or the water, in breach of existing rules? Why should the inertia, passivity or open disregard of public authorities concerning compliance with existing EU environmental protection rules not be subject to control or investigation? EU inspectors are entitled to act in the areas of fisheries, agriculture, food and feed law, competition, customs, issues etc., why then should they not be allowed to act in the area of environmental issues? This different treatment reveals the approach as purely ideological, influenced by the joint interests of farmers, transporters, economic operators and (local, regional and national) public authorities.

---

[67] Regulation 1367/2006 on the application of the provisions of the Aarhus Convention on Access to Information, Public Participation in Decision-making and Access to Justice in Environmental Matters to Community institutions and bodies, OJ 2006, L 264/13, Article 4(4).

[68] Directive 2010/75 on industrial emissions, OJ 2010, L 334/17.

[69] It is true that Regulation 401/2009 on the European Environment Agency, OJ 2009, L 126/13, Article 2(h), provides for a publication of such a report every five years. However, the four-year-provision of Regulation 1367/2006 finds its origin in Article 5(4) of the Aarhus Convention, which requires the publication of such a report at regular intervals "not exceeding three to four years". As the Aarhus Convention was ratified by the EU, it binds the Member States *and* the EU institutions (Article 216(2) TFEU) and thus prevails over Regulation 401/2009.

[70] This concerns for example the agencies for cooperation of energy regulators, for aviation safety, for banking, for chemicals, for fisheries control, for maritime safety, for railways, or Euratom agencies.

Even without formal investigation powers and environmental inspectors, the Commission has the means to improve its investigations – if it so wished. The Commission may already at present undertake fact-finding missions in Member States, in order to find out and assess possible cases of environmental impairment. It did so in the past,[71] but limited such fact-finding visits to cases of nature conservation and to smaller countries – and never gave an account of such activities (for example by publishing mission reports, organising meetings at the place in question, hearing complainants, NGOs or other members of the public, communicating with the local media on the issue in order to raise awareness, etc.).

Another tool which is available to the Commission is the EU pollution register, which was established under Regulation 166/2006,[72] where Member States shall provide information, every three years, on the emissions of specific, individual industrial installations. The register was designed after the US model on the release of toxic substances. The difference between the EU model and that of the United States, however, is that the US Environment Protection Agency (EPA) more or less systematically addresses those installations that are found to exceed existing emissions limits or which emit significantly more pollutants than comparable installations; the EPA then asks these installations to review their practice, reduce emissions or take other appropriate measures to protect humans or the environment. In contrast, the EU publication of polluting industrial installations is not taken up and discussed with the installations responsible. Rather, the data are published and then allowed to lie around, until the publication of the next dataset three years later, as Member States do not feel responsible for the implementation of an EU regulation and the Commission has no strategy with regard to the application of Regulation 166/2006. Here, the Commission itself or via one of its agencies and together with the Member State concerned would have a wide scope of investigating, monitoring, controlling and proposing improvements – for example, by obliging individual installations or groups of installations to avoid emitting pollutants above the average of installations or by suggesting to national public authorities to amend the individual permit conditions etc. Where necessary, targeted financial support could be used to obtain such improvements.

Overall, the investigation powers of the Commission are certainly capable of being widened. However, the existing possibilities are already not used systematically to address cases of environmental impairment in breach of

---

[71] See Court of Justice, cases C-103/00, Commission v. Greece, ECLI:EU:C:2002:60, para. 8; C-504/18, Commission v. Greece, ECLI:EU:C:2016:847, para. 15, where such missions are mentioned.

[72] Regulation 166/2006 concerning the establishment of a European Pollution Release and Transfer Register, OJ 2006, L 33/1.

existing rules. As mentioned, this neither increases the credibility of the EU Commission, nor the respect for EU environmental law, nor the confidence in the political undertaking of European integration as such.

As the Commission and the Member States are so reluctant to hold polluters and other persons who cause environmental impairment liable or to require them to restore the damaged environment, there should be an option for civil society representatives to bring cases before the courts, where the public authorities, for legitimate or less legitimate reasons, do not take action. The present quasi-monopoly of public authorities to initiate or not to initiate court proceedings in order to protect the environment is outdated, anti-democratic and increasingly perceived as an example of bad governance.

7.3. ENVIRONMENTAL LIABILITY

Could or should Directive 2004/35 be improved? There should be no illusions as regards the difficulty of amending that Directive: a large majority of EU Member States are quite satisfied with the present state of affairs, having a so-called environmental liability system that is only very modestly effective. In large parts of the EU Member States, the protection of the environment continues to be perceived as a threat to economic development, job creation and the well-being of citizens.

Why has the Environmental Liability Directive only had limited success? One of the main reasons was mentioned already at the beginning of this chapter: the environment is sick, but the Directive is based on the model of an "accident/ incident", i.e. a single event that causes damage and can be attributed to one of the activities mentioned in Annex III to the Directive. Addressing the "sickness" of the environment is not possible through one piece of environmental legislation, even if it were as sophisticated as possible. Some 25 years ago, the Council declared that "many current forms of activity and development are not environmentally sustainable ... the achievement of sustainable development calls for significant changes in current patterns of development, production, consumption and behaviour".[73] This statement remains valid even today. Few such "significant changes" have been undertaken so far.

Liability provisions have the objective of granting compensation to victims and of preventing, through their deterrent effect, future incidents. Directive 2004/35 does not provide for the compensation of the environment, for example through penalty payments into an environmental fund. It does not hold responsible public authorities that authorise damaging activities or tolerate

---

[73] Council Resolution of 1 February 1993, OJ 1993 C 138/1.

them by not supervising, monitoring and sanctioning. It is limited as regards the restoration of the impaired environment. It does not give incentives to civil society representatives to identify cases of environmental impairment and enforce restoration, even when public authorities are reluctant.

In their assessment of the effects of Directive 2004/35, Faure and De Smedt conclude, *inter alia*, that:[74]

> the ELD did very little to create equal competitive conditions. In these respects, the ELD has not delivered any significant benefit ... [A]s the ELD provides a flexible framework, it has resulted in less harmonisation than some initially thought. There are differences in the ELD implementation by the Member States, and the burden for industry in various Member States might well differ significantly, so that there is no reason to believe that the ELD will level the playing field or realise a reduction in transaction costs.

7.4. MORE EFFECTIVE PROTECTION OF THE ENVIRONMENT?

Much would be won if the EU were to take the "polluter pays" principle more seriously. The direct and indirect damage that cars continuously cause to the environment, that the use of chemical pesticides and fertilisers cause to the soil and to biodiversity, etc., are almost not at all paid by the polluter. Water and soil pollution through agricultural activities, damage caused by excessive noise levels, the disposal of waste on land and at sea, the pollution of marine waters and – to mention the most important aspect – the pollution of the whole planet through excessive greenhouse gas emissions: if the "polluter pays" principle were correctly applied, environmental damage would be significantly reduced, meaning that there would be less concern about liability, compensation and restoration.

An already very significant improvement that could be quickly achieved in this area is the full and precise application of existing environmental provisions. Environmental sickness cannot be remedied by one or two miraculous measures. A reduction of the symptoms instead requires the long and patient enforcement of existing rules. This would also include legal interpretations of what "sustainable development", "the polluter shall pay" and the obligation to prevent environmental impairment by economic or other activities mean in a concrete case. It is easy simply to repeat in political resolutions or even in legal

---

[74]   *M. Faure & K. De Smedt*, The ELD's effects in practice, in L. Bergkamp & B. Goldsmith (eds.), The EU Environmental Liability Directive, Oxford University Press 2013, chapters 13.30 and 13.33.

acts that there should be sustainable development: as long as it is not clarified what this means in practice, the use of such terms constitutes "greenspeak" with no legal consequences. Environmental lawyers, academics, attorneys, judges and prosecutors have their obligations in making such general terms of environmental law and policy operational in specific cases. As long as in particular judges continue to believe that they should be discreet and not act seriously as regards the protection of the environment, there will continue to be general phraseology on the need to protect the planet and its biodiversity, its resources, oceans and humans, but limited effective legal action. The best way to fight environmental loss and damage is therefore to prevent that loss and damage from occurring, by fully enforcing the numerous provisions of international, European, national, regional and local level.

8. CONCLUSION

It is unrealistic to expect a significant amendment of the provisions on environmental liability within the EU. It is also unrealistic to expect that the Directive on the protection of the environment through criminal law will be significantly improved. The way forward in the area of loss and damage, liability and restoration will thus be greater transparency, greater accountability of public authorities, the full application of existing rules and the possibility for civil society and its representatives to have access to the courts.

TOWARDS A BETTER ENVIRONMENTAL LIABILITY DIRECTIVE?

Anna VANHELLEMONT

1. INTRODUCTION

After many years of deliberations, the EU Environmental Liability Directive (EU Directive 2004/35/EC, ELD) entered into force in 2004. The Member States had until 2007 to transpose the Directive; however, due to difficulties in the process, full transposition was ultimately reached in 2010. As the ELD was first introduced over 10 years ago, it has already proven its added value and positive impact on the development of environmental policies in the EU. However, several implementation issues have arisen, and it is time to consider the future of the Directive and how to unlock its full potential.

As part of the Regulatory Fitness and Performance (REFIT) programme, the EU Commission has carried out an evaluation of the ELD. The results of this check were published in a 2016 report on the relevance, effectiveness, efficiency, coherence and EU-added value of the Directive. The evaluation showed, amongst other things, that the Directive remains relevant, but its effectiveness is still hampered by several challenges.

The main focus of this chapter will be on the future of the ELD: what challenges does the Directive face, and how can we start finding solutions in order to ensure its effectiveness? This mostly entails questions on the Member States' application of the Directive and its relation to other EU environmental legislation.

Following several more general criticisms of the ELD, we will take a look at the evaluation of the Directive by the Commission. This includes both the general implementation reports and the most recent evaluation in the context of the REFIT programme. After finalising this last report in 2016, the Commission adopted a Multi-Annual Work Programme for 2017–2020, with the intention of making the ELD more fit for purpose. The relevant objectives in this work programme will be taken into consideration, including steps that have already been taken. We will mostly take a critical view on the measures intended to improve the implementation of the ELD. This will result in some ideas and suggestions for the future development of the ELD. The last part of the chapter will consist of this look forward, searching for opportunities and ways to counter the current challenges and imagining a better European framework for environmental liability.

2. EVALUATING THE ENVIRONMENTAL LIABILITY DIRECTIVE

With the introduction of the ELD, even before there had been any evaluations by the Commission, there already were various criticisms of the European framework for environmental liability. In the first place, the question was posed as to why it was necessary to establish such a regime, and why the same objective could not be achieved by the Member States (i.e. questions on subsidiarity). Moreover, if EU action was deemed necessary, why were several crucial aspects (e.g. precise definitions of certain concepts, the scope of the regime and the insertion of defences) left up to the Member States?[1] The framework established by the ELD was considered uncertain and it was suggested that the EU environmental liability regime would be a less harmonised regime than expected.[2] Furthermore, questions arose regarding the supposedly limited scope of the Directive, including criticisms of the provided exemptions and defences from the liability regime.[3]

The Commission first reported on the effectiveness of environmental remediation and the availability of financial security under the ELD in 2010.[4] In this report, the Commission noted difficulties in the transposition process and a broad divergence with regard to the key provisions, due to the framework character of the Directive. As a result of the slow transposition of the Directive, the Commission found only a limited implementation, which made it nearly impossible to examine its effectiveness. However, the report mentions that the limited number of cases could also be due to the preventive effect of the Directive, or the fact that Member States maintained existing, more stringent liability legislation. The Commission concludes this report by

---

[1]   *K. De Smedt*, Is Harmonisation Always Effective? The Implementation of the Environmental Liability Directive, EELR 2009, p. 2.

[2]   *K. De Smedt*, Environmental Liability in a Federal System. A Law and Economics Analysis, Intersentia, 2007, p. 195.

[3]   See for example: *P. Wennerås*, A Progressive Interpretation of the Environmental Liability Directive, JEEPL 2005 (4), p. 257; *G. Winter, J.H. Jans, R. Macrory & L. Krämer*, Weighing up the EC Environmental Liability Directive, Journal of Environmental Law 2008, p. 163.

[4]   Commission Report COM(2010) 581 final under Article 14(2) of Directive 2004/35/CE on the environmental liability with regard to the prevention and remedying of environmental damage.

saying that there is not enough information available to allow for concrete conclusions on the effectiveness of the Directive in remedying environmental damage. In order to remediate these findings, several measures for improved implementation and effectiveness are suggested. These measures include the promotion of information exchange and communication, the improvement of awareness and interpretation guidance from the EU level on key definitions and concepts.

On 14 April 2016, the Commission published its REFIT evaluation of the ELD, together with a second implementation report as provided for in Article 18(2) ELD.[5] The aim of the REFIT evaluation was to examine to what extent the ELD remains fit for purpose.

First, the ELD still has clear added value at the EU level. In comparison to pre-existing (national) legislation, the Directive establishes more and better restoration of damaged natural resources. It has the potential to significantly increase the level of environmental protection, by constituting a more coherent and efficient strict liability system for all Member States. Second, it is specifically valuable for transboundary water and biodiversity damage. Of course, these positive effects of the ELD could be better and might be enhanced through stricter enforcement, practical support and capacity building measures, as there are still some issues related to implementation of the Directive.

Regarding the scope of the Directive for environmental damage, the Commission answers several concerns. The exclusion of for example health and property damage can be justified by the fact that the ELD only aims to remedy purely ecological damage. However, it is argued that the scope of this ecological damage under the ELD has not entirely reached its full potential, as damage to air is not included. Extension of the scope to damage to air may help in promoting the "polluter pays" principle and could result in harmonisation with existing national legislation. Nevertheless, the Commission finds that such an extension would be technically challenging due to the nature of air pollution (i.e. it may represent diffuse pollution that cannot easily be attributed to identifiable individual polluters) and would have detrimental implications for insurance and other financial security instruments.[6]

Several detected issues can be attributed to the framework character of the ELD, which is characterised by vague provisions that leave room for flexibility and integration. Framework directives often provide for many exceptions and different options. In regard to the ELD, the divergent interpretations and

---

[5]   Commission Staff Working Document SWD(2016) 121 final on REFIT Evaluation of the Environmental Liability Directive (REFIT report).

[6]   REFIT report, *supra*, note 5 at p. 41.

application of the concept of the "significant threshold" for environmental damage should be mentioned. This is considered the main reason for the uneven application of the Directive.[7] Currently, there is a patchwork of environmental remediation across the EU, while the number of cases where the regime is applied differs greatly among Member States. Divergent application of the three significance thresholds (i.e. for biodiversity, water and land damage) might, besides hindering the overall effectiveness of the Directive, also hamper the level playing field for industries in the EU and the development of adequate financial security instruments and markets.[8]

The Commission also examines the coherence of the Directive with other parts of EU environmental law. As the ELD is a horizontal measure, i.e. a cross-cutting instrument, coherence with other pieces of EU environmental legislation is very relevant and necessary. The Commission concludes that the ELD is mostly coherent with other pieces of EU environmental legislation. However, several potential coherence issues should be investigated further, particularly in regards to the Habitats Directive. These particular problems could be found in the relationship between the significance threshold (as provided in the ELD) and the habitat deterioration and significant species disturbance (as provided in Article 6(2) Habitats Directive), and between the geographical reference and similar concepts of "favourable conservation status" in both Directives.[9]

In the REFIT check, the Commission already mentions the need to clarify the notion of the significance threshold or to be more precise about the three significance thresholds for biodiversity, water and land damage. This could resolve the wide differences that currently exist due to the lack of common understanding and uniform application.[10] Besides meeting the need for clarification and more even application of the Directive, this could also counter the potential coherence issues.

We could summarise that the main challenges that remain for the ELD concern both practical issues, i.e. the low availability of data on ELD cases and the low awareness of the Directive, and content-related issues, i.e. ambiguity around key concepts and definitions, potential coherence problems and exceptions and defences to the scope of environmental damage and strict liability. Furthermore, the evaluations note the insolvency of operators in cases of costly environmental remediation. In addition, it is interesting to note that the issues that came to light in the 2010 evaluation still existed during the REFIT check, and no remedial actions had been taken yet.

---

[7]   Commission Report COM(2016) 204 final under Article 18(2) of Directive 2004/35/EC on environmental liability with regard to the prevention and remedying of environmental damage, p. 5.
[8]   REFIT report, *supra*, note 5 at p. 43.
[9]   Id. at pp. 52–53.
[10]   Id. at p. 42.

3. THE MULTI-ANNUAL WORK PROGRAMME: CHALLENGES AND OPPORTUNITIES

Based on the findings in the REFIT evaluation, the Commission adopted a Multi-Annual Work Programme (MAWP) for the period 2017–2020. The aim of this programme is to address the issues that were identified in the REFIT check, such as clear knowledge gaps and implementation deficiencies, and boost the application of the ELD. The ultimate goal is of course the reduction and possibly the prevention of future environmental damage. The three priority working areas of the MAWP are improvement of the evidence base for the evaluation of the ELD, support of the implementation of the ELD and promotion of the availability of financial security for ELD liabilities across the EU.[11]

First, improving the evidence base should allow for a better assessment of the implementation of the ELD and whether it achieves its objectives. Furthermore, it can show how Member States implement the provisions and aid in discovering existing implementation gaps. This includes questions on the scope of strict liability and environmental damage and the definitions and concepts (to ensure coherence with other EU legislation).[12] It will also contribute to the next REFIT evaluation which will take place between 2021 and 2023. Specific action that has been taken is the development of a concept for evidence gathering, with the objective to develop a comprehensive information system, including environmental liability cases from across the EU.[13] This concept was to be tested in several Member States in 2017 and implemented in 2018; however, it is unclear whether further steps have been taken.

Second, the Commission intends to support tools and measures for more even and increasing implementation of the ELD. In this work area, the focus is on the following EU measures: guidance or interpretative notice of key issues, training programmes and helpdesks for practitioners. These measures should be complemented by national efforts in the Member States, for example supporting implementation with proactive initiatives, reviewing the interpretation of the key provisions and exchanging experiences, data and practices.[14] In light of this second working area, a Common Understanding Document has been drafted, which investigates the different interpretations of the key concepts and puts forth best practices in Member States.[15]

---

[11]   Multi-Annual ELD Work Programme for the period 2017–2020, Making the Environmental Liability Directive More Fit for Purpose (rev. version 28 February 2017), p. 8 (MAWP).
[12]   Id. at p. 9.
[13]   See section 4 of this chapter.
[14]   MAWP, *supra*, note 11 at p. 10.
[15]   See section 4 of this chapter.

The third work area focuses on ensuring sufficient availability and demand for financial security to cover ELD liabilities.[16] This third aspect will not be examined further in this chapter.

On a positive note, the MAWP clearly defines the issues found in the REFIT evaluation and suggests practical initiatives to resolve them. It is a collaborative effort between the Commission, the Member States and other stakeholder experts, combined with the ELD Expert Group.[17] This shows both the willingness for action at the EU level, and the consideration of Member States' interests and input. Concerning the proposed actions, the work programme does not currently provide a revision of the text of the Directive, as this was not yet deemed necessary based on the findings in the 2016 evaluation. It is possible that a review will be found useful based on future evaluations; however, the Commission has chosen to capitalise on existing legislation, without introducing substantive changes or costly new requirements.

On the other hand, several criticisms can already be brought up. The MAWP is non-binding and informal, which allows for a flexible and pragmatic approach, but may also diminish its value and practical implications. The work programme covers the entire period from 2017 to 2020, but it only provides an overview of the activities for 2017 and 2018. The original intent was to lay down the activities for 2019 and 2020 in a later document, building upon the first results. This is a logical decision, seeing as it is a rolling work programme that is open for annual review and can be adapted according to interim results and discovered needs. However, this type of programme requires timely action in order to attain its objectives. Currently, the specific activities for the years 2019 and 2020 have not yet been communicated.[18] Furthermore, no reports are available that contain results of previous actions, or show any (positive) developments in the implementation of the ELD.[19] In addition, no yearly revisions of the MAWP have been published, even though the initial idea was to update the programme annually to adapt to changing developments, growing knowledge and new needs.

4. UNLOCKING THE DIRECTIVE'S FULL POTENTIAL

Based on the Commission's evaluations, we can conclude that the ELD has aided in improving the level of environmental protection in the EU to a limited

---

[16] MAWP, *supra*, note 11 at p. 12.
[17] This informal expert group has been meeting twice a year since the adoption of the ELD, with the intention to support the implementation process of the ELD.
[18] This chapter was finalised on 1 March 2019.
[19] However, several studies resulting from an external service contract were published in 2017. They are discussed in section 4 of this chapter.

degree in comparison to the situation before transposition. However, the Directive has not yet fulfilled its potential. The varying interpretations of definitions and specific terms affect the implementation of the Directive, including its effectiveness and coherence with other EU (environmental) legislation. In its MAWP, the Commission provides several options to improve the application of the ELD and aid in attaining its goals.

In order to support the implementation of the MAWP during the first two years, the Commission has carried out a study, based on an external service contract.[20] This project was aimed at addressing the three main barriers for implementation of the ELD (i.e. insufficient evidence base for evaluation, lack of clarity regarding key concepts and lack of knowledge on the ELD at the national level). In order to resolve these issues and attain better implementation, the main objectives of the project were the development of a prototype for a register to gather information on ELD cases across the Member States, the development of a Common Understanding Document on key concepts and the review and suggestions for training and capacity building measures.[21] The results of this project can be consulted online.[22]

In order to reach the first objective, an ELD information system was developed to gather and present information on the implementation of the Directive in all its aspects. The proposed system goes further than the initial scope, which only included present data on ELD cases. Indeed, setting up such an information system at the EU level could lead to a more harmonised approach to collecting information, which may be beneficial to the Member States and help in implementing the ELD correctly. Available information is currently scarce at the national level and the collection efforts are lacking.[23] This information system would certainly be a step in the right direction, but it would be very ambitious to hope for short-term positive effects. However, it will aid the Commission in its next evaluations of the ELD.[24]

To tackle the aforementioned problems of effectiveness and coherence, caused by the various interpretations of definitions and specific terms among

---

[20] Support in the implementation of the REFIT actions for the Environmental Liability Directive (ELD), Specific Contract No 07.0203/2016/745366/SER/ENV.E4 implementing framework contract No ENV.D.4/FRA/2016/0003.

[21] Support for the REFIT actions for the ELD – phase 1, Annex I.A – Task 1: Conceptual and Assessment framework and ELD Information tool – Background document, 2017, p. 6 (Annex I.A).

[22] The results and conclusions of the ELD Implementation Support Contract in 2017 can be consulted on the CIRCABC website: https://circabc.europa.eu/faces/jsp/extension/wai/navigation/container.jsp.

[23] Annex I.A, *supra*, note 21 at p. 15.

[24] As mentioned above, the next evaluation of the ELD is expected to take place between 2021 and 2023.

Member States, the project aimed at developing a Common Understanding Document. This document provides a clear and objective overview of the key terms and concepts included in the ELD. It addresses those terms and concepts that either have been interpreted inconsistently across the EU, or lack coherence with related terms in other EU environmental legislation. The main aim is to give an understanding, without constituting an authoritative interpretation of EU law. The nine selected key terms and concepts are clarified and analysed, in order to reach a common understanding, while taking into account the objectives of the ELD and the current practices in the Member States.[25] This Common Understanding Document seems to be very valuable for further implementation of the Directive. It examines every concept thoroughly, scrutinising the provisions of the ELD and other pieces of EU legislation, including interpretations of the provisions by Member States, consulting the views of the Commission and combining these with examples of cases. For every concept, good practices and recommendations are provided, aiming at a more harmonised application of the ELD. Even though this document has no authoritative value, it would be useful to review and adapt it where necessary, and publish it as official guidelines helping in the interpretation of the main ELD provisions.[26] The Commission could easily incorporate this in its Environmental Implementation Review, an initiative announced in 2016, and its Better Regulation Agenda.[27] Such an initiative would address both the interpretation issues noted in the evaluation, and the possible incoherencies with other EU environmental legislation. However, providing a legally binding interpretation of EU legislation is still the exclusive competence of the European Court of Justice, as it is ultimately the Court that will ensure the uniform interpretation of EU law.[28]

A final comment can be made on the framework character of the ELD, which is seen as the source of most interpretation and application issues. The use of framework directives is central in the EU's Better Regulation Agenda and many positive traits can be attributed to this type of instrument. Framework directives offer great flexibility, including concerning their national implementation, which is necessary in the field of environmental liability, as this regime coexists with other liability instruments and provisions, both at EU and Member State level. Furthermore, flexibility when regulating environmental issues is necessary due to ecological diversity across the Member States. In environmental policy

---

[25]   Support in the implementation of REFIT actions for the ELD – phase 1, Annex II – Task 2: Common Understanding Document ELD key terms and concepts, 2017, p. 6 (Annex II).

[26]   For example: the Commission has published several guidance documents in the past, e.g. on the interpretation of key provisions of the Waste Directive, on the interpretation of project categories in annexes of the EIA Directive, etc.

[27]   Tool #39 of the Better Regulation Toolbox explicitly concerns guidance documents containing legal interpretation of EU law. See: https://ec.europa.eu/info/sites/info/files/file_import/better-regulation-toolbox-39_en_0.pdf.

[28]   Id. at p. 297.

specifically, framework directives are also seen as an instrument to establish a coherent approach, aiding in the development of an integrated environmental policy.[29] However, the ultimate implementation of the directive cannot suffer from its versatility, and the framework provided, including its broad concepts and terms, should be clear and applied evenly in all Member States. In this sense, it is a balancing act between ensuring the effective application of the environmental liability regime and leaving adequate room for national implementation of the directive. In light of this idea, it is necessary to focus current actions on the Member State level, and refrain (for now) from adapting the current EU regime.

5. CONCLUSION: TOWARDS A BETTER ENVIRONMENTAL LIABILITY DIRECTIVE?

Since the conception of the ELD and throughout the evaluations of the Directive, we can notice the same concerns and issues. Due to its framework character and lack of definitions of key concepts, the Directive has not yet achieved a harmonised environmental liability regime across the EU Member States. Furthermore, it is difficult to assess the level of implementation in the different Member States, as the knowledge base is lacking and shows a great variation in the reporting of environmental liability cases between Member States.

We can conclude that the Directive itself still seems to be very relevant and should be able to attain its goal of reducing and preventing environmental harm. Currently, there does not seem to be a need for substantive changes, such as an extension of the scope of environmental damage, as this would be very difficult to attain. However, it is mostly the implementation (including the interpretation, application and information) of the Directive that should be bettered. There are several ways in which this can be achieved.

In first place, there is a need for more information on the current implementation of the Directive, potentially including cases from all Member States. The ELD information system which was adopted in the context of the first phase of the MAWP is an ambitious step in the right direction. If the collection of information runs smoothly, it would surely benefit the knowledge on the ELD implementation, and be a good basis for further evaluations and actions.

Second, the interpretation of key terms and concepts should be harmonised across the EU. An interpretative guidance document or manual with interpretation

---

[29]   M. Bogaart, The emergence of the Framework Directive in EU environmental policy: An exploration of its function and characteristics, in M. Peeters & R. Uylenburg (eds.), EU Environmental Legislation. Legal Perspectives on Regulatory Strategies, Edward Elgar, 2014, pp. 48, 58–68.

guidelines from the Commission could help in attaining this goal. Currently, there is a comprehensive Common Understanding Document, though without any authoritative value. Publishing and disseminating a similar document with greater policy value among all Member States would be very valuable for the further implementation of the ELD. Primarily, the focus on the best practices in Member States could help in attaining a harmonised application of the Directive.

Ensuring better information and understanding of the ELD may lead to an improved and more harmonised implementation of the environmental liability regime. In addition, the proposed actions may facilitate further evaluations of the Directive, as more data on environmental liability cases would be available. This could enable the Commission to start asking different questions and, if deemed useful or necessary, research the possibility of revising the ELD. We can conclude that, although the ELD offers a decent basis and framework for an EU environmental liability regime, it is not yet possible to answer questions on a potential substantial reform of the Directive. Right now, the focus should be on the correct application of the Directive in the Member States. Looking forward, questions on revision at the EU level could be central in further evaluations, when there is more data readily available to make such a decision.

THE PERMIT DEFENCE BETWEEN THE EU ENVIRONMENTAL LIABILITY DIRECTIVE AND NATIONAL PRIVATE LAW

Some Comparative Law Remarks

Carlo MASIERI

1. INTRODUCTION: AIM AND SOME VOCABULARY

"Permit defence" is a common way of addressing Article 8(4)(a) Directive 2004/35/CE,[1] according to which:

> The Member States may allow the operator not to bear the cost of remedial actions taken pursuant to this Directive where he demonstrates that he was not at fault or negligent and that the environmental damage was caused by: (a) an emission or event expressly authorised by, and fully in accordance with the conditions of, an authorisation conferred by or given under applicable national laws and regulations which implement those legislative measures adopted by the Community specified in Annex III, as applied at the date of the emission or event.

The expression "permit defence" is clearly inspired by private law language. In particular, defences in civil trials are submissions made by the defendant, according to which "for some particular reason, plaintiff's claim did not arise, has in the interim been lost, or is barred" or through which "defendant raises an individual right which he enjoys against plaintiff".[2] In legal English, especially

---

[1] See for instance the European Commission, Report From the Commission to the Council, the European Parliament, the European Economic and Social Committee and the Committee of the Regions Under Article 14(2) of Directive 2004/35/CE on the Environmental Liability With Regard to the Prevention and Remedying of Environmental Damage, COM(2010) 581 final.

[2] See *A. Blomeyer*, Types of Relief Available, in M. Cappelletti (ed.), International Encyclopedia of Comparative Law, Volume XVI: Civil Procedure, Brill, 2014, para. 4–118, p. 58.

American legal English, there is also a "partial defence", which goes "either to part of the action or toward mitigation of damages".[3]

This chapter analyses Article 8(4) Directive 2004/35/CE in order to ascertain the relationship between EU law and private law.

After a short drafting history, the effects of the EU permit defence will be examined, highlighting the problem of distinguishing between legal and illegal activities. The chapter will then explore how private law liability systems of Member States deal with the same problem, paying particular attention to select rules of tort law and nuisance in Germany, France and Italy. Finally, national transposition and implementation measures of the EU Directive will be studied and compared with national private law rules, with the intention of measuring their coherence with the legal traditions of the respective Member States.

2. SOME DRAFTING HISTORY

The original Proposal of this Directive drafted by the European Commission (COM/2002/0017 final – COD 2002/0021) would have allowed a very broad "permit defence", as its Article 9(1)(c) merely stated that "this Directive shall not cover environmental damage or an imminent threat of such damage caused by an emission or event allowed in applicable laws and regulations, or in the permit or authorisation issued to the operator". This was partially due to lobbying efforts of industry and professional associations.

The European Parliament proposed amendments,[4] among which a new Article 11(3) stated that:

> when deciding the level of responsibility and the amount of financial compensation in respect of liability to be recovered from an operator, the competent authority and a reviewing court or tribunal shall take into account the following mitigating factors: (a) an emission or activity specifically and explicitly allowed in applicable laws and regulations, or in the permit or authorisation issued to the operator. An emission or activity and its foreseeable effects, specifically and explicitly allowed in the permit or authorisation issued to the operator, can be considered as an exemption, so far as the usual risks within the framework of the authorisation are concerned. In case of damage, the responsibility shall lie with the issuing authority.

---

[3] See Defense, in B.A. Garner (ed.), Black's Law Dictionary, Thomson Reuters, 10th ed., 2014.

[4] See Position of the European Parliament Adopted at First Reading on 14 May 2003 With a View to the Adoption of European Parliament and Council Directive 2003/ ... /EC on Environmental Liability With Regard to the Prevention and Remedying of Environmental Damage, EP-PE_TC1-COD(2002)0021.

This formulation shows the clear intent to hold someone liable in any event, whether the operator or the administrative authorities of Member States. However, it must be stressed that – notwithstanding the fact that the final text of the Directive also ultimately attaches the costs of remedial measures to EU countries – such explicit assignment of liability might not have been well received by the states.[5] Additionally, this amendment would have directly charged the government or the judiciary with the task of setting general criteria to establish liability, effectively bypassing state legislatures. As such a solution would potentially violate the principle of separation of powers in some legal systems, it would unlikely have been accepted, especially by civil law countries.

Over the course of an EU law-making co-decision process, the Council's common position[6] (positively commented by the Commission[7]) took a different path. Specifically, the Council rejected the expression providing residual liability of single public authorities, clearly established a specific reference to European legislation as the basis for the permit defence, and assigned more general power to the Member States (rather than single authorities or courts).[8] Despite the European Parliament criticising this approach – lamenting that too much discretion would have been given to the Member States[9] – the final text of the Directive allows individual Member States to adopt or reject the permit defence.

Indeed, in addition to the final version of the defence, which is written into Article 8(4)(a) Directive 2004/35/CE, Recital 20 of the very same Directive also states that "Member States may allow that operators who are not at fault or negligent shall not bear the cost of remedial measures, in situations where the damage in question is the result of emissions or events explicitly authorised".

---

5   See *A. Gouritin*, EU Environmental Law, International Environmental Law, and Human Rights Law, Brill, 2016, p. 264.

6   See Common Position 10933/5/03 REV 5.

7   See Communication SEC(2003) 1027 final.

8   See SEC(2003) 1027 final: "Article 8(4) replaces Articles 9(1)(c) and (d) and (2) of the Commission proposal and provides that Member States may allow the operator not to bear the costs in two types of situation which can be succinctly described as follows: when the damaging emission or event is expressly authorised under Community law or was not considered likely to cause environmental damage according to the state of scientific and technical knowledge." The Commission observed that "the thrust of Parliament's amendment seems to be reflected" in the new proposal, but the different setting of the rules is almost self-evident; see also Gouritin, supra, note 5 at pp. 268–269. Instead, the Commission admitted that "parts of the amendment on the liability of competent authorities and on the use of an environmental audit and management system by operators have not been incorporated in the Common Position".

9   See Recommendation for 2nd Reading Issued by the Committee on Legal Affairs and the Internal Market of the European Parliament, Document A5-0461/2003, RR/332617EN, saying that "the broad margin of discretion given to Member States by the Council will have serious repercussions on the functioning of the internal market".

3. THE EFFECTS OF THE PERMIT DEFENCE

It is undisputed that environmental damage – which is defined under this EU Directive as a harm caused by the operator to the environment – can be split into two parts. On the one hand, "'damage' means a measurable adverse change in a natural resource or measurable impairment of a natural resource service which may occur directly or indirectly" (Article 2(2) Directive 2004/35/CE). On the other, an "imminent threat of damage" is also relevant. This means that legal consequences may arise where there is "sufficient likelihood that environmental damage will occur in the near future" (Article 2(9) Directive 2004/35/CE).

This twofold nature of damage thus produces two distinct legal effects. First, "where environmental damage has not yet occurred but there is an imminent threat of such damage occurring, the operator shall, without delay, take the necessary preventive measures" (Article 5(1) Directive 2004/35/CE). It is noteworthy that such preventive measures are defined as "any measures taken in response to an event, act or omission that has created an imminent threat of environmental damage, with a view to preventing or minimising that damage" (Article 2(10) Directive 2004/35/CE). Second, only when "environmental damage has occurred" (Article 6(1) Directive 2004/35/CE), i.e. only when an "adverse change ... or a measurable impairment of a natural resource" has already effectively resulted, shall remedial measures be taken (see Articles 6(1) (b) and 7(2) Directive 2004/35/CE). Such remedial measures are "any action, or combination of actions, including mitigating or interim measures to restore, rehabilitate or replace damaged natural resources and/or impaired services, or to provide an equivalent alternative to those resources or services as foreseen in Annex II [of the Directive]" (see Article 2(1) Directive 2004/35/CE).[10]

A careful reading of the provisions reveals that the choice to employ the expression "to be liable" may prove problematic as, in common law systems, this expression typically recalls tort law remedies (in particular the obligation to pay monetary compensation in the form of damages). Here, the aims and the legal effects of environmental liability are very different from tortious liability, as long as the "remedy" means to cure rather than "to pay damages". In any event, the liable party "pays", but the form of payment changes.

Since Article 8(4) Directive 2004/35/CE makes mere reference to "remedial actions", the permit defence "allows the operator not to bear the costs of restoration, but does not exempt the operator from prevention costs".[11]

---

[10] On remedial measures see also Case C-379/08, ERG and Others [2010] ECLI:EU:C:2010:127; Case C-478/08, Buzzi Unicem and Others [2010] ECLI:EU:C:2010:129, in particular Ruling 2.

[11] See *Gouritin, supra*, note 5 at p. 263; similarly, *A. Di Landro*, La responsabilità per l'attività autorizzata nei settori dell'ambiente e del territorio, Giappichelli, 2018, p. 227. It has

An analysis of Article 5 and Recital 21 Directive 2004/35/CE is necessary to better understand how preventive measures work. Article 5(1) provides that the operator must take necessary preventive measures "[w]here environmental damage has not yet occurred but there is an imminent threat of such damage occurring, ... without delay". Paragraph 3 allows "[t]he competent authority ... at any time [to] (a) require the operator to provide information on any imminent threat of environmental damage or in suspected cases of such an imminent threat; (b) require the operator to take the necessary preventive measures; (c) give instructions to the operator to be followed on the necessary preventive measures to be taken; or (d) itself take the necessary preventive measures". Then, according to paragraph 4, "[t]he competent authority shall require that the preventive measures are taken by the operator. If the operator fails to comply with the obligations laid down in paragraph 1 or 3 (b) or (c), cannot be identified or is not required to bear the costs under this Directive, the competent authority may take these measures itself". Moreover, Recital 21 states that "[o]perators should bear the costs relating to preventive measures when those measures should have been taken as a matter of course in order to comply with the legislative, regulatory and administrative provisions regulating their activities or the terms of any permit or authorisation".

Finally, it has to be noticed that Article 8 establishes an exception to the "polluter pays" principle, as long as – pursuant to Recital 18 of the Directive – the polluter is an "operator causing environmental damage", which "should, in principle, bear the cost of the necessary ... remedial measures". At the same time, as environmental law scholars have adopted language similar to that used in private law, the EU "permit defence" and "partial defence" have the same meaning, as both only partially shield the operator from legal effects. Indeed, the operator always bears some consequences in any case, like the obligation to take preventive measures. In addition, even the obligation of taking remedial measures could initially bind the operator, as Article 8 speaks about "costs" that can also be shifted after the measures are taken.

---

to be said that the Committee on Legal Affairs and the Internal Market of the European Parliament, Document A5-0461/2003, RR/332617EN warned about this: "Operators who cannot be held liable should not be asked to take preventive or remedial action nor to advance the costs of such measures. Exceptions based on permit compliance or state of the art knowledge should have the same standing as those based on third party causation and compliance with a compulsory public order or instruction. The wording of the common position risks undermining the current permit system and the development of appropriate financial security instruments. The downgrading of the exceptions originally provided for by the Commission to factors that would diminish the costs would introduce an unacceptable element of uncertainty into production related costs (which will affect the operator's financial exposure)".

4. SOME COMPARATIVE LAW QUESTIONS ARISING FROM THE EU "PERMIT DEFENCE"

Scrutiny of permit defence under Directive 2004/35/CE raises several questions. For example, the wording of the permit defence recalls the distinction between strict liability and negligence. If the European model, generally speaking, adheres to a strict liability framework,[12] the fact that Article 8 Directive 2004/35/CE clearly refers to negligence and fault, implying that there still can be negligence even if the operator has acted according to the permit,[13] is problematic. Although this topic warrants further discussion, it is too complicated to be addressed, even superficially, in the present chapter. Instead, this chapter will focus on another aspect of the "permit defence".

The term "defence" pursuant to Article 8 is obviously related to the problem of distinguishing between legal and illegal activities. The following paragraphs will illustrate how traditional private law liability rules address this problem, highlighting the differences between Member States' legal systems. Moreover, it will be discussed whether European environmental law and private law adopt similar provisions in response to this "legality problem". Finally, national transposition and implementation measures in select national jurisdictions – specifically, in Germany, France and Italy – will be analysed to better understand if, and eventually how, the "permit defence" is applied in each of these jurisdictions.

4.1. THE GERMAN SYSTEM

Under §823 BGB, unlawfulness is a requirement of German tort law. This means that compensation depends on the establishment of harm, which must result from either a violation of a right of the defendant or of a statutory provision. Property violations provide a prime example of how such requirement is assessed, especially when it interacts with other areas of law.

For instance, §1004 BGB establishes remedies of injunction and removal in cases of interference with property. At the same time, a claim may be rejected when a duty to tolerate the interference has been established. Although the text

---

[12] Cfr. *B. Pozzo*, La nuova direttiva 2004/35 del Parlamento Europeo e del Consiglio sulla responsabilità ambientale in materia di prevenzione e riparazione del danno, Riv. giur. amb. 2006 (1), p. 6; Case C-378/08, ERG and Others [2010] ECLI:EU:C:2010:126, para. 63: "In the case of the occupational activities falling within Annex III to Directive 2004/35, environmental liability on the part of operators active in those areas is strict liability".

[13] See *L. Bergkamp & A. van Bergeijk*, Exceptions and defences, in L. Bergkamp & B. Goldsmith (eds.), The EU Environmental Liability Directive: A Commentary, Oxford University Press, 2013, paras. 4.45–4.46.

of this paragraph does not refer directly to unlawfulness, according to most scholars, the interference is deemed illegal when these remedies are issued.[14] Compliance with public law by the defendant is not always relevant. Thus, some activities – despite having been performed after a permit has been issued – are not protected by a consequential defence from actions arising from §1004 BGB. For example, industrial property permits, building permits and police permits did not shield a club from the application of §1004 BGB.[15]

The introduction of gases, steam, smells, smoke, soot, warmth, noise, vibrations and similar influences emanating from another plot of land is regulated by §906 BGB. If these phenomena significantly interfere with the owner's property, such owner is entitled to damages or may seek an injunction. German courts have been assessing these nuisance cases in a way that does not put their decisions in excessive conflict with public law legality thresholds.[16] In addition, the legislature takes into great consideration statutes, statutory orders and administrative provisions that have been issued under §48 of the Bundes-Immissionsschutzgesetz (BImSchG, Federal Environmental Impact Protection Act) and represent the state of the art. If the wording of §906(1) does not automatically imply shifts of the burden of proof, compliance with public law thresholds is considered strong evidence for dismissing the case. On the other hand, non-compliance is considered strong evidence in favour of the plaintiff's case.[17] Even if the defendant shows that he has complied with public law regulations, the plaintiff may nonetheless offer further evidence of the significance of the impairment. Accordingly, there is no defence in such cases. If the defendant uses the land in compliance with local custom, a duty to tolerate alleged interference pursuant to §906 (2) BGB[18] may be established. In these cases, even if the activity is held to be perfectly legal under private law[19] and no injunction is issued, a defendant may nonetheless be ordered to compensate the plaintiff. Once again, public law thresholds play a relevant role in decisions whether to issue the aforementioned compensation.[20] And once again, a permit does not exclude application of any specific remedy. Indeed, this was the case when a shooting range, which was built in compliance with the required building permit, polluted the ground with lead powder.[21] These rules are also applied

---

[14] See *C. Baldus*, §1004 BGB, in R. Gaier (ed.), Münchener Kommentar zum BGB, Volume 7, 7th ed., 2017, Rn. 192–198.

[15] See BGH, urt. vom 27.5.1959 – V ZR 78/58 (KG), in NJW 1959, 2013.

[16] See *B. Brückner*, §903 BGB, in R. Gaier (ed.), Münchener Kommentar zum BGB, Volume 7, 7th ed., 2017, Rn. 60; *B. Brückner*, §906 BGB, in R. Gaier (ed.), Münchener Kommentar zum BGB, Volume 7, 7th ed., 2017, Rn 8, 19.

[17] See *B. Brückner*, §906 BGB, *supra*, note 16 at Rn. 219.

[18] Id. at Rn. 93.

[19] Id. at Rn. 183.

[20] Id. at Rn. 186.

[21] See BGH, urt. vom 20.4.1990 – V ZR 282/88 (Stuttgart), in NJW 1990, 1910.

in tort actions arising from the very same facts, in order to run the illegality check under §823 BGB.[22]

According to other statutory provisions, a number of permits works as defence from some private law effects. Among these,[23] §14 BImSchG shields the defendant that has been issued with a permit that allows installations on his property from injunctions by private law courts to cease activity.[24] However, the plaintiff may still bring action against the defendant for forcing him to take some precautions, or at least for damages. This kind of provision stems from a traditional idea of German law that investments in activities that have already been deemed legal by public authorities must be protected.[25] A defence seldom excludes damages claims; §16 Wasserhaushaltsgesetz (WHG, Federal Water Management Act) is an exception.

Lastly, §1 Umwelthaftungsgesetz (UmweltHG, Environmental Liability Act) is a major statute that regulates damages under private law. In particular, it applies to damages arising from certain types of installations, providing for strict liability when the environmental impacts caused by specific plants result in the death or personal injury, or in damage to individual property.[26] Permits are also influential under this statute. Specifically, they do not conclusively exclude liability, but set aside the presumption of causation in favour of the plaintiff that would have otherwise been granted by §6 UmweltHG. In other words, an installation that is likely to have caused harm is presumed to have effectively caused such harm where its operation was not performed in compliance with the permit conditions.[27]

In 2007, Germany took measures to transpose and implement the EU Directive by enacting the Gesetz über die Vermeidung und Sanierung von Umweltschäden (Law on the Prevention and Remedying of Environmental Damage, also referred to as the Umweltschadensgesetz, USchadG). An official EU Commission report indicates that German legislature decided not to expressly allow the permit defence from environmental liability.[28] This is at least questionable. The Umweltschadensgesetz establishes that a "liable person" is "any natural or legal person who carries on or is in charge of a professional

---

22 See *Brückner, supra*, note 17 at Rn. 224.
23 For a list, see E. *Rehbinder*, §14 BImSchG, in M. Beckmann et al. (eds.), Landmann/Romer Umweltrecht, 85. EL Dezember 2017, Rn. 4–7.
24 Even if it is not mentioned by the statute, the activity should comply with the permit as a condition for these private law effects, see id. at Rn. 22–25.
25 For the historical background of §14, see id. at Rn. 3.
26 See id. at Rn. 1, 4.
27 See G. *Hager*, §6 UmweltHG, in M. Beckmann et al. (eds.), Landmann/Romer Umweltrecht, 85. EL Dezember 2017, Rn. 3, 14, 39 ff.
28 See European Commission, Report from the Commission to the Council, the European Parliament, the European Economic and Social Committee and the Committee of the Regions Under Article 14(2) of Directive 2004/35/CE on the Environmental Liability With Regard to the Prevention and Remedying of Environmental Damage, COM(2010) 581 final.

activity, including the holder of an authorisation or a permit for such activity" (§2 no. 3 USchadG), but some "permit defence" seems to be allowed. According to §9(1) USchadG, the Federal Government has attributed the application of Article 8(4) EU Directive to the *Länder*. This means that the "permit defence" provided by EU environmental liability law may be granted at a local level. Thus, we cannot clearly affirm that Germany, as a federation of *Länder*, applies Article 8: it depends on the specific locality. Moreover, it is noteworthy that German legal scholars find that this defence does not amount to a full legalisation of the operator's acts, which cause some effects anyway (e.g. information and avoidance obligations).[29]

4.2. THE FRENCH SYSTEM

Article 1240 of the current version of the Code civil states that "Any act of man, which causes damage to another, shall oblige the person by whose fault it occurred to repair it". Additionally, Article 1241 provides that "Everyone is responsible for the damage he has caused not only by his own actions, but also by his negligence or imprudence". French statutory law does not expressly require unlawfulness as a requirement of torts. Still, scholars believe that *illicéité* is an objective element that implies *faute* under Article 1240. However, when it comes to identifying it, such unlawfulness stems from the violation of either single legal obligation or a general duty of care.[30] Nonetheless, the violation of any right or interest protected by the law may result in tort action.

When it comes to property, it is interesting that the French legislature has not enacted any specific provision regulating nuisance cases. Consequently, scholars and courts have had to develop doctrines without referring to the Civil Code or to a specific statute.[31] Under the *trouble de voisinage* doctrine, the acts of a defendant who abnormally disturbs his neighbour can be perfectly legal – in the sense that they represent a legal way of exploiting his piece of land – and not characterised by *faute*.[32] However, the same defendant may still be held liable.[33] This is because, to use French legal reasoning, the "chain of legality" that connects public and private law (public law > individual permit > general lawfulness of the acts compliant with the permit) is broken. Indeed,

---

29 See *A. Wittmann*, §1 USchadG, in M. Beckmann et al. (eds.), Landmann/Romer Umweltrecht, 85. EL Dezember 2017, Rn. 25.
30 See *P. Jourdain*, Art. 1382 à 1386 – Fasc. 120-10: DROIT À RÉPARATION – Responsabilité fondée sur la faute – Notion de faute: contenu commun à toutes les fautes, in JCl. Civil Code, 2011, para. 13.
31 See *V. Gaillot-Mercier*, Troubles de voisinage, in Dalloz.fr – Répertoire de droit civil, 2002 (act. Janv. 2019), paras. 24–25.
32 Id. at paras. 23, 27–28.
33 Id. at paras. 3–4.

case law illustrates that permits are always issued subject to the rights of third parties,[34] as recalled also by particular statutes, like Article L. 514-19 of the Environmental Code.

Therefore, building permits do not grant defence from nuisance claims.[35] Even if a permit has been issued for the construction of a garage, its building could nonetheless represent an abnormal disturbance for neighbours.[36] Likewise in cases of industrial authorisations. Thus, a pig farm that had been authorised under administrative law can nonetheless be liable from a private law point of view for olfactory nuisance.[37] The remedies issued by the courts in these cases are many: compensation, injunction, *astreintes*, etc.

Article L. 112-16 of the Code de la construction et de l'habitation (Construction and Housing Code) provides an exception. Under this article no compensation should be given to the plaintiff where some activities that are legal under public law are already being performed by the defendant. This is the so-called "pre-occupation exception", which the defendant can enjoy if his activity started before the plaintiff began dwelling there, and if the very same activity has always been deemed to be legal. But when it comes to the environment, the aforementioned provision should be interpreted as it "does not preclude an action in liability based on fault",[38] due to the higher level of protection granted by the Charte de l'environnement (Environmental Chart).[39]

As regards French law deriving from the EU Environmental Liability Directive, only Law no. 2008-757[40] and Decree n° 2009-468[41] are official French "transposition measures communicated by the Member State" to the European Union. Notably, these statutes do not mention the permit defence pursuant to Article 8(4) EU Directive at all. Finally, further relevant environmental legislation has been enacted in the field of private law: Law no. 2016-1087 inserted a new *Titre* (Title) on the *réparation du préjudice écologique* (ecological damage remediation) into the Code civil, and the *"préjudice écologique"* regulated thereby seems very similar in some aspects to environmental damage in Directive 2004/35/CE.[42] However, not even this statute mentions the permit defence.

---

[34] See cases referred to by G. *Courtieu*, Art. 1382 à 1386 – Fasc. 265-10: RÉGIMES DIVERS. – Troubles de voisinage, in JCl. Civil Code, para. 84.

[35] See *Gaillot-Mercier*, *supra*, note 31 at paras. 17, 56.

[36] See Cass. 3e civ., 20 juill. 1994, no. 92-21.801, Numéro JurisData: 1994-001365.

[37] See Cass. 1re civ., 13 juill. 2004, no. 02-15.176, Numéro JurisData: 2004-024670.

[38] See Cons. const., 8 avr. 2011, no. 2011-116 QPC, ECLI:FR:CC:2011:2011.116.QPC.

[39] Loi constitutionnelle no. 2005-205 du 1er mars 2005 relative à la Charte de l'environnement.

[40] Loi no. 2008-757 du 1er août 2008 relative à la responsabilité environnementale et à diverses dispositions d'adaptation au droit communautaire dans le domaine de l'environnement.

[41] Décret no. 2009-468 du 23 avril 2009 relatif à la prévention et à la réparation de certains dommages causés à l'environnement.

[42] See L. *Neyret*, La consécration du préjudice écologique dans le code civil, in Rec. Dalloz 2017 (17), p. 924.

4.3. THE ITALIAN SYSTEM

Article 2043 of the Italian Civil Code represents a general tort law provision and establishes that, in order to grant compensation, an illicit harm must be caused by the defendant. Furthermore, such harm must be committed with either negligence or intent. Still, it is significant that several strict liability rules are established by other articles of the Code, or by additional statutes. Italian scholars and courts have construed the *danno illecito* requirement so that a violation of any interest protected by the law implies tort liability.[43] Again, property violations may give rise to a number of remedies under private law.

It is undisputed that the Italian Civil Code was greatly influenced by the French Civil Code, which does not expressly govern nuisance cases. Thus, the Italian discipline drew from the German experience and the ideas of von Jhering.[44] According to Article 844 Civil Code, *immissioni* (nuisance) that are considered tolerable according to a "usual" standard are deemed legal and may persist as long as they do not exceed the threshold of "normal tolerability". If *immissioni* exceed this threshold, aggrieved parties may be entitled to compensation and/or injunction.[45] In any case, Italian scholars[46] do not consider these "intolerable *immissioni*" illegal, especially when they just end in compensation for the plaintiff: in this case, defendant has to pay a sum for the taking of another's property or – which is the same – give compensation for externalities.

When activities also endanger human health and the environment, there is a tendency in current case law to regard the violation of public law thresholds as intolerable,[47] and to issue injunctions under the nuisance doctrine. Still, compliance with thresholds does not mean that the defendant is shielded from private law remedies.[48] The authorisation of an activity under public law is not relevant for the application of Article 844.[49] Thus, a properly

---

[43] See *C. Salvi*, Responsabilità extracontrattuale (dir. vig.), in Enciclopedia del diritto, Volume XXXIX, Giuffrè, 1988, p. 1189. On *ingiustizia del danno* see also *R. Sacco*, L'ingiustizia di cui all'art. 2043, in Foro pad. 1960, I, p. 1420; *P. Schlesinger*, L'ingiustizia del danno, in Jus 1960, p. 366; *S. Rodotà*, Il problema della responsabilità civile, Giuffrè, 1964; *G. Cian*, Antigiuridicità e colpevolezza, Cedam, 1966; for some examples of *ingiustizia*, see *F. Gazzoni*, Manuale di diritto privato, Edizioni Scientifiche Italiane, 2013, pp. 716–722.

[44] See *A. Gambaro*, Il diritto di proprietà, in Trattato Cicu-Messineo, Giuffrè, 1995, pp. 498–501; *A. Gambaro*, La proprietà: beni, proprietà, possesso, in Trattato Iudica-Zatti, Giuffrè, 2017, p. 274.

[45] See *A. Gambaro*, Il diritto di proprietà, *supra*, note 44 at p. 505; *A. Gambaro*, La proprietà: beni, proprietà, possesso, *supra*, note 44 at pp. 276–277.

[46] See *A. Gambaro*, Il diritto di proprietà, *supra*, note 44 at p. 521.

[47] See *A. Gambaro*, La proprietà: beni, proprietà, possesso, *supra*, note 44 at pp. 282–283.

[48] See Cass. civ., sez. III, 16 ottobre 2015, no. 20927, in *DeJure*.

[49] See *Gambaro*, Il diritto di proprietà, *supra*, note 44 at pp. 511–512.

authorised heliport[50] or bakery[51] can still cause *immissioni intollerabili* to the neighbours according to private law standards. From this perspective, the Italian solution seems to be more similar to the French experience rather than to the German one.

Article 308 para. 5 of the Codice dell'ambiente (Environmental Code) contains a "permit defence". This part of the Italian transposition and implementation measure of the EU Directive has been poorly drafted, as it reads:

> The operator may not bear the cost of *comma* 5 measures ... where he demonstrates that he was not at fault or negligent and that the preventive measure has been taken due to: a) an emission or event expressly authorised by an authorisation given under applicable laws and regulations which implement those of the Community specified in Annex 5 to Part VI of this decree, as applied at the date of the emission or event, and fully in accordance with the conditions thereby stated.

Firstly, "*comma* 5 measures" means "the measures regulated by paragraph 5" of Article 308 itself, not of a different article. Thus, the costs that "the operatory may not bear" are not expressly defined. Second, the paragraph refers to a "preventive measure" that "has been taken". This has led some commenters to believe that this "permit defence" works as a shield from the costs of preventive measures,[52] whereas other scholars seem to relate the defence only to remedial measures.[53] Even if the latter interpretation is inconsistent with the wording of Article 308, it is preferable because any other interpretation would conflict with Article 8(4) of the EU Directive (which expressly and exclusively refers to "remedial actions"). It is common knowledge that Italian national law cannot contrast with EU law, and that, should contrast between national and EU law exist, Italian judges must apply EU law over national law.

5. CONCLUSION

The idea that compliance with public law excludes legal consequences under the private law of EU Member States is unpersuasive, as property remedies issued

---

[50] See Cass. civ., sez. II, 14 agosto 1990, no. 8271, in *DeJure*.

[51] See Cass. civ., sez. II, 18 maggio 2015, no. 10169, in *DeJure*.

[52] For *M. Benozzo*, La disciplina del danno ambientale, in A. Germano et al., Commento al codice dell'ambiente, Giappichelli, 2013, pp. 994, 996 this defence would be related only to preventive measures; *S. Masini*, Art. 308 cod. amb., in L. Costato & F. Pellizzer (eds.), Commentario breve al codice dell'ambiente, Cedam, 2012, p. 1118 seems to exonerate the operator from all the legal consequences of environmental liability, and in any case from costs related to preventive measures.

[53] See *B. Pozzo*, La responsabilità per danno ambientale, in S. Nespor & A.L. De Cesaris (eds.), Codice dell'ambiente, Giuffrè, 2009, p. 875.

under private law and environmental public law differ in aim and instrument. When it comes to protecting the individual property of neighbours, private law courts do not base their judgments only on the fact that the harming activity has been authorised. It must be stressed that the public administration cannot authorise an operator to damage neighbours and at the same time exempt him from liability, as such allowance would result in expropriation without compensation (which is frowned upon in European legal culture). Thus, private law provides different standards from those of public law: "relevant interference" or "abnormal disturbance" or "intolerable nuisance". In these cases, permits do not usually play a significant role, as thresholds are frequently set directly by statutes or regulations. On the other hand, permits are very relevant under public law because they require the public administration to assess standards directly related to the environment, not to individual properties. This separation between private law and public law functions differently in each of the legal systems that have been analysed here. Germany is characterised by a very strong importance of unlawfulness as a basis for private law remedies; nonetheless, the "permit defence" seldom shields the defendant from each and any private law consequences, and this is notably due to public law statutes.[54] In the French and Italian systems, public law and private law standards run on parallel lines, except for Italian cases in which health and the environment tend to be protected with property remedies.

In any event, national private law and the EU Environmental Liability Directive seem to share a common aspect: neither appear to consider permits a general exemption from any legal consequences provided by their respective liability schemes. Additionally, given the differences between private law legislation in the aforementioned European countries, allowing Member States to decide whether to adopt the Article 8 "permit defence" is laudable.

Finally, as for transposition and implementation measures, while the German and French statutes are consistent with their legal traditions, the Italian solution seems to be rather innovative, albeit full of interpretative problems.

---

[54] E.g. §14 BImSchG.

THE JURISPRUDENTIAL CONFIGURATION OF THE "POLLUTER PAYS" PRINCIPLE

A Critical Assessment

Theodoros G. Iliopoulos

1. INTRODUCTION

Almost 15 years after the enactment of the Environmental Liability Directive (ELD),[1] quite a few lacunae in the established Union liability regime have been highlighted. One can observe significant discrepancies among national environmental liability frameworks that implement the ELD, which to a large extent can be attributed to a certain confusion about how the ELD applies, as well as about the meaning of the concepts and the scope of the exceptions.[2]

Within this context, an important issue that remains unsettled is the potential extension of liability beyond the operators of the activity that brought about the pollution and the environmental damage. More specifically, the Court of Justice of the European Union (CJEU) has recently dealt with the question whether national legislation that holds the owners of contaminated sites liable for the pollution that occupational operators caused while using their land can be in accordance with the ELD.

This problem has its roots in the fact that the ELD is explicitly based on the "polluter pays" principle (PPP).[3] In this regard, it is controversial to decide whether, and for the sake of a more stringent system of environmental protection, Member States are allowed to extend liability beyond the apparent polluters so as to cover more actors. Of course, as might be expected, the problem is exacerbated if the actual polluters are untraceable or insolvent.

---

[1]   Directive 2004/35/CE of the European Parliament and of the Council of 21 April 2004 on environmental liability with regard to the prevention and remedying of environmental damage, OJ 2004 L 143/56.

[2]   *K. Pouikli*, Overview of the Implementation of the Directive 2004/35/EC on Environmental Liability with Regard to the Prevention and Remedying of Environmental Damage in Europe, Desalination and Water Treatment 2016 (25), p. 11520.

[3]   See Directive 2004/35/CE, Articles 1 and 3; see also Recitals 2 and 18.

Accordingly, this chapter examines whether national environmental liability regimes that extend liability are in conformity with the PPP, as enshrined in the ELD.

In dealing with this topic, this chapter adopts a jurisprudence-based approach. The case law of the CJEU is examined so as to elucidate the notion of the PPP in the field of environmental liability. The emphasis is placed on a triad of relatively recent CJEU cases that deal with the PPP and the extension of environmental liability. This triad consists of the landmark case *ERG*,[4] the *Fipa* case,[5] and the most recent case, *TTK*.[6] Particular attention is called to the judgment in *TTK*, which raises significant issues, but is still not as thoroughly scrutinised by scientific legal literature.

In terms of structure, section 2 presents the PPP as an economics principle that is translated into EU law. Section 3 presents the core content of the PPP, as clarified by landmark CJEU cases. Next, section 4 analyses the possibility of extending environmental liability beyond polluters and holding landowners liable for the pollution that occupational operators caused while using their land. Section 5 assesses whether Member States can diverge from the PPP and section 6 examines certain legal problems associated with the application of the PPP. Last, section 7 concludes the chapter.

2. THE PPP, A LAW AND ECONOMICS PRINCIPLE TRANSLATED INTO EU LAW

The PPP originates from the environmental economics and, more specifically, from the negative externalities theory. The concept of negative externalities relates to the fact that economic activities might entail unintentional negative effects, to wit costs, for parties not involved in them and for society in general.

Pollution is a typical example of a negative externality. Indeed, the polluters' actions impose a certain harm on third parties; for instance, an economic operator runs a factory in order to produce a certain good, but the emissions this activity entails also lead to the deterioration of the quality of the air, to the deterioration of the health of the area's residents, to the decrease in the value of the land near the factory, etc. What is particularly interesting from an economics point of view is that such social costs are often "unaccounted for by market

---

4   Case C-378/08, ERG and Others [2010] ECR I-1919.
5   Case C-534/13, Fipa Group and Others [2015] published in the electronic Reports of Cases, ECLI:EU:C:2015:140.
6   Case C-129/16, Túrkevei Tejtermelő Kft. [2017] published in the electronic Reports of Cases, ECLI:EU:C:2017:547.

valuations",[7] which means they are not reflected in the price, the demand and the supply taking place in the market. Therefore, these costs are external in the sense that they are not borne by the polluters, but by the citizens, the taxpayers or the society. Still, they should be internalised into the structure of the costs of the polluters' economic activity.[8] This internalisation of negative externalities serves equity, but also serves social welfare. If polluters are burdened with the full costs accompanying their activity, they are expected to adjust their activities accordingly (output, use of resources, production techniques and technologies, investments in research and development, etc.).

This internalisation of external costs is what the PPP aims for, by requiring the polluters to compensate for the external costs they cause. In this regard, the PPP can be put into practice through *ex ante* means, like taxation, or through *ex post* means.[9] An environmental liability regime belongs to the latter group, but it can also contribute to prevention. This is because potential polluters are expected to be more cautious in order to avoid being held financially liable in the future.[10]

But the PPP is also a legal principle, and a crucial one for environmental liability. As early as since 1985 and the Single European Act, primary EU law has explicitly set down that the PPP is one of the bases of EU environmental policy;[11] this declaration is now found in Article 191(2) of the Treaty on the Functioning of the European Union (TFEU).[12] However, Article 191(2) TFEU does not directly address Member States. Thus, the EU PPP can be applied by a national court only in connection with a specific act of secondary law that gives a concrete expression to it, like *inter alia* the Waste Framework

---

[7] F.M. *Bator*, The Anatomy of Market Failure, The Quarterly Journal of Economics 1958 (3), pp. 351, 358.

[8] E. *Hutchinson*, Principle of Microeconomics, University of Victoria, 2017, pp. 294 et seq.; S.A. *Greenlaw et al.*, Principles of Microeconomics 2e, OpenStax, 2017, pp. 275 et seq.; P. *Dorman*, Microeconomics, Springer, 2014, pp. 315 et seq.; I.A. *Moosa & V. Ramiah*, The Costs and Benefits of Environmental Regulation, Edward Elgar, 2014, pp. 32 et seq.; H.R. *Varian*, Intermediate Microeconomics, W.W. Norton & Company, 8th ed., 2010, pp. 645 et seq.; P. *Bohm*, External Economies, in S.N. Durlauf & L.E. Blume (eds.), The New Palgrave Dictionary of Economics, Palgrave Macmillan, 2008, pp. 1–5; S.C. *Hackett*, Environmental and Natural Resources Economics, M.E. Sharpe, 6th ed., 2006, pp. 391 et seq.

[9] The fathers of the debate about externalities and the means for tackling them are Arthur Pigou and Ronald Coase. They have adopted different stances, with the former arguing in favour of taxation and the latter supporting that the problem will be best solved through transactions that will bring interested parties together and make them reach an agreement about the compensation polluters should pay. See A.C. *Pigou*, Economics of Welfare, MacMillan and Co., 1920; R.H. *Coase*, The Problem of Social Cost, The Journal of Law and Economics, 1960 (3), pp. 1–41.

[10] See also Directive 2004/35/CE, Recital 2.

[11] Single European Act, OJ 1985 L 169/1, Article 130r(2).

[12] Consolidated version of the Treaty on the Functioning of the European Union, OJ 2016 C 202/47.

Directive,[13] the Water Framework Directive,[14] the Industrial Emissions Directive[15] and the ELD.[16]

Focusing on the ELD, it has established "a framework of environmental liability based on the 'polluter-pays' principle, to prevent and remedy environmental damage".[17] The Directive applies to environmental, water or land damage caused by an occupational activity.[18] The operators who cause such damage or the imminent threat of it are to be held financially liable for the cost of the necessary preventive or remedial measures.[19] But, according to Article 4(5) ELD, for the polluter to be identified and the PPP and the liability framework to be applied, a causal link between the activity and the damage or threat should be established.[20] At the same time, according to Article 16 ELD, Member States are allowed to maintain or adopt "more stringent provisions in relation to the prevention and remedying of environmental damage".

At this point, the question raised is whether the above formulations lead to the conclusion that the ELD allows a divergence from the causal link requirement and the PPP. In order to answer this question, the following sections place the emphasis on CJEU case law. Accordingly, section 3 examines the content of the PPP as interpreted by the CJEU.

3. THE PPP THROUGH CASE LAW

The first time the CJEU was asked to interpret the PPP was about 20 years ago, in the *Standley* case.[21] The case related to a preliminary question about the validity of the Directive 91/676/EEC,[22] which required Member States to take action to reduce water pollution caused or induced by nitrates from agricultural sources. The National Farmers' Union of England and Wales argued that the Directive was infringing the PPP, as expressed in primary EU law. More specifically, they argued that while the concentration of nitrates in waters is ascribable to various

---

[13]   Directive 2008/98/EC of the European Parliament and of the Council of 19 November 2008 on waste and repealing certain Directives, OJ 2008 L 312/3.

[14]   Directive 2000/60/EC of the European Parliament and of the Council of 23 October 2000 establishing a framework for Community action in the field of water policy, OJ 2000 L 327/1.

[15]   Directive 2010/75/EU of the European Parliament and of the Council of 24 November 2010 on industrial emissions (integrated pollution prevention and control), OJ 2010 L 334/17.

[16]   See Case C-129/16, *supra*, note 6 at para. 37 and the case law cited.

[17]   Directive 2004/35/CE, Article 1.

[18]   Id., Article 3.

[19]   Id., Recitals 2 and 18.

[20]   See also Recital 13 ELD, which links the establishment of the causal link with the effectiveness of the environmental liability regime.

[21]   Case C-293/97, Standley [1999] ECR I-2603.

[22]   Council Directive 91/676/EEC of 12 December 1991 concerning the protection of waters against pollution caused by nitrates from agricultural sources, OJ 1991 L 375/1.

sources, the Directive at issue put the burden of reducing pollution solely on the agricultural sector. The CJEU found no infringement of the PPP. In point of fact, it was elucidated that the Directive required that farmers, to wit the polluters, should only bear the burden of eliminating the pollution they have contributed to. In accordance with the PPP, they should not bear the costs of the pollution they are not responsible for. In this sense, and as stated by the CJEU, the PPP "reflects the principle of proportionality".[23] Therefore, it was recognised that the extent to which an actor has contributed to the pollution determines the attribution of that actor's responsibility. This can be regarded as implying that the establishment of causality is inherent to the PPP. Still, the CJEU did not refer to causality.

The contribution to pollution as a prerequisite for attributing responsibility has been confirmed in a series of CJEU judgments interpreting the Waste Framework Directive.[24] The question at issue in these cases was not the limitation of an actor's responsibility, like in *Standley*, but the coverage of more actors by the waste management liability regime.

In Article 14, the Waste Framework Directive states that:

1. In accordance with the polluter-pays principle, the costs of waste management shall be borne by the original waste producer or by the current or previous waste holders.
2. Member States may decide that the costs of waste management are to be borne partly or wholly by the producer of the product from which the waste came and that the distributors of such product may share these costs.

In applying this article, national courts have several times submitted preliminary questions to the CJEU in order to clarify who can be considered a "waste producer" and "holder", as well as what the requirements are for applying the waste management liability regime. In this regard, in 2004, in *Van de Walle*, the CJEU held that the manager of a service station was responsible for the contamination caused by the leak of hydrocarbons from the station's storage facilities. This was because the manager was regarded as the producer and the holder of the waste. But if "the leak of hydrocarbons [could be] attributed to a disregard of contractual obligations by the petroleum undertaking, which [supplied] that service station, or to any actions which could render that undertaking liable", then the national judges could hold the hydrocarbons' supplier liable for the contamination; in that case, the supplier would be regarded as the producer and holder of the waste.[25]

A few years later, the CJEU published its judgment in the landmark case *Commune de Mesquer*, which involved an accidental spillage of hydrocarbons at sea.

---

23 Case C-293/97, *supra*, note 21 at para. 52.
24 Directive 2008/98/EC.
25 Case C-1/03, Van de Walle [2004] ECR I-7613, paras. 57–60.

The CJEU explicitly stated that the waste management financial obligation is imposed on the persons mentioned in Article 14 "because of their contribution to the creation of the waste and, in certain cases, to the consequent risk of pollution".[26] In this regard, the national court might consider that, apart from the shipowner, liability could be imposed on the seller of the hydrocarbons and charterer of the ship, as well as on the producer of the product from which the waste thus spread came, if they were found to have contributed to the risk that the pollution caused by the shipwreck would occur.[27] Since *Commune de Mesquer*, the CJEU has constantly affirmed the contribution to the production of that waste as the foundation for the imposition of the waste management financial obligation.[28]

Consequently, the CJEU affirmed that the PPP, as concretely expressed in the Waste Framework Directive and its Article 14, permits the channelling of liability along the production chain to those who contributed to the creation of waste or to the risk that the pollution would occur. The CJEU did not set down any causation requirement for this liability channelling to occur; still, such a requirement might be implied by the constant "contribution" requirement, which is interpreted as a "causation and negligence" test.[29]

The CJEU took a step further and explicitly required the liability to be established on the inference of causality in 2010, in the *ERG* case.[30] The *ERG* case related to the PPP, this time as concretely expressed in the ELD. The dispute concerned the decontamination of the Augusta roadstead in Sicily. Environmental pollution in Augusta dated back to 1960s, since when many companies in the petroleum industry have operated in the region. A few decades later, in the mid-2000s, the national authorities required the undertakings that were operating in Augusta at that time to bear the costs for safety and decontamination measures. The addressees challenged the relevant administrative decisions before the national courts, as imposing disproportionate costs on them and as being out of line with the PPP. Their arguments were founded upon the generally accepted fact that the succession of undertakings over the years had rendered it impossible to determine each one's share of responsibility for the pollution. After a series of judgments, the competent administrative court of Sicily asked the CJEU to clarify whether the PPP and the ELD

> preclude national legislation which allows the competent authority to impose measures for remedying environmental damage on commercial operators on account

---

26 Case C-188/07, Commune de Mesquer [2008] ECR I-4501, para. 77.
27 Id. at paras. 78–82.
28 Case C-335/16, VG Čistoća [2017] published in the electronic Reports of Cases, ECLI:EU:C:2017:242; Case C-254/08, Futura Immobiliare and Others [2009] ECR I-6995.
29 *A. Bleeker*, Does the Polluter Pay? The Polluter-Pays Principle in the Case Law of the European Court of Justice, EEELR 2009 (6), p. 289.
30 Case C-378/08, *supra*, note 4.

of the fact that their installations are located close to a contaminated area, without carrying out any preliminary investigation into the occurrence of the contamination or establishing a causal link between the environmental damage and those operators.[31]

The CJEU started by affirming that for the ELD to apply, it is necessary that a causal link between the damage and the activity is established, as explicitly provided by Article 4(5) ELD. It was also recognised that this article might result in exempting from the environmental liability framework cases of diffuse pollution, where causality is not straightforward.[32] Nevertheless, since the ELD does not contain any rules on how Member States should establish causality, and since the environment is a field of shared competence between the EU and Member States, the latter enjoy a broad discretion in setting down the relevant criteria that will enable them to apply the PPP.[33] In this regard, Member States are entitled to empower national authorities to establish causality between the damage and the activities of one or more operators on the basis of a presumption. But such a presumption should be constructed from plausible evidence. The CJEU mentioned "the fact that the operator's installation is located close to the pollution found and that there is a correlation between the pollutants identified and the substances used by the operator in connection with his activities" as a potentially valid presumption. But of course it was the national court's competence to examine the factual background and to assess the line of reasoning the national authorities used to justify the presumption.[34] In addition, such a presumption should be rebuttable; operators should have the right to prove that the environmental damage was not caused by them, but by third parties, and thus to be relieved of the costs of remedial actions. The CJEU reaffirmed that the PPP does not entail that operators carry "the burden of remedying pollution to which they have not contributed".[35]

In summary, the application of the ELD, as founded upon the PPP, requires the prior affirmation of a causal link between the environmental damage and the activities, be it on the basis of a legally admissible presumption. The possibility to use a presumption ensures the effectiveness of the environmental liability regime, especially in cases of diffuse pollution where it is hard to track down the exact sources of pollution and estimate each source's effect. Nevertheless, the use of a presumption is accompanied by the risk of holding liable not

---

[31] Id. at para. 34.
[32] Id. at para. 54. See also *L. Bergkamp & A. van Bergeijk*, Exceptions and Defences, in L. Bergkamp & B. Goldsmith (eds.), The EU Environmental Liability Directive: A Commentary, Oxford University Press, 2013.
[33] Case C-378/08, *supra*, note 4 at para. 55.
[34] Id. at para. 57.
[35] Id. at paras. 58 and 67.

actual polluters, but rather mere "bystanders".[36] This risk is higher when the actual polluters cannot be traced or held liable, for example because of death or insolvency; in this case, the presumption doctrine might lead to the extension of the liability regime to third parties. The legal issues raised by such a liability extension will be examined in the next sections.

4. THE PPP AND THE EXTENSION OF LIABILITY TO OWNERS OF CONTAMINATED SITES

The extension of liability beyond polluters to also cover bystanders is particularly relevant for owners of contaminated sites. Indeed, it is probable that national laws adjudge them liable for the pollution that other parties caused, like former owners or possessors of the site, or occupational operators while using the land. Nevertheless, it is not clear whether such a liability channelling or extension is compatible with the PPP, and hence with the ELD. This question occupied the CJEU in two recent cases, to wit in *Fipa*[37] and in *TTK*.[38]

Starting with the *Fipa* case, which was the first to emerge, it related to the environmental safety and remedial measures the Italian authorities ordered for the protection of the groundwater table and the rehabilitation of certain contaminated sites in Massa Carrara in Tuscany. The sites at issue were contaminated by insecticide and herbicide undertakings that had been operating in the area from the 1960s to the 1980s. The administrative orders were issued in 2007 and 2011 on the basis of the national environmental code, which enshrined the PPP, and they were addressed to several private companies that were the owners of the land at that time. But these companies did not have any involvement in the contamination; they had only become owners of the contaminated land a few months before the orders were issued. In this regard, the addressees challenged the administrative orders before the national courts, arguing that imposing liability on actors who had not contributed to the pollution that had occurred was not in conformity with the PPP. On the other hand, the authorities saw the PPP in conjunction with the precautionary principle and they claimed that the law allows an extension of the environmental liability to the landowners. The case reached the Council of State (Consiglio di Stato), which found that Italian law does not empower national authorities to require the adoption of measures by landowners who are not the polluters.

---

[36]   L. *Bergkamp*, Comment on Case C-378/08, 9 March 2010; Joined Cases C-379-08 and 380/08, 9 March 2010; Joined Cases C-487/08 and C-479/08, 9 March 2010, JEEPL 2010 (3), pp. 355, 357.

[37]   Case C-534/13, *supra*, note 5.

[38]   Case C-129/16, *supra*, note 6.

Nevertheless, after reaching this conclusion, the Consiglio di Stato wondered whether Italian legislation is compatible with the PPP, as enshrined in the ELD.

Accordingly, the national court asked the CJEU whether the ELD requires Member States to extend environmental liability to landowners who are not responsible for the pollution. In other words, the Consiglio di Stato asked whether national legislators are required to adopt a more stringent environmental liability regime than what the ELD sets down. This was a rather bizarre preliminary reference, in the sense that Article 16 ELD has a clearly non-coercive nature. Indeed, it does not oblige, but explicitly gives Member States the possibility to adopt more stringent environmental liability provisions.[39] Furthermore, the CJEU has constantly emphasised that the establishment of a causal link between the environmental damage and the activity is an essential element of and a prerequisite for the application of the EU environmental liability framework.[40] Therefore, it could not be concluded that Member States are obliged by the ELD to hold non-polluters liable for environmental damage. Besides, in an *argumentum ad absurdum*, if the adoption of more stringent provisions was found to be obligatory for Member States, then Article 16 ELD would be practically meaningless; it would explicitly allow Member States to do something they were obliged to do.[41]

Therefore, the Italian legislation was found to be compatible with EU law.[42] Nevertheless, as straightforward as the judgment was, it sparked a very interesting debate.[43] While the CJEU responded that Member States are allowed to not adopt more stringent provisions, the pivotal legal issue highlighted was whether they were also allowed to adopt the opposite stance. More specifically, the *Fipa* judgment brought to the fore the question whether extending environmental liability to non-polluters would be compatible with the PPP and the ELD.

This question was plainly raised in the *TTK* case.[44] The case started in July 2014, when the environmental protection authority of Hungary found that waste was being illegally incinerated on a site in Túrkeve. This site had been leased to the operator of the incineration by the owner, to wit the company TTK. The national authority confirmed that the incineration had caused an environmental hazard, for which persons who owned or were in possession of

---

[39] Case C-534/13, *supra*, note 5 at para. 61.
[40] Id. at paras. 54–57.
[41] Opinion of Advocate General Kokott in Case C-534/13, *supra*, note 5 at paras. 30, 59.
[42] Case C-534/13, *supra*, note 5 at para. 63.
[43] N. de Sadeler, Case Note Preliminary Reference on Environmental Liability and the Polluter Pays Principle: Case C-534/13, Fipa, RECIEL 2015 (2), p. 232. See also B. Pozzo et al., The Remediation of Contaminated Sites and the Problem of Assessing the Liability of the Innocent Landowner: A Comparative Law Perspective, European Review of Private Law 2015 (6), p. 1071.
[44] Case C-129/16, *supra*, note 6.

the property at the material time were jointly and severally liable, according to the Hungarian environmental law. But since the lessee, to wit the operator of the incineration, had already died at the time the law infringement was detected, the national authority imposed liability on TTK, the owner of the site. In addition, the Hungarian authority fined TTK for the pollution that had occurred. TTK disputed the fine and brought proceedings before the competent administrative court. The court noticed that while establishing causality is a prerequisite for the application of the EU environmental liability framework, the Hungarian authority had not showed that there was any causal link between the damage and TTK's conduct. Moreover, the fine that the national authority imposed on TTK was not a remedial measure, as defined by the ELD. Nevertheless, attention was called to Article 16 ELD, which allows Member States to maintain or adopt "more stringent provisions in relation to the prevention and remedying of environmental damage". Accordingly, the court submitted a preliminary question to the CJEU, asking whether primary and secondary EU law allows Member States to "go beyond" the PPP and to "hold specifically the owner of the property liable to pay compensation for the environmental damage caused, without it first being necessary to determine whether there is a causal link between the conduct of that person (a commercial undertaking) and the pollution caused".[45] In addition, the Hungarian court asked whether Member States are allowed to impose fines, which have a mere punitive nature and are not remedial measures, as the EU liability framework requires.

The CJEU started by recalling that the PPP, in spite of being enshrined by Article 191(2) TFEU, can only be invoked by individuals seeking to exclude the application of national legislation, if it is concretely expressed by a secondary EU legal act that is connected with the Union environmental policy.[46] In this regard, the CJEU examined whether the ELD applied in the case. This was not clear because the illegal waste incineration caused air pollution, while Article 2 ELD explicitly states the Directive only covers damage to protected species and natural habitats, water damage and land damage. Nevertheless, Recital 4 ELD clarifies that environmental damage, defined in Article 2, "also includes damage caused by airborne elements as far as they cause damage to water, land or protected species or natural habitats". Consequently, it was held that if the national court concludes that the waste incineration caused such damage or an imminent threat of it, the ELD applies.[47]

Next, the CJEU proceeded to the interpretation of the ELD. By way of a leitmotif, the CJEU emphatically stated that the application of the PPP, as implemented in the ELD, relates to the establishment of a causal link between

---

[45] Id. at para. 24.
[46] Id. at paras. 37, 38.
[47] Id. at paras. 40 et seq.

the operator's activity and the environmental damage or the imminent threat of such damage. Hence, for the PPP-based Union environmental liability regime to apply, the establishment of such a causal link is required.[48] Still, Article 16 ELD allows Member States to adopt more stringent measures, and this is the case of the Hungarian environmental protection legislation. The latter provides that:

> in the absence of proof to the contrary, the persons who own or are in possession of the land "on which the environmental damage or hazard occurred" are to be held jointly and severally liable; the owner can discharge himself of his liability only if he can identify the actual user of the land and can prove beyond reasonable doubt that he did not cause the damage himself.[49]

The CJEU concluded that the foregoing national legislation serves the objectives of the ELD because it strengthens the prevention of environmental damage. While under a typical environmental liability regime landowners have no incentive to heed the behaviour of the lessees, if they know they will be responsible in the event environmental damage occurs, they will be encouraged to adopt measures and develop practices in order to minimise the risk of damage. For instance, they will monitor the activities performed on their property or they will report polluters to the competent authorities. With this argumentation, the CJEU found that national legislation that holds jointly and severally liable both the operators of the damaging activity and another category of persons, like the landowners, is compatible with EU law, under Article 16 ELD. Nevertheless, three conditions should be respected. First, the objective of the ELD should be attained; second, national law should comply with EU law, and in particular its general principles; and third, the operators should remain liable in principle.[50]

It is also interesting to briefly refer to the Opinion of Advocate General (AG) Juliane Kokott in the case. AG Kokott suggested that it is not the ELD but the Waste Framework Directive that applies, because the waste incineration did not lead to "environmental damage" within the meaning of the ELD.[51] In this regard, the AG examined the PPP as expressed in the Waste Framework Directive and she emphasised that it is not in conformity with the PPP, or with the principle of proportionality, to "penalise persons in respect of breaches for which they are not responsible".[52] Nevertheless, she found that national authorities are allowed to use presumptions for the establishment of liability and the imposition of an administrative fine, as long as the presumption is rebuttable. She also examined the rationale behind a presumption holding the landowners liable for the

---

[48]   Id. at paras. 48, 51.
[49]   Id. at para. 57.
[50]   Id. at paras. 58–63.
[51]   Opinion of Advocate General Kokott in Case C-129/16, *supra*, note 6 at paras. 30–32.
[52]   Id. at para. 43.

damage the land users caused. Accordingly, she stated that such a presumption is an expression of the principle of *bonus et diligens pater familias* and of the landowners' duty of care that is connected to the property.[53] Given the above, it is interesting that although the AG interpreted the PPP as concretely expressed in another legal act and not the ELD, she used similar arguments and reached similar conclusions to the CJEU.

This judgment has – for the moment – culminated a series of environmental liability cases that relate to the extent of liability and the conditions for imposing it. Still, the questions that have been raised have not been satisfactorily answered. There are still many points of confusion that have not been clarified, but have perhaps been even further obfuscated. These points will be presented in sections 5 and 6, which more thoroughly assess the judgment in *TTK*.

5. DECONSTRUCTING *TTK*: PROBLEMS ASSOCIATED WITH A DEROGATION FROM THE PPP UNDER THE ELD

The *TTK* judgment, albeit apparently consistent with previous CJEU case law, ends up highlighting the complexity accompanying the EU environmental liability framework.

To begin with, the judgment raises some questions as regards the requirement of causality. As mentioned in section 4, the CJEU affirmed that the establishment of causality is a requirement for the application of the ELD. Yet the Hungarian law at issue imposed liability without firstly establishing causality. Nevertheless, it was still regarded as compatible with the ELD, under its Article 16, because it contributed to the attainment of the objective of the ELD. The objective of the Directive was defined as the prevention and remedy of environmental damage as well as the compliance with EU law and its general principles.[54] But these conclusions did not answer the question whether invoking the objectives of the ELD, in conjunction with Article 16 ELD, allows Member States to derogate from the causality requirement and, consequently, from the PPP in itself.

Accordingly, it should be noted that there are cases where environmental protection can be ensured if environmental liability regimes diverge from the PPP. For instance, and similarly to the factual background of the *TTK* case, if the actual polluter is untraceable or insolvent, then strictly applying the PPP entails the risk of nobody bearing the costs. It can be argued that in such cases national authorities should be able to resort to the "beneficiary pays" principle, which

---

[53]   Id. at para. 54.
[54]   Id. at paras. 56, 61.

is independent of causality considerations. Applying the "beneficiary pays" principle can lead to the affirmation of liability of either those persons who benefit from the actions that cause the environmental damage or those who benefit from the prevention of pollution and from the restoration of the site. In the latter case, the "beneficiary pays" principle turns in essence into a "community pays" principle because it will normally be society, citizens and taxpayers who will mostly care for and benefit from an intact environment, and they will be those who will have to bear the relevant costs.[55] In another deviation from the PPP, in the event that the polluter cannot afford to bear the whole costs of the necessary preventive or remedial measures, Member States could apply the "ability to pay" principle and extend liability to more actors, each of whom will in the end cover a part of the total cost, depending on their economic capacities.[56]

As meritorious as turning to alternative solutions might be,[57] there are certain important counter-arguments. First, the ELD is explicitly based on the PPP, which is also enshrined in Article 191(2) TFEU; EU law does not contain any references to other principles and does not provide for exceptions from the PPP. Therefore, interpreting the ELD as allowing Member States to shift towards the "beneficiary pays" principle or other principles is not founded on a solid legal basis. Besides, even if one holds that the ELD leaves room for derogation from the PPP, neither the ELD nor the CJEU has provided any conditions under which such a derogation from the PPP is allowed.

Still, the Commission adopts the stance that:

[d]epending on the individual position of each [Member State], Member States could act as they deem appropriate and may lower or abolish the prevention and remediation requirements or replace the polluter pays principle by another principle of cost allocation (beneficiary-pays principle, community pays principle, ability-to-pay principle).[58]

However, if one accepts that Article 16 ELD means that Member States are empowered to decide at will when they apply the PPP and when they turn to

---

55   J. Wündisch, Does excusable ignorance absolve of liability for costs?, Philosophical Studies 2017 (4), p. 837; Commission Staff Working Document, REFIT Evaluation of the Environmental Liability Directive, SWD(2016) 121 final, pp. 11, 97.

56   N.S. Dufau, Too Small to Fail: A New Perspective on Environmental Penalties for Small Businesses, The University of Chicago Law Review 2014 (4), p. 1795; Commission Staff Working Document, supra note 55, p. 97.

57   See also C. Barry & R. Kirby, Scepticism about Beneficiary Pays: A Critique, Journal of Applied Philosophy 2017 (3), p. 285; D. Butt, "A Doctrine Quite New and Altogether Untenable": Defending the Beneficiary Pays Principle, Journal of Applied Philosophy 2014 (4), p. 336.

58   Commission Staff Working Document, supra note 55, p. 59.

another principle, there is the possibility of the ELD leading to a mosaic of very different national environmental liability regimes. It goes beyond the scope of this chapter to discuss whether the environmental liability rules should be harmonised or not.[59] Still, if the Union legislator wishes to allow Member States to deviate from the PPP, the safest path would be an amendment to the ELD so that the Directive either explicitly states that there can be no divergence from the PPP or explicitly refers to other principles that may govern a national environmental liability regime. Furthermore, it is particularly important to explicitly set down the conditions that legitimise a certain deviation from the PPP.

Second, extending the liability framework to cover more persons than the operators of the damaging activity almost necessarily has a certain degree of arbitrariness. In this regard, one might have difficulties in fairly applying the "beneficiary pays" principle. Indeed, it is particularly difficult to determine who the persons benefiting from a polluting activity are. Thus, liability could extend to cover the landowners of the site where the polluting activity took place, but also the lenders that finance that activity, or even the consumers who enjoy the goods produced by it.[60] Of course, holding liable one category or the other leads to a very different outcome both from a legal and from a fairness point of view.[61] But even if beneficiaries are identified, it will be hard to correctly decide about the fair share of liability they should bear, given that various beneficiaries are not benefiting to exactly the same extent from the activity that causes pollution. And the same lines of criticism stand *mutatis mutandis* for the "ability to pay" principle.

Third, although a divergence from the PPP enlarges the coverage of the liability regimes, it is debatable if it is indeed more effective for environmental protection. Polluters may be less constrained by the preventive character of the ELD if they have a way to dodge liability, by transferring liability to other persons and hiding behind bystanders.

In conclusion, it seems that the liability of the landowners or other persons can be better established under the "beneficiary pays" principle or the "ability to pay" principle. Still, in the *TTK* judgment the CJEU did not examine whether the ELD allows any derogation from the PPP. In point of fact, the CJEU assessed the compatibility of the Hungarian legislation with the ELD, without even referring to any principles, except of course for the PPP.

---

[59]   For more about this issue see *K. De Smedt*, Is Harmonisation Always Effective? The Implementation of the Environmental Liability Directive, EEELR 2009 (1), p. 2 and the literature cited.

[60]   *R. Hooley*, Lender Liability for Environmental Damage, Cambridge Law Journal 2001 (2), p 405; *D. Fullerton & S. Tsang*, Environmental Costs Paid by the Polluter or the Beneficiary? The Case of CERCLA and Superfund, 1993 National Bureau of Economic Research Working Paper No. 4418.

[61]   See also *Pozzo et al., supra*, note 43.

Given the above, the CJEU has not settled the issue whether Member States are entitled to enact environmental liability regimes derogating from the PPP. This section has also highlighted a number of issues that would derive from such a derogation. Next, section 6 accepts that the judgment in *TTK* did not derogate from but applied the PPP. In this respect, it focuses on the application of the PPP as enshrined in the ELD and notices that there are certain legal problems that emerge when a national environmental liability framework is compatible with the PPP and the ELD, but it mostly appertains to systems that deviate from the PPP.

6. DECONSTRUCTING *TTK*: PROBLEMS ASSOCIATED WITH THE APPLICATION OF THE PPP

The question whether the PPP or other liability principles apply is not the only problematic point of the ELD. This part elaborates on the *TTK* judgment in order to examine certain complex issues that derive from the application of the PPP in itself. More specifically, it critically examines how the environmental liability of landowners was established.

According to Recital 18 ELD, the PPP dictates that "an operator causing environmental damage or creating an imminent threat of such damage should, in principle, bear the cost of the necessary preventive or remedial measures". The words "in principle" denote that the application of the PPP might lead to other persons being held liable, as long as this does not absolve the operators of liability. This seems to be implicitly confirmed by the CJEU in *TTK*, where the fact that national legislation did not affect "the liability in principle of the operator", but only created a regime of joint and several liability, proved a decisive criterion for the Court's decision. Nevertheless, it is not clear how this "liability in principle of the operator" requirement should apply in practice; more specifically, this requirement can be read in two ways, either as creating an obligation for Member States or as just granting a right to those who are jointly and severally liable with the operator. In the former interpretation, the PPP compels Member States to firstly impose liability on the operator and to only proceed to imposing liability on landowners or other persons under conditions that render the operator's liability meaningless, like death, dissolution or insolvency of the operator. The second possible interpretation means that national authorities are not constrained when it comes to whom they hold liable for environmental damage; they can charge either the operator or other persons, like landowners, to take the necessary preventive or remedial measures. But the landowners should have the right to identify the actual polluter and thus to be relieved from environmental liability or to have a recourse claim against the operator who, thus, remains liable in principle.

The CJEU did not clarify what the meaning of the ELD is. The first interpretation strengthens the PPP, as it limits the possibilities for operators to avoid liability. Nevertheless, it also restricts the discretion that Member States enjoy when they enact their national environmental liability regime. Contrariwise, the second interpretation gives more power to national authorities to deal with environmental damage as they deem appropriate. In this sense, and also given the fact that environment is a field of shared competence, it seems more pragmatic to read the CJEU judgment as adopting this second interpretation, which does not entail a teleological restriction of the Member States' powers. Nevertheless, such an interpretation opens the way for a divergence from the PPP, which is problematic in itself, as was shown above in section 5.

In addition, in accordance with Recital 18 ELD, it is possible that a framework applies and imposes liability on other persons and not on the operators, but it still follows the terms of the PPP. In this case, a causal link should be established between the damage that occurred and the conduct of those held liable. This causality requirement is missing when the environmental liability regime extends to more persons after the application of the "beneficiary pays" principle or the "ability to pay" principle. In the *TTK* judgment, it was not made clear how the causal link between the environmental damage and landowners' conduct was established. Reading between the lines of the judgment, it seems that the CJEU has implicitly affirmed that it is compatible with the ELD to use a causality presumption, which derives from the fact that national laws assign to landowners a duty to care. More specifically, the CJEU noticed that according to the Hungarian law at issue, landowners are regarded as in general liable, but they are absolved from liability if they prove "beyond reasonable doubt" that they did not cause the damage themselves.[62] The CJEU avoided making any reference to the power of national authorities to presume causality, but the national law under examination can be interpreted as introducing in essence a rebuttable presumption about landowners' liability. Then, the CJEU stated that:

> [t]o the extent that, without affecting the liability in principle of the operator, such national legislation seeks to prevent a lack of care and attention on the part of the owner, as well as to encourage the owner to adopt measures and develop practices likely to minimise the risk of damage to the environment, it contributes both to the prevention of such damage and, as a result, to the attainment of the objectives of Directive 2004/35.[63]

Both the foregoing inferences are accompanied by complexities. In terms of presuming liability, this has already been deemed to be in line with the ELD

---

[62]   Case C-129/16, *supra*, note 6 at para. 57.
[63]   Id. at para. 58.

since the *ERG* judgment, as long as the presumptions are rebuttable and justified by plausible evidence. However, the only evidence the Hungarian authority used to hold TTK liable was the fact that the company had ownership of the polluted site. But, as a matter of fact, it is rather far-fetched to argue that the mere fact of owning the land where the pollution occurred constitutes plausible evidence of contribution to the environmental damage. Given the above, one would wonder whether the *TTK* judgment paves the way for a relaxation of the "plausible and rebuttable presumption" doctrine, as pronounced in the *ERG* judgment.

The identification of the causal link becomes even easier if the presumption is complemented by a liability for omission regime, as introduced by the Hungarian law. But it is debatable whether an environmental liability framework that is founded upon certain persons' *culpa in vigilando*, to wit fault in supervising, complies with the principle of the PPP.[64] Indeed, an omission-based liability framework starts from a "duty of care and attention", assigned to certain persons by the national law. But if this assignment sufficed on its own to render someone liable for environmental damage under the ELD, then the PPP would end up covering as many persons as the national legislators wished. For instance, just like the Hungarian law at hand considers the landowners bear a duty of care and attention, another legislator could extend responsibility to the neighbours of the site where pollution occurs and require them to monitor and report to the competent authorities. Similarly, consumers of the goods or services that an operator produces or provides can be regarded as having considerable disciplining powers, which can lead to the attribution of supervision tasks to them. This *argumentum ad absurdum* denotes that liability based on the mere fact of a duty of care and attention does not seem compatible with the PPP. Besides, the PPP reflects the principle of proportionality. But it does not seem proportionate to impose liability on persons solely on the basis of a "duty of care and attention", without showing how a lack of care caused the environmental damage, the more so if this "duty of care and attention" is vague and not translated into specific requirements. This is not in conformity with the PPP, as interpreted in the light of the principle of legal certainty; the supervising obligations should be clearly set down before a person is held liable for breaching them.

In conclusion, it is suggested that the CJEU should clarify that such an omission-based liability regime can be compatible by the PPP if the national legislators establish a special link between those bearing the burden of "duty and attention" and the operator and, perhaps most importantly, if the contribution of the omission to the environmental damage is affirmed.

---

64   *F. Goisis & L. Stefani*, The Polluter-Pays Principle and Site Ownership: the European Jurisprudential Developments and the Italian Experience, JEEPL 2016 (13), p. 218.

7. CONCLUSION

A series of cases that have recently reached the CJEU have highlighted that Member States often seek to derogate from the "polluter pays" principle, and they have good reasons for this. If the actual polluter, to wit the operator of the activity that causes the environmental damage, is untraceable or insolvent, then somebody has to bear the costs. Accordingly, Member States have in theory a plethora of choices. More specifically, a national environmental liability framework could impose liability on those who are financially able to bear the costs, or on those who benefit from the pollution and the polluting activity, or on those who benefit from the integrity of the environment and from the restoration of the polluted sites. Another solution is that liability is imposed on persons who are regarded as capable of disciplining potential polluters and, thus, of preventing the environmental damage. Intuitively, one could argue in favour of the widest possible extension of the environmental liability framework so that the environmental protection becomes as stringent as possible.

Nevertheless, the foregoing solutions are not always satisfactory either from a fairness or from a legal point of view. A wide environmental liability framework creates the risk of imposing liability on bystanders who had not contributed to the pollution or to the threat of it. And seen from a more strictly legal point of view, EU law explicitly enshrines the PPP as governing the environmental liability regime and it is unclear if and under what conditions Member States can diverge from it. Complexity is rather exacerbated by the fact that the Commission in soft law vaguely accepts that Member States can decide to extend environmental liability to more categories of persons than just the operators of the polluting activity. Similarly, the CJEU has proved quite lenient when assessing national environmental liability frameworks that go beyond the PPP. Nevertheless, the content of the PPP as expressed in the ELD is not consolidated. There is still certain confusion about the exact content of the PPP and it is expected that more problems will arise if Member States decide to take even more stringent environmental protection measures.

Given the above, it is suggested that a solution might be the enactment of a more comprehensive EU environmental liability framework. An amended ELD that will *inter alia* elaborate on the PPP and will delineate the conditions justifying a deviation from it is expected to soften to a large extent the problems of confusion and uncertainty and to result in clearer and more stable national frameworks.

"CAUSAL LINK" AS A CONDITION OF LIABILITY IN THE ENVIRONMENTAL LAW

The Example of the Liability Mechanism in Directive 2004/35/EC*

Mariusz Baran

1. INTRODUCTION

In accordance with the classic principles of legal liability understood as "a situation in which a given entity bears the negative consequences specified by law for an event or a state of things that is normatively qualified as negative and attributed in law to a specific entity in a given legal order",[1] it is necessary to determine whether there exists a causal link between the act (action/omission) and the damage to the environment.

In the context of the liability mechanism introduced by Directive 2004/35/EC on environmental liability with regard to the prevention and remedying of environmental damage,[2] the question arises whether establishing a causal link is always a *sine qua non* condition in determining a given business operator's liability.

The aforementioned assumption requires verification through analysis of the case law of the Court of Justice of the European Union (CJEU), especially regarding the interpretation of Directive 2004/35. Should only those operators

---

*   This study was prepared as part of the scientific project carried out under the contract concluded with the National Science Centre in Krakow, Poland on the basis of agreement no UMO-2016/21/D/HS5/03841, registration number of the research project 2016/21/D/HS5/03841.

1   *W. Lang*, Struktura odpowiedzialności prawnej. Studium analityczne z dziedziny teorii prawa (The structure of legal responsibility. Analytical study in the field of legal theory – in Polish), Zeszyty Naukowe Uniwersytetu Mikołaja Kopernika w Toruniu (Research Journal of the Nicolaus Copernicus University in Toruń – in Polish), no. 31, 1968, p. 12.

2   Directive 2004/35/CE of the European Parliament and of the Council of 21 April 2004 on environmental liability with regard to the prevention and remedying of environmental damage, OJ 2004 L 143/56.

who have contributed to the emergence of damage be held liable, or are the parties that own land in a given area or conduct their business operations there also be considered potentially liable? This is the question that the author has set out to answer.

Before we move any further, we need to have a look at the case law of the CJEU in the relevant matter, as it will unveil numerous faces/facets of "causal link" in environment law.

For example, in Case C-378/08 *Raffinerie Mediterranee (ERG) I*,[3] it was claimed in the proceedings before the national court that the competent public authorities had required the business enterprises operating in a specified area to remedy the damage done to the natural environment without investigating or even demonstrating the existence of any causal link between the conduct of the enterprises and the damage occurring in the natural environment or whether any of the enterprises were at fault in the case in question.

2. "CAUSAL LINK" AS THE NECESSARY CONDITION OF LIABILITY?

In order to establish/find the existence of "a causal link", as well as to indicate its facets as the conditions of liability in environment protection, it is above all necessary to specify the principles of liability for damage required by Directive 2004/35.

The purpose of Directive 2004/35 is to establish a framework of environmental liability based on the "polluter pays" principle, to prevent and remedy environmental damage (Article 1 of the Directive). One of the primary conditions for pursuing the application of the liability mechanism established in the provisions of Directive 2004/35 is to identify the business operator that could be considered responsible.[4]

---

[3]   Case C-378/08, ERG and Others, ECLI:EU:C:2010:126, para. 41; see *S. Casotta &
       C. Verdure*, Recent Developments Regarding the EU Environmental Liability for Enterprises:
       Lessons Learned from the Italian Implementation With the Raffinerie Mediterranee Cases,
       Jean Monnet Working Paper 2012 (2) and *S. Casotta & C. Verdure*, Recent Developments
       Regarding the EU Environmental Liability for Enterprises: Lessons Learned from Italy's
       Implementation of the "Raffinerie Méditerranée" Cases, EEELR 2012 (4), pp. 156 et seq.

[4]   See Article 3(1) of Directive 2004/35 in conjunction with Recitals 2 and 18, and with
       Article 2(6) and (7), and with Articles 5, 6, 8 and 11 (2) – directly along this line: Case
       C-534/13, Fipa, ECLI:EU:C:2017:419, para. 48; also Case C-129/16, Túrkevei Tejtermelő,
       ECLI:EU:C:2017:547, para. 48; see also: *L. Bergkamp & B.J. Goldsmit* (eds.), The Environmental
       Liability Directive. A Commentary, Oxford University Press, 2013; *G. Roller*, Liability, in
       R. Macrory (ed.), Principles of European Environmental Law, Europa Law Publishing,
       2006, pp. 134 et seq.; *G. Winter, J.H. Jans, R. Macrory & L. Krämer*, Weighing up the EC
       Environmental Liability Directive, Journal of Environmental Law, 2008 (20) pp. 163–191;
       S. Casotta, Environmental Damage and Liability Problems in a Multilevel Context: The Case

If we examine the issue from the perspective of the *ratione materiae* application of the liability mechanism established by Directive 2004/35, it is fundamental to underline that it may be applied to the damage done to the natural environment[5] through occupational activities, as well as to the imminent threat of such damage occurring by reason of the aforementioned activities (Article 3(1) of the Directive). It follows that entities other than those identified in Article 2(6) of Directive 2004/35, namely entities that do not carry out occupational activities as defined in Article 2(7) of this Directive, fall outside the scope of the Directive's application, as defined in Article 3(1)(a) and (b) thereof,[6] unless the matter refers to damage that occurred in carrying out activities other than those listed in Annex III, regardless of the business operator being at fault or negligent (and unless it falls within the scope of the Directive based on Article 3(1)(b)).[7]

In compliance with Article 17 of Directive 2004/35, the liability mechanism applies to damage done by an emission, event or incident taking place after 30 April 2007, if the damage results from an activity carried out subsequently to this date or an activity carried out prior to this date which, however, was not yet over.[8] Additionally, as the Court precisely defined in Case C-529/15 *Folk*, the Directive applies *ratione temporis* also to damage to the natural environment that occurred after 30 April 2007 but that was caused by the operation of an installation the permit for which had been issued under the national water law before that date and the installation had been approved for operation before that date.[9] The fact that the damage started to occur prior to 30 April 2007 and results from an activity for which the permit was issued before that date is irrelevant in establishing the temporal scope of application of Directive 2004/35.[10]

The business operator responsible for such actions (omissions) is obliged, under Articles 5–7 of Directive 2004/35, to take the necessary preventive and

---

of the Environmental Liability Directive, Kluwer Law International, 2012, pp. 141–216; N. de Sadeleer, Case Note Preliminary Reference on Environmental Liability and the Polluter Pays Principle: Case C-534/13, Fipa, RECIEL 2015 (2), pp. 232–237; G. Betlem & E.H.P. Brans (eds.), Environmental Liability in the EU. The 2004 Directive compared with U.S. and Member State Law, Cameron May, 2006; E.H.P. Brans, Liability for Damage to Public Natural Resources under the 2004 EC Environmental Liability Directive – Standing and Assessment of Damages, Environmental Law Review 2005 (7), pp. 91 et. seq.; B. Pozzo, Liability for environmental harm in Europe: towards a harmonised regime?, Hitotsubashi Journal of Law and Politics 2016 (44), pp. 43–65.

5   Defined in Article 2(1) Directive 200/35.
6   Case C-534/13, *supra*, note 4 at para. 52.
7   Id. at paras. 52–53.
8   See Case C-378/08, *supra*, note 3 at para. 41 and Cases C-379/08 and C-380/08, ERG and Others, ECLI:EU:C:2010:127, para. 34; also Case C-529/15, Folk, ECLI:EU:C:2017:41, para. 22.
9   Case C-529/15, *supra*, note 8 at para. 25.
10   Id. at para. 24; see the Opinion of Advocate General Bobek in Case C-529/15, Folk ECLI:EU:C:2017:1, paras. 22–26.

remedial measures, or, pursuant to Articles 8–10 and Recital 18, to bear the cost of the measures taken by national authorities.[11]

Pursuant to Articles 4(5) and 11(2) of Directive 2004/35, and in conjunction with Recital 13 thereof, the liability mechanism provided for in the Directive may be effectively applied only if:

- first, it is possible to identify at least one polluter (perpetrator);
- second, the damage is concrete and quantifiable; and
- third, there exists (must be found) a causal link between the damage and the identified polluter(s).[12]

The key concept for attributing liability to a business operator, as follows from Article 8(3)[13] and Recital 20 of the Directive,[14] is the notion of preparation (causing the pollution), i.e. the existence of (any?) causal link.

The consequence of the above is that national authorities are required, within the framework of the objective liability mechanism (which refers to damage to the natural environment done by business operators whose activity falls within the scope of Annex III to the Directive), to do the following:

- identify the causes of a confirmed occurrence of pollution; national authorities are free as to the selection of the procedures necessary for taking

---

[11] Opinion of the Advocate General Kokott in Case C-534/13, Fipa, ECLI:EU:C:2014:2393, para. 31.

[12] See Recital 13 of the Directive: "Not all forms of environmental damage can be remedied by means of the liability mechanism. For the latter to be effective, there need to be one or more identifiable polluters. The damage should be concrete and quantifiable, and a causal link should be established between the damage and the identified polluter(s). Liability is therefore not a suitable instrument for dealing with pollution of a widespread, diffuse character, where it is impossible to link the negative environmental effects with acts or failure to act of certain individual actors." See also: L. Bergkamp, The Proposed Environmental Liability Directive, European Environmental Law Review 2002, pp. 294–314 and 327–341; G. Betlem, Scope and Defences of the 2004 Environmental Liability Directive: Who is Liable for What?, ERA-Forum 2005 (3), pp. 376–388.

[13] See Article 8(3) of the Directive: "An operator shall not be required to bear the cost of preventive or remedial actions taken pursuant to this Directive when he can prove that the environmental damage or imminent threat of such damage: (a) was caused by a third party and occurred despite the fact that appropriate safety measures were in place; or (b) resulted from compliance with a compulsory order or instruction emanating from a public authority other than an order or instruction consequent upon an emission or incident caused by the operator's own activities."

[14] Recital 20 of the Directive: "An operator should not be required to bear the costs of preventive or remedial actions taken pursuant to this Directive in situations where the damage in question or imminent threat thereof is the result of certain events beyond the operator's control. Member States may allow that operators who are not at fault or negligent shall not bear the cost of remedial measures in situations where the damage in question is the result of emissions or events explicitly authorised or where the potential for damage could not have been known when the event or emission took place."

appropriate measures, as well as to the duration of such investigation, because the identification must be done pursuant to national procedural regulations (rules of evidence proceedings); and

- demonstrate – "pursuant to the national rules on evidence proceedings – that there exists a causal link between the activities of business operators obliged to take preventive measures and the occurrence of pollution".[15]

When the obligation to remedy the damage rests on several business operators following their contribution (various degrees of contribution) to the occurrence of pollution or an imminent threat of such occurrence, national authorities are required, insofar as possible, to determine the degree of contribution of each of these operators to the pollution which they are obliged to remedy, as well as to administer – pursuant to the requirements of Article 9 of Directive 2004/35 – the suitable apportionment of the remedy costs which the operators are to bear.[16]

On the basis of the environmental liability mechanism provided for in the Directive, competent national authorities must demonstrate the existence of a causal link "between the activity of one or more identifiable operators and concrete and quantifiable damage so that remedial measures could be required of this operator, irrespective of the type of pollution at issue".[17]

Finding the causal link is necessary both:

- within the framework of the objective business operators' environmental liability mechanism, pursuant to Article 3(1)(a) of the Directive;[18] and
- within the framework of the subjective liability mechanism arising from fault or negligence on the part of a business operator, pursuant to Article 3(1)(b) in conjunction with Article 4(5) of the Directive, with reference to types of activities other than those listed in Annex III.[19]

3. CONSEQUENCES OF THE ABSENCE OF A CAUSAL LINK FOR THE LIABILITY MECHANISM

In Case C-534/13 *Fipa*, the Italian court (Consiglio di Stato) was in doubt as to whether the principles originating from Article 191(2) of the TFEU and

---

[15]   Cases C-478/08 and C-479/08, Buzzi Unicem and Others, ECLI:EU:C:2010:129, para. 45; see also Case C-378/08, *supra*, note 3 at para. 65.

[16]   Cases C-478/08 and C-479/08, *supra*, note 15 at para. 47.

[17]   Case C-534/13, *supra*, note 4 at para. 54; see also a similar Case C-378/08, *supra*, note 3 at paras. 52–53 and Cases C-478/08 and C-479/08, *supra*, note 15 at para. 39.

[18]   Along this line: Case C-378/08, *supra*, note 3 at paras. 63–65; also Cases C-478/08 and C-479/08, *supra*, note 15 at para. 45; also Case C-534/13, *supra*, note 4 at para. 55; also Case C-129/16, *supra*, note 4 at para. 49.

[19]   Case C-534/13, *supra*, note 4 at para. 56; also Case C-129/16, *supra*, note 4 at para. 50.

Directive 2004/35 on environmental liability preclude national legal regulations which, in circumstances when it is established that a site is contaminated and it is impossible to identify the polluter or to have that polluter adopt remedial measures, do not permit the administrative authority to require the owner, who is not responsible for the pollution, to implement emergency safety and rehabilitation (restoration) measures, merely attributing to that person financial liability limited to the value of the site once the rehabilitation measures have been carried out.

A question then arises in relation to the above about the legal consequences of the absence of a causal link with pollution or imminent threat thereof for the liability mechanism established by Directive 2004/35: whether EU law (principles laid down in Directive 2004/35) requires Member States to impose certain safety and rehabilitation (restoration) measures upon the owner of contaminated land, even if he/she is not responsible for the contamination (there is no causal link). The question may seem a little surprising, as responsibility for causing damage to the environment appears to be a necessary condition for imposing the obligations specified in the Directive on operators (physical or legal persons).

An analysis of the provisions laid down in Directive 2004/35 leads to the conclusion that where there is no causal link between the activities of a business operator and the damage done to the natural environment:

- first, it is not required that the business operator bear the cost of the remedial measures taken under the Directive if he/she is able to prove that the damage done to the natural environment is the result of actions of a third party and has occurred in spite of the fact that appropriate safety measures were in place, or the damage has resulted from a compulsory order or instruction emanating from a public authority (pursuant to Article 8(3)(a) of Directive 2004/35 in conjunction with Recital 20 thereof);[20]
- second, such situation as the one described above falls within the scope of application of national legislation (the liability mechanism under Directive 2004/35 is not applicable[21]), which, nevertheless, must respect the provisions of the Treaty and remain without prejudice to other acts of secondary law.[22]

---

[20] Case C-534/13, *supra*, note 4 at para. 58; similarly, Case C-378/08, *supra*, note 3 at para. 67 and the case law cited there; also Cases C-478/08 and C-479/08, *supra*, note 15 at para. 46.

[21] Common owners of sites affected by damage, who have not caused that damage, will not – in principle – be burdened with the obligation to undertake remedial or preventive measures within the liability regulations laid down in Directive 2004/35 (the Directive has no applicability whatsoever in such cases). This is to be considered valid given the fact that they do not carry out business operations of the types listed in Annex III to the Directive – see, along a similar line, Case C-378/08, *supra*, note 3 at para. 58; for the same see Advocate General Kokott in Opinion in Case C-534/13, *supra*, note 11 at para. 37.

[22] Case C-534/1, *supra*, note 4 at para. 59; see, along a similar line, Case C-378/08, *supra*, note 3 at para. 59; also Cases C-478/08 and C-479/08, *supra*, note 15 at paras. 43 and 48.

Looking at the matters from the negative side, a business operator should not bear the cost of preventive or remedial measures taken under Directive 2004/35 in situations where the damage or the imminent threat thereof results from events remaining beyond the control of the operator.

Liberation from liability (exoneration) is possible even when it is the activity of a given business operator that caused the damage. However, the operator must demonstrate that the damage done to the natural environment or the imminent threat thereof has been caused by a third party and has occurred in spite of the fact that appropriate safety measures were in place (Article 8(3)(a) of the Directive).

In opposition to the hypothesis presented by the Italian Consiglio di Stato in case C-534/13 *Fipa*, Advocate General J. Kokott points out that Article 8(3) of Directive 2004/35 must not be interpreted as if it meant that it could be assumed, without finding any additional circumstances (e.g. under more stringent national provisions introducing the construct of presumed "causal link", which will be discussed further on), that an operator using a polluted site caused that pollution, until there is proof of a different cause. On the contrary, this provision exonerates the operator in spite of the proof that the damage is related to its business activities.[23]

4. CAUSAL LINK AND PRESUMPTION OF ITS EXISTENCE – DOES IT MEAN PRESUMPTION OF LIABILITY?

Regardless of the previous observations, it must be pointed out that – in its judgment in Case C-378/08 *Raffinerie Mediterranee (ERG) I* – the CJEU considered it admissible for Member States to introduce the presumption in question to the detriment of business operators, as Member States have a broad discretion, particularly with reference to establishing the causes of widespread and diffused pollution, and they may – for the purpose of establishing liability for environmental pollution – introduce the notion of the presumed causal link.[24] This means that, in the case of widespread or diffused pollution, it is admissible to construe the condition of a causal link on the grounds of a legal presumption related to causing the pollution, if there is plausible evidence justifying this reasoning, such as the fact that the operator's installation is located close to the pollution and that there is a correlation between the pollutants identified and the substances used by the operator in connection with his/her activities.[25]

---

[23] Opinion of Advocate General Kokott in Case C-534/13, *supra*, note 11 at para. 34.
[24] Case C-378/08, *supra*, note 3 at para. 55.
[25] Case C-378/08, *supra*, note 3 at para. 57; also see Cases C-478/08 and C-479/08, *supra*, note 15 at paras. 42–43.

It must be emphasised, however, that the limitation of the national legislator's discretion in construing this detrimental legal presumption is the possibility of rebuttal of operator and exoneration from liability where the "causal link" has not been proved but is only based on legal presumption. This limitation is justified by at least three considerations:

- first, the "polluter pays" principle (as well as the "preparation" principle) does not mean that business operators are obliged to take on the burden of remedying pollution to which they have not contributed (through their actions or omissions);[26]
- second, the necessity of taking into account the principle of proportionality, which should be applied in conjunction with the principle that damages done to the environment should "as a priority be rectified at source";[27]
- third, in accordance with Article 11(4) of the Directive, business operators also have available to them legal remedies to challenge remedial measures adopted on the basis of this Directive when it comes to the existence of any causal link between their activities and the pollution found;[28] the legal remedies also allow them to rebut the presumption introduced in national legislation that they have caused the damage (presumed causal link).[29]

The limitations – indicated above – of the possibility of introducing presumption of a business operator's liability ("causal link") into national legislation may not be modified by using an extensive interpretation of the presumption of a business operator. Likewise, it should not even be modified by invoking the precautionary and preventive principles or the principle that environmental damage should be rectified at source as a matter of priority,[30] or the requirement of effective implementation of the Directive.[31] As has been rightly pointed out by Advocate General J. Kokott, the aforementioned principles must be taken into account in interpreting Directive 2004/35, yet they may not per se establish any

---

[26]   Article 191(2) TFEU, which invokes the "polluter pays" principle, concerns the actions at the EU level; individuals may not rely on this provision in order to exclude the application of national regulations if there is no EU legislation applicable under Art. 192 TFEU, referring specifically to the situation in question (see Case C-378/08, *supra*, note 3 at para. 46; Cases C-379/08 and C-380/08, *supra*, note 8 at para. 39, and also Cases C-478/08 and C-479/08, *supra*, note 15 at para. 36). Similarly, the competent environmental authorities cannot rely on Article 191(2) TFEU, in the absence of any national legal basis, for the purposes of imposing preventive and remedial measures – see Case C-534/13, *supra*, note 4 at paras. 40–41; see Case C-293/97, Standley and Others, ECLI:EU:C:1999:215, para. 50; Case C-378/08, *supra*, note 3 at para. 67.

[27]   Case C-293/97, *supra*, note 26, paras. 52 and 53.

[28]   Case C-378/08, *supra*, note 3 at para. 67.

[29]   Id. at para. 58.

[30]   Opinion of Advocate General Kokott in Case C-534/13, *supra*, note 11 at para. 38.

[31]   Id. at para. 39.

obligations – grounds for liability – going beyond the conditions derived from the provisions of the Directive.[32]

The principle that remains valid within the framework of environmental liability established by Directive 2004/35 is that business operators are obliged to undertake remedial actions only when they have contributed to the pollution in question or to the risk of pollution, i.e. when there is a causal link between their actions and the damage/imminent threat thereof.[33] It is so because the "polluter pays" principle, which implements the notion of liability established by Directive 2004/35, does not itself require business operators to take on the burden of remedying the pollution of which they have not contributed to the occurrence.[34]

As Advocate General J. Kokott points out quite rightly in her opinion in case C-534/13 *Fipa*, in exceptional circumstances the competent authorities may require site owners to take on themselves remedial measures if they perform – on this site – occupational activities within the meaning of this Directive.[35] However, imposition of such an obligation (and this is how the judgment in joint Cases C-379–380/08 *Raffinerie Mediterranee (ERG) II* is to be understood) must be dependent on the "causal link" condition (contribution), even if its existence results from a legal presumption that has not been rebutted.[36]

5. CAUSAL LINK AS THE CONDITION OF LIABILITY AND MORE STRINGENT NATIONAL PROVISIONS

The content of Article 16 of Directive 2004/35 clearly states that the Directive does not prevent Member States from maintaining or adopting more stringent provisions in relation to the prevention and remedying of environmental damage. What is more, it clearly indicates that they have the right to establish additional liable entities (bearing responsibility) for damage. It means that, pursuant to national regulations, other entities (owners who have not caused environmental damage on their sites) may nevertheless be also held liable for damage. There is one reservation, though, namely that Member States,

---

[32] Id. at para. 38.

[33] Case C-378/08, *supra*, note 3 at paras. 52–59 and 64–67; and also Case C-188/07, Commune de Mesquer, ECLI:EU:C:2008:359, para. 77.

[34] Case C-378/08, *supra*, note 3 at para. 6; and also Case C-293/97, *supra*, note 26 at para. 51; see also: A. Bleeker, Does the Polluter Pay? The Polluter-Pays Principle in the Case Law of the European Court of Justice, EEELR 2009 (6), pp. 289 et seq., and N. De Sadeleer, Environmental Principles: From Political Slogans to Legal Rules, Oxford University Press, 2002.

[35] Cases C-379/08 and C-380/08, *supra*, note 8 at para. 78 and also para. 82.

[36] Opinion of Advocate General Kokott in Case C-534/13, *supra*, note 11 at para. 46.

in executing this competence (i.e. adopting more stringent regulations), are limited by the objectives of Directive 2004/13, which may not be undermined by Member States.[37] For this reason, Member States may establish additional liable entities, but only alongside (with secondary or joint and several liability[38]) and never instead of (in the place of) the operators liable on the basis of the Directive.[39] The option of adopting more stringent protective provisions is not restricted to specifying additional liable parties (adding more entities), but it also refers to the identification (indication) of additional types of activities that would be subject to the requirements of the Directive related to prevention and remedy of damage in the environment.[40]

As Advocate General J. Kokott observes, a doubt arises here whether the option, provided for in Article 16 of Directive 2004/35, to adopt more stringent regulations in national legislation, entails the obligation on the part of Member States to hold liable site owners who have not caused damage (thus extending the subjective scope of liability) in order to ensure that the objectives of the Directive are achieved,[41] other than results from the literal wording of the Directive provisions.

There is no doubt that Member States enjoy discretion in this area. The question thus refers to whether the objectives of the Directive do not reduce this discretion in adopting national regulations identifying further parties liable for damage. Neither Article 16 nor any other provisions of Directive 2004/35 formulate guidelines that would reduce the scope of Member States' regulatory discretion in this respect, particularly by requiring them to call on site owners to remedy environmental damage where they did not cause that damage. At most, Directive 2004/35 contains an unspoken assumption that Member States may oblige site owners (who have not caused the damage) to accept the necessary measures undertaken on their sites by other operators and, to the necessary extent, to cooperate in their implementation. Therefore, Article 12(4) makes provision for the views of such owners to be heard.[42]

---

[37]   Cases C-379/08 and C-380/08, *supra*, note 8 at paras. 65–66; also see Opinion of Advocate General Kokott in Cases C-378/08 and C-379/08 and C-380/08, ERG and Others, ECLI:EU:C:2009:650, paras. 96–115.

[38]   Thus Case C-129/17, *supra*, note 4 at para. 60.

[39]   Cases C-379/08 and C-380/08, *supra*, note 8 at paras. 65–66.

[40]   Case C-129/17, *supra*, note 4 at para. 56.

[41]   As an example, Advocate Kokott invokes the content of Article 4(2) of Directive 2011/92/EU on the assessment of the effects of certain public and private projects on the environment, which states that it is at the discretion of Member States whether the environmental impacts of projects listed in Annex II have to be assessed. However, in the case law of the Court, this discretion of Member States has been significantly restricted, as the Court has ruled that such an assessment is obligatory if a given project is likely to have significant effects on the environment – see Opinion of Advocate General Kokott in Case C-534/13, *supra*, note 11 at para. 51; see also Case C-72/95, Kraaijeveld and Others, ECLI:EU:C:1996:404, para. 55; Case C-435/97, WWF and Others, ECLI:EU:C:1999:418, para. 36; and Case C-244/12, Salzburger Flughafen, ECLI:EU:C:2013:203, para. 29.

[42]   Opinion of Advocate General Kokott in Case C-534/13, *supra*, note 11 at para. 52.

Additionally (as already discussed here), the principles of environmental protection laid down in Article 191 (2) TFEU[43] do not reduce the discretion left to the Member States in this respect. Article16 of Directive 2004/35 must be viewed as aiming to achieve "a high level of protection taking into account the diversity of situations in the various regions of the Union; it is based on the precautionary principle and on the principles that preventive action should be taken, that environmental damage should as a priority be rectified at source and that the polluter should pay".[44] As regards the principles of environmental protection laid down in Article 191(2) TFEU considered in the context of interpretation of Article 16 of Directive 2004/35, it must be pointed out that:

– first, the remaining liable entities (other than the polluters) may therefore only have secondary (or potentially joint and several) liability, as considering such additional entities to be exclusively liable besides the polluters would undermine the "polluter pays" principle (and thus the objective of the Directive);[45]

– second, the primary principle about the assumption that the polluting operator is the one that has liability still complies with the principle of preventive action, which requires that operators, realising their liability, undertake preventive measures, and, naturally, the polluting operators are the ones able to take the most effective preventive action;[46]

– third, the principle of preventive action, as well as the principle that damage should be repaired as a priority at source, require that, regardless of whether the owner is responsible/co-responsible for the damage on the polluted site, it must be possible to undertake measures to prevent further spread of the damage. Not infrequently, the current owner has better knowledge of the site than the operator that caused the damage, which means that it would be much more difficult, if not impossible, to prevent the spread of pollution without the cooperation of the current owner of the site, who, at the very least, may have to provide access to the site. However, the obligation of rehabilitation must be considered to be a different matter (the above principles do not justify imposing such obligation on the site owner who is not responsible for the damage),[47] although the principle of preventive action may suggest that it could sometimes be justifiable to call on site owners, in certain cases,

---

[43] See Cases C-188/07, *supra*, note 33 at para. 38; Case C-301/10, Commission v. UK, ECLI:EU:C:2012:633, para. 49; Cases C-241/12 and C-242/12, Shell Nederland, ECLI:EU:C:2013:821, para. 38; Case C-237/12, Commission v. France, ECLI:EU:C:2014:2152, para. 30.

[44] Article 191(2) TFEU.

[45] Opinion of Advocate General Kokott in Case C-534/13, *supra*, note 11 at para. 54.

[46] Id. at para. 55.

[47] Id. at para. 56.

to take preventive safety measures against risks for which third parties are essentially responsible;[48]

- fourth, the principle of a high level of protection does not require Member States to adopt far-reaching secondary liability of site owners for environmental damage on their sites, as the objective of the environmental regulations must be balanced with other objectives, for example the fundamental rights of site owners who are not responsible for the pollution (the requirement of balancing objectives).[49]

As the judgment in case C-129/16 *Túrkevei Tejtermelő* confirms, it is possible, through more stringent national protection regulations, to create such environmental liability that identifies (introduces) another category of subjects with joint and several liability, besides business operators carrying out operations on unlawfully polluted sites, namely the owners of such sites, without requiring the causal link between the owners' conduct and the damage to be demonstrated. There is one condition, however, namely that such regulation must comply with the general principles of EU law, as well as with all relevant provisions of the TEU and TFEU and of the acts of secondary law of the European Union.[50]

In the *Túrkevei Tejtermelő* case, Hungarian authorities held the company liable not in its capacity as a business operator but as the owner of the site on which the pollution occurred. Moreover, the national authority imposed a fine on the site owner but did not require the company to take any preventive or remedial action.[51] Both attributing (assigning) the liability to the site owner, who was not the polluter, and imposing a fine on him was done under national provisions, which were not part of the provisions implementing the liability mechanism established by Directive 2004/35 (foundation of liability), but rather were part of the mechanism provided for in Hungarian provisions falling within the scope of Article 16 of Directive 2004/35, which – in conjunction with Article 193 TFEU[52] – permits adoption of more stringent protective measures, for the following reasons:

- the liability mechanism provided for in the national legislation (liability of the site owner without the requirement to prove a causal link, as well as the possibility of imposing a fine on the site owner jointly and severally liable with

---

48   Id. at para. 57.
49   Id. at para. 61.
50   Case C-129/16, *supra*, note 4 at para. 63.
51   Id. at para. 54.
52   Although it is true that Art. 193 TFEU allows adoption of more stringent protective measures provided that they comply with the Treaties and have been previously notified to the European Commission, yet in the case of failure to comply with the obligation to notify, provided for in Art. 193 TFEU, the failure itself does not render the more stringent protective measures unlawful – along this line Case C-2/10, Azienda Agro-Zootecnica Franchini i Eolica di Altamura, ECLI:EU:C:2011:502, para. 53 and the case law cited therein.

the polluter) helps to prevent (minimise) lack of care and attention on the part of the owner, as well as to encourage the owner "to adopt measures and develop practices likely to minimise the risk of damage to the environment, which contributes both to the prevention of such damage and, as a result, to the attainment of the objectives of Directive 2004/35";[53]

- site owners, under such national legislation, are "to monitor the conduct of business operators carrying out activities on their sites and to report such operators to the competent authority in the event of environmental damage or the threat thereof, failing which they will themselves be held jointly and severally liable",[54] which helps reinforce the liability mechanism provided for in Directive 2004/35;

- an administrative fine imposed on a site owner for unlawful pollution which the owner has not prevented or for which he/she has not reported the responsible party may, under more stringent national provisions, contribute to the attainment of the objective of protection defined by the more stringent national legislation prescribing joint and several liability, with the reservation, however, that the method of determining the amount of the fine does not go beyond what is necessary to attain that objective.[55]

The requirement that more stringent protection measures adopted in national legislation are to comply with EU law entails the necessity, first, to seek to attain "the objective of Directive 2004/35 as defined in Article 1 thereof, namely to prevent and remedy environmental damage, and, second, to comply with EU law, in particular with its general principles, which include the principle of proportionality".[56]

6. CONCLUSIONS

The problem of "causal link" is of great theoretical and practical significance, as it is related to the fundamental principles of liability in environment protection law. In fact, the condition of "causal link" – as one of the conditions of legal liability – directly concerns the rights or obligations of business operators. Finding the "causal link" is necessary to impose subjective or objective liability for the environmental damage/threat of damage in question. However, as the analysis of the case law of the CJEU related to the liability mechanism established

---

[53] Case C-129/16, *supra*, note 4 at, para. 58.
[54] Id. at para. 59.
[55] Id. at para. 66; see, by analogy; also Case C-69/15, Nutrivet, ECLI:EU:C:2016:425, para. 51 and the cited case law.
[56] Case C-129/16, *supra*, note 4 at para. 61; see, to that effect, Cases C-379/08 and C-380/08, *supra*, note 8 at para. 79.

by Directive 2004/35 demonstrates, it is not necessary each time to imposing on a given party (particularly the owner of the site) the obligation to take preventive or remedial measures. It is so because there may occur situations in which:

- the condition of "causal link" within the framework of the liability mechanism provided for in Directive 2004/35 is based on the concept of presumption, which would then require that the party who is not at fault, in order to exonerate themselves from liability, would have to bear the burden of proving so (reversed burden of proof); or
- under national protection regulations that are more stringent than the measures provided for in Directive 2004/35, the national regulation identifies another category of subjects with joint and several liability, besides business operators carrying out operations on unlawfully polluted sites, without the requirement to demonstrate the "causal link" between the owners' conduct and the damage that has occurred, on the condition, however, that such regulation complies with the general principles of EU law, as well as with all the relevant provisions of the Treaties and of the acts of EU secondary law.

The condition of a "causal link" is absent where the owner is not responsible for the pollution, and – as a consequence – his/her liability is based on his/her capacity as the owner of the site, as the pollution may not be attributed to him/her either subjectively or objectively.

The situation in which a given entity is held liable without the requirement of prior demonstration of the "causal link" between the conduct and the damage may raise doubts from the point of view of protection of the rights and freedoms of individuals, the right to access to court, protection of ownership rights or the principle of proportionality. Nevertheless, in certain cases and within certain limits, it may be justified by the specific character of environmental damage and problems with prevention and remedy thereof, such as:

- the necessity to take measures to prevent the spread of damage; not infrequently the current owner has better knowledge of the site than the operator that has caused the damage;
- the requirement of cooperation with the current owner (in fact governing the site where the damage has occurred), who – at the very least – may have to provide access to the site so that preventive or remedial measures can be taken;
- the necessity, due to the scale of the danger for the natural environment, of taking immediate action, which, in certain cases, may speak for imposing an obligation (at least temporarily) on the site owners to take protective preventive measures against the risk for which third parties are responsible;
- the need to take appropriate preventive or remedial measures in cases of diffuse or widespread damage; and

– the necessity to make a significant change to remedial measures against the damage to the natural environment which the liable party has been obliged to take, due to the scale of the danger to the natural environment.[57]

The analysis of the liability mechanism established in Directive 2004/35 confirms that the notion of liability for environmental damage constructed by the Directive constitutes *sui generis* "a public legal type of liability of the economic character". It is not insignificant in certain special cases, like the ones presented above, that the requirement of demonstrating the "causal link" as a condition for liability in the environment protection law is subject to limitation if necessary, due to the specific characteristics and principles governing this legal area (such as, in particular, the protection of the environment as a common good, the "polluter pays" principle, the preventive principle and the precautionary principle). The provisions regulating liability for environmental damage are characterised by at least two fundamental features: first, they view environmental resources as "common goods" rather than as "resources which may be subject to individual appropriation"[58] and, second, they are to ensure (enable) that measures are taken, in fact, in order to remove the threat or remedy the environmental damage.

---

[57] See Cases C-478/08 and C-479/08, *supra*, note 15 at paras. 51–53.
[58] Expression taken from A. *Wasilewski*, Administracja wobec prawa własności nieruchomości gruntowych: rozważania z zakresu nauki prawa administracyjnego (Administration over ownership of land real estate: considerations in the field of administrative law – in Polish), Krakow, 1972, p. 64.

ACCUMULATION OF POTENTIALLY TOXIC ELEMENTS IN AGRICULTURAL SOILS

Iain GREEN, Tilak GINIGE,
Merve DEMIR and Patrick Van CALSTER

1. INTRODUCTION

Over recent decades, it has become evident that certain anthropogenic activities have drastically changed the composition and organisation of our soil,[1] reducing its ability to function[2] and generating a downward spiral in both organic matter (OM) and biodiversity. The increase in contamination, compaction, salinisation, floods and landslides, which soils have faced, has reduced the ability of soil to support life systems.[3] With the world population predicted to reach 9.7 billion people by 2050,[4] the pressure on soil is going to increase considerably, hence soil conservation is vital to achieving sustainability.

Although in 1996 the Royal Commission for Environmental Pollution (RCEP)[5] acknowledged the need to protect and conserve the sustainability of soil, since then very little has been done to effectively prevent its degradation.[6] Indeed, soil health has failed to capture both society's attention and politicians' interests,[7] which has led some academics to compare its situation to that of "the Cinderella of environmental media",[8] highlighting the lack of attention towards it and its weak legal protection.[9] Moreover, at a global level, the

---

[1]   *European Commission* The Implementation of the Soil Thematic Strategy and Ongoing Activities, COM(2012) 46..

[2]   *S.M. Rodrigues et al.,* A Review of Regulatory Decisions for Environmental Protection: Part I Challenges in the implementation of national soil policies, Environ. Int. 2009 (35), p. 202.

[3]   Id. at p. 1.

[4]   *UN, Department of Economic and Social Affairs,* Population Division. World Population Prospects: Highlights, ST/ESA/SER.A/423 (2019), p. 5.

[5]   *S. Owens,* Knowledge, Policy, and Expertise: The UK Royal Commission on Environmental Pollution 1970–2011, Oxford University Press, 2015, p. 336.

[6]   *Royal Commission on Environmental Pollution,* Sustainable Use of Soil – Nineteenth Report, 1996.

[7]   *S. Bell,* A Slow Train Coming? Soil Protection Law and Policy in the UK, JEEPL 2006 (3), p. 227.

[8]   Id.

[9]   Id.

promotion of soil health has repeatedly been overlooked by governments in comparison with other environmental concerns.[10] This seems odd, as the need to maintain healthy soil was known as far back as 1500 BC, with the Vedas Sanskrit Scripture stating, "Upon this handful of soil our survival depends. Husband it and it will grow our food, our fuel and our shelter and surround us with beauty. Abuse it and the soil will collapse and die, taking humanity with it." This acknowledges the underlining symbiotic relationship between nature and man, where if one suffers, the other suffers as well. Consequently, humanity must act on the need to re-address the value of nature and more specifically soil. There are, as one may suspect, a few hurdles preventing this from happening.

The 19th century development into the industrialised, self-centred, market-based economic model that instigated the neglect of the symbiotic relationship between man and nature that ancient wisdom emphasised.[11] This economic model prioritises the need to exploit nature for short-term gains and immediate prosperity,[12] with policy and legislation as its co-conspirator. This had led to an agricultural economy where the introduction of chemicals into the soil is a necessity to guarantee the viability of food production levels.[13] This model may explain why soils have not received the attention they truly deserve in environmental policy and law. This omission intensifies the effects of the global challenge posed by soil degradation, which is one of the most serious threats to ecosystem functionality[14] and ultimately sustainability.[15] As Jannes Stolte and colleagues have suggested, extensive degradation leads to a decline in the capability of soil to provide vital functions and ecosystem services (ES).[16] ES are the benefits humans obtain from ecosystems for their survival and well-being, such as food production,[17] making the prevention of soil degradation a priority. Food production is considered one of the most important ES provided by agro-ecosystems and 72 per cent of the

---

[10]   M.G. Kibblewhite et al., Soil Health in Agricultural Systems, Philos. Trans. R. Soc. Lond. B Biol. Sci. 2008 (363), p. 685.

[11]   C.L. Spash, Bulldozing Biodiversity: The Economics of Offsets and Trading-in Nature, Biol. Conserv. 2015 (192), p. 541.

[12]   N.C. Brady & R.R. Weil, The Nature and Properties of Soils, 11th ed., Prentice-Hall, 1996.

[13]   E. Plaas et al., Towards Valuation of Biodiversity in Agricultural Soils – A Case for Earthworms, Ecol. Econ. 2019 (159), p. 291.

[14]   G.V. Dobrovol'skii & E.D. Nikitin, Ecological Functions of Soils, Izd. Mosk. Gos. Univ., 1986 [in Russian].

[15]   L.R. Oldeman, Soil Degradation: A Threat to Food Security, 1998, http://www.isric.org/sites/default/files/isric_report_1998_01.pdf; K. Adhikari & A.E. Hartemink, Linking Soils to Ecosystem Services – A Global Review, Geoderma 2016 (262), p. 101.

[16]   J. Stolte et al., Soil Threats in Europe: Status, Methods, Drivers and Effects on Ecosystem Services, European Commission Joint Research Centre Technical Reports, European Union, 2016.

[17]   Millennium Ecosystem Assessment, Ecosystems and Human Well-being: Synthesis, Island Press, 2005.

UK land area is given over to farming.[18] In many parts of the world, maximising food production is still the overriding motivation due to a lack of food security,[19] which seems to be increasingly overlooked. Implementations of ES into economic systems will hopefully lead to the promotion of a more sustainable future. However, developing effective policy measures and effective legal instruments in regards to sustainable ES is proving to be incredibly difficult.[20]

The challenge faced by both scientists and policy makers, therefore, is to find methods to effectively protect soil functionality,[21] whilst at the same time guaranteeing existing economic benefits. This chapter aims to contribute to the debate by critically discussing the weaknesses of both UK and EU soil pollution regulation.

The first part of the chapter will focus on the scientific exploration of soil biodiversity and the threats it faces. The scientific perspective will enable us to better understand the irregularities in current environmental policies and legislation. We will then develop the argument that ES must be taken into consideration in addressing the problems faced by policy makers and legislators.

2. SOIL BIODIVERSITY AND THE THREATS TO IT

As soil biodiversity is crucial to soil health,[22] there is a fundamental need to understand biodiversity.[23] In this section, we will first address the manifestation of soil biodiversity, after which we will look at the threats it has to face.

2.1. SOIL BIODIVERSITY

Soil consists of a range of minerals, such as silica, in differing proportions, a variety of organic matter (OM), chiefly of plant origin, atmospheric gases, water

---

[18]   *United Kingdom National Ecological Assessment (UKNEA)*, Understanding Nature's Value to Society – Synthesis of the Key Findings, 2011; "Enclosure (sometimes inclosure) was the legal process in England of consolidating (enclosing) small landholdings into larger farms. … In England and Wales the term is also used for the process that ended the ancient system of arable farming in open fields": Managing and Owning the Landscape, https://www.parliament.uk/about/living-heritage/transformingsociety/towncountry/landscape/overview/enclosingland/.

[19]   *D.S. Powlson et al.*, Soil Management in Relation to Sustainable Agriculture and Ecosystem Services, Food Policy 2011 (36), p. 572.

[20]   *C.L. Lant et al.*, The Tragedy of Ecosystem Services, Bioscience 2008 (58), p. 969.

[21]   *Dobrovol'skii, supra*, note 14.

[22]   *Environment Agency*, The State of Soil in England and Wales, 2004, http://www.adlib.ac.uk/resources/000/030/045/stateofsoils_775492.pdf.

[23]   *S. Jeffery et al.*, European Atlas of Soil Biodiversity, Office of the European Union, 2010.

and billions of organisms.[24] Living within the soils are plant roots, viruses, bacteria, fungi, algae, protozoa, mites, nematodes and oligochaete worms.[25] It is estimated that one quarter of all the species on the planet live within the soil.[26] Species abundance, however, varies from soil to soil, depending on OM content, pH, soil texture and water content.[27]

Anne Turbe and colleagues[28] have suggested the following classification as a means to better understand soil biodiversity. First, there are chemical engineers. These are microorganisms, such as bacteria, fungi and protozoa.[29] Micro-organisms are major agents by which carbon and energy move though soil food webs, and are responsible for the decomposition of OM and concomitant recycling of nutrients, which is a fundamentally important process for plant growth. Secondly, biological regulators such as nematodes, pot worms, springtails and mites that feed on plants. Unfortunately, very little is currently known about how these invertebrates contribute to the emergence of soil biodiversity.[30] Soil structure is enhanced by the different organisms within the soil that are considered ecosystem engineers, which impact on the environment physically, chemically and microbiologically.[31] Larger ecosystem engineers, such as oligochaete worms, ants, termites and small mammals, create or modify habitats for smaller soil organisms by building resistant soil aggregates and pores.[32] Earthworms, in particular, are hugely beneficial to the environment and structure of the soil as they produce casts at the soil surface that affect its roughness and the distribution of macrospores.[33] Stephane Boyer and Stephen Wratten[34] have argued that these soil processes are likely to accelerate soil restoration. Indeed, this classification provides a good framework for better management initiatives in preserving soil biodiversity as it highlights critical groups of organisms to be protected. However, there is still insufficient knowledge on the role soil microbes play in the establishment of soil health.[35]

---

[24] J. Clapperton, Managing the Soil as a Habitat, Proceedings of the 2006 Indiana CCA Conference, 2006, https://www.agry.purdue.edu/cca/2006/pdf/clapperton.pdf.

[25] M. Blouin et al., A review of earthworm impact on soil function and ecosystem services, Soil Sci. 2013 (64), p. 161.

[26] Jeffery, supra, note 23.

[27] R. Bardgett, The Biology of Soil: A Community and Ecosystem Approach, Oxford University Press, 2005.

[28] A. Turbe et al., Soil Biodiversity: Functions, Threats and Tools for Policy Makers, Bio Intelligence Service, IRD and NIOO. Report for European Commission (DG Environment), 2010, http://ec.europa.eu/environment/archives/soil/pdf/biodiversity_report.pdf.

[29] Id.

[30] Id.

[31] Jeffery, supra, note 23.

[32] Turbe, supra, note 28 at p. 4.

[33] L. Thyug & L.N. Kakati, Earthworm – The Soil Architect, IOSR-JESTFT 2018 (12), p. 77.

[34] S. Boyer & S.D. Wratten, The Potential of Earthworms to Restore Ecosystem Services After Opencast Mining – A Review, Basic Appl Ecol. 2010 (11), p. 196.

[35] Environment Agency, supra, note 22 at p. 4.

2.2. POTENTIALLY TOXIC ELEMENTS THREATING SOIL BIODIVERSITY

As Simon Jeffery and colleagues argue, there is increased concern with regard to the potential decline of soil biodiversity.[36] Especially within England, there is a high level of potential threats to soil biodiversity, mainly due to inappropriate management practices.[37] These threats are damaging agricultural soils by reducing their functioning capacity through compaction, which in turn lessens water infiltration, eventually increasing soil erosion and surface runoff.[38] Soil erosion affects soil biodiversity both directly and indirectly: directly though the removal of soil biota and its habitat, and indirectly through changes in the vegetation, which is linked to biodiversity.[39] Other key impacts caused by inappropriate management, especially in agricultural contexts, are OM loss and contaminant accumulation. Soil is a major store of OM[40] and its loss reduces soil fertility, which is a key indicator of soil health.[41] A reduction in soil OM also results in a decrease in soil organism abundance and diversity.[42] Soil contaminants, such as heavy metals and hydrocarbons, affect soil biota by reducing abundance and thus soil biodiversity.[43] Heavy metals, more appropriately described as PTEs ("potentially toxic elements"), include zinc (Zn), copper (Cu), nickel (Ni), lead (Pb), cadmium (Cd), chromium (Cr) and mercury (Hg). Some PTEs, such as Zn, Cu, Ni and Cr, are important nutrients that are required for proper metabolic function, whilst other PTEs, such Cd, Hg and Pb, have no known function and are highly toxic. All PTEs, however, can be toxic to soil health if the detoxification systems at the organism or cellular level are overwhelmed by the concentration of PTEs the organism is exposed to.[44] PTEs enter the agro-ecosystem through a variety of sources, such as animal slurries/manures, sewage sludge, pesticides, fertilisers and depositions from air and water.[45]

---

[36]   *Jeffery, supra,* note 23 at p. 4.
[37]   C. Gardi *et al.,* An estimate of potential threats levels to soil biodiversity in EU, Global Change Biol. 2013 (19), p. 1538.
[38]   *Department for Environment, Food & Rural Affairs (DEFRA),* Safeguarding Our Soils – A Strategy for England, 2009, https://assets.publishing.service.gov.uk/government/uploads/system/uploads/attachment_data/file/69261/pb13297-soil-strategy-090910.pdf.
[39]   *Jeffery, supra,* note 23 at p. 4.
[40]   B. Bolin *et al.,* The Global Perspective, in R.T. Watson, I.R. Nobel & B. Bolin (eds.), IPCC Special Report on Land Use, Land-Use Change And Forestry, Cambridge University Press, 2001.
[41]   *Kibblewhite, supra,* note 10 at p. 2.
[42]   *Jeffery, supra,* note 23 at p. 4.
[43]   Id.
[44]   M. Braungart *et al.,* Cradle-to-cradle design creating healthy emissions – a strategy for eco-effective product and system design, J. Clean Prod. 2006 (15), pp. 1337–1348.
[45]   F.A. Nicholson *et al.,* Quantifying heavy metal inputs to agricultural soils in England and Wales, Water Env. J. 2006 (20), p. 87.

Contamination occurs when PTEs are introduced to the environment in amounts that increase the natural levels in the soil. Over time, this may impose serious health problems for soil organisms, plants and thus the people and livestock that feed on the plants.[46] These elevated concentrations of PTEs can be sustained for very long periods.[47] The half-life of a PTE varies among the different elements; Cd, Ni and Zn remain in soils for a relatively shorter time in comparison to Pb and Cr.[48] However, for all PTEs, half-lives are measured in hundreds of years. Furthermore, PTEs are difficult to remove as soil has a natural ability to retain metals[49] and they do not breakdown like organic contaminants. Due to their toxicological impact on ecosystems, agriculture and human health,[50] the reduction of heavy metals in soils has been made a strategic aim by the UK.[51] Before we explore the control of PTEs, we would like to delve further into the way PTEs endanger soil health.

2.3. SOILS AND POTENTIALLY TOXIC ELEMENTS

Soil fertility depends on ecosystem processes within the soil, especially those driving the provision of nutrients into crop-available forms. These processes are largely driven by the action of soil microorganisms. The three main microbially mediated processes delivering nutrients to plants are: decomposition of OM and concomitant release of plant-available nutrients;[52] fixation of atmospheric nitrogen (N);[53] and acquisition of nutrients from the soil for plants by fungal symbionts.[54] The decomposition of OM is driven by free-living microorganisms

---

[46]   V. Grubinger & D. Ross, Interpreting the results of soil tests for heavy metals, 2011, https://www.uvm.edu/vtvegandberry/factsheets/interpreting_heavy_metals_soil_tests.pdf.

[47]   P.C. Brookes, The use of microbial parameters in monitoring soil pollution by heavy metals, Biol. Fert. Soils 1995 (19), p. 269.

[48]   B.J. Skinner et al., Dynamic Earth – An introduction to Physical Geology, John Wiley and Sons, 2004; S. Dudka & D.C. Adriano, Environmental impacts of metal ore mining and processing: a review, J. Envi. Qual. 1997 (26), p. 590.

[49]   R. Sanghi & K.S. Sasi, Pesticides and heavy metals in agricultural soil of Kanpur, India, Bull. Env. Contam. Toxicol. 2001 (67), p. 446.

[50]   L. Popescu & A. Stanca, Monitoring of heavy metals soil contents in the area of thermal power plants in Romania, Proc. World Acad. Sci. Eng. Technol. 2008 (46), p. 382.

[51]   DEFRA, The First Soil Action Plan for England: 2004–2006, 2004, https://webarchive.nationalarchives.gov.uk/20081023175603/http://www.defra.gov.uk/environment/land/soil/pdf/soilactionplan.pdf; European Commission, Communication from the Commission to the Council, the European Parliament, the Economic and Social Committee and the Committee of the Regions – Towards a Thematic Strategy for Soil Protection, COM(2002) 179.

[52]   D.B. Alexander, Bacteria and Archaea, in D.M. Sylvia et al. (eds.), Principles and Applications of Soil Microbiology, 2nd ed., 2005, pp. 101–140.

[53]   P.H. Graham, Biological dinitrogen Fixation: Symbiotic, in D.M. Sylvia et al. (eds.), Principles and Applications of Soil Microbiology, 2nd ed., 2005, pp. 405–432.

[54]   S.E. Smith & D.J. Read, Mycorrhizal symbiosis, 3rd ed., Academic Press, 2008.

in the soil and specifically in agricultural soils bacteria are mainly responsible for this process. The fixation of N and direct acquisition of nutrients are both largely driven by symbiotic relationships between plants and microorganisms. Fixation of atmospheric N is achieved by bacteria of the *Rhizobium* and *Frankia* genera, which form nodules in the roots of plants belonging to members of several families and most notably the *Fabacea* (e.g. field peas, broad beans, etc.). The fixed N provided to the plant reduces the need for fertiliser inputs and leakage of the fixed N into the soil surrounding the roots can supply N to subsequent crops not involved in the symbiosis. Over 80 per cent of terrestrial plant genera form symbiotic relationships with soil-dwelling mycorrhizal fungi to acquire part of their nutrients, especially phosphorus.[55] Mycorrhizal fungi breakdown OM, releasing nutrients and passing them on there their plant hosts and receive carbon (C) sources from the plant in return.[56] This relationship is less important in intensive agriculture because the nutrient demands of modern crop cultivars are met through the use of inorganic fertilisers. However, the mycorrhizal relationship may be of greater importance in less intensive agriculture, where it potentially plays an important role in nutrient acquisition, particularly in the future as sources of phosphorus for fertiliser production become limited.

In the UK, the concentration limits for PTEs applied by the EU laws were reviewed to ensure soil fertility was protected.[57] It was agreed that the limit set for the concentration of Zn in soil was insufficient to protect some aspects of the fertility pertaining to soil microorganisms, especially *Rhizobium* spp. and possibly mycorrhizal fungi. The recommendation of the review was to lower the limits of Zn from 300 mg kg^{-1} to 200 mg kg^{-1} for soils with a pH < 7.0.[58] Further, a series of field experiments demonstrated that where soil Zn concentrations have been elevated by sewage sludge additions, the mean probable number (a statistical estimate of the number of microorganisms in a substance) of *Rhizobium* in the soil was significantly decreased and in some instances, no *Rhizobium* were detectable.[59] Significant decreases in the soil microbial biomass carbon have also been shown at or close to the limit concentrations for both Cu and Zn, indicating that wider change in the soil microbial community can also occur.[60] This work has also shown that Cu and Zn affect the soil microbiology at lower

---

[55] Id. at pp. 145 et seq.

[56] Id.

[57] *MAFF/DoE*, Review of the Rules for Sludge Application to Agricultural Land: Soil Fertility Aspects of Potentially Toxic Elements: Report of the Independent Scientific Committee, MAFF/DoE, 1993.

[58] Id.

[59] *UK Water Industry Research (UKWIR)*, Effects of sewage sludge applications to agricultural soils on soil microbial activity and the implications for agricultural productivity and long-term soil fertility: Phase III, October 2007, Report Ref: SP0130; CSA 6222.

[60] *D.A. Abaye et al.*, Changes in the microbial community of an arable soil caused by long-term metal contamination, Euro J. of Soil Sci. 2005 (56), p. 93.

concentrations than the more notoriously toxic element Cd.[61] These findings clearly demonstrate both the potential for Cu and Zn to detrimentally affect soil health through their impact on soil microorganisms and that the current limits on Cu and Zn concentration in sewage sludge amended soil represent a value beyond which Cu and Zn accumulation should not be allowed to pass.

Let us now address the way PTEs are controlled by both UK and the EU regulation.

3. CONTROLS ON POTENTIALLY TOXIC ELEMENTS

Up to now, we have been discussing the threats to soil, focusing on PTEs, specifically Cu and Zn. To truly appreciate the gravity of the situation, we will now turn our focus on the use of organic by-products such as sewage sludge and animal manures/slurries as fertilisers,[62] which are applied to the UK's agricultural landscape.[63]

3.1. ORGANIC BY-PRODUCTS

Sewage sludge is formed during the process of initial settlement treatment of wastewater. The solids falling out of the water column are collected and transferred to an anaerobic digester for treatment. Once treated, sludge is a significant source of plant nutrients and OM,[64] rendering it a valuable fertiliser and soil conditioner and thus creating a product suitable for beneficial use in agriculture.[65] However, the bulk of PTEs in the wastewater are associated with the solid phase,[66] hence sewage sludge is enriched with PTEs. Due to presence of PTEs, the agricultural use of sewage sludge is controlled by the Sewage Sludge Directive,[67] which sets out how it should be used in agriculture; incorporating protection to soil; focusing on the known threats of PTE contamination;[68]

---

[61]   Id.; UKWIR, *supra*, note 59.

[62]   *L.H. Moss et al.*, Evaluating Risks and Benefits of Soil Amendments Used in Agriculture, Water Environment Research Foundation, 2002.

[63]   Id.

[64]   *B.J. Alloway*, Heavy Metals in Soils, 2nd ed., Springer, 1995.

[65]   *DEFRA*, Fertiliser Manual (RB209), http://www.defra.gov.uk/publications/files/rb209-fertiliser-manual-110412.pdf.

[66]   *S.P. McGrath et al.*, Land application of sewage sludge: scientific perspectives of heavy metal loading limits in Europe and the United States, Environ. Rev. 1994 (2), p. 108.

[67]   Council Directive 86/278/EEC of 12 June 1986 on the protection of the environment, and in particular of the soil, when sewage sludge is used in agriculture, OJ 1986 L 181/6 (Sewage Sludge Directive).

[68]   *A. Charlton et al.*, Long-term impact of sewage sludge application on soil microbial biomass: An evaluation using meta-analysis, Environ. Pollut. 2016 (219), p. 1021.

covering record keeping, soil and sludge testing requirements, and maximum contaminants concentration in sludge and soil; with requirements for treatment and timing of application.

However, as Cieślik and colleagues have suggested, there are concerns that large amounts of harmful chemical compounds that may occur in processing of sewage sludge lie outside the control of current established legal regulations.[69] Furthermore, EU regulations allow Member States to put limits on organic contaminants in reaction to public concerns rather than scientific research[70] where the latter would ideally be the starting point for environmental policy.[71,72,73] The UK government implemented the Sewage Sludge Directive untouched,[74] in the midst of ongoing legal research and debates which saw proposed amendments translated into guidance.[75] It was felt that agricultural land was the best disposal route and that the legal controls in place were sufficient to manage the hazards[76] from a risk assessment perspective.[77] Sludge quality is ensured by controlling inputs and treatment.[78,79] Organic wastes are in the main seen as an energy resource resulting in marketisation, which causes legal uncertainty for combined waste streams and potentially creating loopholes.[80]

To secure quality, sludge analysis is required to be performed every six months, and more frequently where composition varies significantly. However,

---

[69] B.M. *Cieślik et al.*, Review of sewage sludge management: standards, regulations and analytical methods, J. Clean Prod. 2015 (90), p. 1.

[70] *K. Jones & J. Stevens*, Organic Contaminants in Sewage Sludge Applied to Agricultural Land: A Critical Evaluation of the Proposed Limit Values for Organics in the EU Working Document on Sludge and Development of a Tiered Screening Process to Identify Priority Pollutants in Sewage Sludge, UK Water Industry Research, 2002, https://www.ukwir.org/reports/02-SL-04-2/66964/Organic-Contaminants-in-Sewage-Sludge-Applied-to-Agricultural-Land.

[71] *G. Mininni et al.*, EU policy on sewage sludge utilization and perspectives on new approaches of sludge management, Environ. Sci. Pollut. Res. 2015 (22), p. 7361.

[72] The Sludge (Use in Agriculture) Regulations 1989, SI 1989/1263.

[73] *A. Christodoulou & K. Stamatelatou*, Overview of legislation on sewage sludge management in developed countries worldwide, Water Sci. Technol. 2016 (73), p. 453.

[74] The Sludge (Use in Agriculture) Regulations, *supra*, note 72.

[75] *B. Crathorne et al.*, Implementation of HACCP controls under the new Sludge (Use in Agriculture) Regulations, in Proceedings of CIWEM/Aqua Enviro 7th European Bio Solids and Organic Residuals Conference, 18–20 November 2002.

[76] DEFRA, Review of Research on Recycling of Sewage Sludge to Agricultural Land, 2006 <http://sciencesearch.defra.gov.uk/Document.aspx?Document=WT03051_4104_FRP.doc.

[77] *R.D. Davis*, The impact of EU and UK environmental pressures on the future of sludge treatment and disposal, Water Environ. J. 1996 (10), p. 65.

[78] *H. Kirchmann et al.*, From agricultural use of sewage sludge to nutrient extraction: A soil science outlook, Ambio 2017 (46), p. 143.

[79] *I. Thornton et al.*, Pollutants in urban waste water and sewage sludge – Final report prepared for European Commission Directorate-General Environment, European Commission, 2001, http://ec.europa.eu/environment/archives/waste/sludge/pdf/sludge_pollutants_2.pdf.

[80] OFWAT, The Fifth Sludge Working Group Meeting, 2016 https://www.ofwat.gov.uk/wp-content/uploads/2016/08/sludge-working-group-consolidated-slides-20160720.pdf.

---

a lack of clear definition makes enforcement of the procedure highly problematic.[81] Similarly, soil testing is required every 20 years for soils subject to sewage sludge amendment; however, it commonly occurs every three to five years to inform nutrient management planning.[82] There is an ongoing debate as to whether this is sufficient, as soil parameters including heavy metal concentration do not vary greatly between applications.[83] However, 10 years of repeated application have brought to the surface several adverse effects.[84] Although guidance regarding sampling depth and limits was updated, it was not translated into law. Research indicates that concentrations of metals are misleading as they may be affected by underlying geology, and the bioavailability (and therefore toxicity) of metals is not necessarily reflected by the total concentration. Moreover, metal toxicity can increase with time after sludge application as the protective effect of OM diminishes (the "sludge time bomb"); therefore care is required in determining safe thresholds.[85] Metals in sewage sludge can also increase environmental damage from pesticides, so other factors should also be considered.[86] This clearly calls for regular monitoring in support of current government policy,[87] which in turn will improve scientific understanding of long-term effects, as well as the emerging pollutants and farmers' understanding of their soil.

As discussed above, when used as fertiliser, slurries and manures (hereafter combined as manures) can also damage soil, if not managed responsibly. However, direct legislation is lacking. Metals such as Zn, Cu and arsenic (As) are added to animal feed as antimicrobial and bulking agents, especially in intensive pig and poultry systems. Application of manure from these sources can negatively affect soil health,[88] being implicated in antibiotic

---

[81] P.H.T. Beckett, The Statistical Distribution of Sewage and Sludge Analyses, Environ. Pollut. (Series B), 1980 (1), p. 27.

[82] DEFRA, Sewage Sludge on Farmland: Code of Practice for England, Wales and Northern Ireland, 2017, https://www.gov.uk/government/publications/sewage-sludge-on-farmland-code-of-practice/sewage-sludge-on-farmland-code-of-practice#sludge-treatment.

[83] A. Cundill et al., Review of the application of organic materials to land, Natural Scotland and SEPA, 2012, https://www.sepa.org.uk/media/163500/review_application_-organic_materials_to_land_2011_12.pdf.

[84] B.J. Chambers et al., Effects of sewage sludge applications to agricultural soils on soil microbial activity and the implications for agricultural productivity and long-term soil fertility: Phase III – SP0130; CSA 6222 DEFRA, 2007, https://randd.defra.gov.uk/Document.aspx?Document=SP0130_6505_FRP.pdf.

[85] M.B. McBride, Toxic metal accumulation from agricultural use of sludge: are USEPA regulations protective?, J. Environ. Qual. 1995 (24), p. 5.

[86] R.P. Singh & M. Agrawal, Potential benefits and risks of land application of sewage sludge, Waste Manage. 2008 (28), p. 347.

[87] B. Petri et al., A review on emerging contaminants in wastewaters and the environment: current knowledge, understudied areas and recommendations for future monitoring, Water Res. 2015 (72), p. 3.

[88] W. Tian et al., Short-term changes in total heavy metal concentration and bacterial community composition after replicated and heavy application of pig manure-based compost in an organic vegetable production system, Biol. Fert. Soils 2015 (51), p. 593.

resistance[89] and increased pesticide toxicity.[90] This is in the face of Soil Association standards[91] prohibiting usage of these elements and the progressive tightening of limits.[92] However, these elements can still be prescribed separately to treat infections,[93] thus polluting the soil.

Levels of heavy metals and other pollutants are regulated through the concentration in food,[94] although this is not necessarily reflected in soil or manure concentration. Additionally, there are voluntary soil concentrations of Zn and Cu to provide warnings when using manure, whilst mandatory limits remain only a recommendation for all organic fertilisers.[95] Moreover, determining responsibility for contamination is ambiguous except in the case of on-site manure application. The code of practice states that it is the sludge producer's responsibility, according to the "polluter pays" principle, in line with the Waste Framework Directive,[96] but it is not explicit. Furthermore,

---

[89]   Y. Kang et al., High diversity and abundance of cultivable tetracycline-resistant bacteria in soil following pig manure application, Scientific Reports 2018 (8), art. no. 1489; S. Peng et al., Prevalence of antibiotic resistance genes in soils after continually applied with different manure for 30 years, J. Hazard. Mat. 2017 (340), p. 16; M. Wang et al., Fate of antimicrobial resistance genes in response to application of poultry and swine manure in simulated manure-soil microcosms and manure-pond microcosms, Environ. Sci. Pollut. Res. 2017 (24), p. 20949.

[90]   Y.X. Chen et al., Behavior of Cu and Zn under combined pollution of 2, 4-dichlorophenol in the planted soil, Plant and Soil 2004 (261), p. 127; B. Sharma et al., Synergistic effects of heavy metals and pesticides in living systems, Front. Chem. 2017 (5), p. 70.

[91]   Soil Association, Soil Association organic standards farming and growing, 2016, https://www. soilassociation.org/what-we-do/organic-standards/our-standards/.

[92]   Commission Implementing Regulation (EU) No. 2016/1095 of 6 July 2016 concerning the authorisation of Zinc acetate dihydrate, Zinc chloride anhydrous, Zinc oxide, Zinc sulphate heptahydrate, Zinc sulphate monohydrate, Zinc chelate of amino acids hydrate, Zinc chelate of protein hydrolysates, Zinc chelate of glycine hydrate (solid) and Zinc chelate of glycine hydrate (liquid) as feed additives for all animal species and amending Regulations (EC) No. 1334/2003, (EC) No. 479/2006, (EU) No. 335/2010 and Implementing Regulations (EU) No. 991/2012 and (EU) No. 636/2013, OJ 2016 L 182/7; Commission Regulation (EC) No. 1334/2003 of 25 July 2003 amending the conditions for authorisation of a number of additives in feeding stuffs belonging to the group of trace elements, OJ 2003 L 187; G. Aquilina et al., Revision of the currently authorised maximum copper content in complete feed EFSA Panel on Additives and Products or Substances used in Animal Feed (FEEDAP), EFSA Journal 2016 (14), p. 4563.

[93]   F.A. Nicholson & B.J. Chambers, Sources and impacts of past, current and future contamination of soil Appendix 1: Heavy Metals. Final Report to DEFRA, 2007, http://randd.defra.gov.uk/ Document.aspx?Document=SP0547_7265_FRA.pdf.

[94]   Commission Regulation (EC) No. 1334/2003 of 25 July 2003 amending the conditions for authorisation of a number of additives in feeding stuffs belonging to the group of trace elements, OJ 2003 L 187; Commission Regulation (EC) No. 1881/2006 of 19 December 2006 setting maximum levels for certain contaminants in foodstuffs, OJ 2006 L 364; Commission Regulation (EC) No. 629/2008 of 2 July 2008 amending Regulation (EC) No. 1881/2006 setting maximum levels for certain contaminants in foodstuffs, OJ 2008 L 173.

[95]   Cundill et al., supra, note 83.

[96]   Commission Directive 2008/98/EC of the European Parliament and of the Council of 19 November 2008 on Waste and Repealing Certain Directives, OJ 2008 L 312/3.

complications could arise where multiple producers supply a farm. In this scenario, the farmer is responsible for ensuring sludge comes from a reputable source and must keep their accounts up to date concerning, for example, imports and exports of sludge and the usage of all fertilisers. Furthermore, the possibility still exists for the landowner to be prosecuted as the liability rests with the owner if they "knowingly permitted" contamination.[97] Finally, these procedures do not eliminate the problem of identifying the sources of pollution and it could lead to a lack of trust in environmental protection legislation and may cause financial problems to businesses as the true source goes unnoticed.

3.2. LEGISLATION AND ORGANIC FERTILISERS

Large amounts of animal faecal wastes are applied to agricultural land in the UK,[98] both to dispose of this by-product of animal husbandry and to derive fertiliser value from the essential micro- and macro-elements they contain.[99] It is well known that farmers have supplemented soils with animal manures/slurries for more than 2,000 years in order to increase crop yields, provide plant nutrients, and to enrich soils.[100] However, it can also elevate levels of PTEs, including Cu and Zn, which in the long term may lead to undesirably high levels in the soil[101] and detrimental health effects, as discussed above. Nicholson and colleagues[102] estimated that 2,000t of Zn is spread onto agricultural land from animal manures each year, while in the total agricultural area of England and Wales, livestock manures are responsible for around 40 per cent of the total input of Zn. It is therefore not surprising that, with current large-scale livestock production and increasing globalisation, there is a growing need to protect soil health, especially with regard to the food chain. Although there are measures that set limits for levels of heavy metals found in animal feed, they are regulated in a very indirect way. Directive 2002/32/EC[103] on undesirable substances in animal feed provides for the maximum allowable concentration in feeding stuff of elements such as As, Cd,

---

[97] The Environmental Permitting (England and Wales) Regulations 2016, SI 2016/1154, ss. 12 and 38.

[98] F.A. Nicholson et al., A study on farm manure applications to agricultural land and an assessment of the risks of pathogen transfer into the food chain, A Report to the Ministry of Agricultural Fisheries and Food, 2000.

[99] A.A. Araji et al., Efficient use of animal manure on cropland – economic analysis, Bioresour. Technol. 2001 (79), p. 179.

[100] Moss, supra, note 62 at p. 8.

[101] DEFRA, supra, note 65 at p. 8.

[102] Nicholson, supra, note 45 at p. 6.

[103] Commission Directive 2002/32/EC of the European Parliament and of the Council of 7 May 2002 on undesirable substances in animal feed, OJ 2002 L 140/10.

Pb and Hg. Other legislation that indirectly protects the soil from contamination due to animal manure is the Commission Regulation (EC) No. 1881/2006,[104] setting the maximum levels for certain contaminants in foodstuffs. Nicholson and Chambers found that reducing levels of Zn and Cu in livestock feeds would substantially reduce manure Zn and Cu concentration and decrease inputs to agricultural land and loadings to individual feeds.[105] The EU Animal By-products Regulation[106] applies a light touch to the use of manure and digestive tract content, and seeks to control its use only where necessary. The transposition of the EU law in the UK through the Animal By-products Regulations 2013[107] makes provision for the administration and enforcement of Regulation 1069/2009 in England but it is silent on levels of soil improvers. It suggests significant gaps in the EU and UK legislation in regards to animal manures and inorganic fertilisers.

3.3. INORGANIC FERTILISERS

There has been an increase in the use of inorganic fertilisers, which are essentially synthetic chemicals that help to supply the plants with the nutrients required, promoting plant growth when applied to agricultural soils. Currently Regulation (EC) No. 2003/2003 of the European Parliament and of the Council of 13 October 2003 related to fertilisers does not provide for heavy metal limits associated with inorganic fertilisers, even though they have known to have serious impacts.[108] It follows from the above that the UK has no specific limits on heavy metals in animal manures and inorganic fertilisers, and that the country's agro-ecosystem is inadequately protected.

The EU Commission Regulation setting maximum levels for certain contaminants in foodstuffs (No. 1881/2006)[109] represents an "end of pipe" regulation by setting a limit on the concentration of selected metal PTEs (Cd, Hg, Pb and Sn) in foodstuffs. This may have the consequence of protecting the food produced by rendering a crop unsalable if PTE levels have reached concentrations exceeding statutory limits. However, end of pipe control is of dubious efficacy in protecting soil fertility due to the disconnect between produce and soil concentrations,

---

[104] Commission Regulation (EC) No. 1881/2006 of 19 December 2006 setting maximum levels for certain contaminants in foodstuffs, OJ 2006 L 364/5.
[105] *Nicholson, supra,* note 93 at p. 11.
[106] Commission Regulation (EC) No. 1069/2009 of the European Parliament and of the Council of 21 October 2009 laying down health rules as regards animal by-products and derived products not intended for human consumption and repealing Regulation (EC) No. 1774/2002, OJ 2009 L 300/1.
[107] The Animal By-Products (Enforcement) (England) Regulations 2013, SI 2013/2952.
[108] Commission Regulation (EC) No. 2003/2003 of the European Parliament and of the Council of 13 October 2003 Relating to Fertilisers, OJ 2003 L 304/1.
[109] Commission Regulation (EC) No. 1881/2006 of 19 December 2006 setting maximum levels for certain contaminants in foodstuffs, OJ 2006 L 364/5.

i.e. safe food can potentially be produced from polluted soil. Other aspects of soil health are dealt with sporadically through 24 European Union laws that in some way address elements of soil "contamination" in the relation to air, water, waste, chemicals, impact assessment and environmental liability.[110] For example, the Water Framework Directive (2000/60/EC)[111] seeks to achieve good ecological status of water resources/bodies, thus indirectly mitigating soil health through reduced erosion, runoff, phosphate and nitrate levels. While the Common Agricultural Policy seeks to reduce erosion and maintain OM and structure, it only provides guidelines to avoid contamination, which are typically in line with existing legislation. Other sources of Cu and Zn within agro-ecosystems can be applied through the addition of composted "wastes", which are controlled through a voluntary code of conduct that details heavy metal concentrations. Separated biodegradable wastes "compost" is controlled in England and Wales by BSI PAS 100,[112] which sets target concentrations and upper limits for metals, including Cu and Zn, that can be applied without permit. Although this standard is targeted at the horticultural industry, there is opportunity for small holders to use such fertiliser material. Another source for concern has to do with the Environmental Permitting Regulations 2016[113] and its amendments, which permits the application of waste where it can be shown that there is an agricultural benefit or ecological improvement. There is a possibility that this waste could contain high levels of PTEs.

3.4. THE POTENTIAL FOR ORGANIC FERTILISERS TO HARM SOILS

The lack of legal controls on the addition of PTEs to soil in forms other than sewage sludge clearly leaves soil health vulnerable. Amongst the chemicals categorised as PTEs, Cu and Zn are the least controlled and have the greatest potential to affect soil health and fertility due to their potential to cause toxicity to important soil microbes at relatively low concentrations. Whilst organic by-products such as manures have a sufficient nutrient content to act as fertilisers and can replace lost organic carbon from the soil, they can also contain significant levels of Cu and Zn.[114]

---

[110]   *Rodrígues, supra*, note 2 at p. 1.
[111]   Commission Directive 2000/60/EC of the European Parliament and of the Council of 23 October 2000 establishing a framework for Community action in the field of water policy, OJ 2000 L 327/1.
[112]   WRAP, The Waste and Resources Action Programme, BSI PAS 100 FAQs, 2016, http://www.wrap.org.uk/collections-and-reprocessing/organic-waste/composting/guidance/BSI-PAS-100-FAQs.
[113]   The Environmental Permitting (England and Wales) Regulations 2016, SI 2016/1154.
[114]   *Nicholson, supra*, note 45 at p. 6.

The authors therefore estimated the time required for the application of these materials to raise the concentration of Cu and Zn in an average agricultural soil to the limit levels enshrined in the Sewage Sludge Directive. Calculations were based on the mean metal concentrations for rural soils in the UK[115] and the mean bulk density (1.24 g cm^{-3}) for arable soils in England and Wales.[116] Metal concentrations in organic by-products used to derive the estimates were those reported by Nicholson et al. (2006)[117] and the assumption was made that the organic fertiliser was evenly distributed throughout a plough layer 25 cm deep. Applications of organic fertilisers are limited to 170 kg N ha^{-1} yr^{-1} in nitrate vulnerable zones and 250 kg N ha^{-1} yr^{-1} outside these zones. Consequently, estimates were made at both N application rates using the values for N content quoted by MAFF[118] to determine the amount of each organic fertiliser that represented the appropriate N application. A dry matter content of 6 per cent and a specific gravity of 1.038 was assumed for dairy slurry, whilst the respective values for pig slurry were 4 per cent and 1.026.

Table 1. Estimated time required (years) to reach the current EU limit for Cu soils with a pH < 7.0, for an average rural UK soil when organic fertilisers with mean and the high levels of contamination are applied at rates permitted in nitrate vulnerable zones (NVC) and outside of such zones

	Mean conc. fertiliser		High conc. fertiliser	
	In NVZ	Outside	In NVZ	Outside
Sewage sludge	153	110	115	83
Diary slurry	1527	1100	270	195
Dairy manure	1261	908	847	610
Pig slurry	546	394	238	171
Pig manure	147	106	71	51
Layer manure	1619	1167	1403	1011
Broiler manure	1018	733	569	410

Source: Authors.

The result of these calculations demonstrated that sewage sludge application could most rapidly increase soil concentrations of both Cu and Zn to limit

115   *Environment Agency*, UK soil and herbage pollutant survey – UKSHS Report No. 1, 2007.
116   *Environment Agency*, The development and use of soil quality indicators for assessing the role of soil in environmental interactions – Science Report SC030265, 2006.
117   *Nicholson, supra*, note 45 at p. 6.
118   *MAFF*, Fertiliser recommendations for agricultural crops and horticultural crops (RB209), 7th ed., The Stationary Office, 2000.

values; therefore, the level at which soil microbial processes important to fertility may be affected. However, pig manure may increase soil Cu concentrations slightly quicker than sewage sludge (Table 1). The time taken for dairy and pig slurries to raise soil Cu concentrations to the limit value can also come close to sewage sludge if the most contaminated slurries are applied at a high rate. Where organic fertilisers have a mean concentration of Zn, pig manure is again the only fertiliser that is close to sewage sludge in ability to increase soil concentrations (Table 2). However, dairy, layer and broiler manure can also increase soil Zn concentrations at rate that could lead to limit values being reached within a time scale short enough to suggest that their application could impact soil quality. When organic fertilisers with high concentrations of Zn are considered, pig slurry and manure could potentially raise the Zn concentration in an "average" soil to the limit value within a human lifetime. Moreover, dairy slurry, dairy manure, layer manure and broiler manure could potentially raise soil concentrations to the limit value within 200 years.

Table 2. Estimated time required (years) to reach the current UK code of practice limit for Zn (200mg kg^{-1} for soil with a pH < 7.0) for an average rural UK soil when organic fertilisers with mean and the high levels of contamination are applied at rates permitted in nitrate vulnerable zones (NVC) and outside of such zones

	Mean conc. fertiliser		High conc. fertiliser	
	In side NVZ	Out side	In side NVZ	Out side
Sewage sludge	112	81	83	60
Dairy slurry	473	340	136	98
Dairy manure	321	231	206	149
Pig slurry	346	250	80	57
Pig manure	133	96	80	58
Layer manure	237	171	172	124
Broiler manure	271	195	216	156

Source: Authors.

The scenarios used in these calculations are not unrealistic. For example, maximal applications of dairy manure/slurry are applied to soil to drive maize production to feed to cows and the need to dispose of manures/slurries frequently requires their application at the maximum permission N loading rate. Moreover, whilst organic fertilisers are frequently applied annually, sewage sludge amendments are typically made every third year. Consequently, the use of organic fertilisers can elevate soil Cu and Zn concentrations with similar, and in some case higher, rates than sewage sludge under conditions of normal use. However, the extent of the problem of PTE enrichment in European soils is not well researched and there is a very real risk that soil health could to be damaged within a human lifetime.

It is clear that the application of manures/slurries can elevate soil PTE concentrations in the plough layer to levels that could affect the functionality of the microbial soil community, which in turn will have a negative impact on soil health and fertility. Thus, current agricultural practices are not compatible with sustainable food production and lowered crop production may occur in a time scale as short as decades. To date, legal controls on the accumulation of PTEs, particularly from the use of organic by-products, are insufficient to prevent this and urgent action is required to address this.

It is surprising, therefore to realise that currently there are no specific legislative controls on the accumulation of PTEs applied to agricultural soils via animal manure and inorganic fertilisers. Sewage sludge indicator pathogen concentrations are regulated, but no such regulations exist for manures. Furthermore, Regulation (EC) 2003/2003 relating to fertilisers[119] does not provide for heavy metal limits.

At this point, we may perhaps introduce a synergetic approach[120] to the topic addressed, as it could bring some clarity and flexibility that may help with integrating the variety of legal instruments, ensuring the return of valuable nutrients and OM to the contaminated soil and thus undoing the current unbalanced relationship between economics and soil health.[121]

4. ECOSYSTEM SERVICES

So far, we have argued that for decades, science, policy and legal initiatives installed to protect soil from degradation are, at least in part, inadequate. We would like to suggest that novel ways need to be explored in order to address the problems at hand.

One way is the application of ES within soil policy and legislation to provide management practices that avoid damage to soils and therefore promote sustainable agricultural systems. If ES were to become an imperative, it would be a substantial addition to current soil protection policy and legislation. It may be beneficial in supporting the continuous flow of ES, which would secure

---

[119] Commission Regulation (EC) No. 2003/2003 of the European Parliament and of the Council of 13 October 2003 Relating to Fertilisers, OJ 2003 L 304/1.

[120] A.C. Singer et al., Review of antimicrobial resistance in the environment and its relevance to environmental regulators, Front. Microbiol. 2016 (7), p. 1728.

[121] J. Hall, Ecological and economical balance for sludge management options, in European Commission Joint Research Centre, Workshop on Problems Around Sludge, 2000.

the availability of natural capital (NC), i.e. the world's stocks of natural assets, which includes air, water, and all living entities.[122] A decrease in NC would create a situation in which substitutes such as manufactured or human capital would be used.[123] A common example of this situation is seen when farmers add fertilisers to the soil to offset the decrease in fertility.[124] However, situations where substitution is possible are highly unlikely in some cases, for example where there is loss of important species that hold cultural importance and where there are economical impracticalities due to the loss of services like erosion control.[125] The original public good is free; therefore, difficulties arise when the use of substitutes become too costly, or when available substitutes for that particular service are absent.[126] In addition, it is important to note that many ES do not have feasible substitutes.[127]

As Daily has argued, when economic activities are limited, ES is under less pressure.[128] The more our economy develops, the more societal wants and needs create a situation that causes pressures to be brought to bear on vital ES.[129] When demand for a service reaches the limits of its capacity/availability or where its supply decreases to the minimum level for survival, the price of that service can become infinite.[130] This may potentially create difficulties for obtaining access to these vital services, thus threatening human well-being.[131]

Protecting soil ES and NC is important and challenging at the same time. These concepts have been undervalued by governments, businesses and society, which may be one explanation as to why they have been inadequately protected. Governments seem to invest in protection of certain ES if the benefits obtained from those services are apparent,[132] for example drinking water. However, this is not the case with less apparent ES, such as erosion control or nutrient cycling.

---

[122] *World Forum on Natural Capital*, What is Natural Capital?, https://naturalcapitalforum.com/about/.

[123] R. Costanza, The value of the world's ecosystem services and natural capital, Nature 1997 (387), p. 253.

[124] *Millennium Ecosystem Assessment (MEA)*, Ecosystems and Human Well-being: A Framework for Assessment, Island Press, 2003, p. 14.

[125] Id.

[126] G.C. Daily, Management Objectives for the Protection of Ecosystem Services, Environ. Sci. Pol. 2000 (3), p. 333.

[127] *Costanza, supra*, note 123.

[128] *Daily, supra*, note 126.

[129] Green Facts, Biodiversity & Human Well-being https://www.greenfacts.org/en/biodiversity/index.htm#2.

[130] M.A. Finvers, Application of e²DPSIR for analysis of soil protection issues and an assessment of British Columbia's soil protection legislation, MSc Thesis, Cranfield University; *Costanza, supra*, note 123.

[131] *Daily, supra*, note 126.

[132] H. Tallis et al., An Ecosystem Services Framework to Support Both Practical Conservation and Economic Development, PNAS 2008 (105), p. 9457.

Even though there is a movement towards the integration of ES into soil policy,[133] fundamental issues need to be dealt with in order to achieve robust soil protection. To begin with, there is a lack of information regarding the concept of ES.[134] The science of ES is equally complex[135] and practical problems such as classification and calculation of ES and their valuation are yet to be addressed.[136] Furthermore, it is argued that, without legal status, these services will continue to diminish.[137] Integrating ES into the current environmental policy and law cannot be addressed through minor alterations of legal instruments.[138] Thus, a radical shift in this approach is required.[139] One such approach has been suggested by Salzman and colleagues, who propose that this ES approach can be operationalised through a four-step process which involves the following aspects: education, science, law and economics.[140]

Applying Salzman and colleagues' approach to soil ES, firstly, it is argued that awareness and education are crucial for understanding the importance of ES for humans.[141] Humans do not appreciate the potential threats to ES,[142] owing to the fact that there is disconnect between them and the natural world. ES helps to make the soil functions visible, resulting in more human appreciation of their role.[143]

Following on, knowledge of the linkages between functions of ecosystems and the provision of ES should be strengthened through science.[144] There are numerous aspects missing within the existing soil ES classification frameworks, such as: the complexity and characteristics of soil functioning;[145] the link between soil NC, functions and ES;[146] the categorisation of different services;

---

[133]   L. Greiner et al., Soil Function Assessment: Review of Methods for Quantifying the Contributions of Soils to Ecosystem Services, Land Use Pol. 2017 (69), p. 224.

[134]   D. Markell, Symposium – Ecosystem Services, Stan. Envtl. L.J. 2001 (20), p. 309.

[135]   K.M.A. Chan et al., Conservation Planning for Ecosystem Services, PLoS Biology 2006 (4), p. 2138.

[136]   K. Grunewald & O. Bastian, Ecosystem Services – Concept, Methods and Case Studies, Springer, 2015.

[137]   B. Pardy, Book Review: The Law and Policy of Ecosystem Services, by J.B. Ruhl, Steven E. Kraft and Christopher L. Lant. OHLJ 2008 (46), p. 445.

[138]   Id.

[139]   Id.

[140]   J. Salzman et al., Protecting Ecosystem Services: Science, Economics and Law, SELJ 2001 (20), p. 309.

[141]   Id.

[142]   Id.

[143]   A. Grêt-Regamey et al., Soils and Their Contribution to Ecosystem Services, National Research Programme NRP 68, 2016.

[144]   Salzman, supra, note 140.

[145]   E. Garrigues et al., Soil Quality in Life Cycle Assessment: Towards Development of an Indicator, Ecol. Indic. 2012 (18), p. 434.

[146]   E. Dominati et al., A Soil Change-Based Methodology for the Quantification and Valuation of Ecosystem Services From Agro-Ecosystems: A Case Study of Pastoral Agriculture in New Zealand, Ecol. Econ. 2014 (100), p. 119.

the potential beneficiaries of soil ES;[147] and a standardised definition for each soil ES.[148] To operationalise the aforementioned aspects, it is necessary to overcome the lack of consensus in the scientific literature regarding the classification of soil ES.[149] In addition, sustainable soil management[150] and governance based on ES can only be achieved through interdisciplinary approaches.[151] It is not possible to generate an effective environmental policy without validating it with scientific information.[152] Hence, soil scientists should engage with stakeholders from other disciplines, policy makers, communities and the public, and communicate more productively to improve the legal regime.[153]

The third step of this ES approach deals with the operationalisation of ES in order to promote the importance of soils in policy and law.[154] The integration of ES within institutional and regulatory frameworks is required in order to avoid ES remaining as an abstract idea.[155] It is opined that creating effective soil protection laws from an ES perspective requires ecological consciousness and the concepts of natural rights of soil being embedded into the legal instruments.[156] Furthermore, these laws should be underpinned by monitoring and valuation of soil ES to promote effectiveness.[157]

The final step of ES integration requires the valuation of ES.[158] Appreciation of the actual monetary value of ES[159] enables appropriate consideration of the

---

[147] J. Örvar et al., Classification and valuation of soil ecosystem services, Agri. Sys. 2016 (145), p. 24.

[148] Dominati, supra, note 146.

[149] G.C. Daily, Nature's Services: Societal Dependence on Natural Ecosystems, Island Press, 1997; P. Lavelle et al., Soil Invertebrates and Ecosystem Services, Eur. J. Soil Biol. 2006 (42), S3; E. Barrios, Soil Biota, Ecosystem Services and Land Productivity, Ecol. Econ. 2007 (64), p. 269; S.M. Swinton et al., Ecosystem Services and Agriculture: Cultivating Agricultural Ecosystems for Diverse Benefits, Ecol. Econ. 2007 (64), p. 245; W. Zhang et al., Ecosystem Services and Dis-services to Agriculture, Ecol. Econ. 2007 (64), p. 253; H.S. Sandhu et al., The Future of Farming: The Value of Ecosystem Services in Conventional and Organic Arable Land – An Experimental Approach, Ecol. Econ. 2008 (64), p. 835; E. Dominati et al., A Framework for Classifying and Quantifying the Natural Capital and Ecosystem Services of Soils, Ecol. Econ. 2010 (69), p. 1858; Örvar, supra, note 147.

[150] Y.-G. Zhu & A.A. Meharg, Protecting global soil resources for ecosystem services, Ecosys. Health Sustain. 2017 (1), p. 11.

[151] R.B. Prado et al., Current Overview and Potential Applications of the Soil Ecosystem Services Approach in Brazil, Pesq. Agropec. Bras. 2016 (51), p. 1021.

[152] MEA, supra, note 124 at p. 17.

[153] A.M. Wyatt, The Dirt on International Environmental Law Regarding Soils: Is the Existing Regime Adequate?, DELPF 2008 (19), p. 165.

[154] Grêt-Regamey, supra, note 143 at p. 18.

[155] Salzman, supra, note 140 at p. 18.

[156] I. Hannam & B. Boer, Legal and Institutional Frameworks for Sustainable Soils: A Preliminary Report, IUCN, 2002.

[157] B.B. Ghaley et al., Quantification and valuation of ecosystem services in diverse production systems for informed decision-making, Environ. Sci. Pol. 2014 (39), p. 139.

[158] Salzman, supra, note 140 at p. 18.

[159] Id.

overall effects of changes in soil functionality.[160] A fundamental weakness of the existing frameworks is that soil is normally valued from the perspective of land or production[161] and rarely is the economic valuation of soil ES considered.[162] These schemes focus on the above-ground component of ES, rather than the less visible ones, for example nutrient cycling,[163] which are overlooked in decisions regarding land use and management as these are commonly non-marketable.[164] However, more rational decisions require marketable and non-marketable ES to be taken into consideration by decision-makers.

Overall, it is argued that the main aim of adopting an ES approach is to protect and restore services that function for the benefit all edaphic organisms and human existence. Implementing this into policy and legislation, and more importantly creating a paradigm shift, is crucial for the protection of soil and the ES it provides.

5. CONCLUSION

It is clear from the above discussion that the accumulation of Zn and Cu in agricultural soil has serious implications for soil biodiversity. The more serious issue is the fact that it highlights the inadequacies of the current direct and indirect legal instruments used to protect soils. Legal controls on PTEs within agro-ecosystems are minimal in Europe and the UK. Their control is largely through codes of practice, incentive schemes and infrequently legislation. This serves as an example of the ineffectiveness of the current legislation to protect soils. If we are to preserve the fragile balance between the human need to exploit our natural capital and maintaining the delicate soil ecosystems, it is crucial to adopt a synergetic approach through the application of ES to halt the deterioration of our Earth.

---

[160] *D.A. Robinson et al.*, Natural Capital, Ecosystem Services, and Soil Change: Why Soil Science Must Embrace an Ecosystems Approach, Vadose Zone J. 2012 (11), p. 5.
[161] Id.
[162] *Örvar, supra*, note 147 at p. 19.
[163] *Dominati, supra*, note 149 at p. 19.
[164] *Ghaley, supra*, note 157.

PART II
PRIVATE AND CORPORATE
ENVIRONMENTAL LIABILITY

CORPORATE SOCIAL RESPONSIBILITY AND CORPORATE LIABILITY FOR ENVIRONMENTAL DAMAGE

Carola GLINSKI

1. INTRODUCTION

For decades, transnational corporations have been involved in environmental disasters or continuous environmental degradation, in particular in the "Global South" where public law standards and/or enforcement are weak. The chemical accident in Bhopal, chemical and asbestos contamination in South Africa or oil pollution in Nigeria have led to spectacular transnational tort liability cases against parent companies in the "Global North", such as Union Carbide, Thor Chemicals, Cape plc or Royal Dutch Shell, which however have had very limited success. Whereas some environmental liability laws, especially in the US and in Europe, have established a certain parallelism between control (of operations) and liability, and therefore parent companies can be regarded as "operators" of a polluting production site,[1] their geographical spread is limited and traditional tort law has for a long time been reluctant to assign liability to parent companies.

While no international agreement on the environmental (and social) responsibility of transnational corporations could be reached until now, private standards on the subject matter have emerged in many industries, today often referred to as corporate social responsibility (CSR) standards. They were, however, largely regarded to be voluntary and outside the legal sphere.

Recently, the picture has begun to change. On the one hand, public (international) law is increasingly assigning responsibility to parent companies and to "leading" companies in transnational production chains. In particular, the UN Guiding Principles on Business and Human Rights, although formally soft law, are in the process of being implemented in a number of European jurisdictions.

---

[1] See *infra*, section 3.2.1.

On the other hand, recent developments in tort law, most importantly in the English cases of *Chandler v. Cape* (concerning asbestos exposure of a subsidiary's employee) and *Vedanta* (concerning serious environmental degradation resulting from a copper mine in Zambia) point towards increased liability of parent companies. In this context, the tort law relevance of CSR or environmental self-regulation has explicitly been discussed in the two recent cases of *Vedanta* and *Okpabi* (the latter concerning serious environmental degradation resulting from oil spills in Nigeria).

This chapter analyses the legal relevance of transnational CSR or environmental self-regulation and best practices for the liability of parent companies in the light of recent tort law developments, and in particular for the establishment of a duty of care of parent companies towards the neighbours of industrial production of subsidiaries or supplies in the Global South. It starts by briefly presenting the background of CSR instruments (section 2) and by setting out principled requirements for the tort liability of parent companies (section 3) before it turns to the discussion of the relevance of CSR self-regulation for the tort liability of parent companies with the cases of *Vedanta* and *Okpabi* (sections 3.1 and 3.2). It then presents a proposal for a more principled duty of parent companies to organise the corporation in such a way that damage by subsidiaries or suppliers to third parties is avoided (section 3.3) before it offers conclusions (section 4).

2. CORPORATE SOCIAL RESPONSIBILITY INSTRUMENTS

2.1. BACKGROUND

Transnational economic activities based on environmentally sensitive production in the Global South where protection and/or enforcement standards are low have attracted attention for a long time. Concerns follow from the observation that production abroad often is either based on resource extraction in countries where standards are low or constitutes the (mere) outsourcing of production to countries where production costs are low. This is often accompanied by the transfer (and operation) of risk technologies to subsidiaries and societies which are often legally, administrative, technically and/or financially poorly equipped to deal with these technologies. Frequently, the subsidiary (or supplier) is financially dependent, whereas superior knowledge and means concerning risk prevention rest with the parent (or leading) company.

At the same time, corporate groups have always been characterised by the legal separation of the parent company from its subsidiaries, and even more so the leading companies in supply chains from the individual suppliers.

In the words of John Ruggie: the challenge is to change the "fact that each legally distinct entity is subject to the laws of the countries in which it operates, but the corporate group as a whole is not governed directly by international law".[2]

2.2. PUBLIC INTERNATIONAL LAW

Since the 1970s, there have been attempts to introduce human rights, social and environmental responsibilities for (transnational) corporations, which more recently have been extended to (transnational) supply chains. Nevertheless, the current situation is still characterised by the absence of binding public international law instruments. Previous international attempts to introduce human rights, social and environmental obligations for transnational corporations through classical international law mechanisms have either failed,[3] remained soft law[4] or been built upon the voluntary cooperation of transnational corporations.[5] It remains to be seen whether or not the Human Rights Council's attempt to set up a binding treaty on business and human rights[6] will be more successful. However, in particular, the UN Guiding Principles on Business and Human Rights[7] have gained significant importance and are in the process of being implemented in a number of European jurisdictions.[8] They can by now be regarded as the "state of the art" on the subject matter of business responsibility.

---

[2] *J. Ruggie*, Business and Human Rights: The evolving international agenda, The American Journal of International Law 2007 (101), p. 818, 824.

[3] See UN Intergovernmental Working Group on a Code of Conduct, Draft UN Code of Conduct on Transnational Corporations, UN Doc. E/1990/94, 12 June 1990; Norms on the Responsibilities of Transnational Corporations and Other Business Enterprises with Regard to Human Rights (Draft Norms), UN Doc. E/CN.4/Sub.2/2003/12/Rev.2, 26 August 2003.

[4] See, for example, the OECD Guidelines for Multinational Corporations as first adopted in 1976, available at http://mneguidelines.oecd.org/text; the revised OECD Guidelines for Multinational Enterprises of 2011 have at least been equipped with certain enforcement and sanction mechanisms, see http://www.oecd.org/corporate/mne/48004323.pdf. Another example would be the Tripartite Declaration of Principles Concerning Multinational Enterprises and Social Policy of the ILO, available at http://www.ilo.org/empent/Publications/WCMS_094386/lang--en/index.htm.

[5] See e.g. the UN Global Compact, available at http://www.unglobalcompact.org.

[6] *Human Rights Council*, Elaboration of an International Legally Binding Instrument on Transnational Corporations and Other Business Enterprises with Respect to Human Rights, 24 June 2014, A/HRC/26/L.22/Rev.1; *Human Rights Council*, Human Rights and Transnational Corporations and Other Business Enterprises, 23 June 2014, A/HRC/26/L.1.

[7] *J. Ruggie*, Guiding Principles on Business and Human Rights: Implementing the United Nations "Protect, Respect and Remedy" Framework, UN Doc. A/HRC/17/31, 31 March 2011, http://www.ohchr.org/documents/issues/business/A.HRC.17.31.pdf.

[8] See, most prominently, the French Loi no. 2017-399 du 27 mars 2017 relative au devoir de vigilance des sociétés mères et des entreprises donneuses d'ordre. See also *M. Krajewski*, Regulierung transnationaler Wirtschaftsbeziehungen zum Schutz der Menschenrechte: Staatliche Schutzpflichten jenseits der Grenze?, in M. Krajewski (ed.), Menschenrechte in globalen Lieferketten, FAU University Press, 2018, p. 103, 114 et seq.

They rest on three pillars: first, the states' duty to protect human rights against abuse by third parties, including business actors, requiring "appropriate steps to prevent, investigate, punish and redress private actors' abuse through effective policies, legislation, regulations and adjudication" (Principles 1 et seq.); second, the corporations' responsibility to respect human rights in their own activities as well as in business relationships directly linked to their operations (Principles 11 et seq.), which requires (parent or "leading") companies to carry out corporation-wide or supply-chain-wide "due diligence", which includes a related business self-commitment at the most senior level of the enterprise, a detailed risk assessment and preventive as well as remediation measures; and third, access to effective judicial and non-judicial remedies (Principles 25 et seq.).

2.3. PRIVATE CSR INITIATIVES

The public international law regimes are complemented by a multitude of hybrid or private transnational regimes addressing human rights, social and environmental issues. The latter range from arrangements between public or international bodies and private stakeholders over purely private multi-stakeholder approaches[9] to unilateral self-regulatory instruments adopted by business organisations or individual businesses. Self-commitments accompanied by management systems have often been elaborate and detailed, in particular those related to the health, safety and environmental management of corporations, including their subsidiaries. In fact, in branches with increased potential of risk, the parent company often does not delimit itself to mere financial control; instead, there is often a special department within the parent company that exercises intense control over the production structures in subsidiaries abroad, partly by issuing very detailed internal guidelines and handbooks, compliance with which is regularly monitored by auditors.[10]

Examples of such self-regulatory systems are the Shell Commitment and Policy on Health, Security, Safety, Environment and Social Performance, which applies across the Shell group and contains mandatory standards and accompanying manuals, and the Vedanta Health, Safety and Environment Charter, which is titled "zero harm, waste and discharge" and which refers to the corporation-wide implementation of "world class standards", risk management and control of effectiveness (see also below, section 3.2).

---

[9] The most prominent private regime is the Forest Stewardship Council, on which see, for example, *E. Meidinger*, Multi-Interest Self-Governance through Global Product Certification Programmes, in O. Dilling, M. Herberg & G. Winter (eds.), Responsible Business: Self-Governance and the Law in Transnational Economic Transactions, Hart Publishing, 2007, pp. 259 et seq.

[10] On the transnational German chemicals industry see *M. Herberg*, Codes of Conduct und kommunikative Vernunft, Zeitschrift für Rechtssoziologie 2001, pp. 25 et seq.

3. TORT LAW AND THE DUTY OF CARE OF PARENT COMPANIES

The tort laws of the various countries even within the European Union differ, as they have scarcely been harmonised by EU law or other supranational law. Still, there are common principles that allow, with all caution, an analysis of whether parent companies may incur liability for damage that their subsidiaries have caused to third parties, and whether leading companies in a supply chain may be liable for damage caused by their suppliers. In the following, this chapter mainly focuses on English law, as this is the most important legal order for transnational tort law claims due to its wide influence throughout the common law world, but it also makes comparative references to other legal systems. It focuses on the tort of negligence, which is the basis of recent case law and where CSR instruments can have a significant impact on the *duty of care* of the parent company as well as on the *standard of care*.

An indispensable requirement of the tort of negligence in many, if not all, legal systems is a duty of care that the alleged tortfeasor owes to the victim. For example, the English tort of negligence is based on the rule "you must not injure your neighbour".[11] Under German law, tort law liability under §823 para. 1 of the German Civil Code (*Bürgerliches Gesetzbuch*, BGB) arises where a person, intentionally or negligently, unlawfully injures the life, body, health, freedom, property or another right of another person. Then there must be a breach of that duty of care, and that breach must have caused harm to the victim.

Doctrinally, the major challenge for establishing the parent or leading company's liability is the fact that usually the subsidiary or supplier, which has directly caused the damage, is a legally independent entity and thus a "third party". Liability for damages caused by third parties is not a natural element of tort law but requires specific justification. However, corporate structures (and to a certain extent also supply chains) often involve a complex allocation of responsibilities, resources and control. Therefore, tort law criteria such as the (co-)generation and the maintenance of a risk and/or (the potential for) risk control could apply to the parent or leading company. In addition, previous dangerous actions or an assumption of responsibility for certain (dangerous) management or monitoring tasks could lead to relevant proximity of the parent or leading company to victims and/or the endangered environment and their dependence on the care of the parent or leading company.[12]

---

[11] See Donoghue v. Stevenson [1932] AC 562, 580.

[12] For an overview of relevant criteria in German tort law see e.g. G. *Spindler*, § 823 BGB Schadensersatzpflicht, in B. Gsell et al. (eds.), Beck-online Großkommentar, C.H. Beck, 2018, paras. 385 et seq.

Thus, in principle and depending on the circumstances of the individual case, parent or leading companies could be held liable, for example, and rather obviously, for direct orders to the subsidiary or supplier that have led to damage to third parties, but also for the breach of a duty in a relevant sector for which the parent or leading company has voluntarily assumed responsibility, or perhaps even for the infringement of a general corporation-wide duty of care.[13]

3.1. DIRECT ORDERS OF THE PARENT OR CORE COMPANY

If the parent company has had an active role in the detrimental action or event, for example by giving instructions or by issuing management handbooks, and the subsidiary causes damage while following these instructions, the parent company is liable if the procedures followed were below the standard of a "reasonable enterprise".[14] This result should be obvious in all legal systems and has just been confirmed by the UK Supreme Court in *Vedanta*, where the Court explicitly refers to group-wide policies and guidelines of a corporation that have created an unsafe system of production as one possibility where CSR instruments could lead to parent liability.[15]

3.2. ASSUMPTION OF RESPONSIBILITY

3.2.1. The General Doctrine

In principle, tort liability resulting from a *de facto* or contractual assumption of responsibility for certain (safety) tasks is common to many legal orders.[16] For example, in the US *Amoco Cadiz* case the State Court of Illinois found that the oil spill was caused negligently by the parent company that had been

---

[13] See, generally, *C. Glinski*, Die rechtliche Bedeutung der privaten Regulierung globaler Produktionsstandards, Nomos, 2010, pp. 332 et seq.

[14] See e.g. *R. Mares*, A Gap in the Responsibility to Respect Human Rights, http://rwi.lu.se/app/uploads/2012/08/A-Gap-in-the-Corporate-Responsibility.pdf, p. 48 (also published in Monash University Law Review 2010 (36), pp. 33–83); *H.P. Westermann*, Umwelthaftung im Konzern, Zeitschrift für das gesamte Handelsrecht 1991 (155), p. 223, 239 et seq.; *G. Wagner*, Haftung für Menschenrechtsverletzungen, Rabels Zeitschrift für ausländisches und internationales Privatrecht 2016 (80), pp. 717 et seq. Regarding the relevant standard of a "reasonable enterprise", see *infra*, section 3.3.5.

[15] Vedanta Resources PLC and another v. Lungowe and others [2019] UKSC 20, para. 52. For details of the case, see *infra*, section 3.2.2.1.

[16] For Germany, see *Spindler, supra*, note 12 at paras. 392 et seq., 427 et seq.; *G. Wagner*, § 823 Schadensersatzpflicht, in M. Habersack (ed.), *Münchener Kommentar zum Bürgerlichen Gesetzbuch*, vol. 6, 7th ed., C.H. Beck, 2017, paras. 464, 466 et seq.

responsible for the safety and the maintenance of the whole fleet and thus of the ship, according to the contract between the parent company and its subsidiary.[17] This principle is also reflected in the environmental liability laws in many countries, where a parent company that controls the environmental management of the subsidiary can be regarded as the (joint) operator of the plant and be held directly liable for the damage.[18] In English law, an assumption of responsibility creates the doctrinally necessary proximity between the one who has assumed responsibility and the victim. In particular, this applies to experts[19] and others with special abilities who support those that are primarily responsible in relation to safety tasks.[20] An assumption of responsibility does not rely on the will of the one who assumes responsibility, but is objectively imposed by law according to certain criteria[21] and depending on the concrete circumstances.[22]

Concerning production and corporate structures, the landmark decision of the English Court of Appeal in the case of *Chandler v. Cape*[23] was a breakthrough. The Court of Appeal held the parent company Cape plc liable towards Mr Chandler, an employee of its wholly owned subsidiary Cape Products who had developed asbestosis due to defective health and safety standards. Summarising the judgment, Arden LJ stated that:

> in appropriate circumstances the law may impose on a parent company responsibility for the health and safety of its subsidiary's employees. ...

---

[17] See *J.E. Antunes*, Neue Wege im Konzernhaftungsrecht – Nochmals: Der "Amoco Cadiz"-Fall, in U.H. Schneider et al. (eds.), Festschrift für Marcus Lutter zum 70. Geburtstag, Otto Schmidt Verlag, 2000, p. 1007.

[18] On German environmental liability law, see *P. Salje*, Umwelthaftungsgesetz, C.H. Beck, 1990, p. 50; *Westermann, supra*, note 14 at p. 240; *U.H. Schneider*, Die Überlagerung des Konzernrechts durch öffentlich-rechtliche Strukturnormen und Organisationspflichten, Zeitschrift für Unternehmens- und Gesellschaftsrecht, 1996, p. 225, 239 et seq.; *A. Hucke & H. Schröder*, Umwelthaftung von Konzernen, Der Betrieb, 1998, pp. 2205, 2206. On US American environmental liability law, namely the Comprehensive Environmental Response, Compensation and Liability Act (CERCLA), 42 U.S.C. §§9601–9675 (1991), and related case law, see *U. Vettori*, Haftung für Ökoschäden im Recht der USA, Lang, 1996, pp. 100 et seq.; *W. Meier*, Grenzüberschreitender Durchgriff in der Unternehmensgruppe nach US-amerikanischem Recht, Lang, 2000, pp. 585 et seq.; *M. Landwehr*, Die Durchgriffshaftung in konzernverbundenen Gesellschaften, Lang, 2002, pp. 113 et seq.

[19] See the landmark decision of Hedley Byrne v. Heller [1964] AC 465 (HL).

[20] See Phelps v. Hillington LBC; Anderton v. Clwyd CC; G (A Minor) v. Bromley LBC; Jarvis v. Hampshire CC [2000] 4 All ER 504 (HL); Capital & Counties plc v. Hampshire County Council [1997] QB 1004, 1034.

[21] See the clear statement by Lord Bingham in Customs and Excise Commrs v. Barclays Bank plc [2007] 1 AC 181, para. 5.

[22] See only Customs and Excise Commrs v. Barclays Bank plc [2007] 1 AC 181, para. 8.

[23] [2012] EWCA Civ 525. For detailed analysis, see *M. Petrin*, Assumption of Responsibility in Corporate Groups: *Chandler v. Cape plc*, Modern Law Review 2013 (76), p. 589, 603 et seq.; *S. Demeyere*, Liability of a Mother Company for its Subsidiary in French, Belgian, and English Law, European Review of Private Law 2015, p. 385, 402 et seq.

(1) the businesses of the parent and subsidiary are in a relevant respect the same;

(2) the parent has, or ought to have, superior knowledge on some relevant aspect of health and safety in the particular industry;

(3) the subsidiary's system of work is unsafe as the parent company knew, or ought to have known; and

(4) the parent knew or ought to have foreseen that the subsidiary or its employees would rely on its using that superior knowledge for the employees' protection.

For the purposes of (4) it is not necessary to show that the parent is in the practice of intervening in the health and safety policies of the subsidiary. The court will look at the relationship between the companies more widely. The court may find that element (4) is established where the parent has a practice of intervening in the trading operations of the subsidiary, for example production and funding issues.[24]

In substance, it was crucial that Cape plc had omitted to advise the subsidiary as to what precautionary measures it should take.[25] However, already in *Thompson v. Renwick*,[26] the same court applied these criteria more restrictively and emphasised the importance of the parent being in the same business and having superior knowledge, which does not apply to a pure holding company. That basic distinction has been pursued in recent case law, including the cases of *Vedanta* and *Okpabi* that are discussed below (section 3.2).

Chandler v. Cape, although a judgment under English law, had significant influence on the legal development in other countries, in particular in the common law world. For example, the District Court of The Hague regarded *Chandler v. Cape* to be a part of Nigerian law,[27] and in *Vedanta*, one of the issues was whether this judgment would be followed under Zambian law.[28] In the German case of *Jabir and Others v. KiK*, the logic of *Chandler v. Cape* has been tried under the law of Pakistan.[29] Even beyond the common law world, *Chandler v. Cape* revived the discussions around parent company liability.[30]

Chandler v. Cape has been applied since to other situations where the criteria that the Court of Appeal had developed also appeared to fit. First, whereas *Chandler v. Cape* was a domestic case, the subsidiary being domiciled near

---

24 Chandler v. Cape [2012] EWCA Civ 525, para. 80.

25 On this, see *infra*, section 3.3.4.

26 [2014] EWCA Civ 635.

27 District Court of The Hague, 30 January 2013, Fidelis Ayoro Oguru et al. v. Royal Dutch Shell plc et al., paras. 4.30 and 4.34 et seq. See also L. *Enneking*, The Future of Foreign Direct Liability? Exploring the International Relevance of the *Dutch Shell Nigeria* Case, 10 Utrecht Law Review (2014), pp. 44 et seq.

28 Lungowe and others v. (1) Vedanta Resources plc (2) Konkola Copper Mines plc [2016] EWHC 975 (TCC), para. 124.

29 See P. *Wesche & M. Saage-Maaß*, Holding Companies Liable for Human Rights Abuses Related to Foreign Subsidiaries and Suppliers before German Civil Courts: Lessons from *Jabir and Others v. KiK*, Human Rights Law Review 2016 (16), p. 370, 372 et seq.

30 For the German discussion, see *infra*, section 3.3.3.

London, courts saw no problem with extending its criteria to transnational situations.

Further and most importantly for this chapter, whereas *Chandler v. Cape* dealt with a duty of care towards employees of the subsidiary, courts also found that a parent duty of care "may be owed in analogous situations, not only to employees of the subsidiary but to those affected by the operations of the subsidiary",[31] which includes, in particular, the victims of pollution and environmental degradation.[32] This latter extension was expressly confirmed by the UK Supreme Court in *Vedanta*.[33] Discussing *Chandler v. Cape*, the Supreme Court stated that "the result would surely have been the same if the dust had escaped to neighbouring land where third parties worked, lived or enjoyed recreation".

Finally, in *Jabir and Others v. KiK*, the claimants, four victims of the Ali Enterprises factory fire in Karachi sued the garment discounter KiK, the main customer of Ali Enterprises, thereby applying the *Chandler* considerations to a supply chain rather than a corporation. They argued that there was a sufficiently close relationship between the buyer and the producer company as the Pakistani factory produced almost exclusively for KiK, and that KiK had assumed responsibility for health and safety issues because it had adopted a code of conduct requiring suppliers to ensure safe working conditions, which formed part of its supply chain contracts, had developed correction plans and conducted on-site qualification programmes, and in particular, because employees of KiK's CSR, purchasing and quality assurance departments had regularly visited the supplier site. Moreover, an auditing company had been hired to review safety and other working conditions at the factory on a regular basis. Thus, they argued that KiK knew or ought to have known about the working conditions, as well as construction details, such as the barred windows.[34] Unfortunately, no decision on the merits of the case was taken, because the court found that under the applicable law of Pakistan the claim was already time-barred.[35]

In April 2019, the UK Supreme Court may have introduced even more flexibility in the assessment of the potential liability of parent companies by emphasising that the *Chandler v. Cape* criteria did not impose a straitjacket on other courts but that the *Chandler v. Cape* indicia were no more than particular

---

[31]   Lungowe and others v. (1) Vedanta Resources plc (2) Konkola Copper Mines plc [2017] EWCA Civ 1528, para. 83 (per Simon LJ); on which see *infra*, sections 4.1 and 4.4.

[32]   See also Appeal Court of the Hague, 18 December 2015, Dooh et al. v. Royal Dutch Shell et al., ECLI:NL:GHDHA:2015:3586, para. 3.2, available at https://uitspraken.rechtspraak.nl/inziendocument?id=ECLI:NL:GHDHA:2015:3586.

[33]   UK Supreme Court, *Vedanta, supra*, note 15 at para. 52.

[34]   See *Wesche & Saage-Maaß, supra*, note 29.

[35]   LG Dortmund, 10.1.2019, 7 O 95/15, Beck-Rechtsprechung 2019, 388.

examples of circumstances in which a duty of care may affect a parent company.[36] The more general principles of whether A owes a duty of care to C in respect of the harmful activities of B could easily be traced back as far as the decision of the House of Lords in *Dorset Yacht Co. Ltd v. Home Office*,[37] in which the negligent discharge by the Home Office of its responsibility to supervise borstal boys working on Brownsea Island in Poole Harbour led to seven of them escaping and causing serious damage to moored yachts in the vicinity, including one owned by the plaintiff.[38] In relation to parent/subsidiary relationships, though, the Supreme Court confirmed the relevance of control: "Everything depends on the extent to which, and the way in which, the parent availed itself of the opportunity to take over, intervene in, control, supervise or advise the management of the relevant operations (including land use) of the subsidiary."[39]

3.2.2. Vedanta *and* Okpabi: *CSR Self-Commitments and Assumption of Responsibility*

Following *Chandler v. Cape*, in *Vedanta* as well as in *Okpabi*,[40] the tort law relevance of Vedanta's and Royal Dutch Shell's CSR and environmental self-commitments played a major role in the assessment of their (potential) duty of care towards victims in Zambia and Nigeria, due to their (potential) assumption of responsibility. The rulings only dealt with the jurisdiction of the English courts, but still went deep into the merits of the cases while deciding the procedural question of whether "there is a real issue" between the claimants and the parent company.

3.2.2.1. *Vedanta*

Vedanta is a financially wealthy UK incorporated mining company and parent of a number of mining companies. It held 79.42% of the shares of Konkola Copper Mines plc (KCM), a Zambian company which operates a copper mine in Zambia that has discharged extremely harmful effluents into the local waterways and the local environment and caused other serious pollution issues – and which got into financial difficulties. The claimants were subsistence farmers who lived in the vicinity of Konkola's copper mines and relied on the land and the waterways

---

[36] UK Supreme Court, *Vedanta*, *supra*, note 15 at para. 56. Similarly AAA and Others v. Unilever plc and another [2018] EWCA Civ 1532, para. 36, where the Court of Appeal ultimately saw no arguable case for the liability of the parent company.
[37] [1970] AC 1004.
[38] UK Supreme Court, *Vedanta*, *supra*, note 15 at para. 54.
[39] Id. at para. 49.
[40] Okpabi and others v. Royal Dutch Shell plc and another [2017] EWHC 89 (TCC); [2018] EWCA Civ 191.

to sustain basic agrarian livelihoods and for drinking, cooking, bathing and cleaning. Vedanta's health, safety and environmental self-commitment refers to a corporation-wide environmental management based on "world class standards", the effectiveness of which is controlled by Vedanta itself. According to Vedanta's sustainability report, called "Embedding sustainability", the oversight of the environmental performance of all Vedanta's subsidiaries rests with the Board of Vedanta itself. The mine was explicitly mentioned in the report. Moreover, the claimants had submitted proof of monitoring activities of Vedanta with a respect to the mines.[41]

On that basis, the English High Court saw a real tort law issue of *foreseeability*, *proximity* and *reasonableness* on the basis of the *Chandler* criteria and granted jurisdiction for the claims against Vedanta.[42] This was further detailed by the Court of Appeal, which held that:

(2) A duty may be owed by a parent company to the employee of a subsidiary, or a party directly affected by the operations of that subsidiary, in certain circumstances.

(3) Those circumstances may arise where the parent company (a) has taken direct responsibility for devising a material health and safety policy the adequacy of which is the subject of the claim, or (b) controls the operations which give rise to the claim.[43]

The Court concluded that both alternatives could correctly have been regarded as arguable by the High Court on the basis of the sustainability report (and the proof of control submitted by the claimants).[44]

Thus, CSR mechanisms were regarded to be an important or even decisive factor with regard to the decision whether the parent company has assumed responsibility for devising the health, safety and environmental policy of the subsidiary. The courts looked at CSR instruments as a mechanism for and an indication of control.

3.2.2.2. Okpabi

In *Okpabi*, 42,500 claimants are seeking damages arising as a result of serious and ongoing pollution and environmental damage caused by oil spills leaking from oil pipelines and associated infrastructure of the Shell Petroleum Development Company of Nigeria (SPDC) in and around the Ogale Community in Nigeria.

---

41   See e.g. Court of Appeal, *Vedanta, supra*, note 31 at para. 84.
42   High Court, *Vedanta, supra*, note 28.
43   Court of Appeal, *Vedanta, supra*, note 31 at para. 83.
44   Id. at para. 84.

Royal Dutch Shell plc (RDS) holds shares in Shell Petroleum NV, which for its part holds shares in SPDC. SPDC is part of a Nigerian joint venture where RDS is not a direct member. RDS is, after internal restructuring, no longer itself directly in the extracting business but is rather an investment company incorporated in the UK.

Undisputedly, RDS had a mandatory and corporate-wide system of health, safety, environmental and social self-regulation which included mandatory environmental policies and standards and accompanying manuals and a centralised system of supervision and oversight of the implementation of these standards. In addition, there were mandatory centralised design and engineering practices, an overall budgetary control which was also relevant for investment in pipeline infrastructure, and centralised direction and oversight of the security of operations (for example, against third-party interference).[45]

Nevertheless, unlike in *Vedanta*, the High Court and the Court of Appeal denied jurisdiction and dismissed the claims against RDS. The High Court focused on the corporate structure and the fact that RDS itself does not conduct any operations in Nigeria so as to deny the elements of proximity and reasonableness. The latter was also supported by the fact that SPDC was subject to strict liability in Nigeria. As opposed to *Chandler*, RDS was regarded as the "ultimate holding company" with no specialist or superior knowledge as compared to SPDC. Notwithstanding RDS's centralised CSR self-commitments and environmental management and control system, the High Court argued that – regarding the amount of its subsidiaries – RDS could only have very superficial knowledge of individual production risks and issues. In addition, it was argued that SPDC had enough of its own expert knowledge as established by the Nigerian licence and did not rely on RDS.[46]

The Court of Appeal denied jurisdiction and dismissed the appeal as well, by a majority of two to one, although it followed different lines of argument: whereas Sir Geoffrey Vos C also denied proximity due to the indirect corporate structure of the RDS group, which allows much less direct involvement than the corporation structure of Vedanta,[47] the other two judges did not regard the corporate structure as decisive. With a view to CSR mechanisms, Simon LJ[48] and Sir Geoffrey Vos C[49] rejected the claimants' arguments that these self-regulatory instruments would indicate an assumption of responsibility and thus proximity. In particular, they argued that centralised CSR policies only have the purpose of informing shareholders, addressing reputational concerns, avoiding loss

---

[45] See e.g. Court of Appeal, *Okpabi, supra*, note 40 at paras. 41 et seq.
[46] High Court, *Okpabi, supra*, note 40.
[47] Court of Appeal, *Okpabi, supra*, note 40 at paras. 197 et seq.
[48] Id. at paras. 84 et seq.
[49] Id. at paras. 191 et seq.

of oil and environmental damage, and ensuring proper functioning systems instead of taking over responsibility. In addition, a centralised system of RDS's own developed best practice throughout the whole Shell group, which is based on expertise and experience and ensured via audits, did not prove sufficient material control over operations to establish proximity. Quite to the contrary, centralised management that applies corporation-wide did not lead to an assumption of responsibility for an individual subsidiary. The same applied to a closer information and control structure with SPDC as this was only due to the particular risks of SPDC operations. The judges held that it would have been necessary for the claimants to prove control of day-to-day operations in order to establish proximity, which they were not able to do.

At the same time, they argued that it would not be fair, just and reasonable to impose liability on RDS on the basis of international CSR standards as they only constituted abstract principles.

Sales LJ, in contrast, proposed to allow the appeal.[50] According to him, the fact that there could be thousands of neighbours (of hundreds of subsidiaries) provides no obstacle to proximity as the claimants are nevertheless a determinate group of neighbours affected by the operations of a subsidiary under the practical control of the management of RDS. Regarding CSR instruments, he distinguished CSR standards as pure guidelines, where control and responsibility remains with the subsidiary, from real control or joint control of parent with a direct and substantial involvement in the operations of the subsidiary beyond group-wide standards. Here, the Shell CSR literature together with other evidence (for example witnesses) reflected the assumption of responsibility for reputational and business reasons, which was supported by a high degree of centralised control from headquarters and departments with global oversight who are in fact involved in the implementation of standards abroad. These standards at the same time reflected a high degree of expertise; thus, local knowledge and expertise of SPDC were not an obstacle to the criterion of superior or equal knowledge. Overall, Sales LJ thought that the claimants had sufficiently submitted proof of centralised control and thus of proximity. He also regarded it as fair, just and reasonable to impose liability on RDS. In particular, he saw neither the exact corporate structure nor the fact that SPDC was subject to strict liability in Nigeria as relevant obstacles.

To summarise, in *Okpabi* the Court of Appeal distinguished between corporate-wide CSR and environmental standards as "pure guidelines" (although mandatory!), which leave the implementation to the subsidiary, and *de facto* control. However, whereas Sales LJ – in line with *Vedanta* – regarded

---

[50]   Id. at paras. 134 et seq.

centralised management systems with centralised oversight, involvement in implementation and audits as sufficient control, the majority required direct and substantial involvement in concrete operations on a day-to-day-basis. As a result, mandatory CSR and environmental standards, guidelines and handbooks, centralised implementation control and regular audits were regarded as insufficient for an assumption of responsibility. The ruling has been qualified as a serious step back in the light of contemporary international discussions on corporate human rights and environmental responsibility.[51]

3.2.2.3. The Position of the UK Supreme Court

Vedanta and *Okpabi* were both appealed to the Supreme Court. Whereas *Okpabi* is still pending before the Supreme Court, which decided to stay the proceedings until the judgment in *Vedanta* was handed down, the Supreme Court gave judgment in *Vedanta* on 10 April 2019, dismissing the appeal and upholding the decision of the High Court to grant jurisdiction to the claimants.[52] The most interesting aspect of the judgment for the purpose of this chapter relates to the relevance of Vedanta's CSR materials.

Lord Briggs (with whom the other judges concurred) mentioned several ways in which group-wide CSR instruments about minimising the environmental impact of inherently dangerous activities might be relevant for establishing a duty of care.

Firstly, they might contain errors that, when implemented by the subsidiary, cause harm to third persons.[53] Secondly, the parent company "does not merely proclaim group-wide policies, but takes active steps, by training, supervision and enforcement, to see that they are implemented by relevant subsidiaries".[54] Thirdly, the parent company "might incur the relevant responsibility to third parties if, in published materials, it holds itself out as exercising that degree of supervision and control of its subsidiaries, even if it does not in fact do so. In such circumstances its very omission may constitute the abdication of a responsibility which it has publicly undertaken."[55]

---

[51]   See, for example, G. *Quijano*, Okpabi v Royal Dutch Shell: An opportunity to honour international standards or another instance of corporate impunity?, available at https://www.business-humanrights.org/en/okpabi-v-royal-dutch-shell-an-opportunity-to-honour-international-standards-or-another-instance-of-corporate-impunity; N. *Bernaz*, Okpabi v. Shell on Appeal: Foreign Direct Liability in Troubled Waters, available at http://rightsasusual.com/?p=1194.

[52]   UK Supreme Court, *Vedanta, supra*, note 15.

[53]   Id. at para. 52. Similarly, Court of Appeal, *Okpabi, supra*, note 40 at para. 196 (per Sir Geoffrey Vos C); Court of Appeal, *Unilever, supra*, note 36 at para. 37 (per Sales LJ).

[54]   Id. at para. 53.

[55]   Id. at para. 53.

In the instant case, Lord Briggs regarded

> the published materials in which Vedanta may fairly be said to have asserted its own assumption of responsibility for the maintenance of proper standards of environmental control over the activities of its subsidiaries, and in particular the operations at the Mine, and not merely to have laid down but also implemented those standards by training, monitoring and enforcement, as sufficient on their own to show that it is well arguable that a sufficient level of intervention by Vedanta in the conduct of operations at the Mine may be demonstrable at trial, after full disclosure of the relevant internal documents of Vedanta and KCM, and of communications passing between them.[56]

To summarise, he particularly referred either to a situation where the parent does not merely proclaim group-wide standards but also takes active steps to implement them, or to a situation where published CSR instruments assert an assumption of control even though the parent does not live up to this assertion, although the threshold for such an assertion to be taken seriously as an assumption of responsibility remains unclear.

3.3. CORPORATION-WIDE (OR SUPPLY-CHAIN-WIDE) DUTIES OF CARE IN LINE WITH CSR STANDARDS?

The discussion of the cases of *Vedanta* and *Okpabi* leaves us with the dilemma that a parent company that does nothing seems to be better off than a parent company that takes responsibility for and has an influence on the operations of its subsidiary, perhaps with good intentions, but acts negligently in doing so. A corporation-wide duty of care in line with international CSR standards and corporate best practices instead of an individual assumption of responsibility could provide a solution to that problem.

The establishment of corporation-wide duties of care would not only cover parent companies that engage in the operations of their subsidiaries but also those that simply leave the responsibility to a subsidiary that is not capable of dealing with risks appropriately, be it for lack of financial resources or for lack of technical knowledge and experience, whereas the parent company avails of the necessary means. This is a situation which frequently arises in transnational corporations with subsidiaries in the Global South, but also in transnational supply chains. Here, the law would impose on parent companies the duty to organise the corporation or the supply chain so as to avoid damage. Thus, duties of care would also arise *vis-à-vis* those that are (potentially) affected by the

---

[56] Id. at para. 61.

operations of the subsidiary of the supplier, independently of any individual assumption of responsibility by the parent company. In fact, the parent (or buyer) company would become liable for the *omission* to take responsibility and to act accordingly.[57]

3.3.1. UN Guiding Principles on Business and Human Rights

A tort law duty to organise a business, corporation or production chain so as to avoid damage would be well in line with the business-wide "due diligence" requirements that were originally detailed in the UN Guiding Principles on Business and Human Rights[58] and that are now widely used in many CSR instruments.[59] Apart from a CSR self-commitment, due diligence requires enterprises to carry out comprehensive and detailed business-wide proactive steps to identify, prevent and mitigate violations, and in particular a detailed risk assessment.[60] Responsibilities must be assigned to the appropriate levels and functions within a business (including subsidiaries and other business relationships).[61] In principle, this duty applies "to all enterprises regardless of their size, sector, operational context, ownership and structure"; however, scale and complexity of these responsibilities may vary in accordance with the size and capacity of the enterprise and to the severity of potential impacts.[62] In this context, leverage in addressing the wrongful doings of other entities should be used.[63] This, however, depends *inter alia* on the extent of the enterprise's leverage on the entity concerned, how crucial the relationship is and the severity of the abuse.[64] In this regard, it has been argued that the UN Guiding Principles justify and fortify the recognition of corporation-wide or supply-chain-wide duties of

---

[57] See also *Mares, supra*, note 14 at p. 47.

[58] For a comparison of tort law principles and the Guiding Principles see *C. Glinski*, The Ruggie Principles, business human rights self-regulation and tort law: Increasing standards through mutual impact and learning, Nordic Journal of Human Rights 2017 (35), pp. 15 et seq.

[59] Moreover, corporation-wide due diligence requirements are laid down in other legal instruments, such as international, European and national anti-bribery laws, money laundering laws including Directive 2015/849/EU on the prevention of the use of the financial system for the purposes of money laundering or terrorist financing, OJ 2015 L 141/73, and accounting laws. In the area of cartel law, the European Court of Justice has overplayed the legal separation of companies in the case of *Akzo Nobel*, see Case C-97/08 P, Akzo Nobel NV v. Commission, ECLI:EU:C:2009:536, paras. 58 et seq. For an account, see *C. Glinski*, UN-Leitprinzipien, Selbstregulierung der Wirtschaft und Deliktsrecht: Alternativen zu verpflichtenden Völkerrechtsnormen für Unternehmen?, in M. Krajewski (ed.), Menschenrechte in globalen Lieferketten, FAU University Press, 2018, p. 44, 70 et seq.

[60] *Ruggie, supra*, note 7, Principles 16–21.

[61] Id., Principle 19. See also *Mares, supra*, note 14 at pp. 8 et seq.

[62] *Ruggie, supra*, note 7, Principle 14.

[63] Id., Principle 19.

[64] Id., Commentary on Principle 19.

care in tort law as they reflect relevant social norms and expectations on the subject matter, which are equally relevant in tort law.[65]

3.3.2. Tort Law Doctrine

Indeed, the duty to organise a corporation in such a way that the subsidiaries do not cause harm to third parties could, in principle, be based upon traditional tort law criteria such as the (joint) creation of risk, risk control and reliance of victims (or the environment) on certain entities to take over responsibility. A number of legal systems do recognise the concept of "organisational torts" or "organisational negligence".[66] For example, in German enterprise liability, the original tort law duty of the principal to secure safety in a company's operations has been transformed into the duty to organise the company and processes, to allocate responsibilities and to supervise the activities in such a way as is required to prevent damage.[67] Comparably, product liability law is based on the consideration that the producer is best suited to instruct users and to monitor the functioning of the product in practice.[68] Translated into production processes, this could mean that the parent company that develops technology and makes it available to a subsidiary has to take responsibility for its proper functioning and use. This includes the duty to instruct and educate the employees of the subsidiary on safety and environmental issues.

In terms of transnational corporate structures or supply chains, this could mean that parent (or leading) companies in transnational production chains are obliged to introduce a corporation-wide (or supply-chain-wide) safety and environmental management system that allocates responsibilities where they can best be exercised. Usually, the burden of proof for such a structure would lie with the company.[69]

---

[65] See *A. Sanders*, The Impact of the "Ruggie Framework" and the United Nations Guiding Principles on Business and Human Rights on Transnational Human Rights Litigation, LSE Law, Society and Economy Working Papers 18/2014, p. 1, 22 et seq. See also *Glinski*, *supra*, note 55 at pp. 31 et seq.

[66] See *G. Brüggemeier*, Common Principles of Tort Law, BIICL, 2004, pp. 117 et seq., 132 et seq. concerning enterprise liability in US tort law. Case law based on the same line of reasoning can also be found in legal systems that have not explicitly formulated the principle of "organisational torts". See also *P. Rott & V. Ulfbeck*, Supply Chain Liability of Multilateral Corporations?, European Review of Private Law 2015, p. 415, 426 et seq., with further references.

[67] See *A. Matusche-Beckmann*, Das Organisationsverschulden, Mohr Siebeck, 2001, pp. 37 et seq.; *G. Brüggemeier*, Prinzipien des Haftungsrechts, Nomos, 1999, pp. 116 et seq.; *G. Spindler*, Organisationsverschulden, Heymann, 2001.

[68] See *P. Hommelhoff*, Produkthaftung im Konzern, Zeitschrift für Wirtschaftsrecht 1990, p. 761, 763 et seq. See also *Spindler*, *supra*, note 67 at pp. 945 et seq.

[69] See *G. Brüggemeier*, Enterprise Liability for Environmental Damage: German and European Law, in G. Teubner, L. Farmer & D. Murphy (eds.), Environmental Law and Ecological Responsibility, Wiley, 1992, p. 75, 90 et seq., for the organisation of enterprises. See also *Glinski*, *supra*, note 13 at pp. 346 et seq., with further references.

3.3.3. German Case Law

German courts have recognised duties of care and liability with regard to damages caused by third parties, namely contractors. One example is the liability of a tour operator for the insecure balcony of a contractor's hotel.[70] Relevant considerations were the contractual proximity between the tour operator and the victim as well as the reliance of the victim on the safety precautions taken by the operator. Even more relevant is the liability of a waste producer for the inappropriate disposal of waste oil by a contractor.[71] Here, the ruling was based on the continuing responsibility of the waste producer for a risk that he created and the fact that he could not simply get rid of it by transferring it to an insufficiently competent third party. Thus, identifiable risks related to waste treatment or disposal must be prevented either through supervision of the treatment or through careful selection of the contractor. The less influence on the contractor, the higher the requirements for his selection.[72]

These arguments could be easily transferred to often far more intensively amalgamated competences and spheres of influence in transnational corporations or production chains,[73] where production technology developed by the parent or leading company has been made available to a subsidiary or producer with far less know-how, expertise and/or financial and technical means. In addition, in particular in countries with a different socio-economic situation, adaption difficulties may be expected, for example with a view to infrastructure and adequate administrative control of the expertise within and the operations of the subsidiary or producer. A frequent problem of many industries in this regard, be it in the extractive, chemical or textile production industries, is inadequate waste disposal and wastewater treatment, which leads to serious environmental and health damage. Applying the considerations of the above-mentioned waste oil decision of the German Supreme Court, parent or leading companies would be obliged to deal adequately with expectable difficulties in this regard. One could also argue that (potential) victims of unsafe or unhealthy working conditions, resulting from a financial and timeframe that is determined by the buyer, *have to rely* on the responsibility of the (influential main) buyer.[74]

---

[70]   BGH, 25.2.1988, VII ZR 238/86, Entscheidungen des Bundesgerichtshofs in Zivilsachen 103, p. 298.

[71]   BGH, 7.10.1975, VI ZR 34/74, Neue Juristische Wochenschrift 1976, p. 46; on which see W. *Oehler*, Produzentenhaftung im Konzern – Deliktsrecht und Haftungsbeschränkung, Zeitschrift für Wirtschaftsrecht 1990, p. 1445, 1451.

[72]   See also *Wagner, supra*, note 14 at pp. 775 et seq.

[73]   Against M.-P. *Weller*, L. *Kaller* & A. *Schulz*, Haftung deutscher Unternehmen für Menschenrechtsverletzungen im Ausland, Archiv für civilistische Praxis 2016 (216), p. 387, 401 et seq., who want to limit liability to cases of true delegation of duties.

[74]   See also M. *Saage-Maaß* & C. *Leifker*, Haftungsrisiken deutscher Unternehmen und ihres Managements für Menschenrechtsverletzungen im Ausland, Betriebs-Berater 2015, p. 2499, 2502.

Still, German authors have traditionally been reluctant to recognise corporation-wide duties of care. The main concern has been the incompatibility of such a tort law doctrine with the limited liability of companies under company law, on the basis of which corporations usually take financial decisions. In the light of contemporary public discussions on the subject matter, this is however gradually changing towards a more progressive approach.[75]

3.3.4. English Case Law

English case law shows aspects of business-wide organisational duties as well. As early as in *Lubbe v Cape plc*,[76] the claimants had argued that the export and erection of a dangerous industrial facility as such leads to a duty of care of the exporting parent company *vis-à-vis* workers and neighbours; the subsequent non-safeguarding of the plant's proper operation constitutes a breach of the duty of care with the consequence of tort law liability.[77]

In particular, although on the facts of *Chandler v. Cape*, Cape plc had indeed assumed responsibility for the health and safety management of its subsidiaries, the criteria of the ruling go further in the direction of a legal duty to take that responsibility, as the Court not only referred to an actual assumption of responsibility and the *de facto* knowledge of the parent but also included the normative element that the parent *ought to have* superior or similar risk knowledge and *ought to have known* that the subsidiary's system of work is unsafe and that those (potentially) affected by the operations would rely on the parent's protection. This is further supported by the explanation that for the latter a "practice of intervening in the health and safety policies of the subsidiary" is not necessary, but it would for example be sufficient that "the parent has a practice of intervening in the trading operations of the subsidiary, for example production and funding issues".[78]

In line with that, the meaning of the criteria of "same business" and "superior knowledge" had been further elaborated in *David Thompson v. Renwick Group*[79] and in *Vedanta* in the sense that it is decisive whether the "parent is well placed, because of its knowledge or expertise, to protect the employees or others

---

[75]   See *Wagner, supra*, note 14 at pp. 756 et seq.; cautiously assenting *M.-P. Weller & C. Thomale*, Menschenrechtsklagen gegen deutsche Unternehmen, Zeitschrift für Unternehmens- und Gesellschaftsrecht 2017, p. 509, 520 et seq.

[76]   [2000] UKHL 41.

[77]   When the English courts had decided to have jurisdiction for the cases, the defendants moved to settle the claims. For details, see *H. Ward*, Towards a New Convention on Corporate Accountability? Some Lessons from the Thor Chemicals and Cape PLC Cases, Yearbook of International Environmental Law 2001, p. 105, 113 et seq.; *P. Muchlinski*, Corporations in International Litigation: Problems of Jurisdiction and the United Kingdom Asbestos Cases, International & Comparative Law Quarterly 2001 (50), p. 1, 3 et seq.

[78]   Court of Appeal, *Chandler v. Cape, supra*, note 24 at para. 80.

[79]   [2014] EWCA Civ 635. See also *Demeyere, supra*, note 23 at pp. 405 et seq.

affected by the operations of the subsidiary".[80] "If both parent and subsidiary have similar knowledge and expertise and they jointly take decisions about mine safety, which the subsidiary implements, both companies may (depending on the circumstances) owe a duty of care to those affected by those decisions."

From this, one could have concluded that *Chandler* and *Vedanta* establish corporate-wide duties of care not only in the case of a *de facto* assumption of responsibility but also where the parent has (or ought to have) superior (or equal) risk knowledge and the (potential) victims rely on the parent's use of that knowledge, and where the parent has leverage to impact upon health, safety and environmental issues in the subsidiary. In addition, *Okpabi* did not rebut this finding as it explicitly confirmed the *Chandler* and *Vedanta* criteria in principle, but rejected an assumption of responsibility namely due to insufficient control on the basis of the facts of the case.

The Supreme Court in *Vedanta*, however, appears to be more cautious. Having confirmed that direct or indirect ownership by one company of all or a majority of the shares of another company may enable the parent to take control of the management of the operations of the business or of land owned by the subsidiary, but it does not impose any duty upon the parent to do so, Lord Briggs held:

> Everything depends on the extent to which, and the way in which, the parent availed itself of the opportunity to take over, intervene in, control, supervise or advise the management of the relevant operations (including land use) of the subsidiary. All that the existence of a parent subsidiary relationship demonstrates is that the parent had such an opportunity.[81]

However, he went on to elaborate that:

> In the Chandler case, the subsidiary inherited (by taking over a business formerly carried on by the parent) a system for the manufacture of asbestos which created an inherently unsafe system of work for its employees ... As a result, ... the parent was found to have incurred a duty of care to the employees of its subsidiary, and the result would surely have been the same if the dust had escaped to neighbouring land where third parties worked, lived or enjoyed recreation.[82]

Thus, even the Supreme Court – although not embracing corporation-wide duties of care in general – seems to acknowledge that there might be situations which lead to corporate-wide duties of care, namely in case of (joint) creation of risks, and particularly of those related to risky production methods.

---

80 Court of Appeal, *Vedanta, supra,* note 31 at para. 83.
81 UK Supreme Court, *Vedanta, supra,* note 15 at para. 49.
82 Id. at para. 52.

3.3.5. CSR Instruments and the Standard of Care

In situations where tort law acknowledges corporation-wide or supply-chain-wide duties of care, in particular in scenarios where the parent or leading company has (jointly) created a risk or avails of specific or superior expertise concerning the control of that risk, or where the (potential) victims particularly rely on the protection of the parent or leading company, CSR instruments such as corporation-wide safety and environmental management systems would play an important role. However, their role would be less in establishing the duty of care (as in *Vedanta*) but instead in determining the required *standard of care*, in particular the necessary corporation-wide environmental management and control system.

Thus, the ability of the tort of negligence to build upon legal and social norms of a variety of sources, including CSR self-regulation and environmental best practices, and transform them into binding legal minimum standards plays a crucial role. The standard of care is constantly developing and integrating new technical and organisational knowledge. CSR self-regulation and environmental best practices reflect what can be regarded as foreseeable and avoidable in a given situation and thus either reflect the relevant duty of care of the individual enterprise (in particular when these instruments reflect specific experience or expertise)[83] or of a comparable "reasonable enterprise" in a comparable situation.[84] The legal consequence of the latter would be that producers in the same trade or industry who do not adhere to comparable practices or rules would still be bound by this standard of care as defined by the practice or regulation of others. Vice versa, compliance with any CSR or environmental self-commitments, standards or best practices does not necessarily lead to a "safe harbour" in the tort of negligence as the duty of care is normative rather than empirical and these self-commitments or standards could be too lax, outdated or inadequate in a given situation.[85] The German Supreme Court has held in established case law that standards do not always determine the ultimate care that can be expected in a particular case and do not discharge the judge from his duty to take account of the safety interests of potential victims.[86]

---

[83]   See, for example, the US American case of Toussaint v. Blue Cross & Blue Shield, 408 Mich. 579, 614 f. 292 N.W.2d 880, 892 (1980). See also *Glinski, supra*, note 13 at pp. 265 et seq.

[84]   For German law, see e.g. OLG Dusseldorf, 15.1.1999, 22 U 160/98, Neue Juristische Wochenschrift – Rechtsprechungsreport 2000, p. 168; for English law, see e.g. Ward v. The Ritz Hotel (London) [1992] PIQR 315; for US American law, see *Meidinger, supra*, note 9 at p. 282. See also *Glinski, supra*, note 13 at pp. 266 et seq.

[85]   See *Brüggemeier, supra*, note 66 at pp. 66 et seq. For US tort law see e.g. Texas and Pacific Ry Co. v. Beymer, 189 US 468, 470 (1903, per Holmes, J); "The TJ Hooper", 60 F 2d 737 (2d Cir 1932, per Learned Hand, CJ). For the position of English law see e.g. Edward Wong Finance Co. Ltd v. Johnson Stokes and Master [1984] AC 296. For detailed analysis, see *Glinski, supra*, note 13 at pp. 270 et seq.

[86]   BGH, 29.11.1983, VI ZR 137/82, Neue Juristische Wochenschrift 1984, p. 801.

In conclusion, this would mean that parent or leading companies are obliged to introduce a corporation-wide safety and environmental management system that allocates responsibilities where they can best be exercised. Thus, the relevant standards could be defined by CSR and environmental management best practices (e.g. of comparable corporations). If the parent company has no adequate system in place, it is liable for damage that occurs from insufficient management and control. If, however, a reasonable structure has been established, and a subsidiary still causes damage, the parent company is not liable but only the subsidiary in question. Usually, the burden of proof for such a structure would lie with the parent company.[87] Self-regulatory instruments would then become an important tool for establishing a corporation-wide safety and environmental management system. Tort law would then serve as an incentive to introduce environmentally friendly corporate structures and production schemes.[88]

4. CONCLUSION

This chapter has shown that recent developments in tort law, namely in the English tort of negligence, point towards increased liability of parent companies for damage caused by their subsidiaries, and perhaps also of leading companies in supply chains for damage caused by their suppliers. The particular role of CSR and environmental self-regulation and best practices for the establishment of a parent company's duty of care has been discussed controversially in the cases of *Vedanta* and *Okpabi*.

The chapter has demonstrated that CSR instruments play an important role with regard to the assumption of responsibility in the individual case, resulting in a duty of care towards, for example, neighbours of a factory. Moreover, it has pinpointed their influence on the determination of the required standard of care when it comes to more general corporation-wide (or supply-chain-wide) duties of care that require the introduction of a corporation-wide environmental management and control system. The recognition of such more general duties of care indeed appears necessary, be it only to solve the dilemma that otherwise parent companies that make an honest attempt to introduce corporation-wide CSR are more at risk of being held liable than those who do not even try.

---

[87] See *Brüggemeier, supra*, note 69 at pp. 90 et seq., for the organisation of enterprises.
[88] Id. at pp. 91 et seq.

EXTENDED PRODUCER RESPONSIBILITY IN THE EU

Achievements and Future Prospects

Susanna PALEARI

1. INTRODUCTION

The rationale behind extended producer responsibility (EPR) is to make producers responsible for the environmental impacts of their products from design to the post-consumer phase.[1] EPR was, therefore, expected to stimulate design for the environment (DfE); reduce the amount of waste destined to final disposal, while increasing separate collection and recycling; and internalise the costs of waste collection and management,[2] in accordance with the "polluter pays" principle.[3]

Countries around the world have defined and applied EPR in very different ways. However, it is usually recognised that the principle comprises, at least, a physical and a financial dimension, which can be implemented through different instruments, sometimes used in combination.[4] In the EU, the principle has been incorporated into several pieces of waste legislation. In particular, it is stated as a

---

[1]   *T. Lindhqvist*, Extended Producer Responsibility in Cleaner Production: Policy Principle to Promote Environmental Improvements of Product Systems, International Institute for Industrial Environmental Economics, Lund University, 2000, p. v.

[2]   In this chapter, the expression "waste management" is used to indicate waste transport and treatment, once waste has been (separately) collected.

[3]   *OECD*, Extended Producer Responsibility – Updated Guidance for Efficient Waste Management, OECD Publishing, 2016, p. 13.

[4]   *Lindhqvist, supra*, note 1 at p. iii; *OECD, supra*, note 3 at p. 21; *N. Tojo*, Extended Producer Responsibility as a Driver for Design Change – Utopia or Reality?, Doctoral Dissertation, International Institute for Industrial Environmental Economics, Lund University, 2004, pp. 12–14; *C. Van Rossem, N. Tojo & T. Lindhqvist*, Extended Producer Responsibility. An Examination of its Impact on Innovation and Greening Products, International Institute for Industrial Environmental Economics, Lund University, 2006, p. 4; *M. Walls*, Extended Producer Responsibility and Product Design. Economic Theory and Selected Case Studies, Discussion Paper, OECD Publishing, 2006, p. 2.

"general requirement" by the Waste Framework Directive (WFD)[5] and is applied by the Packaging Waste Directive,[6] the End-of-Life Vehicles (ELVs) Directive,[7] the Batteries Directive[8] and the Waste Electrical and Electronic Equipment (WEEE) Directive[9] (hereinafter referred to collectively as the EPR directives). The implementation of this legislation has resulted in the flourishing of EPR systems across Europe. A study by the OECD[10] highlights that of over 395 EPR policies adopted globally in the period 1970–2013, 164 have been introduced by EU Member States.

After more than 20 years of experience in the EU with EPR, this chapter evaluates whether the environmental objectives associated with the advocacy of the principle have been met. Secondly, it discusses EPR's future prospects, by considering how its application can be improved to fully reach both its original objectives and, possibly, more ambitious ones.

The remainder of the chapter is structured as follows. Section 2 provides a short overview of EPR systems in the EU. Section 3 describes the environmental results achieved by EU EPR systems. Section 4 focuses on EPR future prospects, in the light of the recent amendments to the WFD.[11] Section 5 concludes.

Most of this work is related to the activities of the European Topic Centre on Waste, Materials and the Green Economy (ETC/WMGE), funded by the European Environment Agency.

2. EPR SYSTEMS IN THE EU: AN OVERVIEW

Member States' experience with EPR is mainly driven by the EPR directives, which establish waste collection/management requirements to be met by producers, in order to achieve binding collection, recycling and recovery targets. EPR requirements address the physical and financial dimensions of the principle.

---

[5]   Directive 2008/98/EC of the European Parliament and of the Council on waste and repealing certain directives, OJ 2008 L 312/3.

[6]   Directive 94/62/EC of the European Parliament and of the Council on packaging and packaging waste, OJ 1994 L 365/10.

[7]   Directive 2000/53/EC of the European Parliament and of the Council on end-of life vehicles – Commission Statements, OJ 2000 L 269/34.

[8]   Directive 2006/66/EC of the European Parliament and of the Council on batteries and accumulators and waste batteries and accumulators and repealing Directive 91/157/EEC, OJ 2006 L 266/1.

[9]   Directive 2012/19/EU of the European Parliament and of the Council on waste electrical and electronic equipment, OJ 2012 L 197/38.

[10]   OECD, What Have We Learned About Extended Producer Responsibility in the Past Decade? A Survey of the Recent EPR Economic Literature (prepared by D. Kaffine & P. O'Reilly), OECD Publishing, Paris, 2013.

[11]   Directive 2018/851/EU of the European Parliament and of the Council amending Directive 2008/98/EC on waste, OJ 2018 L 150/109.

In theory, both the physical and the financial responsibility for collecting/ managing waste can be set at the individual or collective level.[12] However, only a few provisions of the EPR directives explicitly allocate an individual or collective responsibility to producers. Since producers are mainly required to "set up systems" for collecting/managing waste, they are generally allowed to meet their EPR obligations both individually and collectively. Producers have mostly chosen the latter option and have set up producer responsibility organisations (PROs), which, through shared infrastructure, take advantage of economies of scale in collection and treatment.[13] PROs have been designed and operated in different ways across Europe, for example with reference to their legal status, scope, functions and financing. As regards this last aspect, PROs usually apply a collective financial responsibility, i.e. they allocate the cost of waste collection/management to member producers, based on their market shares.

Individual compliance schemes and PROs managing the same waste stream in a Member State are part of a larger system (that the author calls "EPR system"), which includes roles for several actors (see Figure 1). Considering their governance structure, EPR systems can be classified as monopolistic or competitive. Within the former, there is generally a single PRO that implements EPR obligations. Monopolistic PROs offer administrative simplicity for producers and public authorities, may reflect an effort to capture economies of scale and may be appropriate to stimulate investments, but they are subject to diminished incentives for efficiency.[14] Instead, within competitive EPR systems, multiple PROs operate in competition and, often, a clearinghouse is established to allocate the amounts of waste to be collected/managed and ensuring that collection is provided everywhere that is needed. A third possible governance structure is that of EPR systems using tradable credits. In the UK, for example, actors along the packaging supply chain are required to reach specific recycling rates. When a ton of packaging waste is processed or exported for recycling by an accredited processor/collector, credits are generated, which can be traded on the market.[15]

Apart from producers, PROs, and clearinghouses, EPR systems also involve: (1) government agencies, which are in charge of formulating EPR policies, registering producers, accrediting PROs, monitoring and enforcing EPR systems, etc.; (2) municipalities and commercial waste operators, interacting with

---

[12] S. *Paleari*, The EU Waste Electric and Electronic Equipment Directive: the Implementation of Producer Responsibility across the EU-27, JSWTM 2015 (41/2), p. 177.

[13] *OECD, supra*, note 3 at p. 28.

[14] *INSEAD–EPR*, Extended Producer Responsibility: Stakeholders Concerns and Future Developments – White Paper (prepared by N. Kunz et al.), 2014, p. 12.

[15] *OECD, supra*, note 3 pp. 73–74.

producers/PROs within "shared" or "dual" systems;[16] (3) consumers, who provide for the separate collection of waste; and (4) retailers, who can take part in waste collection.[17] It has to be added that, especially in middle-income countries, the informal sector traditionally performs waste collection/management functions. The potentially positive contribution of informal waste pickers is increasingly recognised, so that the failure to integrate them into new formal EPR systems is an issue (as the dysfunctionality of the EPR packaging system in Bulgaria, for instance, demonstrates).[18]

Figure 1. Role of stakeholders in EPR systems

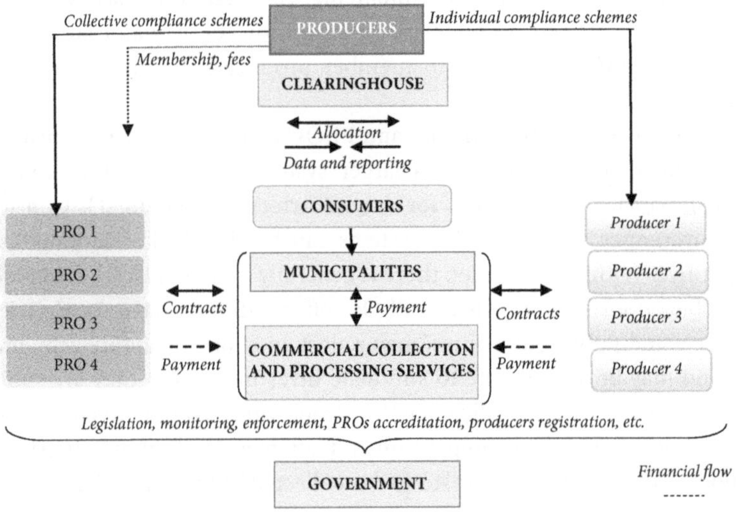

Source: Author.

3. RESULTS ACHIEVED BY EPR SYSTEMS

This section evaluates whether EU EPR systems have met their environmental objectives, focusing, in particular, on results related to waste collection/ management and DfE. The analysis is based on Eurostat data and on a broad review of the empirical literature on EPR systems in EU Member States, which has been undertaken within the activities of the ETC/WMGE.

---

[16] *J. Quoden*, Experience from Packaging Recovery Organizations in Europe – Key Outcomes of the OECD EPR Forum Moving Forward & Next Steps, Presentation at Global Forum on Environment: Promoting Sustainable Materials Management through EPR, Tokyo, 17–19 June 2014.

[17] *Y. Gupt & S. Sahay*, Review of Extended Producer Responsibility: a Case Study Approach, WM&R 2015 (33/7), p. 609.

[18] *OECD, supra*, note 3 at p. 203.

3.1. THE IMPACT OF EPR SYSTEMS ON WASTE COLLECTION AND MANAGEMENT

Except for ELVs, all the waste streams regulated by the EPR directives are part, to a certain extent, of municipal solid waste (MSW). MSW generation in the EU-28 slightly declined in 2018 relative to 2000, both in absolute (−1%) and relative terms (−6%).[19] As regards MSW treatment (kg per capita), over the 1995–2018 period, the EU-28, on average, has experienced (see Figure 2) a considerable reduction in landfilling (−63%), a progressive and impressive increase in material recycling and composting (+183% and +186%, respectively), and a significant rise in incineration (+103%).[20] Wide differences exist, however, between Member States.

Figure 2. MSW generation and treatment, EU 28 (1995–2018)

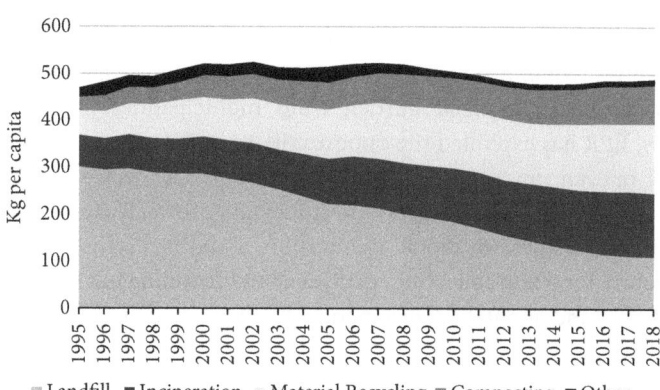

Note: The "other treatment" category is calculated as the difference between the sum of the amounts treated and the amounts of waste generated (this difference mainly arises in countries that report more waste generated than treated). The whole area of the graph covered by different waste treatment operations corresponds to the amount of waste generated.

Source: *Eurostat*, Municipal waste statistics, 2020, available at https://ec.europa.eu/eurostat/statistics-explained/index.php/Municipal_waste_statistics#Municipal_waste_treatment.

The collection, recycling and recovery of EPR waste streams has improved, following the adoption of the related legislation. Based on Eurostat data, apart from a few exceptions, all the targets set by the EPR directives that are currently applied have been reached, on average, by the EU (with again, however, wide

---

[19]　*Eurostat*, Database – Municipal waste by waste management operations, 2020, available at https://appsso.eurostat.ec.europa.eu/nui/show.do?dataset=env_wasmun&lang=en.

[20]　*Eurostat*, Municipal waste statistics, 2020, available at https://ec.europa.eu/eurostat/statistics-explained/index.php/Municipal_waste_statistics#Municipal_waste_treatment.

differences between Member States).[21] In some cases, targets set for the future have also already been met (e.g. the 2030 recycling targets for paper and wood packaging).

Assessing the extent to which EPR systems have contributed to reaching the above-mentioned results is hampered by a considerable lack of data (sharing information within competitive EPR systems is problematic), the analytical difficulties in distinguishing the effects of EPR from those generated by other policy instruments, and the scarce comparability of EPR systems.[22] There is, however, mounting evidence from the empirical literature about the relationship between the advent of EPR and the remarkable increases in separate collection and recycling of waste.[23]

Recycling markets existed before the 1980s, but they were limited in scope and operated with many imperfections. Downstream markets were underdeveloped, the cost of collection and sorting was high, and the low value of some waste made recycling not profitable. According to Massarutto,[24] in the last 20 years, we have witnessed a gigantic exercise of market creation, which has been facilitated by the involvement of producers and PROs in waste management.

By shifting the financial burden from municipalities and taxpayers to producers, EPR has exploited the opportunity to mobilise technical/managerial skills and relevant financial resources from the private sector.[25] This, in turn, has affected a range of correlated issues, including infrastructure development and technological/organisational innovation. Funding, setting or expanding infrastructure for waste collection, treatment and recycling has been pointed out as one of the fundamental achievements of EPR.[26] Specific collection channels

---

[21] These are the author's own calculations, based on the latest Eurostat data available as of May 2020 (2016–2017 data, depending on the waste stream and the target considered). The EU average has been directly provided by Eurostat (EU-28) or calculated as the average of the Member States providing data. The only target currently applying that has not been achieved is the reuse and recovery rate for ELVs (94% instead of 95%, 2017).

[22] *Bio by Deloitte*, Development of Guidance on Extended Producer Responsibility, Final Report (prepared for the European Commission by V. Monier et al.), 2014, p. 19; *OECD*, The State of Play on Extended Producer Responsibility: Opportunities and Challenges, Global Forum for the Environment: Promoting Sustainable Materials Management through EPR, Issues Paper, Tokyo, 17–19 June 2014, p. 8; *OECD, supra*, note 3 at p. 13.

[23] *Bio by Deloitte, supra*, note 22 at p. 2; *A. Massarutto*, The Long and Winding Road to Resource Efficiency – An Interdisciplinary Perspective on Extended Producer Responsibility, Resource, Conservation & Recycling 2014 (85), p. 19; *OECD, supra*, note 22 at p. 8; *OECD, supra*, note 3 at p. 23; *Walls, supra*, note 4 at p. 21.

[24] *Massarutto, supra*, note 23 at p. 19.

[25] *OECD, supra*, note 3 at p. 21.

[26] *Bio Intelligence Service*, Use of Economic Instruments and Waste Management Performances (final report prepared E. Watkins et al.), 2012, p. 150; *R. Lifeset, A. Atasu & N. Tojo*, Extended Producer Responsibility – National, International, and Practical Perspectives, J. Ind. Ecol. 2013 (17/2), p. 162; *A. Santini et al.*, End-of-Life Vehicles Management: Italian Material and Energy Recovery Efficiency, Waste Management 2011 (31), p. 492.

have been put into operation for different EPR waste streams, such as separate collection systems for various packaging waste fractions (paper, plastic, glass and metals) and the collection of household WEEE and portable waste batteries by retailers. In many Member States, waste treatment and recycling capacity has significantly improved, following the implementation of EPR directives, as in the cases of Spain[27] and Romania[28] with regard to WEEE.

EPR has generated an "induced innovation" effect, relative to treatment technologies.[29] For instance, in order to meet the 2015 ELVs recycling/recovery targets, many Member States (Austria, Belgium, France, the Netherlands, Sweden and the UK)[30] have developed new technologies for treating auto shredder residue (traditionally destined for landfill).[31] Similarly, following the adoption of the WEEE Directive,[32] technologies have been introduced to treat complete WEEE fractions (without removal of components) or even complete products, whilst achieving high recovery rates for valuable materials and ensuring that hazardous substances are controlled, at a lower cost compared to disassembly.[33]

Massarutto,[34] however, argues that the extraordinary increase experienced by waste recycling and recovery in the EU is actually more the fruit of organisational than technical innovation. The implementation of EPR, as illustrated in section 2, has resulted in the setting up of PROs and in the definition of new roles and relationships between stakeholders in waste management. In EPR systems, the link between production and post-consumer treatment has been strengthened, or even sometimes created,[35] contributing to a better connection of upstream and downstream decisions and to closing the waste-resources loop.

---

27 *D. Queiruga, J.B. González & G. Lannelongue*, Evolution of the Electronic Waste Management System in Spain, J. Clean. Prod. 2012 (24), p. 57.

28 *N. Ciocoiu & V. Târțiu*, The Role of Informal Sector within WEEE Management Systems: a Romanian Perspective, Theoretical Empirica 2012 (7/1, February), p. 33; *Eco Logic & IEEP*, A Report on the Implementation of Directive 2002/96/EC on Waste Electrical and Electronic Equipment (WEEE), 2009, p. 51.

29 *M. Mazzanti & R. Zoboli*, Economic Instruments and Induced Innovation: the European Policies on End-of-Life Vehicles, Ecol. Econ. 2006 (58), pp. 318–337.

30 *Bio Intelligence Service, Arcadis & IEEP*, Ex-post evaluation of certain waste stream Directives (final report prepared by S. Mudgal et al.), 2014, p. 128.

31 *C. Rinaldi et al.*, Life-Cycle Assessment of Innovative Technology for Energy Production from Automotive Shredder Residue, Integr. Environ. Assess. Manag. 2015 (11/3), p. 435.

32 Directive 2012/19/EU, *supra*, note 9.

33 *United Nations University et al.*, 2008 Review of Directive 2002/96/EC on WEEE (final report prepared by J. Huisman et al.), 2007, p. 13.

34 *Massarutto, supra*, note 22 at p. 19.

35 *Mazzanti & Zoboli, supra*, note 29 at p. 322.

3.2. THE IMPACT OF EPR SYSTEMS ON DESIGN FOR THE ENVIRONMENT

DfE is a broad concept that includes different dimensions, such as the selection of low-impact materials, the reduction in material use and the optimisation of initial lifetime and of end-of-life system (e.g. design for disassembly).[36] Assessing the impacts of EPR systems on DfE is challenging for several reasons:[37] DfE often generates trade-offs between environmental impacts (e.g. a car made of steel can be easily recycled, but it consumes a lot of energy during its use phase);[38] companies may have many incentives to implement DfE, meaning that it is difficult to determine the contribution of EPR as a single driver; and there is a lack, at EU level, of DfE targets, indicators and data.[39]

The empirical literature illustrates some success stories of DfE. For instance, the phasing-out of hazardous substances in EPR waste streams is widely documented.[40] However, specific EU waste and chemical legislative provisions[41] may have contributed to this change, more than EPR. A significant decrease in the weight of packaging is also reported (see Table 1). But heavier materials are not necessarily less environmentally friendly (e.g. glass compared to plastics) and light-weighting can affect the lifespan of packaged goods.[42]

---

[36]   *OECD, supra*, note 3 at p. 162.

[37]   Id. at p. 163.

[38]   A. Gottberg et al., Producer Responsibility, Waste Minimisation and the WEEE Directive: Case Studies in Eco-design from the European Lighting Sector, Sci. Total. Environ. 2006 (359), p. 41.

[39]   *Bio by Deloitte, supra*, note 22 at p. 93.

[40]   *J. Gerrard & M. Kandlikar*, Is European End-of-Life Vehicle Legislation Living up to Expectations? Assessing the Impact of the ELV Directive on "Green" Innovation and Vehicle Recovery, Journal of Cleaner Production 2007 (15), p. 26; *Y. Gupt & S. Sahay*, Review of Extended Producer Responsibility: a Case Study Approach, Waste Manage. Res. 2015 (33/7), p. 604; *J. Lambert*, The Influence of Extended Producer Responsibility on Eco-Design Practices: Insights from Six Producer Case Studies in the European ICT Sector, Master Thesis, University of Utrecht, 2012, p. 76.

[41]   See e.g. Directive 94/62/EC, *supra*, note 6, Article 11; Directive 2000/53/EC, *supra*, note 7, Article 4; Directive 2011/65/EU of the European Parliament and of the Council on the restriction of the use of certain hazardous substances in electrical and electronic equipment, OJ 2011 L 174/88; Directive 2006/66/EC, *supra*, note 8, Article 4; Regulation (EC) No. 1907/2006 of the European Parliament and of the Council concerning the Registration, Evaluation, Authorisation and Restriction of Chemicals (REACH), establishing a European Chemicals Agency, amending Directive 1999/45/EC and repealing Council Regulation (EEC) No. 793/93 and Commission Regulation (EC) No. 1488/94 as well as Council Directive 76/769/EEC and Commission Directives 91/155/EEC, 93/67/EEC, 93/105/EC and 2000/21/EC, OJ 2006 L 396/1.

[42]   *Bio Intelligence Service et al, supra*, note 26 at p. 31.

Table 1. Trends in packaging weight (grams)

Type of packaging	1990s	2000	2008	2010	% change
Washing up liquid bottle (1 litre)	67	50	43		−36%
Cardboard boxes for dry food (500 gr)		13.88		11.32	−18%
Soup can (400 g)	579	559	49		−92%
Yoghurt pot (165 gr)	5		4		−20%
Plastic fizzy drinks bottle (2 litre)		43	40		−7%
Plastic bag for 1 kg of pasta		9.03		7.85	−13%
Metal drinks can (330 ml)	21	15	14	13	−38%
Glass beer bottle (275 gr)		325	176		−46%
Glass milk bottle (1 pint)	230		186		−19%

Note: The percentage change measures the weight reduction in the last year compared with the first year of data reporting for the product in the table.

Source: created by the author based on *Bio Intelligence Service*, Use of Economic Instruments and Waste Management Performances (final report prepared E. Watkins et al.), 2012 and *OECD*, Extended Producer Responsibility – Updated Guidance for Efficient Waste Management, OECD Publishing, 2016.

With regard to WEEE, Lambert argues that the use of recycled materials is increasing in the ICT sector.[43] Several studies have found evidence of design for dismantling and recycling of ELVs.[44] According to ACEA,[45] the amount of waste produced by the car industry in total and per vehicle, excluding recycled scrap metal, decreased in the period 2005–2007 by 0.8% and 4.8% respectively.

Notwithstanding the above-mentioned results, the effectiveness of EPR with respect to DfE is disputed and lower than expected.[46] Individual producer responsibility is generally advocated by scholars as having positive effects on DfE, since it fully internalises the related economic benefits.[47] However, few individual compliance schemes exist in the EU. PROs, on the contrary, tend to dilute incentives for DfE, as they usually allocate costs based on producers' market shares.

---

[43] *Lambert, supra*, note 40 at p. 26.

[44] *Bio Intelligence Service et al., supra*, note 26 at p. 126, *Gerrard & Kandlikar, supra*, note 40 at p. 26; *Tojo, supra*, note 4 at p. ix; *R. Zoboli et al.*, Regulation and innovation in the area of end-of-life vehicles, Leone F. and DG JRC-IPTS (eds.), 2000, p. 15.

[45] Quoted by *Bio Intelligence Service et al, supra*, note 26 at p. 150.

[46] *Bio by Deloitte, supra*, note 22 at p. 23; *Massarutto, supra*, note 23 at p. 14; *Walls, supra*, note 4 at p. 40.

[47] *A. Atasu & R. Subramanian*, Extended Producer Responsibility for E-Waste: Individual or Collective Producer Responsibility?, Production and Operations Management 2012 (21/6), pp. 1042–1059; *G. Esenduran & E. Kemahlioglu-Ziya*, Complying with Takeback Legislation: A Cost-Benefit Comparison of Three Compliance Schemes, Working Paper, Ohio State University, 2011; *E.L. Plambeck & Q. Wang*, Effects of E-Waste Regulation on New Product Introduction, Manage. Sci. 2009 (55/3), pp. 333–347.

However, when collective financial responsibility also applies, DfE can be encouraged, to a certain extent, by the fee structure. In particular, incentives for DfE are strong when PRO fees show a high degree of differentiation with respect to product groups (so that cross-subsidisation is limited) and are related to future waste costs.[48] Further, since the magnitude of the fee affects DfE,[49] fees may be modulated according to design features that make products more easily recyclable and penalise "dirty" products. For instance, in France, a *bonus-malus* system has been introduced by the EPR scheme Eco-Emballages (now CITEO), since 2012, for packaging waste. Under this model, for example, producers can be penalised by up to 100% of the fee for non-recyclable packaging put on the market.[50]

4. FUTURE PROSPECTS FOR EPR: FINANCIAL ISSUES AND MECHANISMS TO IMPROVE EFFECTIVENESS

This section analyses how EPR systems can be improved in order to make the principle achieve its original environmental objectives (which have been only partially met) and, possibly, more ambitious ones. There is, indeed, in the EU, a growing awareness of the opportunity to widen the application of EPR and better exploit its potential (see for instance the EU Strategy for Plastics in the Circular Economy[51] and the 2019 Directive providing for the establishment of EPR systems for certain single-use plastic products).[52]

The performance of EPR systems varies significantly between Member States. Therefore, ensuring a certain degree of harmonisation, based on best practices, represents an important first step to improve the application of the principle. To this end, the EU has recently introduced a set of new operating requirements for EPR systems (to be applied by Member States to existing systems from 2023), which should positively affect the costs and effectiveness of EPR systems, while avoiding obstacles to the functioning of the internal market.[53]

In particular, in this harmonisation process, both financial issues and issues related to the monitoring and enforcement of EPR systems deserve special

---

[48] See e.g. *C. K. Mayers et al.*, Implementing Individual Producer Responsibility for Waste Electrical and Electronic Equipment through Improved Financing, J. Ind. Ecol. 2013 (17/2), p. 196.
[49] *OECD, supra*, note 3 at p. 171.
[50] *OECD, supra*, note 22 at p. 14.
[51] European Commission Communication, A European Strategy for Plastics in a Circular Economy, COM(2018) 28 final.
[52] Directive (EU) 2019/904 of the European Parliament and of the Council on the reduction of the impact of certain plastic products on the environment, OJ 2019 L 155.
[53] Directive 2018/851/EU, *supra*, note 11.

attention. With regard to the former, although PROs generally apply a collective financial responsibility, important differences exist in terms of the type of costs that they cover, the extent of coverage and fees modulation. Apart from the cost of waste collection and management, some PROs already finance other waste-related costs, such as the costs of waste prevention measures or the costs of the collection/management of waste that is not pre-sorted by households.[54] The extent of costs coverage is increasing, even if full cost coverage is not always applied, for instance with regard to collection. As stated above, fees may be modulated based on product characteristics, which may stimulate DfE. However, eco-modulation is neither a common practice among PROs nor it is harmonised across Europe (while internationally harmonised incentives are especially important to encourage DfE for global consumer products).

The new requirements shaped by Directive 2018/851/EU provide for a certain degree of harmonisation of PRO financing. According to the Directive, fees paid by producers shall cover the net costs of separate collection, subsequent transport and treatment of waste, as well as the costs of data reporting and those related to consumer information (Article 4). This article, however, does not apply to EPR systems managing WEEE, ELVs and waste batteries and accumulators (which are regulated by specific directives). Moreover, Member States are allowed to depart from Article 4 under certain conditions and special rules apply to EPR systems only established based on Member State legislation. Finally, eco-modulation is recommended by the Directive, but it is not strictly binding.

Moving to monitoring and enforcement of EPR systems, both of these are important to avoid unfair advantages being created for those who do not meet their obligations and to make EPR systems work and be financially viable. Obviously, since EPR systems include a lot of stakeholders with different interests and obligations, ensuring their adequate monitoring and enforcement has proved challenging. The extent of non-compliance problems depends on the governance structure of the EPR system and the type of products it concerns. In particular, the larger the number of producers and PROs involved and the longer the production chains, the higher the potential for non-compliance.[55] Enforcement is mainly concerned with free-riding by producers, compliance by PROs with licence/accreditation rules, conformity of waste collectors and processors with environmental requirements, and the failure by EPR systems to achieve collection, recycling and recovery targets.[56]

Here too there are wide differences between Member States in terms of the monitoring and enforcement mechanisms in place and their effectiveness. Audits, penalties and sanctions often exist in national laws to fight free-riding

---

[54]   *Bio Intelligence Service, supra*, note 26 at pp. 11 and 91.
[55]   *Bio by Deloitte, supra*, note 22 at p. 10; *OECD, supra*, note 3 at p. 88.
[56]   *OECD, supra*, note 3 at p. 88.

and regulate PROs' activities, but they are seldom applied.[57] The number of unregistered producers is reported to be high in some countries. For instance, of the 10,000 EEE producers estimated to exist in Spain, only around 1,000 have been registered.[58] The financial viability of EPR systems is also threatened by leakage, occurring when the valuable fractions of the regulated waste stream are diverted, often in an illegal way, to other destinations. Available information suggests that the scale of "leakage" has reached a significant level for some waste streams. According to Huisman et al.,[59] for example, only 35% of all the e-waste discarded in 2012 in the EU ended up in the official collection/recycling systems, and, on average, it has been estimated that 25% of all ELVs in the EU are not managed in authorised treatment facilities.[60]

The minimum requirements for monitoring and enforcement of EPR systems, shaped by Directive 2018/851/EU, are stated in very general terms, since the responsibility for applying and enforcing EU law rests primarily with the Member States. Member States are required to establish an adequate monitoring and enforcement framework and to set up a clearinghouse when competitive EPR systems exist. Any PRO must put in place a self-control mechanism, supported by regular independent audits, to appraise its financial management and the quality of data reported. The obligation for Member States to ensure a regular dialogue between all the relevant stakeholders involved in the implementation of EPR systems (producers, distributors, waste operators, local authorities, civil society, etc.) is perhaps the most interesting requirement introduced by the Directive.

5. CONCLUSIONS

The EPR principle was incorporated into the EU waste legislation to improve waste management. EPR waste streams show very positive collection and recycling trends. In particular, by shifting the responsibility for waste collection/ management to producers, EPR has fostered infrastructure development, technological innovation and organisational innovation, resulting in the creation or consolidation of recycling markets. This, in turn, has generated wider environmental benefits, such as a reduction in GHG emissions,[61] less contamination of land and water, and more availability of secondary raw

---

[57] *Bio by Deloitte, supra*, note 22 at p. 108.
[58] *Queiruga et al., supra*, note 27 at p. 62.
[59] J. *Huisman et al.*, Countering WEEE Illegal Trade (CWIT) Summary Report, Market Assessment, Legal Analysis, Crime Analysis and Recommendations Roadmap, Lyon, 2015, p. 6.
[60] *Bio Intelligence Service, supra*, note 26 at p. 122.
[61] See e.g. https://www.eea.europa.eu/data-and-maps/daviz/ghg-emissions-from-municipal-waste-1#tab-chart_1.

materials. However, the effectiveness of EPR with respect to DfE is disputed and, in any case, is lower than expected. The market share approach, currently applied by most PROs without any eco-modulation of the fees, provides weak incentives to engage in DfE.

A certain degree of harmonisation between EPR systems, based on best practices, could positively affect their performance (which also depends on several external factors, such as population density, the value of secondary materials and the existence of other policy instruments). With regard to financial issues, the requirements introduced by Directive 2018/851/EU only provide for partial harmonisation. The new rules, indeed, do not apply to EPR systems managing WEEE, ELVs and waste batteries and accumulators. The directives addressing these waste streams, in turn, rarely indicate (apart from the costs of waste collection/management) other costs that PROs must cover and the extent of that coverage. Further, Directive 2018/851/EU suggests that producers' fees should be modulated, where possible, based on environmental criteria. Although it is indeed recognised that eco-modulation could in principle encourage DfE, there are still no strict and uniform requirements for Member States.

With regard to the monitoring and enforcement of EPR systems, the requirements set by Directive 2018/851/EU are stated in very general terms and mainly reflect the status quo, except for the obligation for Member States to ensure a regular dialogue between all the actors involved in EPR systems. The creation of multi-stakeholder dialogue platforms, by providing adequate incentives to all the actors involved to meet their obligations could positively affect compliance, making it less dependent on enforcement.

Based on the above, the harmonising effect of Directive 2018/851/EU is expected to be limited. Since Member States still enjoy a high degree of flexibility about how to design, implement and enforce EPR systems, differences in the performance of EPR systems will not disappear.

FINANCING SUSTAINABLE GROWTH IN EUROPE

The Key Role of Sustainable Finance in Preventing Environmental Damage and Implementing Adaptation Strategies

Letizia CASERTANO

1. INTRODUCTION

This analysis will develop along three main lines: after some preliminary comments on sustainable finance (its origins and recent development), the analysis will turn to the current situation on the financial markets in the light of the choices made by European lawmakers after the 2007–2008 crisis. Finally, the main critical issues related to green finance will be pointed out and briefly illustrated, with a particular focus on the disclosure of climate risks.

Within industrial and post-industrial societies, the uncontrolled appropriation of natural resources has led to the realisation of the so-called "tragedy of the commons",[1] the actual scenario which current and future generations will have to deal with for years to come. Climate change and the attendant climate change mitigation and adaptation strategies are one of the major challenges ahead, in particular since their complexity and possible scale and consequences are still difficult to foresee. Climate change and related issues are now globally recognised

---

[1]   G.J. *Hardin*, The Tragedy of the Commons, Science 1968 (162), pp. 1243–1248. In his famous article the author argues that open access to natural resources such as the air, the oceans and waters, which are generally recognised and perceived as being common to humankind and as such appropriable without specific limitations, has led to their over-use, over-exploitation and abuse to the point of compromising their ability to renew and regenerate themselves (regeneration capacity). Their scarcity and possible exhaustion is today the reality we are confronted with, as against the previous notion of the overwhelming abundance of the Earth's infinite stock. For a modern, courageous and brilliant analysis on reassessing values, rethinking the law, regenerating the commons and reshaping our societies into communities of peoples working together in order to build a life in tune with nature, see F. *Capra & U. Mattei*, The Ecology of Law. Towards a Legal System in Tune with Nature and Community, Berrett-Koehler Publishers, Inc., 2015, passim.

as a major priority on the sustainability agenda due to the potentially enormous disruptive impact they may have on global economies as a whole. A lack of preparedness on this front is no longer acceptable or sustainable. The rapidly changing scenario has made it clear that radical changes need to be implemented now without further delay.

Following the adoption of the Paris Agreement on Climate Change on 1 January 2016 and the related UN 2030 Agenda for Sustainable Development,[2] on March 2018 the EU Commission launched the "Action Plan: Financing sustainable growth". The aim of this Plan is to refocus capital flows on sustainable development, assessing and managing climate-related financial risks and fostering transparency and long-termism within financial and economic activities.

Strategies in a field such as this are extremely complex due to the incredibly broad scope of the changes required: cross-sectoral planning, coordination and consistency need to be pursued as priority methodological targets, while at the same time implementing the change will require a huge mobilisation of financial resources which are currently unavailable within a market that is busy financing non-sustainable activities.

Major interests are affected by the new trend, which means that it is only by involving the major economic actors in the transition towards low-carbon economies that there can be any chance of the expected changes taking place. The fact that key market stakeholders have already become involved has positive aspects, but is also a cause for concern. Once again, the core issue is who will be in charge and at what pace they will proceed. That should be an issue of major concern for the entire international community.

As a consequence, the international community should cooperate by engaging in specific collective efforts. Roundtables for debate, strategic analysis and planning should become core, priority instruments for developing and implementing the transition towards a new concept of sustainable growth in practice. However, at this stage of the process, this concept must not be left up to isolated initiatives, but must be implemented in practice through far-reaching and substantial change to finance and funding with the overall aim of precluding any further support for and development of dangerous and ineligible activities. The market should become virtuous as soon as possible by creating barriers to activities that are per se dangerous for the planet's ecology.

---

2   The UN 2030 Agenda for Sustainable Development identifies 17 Sustainable Development Goals (SDGs): (1) no poverty; (2) zero hunger; (3) good health and well-being; (4) help children in your community to read; (5) call out sexist language and behaviour; (6) clean water and sanitation; (7) affordable and clean energy; (8) decent work and economic growth; (9) industry, innovation and infrastructure; (10) reduced inequalities; (11) sustainable cities and communities; (12) responsible production and consumption; (13) climate action; (14) life below water; (15) life on land; (16) peace, justice and strong institutions; and (17) partnerships for the goals.

The only way of triggering this kind of virtuous change is to foster awareness by providing relevant information and risk disclosure. Transparency and proper information offer the only reliable leverage for pursuing the transition at the necessary speed. If we as a community recognise that we have a common problem, which is also a common priority target, we also recognise that we must force the system as a whole to embrace and implement the new trend.

2. NEW BUSINESS MODELS ROOTED IN FACT-BASED PRIORITIES AND RELATED LEGAL ISSUES

The introduction of new business models will depend upon the risk assessment and risk management solutions adopted. This in turn shows how important having the right information concerning climate related risks is, as well as the key role it is destined to play.

The need to manage emerging mega-risks by involving science through predictability models, as well as businesses and legal expertise, is as important as ever, and will become increasingly more important, with profound implications for insurance, financial stability and the economy.

As is known, the legal response to the so-called "tragedy of the commons" involves both private ownership and liability schemes. Nonetheless due to the scale of the risk, these instruments may not be sufficient unless the public sector becomes seriously involved in the process. This also means that policy makers and regulators should be able to support private initiatives and cooperate in order to boost the expected changes.

This enormous effort started in Europe with the adoption of the 2018 Action Plan and related initiatives. In particular, as we shall see, on 24 May 2018 the Commission adopted a package of measures on sustainable finance with proposals aimed at establishing an EU taxonomy, at improving the disclosure requirements that should be integrated into risk assessment and risk management by economic and financial actors as well as by institutional investors, and also at creating a new category of environmental, social and governance (ESG) benchmarks to orient investors' choices. Moreover, a new regulation setting out sustainable finance disclosure requirements is currently being drafted by EU co-legislators.[3]

---

[3] On 7 March 2019, in a press release entitled "Capital Markets Union: Commission welcomes agreement on sustainable investment disclosure rules", the Commission welcomed "the political agreement reached by the European Parliament and EU Member States on new rules on disclosure requirements related to sustainable investments and sustainability risks". See European Commission Press Release (IP/19/1571), available at http://europa.eu/rapid/press-release_IP-19-1571_en.htm.

As one of the strategic stakeholders involved in the changing scenario, insurance companies have much to say, as they are being increasingly affected by climate and weather-related loss events. As Mark Carney stated in a speech given on 29 September 2015, one needs only consider that, based on research analysis and available data, "insurance losses from these events have increased from around 10 billion per year during the 1980s to around 50 billion annually over the past decade, but the challenges currently posed by climate change are pale in significance compared with what might come".[4] Moreover, although we still do not know how serious and disruptive the incidence of catastrophic natural events may prove to be, we can still envisage some possible scenarios.

As mentioned above, the legal response to the new challenges will come from proprietary models and liability schemes, which will need to adapt to the new threats posed by climate change. Physical risks and damage to property and businesses will be insured under conditions that will have to include risk assessment and risk management as part of a shared liability/ownership scheme. Private ownership will increasingly become an issue of collective and public concern, and as such will be affected by new responsibilities, which will need to take into account both the context and the related risks.

3. ESG FINANCE AS THE NEW "ELIGIBLE" FINANCE

Enormous challenges will need to be overcome in order to ensure a successful and rapid transition to low-carbon economies, and various conditions will need to be met in order to ensure that the new economic and financial trend will be the winning one. As a reminder, and a lesson from the past, it should never be forgotten that final and critical choices in financial markets are ultimately made by investors, who may be either be institutional investors or retail investors. Considered from this perspective, it is sufficiently clear that only high-quality planning and high-quality implementation and performance will be able to achieve long-term results. The success of ESG finance access will require the implementation, joint planning and coordination of strategies as part of a process of continuous learning by doing, monitoring, revising, adjusting, etc.

The complex issues at stake here can also be approached from a dual causal perspective that takes into account both economic failure and environmental failure as global issues which are strictly interconnected.

Based on such a perspective, it can reasonably be argued that, as the impact of financial crises on the real economy has shown (a lesson learned?), monetary and

---

4   Speech by Mr Mark Carney, Governor of the Bank of England and Chairman of the Financial Stability Board, at Lloyd's of London, London, 29 September 2015, available at https://www. fsb-tcfd.org/about/ and also at https://www.bis.org/review/r151009a.pdf.

financial stability should be pursued globally as a precondition for sustainable economic growth. The pursuit of globally sustainable economic growth has been widely acknowledged to be the only reasonable, adequate response to the global risks to which the entire planet is now exposed. There is no doubt that the transition to low-carbon economies represents per se a general public order issue, with both economic and social public (state security) implications. As such, its governance is also a matter for public institutions. Public and private governance mechanisms need to work more in tandem in studying and developing sound instruments and turning the new green economy into the leading sector for reversing the trend.

4. THE TRANSITION TO LOW-CARBON ECONOMIES AS A PUBLIC ORDER ISSUE

The involvement of finance and financial markets in the achievement of ESG goals represents a huge opportunity for reversing the current trend, provided that public and private efforts can join forces and progress together. This will require adequate strategic planning and major efforts at implementation. A key aspect in pursuing this ambitious goal is an increased awareness that the transition to low-carbon economies *is* a public order issue just as much as market stability is. As such, the achievement of this goal through all related initiatives is implicitly endowed with a potential authoritative foundation which must not be underestimated.

Some important lessons can be drawn in this regard from the ongoing process of financial markets reform at the EU level. The need to protect investors from toxic products has become a priority issue following the major financial frauds committed by apparently solid and prestigious commercial banks and financial institutions. These frauds are facts that contributed to raising awareness of dangers and risks, as well as of the responsibilities of the various actors. They also made it clear that the implementation of protective measures is necessary, legitimate and even justified, as we shall see, where they are extreme in nature. The reform trend currently sweeping through Europe offers clear evidence of this new awareness. The initiatives pursued by European lawmakers have turned Europe into one of the most regulated financial markets in the world.[5]

---

[5]   The reform focused on four critical objectives: making financial institutions more resilient; ending the problem of financial institutions being too big to fail; making over-the-counter (OTC) derivatives markets safer; and transforming shadow banking into resilient market-based finance. *M. Carney*, Ten years on: fixing the fault lines of the global financial crisis, in Banque de France, Financial Stability Review no. 21, April 2017, The impact of financial reforms.

Against this backdrop, scholars are significantly contributing to highlighting the role that fundamental principles may play in ensuring sound and sustainable governance for financial markets.[6] This is apparent in particular within the principle of disclosure of relevant conflicting interests under the EU financial services regime, as a core requirement for investor protection, which applies to all issuers irrespective of their country of origin. As has been pointed out by scholars, investors within the EU, as the targeted market, should be protected. First of all, the investor should be warned

> to be aware that the information given may by no means be neutral but instead tainted by bias and to take appropriate additional measures of precaution. If, for instance, US rating agencies did not disclose in their (triple-A) ratings that they had been actively engaged in the design of the financial products rated (and compensated typically more than for the rating itself), the EU rule violated would seem to apply to any such non-disclosure with respect to products marketed on the EU markets ... Again the effect principle would require application of the EU regime, and therefore liability for international violation of disclosure rules which amounts to a common law tort to most jurisdictions (see for example, section 826 Civil Code in Germany).[7]

5. SUSTAINABLE DEVELOPMENT AND SUSTAINABLE FINANCE AS PUBLIC COLLECTIVE ISSUES OF GLOBAL CONCERN

Having been recognised as a collective issue of global concern, sustainable development has been largely addressed by the international community as a priority target, which must be met within all policies and sectors of human activity.[8] This is in particular the case under the following international law instruments: the UN Conference on the Human Environment (Stockholm 1972);

---

[6]   *S. Grundmann*, Do EU Contract and Company Law have Global Reach?, in M. Cremona & H.-W. Micklitz (eds.), Private Law in the External Relations of the EU, Oxford University Press, 2016, pp. 166–168.

[7]   Id.

[8]   It is sufficient to quote the United Nations 2030 Agenda for Sustainable Development and the UN 17 Sustainable Development Goals which include: poverty, hunger, health, education, gender, water, energy, jobs, infrastructure, inequalities, cities, consumption, climate, oceans, the environment, peace, institutions and partnerships. The Agenda was adopted at the Sustainable Development Summit, held on 25–27 September 2015 at the UN Headquarters in New York and officially entered into force on 1 January 2016 (see World Bank Atlas of Sustainable Development Goals 2018, the World Bank compilation of internationally comparable statistics concerning global development and the quality of people's lives based on the World Development Indicators. See the WDI World Bank, Atlas of Sustainable Development Goals 2018: From World Development Indicators, World Bank, 2018.

the Brundtland Commission (1983) Report, *Our Common Future* (1987); the Earth Summit (1992); the Rio Declaration on Environment and Development, Agenda 21 (1992); the Convention on Biological Diversity (1992); the ICPD Programme of Action (1994); the Earth Charter; Lisbon Principles; UN Millennium Declaration (2000); the Earth Summit (Rio+10, 2002); the United Nations Conference on Sustainable Development (Rio+20, 2012); the Paris Agreement (2015); and the United Nations 2030 Agenda for Sustainable Development.

Moreover, in the aftermath of 1992 Earth Summit,[9] the key role played by finance in achieving sustainable growth was first enshrined in the United Nations Environment Programme – Finance Initiative (UNEP FI), which provided for close cooperation between financial institutions, including banks, insurers, investors and the UN Environment Programme, aimed at integrating finance into environmental, social and governance challenges of our times (ESG factors). In other words, the transition towards a low-carbon economy will have to be financed by the issuing of bonds, i.e. long-term debt repayable at pre-agreed rates and guaranteed by governments. The 17 Sustainable Development Goals and the Paris Agreement on climate change acknowledged the need to integrate *sustainable finance* into the economic system *much more quickly and effectively than previously*, thanks also to innovation and the strategic planning of targeted measures and initiatives.

The task ahead is extremely complex. Mobilising huge capital for sustainable development first requires "sustainable investment sectors" and, where applicable, new areas of sustainable growth to be identified. For this purpose, it will be necessary to identify a *common taxonomy* in order to create and strengthen a reliable market characterised by high quality standards. In order to achieve this goal, *disclosure obligations* will be introduced, along with control mechanisms and remedies in the event of non-compliance. Moreover, supervisory powers will need to be delegated to special authorities as guarantors of economic public order. As regards the creation of a harmonised taxonomy, there has been discussion concerning the need to agree on what should be regarded as "sustainable" (bearing in mind the three sectors identified by ESG). Criteria and standards of compliance will be subject to verification according to procedures intended to monitor and supervise consistency between disclosures made and the specific implementation of related activities. As a result, supervisory authorities will carry out checks to ensure that the money borrowed from

---

[9]   The United Nations Conference on Environment and Development (UNCED), also known as the Rio de Janeiro Earth Summit, the Rio Summit, the Rio Conference, and the Earth Summit (Portuguese: ECO92), was a major United Nations conference held in Rio de Janeiro on 3–14 June 1992.

investors is actually being used to fund sustainable projects. As was stressed in ESMA's responses to public consultations:[10]

> ESMA agrees on the importance of having clarity on the terminology used for the correct implementation of the new requirements. ESMA also believes that the development of any binding definitions needs to consider all legislative initiatives developed on the topic of sustainable finance in order to ensure a harmonised approach across sectors.[11]

Another issue related to the creation and implementation of a common ESG taxonomy is legal certainty. In fact, as has been noted by the Securities and Markets Stakeholders Group (SMSG), the lack of a common EU taxonomy might lead to misleading information claiming the "ESG label" for products that do not meet ESG requirements, thereby giving rise to inconsistencies, bubble effects within certain assets classes, increased litigation between clients and investment firms, etc.[12] Developing labelling schemes for green bonds (social bonds and sustainable bonds) is also part of this process. Labelling was started a few years ago on the initiative of some organisations including the CBI (Climate Bonds Initiative), an international organisation whose founders and partners include the biggest banks and financial institutions on the planet.

When discussing strategic planning for financial markets, it is important not to overlook the attendant economic implications. In fact, in order to ensure that the new green/sustainable financial market is sufficiently reliable for investors, the financed activities that are labelled as sustainable will have to be successfully implemented. This in turn requires careful strategic planning, focused on both the macro-economic scenario as well as the micro-economic perspective. Public authorities and private operators will thus need to engage in joint efforts and to cooperate with one another with this aim in mind. Incentives directed both at companies and consumers (such as taxation) will prove to be crucial in prompting green economy and related green investments.

There is a huge need for money in order to fund the transition to a low-carbon economy, which means that a potentially enormous market is waiting to be

---

[10] See ESMA Final Report, "ESMA's Technical Advice to the European Commission on Integrating Sustainability Risks and Factors in MIDIF II", 30 April 2019, ESMA35-43-1737.

[11] Id. The ESMA Response continues by stressing that "ESMA has refrained from suggesting new definitions in its draft technical advice, but is pleased to note that definitions on these topics are indeed included in the new rules on sustainability-related disclosure requirements related to sustainable investments and sustainability risks on which the co-legislators have recently reached political agreement". In particular reference is made to the Disclosure Regulation which includes, amongst others, definitions of "sustainability risk", "sustainability factors" and "sustainable investments".

[12] Id. at p. 7.

launched. This explains why the stakeholders that are currently mobilising with this new development in mind are the same major players that are already present on the market. Consider for example the key role played by insurance companies in insuring new classes of risks and covering modern catastrophic events such as earthquakes, aviation insurance and weather-related events.

This strategic approach for involving the same major players as those already present in the market endorsed on the CBI website is clearly envisaged as a hypothetical pathway. For example, when it is suggested that a slow transition is one possibility, whereas an accelerated transition towards a low-carbon economy will require massive investment with low initial returns, it is necessary to clarify how this effort will be made and by whom. To be honest, this step appears to be rather difficult and will only be strategically feasible if the sacrifice will not have to be made by (inevitably retail) investors. In this regard a great deal of care and attention will have to be paid in order to avoid overly forcing debt financing leverage.

The initiatives aimed at creating *common standards* for ESG finance include: (1) the Action Plan on Sustainable Finance of March 2018, Article 2 of which also envisages the need for harmonised taxonomy;[13] (2) the Disclosure Regulation adopted by the EU Commission on 7 March 2019; (3) the CBI, an international organisation encompassing governments, big banks and insurers,[14] which is working exclusively on mobilising the largest capital market of all, the $100 trillion bond market, for climate change solutions; and (4) the Task Force on Climate-related Financial Disclosure, which is actively working on establishing the necessary conditions for the transition to a low-carbon economy leveraged on ESG finance.

By referring to the need for the wholesale incorporation of finance into "the Change", and even referring directly to the actual amounts of money to be invested (the "$100 trillion bond market for climate change solutions") it is also possible to set targets and measure the scale of the problem. There is no doubt that we must finally engage with the wide-scale involvement of financial instruments within sustainable development as a worldwide priority that cannot

---

[13]   Following the adoption of the Action Plan on Financing Sustainable Growth in March 2018, on 24 May 2018 the Commission presented a series of legislative measures intended to implement the Action Plan. The Disclosure Regulation adopted on 7 March 2019 is part of that package, together with the EU rules on the creation of benchmarks for low-carbon investment strategies approved on 25 February by the European Parliament and Member States. The Commission is now working with co-legislators with the goal to reach agreement on the remaining part of the package: the Commission proposal to establish a unified EU classification system ("taxonomy") of sustainable economic activities. See the European Commission Press Release, *supra*, note 4.

[14]   For a detailed list of partners see https://www.climatebonds.net/about-us/partners.

be postponed. Nonetheless, the final target could be better stated by quoting ESMA chair Steven Maijoor:

> Economic growth needs the willingness to take risks, not the type of risks associated with exotic financial instruments, but the kind of risks that allow companies and entrepreneurs to conduct their business and to innovate, start new projects, and generate new revenues and jobs. The real economy needs capital through channels other than the traditional banking one and it should be more often equity (shares) rather than debt (bonds).[15]

Moreover, as mentioned above, within the context of the new green, sustainable economy, financial market participants (from rating agencies to investors) will need to be informed about specific risks in relation to *all financed activities*. This means that the key factor will prove to be "disclosure of right, faithful, correct, honest ESG related information".

From the regulatory perspective, once more incisive and detailed provision has been made for the disclosure of environmental risks and related risks as a general obligation, this will help to boost the involvement of insurance companies in the process of financing the general turn towards achieving sustainability in practice.

6. SOME GENERAL REMARKS CONCERNING THE CURRENT SITUATION

In the aftermath of the most recent financial crisis in 2008, financial markets around the world have been subjected to more intense regulatory intervention in order to lower the risk exposure of financial institutions by imposing capital caps (capital requirements regimes), regulating OTC platforms (in derivative markets), imposing stricter rules for derivatives, regulating short selling, and introducing new rules for credit ratings agencies, alternative investment fund managers, etc. This includes in particular, under the auspices of Basel III, the Dodd-Frank Act of 2010 in the US, along with the process of reform in Europe that culminated in the adoption of the Markets in Financial Instruments Directive II (MIFID II) and the Markets in Financial Instruments Regulation (MIFIR).[16]

---

[15] Steven Maijoor Keynote Address, "Towards benchmark integrity and stability", 31 May 2018, 50th ICMA Annual General Meeting and Conference in Madrid, ESMA71-99-996, available at https://www.esma.europa.eu/sites/default/files/library/esma71-99-996_towards_benchmark_stability_and_integrity_steven_maijoor_icma_conference_2018_madrid_31_may_1.pdf.

[16] See *M. Comana, D. Previtali & L. Ballardini*, The MiFID II Framework. How the New Standards Are Reshaping the Investment Industry, Springer, 2019.

This wave of stricter regulation ultimately marked the starting point for a new era. We are definitely moving towards the detailed planning and "proceduralisation" of financial activities. The long hand of the regulator is becoming less invisible and is being replaced by a substantive presence made up of rules and standardisations as a means for facilitating controls and supervision by supervisory authorities. Within this context, Europe is one of the most regulated financial markets in the world. The ongoing change is now being driven by the creation of a Capital Markets Union among the EU Member States,[17] which seeks to break down barriers to cross-border investment and to boost sustainable economic growth. This includes in particular the most recent Action Plans adopted on 8 March 2018 by the European Commission in this area, the Action Plan on financing sustainable growth along with the Fintech Action Plan.[18]

The Action Plan on sustainable finance adopted by the European Commission in March 2018 has three main objectives:[19] to reorient capital flows towards sustainable investment in order to achieve sustainable and inclusive growth; to manage the financial risks stemming from climate change, environmental degradation and social issues; and to foster transparency and long-termism in financial and economic activity. The implementation of sustainable finance within the European Capital Markets Union will pose further problems as regards the harmonisation of national laws within the EU, and may also result in the creation of "new, financial markets areas" that are more autonomous from

---

[17] See in particular: (1) Communication from the Commission to the European Parliament, the Council, the European Economic and Social Committee and the Committee of the Regions Action Plan on Building a Capital Markets Union, COM(2015) 468 final; (2) Communication from the Commission to the European Parliament, the Council, the European Economic and Social Committee and the Committee of the Regions on the Mid-Term Review of the Capital Markets Union Action Plan, COM(2017) 292 final; (3) Communication from the Commission to the European Parliament, the European Council, the Council, the European Central Bank, the European Economic and Social Committee and the Committee of the Regions Capital Markets Union: Progress on Building a Single Market for Capital for a Strong Economic and Monetary Union, 15 March 2019, COM(2019) 136 final. As to the contribution that the creation of a European Capital Markets Union is expected to give in boosting sustainable economic growth, see Report by the *Economist Intelligence Unit*, The Road to Action: Financial Regulation Addressing Climate Change, 2017, p. 26. See also the Final Report: Recommendations of the Task Force on Climate-Related Financial Disclosure, June 2017.

[18] Communication from the Commission to the European Parliament, the Council, the European Central Bank, the European Economic and Social Committee and the Committee of the Regions FinTech Action Plan: For a More Competitive and Innovative European Financial Sector, COM(2018) 109 final.

[19] Communication from the Commission to the European Parliament, the European Council, the Council, the European Central Bank, the European Economic and Social Committee and the Committee of the Regions Action Plan: Financing Sustainable Growth, COM(2018) 97 final.

the major international players. The new Keynesian turn within the new era of international finance seems to be made up of a mixture of new elements and critical challenges, which will form part of the future scenario of global market economies.

The spectrum of change introduced in recent decades is extremely broad. Overall protective measures have been envisaged in order to ensure stability for financial institutions and to prevent toxic products from destabilising the market. Depending on the extent of the preventive measures that are adopted and implemented in certain areas, financial markets may end up being regionalised for protective purposes. As is known, economic growth largely depends on the dynamics of capital flows,[20] and thus on investment. Moreover, capital flows are generated not only by investment but also by interest rates, fiscal regulations, etc. With this in mind, financial policies are and should be intended to support economic activities through the direct involvement of public and private investors. Nevertheless, capital investment is not sufficient in order to ensure economic stability since, in order to grow, companies need to secure favourable, balanced economic environment in terms of tax policies, international competition, customs regulations and so forth.

7. TOWARDS MORE TRANSPARENT FINANCIAL MARKETS: THE NEW DISCLOSURE OBLIGATIONS

The adoption of an ESG approach[21] to investment choices was initially introduced by Directive 2014/95/EU, which requires large companies[22] to disclose information about how they operate and manage social and environmental challenges.[23] This is meant to enhance transparency and to put investors, consumers, policy makers and other stakeholders in a condition to better evaluate investments and to encourage companies to develop a responsible approach to business. Under Directive 2014/95/EU, large companies have

---

[20] Since 2012, the global economy has followed a gradual trend towards greater capital account openness.

[21] That is, an approach based on Environmental, Social and Governance criteria as endorsed by EU law (see Directive 2014/95/EU and Directive 2017/828/EU).

[22] EU rules on non-financial reporting only apply to large public-interest companies with more than 500 employees. This covers approximately 6,000 large companies and groups across the EU, including listed companies, banks, insurance companies, as well as other companies designated by national authorities as public-interest entities.

[23] Directive 2014/95/EU of the European Parliament and of the Council of 22 October 2014 amending Directive 2013/34/EU as regards disclosure of non-financial and diversity information by certain large undertakings and groups. Companies have been required to include non-financial statements in their *annual reports* from 2018 onwards (sustainability reports, integrated reports).

to publish reports concerning the policies they implement in relation to: environmental protection; social responsibility and treatment of employees; respect for human rights; anti-corruption and bribery; and diversity on company boards (in terms of age, gender, educational and professional background).

Transparency and disclosure are also at the heart of the 2018 Action Plan on financing sustainable growth. In particular, the Action Plan outlines 10 "actions" in three key reform areas: (1) reorienting capital flows towards sustainable investments, in order to achieve sustainable and inclusive growth;[24] (2) mainstreaming sustainability into risk management;[25] and (3) fostering transparency and long-termism in financial and economic activity.[26]

As early as May 2018, the Commission adopted four legislative proposals aimed at implementing some of the actions announced in its Action Plan on sustainable finance. The four key sectors that need to be regulated and implemented are: taxonomy; disclosure and duties; financial benchmarks; and sustainability preferences (consultation). These are discussed in turn in the following sections.

7.1. TAXONOMY

The importance of establishing a common taxonomy in order to ensure the implementation of a harmonised approach to sustainable finance is clear and is widely accepted by market stakeholders. In fact, legal uncertainty in relation to concepts and terms relating to environmental, social and governance matters can only create confusion, lead to misunderstanding and ultimately result in adverse effects. On the contrary, the identification of a common taxonomy will provide the system with a clear common reference, which can be used in order to assess the sustainability of business activities and to manage information and disclosure, etc. The creation of a common classification system for establishing what can be considered to be environmentally sustainable is thus a basic step towards creating and successfully implementing a bond market for financing sustainable economic activities over the long run. Agreement concerning shared

---

[24] In order to implement reform in this first area it will be necessary to: establish an EU classification system for sustainability activities; create standards and labels for green financial products; foster investment in sustainable projects; incorporate sustainability when providing investment advice; and develop sustainability benchmarks.

[25] In order to implement reform in this first area it will be necessary to: better integrate sustainability into ratings and research; clarify the duties of institutional investors and asset managers; and incorporate sustainability into prudential requirements.

[26] In order to implement reform in this first area it will be necessary to: strengthen sustainability disclosure and accounting rule-making; and foster sustainable corporate governance and attenuate short-termism in capital markets.

definitions, notions and standards is crucial for investors, and the same is true for bond issuer guidelines, information flows for rating agencies and so on. Once again, the key issue will be transparency and the adequacy of the data exchanged.

7.2. DISCLOSURE AND DUTIES

The EU Commission has launched a proposal for a Regulation on disclosure relating to sustainable investment and sustainability risks,[27] which requires asset managers and institutional investors to incorporate ESG factors into their risk processes and to account for that through public reporting (disclosure duties or fiduciary duties). The disclosure regulation includes, amongst others, definitions of "sustainability risks", "sustainability factors" and "sustainable investments",[28] thereby contributing to the creation of a common ESG taxonomy.

As the SMSG clarified when answering a recent public consultation launched by ESMA:[29] "Firms are required to adopt an internal framework designed to incorporate ESG risks and factors where relevant and to ask their clients about their preferences but they are not required to offer products or investments advices/portfolio management that are ESG driven". ESMA's approach to conflicts of interest is however more stringent.[30] In this regard ESMA proposed incorporating the rules on conflicts of interest laid down by MIFID II by introducing into the MIFID II Delegated Regulation "a clear reference to the need for firms to identify conflicts of interests whose existence may damage the interests of a client, and that in doing so such firms should include those that may stem from the distribution of environmentally sustainable investments, social investments or good governance investments." Furthermore, firms "would be expected to include a clear reference in their conflict of interests policy on how they are identified and managed".[31] As ESMA has stressed on several occasions, the need to incorporate ESG factors into financial activities will require a

---

27   Proposal for a Regulation on disclosures relating to sustainable investment and sustainability risks, amending Directive (EU) 2016/2341 (IORP 2 – Pensions).

28   See EMSA Final Report, *supra*, note 11.

29   Id.

30   As ESMA pointed out, due to the timing of the political agreement that led to the adoption of the Disclosure Regulation, in its Technical Advice on integrating sustainability risks and factors into MIFID II of 30 April 2019, it was not able to fully address the issue of disclosure requirements on sustainable finance. Nonetheless in its report, ESMA proposes amendments to MIFID II in order to incorporate into it some of the requirements introduced by the Disclosure Regulation.

31   EMSA Final Report, *supra*, note 11 at pp. 14–15.

continuous reassessment of the results achieved and the consistent amendment of existing legislation.

7.3.   FINANCIAL BENCHMARKS

The proposal for a Regulation[32] amending the existing benchmark regulation of 2016[33] is aimed at creating a new category of benchmark, consisting in low-carbon and positive-carbon-impact benchmarks, in order to help investors better understand the respective carbon impact of their investments.[34] In particular, the Proposal envisages that "introducing a clear distinction between climate transition and Paris-aligned benchmarks and developing minimum standards for each of those, will help facilitate consistency across benchmarks that choose to promote themselves as such".[35]

7.4.   SUSTAINABILITY PREFERENCES (CONSULTATION)

In addition, the Commission has called for feedback concerning proposed amendments to delegated acts under MIFID II and the Insurance Distribution Directive in order to incorporate ESG considerations into the advice that investment firms and insurance distributors offer to their clients. With this in mind, on 4 January 2019, the Commission published updated MIFID rules on how investment firms and insurance distributors should take sustainability issues into account when providing advice to their clients.[36]

---

[32]   The Proposal for a regulation of the European Parliament and of the Council amending Regulation (EU) No. 2016/1011 as regards climate transition benchmarks and Paris-aligned benchmarks.

[33]   Regulation (EU) No. 2016/1011 of the European Parliament and of the Council of 8 June 2016 on indices used as benchmarks in financial instruments and financial contracts or to measure the performance of investment funds and amending Directives 2008/48/EC and 2014/17/EU and Regulation (EU) No. 596/2014.

[34]   The Benchmarks Regulation empowers ESMA to develop draft regulatory technical standards (RTS) and to implement technical standards (ITS) in a number of areas such as: procedures, characteristics and positioning of oversight functions to avoid conflicts of interest; the appropriateness and verifiability of input data; templates for compliance statements for significant benchmarks, etc.

[35]   See Recital 13 of the Draft European Parliament Legislative Resolution on the Proposal for a Regulation of the European Parliament and of the Council amending Regulation (EU) 2016/1011 on low carbon benchmarks and positive carbon impact benchmarks, COM(2018) 355 – C8-0209/2018 – 2018/0180(COD).

[36]   http://ec.europa.eu/finance/docs/level-2-measures/mifid-delegated-act-2018_en.pdf.

8. THE SHAREHOLDERS' RIGHTS DIRECTIVE AND THE LONG-TERM SHAREHOLDER ENGAGEMENT DIRECTIVE

Directive 2017/282 on Long-Term Shareholder Engagement (SRD II) of 17 May 2017, amending Directive 2007/36 known as the Shareholder Rights Directive (SRD), introduced transparency requirements for institutional investors and asset managers with the aim of encouraging long-term investments and the adequate consideration of social and environmental issues. These new rules will be based on a "comply or explain" approach, which means that if the investor decides not to comply with the rules, he needs to provide explanations as to why this is the case.

The measures introduced by the Directive include in particular the following: (1) accountability regarding directors' remuneration (remuneration policies developed by Member States and a requirement to report remuneration) and direct involvement of shareholders by voting on whether to approve directors' remuneration ("say on pay" principle); and (2) increased regulation of intermediaries, institutional investors, asset managers and proxy advisers; in particular, such operators are under a duty to provide the information in their possession to shareholders, who have the right to obtain such information.

9. COOPERATION AND SHARING IN ORDER TO ENSURE BETTER GOVERNANCE

A Corporate Forum for Sustainable Finance was created in January 2019. Sixteen companies joined the Forum with the aim of creating a network of information and financial proposals that could be used to manage green bond emissions linked to green projects with positive impacts on the environment in terms of energy efficiency, energy production from clean sources and sustainable land use.[37] It seems to be a perfect instrument for enhancing inter-corporate best practices and for promoting their circulation. The 16 founding companies, which are active in various sectors from electricity production through transportation to other environmental services,[38] have issued more than two thirds of the total green bonds issued in Europe and are committed to developing sustainable finance as a tool for combating climate change and promoting sustainable development. In particular, low-carbon and sustainable investments play a key role in the industrial strategies of these companies.

---

[37]   See http://www.csroggi.org/nasce-il-corporate-forum-for-sustainable-finance/.
[38]   Including Terna, Enel and Ferrovie dello Stato from Italy, while those from other European countries include EDF, TraEdp, Engie, Iberdrola, RATP, SNCF, SSE, Tennet, Tideway and Vasakronan.

The Forum aims to expand the commitments made in 2017 following the publication of the Paris Green Bond Pledge on the occasion of the Climate Finance Day, when nine of the largest European green bond issuers – EDF, Enel, ENGIE, Iberdrola, Icade, Paprec, SNCF Réseau, SSE and TenneT – publicly announced their promise to further develop one of the most dynamic segments of sustainable finance: the green bond market.

For this purpose it is essential to establish cooperation at the corporate level as this will enable the development of cross-sectoral sustainable projects by involving a considerable number of new stakeholders. By acting in this way, it is clear that the intent is to develop a strategy of horizontal/cross-sectoral implementation which, in order to be successful, will need to involve companies directly. These companies in turn will have to ensure that their activities are "green" and "sustainable" overall if they want to benefit from sustainable financing.

10. THE "ONTOLOGICAL" NEED FOR CROSS-SECTORAL IMPLEMENTATION AND THE NEED FOR A STRATEGY

The cross-sectoral implementation of sustainability is the only effective way ahead. An awareness of the interconnectedness of processes and activities essentially prevents them from being considered in isolation as the sustainability of single segments. The overall purpose of sustainable financing is thus to expand so as to become as inclusive as possible. This goal is inherent in the way financing itself seeks to operate. In fact, the consistency of the activities financed with the goals of sustainability must be evaluated by stakeholders with reference to the whole chain of interconnections with other related activities.

The choice of implementing sustainable finance marks the current stepping stone towards sustainability as a global challenge and a global business. Ultimately, businesses will turn towards sustainable choices and will be financially supported in order to do so. As already noted, they will also have to account for this.

In this perspective it is essential to promote "market awareness". Moreover, this awareness is and will increasingly underlie the very willingness to invest in sustainable activities. Market awareness is itself a priority target since the choices of both institutional investors and retail investors depend on it. The key importance of the issue is apparent from the need to offer a reliable framework to investors. As noted, this calls for sound strategies to be placed at the heart of the entire venture.

The path towards sustainable finance may follow either of two routes: either eco-labelled activities or eco-labelled finance. This is a model which will develop around the role of correct information, accountability issues, the disclosure of risk assessments and risk management.

The role played by new operators that hold relevant information for orienting and guiding investors represents another important stage of development.

The awareness-raising model is going to play a key role in the near future and will have an increasing impact on business activities. The way in which investors' choices can be monitored and labelled as green and more generally as sustainable under the ESG scheme will in fact depend on a series of characteristics and standards that sustainable projects and activities will need to meet (compliance model).

The role of internal auditing and of external controllers is already part of this scenario. Specialist consulting companies already exist in order to provide relevant information to investors, which can thereby verify the overall consistency of activities and businesses that are both directly and indirectly related to those financed as green or sustainable.

11. FINANCIAL GLOBALISATION AND FINANCIAL SUSTAINABILITY FROM THE ILO PERSPECTIVE: MICROFINANCE

The International Labour Organization's (ILO) mandate for the 21st century, "a decent work for all", poses a global challenge for ILO stakeholders. In order to deal with it, ILO Member States will need to implement ongoing strategic planning focused on two main guidelines: macro- and micro-economic critical issues and the related instruments, and strategies for enabling the world community to work through those issues in the long run.

As part of the ILO global strategy, microfinance is gaining ground as a sustainable financial instrument for maintaining economic growth in developing countries. In his introductory speech at the World Micro Finance Forum held in Geneva on 29 November 2007, Juan Somavi pointed to the importance of microfinance within the framework of financial sustainability and institutional viability, stressing that:

> ... the Decent Work concept is also a productive vision based on stimulating entrepreneurship, investment, initiative and sustainable livelihood. ... The idea of locking together innovation, financial markets and social objectives is a powerful one ... provided that governments are ready to work together internationally, implementing policies that can help protect ordinary people, working families and productive enterprises from the financial fallout and looming recession.[39]

---

[39]　"Building fair financial markets for all" – Welcome remarks by Juan Somavia to the World Micro Finance Forum Geneva, 29 November, 2007 at https://www.ilo.org/global/about-the-ilo/newsroom/statements-and-speeches/WCMS_098916/lang--en/index.htm.

The acknowledgment of the key importance of macro- and micro-economic factors by major International Actors involved at the global level (WTO, IMF, BCE, WBI, OEDC, ILO) resulted in the incorporation of finance into the scope of sustainable development as the absolute frontier for both current and future generations.

12. SOME PRELIMINARY CONCLUSIONS

As history tells us, financial crises, like natural disasters, can achieve a global reach. In a changing world that is being threatened by new, hitherto unknown risks, the urgency of reshaping existing models and new thinking has become an issue of common concern for the entire international community. In particular, an awareness of the proximity of the climate change risks nowadays calls for a new chapter on adaptation and mitigation strategies to be written. In other words, the readiness to adapt to unavoidable changes and to their consequences (rising sea levels, intense atmospheric phenomena, desertification) will prove crucial in the years to come. Incorporating finance into the process is the only reasonable step that can be taken in order to finally channel investments and to redirect capital flows towards a sustainable economy.

The legal response to the new challenges will come from proprietary models and liability schemes, which will need to adapt to the new threats posed by climate change. In particular, as private ownership will increasingly become an issue of collective and public concern, insurance of related risks, risk assessments and risk management will become part of a shared liability/ownership scheme.

This is not a simple task. Moreover, in order to make it work, both policies and strategies should be devised and implemented, focusing on both the macro- and the micro-economic perspective, by considering specific contexts without losing sight of the big picture. Long-term strategic planning and coordination among the stakeholders involved will be crucial in order to avoid market failure. This means that investments will need to be supported by a context that is sufficiently favourable to make sustainable growth achievable in the long run. In particular, protective measures should be accurately conceived in order to support the transition towards a low-carbon economy. A strong political will should lead governments and public institutions to increasingly support and cooperate with the major players that are already committed to this ambitious, far-reaching and ultimate attempt to make today's turning point an opportunity to grasp without hesitation and delay.

THE BURDEN OF PROOF IN PROCEEDINGS FOR CORRECTIVE AND PREVENTIVE ACTIONS IN POLISH AND ITALIAN LAW

Bartosz Rakoczy

1. THE BURDEN OF PROOF: DEFINITION AND IMPORTANCE IN PROCEEDINGS

The fundamental term that must first be explained in this chapter is "burden of proof". The term is a borrowing from the German legal terminology,[1] not only differing from the Latin term *onus probandi*, but also, particularly, from its statutory definition adopted in Article 6 of the Polish Civil Code, which mentions the burden of proving a fact. This term [i.e. burden of proof], is easier to communicate. It is undoubtedly a shortcut (simplification) but, since people have used it so commonly in legal language for such a long time, "it became a statutory term in the end ... Thus, it is not a mistake to use it".[2]

In the theory of law, the burden of proof is associated with the application of the law. The application of the law is defined as "making binding and specific legal decisions by a competent state authority pursuant to the generally binding legal norms".[3] On the other hand, Stawecki and Winczorek, combining the application of the law with burden of proof, indicate that:

> The application of law is an action, hence it is a *decision-making process* which can be split into the following stages:
>
> (1) preliminary establishment of the likelihood of occurrence of a legally significant fact;

---

[1]   H. Dolecki, Ciężar dowodu w cywilistyce w latach 1945–1985 (Burden of proof in civil law studies in 1945–1985), Acta Univesitatis Wratislaviensis, Issue 1028, Prawo CLXX (Law CLXX), 1990, pp. 33–53.

[2]   Id. at p. 41.

[3]   L. Leszczyński, Wstęp do prawoznawstwa (Introduction to jurisprudence), in A. Korybski, L. Leszczyński & A. Pieniążek (eds.), C.H. Beck 2007, p. 147.

(2)   proving the occurrence of a fact;
(3)   subsumption of the decision;
(4)   execution of the decision.[4]

These authors associate the burden of proof with the second stage, that is, proving the occurrence of facts. They argue that, "as a rule, proving a fact to the authorities and providing its description is a responsibility of the person (e.g. prosecution, claimant) who believes that specific legal effects result from (are connected with) such a fact. The rule indicates who is bound to have the so-called burden of proof (*onus probandi*)".[5] The principle of burden of proof is expressed by the Latin maxim *ei incumbit probatio qui dicit, non ei qui negat* (the burden of the proof lies upon him who affirms, not him who denies). However, the rule is subject to certain modifications and it cannot be deemed binding throughout the legal system without reservations and exceptions.[6]

The doctrine also notes that burden of proof is not an abstract rule but must follow from a specific legal norm. Wronkowska explicitly claims that such a norm means legal regulations governing the establishment of facts. She remarks "legal regulations governing the establishment of facts also indicate who must show initiative in establishing facts, provide information significant to the settlement of the case and who bears the negative consequences of certain facts not having been proved. Briefly speaking, these regulations govern the *distribution of burden of proof*".[7] However, Morawski also notices the so-called non-statutory regulations of the burden of proof, including factual presumptions, *prima facie* rules of proof and legal actions.[8]

These circumstances are also noted by Wolter, Ignatowicz and Stefaniuk, who indicate, using the example of Polish civil law, that:

> material and legal issues related to burden of proof are regulated mainly by Article 6 of the Civil Code ... In civil law there are numerous special provisions giving a different distribution of the burden of proof; in the Polish codification technique,

---

4   *T. Stawecki & P. Winczorek,* Wstęp do prawoznawstwa (Introduction to jurisprudence), 4th ed., Warsaw 2003, p. 190.
5   Id.
6   Instituzioni di Diritto Romano, 4th ed., 2003, pp. 117 et seq.
7   *S. Wronkowska,* Podstawowe pojęcia prawa i prawoznawstwa (Fundamental terms in law and jurisprudence), 3rd ed., Poznań 2003.
8   *L. Morawski,* Ciężar dowodu – niektóre problemy dowodowe (Burden of proof – selected evidentiary problems), Studia cywilistyczne (Civil law studies), vol. XXXII, 1982, part 206. Morawski emphasises that these issues do not play a major role in practical application of law since they are connected with burden of proof agreements that are inadmissible in the Polish legal regime.

shifting the burden of proof to a party other than the one indicated in Article 6 of the Civil Code, is usually formulated by including the specific circumstances in a side clause starting with 'unless …'.[9]

It is also noted that the burden of proof can be reduced to a short statement that this is an obligation of proving.[10]

Radwański and Zieliński state that "[d]espite Article 6 of CC using the phrase 'burden of proving a fact', the commonly used term is 'burden of proof' – according to the Roman tradition (*onus probandi*) accepted not only within the Polish system, but also in worldwide literature".[11] According to slightly older doctrine:

> In the light of the doctrine, the facts being the objects of the proof are not only specific events happening in a specific time and space in the past or at present, but also the statuses of the external world such as the weather on a given day, mental conditions (intention, will, consent). An object of proof is also the rules of common sense and exceptionally – the law.[12]

The theory of law also notices the material and legal as well as the formal and legal dimension of the burden of proof. Wronkowska discusses the issue of burden of proof in the chapter of her book concerning the establishment of facts in the application of the law. Thus, she combines this issue with the application of the law and one of its elements, that is, the establishment of facts. This is the essence of the burden of proof.[13] In the *formal* (procedural) approach, while talking about the burden of proof, subjects who should show initiative to collect information and prove that certain claims are true are identified. … In *substantive law*, while talking about the burden of proof, it is determined who bears negative consequences of the failure to prove in the proceedings that any facts significant to the settlement of the case did occur.[14]

On the other hand, Kołakowski emphasises that "[a] claim based on entitlement must be proved by means of facts which can substantiate it. Likewise,

---

[9]   A. Wolter, J. Ignatowicz & K. Stefaniuk, Prawo cywilne. Zarys cześci ogólnej (Civil law. An outline of the general part), 2nd ed., Warsaw 2001, p. 383.

[10] A. Keane, The Modern Law of Evidence, Oxford 2008, p. 78.

[11] Z. Radwański & A. Zieliński, System prawa prywatnego. Prawo cywilne – część ogólna (Private law system. Civil law – general part) in M. Safjan (ed.) *System prawa prywatnego. Prawo cywilne – część ogólna*, Warsaw 2007, p. 411.

[12] W. Bryl, Kodeks cywilny. Komentarz (Civil Code. A Commentary), in Z. Resich (ed.) *Kodeks cywilny. Komentarz*, vol. I, Warsaw 1972, p. 66.

[13] Wronkowska, supra, note 7 at p. 151.

[14] Id.

the party denying that such an entitlement exists is required to prove that the facts testifying to such circumstances did exist or they have still existed".[15]

The theory of law indicates that in the case of the burden of proof, regardless of the branch or the division of law, two significant elements occur. According to Morawski, "the burden of proof determines two issues: who should present the proof (burden of proof in the *subjective, formal* sense) and who will bear the risk of not proving (*non liquet*) the specific claims (burden of proof in the *objective, material* sense)".[16] In the case of the first element, this author points to the existence of the subjective aspect and the formal aspect. On the other hand, in the second case, he mentions an objective and material aspect. However, it may be assumed that this is a subjective and objective aspect. From a subjective aspect, it is significant what should be proved and what the consequences will be if the proof is ineffective or doubtful. These two elements are, in the present author's opinion, the most significant issues related to the burden of proof in environmental protection law. In one of his previous papers, Morawski also noted that:

> the burden of proof in the subjective sense regulates the parties' proceedings to take evidence, and namely, it determines which of them should present or indicate evidence to support the specified claims about the facts of the case. On the other hand, in the objective sense, the burden of proof will be only used for legal qualification of the negative outcome of the evidentiary proceedings.[17]

The most important things can be which *subject* bears the burden of proof. The second most important problem is the *scope of proof* and the possible consequences of proving specific circumstances ineffectively.

The burden of proof is defined as identifying the "person obliged to prove the existence of circumstances justifying achievement of a specific legal effect".[18] On the other hand, Schellhammer notes that the burden of proof is the burden occurring in contentious issues that is allocated to the specific subject. The court cannot adopt the claim of the party as true; rather, it must decide against the party to which this burden was allocated when that party did not examine the evidence. He points out that the simplest method of defence – denial – is only apparently an exception from the burden of proof. Only the subject responsible

---

[15]   K. Kołakowski, Dowodzenie w procesie cywilnym. Komentarz do przepisów kodeksu postępowania cywilnego uwzględniający nowelizację z 2000 roku (Presenting evidence in civil proceedings. A commentary on the Code of Civil Procedure including the amendment of 2000), Warsaw 2000, p. 21.

[16]   L. Morawski, Wstęp do prawoznawstwa (Introduction to jurisprudence), 11th ed., Toruń 2008, p. 172.

[17]   Morawski, supra, note 8 at p. 190.

[18]   J. Jezioro, Encyklopedia prawa (The encyclopaedia of law), in U. Kalina-Prasznic (ed.), 4th ed., Warsaw 2007, p. 136.

for examining the evidence changes.[19] The connection between the burden of proof and disputes is also emphasised by Krautstrunk, who considers the dispute between the parties to be the essence of the burden of proof. He notes that each party makes different claims; hence, it is significant that they offer relevant evidence supporting their theses to the arbitration authority.[20] Hov presents a similar position and points to the significance of evidence in evidentiary proceedings.[21] The burden of proof in the formal sense is also indicated in the doctrine of German procedural civil law. It emphasises the significance of evidence for the settlement of civil cases and the relationship between the burden of proof and the principle of disposition.[22] Similarly, the Lithuanian doctrine also strongly emphasises the relationship between the burden of proof and the principle of disposition.[23]

In addition, a view drawing attention to the relationship between the burden of proof and seeking truth must be noted. It is emphasised that the fundamental objective of the burden of proof is seeking truth.[24]

From the point of view of the burden of proof, irrespective of whether or not its formal or material aspect is involved, it is important to establish what circumstances must be proved and who should prove them: "[t]he problems of the burden of proof … include answers to questions which a party must prove and what is to be proved in civil proceedings".[25] In determining the aforementioned, the circumstances connected with certain dynamics that are characteristic of the proceedings and the procedural situation changing consequently must not be neglected. Older literature already recognised this:

> The burden of proof is closely related to the procedural issues for evidence. This institution has two fundamental functions. Firstly, it adds dynamics to evidentiary proceedings in the system in which the principle of adversary trial proceedings (contradictoriness) applies. Secondly, it determines the factual result of the dispute (case) in a critical situation, when the party fails to prove facts significant to the settlement of the case.[26]

When analysing the burden of proof in the context of investigating environmental damage, it must be noted that the latest literature discussing this topic pays

---

19   *K. Schellhammer,* Zivilprozess. Gesetz – Praxis – Fälle, 12th ed., Heidelberg 2007, p. 172.

20   *T. Krautstrunk,* Beeweisverteilung de amissione instrumentorum bis zur Verletzung prozessualer Mitwirkungspflichten, Münster 2004, p. 143.

21   *J. Hov,* Rettergang III, Sivilprocess, Oslo 2008, pp. 272 et seq.

22   *R. Hüßtege,* Zivilprozessordnung, in H. Thomas (ed.), 28th ed., Munich 2007, p. 449.

23   *V. Nekrošius,* Lietuvos Respublikos Civilno proceseo Kodekso. Komentaras, part 1 – Bendrosios Nuostatos, ed. Valančius, Vilnius 2004, pp. 58–59.

24   Id.

25   Id.

26   *K. Piasecki,* Kodeks cywilny z komentarzem (Civil Code with a commentary), in J. Winiarz (ed.), 2nd ed., Warsaw 1989, p. 20.

attention not only to the distribution of the burden of proof, understood as the identification of the party required to prove the relevant circumstances and facts, but also to the order in which they are proved. Andrych-Brzezińska has rightly noted that:

> In consequence to the development of multiple theories concerning the burden of proof a principle was shaped in Polish law according to which each party should prove the facts underlying its claim. Thus, this rule determines who – the claimant or the defendant – should convince the court that their claims are true. It also gives a certain idea about the order in which it should be proved that these claims are true – if the claimant is the party initiating the whole proceedings, they will be in the first place charged with the obligation to present evidence that supports statements underlying their claims. The circumstances quoted in the suit in the statement of reasons already at this stage of proceedings are the starting point for applying relevant norms of substantive law. Furthermore, if the defendant makes a plea precluding or divesting the claimant's right, in order to achieve a positive decision, he/she shall be required to convince the court that the pleas are true. Thus, an advantage of this rule is that it can be applied in proving any facts (investitive, preclusive and divestitive), justifying either the claim stated in the suit or the pleas.[27]

Further, the author indicates that, after the Supreme Court, the distribution of the burden of proof cannot depend on the procedural role of one of the parties. Thus, the burden of proof must not be identified as the claimant's problem only, although without any doubt he/she must prove such investitive facts.[28] In this context, the behaviour of the other party to the proceedings is also significant, and in particular the pleas he/she makes and the circumstances he/she does not challenge.

The above-mentioned general considerations must be fully applied to the burden of proof in the context of environmental damage. However, it must be immediately emphasised that none of the legal acts considered in this chapter – Directive 2004/35 of the European Parliament and the Council of 21 April 2004 on environmental liability with regard to the prevention and remedying of environmental damage,[29] the Polish Act of 13 April 2007 on preventing and remedying environmental damage,[30] or the Decreto Legislativo of 3 April 2006, no. 152, Norme in materia ambientale[31] – directly regulates the burden of proof. Nevertheless, this does not mean that those acts do not regulate issues *related* to the burden of proof.

---

[27]   I. Andrych-Brzezińska, Ciężar dowodu w prawie i procesie cywilnym (Burden of proof in civil law and proceedings), Warsaw 2015, pp. 147–148.

[28]   Id. at p. 148.

[29]   OJ 2004 L 143/56.

[30]   Polish Act of 13 April 2007 on preventing and remedying environmental damage, Journal of Laws Dz.U.2018.954 t.j. of 21.05.2018.

[31]   Gazzetta Uficiale, Serie Gen. no. 88 of 14.04.2006 as amended.

The burden of proof appears in Directive 2004/35 in the context of the obligations the European lawmaker imposes on the subject notifying of an incident of environmental damage or an imminent threat of environmental damage. Although the European lawmaker does not indicate clearly that the burden of proving specific circumstances is allocated directly to the notifying party, such a party is obliged to specify or prove the existence of specific circumstances.[32]

On the one hand, the European lawmaker gives a quite broad treatment to subjectivity of notifying environmental damage or an imminent threat of environmental damage. On the other hand, it deems such a notification a qualified one.

Any legal subject can notify of environmental damage or an imminent threat of environmental damage; there are no limitations on this in Directive 2004/35. Thus, such a notification of environmental damage is a peculiar *actio popularis*.

However, problems occur with reference not only to the entities capable of notifying of environmental damage or an imminent threat of environmental damage but also to the eligibility criteria for a request. Beyond any doubt, a notification of environmental damage or an imminent threat of environmental damage alone is not sufficient. The notifying subject must either indicate the user of the environment who caused the damage or the imminent threat of damage, or offer documents to the authority based on which the latter will be able to establish such circumstances on its own. As a matter of fact, Directive 2004/35 does not regulate the fundamental elements resulting from such an obligation being imposed on the notifying subject.

Considering the *actio popularis* concepts and the broad entitlement to making notifications, the European lawmaker did not regulate the status of the person making such notifications at later stages of the proceedings, if any. It did not determine the existence and identity of such a notifying subject if any proceedings are instituted as a result of the notification.

In addition, Directive 2004/35 does not regulate the legal effects in the situation where the notifying subject fails to prove the facts to the extent stipulated by the Directive.

The above theoretical considerations on the burden of proof lead to the unanimous conclusion that formal and material aspects of the burden of proof can be identified. The Directive does not indicate who will bear the material and legal effects of failure to prove environmental damage or an imminent threat of environmental damage. Nor does it specify whether in the event of insufficient

---

[32]   B. *Rakoczy*, Responsibility for damage to the environment. Directive 2004/35 of the European Parliament and of the Council. Comment, Toruń 2010, in M. Hinteregger (ed.), Environmental Liability and Ecological Damage in European Law, Cambridge 2008; L. Bergkamp & B.J. Goldsmith (eds.), The EU Environmental Liability Directive. A Commentary, Oxford 2013.

evidence the authority is discharged from carrying on with further proceedings or obliged to undertake official action. Assuming that the adjudicating authority must take official actions, why should the notifying subject be responsible for proving the existence of specific circumstances? It would suffice to assume that the notifying subject has the right to inform the authority about environmental damage or an imminent threat of environmental damage. When such a notification is qualified, another question arises, namely whether the notifying subject becomes a party to the proceedings investigating the notification or whether the subject's entitlement is exhausted by the notification alone. The Directive does not offer any normative solutions in this respect either, although, from the point of view of the problem analysed here, these are the key issues. The fact that the European lawmaker remains silent about these key issues can only be interpreted as leaving these problems to be solved by the respective national lawmakers.

The relevance of such an interpretation of Directive 2004/35 is further reinforced by the argument that the Directive in no way determines the procedure to be followed in the case of environmental damage or imminent threat of environmental damage, leaving selection of the mode of proceeding to the discretion of national lawmakers. Indeed, it must be noted that the burden of proof in proceedings for preventing environmental damage or remedying such damage has to be determined solely by the national lawmaker. The determinant of the burden of proof is the selection of the mode of proceeding in the case of such damage. For it should be considered that Directive 2004/35 could not be implemented without taking into account the legal regime as a whole, including the premises and axiology of procedural law. The regimes of Polish and Italian law, which are the focus of this chapter, provide the best examples of how the burden of proof can be regulated in national law. In Poland, Directive 2004/35 was implemented in the Act of 13 April 2007 on preventing and remedying environmental damage.[33] A characteristic feature of the implementation of this Directive in Polish law was that it took place through the adoption of a separate legal act. The implementation of this Directive was also similar in the Czech Republic and Austria.

The Polish act on preventing and remedying environmental damage gave rise to doctrinal disputes referring to the legal nature of such liability. Radecki has pointed out that the liability regulated by the act was in fact civil liability incorporated within the framework and standards of administrative liability.[34] Other authors have claimed it was administrative liability. Indeed, the assessment of the legal nature of this liability determines the burden of proof. If we assume that it is civil liability, the investigation should be by way of civil proceedings

---

[33] Journal of Laws Dz.U.2018.954 i.e. of 21.05.2018.
[34] *W. Radecki,* Ustawa o zapobieganiu szkodom w środowisku i ich naprawie (Act on preventing and remedying environmental damage), Warsaw 2008.

and the burden of proof should be determined by the common standard, that is the above-mentioned Article 6 of the Polish Civil Code. If we assume that it is administrative liability, the Polish Code of Administrative Procedure (the Act of 14 June 1960) applies.[35] To this extent, material significance must be granted to Articles 7 and 77 of the Code of Administrative Procedure, which stipulate respectively that "[i]n the course of the proceedings, public administration authorities shall safeguard the rule of law and undertake, *ex officio* or at request, any actions necessary to accurately clarify the facts of the case and to resolve it, having regard towards the public interest and the legitimate interest of citizens", and that:

§1. A public administration authority is required to comprehensively collect and examine all evidentiary material.

§2. At each stage of proceedings, the authority can amend, supplement or withdraw its rulings regarding the examination of evidence.

§3. The authority conducting the proceedings, at the request of the body in charge of resolving the case (Art. 52) may, *ex officio* or at the request of a party, hear new witnesses and experts with regard to the circumstances being examined in such proceedings.

§4. Universally accepted facts and facts known to the authority *ex officio* do not require proof. Facts known to the authority *ex officio* must be communicated to the party.

According to these provisions, the burden of proof rests on the public administration authority, which is also required to collect and comprehensively examine the evidentiary material. Whereas in the civil law model the burden of proof would rest on the subject notifying of environmental damage or a threat of environmental damage, in the administrative model the burden of proof rests on the authority. It must be emphasised that matters related to preventing or remedying environmental damage are settled in administrative proceedings. This means that the Polish environmental protection authority is required to collect and evaluate the evidentiary material. Thus, it seems that the problem in collecting and evaluating the evidentiary material does not really exist. However, it does exist in connection with obligations imposed on the subject notifying of environmental damage. Pursuant to Article 24 para. 1 of the Polish Act on preventing environmental damage, "[t]he environmental protection authority is required to accept any notification of an imminent threat of environmental damage or of actual environmental damage".[36] According to this provision, the

---

[35] Journal of Laws Dz.U.2017.1257 i.e. of 27.06.2017.
[36] *B. Rakoczy,* Ustawa o zapobieganiu szkodom w środowisku i ich naprawie (Act on preventing and remedying environmental damage), Warsaw 2008.

notifying subject should prove certain circumstances or at least demonstrate that it is not able to prove such circumstances. Polish case law tends to recognise that the burden of proof, with all its formal and material consequences, should be allocated to the person notifying of environmental damage or an imminent threat of environmental damage.

In the Italian legal framework, Directive 2004/35 was implemented in a completely different manner. The Italian lawmaker did not adopt a separate and autonomous legal act implementing the Directive, but rather implemented it in a general legal act on environmental protection, the Environmental Code. Matters regarding the implementation of Directive 2004/35 are regulated in the final section of the Code.

A very significant fact must be taken into account, namely that the normative matter regulating prevention and remedial of environmental damage is a part of a wider legal act regulating environmental protection comprehensively and generally. Thus, the matter is included in other solutions regarding environmental protection. By taking such a course of action, the Italian lawmaker was able to partly, but not completely, avoid the need to adopt general provisions and introduce separate legal definitions. Preventing and remedying environmental damage is such a peculiar matter that at least an individual definition of the term "environmental damage" should be adopted.

However, the Italian Environmental Protection Code alone does not contain any standalone procedural solutions in that respect. The doctrine emphasises the existence of a problem identical to that present in Polish law, namely whether the solution adopted in the Italian Environmental Protection Code should be treated as the notifying party's obligation to prove with evidence that such environmental damage actually occurred or that an imminent threat of such damage does exist. This problem is evaluated in different ways, although in the present author's opinion the Italian legal system does not differ from the Polish law in that respect and it should be consistently recognised that notification of environmental damage or an imminent threat of environmental damage requires proof in the procedural sense.[37]

Both Italian literature and doctrine assume that cases of prevention or remedy of environmental damage are examined in accordance with the rules determined in the act governing administrative proceedings.[38] The Italian model

---

[37]   *M. Benozzo,* Commento al Codice dell'Ambiente, in A. Germanó, E. Rook Basile, F. Bruno & M. Benozzo (eds.), Torino 2008; S. Maglia, Codice dell'ambiente, 21st ed., Piacenza 2011, pp. 263 et seq.; *E. Mariotti,* Il nuovo diritto ambientale, in E. Mariotti & M. Iannantuoni (eds.), Maggioli Editore 2011, pp. 477 et seq.; *B. Rakoczy,* Włoski kodeks środowiskowy – Norme in materia ambientale – Codice dell'ambiente (Italian Environmental Code), in K. Szuma & B. Rakoczy (eds.), Warsaw 2013.

[38]   *L. Delpino & F. del Giudice,* Diritto Amministrativo, 26th ed., Simone 2009.

of administrative proceedings is identical to the Polish one, hence the burden of proof concerning a threat of environmental damage or actual environmental damage rests on the public administration authority, which is required to seek objective truth. Thus, the public administration authority is charged with the legal and material effects of the burden of proof. A significant factor is that in both the Polish and Italian legal systems, liability for a threat of environmental damage or occurrence of environmental damage is borne by a specific subject. In both cases, this subject is a party to the administrative proceedings, with all related consequences. The subject's fundamental procedural right is the possibility of taking an active part in the course of the proceedings. This procedural guarantee also includes the right to present one's own evidence, which, for obvious reasons, will in this case aim at proving that there are no grounds to hold that party liable. The administrative proceedings model in both cases provides for a wide variety of evidence.

However, what is significant is that in this case the subject who is not party to proceedings is not required to prove, and does not bear the negative consequences of failing to prove, the facts in the light of substantive law. This is a significant difference as far as civil and administrative proceedings are concerned.

2. CONCLUSIONS

To sum up, it must be noted that Directive 2004/35 does not regulate the burden of proof. It only imposes certain obligations on the subject notifying of environmental damage to offer specified information or documents to the authority. Thus, the procedural dimension of the burden of proof must be regulated by the national lawmaker. However, it is determined by the models of administrative or court proceedings applicable in the specific legal regime. The author is not aware of any solution related to procedural law where the national lawmaker adopted completely separate formal and legal regulations on preventing or remedying environmental damage. The Polish and Italian legal systems, analysed for the sake of comparison, differ only in their method of implementation of Directive 2004/35. The Polish lawmaker implemented the Directive in a separate legal act, whereas the Italian lawmaker did it as part as a general legal act governing environmental protection matters. However, in neither case was the burden of proof regulated. It means that the burden of proof is determined by the choice of proceedings in which issues related to preventing or remedying environmental damage are examined. In both cases, this is an administrative proceedings model, which means the burden of proof in this respect rests on the public administration authority. Such an authority should seek to establish objective truth *ex officio* by collecting evidentiary material. In both Polish and Italian law, it is disputable how to evaluate the obligations imposed on the subject notifying of environmental damage or an immediate threat of environmental damage. However, in both cases the prevailing opinion is that the burden of proof, including all its consequences, rests on the subject.

De lege ferenda, it would be reasonable if Directive 2004/35 clearly regulated this problem. Of course, the choice of the mode of proceedings depends on the national lawmaker. Nevertheless, the specification of who should prove what requires an intervention of the European lawmaker. In practice, it transpires that Directive 2004/35 was also ineffective with regard to the fact that the subjects in the proceeding have a problem proving the premises for liability by presenting evidence.

PART III
THE ROLE OF CRIMINAL LIABILITY

THE PROTECTION OF THE ENVIRONMENT THROUGH CRIMINAL LAW

Preliminary Remarks

Chiara Perini

1. ENVIRONMENT AS A "WORTHY" AND "NEEDY" GOOD FOR CRIMINAL PROTECTION

The reports presented during the 6th Annual Conference of the European Environmental Law Forum in the sessions dedicated to the role of criminal law in the protection of the environment (in part, collected in this volume) demonstrate, first of all, that the need to also protect the environment with the instrument of criminal law is clearly affirmed at international level with consequent impact on national criminal systems. This appears with particular evidence in the European legal area, where the recognition of the environment as good characterised by "worthiness of punishment" and "need for punishment" has matured thanks first to a jurisprudential and then to a legislative process, that culminated in the Directive 2008/99/EC on the protection of the environment through criminal law.

The reports of Miriam Ruiz Arias ("Enterprises' Environmental Criminal Liability and Compliance Programmes in Spain"), María del Mar Martín Aragón ("The Last Spanish Criminal Code Reform on Environmental Crimes: Legal Construction and Case Studies") and María-Ángeles Fuentes-Loureiro ("The Influence of Directive 2008/99/CE on Spanish Regulation") were devoted to the implementation of this Directive in the Spanish legal system. At this conference, Edoardo Mazzanti ("Environment, ECHR and EU Criminal Law. A Possible Interplay") also underlined the importance of analysing the issue of criminal protection of the environment in the light of the international exchange that takes place between two legal frameworks, firstly of the European Union (now focused in this field on Directive 2008/99/EC) and secondly that revolving around the European Convention on Human Rights (ECHR). The grounds of some judgments of the Court of Justice of the European Union (CJEU) and of the European Court of Human Rights (ECtHR) indicate the presence of a real "dialogue between the Courts" about the recognition of the environment as an important good for criminal law and about how to organise such protection.

From the point of view of regulatory changes, Directive 2008/99/EC holds, as is known, in an intermediate position between, on the one hand, some decisions of the Court of Justice of the European Union that are of central importance for the statement (at international level) of the so-called "worthiness" of criminal protection of the good "environment", as well as – on a more general level – for the possibility of the European legislator to impose criminalisation obligations on Member States' legislators,[1] and, on the other hand, Article 83 of the Treaty on the Functioning of the European Union (TFEU), which currently regulates the competence of the European Union in criminal matters and expressly sets limits on the EU from this point of view.

In the case law of the CJEU, prior to the adoption of Directive 2008/99/EC, the good "environment" was considered deserving of protection under criminal law in the judgment of 13th September 2005 in Case C-176/03. In this context, ordering the annulment of the Framework Decision 2003/80/JHA[2] and recognising the competence of the Community legislator to adopt its *own* policy of criminal law in the environmental field, binding on the Member States, the Court stated:

47 ... As a general rule, neither criminal law nor the rules of criminal procedure fall within the Community's competence ...

48 However, the last-mentioned finding does not prevent the Community legislature, when the application of effective, proportionate and dissuasive criminal penalties by the competent national authorities is an essential measure for combating *serious environmental offences*, from taking *measures which relate to the criminal law of the Member States* which it considers *necessary* in order to ensure that the rules which it lays down on environmental protection are *fully effective*.[3]

---

[1]   See *A. Gargani*, La protezione immediata dell'ambiente tra obblighi comunitari di incriminazione e tutela giudiziaria, in S. Vinciguerra & F. Dassano (eds.), Scritti in memoria di Giuliano Marini, Edizioni Scientifiche Italiane, 2010, pp. 407 et seq.; *L. Siracusa*, La competenza comunitaria in ambito penale al primo banco di prova: la direttiva europea sulla tutela penale dell'ambiente, Riv. trim. dir. pen. ec. 2008, pp. 866 et seq.

[2]   As is widely known, the Council Framework Decision 2003/80/JHA of 27 January 2003 on the protection of the environment through criminal law intended to harmonise the Member States' environmental criminal legislations through means in fact negotiated by each national legislator through its representative in the European Council and without direct effect on national law. Regarding the path that led to the adoption of Directive 2008/99/EC, see *M. Caterini*, Effettività e tecniche di tutela nel diritto penale dell'ambiente, ESI, 2017, pp. 320 et seq.

[3]   Emphasis added.

That judgment immediately appeared significant for the affirmation and development of the so-called "European criminal law":[4] the competence recognised to the European legislator by the Court did include, in fact, not only the choice regarding criminalisation in the strict sense (i.e. the identification of the conduct to be prevented and repressed via criminal law), but also the specification of the type and level of the penal sanction, thus removing any discretion from the national legislator *both* in terms of *crime typification* and in relation to the *imposition of the penalty*. Secondly, it clearly came to light from the Court's argument – and it will be confirmed in the subsequent phases of the evolution in question – how the pivot of the *disvalue* statement (that is, the factor upon which the negative statement expressed on the conduct that damages the environment is based), ascribed to the European legislator, was represented by the fact that the conduct to be incriminated, on the one hand, was related to serious harmful consequences for the environment and, on the other hand, violated or in any case compromised the efficacy of the Community rules already adopted in the environmental field: hence the "accessory" nature of the criminal jurisdiction recognised in this phase to the European Community.

The "worthiness" of criminal protection of the "environment" as a good was then confirmed by the CJEU in the judgment of 23 October 2007 that decided Case C-440/05. In a case similar to the previous one,[5] the Court stated:

66 Although it is true that, as a general rule, neither criminal law nor the rules of criminal procedure fall within the Community's competence ... the fact remains that when the application of effective, proportionate and dissuasive *criminal penalties* by the competent national authorities is an *essential* measure for combating *serious environmental offences*, the Community legislature may require the Member States to introduce such penalties in order to ensure that the rules which it lays down in that field are *fully effective* ...

70 By contrast, and contrary to the submission of the Commission, the determination of the *type* and *level* of the *criminal penalties* to be applied does not fall within the Community's sphere of competence.[6]

In this judgment, the Court therefore carried out a division of competences, assigning to the Community legislator the competence relating to the choice

---

4   See G. *Mannozzi & F. Consulich*, La sentenza della Corte di Giustizia C-176/03: riflessi penalistici in tema di principio di legalità e politica dei beni giuridici, Riv. trim. dir. pen. ec. 2006, pp. 899 et seq.

5   Also in this case, the CJEU cancelled a framework decision of the European Council (Council Framework Decision 2005/667/JHA of 12 July 2005, to strengthen the criminal law framework for the enforcement of the law against ship-source pollution: the CJEU affirmed the competence of the European legislator to promote by directive a European criminal law policy binding for the Member States).

6   Emphasis added.

of criminalisation in the strict sense and reserving to the national legislator the qualitative and quantitative specification of the penalty.[7] Finally, the pivot of the *disvalue* statement is always linked to the fact that the conduct to be repressed is strongly affected by a potential offence against the protected good and contrasts with rules already set by the Community legislator to protect the environment in an accessory regime.

Directive 2008/99/EC brings together the results of this case law, expressly recognising the "worthiness" of criminal protection of the "environment" as a good:

> Experience has shown that the existing systems of penalties have not been sufficient to achieve complete compliance with the laws for the protection of the environment. Such compliance can and should be strengthened by the availability of criminal penalties, which demonstrate a social disapproval of a qualitatively different nature compared to administrative penalties or a compensation mechanism under civil law.[8]

The Directive associates the purpose "to protect the environment more effectively" (Article 1) with the introduction of the obligation for Member States "to provide for criminal penalties in their national legislation in respect of serious infringements of provisions of Community law on the protection of the environment" (Recital 10).[9] From the perspective of the European legislator, the criminalisation obligations specified in Article 3 of the Directive therefore have in common a particular offensive character (in this sense, the reference to the seriousness of the violation), as well as the fact of intervening to support – in order, so to speak, to provide further sanctioning – the observance of EU regulations already in place to protect the environment.

The latter characteristic translates into the requirement of the so-called *unlawfulness* of the criminally relevant conduct,[10] which echoes some passages of the sentences examined above. Given the definition of "unlawful" contained in Article 2(a) of the Directive,[11] the activities subject to the criminalisation obligation must be committed, in fact, in violation of: (i) one of the European legislative acts listed in the Annex to the Directive (i.e. the main Community directives on the protection of the environment in the broad sense); or (ii) the implementing legislation which – at the legislative, regulatory or in any case administrative level – has been implemented in the Member State to comply

---

[7]   See *Siracusa, supra*, note 1 at p. 871.
[8]   Recital 3 Directive 2008/99/EC.
[9]   Emphasis added.
[10] See *Siracusa, supra*, note 1 at pp. 877 et seq.
[11] To be read in conjunction with Article 3, first sentence, Directive 2008/99/EC, according to which: "Member States shall ensure that the following conduct constitutes a criminal offence, when *unlawful* and committed intentionally or with at least serious negligence" (emphasis added).

with the aforementioned Community regulations. From the European legislator's perspective, therefore, the conduct of criminally relevant facts listed in Article 3 Directive 2008/99/EC is characterised by the fact of contrasting not generally with the legal system, but only with the provisions referred to in the aforementioned definition rule.[12]

On the other hand, the offensive significance of the conduct identified at European level as criminally relevant clearly comes to light from the catalogue compiled by Article 3 of the Directive to constrain the Member States' discretion regarding environmental protection through criminal law. The facts thus described dovetail with a "strong model" of environmental protection, which revolves around a material conception of the safeguarded good and includes crimes based on damage or concrete danger to the good itself.[13] One of the outcomes is the indirect conditioning of the specification of the penalty by national legislators, which are required to adopt "effective, proportionate and dissuasive criminal penalties" (Article 5 Directive 2008/99/EC).[14]

Overall, the axis of environmental protection is therefore clearly oriented towards criminal law, marking a shift for national systems that previously also assigned administrative law a central role in this field. The synergy between criminal law and administrative law in environmental protection was highlighted, at the 6th EELF Conference, with regard to the British legal system, by Richard Macrory ("Liability and Sanctions for Breaches of Environmental Regulatory Requirements Integrating Criminal and Administrative Liability").

In order to achieve powerful environmental protection, Directive 2008/99/EC also requires that Member States provide for an accountability system for legal persons, accompanied by "effective, proportionate and dissuasive penalties" (Article 7) when the serious offences against the environment

---

[12] For a more detailed analysis, see *C. Perini*, Tra sicurezza alimentare e sicurezza ambientale: il principio di precauzione nella gestione penale del rischio da OGM, in L. Foffani, A. Doval Pais & D. Castronuovo (eds.), La sicurezza agroalimentare nella prospettiva europea. Precauzione, prevenzione e repressione (atti del Convegno di Modena, 3–5 novembre 2011), Giuffrè, 2014, pp. 592 et seq.; *C. Perini*, The Influence of Directive 2008/99/EC on the Harmonization and Renewal of the Lexicon of Environmental Criminal Law, in F. Ruggieri (ed.), Criminal Proceedings, Languages and the European Union. Linguistic and Legal Issues, Springer, 2014, pp. 145 et seq. See also *Siracusa, supra*, note 1 at p. 894 et seq.

[13] See *Gargani, supra*, note 1 at pp. 411 et seq.

[14] See *Siracusa, supra*, note 1 at pp. 882 et seq. With regard to possible repercussions on the "principles of necessity, proportionality and effectiveness of criminal intervention, which must inspire the EU legislator in the adoption of criminal laws on environmental matters", caused by the European Court of Human Rights jurisprudence pursuant to Articles 2 and 8 of the ECHR as legal basis for a "human right to the environment", see *E. Mazzanti*, La protezione penale dell'ambiente come diritto umano. Inquadramento e rilievi critici, Leg. pen. 25 June 2019, pp. 10 et seq. For a comment on the first phases of the interpretative path cultivated in this direction by the ECtHR, see *C. Perini*, La mediazione dei conflitti nella società del rischio, in G. Mannozzi (ed.), Mediazione e diritto penale. Dalla punizione del reo alla composizione con la vittima, Giuffrè, 2004, p. 210 et seq.

outlined by the Directive are committed "for their benefit" by someone working for them (Article 6). In this regard, the considerations made by Robert Esser ("Confiscation of Assets and Proceeds of Crime in Environmental Criminal Law: New Approaches by the German Legislator") during the conference, and reproduced in this volume, appear significant.

Finally, Article 83 TFEU confirms the ancillary nature (with respect to EU regulations previously adopted in the sector) of the European Union's criminal jurisdiction in environmental matters, in line with the judgments of the CJEU examined here, as well as with the provisions of Directive 2008/99/EC:[15] crime against the environment is not, in fact, among the fields left to the autonomous criminal jurisdiction (albeit always indirect) of the European legislator, strictly listed in Article 83(1), second sentence TFEU. Therefore, it seems to be connected to Article 83(2), according to which: "If the approximation of criminal laws and regulations of the Member States proves essential to ensure the effective implementation of a Union policy in an area which has been subject to harmonisation measures, directives may establish minimum rules with regard to the definition of criminal offences and sanctions in the area concerned".

2. DIRECTIVE 2008/99/EC AND THE CRIMINAL LAW LEGALITY PRINCIPLE

Directive 2008/99/EC establishes within the European legal area obligations to incriminate the most serious offences against the environment using sometimes indeterminate language. This leaves room for the discretion of the national legislators when implementing the Directive itself and, later, if the national laws have not been able to develop a precise description of the fact to be punished, enhances the role of the criminal judge's discretion in the application phase.

Thus there are some twists not only in relation to the principle of legality in criminal law, in terms of the forms that characterise it within some legal systems, such as the Italian one (Article 25, paragraph 2, Italian Constitution), but also in relation to the set of guarantees enshrined in Article 7 ECHR, such as the understandability of the penal precept and the predictability of the penalty.[16]

The vagueness of the language used by the European legislator clearly emerges from the different language versions of the Directive. Within the framework of

---

[15] See L. *Siracusa*, Il transito del diritto penale di fonte europea dalla "vecchia" alla "nuova" unione post-Lisbona, Riv. trim. dir. pen. ec. 2010, pp. 789 et seq.

[16] See F. *Viganò*, Il principio di prevedibilità della decisione giudiziale in materia penale, Dir. pen. cont. 19 December 2016, pp. 5 et seq.; F. *Viganò*, Il nullum crimen conteso: legalità "costituzionale" vs. legalità "convenzionale"?, Dir. pen. cont. 5 April 2017, pp. 13 et seq.; as well as recently G. *Rotolo*, "Riconoscibilità" del precetto penale e modelli innovativi di tutela. Analisi critica del diritto penale dell'ambiente, Giappichelli, 2018.

the criminal protection model conveyed by the Directive, the aim is to limit the area of criminal relevance on the basis of considerations grounded, in a broad sense, on the principle of crime offensiveness. This intent is, however, pursued by resorting to linguistic expressions that sacrifice the legal certainty and precision of the criminalising rule, enhancing the judge's appreciation and discretion. The choice of the EU legislator does not have merely a lexical relevance, but also improperly sets the founding principles of criminal law one against the other in a dialectic opposition – founding principles which have become, thanks to the jurisprudence of the ECtHR, shared heritage in the European legal area: the *principle of legality* (understood in the corollaries of *certainty* and *precision*) and the *principle of crime offensiveness*.

Consider in particular the following expressions: "substantial damage" against the environment, which has the role of a *damage event or concrete danger* (Article 3(a), (b), (d) and (e) Directive 2008/99/EC);[17] "non-negligible quantity" versus "negligible quantity" (Article 3(c), (f) and (g) Directive 2008/99/EC), mentioned to sanction and, respectively, exclude the criminal relevance of the fact in relation to the thing on which the conduct of the offense occurs;[18] "negligible impact" (Article 3(g) Directive 2008/99/EC), used in reference to the conduct's potential offensive power to exclude the criminal relevance of the fact;[19] and "significant deterioration" (Article 3(h) Directive 2008/99/EC), used again in relation to the offensive scope of the conduct's potential offensive power to found the criminal relevance of the fact.[20]

The vagueness of the language used by the European legislator can influence the environmental criminal law of each EU Member State. This happened most recently, for example, in the Italian legal system, where in implementing Directive 2008/99/EC some serious environmental crimes were added to the Criminal Code, but with rules that describe those offences against the environment in very imprecise terms, provoking a great deal of confusion in the doctrine and jurisprudence. This is the case, in particular, of the new crime of environmental pollution (Article 452-*bis* Italian Penal Code), which punishes the causation of "significant and measurable impairment or deterioration of: 1) water or air, or

---

[17] In German, "*erhebliche Schäden*"; in Italian, "*danno rilevante*"; in French, "*dégradation substantielle*"; in Spanish, "*daños sustanciales*". It should be noted that, in the Italian legal system, the seriousness of the damage or danger does not appear as an element of the punished fact, but as a parameter for measuring the penalty (Article 133, paragraph 2, no. 2, Italian Penal Code); in any case, the concept of "serious damage" is less imprecise than that of "substantial damage".

[18] In German, "*in nicht unerheblicher Menge*" vs. "*eine unerheblicher Menge*"; in Italian, "*quantità non trascurabile*" vs. "*trascurabile*"; in French, "*quantité non négligeable*" vs. "*quantité négligeable*"; in Spanish, "*cantidad no desdeñable*" vs. "*cantidad insignificante*".

[19] In German, "*unerhebliche Auswirkungen*"; in Italian, "*impatto trascurabile*"; in French, "*impact négligeable*"; in Spanish, "*consecuencias insignificantes*".

[20] In German, "*eine erhebliche Schädigung*"; in Italian, "*significativo deterioramento*"; in French, "*dégradation importante*"; in Spanish, "*deterioro significativo*".

large or significant portions of the soil or subsoil; 2) an ecosystem, biodiversity, including agriculture, flora or fauna".[21] It is also the case of the new crime of environmental disaster (Article 452-*quater* Italian Penal Code), which punishes the causation of an "environmental disaster" and describes such events in the following terms: "1) the irreversible alteration of the balance of an ecosystem; 2) the alteration of the balance of an ecosystem whose elimination is particularly expensive and achievable only with exceptional measures; 3) the offense against public safety due to the relevance of the fact for the extension of the compromise or its harmful effects or for the number of people offended or exposed to danger".[22]

A second element that makes the model of criminal protection outlined by the European legislator in Directive 2008/99/EC vague is the already quoted requirement of the "unlawfulness" of the conduct. This has an effect that is in some ways paradoxical, since the combination of the definition contained in Article 2, on the one hand, and the regulatory lists in the annexes to the Directive, on the other hand, seemed capable of achieving a certain precision on the point.

During implementation, the choice made by the Italian legislator, for example, expands – as Directive 2008/99/EC allows, since it only "provides for minimum rules" (Recital 12) – the scope of the environment criminal protection, translating the conduct's characteristic of unlawfulness with the term "*abusivamente*". This term is less selective, because it alludes in general to an opposition to the law *tout court*,[23] without a reference to laws, regulations or administrative acts specifically aimed at protecting the environment, nor in itself necessarily already provided by a criminal or administrative penalty.[24]

The potentially extensive scope of the term "*abusivamente*" was immediately grasped by Italian doctrine and jurisprudence, where different interpretative orientations were affirmed. According to one interpretation, a conduct is "abusive"[25] where it happens in the absence of any authorisation which

---

[21]   In Italian: "una compromissione o un deterioramento significativi e misurabili: 1) delle acque o dell'aria, o di porzioni estese o significative del suolo o del sottosuolo; 2) di un ecosistema, della biodiversità, anche agraria, della flora o della fauna".

[22]   In Italian: "1) l'alterazione irreversibile dell'equilibrio di un ecosistema; 2) l'alterazione dell'equilibrio di un ecosistema la cui eliminazione risulti particolarmente onerosa e conseguibile solo con provvedimenti eccezionali; 3) l'offesa alla pubblica incolumità in ragione della rilevanza del fatto per l'estensione della compromissione o dei suoi effetti lesivi ovvero per il numero delle persone offese o esposte a pericolo".

[23]   See M. *Catenacci*, La legge sugli eco-reati ed i suoi principali nodi problematici, in A. Manna (ed.), Il nuovo diritto penale ambientale (legge 22 maggio 2015, n. 68), 2016, p. 15.

[24]   See C. *Ruga Riva*, Diritto penale dell'ambiente, Giappichelli, 3rd ed., 2016, p. 245; M. *Bosi*, Rilevanza delle condotte realizzate abusivamente tra rischio ed evento ambientali, in G. De Francesco & G. Morgante (eds.), Il diritto penale di fronte alle sfide della "società del rischio". Un difficile rapporto tra nuove esigenze di tutela e classici equilibri di sistema, 2017, pp. 57 et seq.; L. *Bisori*, Linee interpretative e nodi problematici della abusività della condotta nei nuovi reati ambientali. Prove tecniche di abusivismo giudiziario?, Criminalia 2015, p. 324.

[25]   The term "abusive" is used as a synonym of the Italian word "*abusivo*".

is required *in abstracto* for the type of activity, and therefore comes to be equivalent to "clandestine". On another interpretation, behaviours carried out in the context of authorised activities, but in defiance of (national or regional) regulations or provisions provided by the specific enabling administrative act, are considered "abusive". And on a third, it is "abusive" to carry out an activity assisted by "clearly ... unlawful authorisations":[26] in this last case, therefore, the penal sanction would apply to a subject who has respected the authorisation obtained from the public administration, trusting *ex ante* that it was legitimate, but where the criminal judge declares the illegality of the act subsequently.

Especially in the latter scenario, the friction of the criminal law with respect to the principle – of European relevance – of penal precept understandability and the predictability of the penalty is evident.

3. ENVIRONMENT AS A CHANGING CONCEPT IN A COMPARATIVE PERSPECTIVE

Finally, a second group of reports presented at the 6th Annual Conference of the European Environmental Law Forum demonstrate multiplicity of interests worthy of criminal protection, which can be traced back to the notion of "environment" from the perspective of comparison between legal systems, including those outside Europe. This is the case of values traditionally included in a broader notion of the "environment", such as fauna and in particular wildlife, examined in the reports of Magdalena Roibu ("Born to be Wild. Stop Wildlife Crime!") and Amanda Whitfort ("Wildlife Crime and Animal Victims: Improving Access to Environmental Justice").

But this is also the case for types of environment criminal protection still in the process of being affirmed, at the crossroads with conflicting interests as they relate to industrial production; in this regard the reflections of Emanuele La Rosa ("Planned Obsolescence and Criminal Law: A Problematic Relationship?"), also reproduced in this volume, on types of environmental damage connected to the planned obsolescence of industrial products deserve attention.

Moreover it seems quite clear that the notion of the "environment" is a complex one that is predestined to be progressively put more and more into focus, especially in view of a protection strategy that is in practice unified across Europe. In the Italian legal system, for example, on the one hand, the same constitutional foundation of the environment as a "good" – namely Article 9, paragraph 2 of the Constitution – evokes a notion at least tripartite, that is,

---

26   See *C. Melzi d'Eril*, L'inquinamento ambientale a tre anni dall'entrata in vigore, Dir. pen. cont. 2018 (7–8), p. 42.

inclusive of the environment understood as the "landscape", of the environment understood as an "ecological good" (i.e. soil, air and water jointly considered), and of the environment understood as an "urban good".[27] On the other hand, the recognition of the environment is part of a constitutional framework of values, partly concurrent, partly discordant (consider for example the right to health enshrined in Article 32 of the Constitution and the freedom of private economic initiative provided for by Article 41 of the Constitution), with respect to which a balancing act is essential.

---

[27]   See *M.S. Giannini*, "Ambiente". Saggio sui diversi suoi aspetti giuridici, Riv. trim. pubbl. 1973, p. 23.

THE LEGAL FRAMEWORK AGAINST PLANNED OBSOLESCENCE

What Role (If Any) for Criminal Law?

Emanuele La Rosa

1. INTRODUCTION

The phenomenon of products with a life cycle pre-set by the manufacturer is now well known to the average consumer, who may often notice the progressive unusability (frequently sudden) of various types of consumer products (especially technological ones). The topic has also become very relevant as a consequence of some recent cases involving major companies (Apple, Samsung, Epson) that have attracted the attention of the competent authorities in Italy and France.

The aim of this chapter is to reconstruct the regulatory framework at the supranational level on planned obsolescence; then we will evaluate the impact of this regulatory framework in some national legal systems. In particular, the case of France will be examined. This is the first (and at the moment the only) country that has adopted a strategy to combat the phenomenon of planned obsolescence that also includes the use of criminal law.

The "planned obsolescence" crime will be assessed from the point of view of the fundamental principles of criminal law, as well as from the point of view of its actual effectiveness. The results of this research may help to answer the following question: can the use of criminal law be considered an "appropriate dissuasive measure" against "planned obsolescence"?

2. "PLANNED OBSOLESCENCE": CONCEPT, HISTORICAL EVOLUTION AND HARMFUL EFFECTS

What is "planned obsolescence"? It is not easy to answer this question. In fact there are several types of "planned obsolescence". The difficulties of definition also derive from the fact that it is a phenomenon that depends to a large extent on the progress of science and technology, particularly technology as applied to the design, production and marketing of products.

Serge Latouche[1] refers to three types of obsolescence: technical, psychological or symbolic, and programmed. Technical obsolescence involves the disuse of machines and appliances due to technical progress, which introduces improvements and innovations of all kinds. Psychological obsolescence refers to disuse of the product caused not by the technical wear and tear or the introduction of a real innovation, but by the product falling out of favour as a result of advertising and fashion, a new look, design or even new packaging. Programmed obsolescence refers to wear or tear arising from an artificial fault, where, from the beginning, the product is conceived by the manufacturer to have a limited life, and this thanks to the introduction systematics of a device that allows for this. Consequently, for the present author there is a true symbiosis between programmed obsolescence, symbolic obsolescence and technical obsolescence. In fact, for a precise choice of industrial policy, the manufacturer introduces a product that will soon become technologically obsolete and, at the same time, perceived as inadequate by consumers.

A classification that only partially overlaps is that accepted by the Opinion of the European Economic and Social Committee, on "Towards more sustainable consumption: industrial product lifetimes and restoring trust though consumer information".[2] This document identifies indirect obsolescence, incompatibility obsolescence, psychological obsolescence (generated by marketing companies), and "planned obsolescence" *stricto sensu*. Indirect obsolescence generally occurs because the components required to repair the product are unobtainable or because it cannot be repaired (e.g. batteries welded into an electronic device). Incompatibility obsolescence occurs, for example, when software no longer works once an operating system is updated. This type of obsolescence is linked to after-sales obsolescence, which encourages consumers to replace rather than repair a product, partly due to the time and cost of repair. Style or psychological obsolescence occurs because marketing campaigns lead consumers to perceive existing products to be out-of-date. It is pointless to make manufacturers produce tablets that last 10 years if our consumption patterns make us want to replace them every two years. For example, mobile phones are replaced every 20 months on average (every 10 months in the 12–17 age group). Despite the importance of this issue, this chapter will only address the first three points. The fourth point warrants a separate approach relating to consumption patterns.

For the purposes of this investigation, we must focus on planned or programmed obsolescence *stricto sensu*. A definition of planned obsolescence

---

[1] S. *Latouche*, Bon pour la casse: Essais sur l'obsolescence programmée, Liens qui libèrent, 2012.

[2] OJ 2014 C 67/05, https://www.eesc.europa.eu/en/our-work/opinions-information-reports/ opinions/towards-more-sustainable-consumption-industrial-product-lifetimes-and-restoring-trust-through-consumer-information.

as synthetic as it is generic could be as follows: it is the production of goods with uneconomically short useful lives so that customers will have to make repeat purchases.

It is not a new phenomenon. In fact it is associated with a form of industrial production that relies on a minimum renewal rate for its products. As an example, let us consider the famous "lightbulbs affair" or "Phoebus cartel", which was one of the first – and certainly the most famous – cases of planned obsolescence in history.

Originally the lightbulbs had been envisaged and designed to last as long as possible: the model designed by Edison lasted on average 1,500 hours; in 1920, lightbulbs were produced that could last up to 2,500 hours. However, at one point, the producers realised that it would be more profitable to reduce the useful life of these products. In 1924, corporations based in Europe and America (Osram, Philips, Tungsram, Associated Electrical Industries, ELIN, Compagnie des Lampes, International General Electric, and the GE Overseas Group) founded a cartel that conventionally lowered operational costs and worked to standardise the life of lightbulbs at 1,000 hours (down from 2,500 hours) and raised prices without fear of competition. The cartel tested their bulbs and fined manufacturers for bulbs that lasted more than 1,000 hours. Each company had to present a monthly report of the average life of lightbulbs, and those that exceeded the limit imposed had to pay a penalty imposed by the members of the cartel: a 1929 table listed the amount of Swiss francs to be paid depending on by how many hours the lightbulb exceeding the cartel's limits. The cartel operated without the knowledge of the public and could point to the standardisation of lightbulbs as an alternative rationale for the organisation.[3]

Clearly, the strategy described above is highly profitable for producers: the production of goods that are fragile or "destined to perish" maintains a constant level of demand for these goods. The production of durable goods is, from a strictly economic point of view, destined to lead to the commercial failure of producers. Proof of this is that after the creation of the "Phoebus cartel", certain lightbulbs were patented that could last up to 100,000 hours, but they were never produced in series since it was not profitable to manufacture them.

Another case, certainly less famous, is the so-called "DuPont case". In the late 1940s, many technological advances achieved during World War II were incorporated into commodity production processes. Such was the case of the

---

[3] *B. London*, Ending the Depression through Planned Obsolescence, New York (self-published), 1932, available at: https://babel.hathitrust.org/cgi/pt?id=wu.89097035273;view=1up;seq=7; *M. Krajewski*, The Great Lightbulb Conspiracy. The Phoebus cartel engineered a shorter-lived lightbulb and gave birth to planned obsolescence, 2014, https://spectrum.ieee.org/tech-history/dawn-of-electronics/the-great-lightbulb-conspiracy.

nylon fibre industry, which had been used for war purposes in the production of tires and parachutes, while in peacetime it had been used as a raw material for the production of women's stockings.

The resilient nature of the nylon allowed the long-lasting use of the items of clothing, causing a slowdown in the increase of consumer demand. This circumstance was noticed by one of the major producers of nylon socks in those years, DuPont Industries. It reacted by gradually reducing the quality of its products. This was felt by consumer associations, who protested against this corporate behaviour of "social unconsciousness".[4] Despite protests, DuPont continued to progressively reduce material quality, converting its production from essentially durable products, as in the past, to essentially single-use products. The company's argument to support this behaviour was to satisfy consumers' demand for the transparency of these garments, a feature that diminished the strength of the material in order to create aesthetically appealing garments. However, this argument does not convince, considering the technological advances of the textile industry that had occurred over the years, which suggests that the real reason for the planned decrease in the quality of nylon stockings was naturally to induce the replacement of these garments by some consumers.

Unlike the Phoebus case, in the DuPont case there is no official evidence of the planned obsolescence practice. However, in the decades since, the engineers who worked at that company have reported that the DuPont leaders specified that changes should be introduced that reduced the quality of ready-made garments. The DuPont case is a paradigmatic example of what today is the general rule in the textile and fashion sector: a strategy for producing seasonal or occasional products, not only based on changes in fashion and styles, but also based on the garments having a short lifespan.

It is true, however, that today the phenomenon is arousing more noise and attention. This is probably because today mass consumption is increasingly interested in technological products, with respect to which planned obsolescence has a different relevance compared to other products. It is no coincidence that the most significant cases of programmed obsolescence that have emerged in recent years have concerned high-tech sectors (Apple, Samsung, etc.). We will return to these cases later.

For a long time it was thought that planned obsolescence was a normal industrial and commercial practice that represents a form of business freedom. Thought of as a strategy to stimulate demand and stimulate consumption, together with advertising and consumer credit planned obsolescence makes up the triad allowed the boom in so-called "consumer society". The expansion

---

4   *J. Soto Pineda*, En torno a la relevancia jurídica de una estrategia empresarial consolidada y subyacente: La obsolescencia programada, Universidad Externado de Colombia, Bogotá, 2013, http://works.bepress.com/jesusalfonsosoto/5/.

of programmed obsolescence has found fertile ground in consumer society, creating a vicious circle in which advertising creates the desire to consume, credit provides the means to do so, and programmed obsolescence renews that need. Consequently, the programmed obsolescence of products is a functional tool in so-called consumer society, which implies a type of society that promotes, encourages or reinforces the choice of a consumer lifestyle, and which disapproves of any alternative cultural option; a society in which to conform to the precepts of the consumer culture and strictly adhere to them is, to all practical purposes, the only choice unanimously approved: a viable option and therefore plausible, and a requirement of belonging.

Even today, there are those who see in the practices of planned obsolescence an effect induced by the competitive dynamics of the market, which lead to the production of goods in continuous updates, improvement and evolution, also and above all in response to the increasingly sophisticated needs of the average consumer. In other words, these practices are the result of competition between the various producers, to provide the end user with increasingly advanced products, which – perhaps not obviously enough – inevitably leads to the obsolescence of previous models.

In the last few years, this hypothesis has been questioned. It has been realised that the negative consequences of planned obsolescence far exceed possible positive effects for the market and the system of production. Later in this chapter, all the possible negative effects of planned obsolescence will be analysed in detail.[5] Here it is sufficient to highlight not only how it causes damage for consumers, who are forced to bear the costs of repairs and the continued new purchase of these goods, but also that it represents a danger to the environment, from the point of view both of the non-rational use of natural resources and of the excessive production of waste.[6]

3. THE ROLE OF EUROPEAN INSTITUTIONS IN COMBATING THE PHENOMENON

In recent years, even the European institutions have become aware of how serious the phenomenon of "planned obsolescence" is. Although product renewal may be necessary, certain abuses need to be addressed. There is a growing political consensus in the European Union that we have to move away from our current

---

[5]   *Infra*, section 5.1.

[6]   *E. Vidalenc & L. Meunier*, Obsolescence des produits: l'impact ecologique, Revue Futuribles 2014, pp. 402 et seq.; *A.N. Martinez & A.M. Porcelli*, Consumo (in)sostenible: nuevos desafios frente a la osolescencia programads como compromiso con el ambiente y la sustentabilidad, Ambiente y Sostenibilidad. Revista del Doctorado Interinstitucional en Ciencias Ambientales 2016, pp. 105 et seq.

linear economic system to one that is based on closing material loops, i.e. a circular economy.[7]

Acting against planned obsolescence also assumes – in the perspective of the European Union – an important economic value. The vast majority of offending companies are in the high-tech sectors and their products are often imported into Europe. By tackling this issue, the European Union would be offering its companies a way to stand out from the rest by effectively putting sustainability into practice.

A first (even if implicit) consideration of the phenomenon of "planned obsolescence" has occurred in some Directives regarding the environment or industrial production. For example, in Directive 2009/125/EC establishes a framework for the setting of ecodesign requirements for energy-related products. This hard law regulatory tool is the main starting point in the context of product durability. With a clear protective effect on the environment, the Directive aims to reduce pollution through the ecological design, or eco-design, of products, which is defined as the "the integration of environmental aspects into product design with the aim of improving the environmental performance of the product throughout its whole life cycle" (Article 2(23)). The Directive draws attention to the durability of the product, as well as to the possibility of maintenance, repair and availability of spare parts, requiring that the following "sustainable" design criteria be used by the manufacturer: minimum guaranteed duration, minimum time for availability of spare parts, modularity, upgrading, and repairability. Taking into account the provisions of the Directive, the duration must be considered by the manufacturer as a measure of the "optimal life cycle of a product", up to the point where it is no longer economically possible to repair the constituent parts.

Directive 2006/66/EC on batteries and accumulators and waste batteries and accumulators does not expressly mention "planned obsolescence", but it but refers to it when it obliges Member States to ensure that manufacturers design appliances in such a way that waste batteries and accumulators can be readily removed (Article 11). This rule has an important impact in the fight against obsolescence as part of commercial practices, in that it attacks both its causes (the manufacture of non-extractable batteries in electronic products) and its consequences (premature wear of the good and the consequent disposal of it by the consumer, as well as the accumulation of waste).[8]

---

[7]   *E. Maitre-Elkern & C. Dalhammar*, Regulating planned obsolescence: a review of legal approaches to increase product durability and reparability in Europe, Review of European Community & International Environmental Law 2016 (3), pp. 378 et seq.

[8]   *L. Tollmer*, L'Obsolescence Programmee, Université de Montpellier 1, Centre du droit de la consommation et du marché, 2011–2012, p. 77, www.europe-consommateurs.eu/fileadmin/user_upload/eu-consommateurs/PDFs/publications/etudes_et_rapports/Memoire_Lydie_Tollemer-2012.pdf.

Greater and more explicit attention to the phenomenon is recorded in two more recent soft law regulatory acts:

- The Opinion of the European Economic and Social Committee entitled "Towards more sustainable consumption: industrial product lifetimes and restoring trust though consumer information" (2014/C 67/05); and
- The Motion for a European Parliament resolution on "a longer lifetime for products: benefits for consumers and companies" (2016/2272).

The first one defines "planned obsolescence" as "the depreciation of a material or piece of equipment before it wears out in that its depreciation or obsolescence has nothing to do with physical deterioration but with technological progress and changes in behaviour, fashion, etc." The second one refers to a series of legislative and soft law acts of the European institutions dedicated to the issues of sustainable development, environmental protection and a prudent and rational use of natural resources.

Among the goals pursued is the adoption of measures against planned obsolescence: the Commission is invited to propose better consumer legal protection and "appropriate dissuasive measures" for producers.

The purpose of this chapter is to identify what "appropriate dissuasive measures" may be, in particular whether the use of criminal law can be considered an "appropriate dissuasive measure".

4. THE ALTERNATIVES TO CRIMINAL LAW: THE RECENT ITALIAN EXPERIENCE

Before answering this question, it may be interesting to consider how some cases of (presumed or effective) "planned obsolescence" have been dealt with in a country that does not provide in its legal system for the possibility of using criminal law against this phenomenon.

The choice to regulate and sanction the phenomenon with administrative measures seems the most immediate and natural. When one thinks of "planned obsolescence", in fact, the need to protect the consumer immediately comes to mind. It is no coincidence, for example, that one of the first legal instruments to combat planned obsolescence considers it as an unfair commercial practice.

This is the solution recently adopted in Italy.

As a result of two complex investigations, the AGCM (Italian Antitrust Authority) has ascertained that the companies of the Apple group and of the Samsung group have carried out unfair commercial practices in violation of Articles 20, 21, 22 and 24 of the Italian Consumer Code in relation to the release of some firmware updates for mobile phones that have caused serious malfunctions and significantly reduced performance, thereby accelerating the process of replacing them.

In fact, these companies have induced consumers – through insistent requests to download the updates and also because of the information asymmetry between consumers and manufacturers – to install updates on devices that are not able to adequately support them, without providing adequate information or any means of restoring the original functionality of the products.

In particular, Samsung has insistently suggested, from May 2016, that consumers who had purchased a Note 4 (placed on the market in September 2014) proceed to install the new Android firmware called Marshmallow prepared for the new model Note 7, without informing consumers of the likelihood serious malfunctions due to the greater stresses placed on the hardware by the new firmware and requiring a high repair cost for out-of-warranty repairs connected to such malfunctions.[9]

Apple, for its part, has insistently suggested, from September 2016, that the owners of the various models of the iPhone 6 (6/6Plus and 6s/6sPlus respectively released in autumn 2014 and 2015) install the new iOS 10 operating system developed for the new iPhone7, without informing consumers of the greater energy demands of the new operating system and the possible inconveniences – such as sudden shutdowns – that such an installation could entail. To limit these issues, Apple released a new update (iOS 10.2.1) in February 2017, without warning consumers that its installation could reduce devices' response speed and functionality. In addition, Apple has not provided any support for iPhones that have experienced operating problems not covered by the legal guarantee, and only in December 2017 did it provide the option of replacing the batteries at a discounted price.

Also in relation to Apple, another behaviour was found to be in violation of Article 20 of the Consumer Code: until December 2017 Apple did not provide consumers with adequate information about some essential characteristics of the batteries, such as their average lifespan and deterioration, as well as about the correct procedures for maintaining, checking and replacing the batteries in order to preserve the devices' full functionality.[10]

The two companies, Samsung and Apple, have had to pay fines equal to the maximum possible fine, taking into account the seriousness of the conduct and the size of the companies: Samsung had to pay €5 million and Apple €10 million (€5 million for each of the two contested practices). Both companies will also have to publish a statement on the Italian page of their website informing them of the authority's decision with the link to the assessment order.

---

[9] http://www.agcm.it/dotcmsdoc/allegati-news/PS11009_scorr_sanz_omi_dichrett.pdf.
[10] http://www.agcm.it/dotcmsdoc/allegati-news/PS11039_scorr_sanzDich_rett_va.pdf.

These decisions are innovative and could be the basis for an evolutionary interpretation of the Consumer Code rules and a reflection on the appropriateness of a reform of some aspects of consumer legislation.[11] In summary, the AGCM has challenged Samsung and Apple with respect to the aggressive, insistent nature of the proposed updates for users (who would not have had real freedom of choice about whether or not to update the software) and the violation of information obligations.

5. THE FRENCH SOLUTION: THE CRIME OF PLANNED OBSOLESCENCE

After this digression, we can try to answer the following question: can the use of criminal law be considered an "*appropriate dissuasive measure*" against planned obsolescence?

The French legislator would seem to think so. In fact, in 2015 (and then in 2016) the French Parliament revised the French *Consumer Code* (*Code de la consommation*) by introducing a specially crafted penal provision.[12]

Previously, the Law on Consumption of 18 March 2014 (the so-called *loi Hamon*) had provided a first legislative response to fight planned obsolescence.[13] Some of its most striking provisions are as follows:

(i)   the extension of the presumption of existence of compliance, from six months to two years; the consumer also has the possibility to avail himself of the legal guarantee of conformity provided for by the Consumer Code without having to prove a defect functional;

(ii) the obligation for manufacturers and importers to indicate the period during which spare parts will be available (if they exist); and

(iii) the obligation for manufacturers and importers to meet their commitment to supply spare parts within two months following the request.

Subsequently, Article 99 of the Law on Energy Transition of 17 August 2015, after a brief definition of the concept of "planned obsolescence", provides for a sentence of two years' imprisonment and a €300,000 fine (which may be

---

[11]   A. Re & G. D'Ippolito, Obsolescenza programmata. L'AGCM sanziona Apple e Samsung, Rivista di MediaLaws 2018, http://www.medialaws.eu/obsolescenza-programmata-lagcm-sanziona-apple-e-samsung.

[12]   N. Jaenne, « Prête à jeter »? À propos du delit d'obsolescence programmée, in J. Alix, M. Jaquelin, S. Manacorda & R. Parizot (eds.), Humanisme et justice. Mélanges en l'honneur de Geneviéve Giudicelli-Delage, Dalloz, 2016, pp. 603 et seq.; C. Boissonnet & J.F. Puget, Légiférer contre l'obsolescence programmée?, in La Seimane Juridique 2017 (29), p. 559.

[13]   V. Legrand, L'amèlioration de l'informationet des droits contractuel des consommateurs dans la loi "Hamon", in Petites Affiches 2014 (91), p. 4.

increased to 5 per cent of the average turnover over the past three years) for all manufacturers or importers guilty of the crime of programmed obsolescence.

Finally, Ordonnance no. 2016-301 moved the crime of "planned obsolescence" into the Consumer Code. Article L. 441-2 states: "The practice of planned obsolescence is prohibited, which is defined as the use of techniques by which the head of the marketing of a product is to deliberately reduce the lifespan to increase the replacement rate".[14] Article L. 454-6 specifies: "It is punishable with two years of imprisonment and fine of €300,000".

France was the first country to adopt a law that expressly refers to and defines planned obsolescence. The definition is the result of a compromise reached by the two chambers of the French Parliament – the National Assembly and the Senate – after months of intense discussions.

The legal regulation model adopted by the French legislature should be evaluated from two points of view. First of all we must verify whether such a solution is compatible with the fundamental principles of criminal law, in particular the principle of offensiveness (or the harm principle) and the principle of strict legality. Second, we need to verify the effectiveness and efficiency of this solution. The French experience is an interesting test to assess the legitimacy and the effectiveness of the use of criminal law. The examination of the French model can provide useful indications for the more general perspective of the use of criminal law against planned obsolescence.

5.1. PLANNED OBSOLESCENCE AND THE PRINCIPLE OF OFFENSIVENESS/HARM PRINCIPLE

This principle must be considered from two different points of view. The first is whether there are – and if so what are – the interests offended by planned obsolescence? In this case the answer is quite simple. Planned obsolescence produces a lot of negative effects, including social, health, cultural, ethical, environmental effects.

From the social perspective, planned obsolescence presents three problems. First of all, in a crisis, the mindset created by the planned obsolescence of consumer goods has contributed to encouraging credit purchases and unprecedented levels of consumer indebtedness. The ones who suffer most are socially disadvantaged groups who cannot afford expensive long-lasting products and often settle for poorer-quality bottom-end products. Then there are the employees of the entire repairs sector, who have to bear the detrimental effects of planned obsolescence.

---

[14] With respect to the originally proposed text, the words "especially in product design" have been eliminated. The solution adopted is preferable: in fact, the planned obsolescence is not limited to the early stages of the life of a product, but can also occur during its use.

The figures from the 2007 ADEME (*Agence de l'environnement et de la maîtrise de l'énergie*; now *Agence de la transition écologique*) report confirm this trend. Only 44 per cent of broken appliances are repaired. Distributors estimate that only 20 per cent of out-of-warranty customer support results in repairs. The 2010 ADEME study also reveals a significant fall in repairs in France between 2006 and 2009, especially in the case of white goods. The repairs sector has the advantage that it cannot be relocated and mainly offers stable jobs. In short, planned obsolescence causes excessive recourse to credit and restriction of access to the best quality products.

Planned obsolescence also causes harm to health, resulting for example from the effect of increased incineration and waste production. The first concerns the direct consequences of incineration for people living nearby, because electronic components are toxic; and the second is international. Infrastructure for IT waste processing is so lacking that many end-of-life products are exported illegally to regions with lower landfill charges, but this has a severe impact on local residents. In Ghana, for example, scrap iron is recovered from waste and sent to Dubai or China. Much of this waste ends up in southern countries where they cause health and environmental problems.

From a cultural point of view, the phenomenon of planned obsolescence leads to less consumer trust in businesses.

Then there are the ethical and symbolic effects. These are less tangible aspects, but very important from the point of view of the affirmation of a greater focus on the theme of sustainable development. In Italy, for example, the poet and writer Pier Paolo Pasolini was one of the first to grasp the negative effects of the phenomenon of "programmed obsolescence", speaking of a "new way of production" based on the irrepressible invention of superfluous and constantly perishable goods and on the hedonistic function of individual consumption.[15]

The foregoing are observations certainly worthy of consideration. But the most important adverse effects of programmed obsolescence are:

- for "consumers", being forced to bear the costs of repairs and the continued new purchase of goods; and
- for the "environment",[16] being exposed to danger:
  - from the point of view of the non-rational use of natural resources; and
  - from the point of view of the excessive production of waste.

The unnecessary replacement of a still-working product or the premature failure of a product can have a strong impact on the consumption of raw materials

---

[15] *P.P. Pasolini*, Lettere luterane. Il progresso come falso progresso, Einaudi, 1976.
[16] *Vidalenc & Meunier, supra*, note 6 at pp. 402 et seq.

necessary for the production of new products to replace those considered obsolete, which in turn will have to be disposed of, with consequences for the generation of waste.

Planned obsolescence, therefore, is multi-offensive, harming two types of common interests: those of consumers and those of the environment.[17]

Recognising that there are interests that deserve to be protected through criminal law, we must ask ourselves if there are any alternatives to the introduction of a crime of planned obsolescence. Can we protect these interests in another way? We could envisage various alternative solutions, discussed in the following.

First of all we must consider "private law remedies" (warranties, class actions). These are legal remedies which entail the right to compensation for damage due to the breach of the manufacturer's contractual obligations towards the consumer.[18]

First of all, information obligations towards consumers could be exploited, interpreting them in the light of the principles of sustainable development.[19] From this perspective, one could imagine a product labelling system that clearly states the lifetime of the product.[20]

Several legislative initiatives undertaken in various European countries reveal how the system is also evolving towards strengthening the current legislation in terms of warranties.[21] The Netherlands has introduced an extended guarantee covering defects based on the average lifetime the consumer is entitled to expect from the product. Finland also allows the duration of the guarantee to be extended under the Consumer Protection Act. According to the preamble, the seller is responsible for non-conformity arising from the manufacture of a product – for example a vehicle, building materials or an electrical appliance – even if

---

[17] From this point of view, the systematic placement of the French norm on the offence of planned obsolescence is not optimal, because it betrays a prevailing consideration given to the protection of consumers' interests.

[18] *P. Mariotti, P. Serpetti, P. Masini & R. Caminiti*, Prodotti difettosi e obsolescenza programmata, Maggioli editore, 2013; *J.A. Soto Pineda*, Reflexiones acerca de la posibles incompatibilidades de la obsolescencia programada con el sistema de defense de los consumidores, Actualidad Civil, 2015, pp. 6 et seq.; *S. Wrbka*, Warranty Law in case of planned obsolescence – The Austrian situation, EuCML 2017, pp. 67 et seq.; *L.V. Bianchi*, La influencia del principio del consumo sustentable en el combate de la obsolescencia programada, la garantía de los "productos durables" y el derecho a la información de los consumidores en Argentina, Revista de derecho privado 2018, pp. 277 et seq.

[19] *Bianchi, supra*, note 18 at p. 289.

[20] *A. Salcedo Aznal*, Las nuevas actitudes hacia el consumo y la producción: las mejores prácticas en el ámbito del consumo colaborativo y la obsolescencia planificada (Un mundo en tránsito). Enfoque integrador basado en la corresponsabilidad, la eficiencia y la sostenibilidad, Report by European Economic and Social Committee, July 2014, http://www.eesc.europa.eu/resources/docs/estudio-vf.pdf.

[21] *Re & D'Ippolito, supra*, note 11.

the lack of conformity comes to light more than two years after delivery of the goods. This model is similar to the system in the Netherlands. An ombudsman is responsible for determining the lifetime of the product, based on criteria such as the price of the product, its parts or usage, such as frequency of use. The legislator has not developed a list of the "expected lifetime" of specific products. Nevertheless, individual cases can be studied in light of the recommendations of the Consumer Dispute Board.

Secondly, as a possible alternative to both civil and criminal law remedies, "administrative regulations" and "non-criminal sanctions" (fine, administrative sanctions) could be considered. We have seen[22] how fines were applied in Italy to punish cases of planned obsolescence committed by Apple and Samsung. Administrative measures also include those of a fiscal nature. For example, in 2017 Sweden introduced a series of fiscal measures aimed at strengthening the sectors of repair, recycling and the circular economy. It intends to:

- reduce the cost of repairs by reducing the VAT rate on certain goods (including bicycles, shoes and clothes) from 25 per cent to 12 per cent;
- allow consumers who choose to repair their domestic appliances to deduct 50 per cent of the labour cost from their taxes; and
- tax products which contain materials that are impossible or difficult to recycle and repair.

Lastly, the decision to introduce a specific offence against planned obsolescence should be subject to an assessment of the inadequacy of the existing criminal laws. Could offences already provided for by the penal codes in force be applied? The answer is affirmative. For example, at least in some cases, fraud could be applied.[23] However, the crime of fraud presupposes that the consumer is not aware of the fact that the purchased product has an artificially reduced life cycle: but this is not so in the case of planned obsolescence. Furthermore, the fraud protects the patrimonial interests of consumers and does not deal with environmental protection.

Each of these legal instruments mentioned in this paragraph does not seem to be enough to counter the phenomenon.[24] Moreover, they favour consumer protection rather than environmental protection. Another flaw in this approach is that consumers are considered to be completely without responsibility with regard to the phenomenon. Effective action must also involve consumers: it must increase their awareness of the need for sustainable development and

---

[22]   See *supra* section 4.
[23]   *Jaenne, supra*, note 12 at pp. 609 et seq.
[24]   Id. at p. 611.

rational use of natural resources. Thus the introduction of a crime of planned obsolescence could be a useful solution.

5.2. PLANNED OBSOLESCENCE AND THE PRINCIPLE OF LEGALITY

The other principle that we must consider is the principle of legality. The contents of this principle are manifold. In the case we are examining here, two main aspects are important: that of "precision" and that of "sufficient definiteness". The first expresses the need for the incriminating norm to describe a fact with sufficiently clear boundaries, so that every citizen can know in advance what the behaviour forbidden by the legal system is. The second highlights the need for the fact described by the incriminating norm to be ascertained and proven in a criminal trial, on the basis of the laws of science.[25]

Let us start with the aspect of "precision". How can we provide a precise definition of such a multifaceted and complex phenomenon as "planned obsolescence"? As we have seen,[26] it is difficult to provide a precise definition of "planned obsolescence". In fact, it is very difficult to draw a clear boundary between normal business practices and behaviours that are worthy of being punished.

The risk is of adopting too generic a definition. Indeed, the French criminal doctrine has highlighted various ways in which the definition provided by Article L. 441-2 Consumer Code is generic. For example, it is unclear whether "planned obsolescence" can be realised with an omission: for example, is the failure to adopt an update that would lengthen the life of the product a technique of programmed obsolescence? Based on the literal interpretation of the rule, it is not easy to answer this question. Even the reference to the product lifespan is rather imprecise. Many studies have shown that it is particularly difficult to define the concept of the "life" of a product and that it would be preferable talk about "durability": however, the first should assessed in practice, the second in the abstract. The choice of the first option connotes the fact punished in psychological terms. In fact, the concept of the "life of a product" is not objective, but depends on the perception of those who use it.

In any case, there would be considerable difficulties with judicial assessment. The crime of "planned obsolescence" therefore poses problems of compatibility with the principle of "sufficient definiteness".[27]

---

[25] G. Marinucci, E. Dolcini & G.L. Gatta, Manuale di Diritti Penali. Parte Generale, Giuffrè, 2018, pp. 77 et seq.

[26] See *supra* section 2.

[27] G. Geissbühler, L'obsolescence programmée: main invisible versus défaut invisible, in O. Hari (ed.), Protection de certains groupements de personnes ou de parties faibles versus libéralisme économique: quo vadis?, Schulthess editions romandes, 2016, pp. 133 et seq.

Notwithstanding the rather wide definition of planned obsolescence in the law, convicting a producer of an infraction will not be easy. In order to prove that the crime was committed, the judge must verify that:

(i)   the product is the result of the implementation of particular technological solutions;
(ii) the product has a deliberately reduced lifespan; and
(iii) the producer has acted intentionally to increase the "substitutability" rate of the product.

To prove the existence of the first condition is relatively easy. In fact, it is a question of demonstrating an objective element: that a technical device or mechanism not necessary for the product's normal functionality has been included in the product. The question becomes much more complex for the remaining two conditions.

Let us start with the second condition. Take, for example, the case in which it is discovered that the manufacturer has included a device or mechanism which reduces the product's performance. This is what would seem to have happened in the so-called "Apple case" discussed above: the company admitted to having reduced the performance of older models of the iPhone following a software update. Are we sure that the performance degradation is similar to a "reduction in product life"? The literal interpretation of the French norm would seem to lean towards a negative answer, but it will be necessary to see how jurisprudence orients itself.

But also in *de iure condendo* perspective we can discuss the opportunity to equate two conditions that are however different from each other, punishing both with the same penalty.

Proving intention (the third condition above) is even more difficult.[28] Consumer and environmental associations have strongly criticised the use of the word "deliberately", which requires proof of intention on the part of the producer. In the famous case of the "lightbulb affair", discussed above, this proof would have been possible, but in most cases producers can argue that there was no intentional design choice. In that case, how can intention be proved? The producer can defend himself by offering a rational justification that could be credible, even if not objectively demonstrable (e.g. safety needs). If, for example, a manufacturer replaces a joint built for years from a certain material with another built from a different material (perhaps of lesser quality), it is quite possible that this may be part of a precise plan of planned obsolescence, but the

---

[28]   *G.P. Demuro*, Il dolo, II, L'accertamento, Giuffrè, 2010; *M. Pierdonati*, Dolo e accertamento nelle fattispecie penali c.d. "pregnanti", Jovene, 2012; *P. Astorina*, L'accertamento del dolo. Determinatezza, normatività e individualizzazione, Giappichelli, 2018.

producer's justification that it is only trying to reduce production costs without compromising quality could be "credible".

Let us once again consider the Apple case: are we sure that the claim that the reduction in performance is designed to protect the battery in older models does not conceal the intention to encourage their replacement? Obviously not; but we also cannot be certain of the opposite. The same was true in the so-called "Epson case". The company was accused of having altered its printing blocking system, programming to report the lack of ink well before the toner was actually used up, in order to push the supply of new toner ahead of time. Epson could justify this by claiming that the printer cartridge chip stops functioning when the cartridge is at 25 per cent capacity because from that point on there is a high risk of the printing coming out paler or uneven on the page.

Even in the famous "lightbulb affair", some have tried to offer a scientific justification to deny that it is a case of the improper practice of planned obsolescence. Some engineers have claimed that a life expectancy of 1,000 hours is reasonable for most bulbs, and that a longer lifespan comes at the expense of efficiency. They have argued that longer bulb life causes increased heat output and reduced light if bulbs last longer than 1,000 hours, resulting in wasted electricity.

In conclusion, whenever there can be a rational alternative explanation (economic, technical or precautionary) it becomes very difficult to say with certainty that we are dealing with a case of planned obsolescence.[29] The scope for producers to demonstrate their good intentions is undeniably great and their rationale is not always inaccurate, though it may cover less worthy objectives.[30]

It is probable that the French legislator wanted to offset the excessive indeterminacy of the objective contours of the incriminating fact with a more meaningful subjective element. However, the result is an incriminating rule that is difficult to apply.

5.3.   IS THE CRIMINAL REPRESSION OF PLANNED OBSOLESCENCE EFFECTIVE?

After highlighting the possible tensions between a crime of planned obsolescence and some principles of criminal law, we must considerate another parameter of evaluation: the effectiveness of the use of criminal law. In short, we must answer other questions.

The first question is whether criminal law is an effective and dissuasive measure in this area? In the French case, the impact of the reform of 2015/16

---

[29]   *Tollemer, supra*, note 8.
[30]   *Maitre-Elkern & Dalhammar, supra*, note 7 at p. 387.

appears to have been rather limited. So far, there have only been two judicial procedures, against Epson and against Apple. The low number of proceedings is probably also linked to the difficulty for the victims (taken individually) to understand the phenomenon. It is no coincidence that the few proceedings were brought on the initiative of the HOP (Stop Planned Obsolescence) Association, which also prompted the intervention of the French legislator.

It is likely that complaints, investigations and proceedings will increase in the coming years. Only then can we assess the attitude of the jurisprudence and the real impact of the French criminal law on "planned obsolescence".

The second question is whether the crime of planned obsolescence affects the behaviour of producers and consumers? Does it play a cultural orientation role? After the introduction of the crime of planned obsolescence in France, Arnaud Gossement, a lawyer specialising in environmental law, claimed that the creation of a crime of obsolescence would have a pedagogical benefit: "It is a strong signal for the market. Because it will force producers to ask the question of obsolescence and induce some to make the life of their products a comparative advantage".[31] However, in reality, no empirical evidence exists to confirm these statements. The real cultural effects of the change on the mentality and the behaviour of consumers continue to be controversial. In any case, they should not be overestimated.

It is possible that the fear of reputational damages could be a deterrent for companies. Damages that occur when the public becomes aware of the fact that a specific company has recourse to the practice of planned obsolescence: consumers would be induced to stop buying that company's products.

All the objections to use of criminal law previously examined are serious and well founded. But does this mean that we have to renounce the use of criminal law? This is not necessarily the case. However, we must create a less ambiguous and more easily enforceable offence. We could incorporate into the criminal norm a non-exhaustive list of the techniques that amount to planned obsolescence, for example: "the voluntary introduction of a defect, a weakness, a planned or premature outage, a technical limitation, an inability to repair, or an incompatibility".[32] We also could specify that "inability to repair" consists in "the fact that a product cannot be dismantled or that spare parts necessary to its functioning missing".[33] This was the phrasing used in an early definition proposed by the French National Assembly.[34]

We could also better specify who the possible perpetrator of the crime may be. The French Consumer Code would seem to identify the offender with the person

---

[31]   This observation is reported by *L. Van Eeckhout*, L'obsolescence programmée des produits désormais sanctionnée, Le Monde, 14 October 2014.

[32]   Article L. 213-4 of the Draft Law on Energy Transition for Green Growth, as adopted by the Assemblée Nationale on 14 October 2014, TA no. 412.

[33]   Ibid.

[34]   Ibid.

responsible for placing the product on the market. But what about the people involved in the design or implementation of the product? Currently they could be punished only for complicity in the crime. It would be preferable to indicate clearly which categories of subjects (engineers, planners, administrators, etc.) can be considered perpetrators of the crime.

Last but not least, to make proving the crime less difficult, we could replace the reference to intention (i.e. acting deliberately) with that to the simple will to carry out the act.

6.   CONCLUSIONS

Against planned obsolescence, we need a model of regulation that integrates soft law instruments, commercial law actions (class actions) and administrative controls (i.e. imposition – if possible – of a minimum useful life for products or a minimum period of availability for spare parts).

The action to combat planned obsolescence must be advanced in a harmonised way. The main objectives should be:

- to develop a methodology to evaluate the life of products in an objective manner, providing for civil or administrative sanctions for producers who do not adopt the instructions emerging from the use of this methodology; and
- to encourage – through tax mechanisms – repairing products instead of replacing them.

The role of criminal law should be limited only to cases of failure of other instruments, according to the *extrema ratio* principle. From this perspective, it is possible to apply the crimes currently provided for consumer protection, such as fraud. The introduction of a crime of planned obsolescence, however, could offer a more complete protection of the various offended interests (not only those of consumers, but also the environment). From this point of view, the solution adopted by the French legislator is not optimal: considering only consumers as systematic victims of the phenomenon means adopting too unilateral a reading of the phenomenon. The inclusion of the crime of planned obsolescence by the French legislator in the Consumer Code produces a gap between the crime and the legal assets that must be protected. Not only that, there is also a risk that the application of the rule to so-called "professional victims" is excluded.[35] In any case, efficient action against the negative effects of planned obsolescence cannot be entrusted only to national legal systems, effective law enforcement can only pass from legal harmonisation at a supranational level.

---

[35]   *Jaenne, supra*, note 12 at p. 613.

CONFISCATION OF ASSETS AND PROCEEDS OF CRIME IN ENVIRONMENTAL CRIMINAL LAW

New Approaches by the German Legislator

Robert Esser

1. INTRODUCTION

The reform of the law on the confiscation of assets of crime in Germany (Sections 73 et seq. Criminal Code) came into force on 1 July 2017.[1]

In the past, the confiscation of assets gained by criminal acts had been rarely applied by German criminal courts since the provisions were regarded as to be too complicated.[2]

Even in cases of environmental criminal law, forfeiture and confiscation of criminal assets did not play a significant role in the past.[3] Yet the courts' actions are of major importance for an effective enforcement regime of environmental offences.[4]

---

[1]   In detail: *M. Korte*, NZWiSt 2018, p. 231; see also *C. Pelz*, NZWiSt 2018, pp. 251 et seq.; *N. Reh*, NZWiSt 2018, pp. 20 et seq.; *O. Mückenberger & F. Hinz*, BB 2018, p. 1435, 1436; *G. Trüg*, NJW 2017, p. 1913, 1914; *M. Köhler*, NStZ 2017, pp. 497 et seq.; *M. Heim*, NJW-Spezial 2017, p. 248; *T. Gebauer*, ZRP 2016, pp. 101 et seq.; *W. Mitsch*, in Karlsruher Kommentar-OWiG, C.H. Beck, 5th ed., 2018, Section 29a, p. 1; *F. Saliger*, in Nomos-Kommentar-StGB, Nomos, 5th ed., 2017, before Sections 73 et seq., p. 3a; *M. Lindemann*, in W. Leitner & H. Rosenau, Wirtschafts- und Steuerstrafrecht, C.H. Beck, 2017, before Sections 73 et seq. StGB, pp. 22 et seq.; to the amendments in the regulatory fining proceedings: *A. Rebler*, DAR 2018, p. 411.

[2]   *M. Korte*, NZWiSt 2018, p. 231; *R. Köllner & J. Mück*, NZI 2017, p. 593; *R. Köllner, V. Cyrus & J. Mück*, NZI 2016, p. 329; see also the draft bill of the Federal Ministry of Justice and Consumer Protection (March 2016), p. 1, http://www.bmjv.de/SharedDocs/Gesetzgebungsverfahren/Dokumente/RefE_Reform_strafrechtliche_Vermoegensabschoepfung.pdf?__blob=publicationFile&v=2.

[3]   See in particular *M. Kracht*, wistra 2000, p. 326; *H. Franzheim*, wistra 1989, p. 87.

[4]   See for example BGH, judgment of 23 October 2013 – 5 StR 505/12, NStZ 2014, p. 89, 93 et seq. = NJW 2014, p. 91, 94 et seq. = StV 2014, p. 549, 550 (only principles); BGH, judgment of 20 February 2013 – 5 StR 306/12, NStZ 2013, p. 401, 402 et seq. = NJW 2013, p. 950, 951 et seq.; see also *B. Hecker & M. Lorenz*, NStZ-RR 2017, p. 33, 37; *M. Pfohl*, in C. Müller-Gugenberger (ed.), Wirtschaftsstrafrecht, 6th ed., 2015, Section 54, p. 347.

A general account of the year 2016 discloses about 16,000 investigation proceedings in Germany in the area of environmental criminal law. About 1,000 of them led to a conviction. Around 97 per cent of the convictions consisted in fines, and – correspondingly – only 3 per cent in convictions to a prison sentence. The great majority of cases, namely more than 75 per cent, concerned Section 326 of the German Criminal Code, that is the illegal handling and disposal of waste. Compared over the last decade, those numbers do not change significantly.[5]

The main aim of the German legislator was therefore to simplify the existing provisions of asset recovery and to remove any inconsistencies and practical shortcomings in order to remedy the former reluctant approach of the criminal courts thereto.[6]

Another reason for the rare application of the provisions on forfeiture in the German Criminal Code was undoubtedly the fact that German criminal law does not so far recognise criminal liability of companies.[7]

On the other hand, the German system of penalties in regulatory offence law (*Ordnungswidrigkeitenrecht*) provides not only for the imposition of fines against companies, but also for the confiscation of proceeds of regulatory offences.[8]

2. TYPE AND CHARACTER OF SANCTIONS FOR ENVIRONMENTAL CRIMES

2.1. WHICH CRIMINAL LAW SANCTIONS DOES DIRECTIVE 2008/99/EC GENERALLY REQUIRE?

The first issue to be determined is which sanctions in law Directive 2008/99/EC[9] generally requires, and particularly whether Directive 2008/99/EC requires the

---

[5]   Cf. for the relevant statistics Antwort der Bundesregierung auf die Kleine Anfrage der Fraktion Bündnis 90/Die Grünen of 25 June 2018, BT-Drucksache 19/2971, pp. 4–6, 16.

[6]   Cf. *R. Köllner & J. Mück*, NZI 2017, p. 593; *R. Köllner, V. Cyrus & J. Mück*, NZI 2016, p. 329.

[7]   *T. Grützner*, CCZ 2015, p. 56; see also *G. Dannecker & C. Dannecker*, NZWiSt 2016, p. 162, 163; *T. Grützner & A. Jakob*, in T. Grützner & A. Jakob (eds.), Compliance von A-Z, C.H. Beck, 2nd ed., 2015; *A. Meyberg*, in BeckOK-OWiG, Section 30, p. 1 (26th ed., state 01.04.2020).

[8]   *K. Rogall*, in Karlsruher Kommentar-OWiG, 5th ed., 2018, Section 30, pp. 1 et seq.; *A. Meyberg*, in BeckOK-OWiG, Section 30, p. 8; *M. von Galen & S. Maass*, in W. Leitner & H. Rosenau (eds.), Wirtschafts- und Steuerstrafrecht, C.H. Beck, 2017, Section 30 OWiG, pp. 1 et seq.; *M. Engelhart, M. Rübenstahl & M. Tsambikakis*, in R. Esser, M. Rübenstahl, F. Saliger & M. Tsambikakis (eds.), Wirtschaftsstrafrecht, Dr. Otto Schmidt Verlag, 2017, Section 30 OWiG, p. 1; *H. Achenbach*, in H. Achenbach, A. Ransiek & T. Rönnau (eds.), Handbuch Wirtschaftsstrafrecht, C.F. Müller, 5th ed., 2019, Chapter 1, p. 29; *W. Bär*, in J.P. Graf, M. Jäger & P. Wittig (eds.), Wirtschafts- und Steuerstrafrecht, C.H. Beck, 2nd ed., 2017, Section 30 OWiG, p. 1 et seq.

[9]   Directive 2008/99/EC of the European Parliament and of the Council of 19 November 2008 on the protection of the environment through criminal law, OJ 2008 L 328/28 (Environmental Crime Directive, ECD).

Member States to implement an effective system of confiscation of assets and proceeds of crime.

This question is *prima facie* to be answered by interpreting the provisions of Directive 2008/99/EC and the proposal for the Directive presented by the Commission.

Directive 2008/99/EC was adopted on the basis of Article 192(1) TFEU (ex Article 175(1) EC Treaty) and aims at ensuring a high level of environmental protection in accordance with the provisions of Article 191(2) TFEU (ex Article 174(2) EC Treaty) as well as Article 3(3) TEU and Article 37 of the Charter of Fundamental Rights of the European Union.

Similarly, both the Preamble of Directive 2008/99/EC[10] and the Commission's proposal for the Directive[11] outline the main objective of the provisions, namely to ensure the full and effective implementation of Community (now Union) rules on environmental protection.[12]

In order to achieve this objective, Article 3 of Directive 2008/99/EC defines, at the level of substantive law, some serious environmental offences that have to be sanctioned by the domestic legislation of the Member States.

Additionally, that is in a second step, the Environmental Crime Directive requires the Member States to ensure that their domestic legislation adopted to transpose the EU environmental *acquis* is effectively enforced.[13]

Accordingly, the Preamble of Directive 2008/99/EC asserts that a more effective protection of the environment may be reached by imposing a system of more dissuasive penalties.[14]

Directive 2008/99/EC thus places particular emphasis on the possible deterrent effect of the penalties for environmental offences.

Therefore, relevant domestic sanctions will have to comply with the specific requirements set out in the provisions of Directive 2008/99/EC.

Article 5 of Directive 2008/99/EC obliges the Member States to ensure that environmental offences are "punishable by effective, proportionate and dissuasive criminal penalties". This notion stems from the case law of the EU Court of Justice.[15]

---

[10]   Directive 2008/99/EC of the European Parliament and of the Council of 19 November 2008 on the protection of the environment through criminal law, OJ 2008 L 328/29.

[11]   Proposal for a Directive of the European Parliament and of the Council on the protection of the environment through criminal law (presented by the Commission), COM(2007) 51, p. 2.

[12]   *F. Saliger*, Umweltstrafrecht, Vahlen, 2012, p. 23; compare also: *S. Kingston, V. Heyvaert & A. Cavoški*, European Environmental Law, Cambridge University Press, 2017, p. 213.

[13]   *A. Farmer, M. Faure & G.M. Vagliasindi*, State of Affairs and Future Perspectives, in A. Farmer et al. (eds.), Environmental Crime in Europe, Bloomsbury, 2017, p. 319, 331.

[14]   Directive 2008/99/EC of the European Parliament and of the Council of 19 November 2008 on the protection of the environment through criminal law, OJ 2008 L 328/28.

[15]   *Inter alia* ECJ, Case C-68/88, Commission of the European Communities v Hellenic Republic, judgment of 21 September 1989, paras. 23, 24.

Indeed, Article 5 thereby merely defines a relatively broad framework of general principles domestic sanctions have to satisfy, leaving a wide margin of discretion to the Member States as to which specific penalties they wish to implement.[16]

Whilst the proposal document of the Commission did contain provisions on prescriped types and levels of criminal penalties, they were not ultimately adopted in the Environmental Crime Directive as such prescriptions were seen as not residing within the legislative competence of the (former) Community.[17] This considerable leeway of the Member States may be criticised as being contrary to harmonisation attempts pursued by the Directive.[18]

Nevertheless, some basic guidelines can still be derived from the Directive's provisions, also by drawing upon the Preamble of the Directive and the Commission's proposal document.

In particular, it can be determined that Directive 2008/99/EC requires national sanctions available for environmental offences to be of a *criminal* nature.

According to Article 1, the subject matter of Directive 2008/99/EC relates to measures established in the area of criminal law.

In its proposal for the Directive the Commission opted to use the term "sanctions", whereas the final version of Directive 2008/99/EC eventually features the term "penalties", arguably for reasons of the slightly narrower notion of the concept.

According to the Preamble of Directive 2008/99/EC, as well as to the Commission's proposal document, only availability of sanctions in criminal law will offer a sufficiently dissuasive effect and strengthen compliance with rules on environmental protection.

Sanctions that specifically operate within criminal law demonstrate a social disapproval of a qualitatively different nature compared to mere administrative sanctions or compensation schemes available under civil law.[19]

From a procedural and arguably more practical point of view, criminal investigation and prosecution are seen to be more effective and powerful than tools of administrative and civil law.[20]

---

[16]   G.M. Vagliasindi, The EU Environmental Crime Directive, in A. Farmer et al. (eds.), Environmental Crime in Europe, Bloomsbury, 2017, p. 31, 49, 50.

[17]   ECJ, Case C-440/05, Commission of the European Communities v Council of the European Union, judgment of 23 October 2007, paras. 29, 36.

[18]   G.M. Vagliasindi, The EU Environmental Crime Directive, in A. Farmer et al. (eds.), Environmental Crime in Europe, Bloomsbury, 2017, p. 31, 50.

[19]   W. Mitsch in Karlsruher Kommentar-OWiG, 5th ed., 2018, Section 17, p. 5; J. Adam, K. Schmidt & J. Schumacher, NStZ 2017, p. 7, 11; H. Landau, NStZ 2015, p. 665, 666; F. Bittmann, NStZ 2016, p. 249, 250.

[20]   Against this background, Section 46(3) OWiG already shows the differences between a criminal investigation and the investigation of regulatory fining proceedings. In the latter, various investigatory powers of the Criminal Procedure Code do not apply; see A. Bücherl

Thus, one essential requirement set out by Directive 2008/99/EC is for domestic sanctions for environmental crimes to be located within the area of criminal law.

Ordinary sanctions that can be considered are of course possible prison penalties and fines. However, the Commission also proposed alternative sanctions, such as the obligation to reinstate the environment.[21]

Even though the alternative sanction of confiscation of assets and proceeds of crime was not explicitly included in Directive 2008/99/EC or in its proposal, the Commission pointed out that in many cases confiscation of crime-related objects may be an essential tool.[22]

Thus, in its essence Directive 2008/99/EC sets out a list of environmental offences and imposes upon Member States the obligation to provide a workable system of penalties – without specifically inserting the need to provide for a confiscation of assets and proceeds of crime.

On the other hand, Member States are of course free to adopt or maintain measures reaching beyond the scope of the Directive, ensuring a *higher* level of environmental protection. In such a case the Member State is, however, still bound by its obligations deriving from Article 4(3) TEU and Article 288 TFEU.

Thus, where such alternative measures are introduced into the domestic legal system, they also need to comply with the requirements of Directive 2008/99/EC and provide for an "effective, proportionate and dissuasive" system of criminal sanctions.

2.2. CONFORMITY OF CURRENT GERMAN CRIMINAL LAW ON CONFISCATION OF ASSETS AND PROCEEDS OF CRIME WITH DIRECTIVE 2008/99/EC

Besides the imposition of fines in regulatory offence law (OWiG),[23] the general sanctioning principles in German criminal law (StGB) provide for complementary *sanctions* in addition to fines and imprisonment (*penalties*). In particular, proceeds of a crime have to be forfeited (Section 73 StGB) and the

---

in BeckOK-OWiG, Section 46, p. 3; *J. Lampe* in Karlsruher Kommentar-OWiG, C.H. Beck, 5th ed., 2018, Section 46, pp. 19 et seq.

[21] Proposal for a Directive of the European Parliament and of the Council on the protection of the environment through criminal law (presented by the Commission), COM(2007) 51, p. 9: "Alternative sanctions are suggested for both natural and legal persons. Such sanctions may be more effective than imprisonment or fines in many cases and include the obligation to reinstate the environment, the placing under judicial supervision, the ban on engaging in commercial activities or the publication of judicial decisions."

[22] Id.

[23] An example of the combat against environmental offences by means of regulatory offence law can be observed in the area of the International Convention for the Prevention of Pollution from Ships: where ships illegally introduce their waste into the sea the relevant

court may order a deprivation order for objects used for and created by criminal activities (Section 74 StGB).[24]

As already mentioned, in 2017 the German legislator opted to reform those provisions on the confiscation of assets and proceeds of crime in Sections 73 et seq. Criminal Code.

The relevant issue is, thus, whether current German law on confiscation of assets and proceeds of crime – being part of the criminal system of sanctions – satisfies the reqirements set out by Directive 2008/99/EC, or, more specifically, whether the German provisions constitute effective, proportionate and dissuasive criminal penalties – whether they are seen as an isolated measure or as being part of the whole criminal law system.

2.2.1. Introduction to the Current Provisions for Confiscation of Assets

A brief outline of the German law on confiscation will serve as a basis for the subsequent analysis.

Sections 73 et seq. of the German Criminal Code (StGB) set out that both assets and proceeds of crime have to be confiscated.[25] This means that things that have been used to commit a crime (*instrumentum sceleris*) or that are the product of a crime (*productum sceleris*), as well as profits that have been achieved by means of commiting the crime, are subject to confiscation.[26]

The legal effect thereof is that the proprietary rights in the assets move to the state.[27]

Where confiscation of the specific asset is not possible, for example because it has been converted, the courts have to order compensation amounting to the value of the asset (Section 73c StGB).[28]

---

provisions enable the responsible administrative authorities to impose administrative fines, with a margin of discretion ranging from €80 to €25,000. Depending upon the kind of violation, the sort of waste and the severity of the illegal activity the average amount of the fines ranges between around €370 and €520. For more detailed information cf. Antwort der Bundesregierung auf die Kleine Anfrage der Fraktion DIE LINKE of 12 June 2018, BT-Drucksache 19/2675, pp. 2–3.

[24] See for example S. Sina, Environmental Criminal Law in Germany, in A. Farmer et al. (eds.), Environmental Crime in Europe, Bloomsbury, 2017, p. 95, 112; see also M. Heuchemer in BeckOK-StGB, 45th ed., state: 01.02.2020, Section 73 StGB, p. 1.

[25] See W. Mitsch in Karlsruher Kommentar-OWiG, C.H. Beck, 5th ed., 2018, Section 29a, pp. 3 et seq.; M. Lindemann in W. Leitner & H. Rosenau (eds.), Wirtschafts- und Steuerstrafrecht, C.H. Beck, 2017, before Sections 73 et seq. StGB, pp. 3 et seq.

[26] M. Lindemann in W. Leitner & H. Rosenau, Wirtschafts- und Steuerstrafrecht, C.H. Beck, 2017, before Sections 73 et seq. StGB, p. 6.

[27] M. Heuchemer in BeckOK-StGB, Section 75, p. 2; M. Lindemann in W. Leitner & H. Rosenau (eds.), Wirtschafts- und Steuerstrafrecht, C.H. Beck, 2017, Section 74e StGB, p. 2; see also M. Köhler & C. Burkhard, NStZ 2017, p. 665, 671 or M. Köhler, NStZ 2017, p. 497, 500 et seq.

[28] See in the context of Section 73c StGB: M. Heuchemer in BeckOK-StGB, Section 73c, pp. 1 et seq.

2.2.2. Compliance with Requirements of Directive 2008/99/EC

When considering the compliance of the current provisions on confiscation and forfeiture of assets and proceeds of crime in Germany with the requirements of the Environmental Crime Directive, it is perhaps worth noting that the German legislator did not consider Directive 2008/99/EC when implementing the reform, but rather merely intended to transpose Directive 2014/42/EU into German domestic legislation.[29]

2.2.2.1. Criminal Sanctions

According to Articles 1 and 5 of Directive 2008/99/EC, sanctions for environmental crimes must be of a *criminal* nature.

There is an intrastate debate revolving around the question of whether the confiscation of assets as set out in Sections 73 et seq. of the German Criminal Code (StGB) amounts to a criminal sanction or is merely a legal, non-criminal instrument by which those assets are forfeited – following the idea of "unjust enrichment" known from civil law.[30]

Generally, the German regime of criminal sanctions is double-tracked. On the one hand, the Criminal Code provides for genuine criminal sanctions, most notably for prison penalties and fines, originating from the individual blameworthiness of the offender. On the other hand, there are measures such as hospital orders, detention orders or care orders which derive from the potential dangerousness of the offender.[31]

Yet the provisions on confiscation fall neither within the first category, nor within the second, so that the confiscation regime is frequently thought to simply be a measure with a special character not comparable to other categories.[32]

---

[29]   Gesetz zur Reform der strafrechtlichen Vermögensabschöpfung of 13 April 2017, Bundesgesetzblatt (BGBl.) I, 872), whereby the reform serves to implement Directive 2014/42/ EU of the European Parliament and of the Council of 3 April 2014 on the freezing and confiscation of instrumentalities and proceeds of crime in the European Union, OJ 2014 L 127/39.

[30]   See in detail: *W. Joecks* in MüKo-StGB, Vol. 2, C.H. Beck, 3rd ed., 2016, Section 73 StGB, pp. 4 et seq.; *M. Heuchemer* in BeckOK-StGB, Section 73 StGB, p. 1.1.; *A. Retemeyer* in H. Achenbach, A. Ransiek & T. Rönnau, Handbuch Wirtschaftsstrafrecht, 4th ed., 2015, Chapter 14, pp. 14 et seq.; or *H. Schilling* in R. Esser, M. Rübenstahl, F. Saliger & M. Tsambikakis (eds.), Wirtschaftsstrafrecht, Dr. Otto Schmidt, 2017, Section 73 StGB, pp. 2 et seq.

[31]   *H. Pollähne* in Nomos-Kommentar-StGB, Nomos, 5th ed., 2017, Section 61, p. 2; *G. van Gemmeren* in MüKo-StGB, Vol. 2, C.H. Beck, Section 61, p. 1; *B. Heinrich*, Strafrecht Allgemeiner Teil, Kohlhammer, 5th ed., 2016, p. 83; *C. Roxin*, Strafrecht Allgemeiner Teil, Vol. 1, C.H. Beck, 4th ed., 2006, Section 1, p. 3; *V. Krey & R. Esser*, Deutsches Strafrecht Allgemeiner Teil, Kohlhammer, 6th ed., 2016, pp. 182 et seq.

[32]   BGH, judgment of 21 August 2002 – 1 StR 115/02, NJW 2002, p. 3339, 3340 = NStZ 2003, p. 37, 38; *M. Heuchemer* in BeckOK-StGB, Section 73, p. 1; *S. Wiedner* in J.P. Graf, M. Jäger & P. Wittig (eds.), Wirtschafts- und Steuerstrafrecht, C.H. Beck, 2nd ed., 2017, Section 73 StGB, pp. 7 et seq.; *K. Tiedemann*, Wirtschaftsstrafrecht, Vahlen, 5th ed., 2017, p. 521.

As the provisions do not fit easily into the traditional classification within the German domestic system of sanctions, this situation offers a broad scope for discussion.

In this context, *German criminal courts* emphasise the strong preventative purpose of confiscation measures following a conviction. According to this opinion, a confiscation order of a criminal court is not of a penal nature and is not part of an overall system of *criminal* penalties. Its sole purpose is to siphon off assets or profits an offender acquired through means of an unlawful act.[33]

On the contrary, only a minority of academics argue that confiscation is not simply an absorption measure, but rather a legal instrument of punitive character reaching beyond the mere reallocation of assets.[34]

One can thus hold as an interim result that the provisions on confiscation of assets in the German Criminal Code are at least *not criminal* in the narrow sense of the word – even though they are part of the Criminal Code and executed by criminal courts.

However, they may still count as *criminal* for the purposes of Directive 2008/99/EC.

As established above, the reason why the Directive requires penalties for environmental crimes to be of a criminal nature is that the social disapproval that accompanies criminal sanctions is qualitatively different from mere administrative or civil compensation schemes. As a result, it is said, the provisions operate as a more efficient deterrent to environmental crimes.

Yet, as a general matter, the additional value of specifically criminal sanctions with regard to their deterrent nature is not uncontroversial in the literature.[35]

An important question in terms of the possible impact of the Environmental Crime Directive is whether sanctions which are criminal in nature are necessarily more dissuasive than administrative or civil measures.

On the one hand, one could argue that the potential deterrent effect of a sanction in environmental law depends very much on the specific circumstances, for example on the severity of the environmentally detrimental activity in question, or on whether the offence is committed within corporate structures or rather by tourists negligently polluting a beach.[36]

---

[33] BVerfG, decision of 14 January 2004 – 2 BvR 564/95, NJW 2004, p. 2073, 2076; BGH, judgment of 16 May 2006 – 1 StR 46/06, NJW 2006, p. 2500 = NStZ 2006, p. 570, 572; BGH, decision of 18 February 2004 – 1 StR 269/03, NStZ-RR 2004, p. 214 et seq.; BGH, judgment of 21 August 2002 – 1 StR 115/02, NJW 2002, p. 3339, 3340 = NStZ 2003, p. 37, 38; see also *W. Joecks* in MüKo-StGB, Section 73, p. 15.

[34] See in detail: *W. Joecks* in MüKo-StGB, Section 73, p. 7; differentiating: *A. Eser* in A. Schönke & H. Schröder, Strafgesetzbuch, 30th ed., 2019, before Section 73 StGB, pp. 13 et seq.

[35] Cf. *G.M. Vagliasindi*, The EU Environmental Crime Directive, in A. Farmer et al. (eds.), Environmental Crime in Europe, Bloomsbury, 2017, p. 31, 45.

[36] *E. Pirjataniemmi*, Desperately Seeking Reason – New Directions for European Environmental Criminal Law, in Stockholm Institute for Scandinavian Law, Scandinavian Studies in Law, Vol. 54, 2009, p. 409, 416–418, 427.

It might therefore be preferable to introduce sanctions which are of a merely administrative nature for some crimes, in order to purposefully address the different motives, different situations and the whole complexity of the problem.[37]

Yet this theoretical analysis collides with empirical evidence. In this sense, a recent study affirms that German environmental criminal sanctions in fact do have a deterrent effect.[38] According to this study, the dissuasive effect does not result from the severity of the sanctions in question, but supposedly rather from its criminal nature. This is because with this nature comes along a certain public element, namely damage to one's personal reputation by standing trial in a court open to the public.

Relying on this study, opinions in the legal literature which deny the additional dissuasive effect of criminal sanctions cannot be entirely confirmed. Beside that, the offences listed in the Environmental Crime Directive are arguably so serious that a majority of academics would consider it necessary to address them with measures of a criminal nature.

Thus, the crucial question still resides in whether the German provisions on confiscation of assets and proceeds of crime can count as criminal for the purposes of the Environmental Crime Directive.

In this context, factual value can be attributed to the issue of where provisions are finally placed in the overall framework of the domestic legal regime.[39]

Accordingly, the relevant German provisions are located within the German Criminal Code (StGB). As such they may have a certain stigmatising effect.

The German provisions may not be criminal in the narrow sense, but neither are they of a merely administrative or civil nature. The above-mentioned categorisation of the confiscation rules is governed by legal niceties of German criminal law. Especially laypersons will rarely note this rather academic distinction. Thus, this somewhat sophisticated classification will probably not lessen the dissuasive effect of the provisions on confiscation of assets and proceeds of crime. The German provisions on confiscation may therefore even count as criminal for the purposes of Directive 2008/99/EC.

2.2.2.2. Effectiveness

The new German provisions on confiscation of assets may also serve as an *effective* sanction for environmental crimes.

---

[37] See in this context: *K. Tiedemann*, Wirtschaftsstrafrecht, Vahlen, 5th ed., 2017, p. 228.

[38] *C. Almer & T. Goeschl*, Environmental Crime and Punishment: Empirical Evidence from the German Penal Code, 2010, p. 708, 709, 717, 718, 721, 722; as cited in S. *Sina*, Environmental Criminal Law in Germany, in A. Farmer et al. (eds.), Environmental Crime in Europe, Bloomsbury, 2017, p. 95, 113, n. 97.

[39] *M. Faure*, Evolution of Environmental Criminal Law in Europe – A comparative analysis, in A. Farmer et al. (eds.), Environmental Crime in Europe, Bloomsbury, 2017, p. 267, 268, 269.

The relevant Sections 73 et seq. Criminal Code are located within the miscellaneous provisions of the German Criminal Code. As such they are applicable to all criminal offences.

They are, however, still subject to their own conditions. The deprivation of objects generated by or used or intended for use in the commission or preparation of an offence is in certain circumstances only possible where the relevant offence has been commited intentionally, cf. Section 74. Yet, by means of the gateway provision of Section 330c[40] of the Criminal Code, deprivation is also applicable to a wider range of specifically environmental offences, for example where they are commited negligently.

In its proposal for Directive 2008/99/EC, the Commission also suggested to the Member States that they could introduce or maintain alternative sanctions other than prison sentences and fines. The Commission made clear that such sanctions in general could even be more effective than ordinary penalties.[41]

Therefore, the question of whether the German rules on confiscation of assets and proceeds of crime are actually effective first and foremost depends on the specific design of the relevant provisions.

The effectiveness of the provisions is partly ensured by the fact that the courts are – since 2017 – *obliged* to order the confiscation of assets of (environmental) crimes.[42] The offender may also be required to restore the value of the relevant asset where the latter cannot be returned anymore, for example because the asset has been converted or consumed.

On the other hand, the effectiveness of the provisions also depends on whether the specific provisions are conceived in such a way that the German courts in fact – that is, effectively – apply them. In particular, this means that the relevant state authorities must have both the capacity and willingness to impose the sanction.

Before the legal reform came into action in July 2017, the provisions on confiscation were only very rarely applied by the German criminal courts. Even in cases of environmental criminal law, forfeiture and confiscation of criminal assets did not play a significant role in the past.[43]

The essential question is therefore whether the reform led to a simpler and more concise regime of confiscation enabling a more effective application of the provisions by the German courts.

The law amendment has brought about a considerable number of changes in the areas of both substantive and procedural law. In particular, the reform was

---

[40]   See relative to Section 73 StGB: *D. Ventura-Heinrich* in C. Momsen & T. Grützner (eds.), Wirtschafts- und Steuerstrafrecht, C.H. Beck, 2013, Chapter 10, F, p. 74.

[41]   Proposal for a Directive of the European Parliament and of the Council on the protection of the environment through criminal law (presented by the Commission), COM(2007) 51, p. 9.

[42]   See in the context of the ministerial draft bill: *V. Bittmann*, NZWiSt 2016, p. 131.

[43]   *M. Kracht*, wistra 2000, p. 326; *H. Franzheim*, wistra 1989, p. 87.

intended to deal with former loopholes in the law of confiscation and overcome practical shortcomings.[44]

The most notable changes shall be briefly set out in the following, so that an assessment can be made of whether they added to a more effective system of the law on confiscation.

A major feature introduced by the amendments consists in a reorganisation of the rules on compensation of victims. The former compensation scheme followed the principle of "first come, first serve". This has now been abolished, so that currently all victims are compensated equally. Thus, the amendment led to a more effective compensation procedure for victims.[45]

Furthermore, confiscation is now possible even where the assets are not free of third party rights.[46] An essential effect thereof is that confiscation of assets will be possible for white-collar crimes in the future.

The law reform also concretised how proceeds of crime are to be assessed and calculated.[47] It thereby provides for a clear guideline for the practice before the courts. In substantive terms, the new rules on calculation considerably expanded the scope of possible confiscation.

The law amendment further introduced *non-conviction-based confiscation*.[48]

It also enables the confiscation of assets which are discovered only subsequent to the investigation proceedings and conviction.[49]

Yet, in order to determine whether the new provisions provide a sufficiently *effective* system of sanctions for the purposes of Directive 2008/99/EC, one has to revert back to the rationale underlying the adoption of the Directive.

According to the Commission document on the proposal for Directive 2008/99/EC, the difficulties in efficiently addressing environmental offences reside to a considerable extent in the differences between the laws of the Member States.[50]

---

[44] *M. Korte*, NZWiSt 2018, p. 231; *G. Trüg*, NJW 2017, 1913 et seq.; *R. Köllner & J. Mück*, NZI 2017, p. 593; *M. Heim*, NJW-Spezial 2017, p. 248; *T. Rönnau* in Beck'sches Formularhandbuch für den Strafverteidiger, Vermögensabschöpfung, C.H. Beck, 6th ed., 2018, Vorbemerkungen.

[45] See *H. Schilling, J. Corsten & Y. Hübner*, StraFo 2017, p. 305, 313 et seq.; *M. Meißner*, NZWiSt 2018, p. 239; *M. Rhode*, wistra 2018, p. 65, 67 et seq.; *S. Barreto da Rosa*, NZWiSt 2018, pp. 215 et seq.; *G. Trüg*, NJW 2017, p. 1913, 1918; *M. Köhler & C. Burkhard*, NStZ 2017, p. 665, 679; *R. Köllner & J. Mück*, NZI 2017, pp. 593 et seq.

[46] *M. Korte*, wistra 2018, p. 1, 5; *M. Korte*, NZWiSt 2018, p. 231, 233; *G. Trüg*, NJW 2017, p. 1913, 1916; *M. Heuchemer* in BeckOK-StGB, Section 73b StGB, p. 2.

[47] *G. Trüg*, NJW 2017, p. 1913, 1914; see also *M. Rübenstahl*, NZWiSt 2018, p. 255, 256; *A. Rettke*, wistra 2018, pp. 234 et seq. or *M. Korte*, wistra 2018, p. 1, 3 et seq.

[48] *H. Schilling & Y. Hübner*, StV 2018, p. 49, 50; *M. Korte*, wistra 2018, p. 1, 8; *G. Trüg*, NJW 2017, p. 1913, 1915.

[49] On further amendments in the criminal procedural law: *G. Trüg*, NJW 2017, p. 1913, 1916 et seq.; see in this context also *D. Ullenboom*, wistra 2018, p. 291 ("forgotten" confiscation).

[50] Proposal for a Directive of the European Parliament and of the Council on the protection of the environment through criminal law (presented by the Commission), COM(2007) 51, p. 5.

Since environmental crimes often are of a transboundary nature, the differing and insufficient sanctions in many Member States enable the perpetrators to circumvent Member States with stricter legislation for their operations.[51]

Hence, one of the main objectives of Directive 2008/99/EC was to ensure the approximation of applicable criminal sanctions for particular environmental crimes among Member States' legislation in order to avoid perpetrators being able to take advantage of looser regulations in some Member States.

This necessity and desire stand behind the Directive's call for an effective regime of criminal sanctions for environmental crimes.

The changes brought about in the German Criminal Code by the law amendment of July 2017 have to be assessed against this background.

From a more abstract point of view, the German reform enhanced the position of victims in both substantive and procedural matters. Equally, it contributed to a considerable extent to closing the loopholes of the law on confiscation discerned prior to the reform.

Thus, the changes may well entail a more frequent application of confiscation of assets by the German criminal courts, as well as a more consistent one.

By not only enabling but *forcing* the courts to take a more proactive position on confiscating assets, the new German rules represent an effective approach to removing the differences in the sanction systems of the EU Member States.

Hence, the reform in fact rendered the law on confiscation more *effective* for the purposes of Directive 2008/99/EC.

2.2.2.3. Proportionality

In order to ensure that Sections 73 et seq. Criminal Code are proportionate, the rules provide for exceptional circumstances in which levying the profit and particularly tracing the assets of crimes may not be ordered by the courts, relying for example on the state of mind of a receiving third party (Section 73e).

Furthermore, where the order of confiscation of assets is not obligatory, but is at the discretion of the court, Section 74f Criminal Code explicitly requires the court to include the principle of proportionality in its deliberations.

2.2.2.4. Dissuasion

Directive 2008/99/EC further stipulates that the system of national sanctions should be of a dissuasive character.

---

[51] See also *A. Farmer, M. Faure & G.M. Vagliasindi*, State of Affairs and Future Perspectives, in A. Farmer et al. (eds.), Environmental Crime in Europe, Bloomsbury, 2017, p. 319, 328–330, stressing the importance of transborder collaboration in terms of fighting environmental crime in Europe.

A measure is dissuasive in nature where after an assessment of possible risks and possible benefits, the risks prevail, either because they are very likey or very prejudicial, and the potential benefits do not outweigh those risks.[52]

In its proposal for Directive 2008/99/EC, the Commission considered that mere financial sanctions may not be dissuasive where offenders are impecunious or on the other hand financially very strong.[53] In such cases, something more than financial sanctions, i.e. prison penalties, may be required.

Yet punishment as one objective of the sanctioning system does not stand alone. Remedies should also aim at the restoration of harm created by the criminal activity, and at the prevention of future harm.[54]

The remedy of forfeiture of illegal gains – which *complements* ordinary penalties such as fines and prison sentences – is, thus, a sanction aiming at *additional deterrence*.

As set out above, the requirement for national sanctions to be dissuasive is also closely linked with the demand for them to be of a criminal nature.

As a measure of a criminal nature for the purposes of Directive 2008/99/EC and as a measure which accompanies ordinary penalties, the confiscation of assets as set out in Sections 73 et seq. Criminal Code may well then act as a deterrent and satisfy the Directive's requirement of being dissuasive.

2.3.   INTERMEDIARY RESULT

According to Article 5 of Directive 2008/99/EC, the Member States of the Union shall take the necessary measures to ensure that the offences referred to in Articles 3 and 4 are punishable by effective, proportionate and dissuasive criminal penalties.

Article 5 does not force the EU Member States to implement rules on the confiscation of proceeds of crime if traditional (criminal) penalties (imprisonment, fine) suffice to represent a framework of "effective, proportionate and dissuasive criminal penalties" for environmental crimes.

Directive 2014/42/EU is applicable to environmental crimes. According to Article 4(1), Member States shall take the necessary measures to enable the confiscation, either in whole or in part, of instrumentalities and proceeds, or

---

[52]   See *H. Satzger* in R. Streinz (ed.), EUV/AEUV, 3rd ed., 2018, Article 325 AEUV, pp. 17 et seq.; in detail: *H.W. Micklitz & P. Rott* in M. Dauses & M. Ludwigs, Handbuch des EU-Wirtschaftsrechts, Verbraucherschutz, 44th supplement 2018, pp. 717 et seq.

[53]   Proposal for a Directive of the European Parliament and of the Council on the protection of the environment through criminal law (presented by the Commission), COM(2007) 51, p. 2.

[54]   See e.g. *M. Faure*, Evolution of Environmental Criminal Law in Europe – A comparative analysis, in A. Farmer et al. (eds.), Environmental Crime in Europe, Bloomsbury, 2017, p. 267, 309.

property the value of which corresponds to such instrumentalities or proceeds, subject to a final conviction for a criminal offence, which may also result from proceedings in absentia. However, Directive 2014/42/EU does not force the states to opt for a punitive (criminal) system of forfeiture.

Statutory rules on the confiscation of proceeds of crime as a "criminal penalty" are obligatory under Directive 2008/99/EC only if ordinary criminal penalties (imprisonment, fine) alone do not represent a framework of "effective, proportionate and dissuasive criminal penalties" as required by Article 5.

Even in that case, neither Directive 2014/42/EU nor Article 5 of Directive 2008/99/EC force the EU Member States to implement rules on the confiscation of proceeds of crime of a purely criminal nature, i.e. as a (criminal) penalty.

If they are part of a system of criminal sanctions, including criminal penalties, rules on forfeiture of the proceeds of crime may contribute to (a system of) "criminal penalties" in the sense of Article 5 of Directive 2008/99/EC even where these rules are themselves not of a criminal nature but have a *close connection* to a system of criminal penalties.

Despite the fact that the new provisions on the confiscation of assets in the German Criminal Code (Section 73 seq. StGB) cannot be characterised as "criminal penalties" in the narrow sense (i.e. punitive penalties), they may serve in the future – as part of the whole German criminal sanction system – as "effective, proportionate and dissuasive" criminal penalties as required by Article 5 of Directive 2008/99/EC.

Since the new provisions on the confiscation of assets in the German Criminal Code (Section 73 seq. StGB) cannot be characterised as "criminal penalties", they do not fall within the ambit of Article 7 ECHR (*nulla poena sine lege*), which means that they can be applied retroactively.

3. CORPORATE LIABILITY

Serious environmental crimes are often committed by corporations or organisations. Therefore, Directive 2008/99/EC not only requires natural persons to be punishable for the commission of environmental crimes; it further stipulates that legal persons shall also be held liable for such offences.

3.1. WHAT IS REQUIRED BY DIRECTIVE 2008/99/EC?

Articles 6 and 7 of the Directive deal with the issue of liability of legal persons for environmental crimes.

According to Article 6(1) of the Directive, the Member States shall ensure that legal persons can be held liable: (a) for offences referred to in Articles 3 and 4 of the Directive *where such offences have been committed for their benefit* by any person who has a leading position within the legal person, acting either individually or as part of an organ of the legal person; and (b) where the lack of supervision or control, by a person having a leading position, has made possible the commission of an offence referred to in Articles 3 and 4 for the benefit of the legal person by a person under its authority.

Consequently only where environmental crimes are committed for the benefit of a legal person by any person having a leading position therein does Article 7 of the Directive require the legal person to be punishable by effective, proportionate and dissuasive penalties.

A comparison with the wording of Article 5 of the Directive concerning natural persons ("criminal penalties") shows that the sanctions for legal persons do not have to be *criminal* in nature.[55]

Article 6(3) of the Directive clarifies that there ought to be cumulative liability of legal and natural persons.

3.2. DOES GERMAN LAW FULFIL THOSE REQUIREMENTS?

The issue is whether the current provisions of German law on confiscation of assets and proceeds of crime are in accordance with the relevant provisions of the Environmental Crime Directive.

3.2.1. What is the Current Position in German Law on Corporate Liability?

In German criminal law, one of the three main criteria which must be established in order to find the defendant liable is blameworthiness, that is, the accused must be personally responsible for his prohibited behavior (individual guilt).

A corollary of the principle of personal culpability is that only natural persons, and not legal ones, can be liable under criminal law.[56] This principle can be described by the Latin expression *societas delinquere non potest*.[57]

As a result, German criminal law does not so far recognise criminal liability of companies. Against this background, voices have been raised calling for a new

---

[55]   See also *G.M. Vagliasindi*, The EU Environmental Crime Directive, in A. Farmer et al. (eds.), Environmental Crime in Europe, p. 31, 43, 49.

[56]   Cf. *S. Sina*, Environmental Criminal Law in Germany, in A. Farmer et al. (eds.), Environmental Crime in Europe, Bloomsbury, 2017, p. 95, 98, 99; *W. Mitsch*, Recht der Ordnungswidrigkeiten, Springer, 2nd ed., 2005, Section 16, p. 1; *J. Bohnert & J. Bülte*, Ordnungswidrigkeitenrecht, C.H. Beck, 5th ed., 2016, Section 2, p. 161; *G. Heine & B. Weißer* in A. Schönke & H. Schröder, Strafgesetzbuch, C.H. Beck, 30th ed., 2019, before Sections 25 et seq., p. 121; *R. Scholz*, ZRP 2000, p. 435; in terms of legal policy this approach is very controversial, see *C. Schmitt-Leonardy* in H. Blum, K. Gassner & S. Seith, Ordnungswidrigkeitengesetz, C.H. Beck, 2016, Section 30 OWiG, pp. 11 et seq.

[57]   See *M. Engelhart*, NZWiSt 2015, p. 201; *W. Mitsch*, NZWiSt 2014, p. 1.

---

interpretation of the concept of *guilt* in terms of legal entities. In this context, Bürger suggests developing a specific term of guilt, which is detached from personal responsibility and therefore, from the concept of (criminal) *acts*.[58] Instead, the basis of criminal allegations can also be the wrongdoing of *systems*, for instance in the form of an inadequate internal organisation of the respective legal entity.[59]

This lack of a specific corporate criminal law in the German legal system is undoubtedly one reason why – even in cases of environmental criminal law – forfeiture and confiscation of criminal assets did not play a significant role in the past.

On the other hand, however, whilst legal persons cannot be liable in criminal law, the German system of penalties in regulatory offence law (*Ordnungswidrigkeitenrecht*, OWiG) provides not only for the imposition of fines against companies for non-compliance with those administrative penal offences (Section 30 OWiG), but also for the confiscation of proceeds of regulatory offences (Sections 22 et seq. OWiG).

Generally, the regular maximum fine is €1,000 (Section 17(1) OWiG). However, for environmental laws the average fine is €50,000. One of the reasons for this is that Section 17(4) OWiG stipulates that in regulatory offence law the fine ought to exceed the financial benefit that the offender achieved by committing the offence.[60]

In contrast to German criminal law, in regulatory offence law, the principle of discretionary prosecution (opportunity principle, *Opportunitätsprinzip*) applies, allowing the courts to impose fines only as a last resort.[61]

In order to establish corporate liability in regulatory offence law, there is the need to identify a leading representative that has committed the offence in question. This means that there is no automatic or autonomous responsibility.[62]

---

[58]   See *S. Bürger*, ZStW 2018; 130(3), p. 704, 741 et seq.

[59]   *S. Bürger*, ZStW 2018; 130(3), p. 704, 732.

[60]   See for this analysis *S. Sina*, Environmental Criminal Law in Germany, in A. Farmer et al. (eds.), Environmental Crime in Europe, Bloomsbury, 2017, p. 95, 114; moreover: *K. Gassner* in H. Blum, K. Gassner & S. Seith, Ordnungswidrigkeitengesetz, C.H. Beck, 2016, Section 17, p. 35; *K. Sackreuther* in BeckOK-OWiG, Section 17, p. 113; *W. Mitsch* in Karlsruher Kommentar-OWiG, 5th ed., 2018, Section 17, pp. 112 et seq.; *D. Klesczewski*, Ordnungswidrigkeitenrecht, 2nd ed., 2016, Section 8, pp. 593 et seq.

[61]   *S. Sina*, Environmental Criminal Law in Germany, in A. Farmer et al. (eds.), Environmental Crime in Europe, Bloomsbury, 2017, p. 95, 114; *J. Bohnert & J. Bülte*, Ordnungswidrigkeitenrecht, Section 1, p. 7; *D. Klesczewski*, Ordnungswidrigkeitenrecht, Vahlen, 2nd ed., 2016, Section 9, p. 675; *A. Bücherl* in BeckOK-OWiG, Section 47, pp. 2 et seq.; *W. Mitsch* in Karlsruher Kommentar-OWiG, C.H. Beck, 5th ed., 2018, Section 47, p. 2.

[62]   *M. Faure*, Evolution of Environmental Criminal Law in Europe – A comparative analysis, in A. Farmer et al. (eds.), Environmental Crime in Europe, Bloomsbury, 2017, p. 267, 283; *A. Meyberg* in BeckOK-OWiG, Section 30 OWiG, p. 46; *K. Rogall* in Karlsruher Kommentar-OWiG, C.H. Beck, 5th ed., 2018, Section 30 OWiG, p. 88; see also *H. Achenbach*, NZWiSt 2012, pp. 321 et seq. or *M. Engelhart*, NZWiSt 2015, p. 201, 208.

Nevertheless, administrative corporate liability is open to all offences, thus also to environmental offences. Finally, it is applied cumulatively with liability of natural persons.

3.2.2. Does the Current German Law Comply with Directive 2008/99/EC?

In determining whether German law complies with the Environmental Crime Directive, the crucial question revolves around whether the administrative nature of corporate liability in Germany is sufficient.

On the one hand, the Environmental Crime Directive does not require domestic corporate liability to be of a criminal nature.

On the other hand, Article 7 of the Directive *does* stipulate that the measures must be effective and dissuasive. The issue is thus whether administrative sanctions fulfil those requirements.

Courts should at least have the possibility to levy substantial fines so that this prospect may act as a serious deterrent to environmental crimes.

In 2011, the OECD published a report questioning the compliance of the German provisions on administrative corporate liability with Article 7 of Directive 2008/99/EC.[63]

Subsequently, the German Parliament increased the maximum fine in regulatory offence law so that the current system now allows the imposition of a quite substantial €10 million fine (Section 30(2) Sent. 1 No. 1 OWiG).[64]

Nonetheless, there are aspirations among academics that corporate sanctions should go beyond the regime provided for by Sections 30, 22 et seq. OWiG.[65] However, there is no agreement on whether criminal or administrative sanctions should be called for.[66]

---

[63] *OECD*, Deutschland: Phase 3. Bericht über die Anwendung des Übereinkommens über die Bekämpfung der Bestechung ausländischer Amtsträger im internationalen Geschäftsverkehr und der Empfehlung des Rats zur weiteren Bekämpfung der Bestechung ausländischer Amtsträger im internationalen Geschäftsverkehr (17 March 2011), 5–6, 45, 83; as cited in *S. Sina*, Environmental Criminal Law in Germany, in A. Farmer et al. (eds.), Environmental Crime in Europe, Bloomsbury, 2017, p. 95, 114, n. 102.

[64] *S. Sina*, Environmental Criminal Law in Germany, in A. Farmer et al. (eds.), Environmental Crime in Europe, Bloomsbury, 2017, p. 95, 114–115; an important case of Section 30 OWiG is Section 130 OWiG, which describes the omission of supervisory measures of the owner of an operation or undertaking, see *J. Bohnert & J. Bülte*, Ordnungswidrigkeitenrecht, C.H. Beck, Section 2, p. 167; in detail: *D. Klesczewski*, Ordnungswidrigkeitenrecht, Vahlen, 2nd ed., 2016, Section 7, pp. 652 et seq.; *M. Cordes & T. Reichling*, NJW 2015, pp. 1335 et seq.

[65] *S. Sina*, Environmental Criminal Law in Germany, in A. Farmer et al. (eds.), Environmental Crime in Europe, Bloomsbury, 2017, p. 95, 115.

[66] Against this background, there is a discussion going on as to whether there should be an individual criminal law for corporations in Germany, see *S. Beukelmann*, NJW-Spezial 2018, p. 184; *C. Beisheim & L. Jung*, CCZ 2018, p. 63; *G. Ortmann*, NZWiSt 2017, p. 241, 249; *T. Schröder*, NZWiSt 2016, p. 452, 453; *T. Grützner*, CCZ 2015, p. 56, 57; *B. Schünemann*,

According to a study conducted by Meinberg, most proceedings in regulatory offence law relating to environmental offences end with the imposition of a fine. However, the severity of the relevant sanction on average remains behind what would be achieved by criminal law.[67]

Yet the probability of a sanction being imposed for a regulatory offence is higher than the probability of the imposition of a sanction in criminal proceedings.[68]

An analysis of these findings supposes that administrative fines may be more efficient for minor violations, whereas criminal sanctions are more appropriate for the most serious of cases.

This conclusion may also have an impact on the German legislator. The currently governing parties in German Parliament included in their coalition agreement the intention to introduce a more effective system of corporate liability.[69] It is, however, still unclear whether this will entail provisions of an administrative or of a genuinely criminal nature.

4. CONCLUSION

The reform of Sections 73 et seq. of the German Criminal Code (StGB) which entered into force on 1 July 2017 will have a significant punitive impact on the criminal courts' jurisprudence on confiscation of assets and proceeds of crime.

Together with ordinary criminal penalties such as prison sentences and fines, the recent reform will contribute to a system of more effective, proportionate and dissuasive sanctions, with the broad variety of measures and remedies balancing out each other's flaws and downsides.

Despite the fact that Germany still has not opted for provisions of corporate liability in criminal law and that the new provisions on the confiscation of assets in the German Criminal Code cannot be characterised as "criminal sanctions" in the narrow sense, they serve as an "effective and proportionate penalty" as demanded by Directive 2008/99/EC.

ZIS 1/2014, p. 1; *T. Kutschaty*, ZRP 2013, p. 74, 75; *K. Leipold*, ZRP 2013, p. 34; *K. Rogall* in Karlsruher Kommentar-OWiG, C.H. Beck, 5th ed., 2018, Section 30 OWiG, p. 129; *C. Momsen & S. Laudien* in BeckOK-StGB, Section 14 StGB, p. 33.

[67] *V. Meinberg*, Empirische Erkenntnisse zum Vollzug des Umweltstrafrechts, Zeitschrift für die gesamte Strafrechtswissenschaft 1998 (100), p. 112, as cited in *S. Sina*, Environmental Criminal Law in Germany, in A. Farmer et al. (eds.), Environmental Crime in Europe, Bloomsbury, 2017, p. 95, 115, n. 109.

[68] *S. Sina*, Environmental Criminal Law in Germany, in A. Farmer et al. (eds.), Environmental Crime in Europe, Bloomsbury, 2017, p. 95, 115.

[69] Koalitionsvertrag of the parties CDU, CSU and SPD of 14 March 2018, p. 126, lines 5895 et seq.

Due to the non-criminal nature of Sections 73 et seq. of the German Criminal Code (StGB), judicial decisions based on these provisions seeking the confiscation of assets gained by environmental criminal law offences can in principle by applied retroactively – also a factor of *effectiveness* in the sense of Article 5 of the Directive.

Additionally, the intended reform of existing provisions on corporate liability in German regulatory offence law will make the fight against environmental crimes more effective in the future – irrespective of its non-criminal nature.

However, in order to enhance such a positive development, it would furthermore be desirable to add to this overall concept first of all efficient control and supervision by administrative authorities in order to prevent environmentally detrimental activites in advance,[70] as well as the necessary measures to raise the general awareness of the public of the importance of the protection of the environment, and to also promote active commitment to the environment.

---

[70] Cf. e.g. Antwort der Bundesregierung auf die Kleine Anfrage der Fraktion Bündnis 90/Die Grünen of 25 June 2018, BT-Drucksache 19/2971, p. 6: according to the German government, the number of environmental offence cases narrowly correlates with the number and quality of responsible supervision authorities.

ENVIRONMENTAL CRIMINAL LIABILITY OF ENTERPRISES AND COMPLIANCE PROGRAMMES IN SPAIN

Miriam Ruiz Arias

1. INTRODUCTION

Writing about environmental protection policy entails referring to the relationship between human beings and the environment, as well as the implications of the market-based anthropocentric model of decision-making. The legal texts of many international and national organisations reflect this perspective, trying to protect the environment while exclusively keeping human beings at the centre and disregarding the role and relevance of our environment.

Damage to the environment (well exemplified by the dramatic consequences of climate change: droughts, floods, desertification, etc.) is embedded in the age of globalisation, a context not only of new risks but also of commodification, privatisation and massive manipulation of natural resources. In this sense, it is necessary to remember that the main environmental damage has its origin in legal commercial and/or industrial activities and that the most serious environmental damage is not illegal.

Moreover, the doctrine has affirmed that a large number of environmental crimes are committed as a result of enterprises and managers not having enough knowledge of the multiple regulations that protect the environment; people also do not consider environmental crimes to be the most serious crimes.[1]

In the same way, it could be said that the Lisbon Treaty[2] does not establish legal direct competencies in criminal law such the European Union has influence over Member States legislation via the European criminal policy. This European criminal policy is reflected in Directives 2008/99/EC and 2009/123/EC and it is worthwhile to point out some features of these two legal texts: on the one

---

[1]   C. Gibbs et al., Introducing Conservation Criminology. Towards Interdisciplinary Scholarship on Environmental Crimes and Risks, British Journal of Criminology 2010 (50), p. 124, 128–129.
[2]   The Lisbon Treaty amending the treaty on European Union and the Treaty Establishing the European Community, OJ 2007 C 306.

hand, they do not contain a definition of environmental crime, although all the criminal codes of the Member States have as an element of the environmental crime illegal behaviour under administrative law;[3] on the other hand, the two Directives use vague terms such as "substantial damage" and "negligible quantity", among others, and this may lead to less protection in Member States that have a low level of protection.[4]

In this chapter, an effective, Spanish environmental policy for enterprises will be presented. This effective environmental policy consists in two main points: on the one hand, the consistency and cohesion between Articles 339 and 340 of the Spanish Criminal Code (SCC) and Legislative Act 26/2007 regarding environmental restoration and protection; and on the other hand, access to environmental justice for environmental non-governmental organisations (ENGOs) and the participation of these organisations in the development and monitoring of environmental criminal compliance programmes.

Firstly, Article 31bis of the Spanish Criminal Law is addressed, which regulates the two ways of generating corporate criminal liability. Secondly, Article 325 of the Criminal Law will be appraised to analyse the most recent changes to the SCC since 2015, in addition to the chief requirements for committing an environmental crime.

Thirdly, considering the *non bis in idem* principle, as well as the protection of the environment by administrative and criminal law, other Spanish laws, such as

---

3 *G.M. Vagliasindi*, The fight against environmental crime in the European Union and its member states: A perspective on the enforcement system, in J.L. de la Cuesta Arzamendi, L. Quackelbeen, N. Persak & G. Vermeulen (eds.), Protection of the Environment through Criminal Law (AIDP World Conference Bucharest, Romania, 18th20th May 2016), 2016, p. 151, 166; *C. Gerstetter et al.*, Environmental Crime and the EU. Synthesis of the Research Project European Union Action to fight Environmental Crime (EFFACE), 2016, pp. 14 and 29; *M. Marquès Banqué & N. Torres Rosell*, Study on the implementation of Directive 2008/99/EC on the Protection of the Environment Through Criminal Law, SEO/BirdLife to create an European Network against Environmental Crime (ENEC) funded by the Criminal Justice Support Programme of the European Union, Centre d'Estudis de Dret ambiental de Tarragona. Universitat Rovira i Virgili, 2017, p. 81; *A. Farmer, A. Ritta Germani & R. Sollund*, Conclusions of the EFFACE Case Studies, 2015, pp. 9–10; and *Milieu Ltd*, Evaluation Study on the Implementation of Directive 2008/99/EC on the Protection of the Environment through Criminal Law by Member States. Spanish National Report, 2012, p. 28. The impact assessment of the 2007 Directive proposal established as environmental crimes acts and omissions that directly or indirectly damage the environment as well as infringe environmental administrative law: COM(2007) 51 SEC (2007); see *R.M. Pereira*, Environmental Criminal Liability and Enforcement in European Union and International Law, Brill Nijhoff, 2015, p. 49.

4 It could be noted, regarding the current European environmental criminal policy, that nowadays, considering the new redaction of Article 83 of the Treaty on the Functioning of the European Union, the discussion is about setting in Directives the minimum quantity or level of the penalty (the minimum amount of the maximum penalty) or continuing with proportional, effective and dissuasive sanctions. The same goes for the criminal liability of enterprises, since Directives refer to proportional, effective and dissuasive sanctions applicable to enterprises; on the contrary, in relation to natural persons it is necessary to add the adjective "criminal" to "penalties".

the Environmental Responsibility Act 26/2007 and Articles 339–340 SCC, which regulate tort liability and environmental restoration, will be discussed to study the coherence of the protected natural resources and some of the practical issues relating to strict liability.

Fourthly, an important trend of the last 40 years – so-called regulated self-regulation in environmental law – is analysed taking into consideration certain legal tools, such as the participation, *inter alia*, of environmental organisations in the development of the best available technique (BAT) regarding integrated environmental authorisation (IEA). Moreover, access to environmental justice for ENGOs is also considered, connecting this with the environmental right of participation.

To sum up, some considerations on the coherence between administrative and criminal law in order to protect the environment will be made, as well as on the participation of ENGOs in the design of criminal compliance programmes and their access to environmental justice.

2. ARTICLE 31BIS SCC AND SPECIFICATIONS OF CRIMINAL COMPLIANCE PROGRAMMES

In Spain, the criminal liability of enterprises is something new, since it was introduced only in 2010[5] and then reformed in 2015.[6] It is based on Italian Legislative Act 231/2001 and this, in turn, is built on US Regulation (United States Sentencing Commission Guidelines).[7] There is a *numerus clausus* catalogue of crimes that can be committed by enterprises; in the case of environmental crimes, this behaviour is addressed by Article 328 SCC.

Furthermore, there are two ways to generate the criminal liability of the enterprises set out in Art. 31bis paragraph 1 SCC. On the one hand, subparagraph (a) of this article refers to line managers who act on behalf of and on account of the enterprise to its direct or indirect benefit. These subjects are legal agents,

---

5   Organic Law 5/2010, of 22 June, amending Organic Law 10/1995, of 23 November (RCL 1995/3170 and RCL 1996/777) on Spanish Criminal Law (Spanish OJ 152 of 23 June 2015).

6   Regarding pollution crimes (discharges of waste in the sea or inland waters or on land, polluting emissions) in Spain there is only one High National Court decision (from 30 June 2016) that refers to the Dieselgate, or Volkswagen, case. The crimes which are being investigated are environmental crime, fraud and subsidy fraud.

7   *J.I. Gallego Soler*, Criminal Compliance y Proceso Penal: Reflexiones iniciales, in S. Mir Puig, M. Corcoy Bidasolo & V. Gómez Martín (dirs.), Responsabilidad de la Empresa y Compliance. Programas de prevención, detección y reacción penal, Edisofer, 2014, p. 195, 199–201; *H.R. Lobo da Costa & M. Pinhao Coelho Araujo*, Compliance e o julgamento da APn 470, Revista Brasileira de Ciências Criminais 2014 (22), p. 215, 216; *G. Quintero Olivares*, La reforma del régimen de responsabilidad penal de las personas jurídicas, in G. Quintero Olivares (dir.), Comentario a la Reforma Penal de 2015, Thomson Reuters Aranzadi, 2015, p. 77, 84; and *P. Crespo Barquero*, La reforma del Código Penal operada por L.O. 1/2015, de 30 de marzo: Responsabilidad penal de las personas jurídicas, Publicaciones de la Fiscalía, 2016, p. 12.

directors, senior management below director level and employees who have delegated management responsibilities.[8] On the other hand, subparagraph (b) covers workers without management responsibility set out in subparagraph (a). The behaviour giving rise to corporate criminal liability is committed in the exercise of corporate activities as well as on behalf of and on account of the enterprise as long as managers have not complied with their commitments of supervision, surveillance and control.[9]

It cannot be ignored that one of the fundamental updates to the SCC, which came into force on 1 July 2015, is the preclusion of criminal liability of legal entities when the company's board of directors introduce a criminal compliance programme before committing a crime. As a consequence, legal entities are exempted from criminal liability when the crime is committed by a manager, so long as the entity meets four legal requirements:[10] (i) the board of directors has effectively implemented and enforced a compliance programme, which must include suitable measures to prevent and detect crimes; (ii) an independent governing body of the enterprise is in charge of monitoring of the functioning and enforcement of the compliance programme; (iii) the individual perpetrator(s) fraudulently evaded the organisational and management structures; and (iv) the independent governing body had not failed to carry out its obligations of supervision, surveillance and control.

Alternatively, if the crimes were perpetrated by workers without management responsibility, enterprises are exempted from criminal liability if they adopted and efficiently enforced a compliance programme suitable to prevent crimes of the same nature, before the commission of the crime.[11]

Many authors have written about what the essential requirements are for criminal compliance programmes, and the International Organization for Standardization (ISO) and the Spanish Organization of Standardization (UNE) 19600–19601 also provide greater detail on the key provisions of a compliance programme.

---

[8]   Judgement of Caceres Provincial Court no. 203/2015, 2nd Section, 08 May 2015, La Ley 57186/2015, Tena Aragón, María Félix, lead magistrate, Legal Foundation (LF) 5th and B. Feijoo Sánchez, El delito corporativo en el Código Penal Español. Cumplimiento normativo y fundamento de la responsabilidad penal de las empresas, Aranzadi, 2nd ed., 2016, pp. 116–117 and Fiscalía General del Estado, Circular 1/2016, sobre la Responsabilidad Penal de las Personas Jurídicas conforme a la reforma del Código Penal efectuada por Ley Orgánica 1/2015, 2016, p. 14.

[9]   It is necessary to understand that "on behalf of and on account of the enterprise or in their exercise of corporate activities" means that the crimes have been committed regarding the specific powers of the enterprise and in the exercise of these competences. In this sense, it is necessary to underline not only that "direct or indirect benefits" are economic benefits but also that these benefits may be strengths over other legal entities, cost savings, social image improvement or the avoidance of economic damage to the enterprise. See in Feijoo, supra, note 8 at p. 28, and Fiscalía General del Estado, supra, note 8.

[10]   Article 31bis second paragraph SCC.

[11]   Article 31bis fourth paragraph SCC.

In a more general a vague way, the SCC points out these six requirements[12] of a criminal compliance programme:

(i)   the identification of activities where the crimes which should be prevented can be committed, analysing the environmental risks;

(ii)   the provision of protocols or procedures to establish the forming of the willpower (intention of the legal person to take its economical, managerial and legal decisions) of the enterprise, and how decisions are adopted and executed by the legal entity; in other words, the provision of protocols to establish an adequate environmental policy, for instance the policy on anything from the recycling of office supplies to the most onerous disposal of waste;

(iii)   the provision of a model of financial management able to avoid the commission of crimes that should be prevented;

(iv)   the duty to report to the compliance officer or compliance board about potential risks and wrongful behaviours; regarding this, there should be an appropriate system of reporting channels where whistleblower rights are protected;

(v)   the implementation of an effective sanctioning system when the compliance programme is not conformed to; concerning this last point, disciplinary sanctions imposed by the manager, which are similar to sanctions relating to non-compliance with health and safety measures, are needed; and

(vi)   regularly assessing the prevention model and the amendments to it when relevant infringements are committed or when there are changes in the organisation, the control structure or the economic activity of the enterprise.

This last stipulation results in the recording and systematisation of the whole compliance structure, considering that there are some private bodies that certify the legitimacy of these programmes. However, it is compulsory for judges to assess the compliance programmes by themselves.

3.   GENERAL REMARKS ON THE SPANISH CRIMINAL CODE REGARDING ENVIRONMENTAL CRIMES

Article 325 SCC, dating to 1995, covers basic environmental crime, but the article was redrafted on 7 July 2015.[13] The protected good is the environment, and more

---

[12]   Article 31bis (5) SCC.
[13]   Organic Law 1/2015, of 30 March, amending Organic Law 10/1995, of 23 November, on Spanish Criminal Law (Spanish OJ 77 of 31 March 2015).

specifically, the balance of the natural world, in other words, the maintenance of the soil, water and the habitats of wildlife and other species.

The article includes a number of essential elements. First of all, it requires European, state, autonomous and local law and regulations to have been breached, on the basis that these regulations and laws arise from legislative and executive powers.

Second, a basic environmental crime must damage the quality of the air, soil or water or cause damage to wildlife (Article 325, first paragraph) and present a potential danger (Article 325, first and second paragraphs) i.e. the polluting act should have the ability to endanger the environment. In this respect, an act is capable of causing pollution based on the composition of the chemical(s) discharged, the extent of the discharge and the duration and effects of the polluting act.[14] It is worth noting that the principles and standards used by judges and courts to verify the act's capacity to pollute are as follows: the extent to which people's health is endangered, the danger to the natural conditions of ecosystems, the features of the discharge as well as the changes on plant and animal life conditions.[15]

Third, the environmental damage should be serious, but not be qualified as irreversible and devastating (an aggravating factor of Article 326 SCC). Additionally, this damage should go beyond substantial damage as defined in European Directive 2008/99/EC. Over and above that, when the polluting act is carried out, it must produce physical results: emissions, discharges, radiation, extractions, digs, siltation, injections, vibrations, deposits and illegal water harvesting. The most widespread crime committed by enterprises that is dealt with by the provincial courts is the crime of noise pollution.

The polluting act must affect transboundary areas. In other words, the polluting act must affect parts of nature: the atmosphere, soil, subsoil, inland and underground waters or the high seas and the transboundary areas. The high seas means adding the definition of the court with jurisdiction into the Criminal Code. Transboundary areas can be added alongside the open sea in the list of natural sites.

In the specific cases of the polluting acts, two links should be identified: first, the behaviour or act must be what created the discharge or emission; and, second, it must be established through an expert opinion that the polluting act results in environmental damage and that this damage causes serious harm to the natural balance (Article 325, second paragraph). In the same way, the first

---

[14]   F. Muñoz Conde, C. López Peregrín & P. García Álvarez, Manual de Derecho Penal Ambiental, Tirant lo Blanch, 2nd ed., 2015, pp. 170–173.

[15]   L.M. Puente Aba, Arts. 325 y 326, in P. Faraldo Cabana (ed.), Ordenación del territorio, patrimonio histórico y medio ambiente en el Código penal y la legislación especial, 2011, p. 235, 250.

paragraph of Article 325 states that the discharge must have the capacity to cause or is causing harm to a natural resource or to wildlife.[16]

Finally, we must remember that this crime can be committed by enterprises; dogmatic discussions are taking place on how the subjective elements of criminal liability could possibly be adapted to enterprises.[17] The crime's subjective element is also recognised in the case of corporate crimes in prevailing Spanish criminal doctrine. Legal entities can commit crimes wilfully (*dolo*, the Spanish concept of intention regarding mens rea) or recklessly (*imprudencia*, the Spanish concept of negligence regarding mens rea) in terms of Article 331 SCC, that is, an environmental crime may be perpetrated not only wilfully (*dolo*) but also through serious negligence (*imprudencia grave*).

4. ENVIRONMENTAL ADMINISTRATIVE LAW VERSUS CRIMINAL LAW

The environment is usually protected by administrative and criminal law through industrial activity regulations and by the enforcement of criminal and administrative law. Regarding the link between administrative environmental law and criminal environmental law, the *non bis in idem* principle aims at achieving a coherent legal system, avoiding overlapping rules and the lawlessness of certain conducts.

It is worth noting that the *non bis in idem* principle is twofold: on the one hand, from a factual perspective, the principle prohibits applying both criminal and administrative sanctions to the same facts when the facts are identical, subject to the action and legal foundations and with the exception of being subject to special legal provisions.[18] On the other hand, from a procedural perspective,

---

[16] C. *Martínez Buján Pérez*, Derecho Penal Económico y de la Empresa. Parte Especial, Tirant lo Blanch, 5th ed., 2015, pp. 945–946; N. *Matellanes Rodríguez*, Derecho Penal del Medio Ambiente, Iustel, 2008, p. 61; *J.M. Silva Sánchez & R. Montaner Fernández*, Los delitos contra el medio ambiente Reforma Legal y Aplicación Judicial, Atelier, 2012, pp. 34–36; and E. *Gorriz Royo*, Delitos contra los recursos naturales y el medio ambiente, Tirant lo Blanch, 2015, p. 54.

[17] Certain sectors within this doctrine claim that when an enterprise wilfully perpetrates a crime, the enterprise is aware that it is causing a damage and committing a reckless crime, implying that the enterprise must have this knowledge. On the other hand, other authors advance that the subjective component of criminal liability may not be understood as in the case of natural persons, but should be inferred from the severity of the enterprise's organisational fault. As a result, the greater the organisational fault is, the more wilful the enterprise's behaviour, and the smaller the organisational fault, the more reckless the behaviour; see A. *Nieto Martin*, La Responsabilidad Penal de las Personas Jurídicas: Un modelo legislativo, Iustel, 2008, pp. 160–162.

[18] M. *Corcoy Bidasolo & J.I. Gallego Soler*, Infracción administrativa e infracción penal en el ámbito del delito medio ambiental: ne bis in ídem material y procesal. Comentario a la STC 177/1999, de 11 de octubre, Actualidad Penal 2000 (1), p. 159, 160–161.

administrative acts are outranked by judgments of the judiciary. In addition, when the administration handles a disciplinary action against a person and observes that the facts could be considered to constitute one or several crimes, the proceedings should be suspended until the court issues a judicial statement regarding that behaviour. Once the judgment is pronounced, the administration should respect the factual approach or acts as they are set out or laid down in the criminal judgment.[19]

One interpretation is that Article 325 SCC, as is the case for a number of environmental crimes in Spain, requires the violation of administrative environmental law, and this could lead to the above-mentioned conflict between these two law orders that would be resolved using the *non bis in idem* principle.

Nevertheless, regarding the link between the administrative and criminal law, two legal measures of environmental protection must be taken into account: on the one hand, the restoration of the ecological balance is recognised in Article 339 SCC for all criminal legal assessments under Title 16 of the SCC and it is not regarded as a penalty;[20] on the other hand, the enforcement of the voluntary compensation included in Article 340 SCC involves one degree less in the severity of the penalty and this measure is recognised as a specific extenuating circumstance of enterprises' criminal liability (Article 31quater (c) SCC).

In this respect, it is worth mentioning the influence of Directive 2004/35/EC[21] and of the Spanish Legislative Act 26/2007[22] on these two measures recognised in the SCC. Firstly, Directive 2004/35/EC and Legislative Act 26/2007 incorporate two European environmental principles (the polluter pays and preventive action principles); these two principles are also reflected in Articles 339 and 340 SCC

---

[19] *Muñoz Conde et al.*, *supra*, note 16 at p. 60, and Spanish Constitutional Judgment 77/1983, 2nd Chamber, 3 October 1983, La Ley 205-TC/1984, Luis Díez Picazo Ponce de León, lead magistrate, LF 3rd and 4th. As for the most recent constitutional case law (Spanish Constitutional Court Judgment 2/2003, Plenary Session, 16 January 2003, La Ley 962/2003, María Emilia Casas Bahamonde, lead magistrate), the Spanish Constitutional Court stated that Article 25 of the Spanish Constitution does not forbid a *double afflictive accusation*, but nor does it forbid the repeated sanctioning of the same facts based on the same legal argument and regarding the same subject. Moreover, the Constitutional Court also mentioned that administration labour is subsidiary; therefore, if the administration establishes an administrative penalty after a final criminal judgment, this labour penalty is illegal since the Spanish Constitution prioritises criminal proceedings over administrative proceedings due to the fact the former offers greater guarantees.

[20] The obligation to restore the ecological balance is considered a precautionary measure or a provision of tort law; see F. *Muñoz Conde et al.*, *supra*, note 16 at p. 332 and *E.M. Souto García*, Art. 339, in P. Faraldo Cabana (ed.), Ordenación del territorio, patrimonio histórico y medio ambiente en el Código Penal y la legislación especial, Tirant lo Blanch, 2011, p. 457, 464.

[21] Directive 2004/35/EC of the European Parliament and of the Council of 21 April 2004 on environmental liability with regard to the prevention and remedying of environmental damage, OJ 2004 143/56.

[22] Legislative Act 26/2007, 23 October, on Environmental Liability (Spanish OJ 255, 24 October 2007), which transposes Directive 2004/35/EC in Spain.

since these articles refer both to the restoration of ecological balance and compensation for the damage caused. In the same way, environmental criminal law aims at preventing environmental offences using a legal formulation that includes hypothetical risks, namely behaviour likely to produce environmental damage according to scientific rules.

Moreover, Directive 2004/35/EC and Legislative Act 26/2007 both target the prevention and remedying of environmental damage, while Directive 2008/99/EC aims at improving the enforcement of European environmental law. The latter Directive includes countless references to a large number of Regulations and Directives that are also relevant to Directive 2004/35/EC. Both Directives should complement each other; however, differences can be found in their enforcement and approach.

This leads to some difficulties: first of all, Directive 2004/35/EC uses indeterminate legal concepts such as "significant damage"; second, Directive 2004/35/EC and Legislative Act 26/2007 do not make it possible to easily establish the causal link between the pollution act and damage when the damage is of a diffuse nature; and lastly, both Directive 2004/35/EC and Legislative Act 26/2007present difficulties in identifying the operator who is liable and resolving the existing scarcity of preventive measures when liable persons file insolvency proceedings themselves and the damage is substantial.[23]

These shortcomings could be overcome if the concepts of environmental damage or significant damage were defined at a European level. Moreover, Directive 2004/35/EC should be modified in terms of the activities in Annex III that result in diffuse damage by adopting this legal presumption or this legal assumption: when operators are situated close to the polluted site, they would be liable for the damage as long as there is credible evidence of their liability.[24]

This latter presumption can only refer to tort liability; in other words, strict criminal liability cannot be found and the burden of proof cannot be reversed. In this sense, in the case of strict liability flowing from activities included in Annex III hat result in diffuse damage,[25] the administrative authority will not examine whether the behaviour has resulted in an administrative offence or a crime, but the causal link between the operator's activity and the damage must always be clear.

---

[23]   *G.M. Vagliasindi*, Contribution to conclusions and recommendations on environmental crime: Environmental Liability, in EFFACE (European Union Action to Fight Environmental Crime), 2016, pp. 4–5, and *T. Fajardo & J. Fuentes*, The Aznalcollar and the Kolontar Mining Accidents: A case study on mining accidents and the criminal responsibility of operators and administrations. A study compiled as part of the EFFACE project, 2014, p. 39.

[24]   *G.M. Vagliasindi, supra*, note 25 at pp. 7–9.

[25]   We must remember that if the activities are other than those listed in Annex III of Directive 2004/35/EC, no strict liability obliges the operator to repair; as a consequence, the remedying of the damage could be requested under this law if the liability is administrative liability, or it also could be requested under Article 339 SCC when the act is an environmental crime. Nevertheless, it is necessary to prove the liability of the enterprise or operator in both cases.

In this regard, concerning the European regulation (Directive 2004/35/CE of the European Parliament and of the Council of 21 April 2004 on environmental liability with regard to the prevention and remedying of environmental damage, Article 14.)on financial guarantees to bear the costs of this liability in cases of operator insolvency, the financial guarantee should be mandatory rather than voluntary, as in the case of Spain. However, this section of Legislative Act 26/2007 has not yet been enforced because insurance companies and the financial sector have established limitations on the costs that should be covered.[26] It would be advisable to insure activities that produce strict liability but do not result in diffuse damage, since these activities are included in Article 325 SCC; insurance should also be mandatory to ensure the remedying of the damage.

Lastly, the same kind of damage should be referred to in both Directive 2004/35/EC and Directive 2008/99/EC. For example, they should incorporate damage to human health, to the environment and the high seas, and danger to biodiversity, soil and water.[27]

5. REGULATED SELF-RULE IN ENVIRONMENTAL LAW AND ENVIRONMENTAL RIGHTS

Self-regulation in administrative environmental law has been particularly relevant due to the considerable number of legal instruments relating to environmental risk and self-regulation that have come into force since the 1990s.[28]

This way, self-regulation is understood as a voluntary normative system that monitors the quality and security of products or services, based on technical standards created by enterprises and it is also understood as organisation or association that enforces and manages this voluntary normative system.[29]

The different procedures for and instruments of self-regulation have public effects over rules created privately; therefore, it may be considered to be a

---

[26]   B. Lozano Cutanda & J. C. Alli Turrillas, Administración y Legislación Ambiental. Adaptado al EEES, Administración y Legislación Ambiental. Adaptado al EEES, Dykinson, 9th ed., 2016, pp. 234–236.

[27]   G.M. Vagliasindi, supra, note 25. It should be recalled that Directive 2004/35/EC only covers danger to wildlife, water, soil, the seashore and riversides; consequently, some places protected by Directives 2008/99/EC and 2009/129/EC and by Article 325 SCC are not protected by Directive 2004/35/EC.

[28]   R. Montaner Fernández, La autorregulación normativa en el Derecho Penal Ambiental: Problemas desde la perspectiva del Principio de Legalidad, in J.P. Montiel (ed.), La crisis del Principio de Legalidad en el nuevo Derecho Penal: ¿Decadencia o evolución?, Marcial Pons, 2012, p. 289, 291.

[29]   J. Esteve Pardo, Derecho del medio ambiente, Marcial Pons, 1st ed., 2005, pp. 135–136 and B. Lozano Cutanda, supra, note 28 at p. 321.

non-coactive compliance method. By contrast, on the penal side, this kind of regulation could lead to a privatisation of the development of laws since big enterprises could select the environmental protection that better fits their purposes, which may not necessarily be the best environmental course of action. In other words, private bodies "settle a social conflict out of court": they both indicate and distribute permitted risks.[30]

One of the most significant recent examples of self-regulation available in the market[31] is the best available technologies (BAT), which act as a reference in fixing the emissions limits of polluting substances found in the norm that regulates integrated environmental authorisation.[32] The BATs try to prevent contamination as much as possible through technologies that aim at the very sources of pollution, replacing "end of pipe" technologies.[33]

The BAT for each branch of industry are provided via the Seville Process, where the Forum for Exchange of Information is located. They are composed by Member States' representatives, ENGOs and technical groups from each corresponding industrial branch. This Forum draws up the BAT Reference Documents (BREF), which are approved and published by the European Commission via Decisions,[34] and which, in turn, are used to draw up the "Conclusions about the BAT".[35]

---

[30] A. Nieto Martín, Autorregulación, "Compliance" y justicia restaurativa, in L. Arroyo Jiménez & A. Nieto Martín, Autorregulación y Sanciones, 2nd ed., Thomson Reuters Aranzadi, 2015, p. 81, 103–105, and *M.G. Bermejo & O. Palermo*, La intervención delictiva del Compliance Officer, in L. Kuhlen, J.P. Montiel & I. Ortiz de Urbina, Compliance y Teoría del Derecho Penal, Marcial Pons, 2013, p. 171, 184–186.

[31] The BAT are established by the most advanced technical standards developed by private entities that fix the limiting values to reduce or avoid pollution, but the BAT never make mandatory any specific kind of technology.

[32] The legal foundation of the integrated environmental authorisation is formed by Directive 2010/75/EU of the European Parliament and of the Council of 24 November 2010 on Industrial Emissions (integrated pollution prevention and control) (Recast) (text with EEA relevance), OJ 2010 L 334/17; Legislative Decree 1/2016, of 16 December, approving the consolidated text of the Law on the Integrated Pollution and Prevention Control (Spanish OJ 316, 31 December 2016); and Legislative Decree 815/2013, of 18 October, approving the Regulation industrial emissions and the development of Legislative Act 16/2002, of 1 July, on the Integrated Pollution and Prevention Control (Spanish OJ 251, 19 October 2013).

[33] B. Lozano Cutanda, *supra*, note 28 at p. 278; *A. Betancor Rodríguez*, Derecho Ambiental, La Ley, 1st ed., 2014, p. 1132; and *B. Lozano Cutanda, A. Lago Candeira & L.F. López Álvarez*, Tratado de Derecho Ambiental, Centro de Estudios Financieros, 1st ed., 2014, p. 448.

[34] A decision, according to Article 288 TFEU, "shall be binding in its entirety. A decision which specifies those to whom it is addressed shall be binding only on them".

[35] These documents have been legally binding since 2013; therefore, enterprises cannot exceed the emission limit values established in the "Conclusions about the BAT". However, this does not imply the use of a specific technology when an industrial activity which is regulated in Legislative Decree 1/2016 is executed. See *B. Lozano Cutanda, supra*, note 28 at pp. 281–284; *A. Betancor Rodríguez, supra*, note 35 at p. 1325; and Article 7(1)(a) Legislative Decree 1/2016.

In this light, it is possible to refer to the enforcement in the EU and in Spain, respectively, of the Aarhus International Convention[36] and the Legislative Act 27/2006.[37] The idea is to change the law to allow ENGOs to receive information about criminal compliance programmes in a suitable way, as well as to consent to their participation in the development of these programmes, similarly to the Seville Process. Moreover, this participation should be accompanied by the supervision of the enforcement of these programmes, granting ENGOs access to environmental justice when environmental crimes and offences are committed.

In other words, this chapter proposes a checks-and-balances system where ecological organisations participate, at an international level, in the development of compliance norms, as well as in the monitoring of the compliance programmes once approved by the Spanish administration. This proposal should be completed by granting ENGOs access to environmental justice under both administrative and criminal law.[38]

Finally, as a consequence, this system would reflect real law enforcement that incorporates the polluter pays and prevention principles, as well as trust in justice.

6. CONCLUSION

To sum up, concerning self-regulation in environmental protection via criminal law, it would be advisable to avoid privatisation of settlements in environmental conflicts. To achieve this objective, regulated self-rule should involve the

---

[36]   The United Nations Economic Commission for Europe (UNECE) Convention on Access to Information, Public Participation in Decision-Making and Access to Justice in Environmental Matters was adopted on 25 June 1998 in the Danish city of Aarhus.

[37]   Legislative Act 27/2006, of 18 July, regulating the environmental rights of access to information, public participation and environmental justice access (incorporating Directives 2003/4/EC and 2003/35/EC) (Spanish OJ 171, 19 July 2006, pp. 27109–27123). A. Peñalver I Cabré, Novedades en el acceso a la justicia y a la tutela administrativa en asuntos medio ambientales, in A. Pigrau I Solé (ed.), Acceso a la información, participación pública y acceso a la justicia en materia de medio ambiente: diez años del Convenio de Aarhus, Atelier, 2009, p. 349, 355–356. Both legal texts pick up the environmental rights of access to information, participation and access to justice on the administrative side and this should be complemented by the Criminal Procedure Code – Royal Decree of 14 September 1882 approving Criminal Procedure Code (Spanish OJ 260, 17 September 1882) – which allows the exercise of popular action in the case of environmental crimes.

[38]   The protection of the environment by environmental organisations in criminal proceedings in Spain is found in Articles 7(3) and 19(1) of the Organic Law of Judicial Power, as well as in Articles 101, 270, 280 and 281 of the Criminal Proceeding Code. See R. Castillejo Manzanares, El ejercicio de la acción penal, in Hacia un nuevo proceso penal. Cambios necesarios, Editorial La Ley, 2010, pp. 6–7, and R. Sánchez Gómez, El ejercicio de la acción popular a tenor de la jurisprudencia del Tribunal Supremo, Revista Jurídica de los Derechos Sociales. Lex Social 2016 (6), p. 284, 286–287.

participation of ENGOs and should be completed with a pyramidal system of private and public penalties, for instance administrative and criminal penalties.

Regarding Annex III liability (Directive 2004/35), one of the solutions could be to establish the presumption of an operator's environmental liability when it operates near the origin of the pollution, provided there is credible evidence of the link between the action of the operator and the polluting act.

Additionally, the voluntary guarantee to repair environmental damage should be mandatory and the meaning of environmental damage should be the same in Legislative Act 26/2007 and the SCC as in Directive 2004/35, and Directives 2008/99/EC and 2009/123/EC, covering damage to human health, the environment, the high seas, wildlife, soil and water.

PART IV

LEGAL TRANSPLANTS IN THE ENVIRONMENTAL FIELD

The Case of Environmental Liability

THE CERCLA MODEL

Past, Present and Future

Marta CENINI

1. INTRODUCTION: CERCLA AS A POINT OF REFERENCE FOR DIRECTIVE 2004/35

The Comprehensive Environmental Response Compensation and Liability Act (commonly referred to as CERCLA or Superfund) is one of the major environmental federal statutes of the United States of America and was passed by Congress on 11 December 1980.[1] Its origin dates back and is linked to the tragedy that occurred in the State of New York on 2 August 1978 (the so-called Love Canal tragedy),[2] and more generally to the ecological disasters that occurred during that decade.[3] At that time, Congress's primary goal was to

---

[1] CERCLA has generated a vast amount of literature; see in particular *J.M. Hyson*, Private Cost Recovery Actions Under CERCLA, Environmental Law Institute, 2003; *M.B. Gerrard & J.M. Gross*, Amending CERCLA: the post-SARA amendments to the Comprehensive Environmental Response, Compensation, And Liability Act, American Bar Association, 2006; *C.S. Switzer & P. Gray*, CERCLA: Comprehensive Environmental Response, Compensation, and Liability Act (Superfund), ABA Book Publishing, 2006. See also the general handbook *T.F.P. Sullivan* (ed.), Environmental Law Handbook, Bernan Press, 23rd ed., 2017, and in particular *R.E. Cardwell & J.O. King*, Comprehensive Environmental Response, Compensation and Liability Act, in id. at pp. 585 et seq.

[2] Between 1941 and 1954 about 20,000 tonnes of toxic waste had been lawfully deposited by a chemical company in a trench called "Love Canal" in the State of New York. Afterwards, the trench had been covered with a clay clap and, even if the wastes had not been securely encapsulated or removed, a school and houses had been built on and around it. Only in 1978 the wastes were discovered: families had been evacuated and the clean-ups started, which costed millions of dollars. As said in the paragraph, after two years the Congress enacted the CERCLA which, bearing in mind this tragedy, addressed for the first time the problem of remediating historic contamination.

[3] For a list of ecological disasters that occurred during the 1970s see *S.M. Wiegard*, The Brownfields Act: Providing Relief for the Innocent or New Hurdles to Avoid CERCLA Liability?, Wm. & Mary Envtl. L. & Pol'y Rev. 2003 (28), p. 127, 130. The Love Canal Tragedy triggered many judicial cases, among which see in particular United States v. Hooker Chemicals & Plastics Corp., 680 F. Supp. 546 (W.D. N.Y. 1988).

clean up inactive and abandoned hazardous waste sites and at the same time to prevent taxpayers from having to bear the related costs; for this reason, CERCLA imposed liability on a long list of "potentially responsible parties" (PRPs).

The list also includes past[4] and current owners and operators of the facility from which the release of hazardous substances occurred, owners and operators of the site or facility where a hazardous substance has come to be located, and even anyone who "arranged for disposal" of the hazardous substance.[5] Until very recently,[6] the liability was considered strict and joint and several;[7] having to deal with historic contamination and abandoned hazardous waste sites, the Act also had retroactive applicability. At the time the Act was issued, any landowners (whether "innocent" or not) who have had a "contractual relationship"[8] with the polluter, as well as any person who exercised any kind of control[9] over the activity or the substance ("operator" or "arranger"), was thus considered responsible for the full costs of clean-up.[10]

The two major legislative reforms that occurred in 1986 and 2002 have not changed the approach; CERCLA's major focus still remains the clean-up of inactive hazardous waste sites and the distribution of clean-up costs among certain parties who had any involvement with the hazardous substances.[11]

---

[4]   The past owner is the owner of the facility at the time the disposal of hazardous substances occurred.

[5]   See §2 on the definition of "potentially responsible parties". The definition of "facility" is so broad that it includes buildings, structures, installations, equipment and pipelines, as well as any site where a hazardous substance has come to be located (42 U.S.C. §9601(9)). See on this *Cardwell & King, supra*, note 1 at p. 591, note 38 for case law.

[6]   See §3 of this Chapter.

[7]   The recent judgment Burlington Northern & Santa Fe Ry. Co. v. United States, 129 S. Ct. 1870 (2009) has actually challenged this statement and recent case law addresses partial liability.

[8]   See §4 of this Chapter.

[9]   See §2 of this Chapter regarding the so-called "control test".

[10] At the time the Act was issued, it was under discussion whether instruments of transfer of ownership or interest in real estate such as deeds, leases, and other forms of conveyance were to be included in the term "contractual relationship"; the courts tended to answer affirmatively and CERCLA was thus used to impose liability for clean-up costs on landowners based solely on their status as landowners. See *C. Nampewo*, CERCLA: Determining Ownership Liability for Possessory Interests in Real Property, 39 B.C. Envtl. Aff. L. Rev. E. Supp. 2012, p. 83. Afterwards SARA clarified this at Section 101(35)(A) but also introduced an exemption from liability for "innocent" landowners. See on this *P.C. Quinn*, The EPA Guidance on Landowner Liability and the Innocent Landowner Defense: The All Appropriate Inquiry Standard: Fact or Fiction, Vill. Envtl. L.J. 1991 (2), p. 143.

[11] CERCLA is specifically designed to address contamination associated with hazardous substances, which are defined by Section 101(14) and consist of hazardous substances as defined by the Clean Water Act, toxic pollutants, hazardous air pollutants and others. Petroleum is expressly excluded from the definition, which means for example that gasoline service stations cannot be subject of CERCLA actions. Generic pollutants or contaminants are also considered, but can be subject to intervention by the EPA only. The majority of CERCLA actions have thus been response actions associated with a release of a hazardous

However, since the very beginning, CERCLA has also contained provisions to protect damages to natural resources; in this case, government claims aim to recover costs associated with the loss of a contaminated area's natural resources (Section 107(a)(4)(C)). As we shall see, considering that the protection of natural resources is granted by the use of trust law principles, this represented and still represents a very innovative approach.[12]

During the discussion that led to the enactment of Directive 2004/35/EC on environmental liability, the European legislator carefully considered the American model.[13] The comparison and the attention was devoted in particular to questions such as the notion of environmental damage and scope of the regime, the nature of liability (strict or for negligence) and related defences, the retroactivity of the new rules and of course the criteria for identifying the liable parties. The European Commission's White Paper on environmental liability,[14] published in 2000, in particular aimed at outlining the pillars of the future European Directive on environmental liability of 2004 and took a position on the debated issues, bearing in mind the US model.

Regarding in particular the criteria for establishing liability, the White Paper indicated that the liable parties should be the "operators" who exercise control over the polluting activity, but also considered the position of the landowners and occupiers of the land and the related so-called "innocent landowner

---

substances into the "environment" in a broad sense: indeed, this includes surface water, groundwater, drinking water, land surface, subsurface strata, and ambient air.

[12] For a comparison with the European approach, see B. Pozzo, Danno ambientale e responsabilità. Esperienze giuridiche a confronto, Giuffrè, 1996, pp. 151 et seq.

[13] Many influential scholars have carried out the comparison between the European model and the American one, underlining the influence of the latter upon the former. See in particular: B. Pozzo, Towards Civil Liability for Environmental Damage in Europe: the "White Paper" of the Commission of the European Communities, Global Jurist 2001 (1), pp. 30 ss.; Pozzo, supra, note 12; B. Pozzo (ed.), Property and Environment. Old and New Remedies to Protect Natural Resources in the European Context, The Common Core of European Private Law, The Trento Project, Mauro Bussani and Ugo Mattei, general editors, Stämpfli/Carolina Academic Press/Sakkoulas/Bruylant, 2007; A. Gambaro (ed.), La responsabilità delle imprese in campo ambientale, IPA-Servizi, 1997; B. Pozzo, B. Vanheusden, L. Bergkamp & E. Brans, The Remediation of Contaminated Sites and the Problem of Assessing the Liability of the Innocent Landowner: A Comparative Law Perspective, ERPL 2015 (6), pp. 1071 et seq.; M.L. Larsson, The Law of Environmental Damage: Liability and Reparation, Kluwer Law International, 1999; V. Fogleman, Landowners' liability for remediating contaminated land in the EU: EU or national law? Part II: National law, Env. Liability: Law, Policy and Practice 2015 (2), pp. 42 et seq.; W.R. Wilkerson & T.W. Church, The Gorilla in the Closet: Joint and Several Liability and the Cleanup of Toxic Waste Sites, Law and Policy 1989 (11), p. 425; M. Tabatabai, Comparing U.S. and EU Hazardous Waste Liability Frameworks: How The EU Liability Directive Competes with CERCLA, Hous. J. Int'l L. 2012 (34), pp. 653 et seq.

[14] White Paper on Environmental Liability, COM(2000) 66 final. See on this Pozzo, Towards Civil Liability for Environmental Damage in Europe, supra, note 13 at pp. 29 et seq. The White Paper was preceded by the Green Paper on remedying environmental damage, which was published by the Commission in 1993.

defence";[15] as said, landowners are primary liable parties according to CERCLA and the "innocent landowner defence" is a creation of US courts, then codified by the first CERCLA amendment Act of 1986. The following 2002 Proposal for a Directive on environmental liability[16] paid specific attention to so-called "orphan sites", which again reveals a consideration for the American model.

During recent decades CERCLA has evolved significantly, thanks in particular to the legislative reform enacted with the Brownfield Act in 2002 and to the interpretation of the courts. It is thus necessary to understand where CERCLA is going and what are the most innovative provisions that still provide a model for European lawyers.

The chapter is divided into 4 sections. Section 2 will discuss the position of PRPs and in particular of the owner of the contaminated site or of the facility where the hazardous substances come to be located; as we shall see, this appears to be one of the most characteristic features of the American model and also one of the most criticised ones. Section 3 will give an overview of the pillars of CERCLA, which are known for imposing a strict, joint and several, and retroactive liability but have been recently called into question; indeed, recent case law has lessened the rigor of some provisions, especially with regard to the idea that the liability must always be joint and several. Section 4 will discuss the defences to liability with an emphasis on the so-called "innocent landowner defence" and the other defences introduced by the Brownfield Act. As we shall see, the initial broad interpretation of these liability provisions has been reconsidered in the light of a more balanced equilibrium between the different interests. The last section will be a sketch of the protection of natural resources through the trust instrument as established by CERCLA. As suggested, since trusts have been object of great attention by civil lawyers in recent decades, especially with regard to protection of environment and cultural heritage, this may represent the future of environmental protection in a European context as well.

2. THE EPA's AUTHORITY TO REMEDIATE AND NOTION OF "POTENTIALLY RESPONSIBLE PARTIES"

CERCLA first and foremost is a nationwide programme designed to address the problems of historical contaminations and the past disposal of hazardous substances. It gives a federal agency, the Environmental Protection Agency (EPA),[17]

---

15   See also on this *Pozzo, Vanheusden, Bergkamp & Brans, supra*, note 13 at p. 1073.
16   Proposal for a Directive of the European Parliament and of the Council on Environmental Liability with regard to the Prevention and Remedying of Environmental Damage, COM(2002) 17 final.
17   The EPA was set up by President Nixon in 1970 and its mission is to protect human health and the environment. It has authority to implement national environmental law through

the authority to clean up hazardous waste sites. These clean-ups are funded by the "Hazardous Substance Superfund", and for this reason, CERCLA is also known by the nickname "Superfund". The Superfund is mainly financed by taxes imposed upon the petroleum and chemical industries and by an environmental tax on corporations; other contributions come from general tax revenue. In 1981, the National Priorities List was established as a part of the National Contingency Plan and the EPA has the duty to determine priorities among the various releases or threatened releases throughout the United States.

In particular, under Section 104(a)(1), the EPA is authorised to remove and provide for remedial actions relating to hazardous substances or pollutants or contaminants whenever any hazardous substance is released, or there is a substantial threat of such release into the environment, or there is a release or substantial threat of release of any pollutant or contaminant that may present and imminent and substantial danger to the public health or welfare. The EPA can undertake two different types of response actions, that is to say removal actions, which specifically deal with environmental emergencies, and remedial actions, which by contrast are long-term, permanent clean-ups.[18]

Section 107 permits the EPA to ask for reimbursement of clean-up costs associated with hazardous substances from a series of PRPs;[19] the EPA has the authority to respond to a release of "any pollutant or contaminant which may present an imminent and substantial danger to public health or welfare",[20] but in this case the EPA cannot recover its clean-up costs from private parties. Under Section 106, the EPA can issue an administrative order[21] and can also seek a judicial injunction requiring a liable party to abate an imminent and substantial endangerment to public health, welfare or the environment (so-called abatement actions); as above, this is possible only with regard to hazardous substances.[22]

---

regulations, which it also has power to enforce. It also sets national standards that states enforce through their own regulations.

[18] For further details, see *Cardwell & King, supra*, note 1 at p. 594.

[19] 42 U.S.C. §9607. These are referred to "cost recovery provisions". As said Section 107 allows the federal state (actually the EPA), individual states and damaged individuals to initiate legal action against one of the PRPs in order to recover the costs that the actors may have incurred in order to repair environmental damage. As we will see, this action has recently created delicate coordination problems with that provided for by Section 113(f), which is mainly dedicated to the right of compensation.

[20] 42 U.S.C. §9604. These are referred to "abatement provisions".

[21] CERCLA permits the EPA to take certain administrative actions to compel private parties to undertake actions necessary to protect public health, welfare or the environment.

[22] See Section 106: "(a) Maintenance, jurisdiction, etc. In addition to any other action taken by a State or local government, when the President determines that there may be an imminent and substantial endangerment to the public health or welfare or the environment because of an actual or threatened release of a hazardous substance from a facility, he may require the Attorney General of the United States to secure such relief as may be necessary to abate such

Especially when there is not an imminent danger to public health,[23] the clean-up procedure should thus be first carried out by the EPA and then reimbursed by the responsible parties; however, most of the time, the EPA starts the proceeding by issuing a letter to these PRPs and then negotiates with them which measure they shall carry out.[24] Consequently, most of the time the remedial measures are performed directly by private parties who fall under the definition of PRPs.[25]

The notion of PRPs is thus crucial. Section 107 (a) CERCLA, entitled "Covered persons; scope; recoverable costs and damages; interest rate; 'comparable maturity' date", reads:

> Notwithstanding any other provision or rule of law, and subject only to the defenses set forth in subsection (b) of this section –
>
> (1) the owner and operator of a vessel or a facility,
> (2) any person who at the time of disposal of any hazardous substance owned or operated any facility at which such hazardous substances were disposed of,
> (3) any person who by contract, agreement, or otherwise arranged for disposal or treatment, or arranged with a transporter for transport for disposal or treatment, of hazardous substances owned or possessed by such person, by any other party or entity, at any facility or incineration vessel owned or operated by another party or entity and containing such hazardous substances, and
> (4) any person who accepts or accepted any hazardous substances for transport to disposal or treatment facilities, incineration vessels or sites selected by such person, from which there is a release, or a threatened release which causes the incurrence of response costs, of a hazardous substance, shall be liable for –
>   (A) all costs of removal or remedial action incurred by the United States Government or a State or an Indian tribe not inconsistent with the national contingency plan;
>   (B) any other necessary costs of response incurred by any other person consistent with the national contingency plan;

---

danger or threat, and the district court of the United States in the district in which the threat occurs shall have jurisdiction to grant such relief as the public interest and the equities of the case may require. The President may also, after notice to the affected State, take other action under this section including, but not limited to, issuing such orders as may be necessary to protect public health and welfare and the environment."

[23] Section 106 abatement actions should be triggered only in case of "imminent and substantial endangerment"; however, courts have had little difficulty in finding that such an endangerment exists since the standard necessary to establish the "imminent and substantial endangerment" is minimal. Consequently, the EPA has routinely filed suits containing both causes of action (Sections 106 and 107). See on this *Cardwell & King, supra*, note 1 at p. 620.

[24] https://www.epa.gov/enforcement/superfund-notice-liability-letters See also on this *Cardwell & King, supra*, note 1 at p. 607.

[25] See on this *Pozzo*, Property and Environment, *supra*, note 13 at pp. 56–57.

(C)   damages for injury to, destruction of, or loss of natural resources, including the reasonable costs of assessing such injury, destruction, or loss resulting from such a release; and

(D)   the costs of any health assessment or health effects study carried out under section 9604 (i) of this title.

According to this section, anyone having some involvement with the creation, handling or disposal of the hazardous substance or who is currently the owner or manager of the site or facility that requires clean-up is considered liable. In particular, the current owner of the site where the dangerous substances come to be found is a PRP even if they bought the contaminated land *after* the release and after all disposal activities have ceased, and regardless of whether they had any involvement in the handling, disposal or treatment of hazardous wastes at the facility or whether hazardous substances were disposed of at the facility during their period of ownership.[26] Ownership must be established with regard to the time a clean-up is performed or the time litigation is initiated.

Those who were owners and operators of the site at the time of the release of the substances are also responsible, even if they have not contributed to the release or disposal of the substances and/or were unaware of the contamination (for example, in the case of migration of contaminants[27]). Finally, the producers of the pollutant or waste are also responsible, as well as those who have organised the disposal or carried out the transport to the site subject to decontamination.

As scholars point out,[28] the extensive definition of current owner and operator has lead courts to find liable even lessees, mining companies, corporate officials, employees, managers, parent corporations[29] and lenders;[30] even banks that gave credit to the corporation were thus found liable, which led to a significant reduction of credit for companies operating potentially polluting activities. Liability has thus been found in situations where the application of traditional notions of corporate liability, and in particular the notion of limited

---

[26]   Ashley 11 of Charleston, LLC v. PCS Nitrogen, Inc., 2010 WL 4025885 (D.S.C. Oct. 13, 2010); United States v. Tyson, 1986 U.S. Dist. LEXIS 21325 (E.D. Pa. 1986). See section 4 of this chapter about the "innocent landowner defence".

[27]   However, see on this the amendment made by the Brownfield Act to the definition of owner or operator; now excluded from these categories is any person who owns property that is "contiguous to or otherwise similarly situated with respect to, and that is or may be contaminated by a release of a hazardous substance from real property that is not owned by that person".

[28]   *Cardwell & King, supra,* note 1 at pp. 613–614 for references of case law.

[29]   On this see *E.L. Yeo,* United States v. Bestfoods: Narrowing Parent Corporation Liability Under CERCLA for the twenty first century, Admin. L. Rev. 1999 (51), p. 1267.

[30]   *J.P. Morgan,* Lender Liability: Civil Liability Regimes for Environmental Harm, ILSA J. Int'l & Comp. L. 1995–1996 (2), p. 139. See also *Lender Liability of Contaminated Land,* United States v. Fleet Factors Corp, Journal of Environmental Law 1992 (4), p. 145; *R. Hooley,* Lender liability for environmental damage, Cambridge L.J. 2001 (139), p. 405.

liability of corporations, would exempt individuals from liability. Based on Sections 101(20)(A) and 107(a)(3), which consider liable also the "arrangers" of the hazardous substances, courts have designed the so-called "control test": any individual corporate officer or a parent corporation can be found liable if either has exercised control over a corporation's hazardous waste handling and disposal activities.

This was one of the key points that the European legislation considered and rejected. The White Paper[31] indicates as liable parties the "operators", which are the "persons who exercise the control of an activity by which the damage is caused", and stressed that "where the activity is carried out by a company in the form of a legal person, liability will rest on the legal person and not on the managers (decision makers) or other employees who may have been involved in the activity". Moreover, the White Paper adds that "lenders not exercising operational control should not be liable". This position was then confirmed in the final version of the Environmental Liability Directive (ELD) which, in Article 2, defines the "operator'" as "any natural or legal, private or public person who operates or controls the occupational activity or, where this is provided for in national legislation, to whom decisive economic power over the technical functioning of such an activity has been delegated, including the holder of a permit or authorisation for such an activity or the person registering or notifying such an activity".

3. STRICT, JOINT AND SEVERAL, AND RETROACTIVE LIABILITY

As mentioned in the introduction, during the early 1980s the most authoritative interpretation of CERCLA provisions established that the liability for remediating contamination is strict, joint and several, and retroactive;[32] furthermore, proof of causation is limited to demonstrating that a dangerous substance has been released: when the decontamination concerns sites where many parties have come in succession, it is not required to track or fingerprint each PRP's hazardous substance.[33]

---

[31] The White Paper on Environmental Liability, COM(2000) 66 final. See on this *Pozzo*, Towards Civil Liability for Environmental Damage in Europe, *supra*, note 13 at pp. 29 et seq. See also *Tabatabai, supra*, note 13 at p. 667.

[32] See on this *Cardwell & King, supra*, note 1 at p. 604 and the following footnotes for further references.

[33] There is no causation requirement with regard to individual defendants at multiparty sites where there has been a release. In CERCLA Section 107 the issue of causation has been reduced to whether a release or threatened release has caused the plaintiff to incur response costs. See on this *Cardwell & King, supra*, note 1 at p. 604.

The idea that the liability is "strict" came from an interpretation of Section 101(32), which reads that "[t]he terms '"liable" and '"liability"' under this title shall be construed to be the standard of liability which obtains under Section 311 of the Federal Water Pollution Control Act". Indeed, as courts have always interpreted the latter Act as imposing strict liability, this understanding was reached regarding CERCLA also; the party cannot thus avoid liability by claiming that they were not negligent.

Joint and several liability means that even if a party is responsible only for a portion of the damage together with other parties, each of them can be individually required to bear the entire cost of restoration. Despite the fact that there is no mandatory rule in CERCLA which suggests this,[34] and despite the fact that common law recognises the so-called divisibility defence,[35] courts have always found such liability under CERCLA until very recently (see below). At multiparty sites, during the liability phase of the case against the EPA, defendants succeed very rarely by arguing that the damage was divisible or capable of apportionment, and thus were always found joint and several liable.[36] Moreover, several courts have established that within the scope of the remedial actions, the operators may also be obliged to bear the costs of remediation connected to so-called "orphan sites", that is, the costs of remediation interventions for pollution attributable to insolvent or unidentifiable or localisable subjects.

Only recently, in response to criticism of this approach by the parties involved and by commentators, the Supreme Court, in the *Burlington Northern & Santa Fe Railway Co. v. United States* case, stated that when the portion of damage is attributable to the conduct of a particular person, the latter may not be subject to joint and several liability (the so-called divisibility defence). This sentence has been amply commented on and amplified by scholars, as it has been seen as an important step towards partial liability.

However, parties can ask courts for equitable allocation of costs in a Section 113 contribution action. Section 113(f) was added by the Superfund Amendments and Reauthorization Act (SARA) in 1986 and governs the rights of contribution against the co-responsible parties. In these actions it is possible to assert the different causal contribution of each PRP, but the final determination of the respective shares of responsibility is assessed by the judge with broad discretion. To this end, a series of parameters have been used, including in particular the Gore Factors (so called because they are based on the legislative

---

[34]   Congress had even deleted provisions imposing joint and several liability from CERCLA before its enactment.

[35]   Traditionally, joint and several liability does not exist where the harm is divisible or reasonably capable of apportionment.

[36]   The divisibility of harm argument and the question of contribution to the damage may eventually be raised during the secondary proceedings among the parties once they have been already deemed jointly and severally liable.

amendment proposals of the then Senator Al Gore); among these factors one find the volume of hazardous substances which each party has contributed to, the degree of toxicity of each party's waste, the extent to which each party was involved in the management of the substances, the degree of care, and finally the degree of cooperation with government officials.

In the famous case *Cooper Industries, Inc. v. Aviall Services, Inc.* the Supreme Court established, on the basis of a literal interpretation of the law, that the claimant could recover the costs of remediation pursuant to Section 113 with respect to other responsible parties only if the interventions had been ordered by the EPA (Section 106), or were the object of a transaction with the EPA itself or with the states, or still ordered by the judicial authority as part of a dispute initiated pursuant to Section 107. Consequently, the right of contribution was excluded in event that the party initiated the clean-up procedure spontaneously.[37]

This ruling created great confusion and led the courts to probe various alternative routes; the subsequent judgment in *United States v. Atlantic Research Corp.* clarified (but at the same time created other discussions) that the operators who has spontaneously carried out the interventions can and must act pursuant to Section 107[38] (and not Section 113) towards the other parties, but in this case they cannot claim for costs such as those arising from settlement agreements, convictions or orders from the EPA.[39]

4. "LANDOWNER DEFENCES"

As mentioned, the current owner is considered a PRP together with other parties, and at the beginning there was no clear distinction among the landowners on the basis of their knowledge of the contamination. SARA in 1986 clarified some ambiguities of the legislation that had led to conflicting interpretation by courts[40] and thus it is only thanks to that Act that landowners may now mount the so-called "innocent landowner defence". This defence was thus the first of the group called "landowner defences".[41]

---

[37]   See on this *J. Paull*, Nor Innocent nor Proven Guilty: the Aviall Services v. Cooper Industries Dilemma, Buff. Envtl. L.J. 2005–2006 (13), p. 31.

[38]   A PRP can thus bring a cost recovery action against other PRPs based upon CERCLA Section 107(a).

[39]   *R.G. Aronovsky*, A Preemption Paradox: Preserving the Role of State Law in Private Cleanup Cost Disputes, N.Y.U. Envtl. L.J. 2008 (16), p. 225; *S.P. Brand*, The Saga Continues – Trying to find a balance in CERCLA's PRP liability suits, N.D. L. Rev. 2012 (88), p. 209.

[40]   For a reconstruction of the history that led to the introduction of the innocent landowner defence, see *Quinn, supra*, note 10 at p. 143.

[41]   In 2002 the Small Business Liability Relief and Brownfields Revitalization Act (Brownfields Act) introduced other landowner defences, in particular the contiguous property owners exception and the bone-fide prospective purchaser exception. See on this in particular *K.A. Hodson & C.H. Oldham*, Defenses to Liability Under CERCLA, Ariz. St. L.J. 2014 (46), p. 459.

The "innocent landowner defence" is an evolution of the so-called "third party defence" provided for by Section 107. Indeed, according to this section, a defendant can prove that the release of hazardous substance was caused solely by an act of God, an act of war, or by "an act of omission of a third party (other than an employee, agent, or party with whom there is a contractual relationship) as long as the defendant exercised due care and took precautions against foreseeable acts of the third party". Case law has interpreted this provision strictly, in particular stressing that the release must have been caused "solely" by the third party; thus any involvement, however slight, of any defendant makes this defence unavailable. Moreover, it has been considered that there is a "contractual relationship" with the defendant anytime the latter has entered into agreements such as leases, employment contracts, waste hauling contracts, and in general real estate sales contracts related to the polluted site.[42]

As mentioned, in 1986 SARA clarified the position of landowners who acquired the land after the contamination and introduced the so-called "innocent landowner defence" (also known as the "innocent purchaser defence") in the federal Act.

This defence allows the owner to avoid liability if he proves that he acquired the land after the disposal or placement of the hazardous substance on, in or at the facility, and that at the time of purchase he "did not know and had no reason to know that any hazardous substance which is the subject of the release or threatened release was disposed of on, in, or at the facility"[43] (in this sense they are "innocent").

CERCLA thus requires the prospective purchaser to carry out so-called "environmental due diligence"[44] in order to be exempt from liability, which means that they have to conduct accurate investigations on the site ("all appropriate inquiries").[45] The assessment is generally carried out in a standardised form, and the prospective buyer often provides the promissory seller with a list of questions of interest to the prospective buyer (a checklist). In particular, environmental due diligence will check compliance with all relevant environmental laws and the presence (or potential presence) of environmental contaminants on the

---

[42]   See *Cardwell & King, supra*, note 1 at p. 626. See also note 10 above.

[43]   See Section 107(b)(3).

[44]   The term "due diligence" usually refers to the level of diligence or care that prospective purchaser must exercise when buying a business, and is generally understood to mean a comprehensive examination of an enterprise or its assets. Indeed, especially during negotiations for mergers and acquisitions of companies, the prospective purchaser – usually represented by qualified professionals – carries out inquiries about legal and tax compliance, and about the entire managerial and operational state of the company (financial, market and also environmental matters). However due diligence, and in particular environmental due diligence, can also be carried out for the individual transfer of an immovable property through a sale contract.

[45]   See Section 101(35)(B).

site. The prospective purchaser and/or his environmental professionals will evaluate current and past property uses and occupancies, current and past use of hazardous substances, waste management and disposal activities, current and past remediation at the subject property, engineering controls (caps, paving) and institutional controls (e.g. restrictions on groundwater for drinking purposes). Finally, they will also try to obtain information concerning adjoining or nearby properties.[46]

However, especially until the 2000s, it was very rare for owners to escape liability because the EPA could always claim that due diligence, which in fact had not identified pollution that was present, had not been sufficiently thorough.

With the 2002 the Small Business Liability Relief and Brownfields Revitalization Act (the so-called Brownfields Act), the boundaries of the notion of "all appropriate inquiry" and therefore of environmental due diligence have been partially clarified, and two new exemptions for innocent owners have been introduced.[47] At the time of the signing, the then President of the United States George W. Bush stated that the new law was aimed precisely at providing protection to those who were not perpetrators of the pollution of the sites but wanted to cooperate in the remediation and restoration, and to the innocent landowners.[48] The intent of the new piece of law was to encourage, also through federal financing and private agreements, the requalification of "brownfields", that is to say of areas, usually located within urban contexts, characterised by low or medium levels of pollution and not requiring urgent interventions.[49]

The Brownfields Act therefore first introduced the so-called "de micromis exception", providing that the PRP is exempt from liability if the contribution to pollution is below a certain threshold; secondly, it created an exemption from liability for the contiguous property owners, which is applied in cases where the pollution derives from the migration of polluting substances from neighbouring lands through the aquifer.

---

[46]   M.E. Gold & M.C. Gross, Environmental Due Diligence in Real Estate Transactions, 78 PA Bar Assn. Quarterly 47 (2007). This paper is about the environmental due diligence under CERCLA but the procedure and the objectives are similar in other legal systems.

[47]   Section 223 of the following Brownfields Act of 2002, which amended CERCLA, clarified the expression "all appropriate inquiries" and charged the EPA with a duty to identify the expression more clearly and to set the required standards. In 2005, the EPA issued the Standards for Conducting All Appropriate Inquiries. See on this Gold & Gross, supra, note 46, and Cardwell & King, supra, note 1 at p. 611.

[48]   Note however that according to Section 201(35)(C) the "innocent purchaser defense" becomes unavailable if the property is later sold to another party without the owner disclosing any knowledge of contamination or waste disposal gained during his ownership.

[49]   S.M. Wiegard, The Brownfields Act: Providing Relief for the Innocent or New Hurdles to Avoid CERCLA Liability?, Wm. & Mary Envtl. L. & Pol'y Rev. 2003 (28), p. 127, 130. See also S. Fox, CE, Institutional Controls, and the Legacy of Urban Industrial Use, Envtl. L. 2012 (42), p. 1211.

Finally, more importantly, the Brownfield Act provided for a limitation of liability for the "*bona fide* prospective purchasers": the latter are those who acquired the ownership of a site while being aware of the fact that it was or could be polluted and with the specific intention to restore it. In this case, the owner, agreeing with the EPA, accepts part of the remediation interventions even though he is not responsible for the pollution. The purpose of the Act in this case was to provide an exemption from liability for those who, having carried out the appropriate investigations on the site, had actually discovered the contamination before the purchase but had deemed it convenient to purchase, taking charge of the remediation interventions (or in any case preventing the contamination situation from worsening) and proving willing to cooperate with the EPA to clear the site.

Notwithstanding the introduction of these defences, CERCLA continues to be based on the assumption that the "owner", regardless whether he contributed to the contamination or not, bears part or all costs of cleaning up and restoring the polluted lands.

By contrast, as known,[50] the ELD sets forth that the "operator"[51] – that is to say the person or undertaking whose activity[52] caused an imminent threat of or actual environmental damage[53] – is liable for preventing and remediating the environmental damage.[54] Advocate General Kokott, in the Opinion released on the occasion of the *Fipa Group* case,[55] has clearly argued that causation of environmental damage is a prerequisite for the duties laid down in the ELD and mere owners of damaged sites, who are not responsible for the damage, play no part in the system of the ELD.

---

[50] For further explanation, see *M. Cenini*, Environmental Liability and Waste: Which Responsibilities for Landowners?, in H. Tegner Anker & B. Egelund Olsen (eds.), Sustainable Management of Natural Resources. Legal Instruments and Approaches, Intersentia, 2018, which came after the 2017 EELF Conference in Copenhagen.

[51] See Article 2 (6), ELD.

[52] See Article 3 ELD; Annex III lists the activities for which an operator is strictly liable. Among these are waste management operations.

[53] The definition of environmental damage includes damage to protected species and natural habitats, water damage and land damage; see Article 2 (1), ELD.

[54] Joined Cases C-378/08 ECLI:EU:C:2010:126, C-379/08 ECLI:EU:C:2010:127, and C-380/08 ECLI:EU:C:2008:582, Raffinerie Mediterranee (ERG) SpA v. Ministro dello Sviluppo economico (see in particular para. 57); Case C-534/13 ECLI:EU:C:2015:140, Ministero dell'ambiente e della tutela del territorio e del mare v. Fipa Group s.r.l. In all the above-mentioned cases, the Advocate General was Kokott; see also her final opinions about the cases available at curia.europa.eu. These two decisions have been commented on in various reviews and journals; see, in particular, concerning the ERG cases: *B. Pozzo*, Note a margine delle recenti iniziative comunitarie in materia di responsabilità ambientale, Riv. quad. dir. amb. 2011, pp. 94 et seq.; concerning the Fipa Group case: *B. Pozzo, Vanheusden, Bergkamp & Brans, supra*, note 13 at pp. 1071 et seq.; *Fogleman, supra*, note 13.

[55] See Opinion of Advocate General Kokott in Case C-534/13, *Fipa Group*, in particular paras. 30, 33, 37, 45.

The Court of Justice, in the *Fipa Group* case, stated that Article 16 of the ELD left the possibility to Member States to introduce or maintain "more stringent provisions"[56] and in particular provisions that identify "additional responsible parties"; the Court of Justice, in the same decision, ruled that this article means that, regarding cases that are under the temporal scope of application of the Directive, whether to include of the landowner among the "responsible" parties is at the discretion of the Member States. The legislation of only three Member States (Austria, Hungary and Poland)[57] contains provisions that impose liability for preventing and remediating contaminated land and other environmental damage on a landowner who did not cause the damage; by contrast, most national legislation considers and applies the so-called "landowner defence". After the *Fipa Group* case, this interpretation has been confirmed by other judgments of the Court of Justice concerning similar cases.[58]

5. NATURAL RESOURCES DAMAGES: THE ROLE OF PUBLIC TRUST DOCTRINE

Joseph L. Sax, in a famous paper published at the end of the 1960s,[59] argued that legal entities such as the federal government and the states are to be considered *public trustees* with regard to natural resources, which would form the object of the fiduciary ownership. The author founded his argument in particular upon the public trust doctrine,[60] suggesting that its scope should cover certain interests like the air and the sea and could be employed in efforts to fight pollution, strip mining, overuse of pesticides and the destruction of wetland

---

[56] On the meaning of "more stringent measures", see *J.H. Jans & L. Squintani et al.*, "Gold plating" of European Environmental Measures?, JEEPL 2009 (4), pp. 417–435, where the authors show that Member States only sparingly and incidentally use their power to lay down or maintain more stringent environmental standards after European harmonisation. See also *H.T. Anker et al.*, Coping with EU environmental legislation: transposition principles and practices, Journal of Environmental Law 2015 (27/1), pp. 17–44.

[57] See on this *Fogleman, supra*, note 13 at p. 9.

[58] See Case C-156/14 ECLI:EU:C:2015:677, Tamoil, and Case C-592/13 ECLI:EU:C:2015:679, Ediltecnica, where the Court considered the question referred identical to that of the *Fipa Group* case and confirmed the same ruling in application of Article 99 of the Rules of Procedure of the Court of Justice of the European Union.

[59] *J.L. Sax*, The Public Trust Doctrine in Natural Resource Law: Effective Judicial Intervention, Mich. L. Rev. 1969 (68), p. 471. See on this also *Pozzo, supra*, note 12 at pp. 151 et seq.

[60] For a preliminary study, see *R.D. Sagarin & M. Turnipseed*, The Public Trust Doctrine: Where Ecology Meets Natural Resources Management, Annu. Rev. Environ. Resour. 2012 (37), pp. 473–496. The public trust doctrine shall be distinguished from the creation of trusts for protecting nature: regarding this, the most renowned example is the British National Trust, but many others have been established with same purposes. Indeed, the National Trust is a charity and its main goal is to preserve "Places of Historical Interest and Natural Beauty". See on this *Pozzo*, Property and Environment, *supra*, note 13 at p. 53.

habitats. The beneficiaries are consequently all citizens, both present and future, and the trustees must manage trust resources for their exclusive benefit. If the trustees (i.e. the government) breach their fiduciary duties, beneficiaries can seek remedy in the courts in application of the common principle of trust law.[61] In a challenging way, this paper thus linked the public trust doctrine, which is a doctrine developed especially in the United States,[62] with environmental law, which at that time was an emerging field; it is also considered to have established the scholarly basis for the 1970 Michigan Environmental Protection Act, which Sax contributed to drafting. The "Saxian vision" was then followed and broadened in its scope by other eminent scholars and embraced within international environmental law.[63]

CERCLA followed the same approach with regard to the protection of natural resources, and in carrying out their legislated duties, various programmes and offices have acknowledged their duties as trustees vested in the public trust doctrine.[64]

Indeed, Section 107(a)(4)(C) provides that responsible parties may be held liable for "damages for injury to, destruction of, or loss of natural resources, including the reasonable costs of assessing such injury, destruction, or loss resulting from such a release". According to Section 101(16), the term "natural resources" means "land, fish, wildlife, biota, air, water, ground water, drinking water supplies, and other such resources belonging to, managed by, held in trust by, appertaining to, or otherwise controlled" by the federal government, any

---

[61] Sax (*supra* note 59) argues that public trust doctrine must contain "some concept of legal right in the general public" and "it must be enforceable against the government". However, citizen standing to bring suits against public trustees as afforded by public trust doctrine varies significantly from state to state: see on this, *Sagarin & Turnipseed, supra*, note 60 at p. 481.

[62] The evolution and scholarship regarding the public trust doctrine has taken place in particular in the United States. However, scholars remark that its roots can be traced back to Roman law's idea of *res communes omnium* and ancient English law: see on this *J. Arnold & A. Jacoby*, Examining the Public Trust Doctrine's Role in Conserving Natural Resources on Louisiana's Public Lands, Tul. Envtl. L.J. 2017 (29), p. 196; *S.M. Fink*, The Public Trust Doctrine: The Development of New York's Doctrine and How It Can Improve, Touro L. Rev. 2018 (34), p. 1201. See also *infra* note 66.

[63] See on this *P.H. Sand*, The Rise of Public Trusteeship in International Environmental Law, Env. Pol and L. 2014 (44), pp. 201–218.

[64] Senate Comm. Environ. Public Works 1980, Environmental Emergency Response Act Rep. No. 96-848, US Senate, US GPO, Washington, DC, p. 84. See on this *Sagarin & Turnipseed, supra*, note 60 at p. 486; *L. Chase*, Remedying CERCLA's Natural Damages Provision: Incorporation of the Public Trust Doctrine into Natural Resource Damage Actions, Virginia Env. L.J. 1992 (11), p. 353; *T. Fox*, Natural Resource Damage: the New Frontier for Environmental Litigation, S. Tex. L. Rev. 1993 (34), p. 521; *P.E. Tolan Jr.*, Natural Resource Damage under CERCLA: Failures, Lessons Learned, and Alternatives, N.M. L. Rev. 2008 (38), p. 409; *B. Pozzo*, The Working Agenda Presented at the Common Core Meeting 1995, in: *B. Pozzo* (ed.), Property and Environment, *supra*, note 13 at pp. 116–119.

state or local government, any foreign government, or a Native American tribe.[65] Section 107(f)[66] provides that "federal or state trustees" are authorised to assess[67] the damage and bring actions to recover funds to restore damage to natural resources when response actions (see above) are insufficient, to replace the resource or to acquire an equivalent one.[68] To begin with, federal and state governments or their representatives[69] initiated very few actions, but the number of natural resource litigations has recently grown.[70]

In other statutes, such as the Clean Water Act Amendments of 1977[71] and the Oil Pollution Act of 1990,[72] Congress invokes notions of trusteeship many times to describe the responsibility of the federal government to assess and recover damage in relation to natural resources.

Although originally the public trust doctrine applied only to specific natural resources and in particular to waters and coastal lands,[73] the doctrine has recently

---

[65]   The European Environmental Directive defines "environmental damage" as damage to protected species and natural habitats, damage to water and land damage; the Directive thus considers specific natural resources as objects of protection and in this way defines its scope of application. Depending on which resource is damaged, the liability is strict or fault-based: indeed, operators carrying out dangerous activities listed in Annex III of the Directive fall under strict liability; operators carrying out other occupational activities than those listed in Annex III are liable for fault-based damage to protected species or natural habitats.

[66]   Section 107(f) reads as follows: "The President, or the authorized representative of any State, shall act on behalf of the public as trustee of such natural resources to recover for such damages. Sums recovered by the United States Government as trustee under this subsection shall be retained by the trustee, without further appropriation, for use only to restore, replace, or acquire the equivalent of such natural resources. Sums recovered by a State as trustee under this subsection shall be available for use only to restore, replace, or acquire the equivalent of such natural resources by the State. The measure of damages in any action under subparagraph (C) of subsection (a) shall not be limited by the sums which can be used to restore or replace such resources."

[67]   Natural resource damages shall be assessed according to the regulations of the Department of the Interior, which has established specific procedures to determine the damage; the trustees, indicated in the National Contingency Plan (see Section 111), are in charge of assessing the damage and restoration costs that will remain upon the Superfund.

[68]   §9607(f)(1). *Tabatabai, supra,* note 13 at pp. 653 et seq.

[69]   One of the first public trustees for natural resources was the National Oceanic and Atmospheric Administration (NOAA). NOAA is part of the Department of Commerce. On NOAA's initiative see in particular *Chase, supra,* note 64.

[70]   See *Tolan, supra,* note 64.

[71]   In 1977 Congress extended the Clean Water Act's jurisdiction to the oceans and seabed, which would become the Exclusive Economic Zone six years later. Section 311 of the same Act requires the President to act "on behalf of the public as trustee of the natural resources for purposes of recovery for the cost of replacing or restoring natural resources that had been damaged or lost". See *Sagarin & Turnipseed, supra,* note 60 at p. 485.

[72]   The Oil Pollution Act requires the President or federal officials designated by the President to act "on behalf of the public, Indian tribe, or foreign country as trustee of natural resources to present a claim for and to recover damages to the natural resources" (§2705 (b)(1)).

[73]   The public trust doctrine was originally used to protect fishing, navigation and commerce in US navigable waters but, as said, its origin can be traced to Roman law and English law. Indeed, especially in the 19th century, courts were strongly concerned with protect interstate

---

come to the attention of scholars[74] as a powerful tool to protect the environment, wildlife resources, the sky[75] and ecosystems in general[76] and has been recalled within the context of climate change litigation.[77] As already outlined by scholars, this doctrine has also some similarities with the continental theory of the "common goods" (*beni comuni*),[78] especially with regard to the battle against the privatisation of such "common goods" (like drinkable water) and the right of access to the natural resources.

In this respect, CERCLA appears to have chosen an innovative approach regarding the protection of natural resources; however, in the US, and in Europe especially, the trust instrument needs to be carefully designed in order to fully carry out the goal of the protection of the environment.

6. CONCLUSIONS

CERCLA represented and still represents a point of reference for European and national legislation regarding clean-ups of contaminated soils and remediation

---

    commerce, much of which took place via barges and boats. See *Sagarin & Turnipseed, supra*, note 60.

[74] See among others, *Z.J.B. Plater, RH Abrams, W. Goldfarb, R.L. Graham, L. Heinzerling & D.A. Wirth*, Environmental Law and Policy: Nature, Law, and Society, Aspen, 2014; *Sand, supra*, note 63; *P.H. Sand*, Public trusteeship for the oceans, in T.M. Ndiaye & R. Wolfrum (eds.), Law of the Sea, Environmental Law and Settlement of Disputes: Liber Amicorum Judge Thomas A. Mensah, Brill-Nijhoff, 2007.

[75] See *P. Barnes*, Who Owns the Sky? Our Common Assets and the Future of Capitalism, Island Press, 2001. Barnes proposes a "Sky Trust" which should hold the sky and atmosphere and would pay each US citizen an annual dividend from a fund created by the annual action of a fixed allotment of greenhouse gas emission permits to polluting firms.

[76] The evolution and scholarship regarding the public trust doctrine has taken place in the United States. For a preliminary study, see *Sagarin & Turnipseed, supra*, note 60; *M.D. Smith Jr.*, A Blast from the Past: The Public Trust Doctrine and Its Growing Threat to Water Rights, Envtl. L. 2016 (46), p. 461.

[77] *M.C. Blumm & M.C. Wood*, "No ordinary lawsuit": climate change, due process and the public trust doctrine, Am. Un. L.R. 2017 (67), pp. 1–87; *M.E. Peloso & M.R. Cardwell*, Dynamic Property Rights: the Public Trust Doctrine and Takings in a Changing Climate, Stand. Envtl. L.J. 2011 (30), p. 51.

[78] See on this *U. Mattei & L. Nader*, Plunder: When the Rule of Law is Illegal, Blackwell Publishing, 2008, especially p. 207. See also *A. Gambaro*, Public and Private Land Property: The Current Meaning of a Traditional Distinction, in B. Pozzo (ed.), Property and Environment, *supra*, note 13 at pp. 63 et seq.; *B. Pozzo*, The Working Agenda Presented at the Common Core Meeting 1995, in B. Pozzo (ed.), id. at pp. 116–119; *G. Winter*, Property and Environmental Protection, in G. Winter (ed.), Environmental and Property Protection in Europe, The Avosetta Series (12), Proceedings of the Avosetta Group of European Environmental Lawyers, Europa Law Publishing, 2016, p. 5; *M. Montini*, Property and Environmental Protection in Italy, in: G. Winter (ed.), id. at pp. 200 et seq. (where the author also narrates the debate on common goods and the proposals of the Commissione Rodotà); *M. Montini, M. Ciacci*, In the Name of "Common Interest"; Framing Environmental Goods as Common Goods, in G. Winter (ed.), id. at pp. 322 et seq.

of damage to natural resources. Almost 40 years has passed since its enactment and it is thus possible to try to evaluate its success and its failures.

Regarding remediation of contaminated soils, what is most remarkable is the impressive evolution of the rules concerning the determination of liable parties and the scope of liability. At the beginning, the interpretation of the liability provisions was so rigorous that any person who accidentally came into contact with the hazardous substances was considered jointly and severally liable for the entire remediation costs. Step by step, through significant legislative reforms and changes in the interpretation of the relevant provisions, this rigor has been lessened and it is now possible to mount several defences, from the landowner defences to the divisibility defence, and thus it has even been possible to call seriously into question the "dogma" that CERCLA imposes joint and several liability. However, CERCLA is still anchored to the idea that the landowner of contaminated land must bear a significant portion of the clean-up costs (and it is still very difficult for landowners to escape liability), which is a position that has been rejected at the European level.

Regarding the protection of natural resources, CERCLA, as well as other US environmental statutes, anticipated a trend that is now gaining more and more importance within international academia, that is to say the idea that public entities such as the government, the states and their representatives are public trustees of natural resources, especially those that are more difficult to manage and protect (for example, the atmosphere and the sky). This approach was innovative for Americans; it is even more challenging for Europeans and poses delicate questions, starting from the admissibility of this instrument in the civil law system and going on to issues – crucial in the US as well – such as the trustee's role and responsibility, the evaluation and assessment of natural resource damage, and the operation of presumptions in judicial litigation. However, the recent interest in the public trust doctrine within climate change litigation has induced civil lawyers, and especially European lawyers, to take a close look at these new instruments in order to ascertain whether they could also be a viable option in Europe.

COMPENSATION FOR ENVIRONMENTAL DAMAGE IN THE CIS COUNTRIES

A Comparative Legal Analysis

Alena Kodolova

1. INTRODUCTION

Despite the fact that different Commonwealth of Independent States Members are currently at different stages of environmental legislation development, many of those countries are experiencing problems that result in insufficiently effective legislation on compensation and assessment of environmental damage.

For example, in most CIS countries legislation does not prioritise compensation for environmental damage through the efforts to restore its components. Specialist funds have been established in the Kyrgyz Republic and in the Republic of Moldova to collect resources from enterprises received as a payment for negative impact on the environment, as well as compensation for environmental damage. As for the other CIS Member States, the lack of regulations on the targeted nature of funds received, including compensation for environmental damage, mitigates the value of provisions in the environmental legislation on compensation for environmental damage.

When it comes to methods for environmental damage assessment in the CIS countries, there is also a general tendency for indirect methods of assessment to prevail.[1] These methods are a legacy of the Soviet past and can be most effectively applied in conditions of state ownership of natural resources.[2]

---

[1]   *M.N. Ignatieva*, Environmental Economics: a textbook, Yekaterinburg, USMU, 2009, p. 55.
[2]   *OECD*, Responsibility for environmental damage in EECCA countries: applying best international practices (in Russian), http://www.oecd.org/environment/outreach/50247963.pdf.

Let us take a closer look at the specifics of the legal and regulatory framework of environmental liability in the context of prevention and elimination of environmental damage in the various CIS states.

2. ANALYSIS OF THE CURRENT LEGISLATION ON COMPENSATION FOR ENVIRONMENTAL DAMAGE IN CIS COUNTRIES

2.1. RUSSIAN FEDERATION

In the legislation of the Russian Federation, the concepts of "harm" and "damage" mainly have an economic, monetary sense.

The term "environmental damage" in the Federal Law of 10 January 2002, No. 7-FZ, on Environmental Protection (hereinafter referred to as "Law No. 7-FZ") has become subject to criticism from scientists and practitioners on multiple occasions.[3] For example, the definition under consideration entails that damage can only be caused as a result of pollution which is not in line with the provisions of Chapter 14 of Law No. 7-FZ. According to paragraph 1 of Article 77, legal entities that have caused harm to the environment as a result of its pollution, as well as depletion, damage, elimination, inefficient use of natural resources, degradation and destruction of natural ecological systems, natural complexes and natural landscapes and other violation of environmental legislation, must compensate it in full in accordance with the law.

It is obvious that according to Article 4 of Law No. 7-FZ pollution is a form of negative environmental impact; however, the term "environmental damage" does not specify any other forms of such impact.

Russian legislation uses the terms "environmental damage" and "harm to the environment", which have a similar meaning but have to be clearly distinguished.

In contrast to the provisions of Law No. 7-FZ dealing with compensation for environmental damage, Article 42 of the Constitution of the Russian Federation contains the right of citizens to compensation for damage (and not harm) caused by an environmental offence.

Articles 77 and 78 of Law No. 7-FZ establish the obligation to compensate for environmental damage, as well as the procedure for its compensation.

---

[3]   G.A. *Misnik*, Legal forms of compensation for environmental damage, State and Law 2006 (7), p. 49; *N.G. Narysheva*, Tendencies of differentiation of the legal regulation of compensation for damage caused to the environment, Environmental Law 2005 (1), p. 53; *M.I. Vasilyeva*, Compensation of environmental damage caused to the health of citizens, www.miningwatch. ru, Legality. 2012 (7). p. 30.

However, these articles contradict each other in terms of the manner and procedure for environmental damage compensation.[4]

Despite the fact that the goals and objectives of compensation for environmental damage are not explicitly provided for in the Russian legislation, Paragraph 1 of Article 77 of Law No. 7-FZ suggests that the main goal is to repair the environmental damage in full in accordance with the legislation. Prevention of environmental damage and elimination of its consequences (restoration of the environment) are not specified in the Russian legislation as the objectives of imposing liability.

2.2. BELARUS

The main legislative act regulating the procedure of environmental damage compensation in the Republic of Belarus is the Law of the Republic of Belarus of 26 November 1992, No. 1982-XII, on Environmental Protection (hereinafter referred to as the "Belarusian Law on Environmental Protection"). Issues of responsibility for violation of environmental legislation are discussed in Chapter 15 of this Law.

A special role is given to the suspension (prohibition) of activities that create a threat of damage to the environment (Article 100 of the Belarusian Law on Environmental Protection). Such suspension (prohibition) is carried out by the state authority exercising control in the field of environmental protection and rational use of natural resources in the manner established by the legislation on control (supervisory) activities in the Republic of Belarus.

Public associations that carry out activities in the field of environmental protection and citizens have the right to take legal action before the court suspends (prohibits) economic and other activities that have a harmful effect on the environment in the event that such activities violate the requirements in the field of environmental protection, cause environmental damage or create a risk of environmental damage in the future.

Article 101 of the Belarusian Law on Environmental Protection establishes the rule of full compensation of damage caused to the environment. The amount of compensation for damage caused to the environment is determined in accordance with the rates established by the President of the Republic of Belarus and, in their absence, according to the actual costs of restoration of the damaged environmental conditions, taking into account the losses incurred, including lost profits. Damage caused to the environment can be compensated by the person

---

[4]   *L.P. Bernaz, I.N. Zhochkina & N.V. Kichigin et al.*, Scientific and practical commentary to the Federal Law of January 10, 2002 No.7-FZ On Environmental Protection, Law Firm Contract LLC, 2018, pp. 446–451.

who caused the damage by restoring the damaged state of the environment at their own expense in accordance with the instructions of the state authority that oversees the environmental monitoring and rational use of natural resources, contained in the claim for compensation caused by the environment, or by court order, taking into account the circumstances of the case.

Just like in the Russian Federation, there is academic discussion in the Republic of Belarus regarding the sectoral affiliation of the institute of compensation for environmental damage. In the view of Belarusian academics, material responsibility in the form of compensation for damage caused to the environment primarily differs from civil liability in terms of protected objects. The list of objects specified in Article 933 of the Civil Code of the Republic of Belarus intersects with the list specified in Article 102 of the Belarusian Law on Environmental Protection, but it does not include the object of Article 101 of the Law, which is the environment.[5]

2.3. KAZAKHSTAN

The Republic of Kazakhstan has the Environmental Code of 9 January 2007, No. 212-III (hereinafter referred to as the "Kazakh Environmental Code"). Article 1 defines the concept of environmental damage as pollution of the environment or withdrawal of natural resources in excess of established standards, which caused or is causing degradation and depletion of natural resources or death of living organisms.

Despite the fact that the term "harm to the environment" is not used in this article, it is repeatedly used in the text of the Kazakh Environmental Code. The absence of a legal definition of harm to the environment in the Kazakh Environmental Code detracts from its content and allows this term to be interpreted arbitrarily in law-enforcement activity.

As a way out, academics propose replacing the term "environmental damage" with the term "harm to the environment" due to the fact that the legislator only uses the concept of "damage" in a narrow civil law context and only uses the economic component of damage.[6]

Of all the CIS countries, the legislation of the Republic of Kazakhstan on the procedure for compensation and assessment of environmental damage is

---

5   *E.V. Zagorovskaya*, Features of compensation for environmental damage, Bulletin of the BSU, 2012 (2), p. 83.

6   *J.A. Bitabarova*, Problems of improving the legislation on compensation for environmental harm in the Republic of Kazakhstan, News of the National Academy of Sciences of Kazakhstan, 2011 (5), p. 45.

the closest to the regulatory framework of the European Union in its content. The Republic of Kazakhstan applies both direct and indirect methods of economic assessment of damage to the environment. Having said this, priority is given to the direct evaluation method. In accordance with Article 109 of the Kazakh Environmental Code, the direct method of economic assessment of environmental damage consists in determining the actual costs required to restore the environment, replenish degraded natural resources and rehabilitate living organisms using the most efficient engineering, organisational, technical and technological measures. Officials of the authorised body in the field of environmental protection primarily consider the possibility of measures to restore the environment being taken by the person who has caused damage to the environment. Appropriate obligations for the implementation of measures to restore the environment are set out in the letter of guarantee by the person who has caused damage to the environment, indicating specific measures and dates for their implementation. The cost of mitigation measures is determined by their market value.

2.4. MOLDOVA

In the Republic of Moldova, the requirements in the field of environmental liability and environmental damage assessment were included in the Law on Environmental Protection of the Republic of Moldova dated 16 June 1993.

In accordance with this legislation, the responsibility of all individuals and legal entities for damage that was caused or is being caused to the environment, for pollution prevention, restriction and abatement, as well as compensation for damage caused to the environment and its components, is carried out at the expense of individuals and legal entities (Chapters IV–VII).

The damage caused to the natural environment is calculated by means of instructions and techniques developed by the Ministry of Environmental Protection and summarised in the "Guidelines for assessing damage to the environment by human activities and the mechanisms for its compensation" (2006).

2.5. KYRGYZSTAN

The Kyrgyz Republic has the Law of 16 June 1999, No. 53, on Environmental Protection (hereinafter referred to as the "Kyrgyz Law on Environmental Protection").

Unlike other CIS countries, the Kyrgyz legislation separates the concepts of "environmental damage" and "harm to the environment" (Article 2 of the Kyrgyz Law on Environmental Protection). Harm is understood as negative changes in the state of the environment caused by human activity as a result of environmental pollution, depletion of natural resources, damage, destruction of ecological systems of nature, creating a real threat to human health and life, flora and fauna, and material values. Damage to the environment is understood as economic and non-economic losses of society resulting from changes in the environment and its pollution, calculated in monetary terms.

Article 36 of the Kyrgyz Law on Environmental Protection establishes the basics of environmental insurance. The possibility of both voluntary and compulsory environmental insurance of legal entities and individuals, their property and income in case of environmental disasters, accidents and catastrophes, as well as liability insurance for environmental pollution, is envisaged. Legal entities and citizens dealing with environmentally hazardous types of economic and other activities are subject to compulsory environmental insurance.

According to Article 54 of the Kyrgyz Law on Environmental Protection, legal entities and individuals, including foreign ones, that cause damage to the environment, health and property of citizens, legal entities and the state via environmental pollution, waste, destruction, damage, irrational use of natural resources, destruction of natural ecological systems and other environmental violations are obliged to compensate it in full in accordance with the Civil Code of the Kyrgyz Republic and other legal acts, for example Resolution No. 668 of the Government of the KR dated 7 September 2004 on Liability for Damage Caused by Land Deterioration.

Compensation for damage caused to the environment as a result of an environmental offence is made in cash, either voluntarily or by a court decision in accordance with the rates and methodologies for calculating the amount of damage approved in the established procedure, and, in their absence, based on actual costs of restoring the disturbed state of the environment, taking into account the losses incurred, including lost profits. The amount of damages recovered by the court order is transferred to the national or local environmental protection funds.

2.6.   ARMENIA

The concept of environmental damage as such is not defined by a separate law in the Republic of Armenia, and issues relating to compensation for damage caused to nature and the environment are regulated by Article 17 of the Civil Code of the Republic of Armenia, adopted by the National Council of the Republic of Armenia on 5 May 1988.

There are a number of laws regulating the environmental damage assessment and environmental liability in Armenia. An example of such law is the Armenian Law on Tariffs for Compensation of Damage Caused to Fauna and Flora due to Environmental Offences adopted in 2005. Article 6 of this Law, which sets out the "[p]rocedure for calculating the measure of compensation for damage caused to fauna and flora due to the environmental violations" determines, for example, that "a measure of compensation for damage to fauna and flora due to the environmental offences ... is calculated based on the number and/or scope of damaged objects of flora or fauna, and tariffs established by the second chapter of this Law". This legal act provides the rates of compensation for damage to fauna and flora, defined by category and based on the economic value of the resources.

The main laws of the Republic of Armenia in the field of environmental protection that regulate, *inter alia*, the issues of environmental liability and damage assessment, include the Law on the Protection of Atmospheric Air (1994); the Law on the Flora (1999); the Law on the Fauna (2000); the Forest Code (2005); the Water Code (2002; Article 114 of this Code, in particular, regulates criminal and administrative responsibility for violation of the requirements of the Water Code in detail); the Law on Waste (2004); the Land Code (2001); and the Law on Tariffs for Compensation of Damage Caused to Fauna and Flora due to Environmental Offences (2005).

2.7. AZERBAIJAN

The fundamental normative legal "environmental" act of the Republic of Azerbaijan is the Law of 8 June 1999, No. 678-IQ, on Environmental Protection, does not contain the terms "harm to the environment" and "environmental damage". This Law establishes general conditions for environmental liability: violation of standards and other regulatory and technical requirements for the protection of nature; non-compliance with the requirements of the state environmental impact assessment; violation of environmental requirements in the planning, design, placement, construction, reconstruction, commissioning, operation and liquidation of enterprises, structures, vehicles and other objects; non-compliance with sanitary norms, rules and hygienic standards; excessive pollution of the environment, or physical and other harmful effects on it; failure to take measures to eliminate the consequences of harmful impact on the environment; failure to comply with the requirements of the authorities exercising state control over nature conservation; violation of environmental requirements during storage, transportation, use, disposal and dumping of industrial, household and other types of waste; violation of environmental requirements when handling radioactive and harmful chemicals; refusal to provide timely, complete and reliable information on the state of the environment, as well as on sources of pollution; concealment of information on excessive discharges and emissions of pollutants, accidents or disasters with harmful environmental consequences; unauthorised seizure of forest land; violation of the norms and procedures for collecting, harvesting medicinal and other wild plants; and refusal to allocate land for planting erosion-resistant forest plantations.

Similarly to other CIS countries, the most valuable method of compensation for damage in Azerbaijan is the "value-for-price" method. In economic terms, the definition of the measure of lost or impacted resources, as well as the economic value of the resource is taken into account, are used for damage assessment and its compensation.

Measures to restore and compensate for damage are carried out by a polluter or a third party whose activities are financed by the polluter. In cases where monetary compensation is applied, the amount of payment is determined by the cost of compensatory measures.

2.8. TAJIKISTAN

The content of the Law of the Republic of Tajikistan of 2 August 2011, No. 760, on Environmental Protection (hereinafter referred to as the "Tajik Law on Environmental Protection") is very similar to the legislation of the Kyrgyz Republic, including in matters of compensation for environmental damage.

The Tajik Law on Environmental Protection may not be sufficiently detailed when it outlines the issues of environmental liability and definition of damage, but, as in the case of Kyrgyzstan, it provides that "holding the guilty persons liable does not exempt them from the obligation to compensate for the damage they caused".

In accordance with Article 1 of the Tajik Law on Environmental Protection, environmental damage is defined as negative changes in the state of the environment caused by human activity, such as pollution, depletion of natural resources, damage and degradation of ecological systems.

In the legislation of the Republic of Tajikistan, the terms "harm to the environment" and "environmental damage" are not distinguished.

In accordance with Article 77 of the Tajik Law on Environmental Protection, enterprises, institutions, organisations and citizens that have caused damage to the environment through pollution, waste, destruction, irrational use of natural resources, degradation and depletion of natural ecological systems, natural complexes and natural landscapes, and other violations of legislation in the field of environmental protection, are obliged to compensate for it in accordance with the normative legal acts of the Republic of Tajikistan.[7]

---

[7] Fundamentals of national water legislation in the field of water quality control in the States of the Central Asia (in Russian), http://cawater-info.net/library/rus/carewib/water_quality_legislation_1.pdf.

Regarding the regulation of damage compensation, the law of the Republic of Tajikistan is almost identical to Kyrgyz legislation: it determines that "compensation for damage caused to the natural environment by violations of environmental legislation is made voluntarily, or by a court order or economic court order in accordance with established rates and methods of calculation of its amount, and in their absence, based on the actual costs of restoring the disturbed state of the natural environment, taking into account the losses incurred".

2.9. UZBEKISTAN

General provisions with respect to compensation for environmental damage are contained in the Law of the Republic of Uzbekistan of 9 December 1992 No. 754-XII on Nature Conservation.

In accordance with Article 49 of this Law, enterprises, institutions, organisations and individuals who have caused harm to the environment are obliged to compensate for it in accordance with the legislation. Bringing those liable for violation of the environmental requirements to administrative or criminal responsibility does not exempt them from the obligation to compensate for environmental damage.

The Republic of Uzbekistan has a Regulation on the procedure of applying compensation payments for environmental pollution and waste disposal on the territory of the Republic of Uzbekistan, approved by the Resolution of the Cabinet of Ministers of the Republic of Uzbekistan dated 1 May 2003, No. 199, which covers the definition of the value of the damage in sufficient detail and regulates how to calculate it. However, it does not contain the necessary guidance on how to identify those responsible for causing damage, and it does not provide a description of the tools for conducting assessment procedures either.

3. SPECIAL LIABILITY REGIMES FOR ENVIRONMENTAL DAMAGE IN THE CIS COUNTRIES

According to Professor Nicholas Robinson, in order to be an effective method of environmental protection, liability regimes should cover not only traditionally recognised forms of compensable damage, but also damage caused to the environment. The main purpose of developing special environmental liability regimes is to help people understand the consequences of negative impact on the environment – a public good that forms the basis of the life support system for people and all living things. However, many countries have not introduced any special liability regimes for causing environmental harm; instead, they rely on traditional standards of civil liability applied in the environmental context.[8]

According to leading foreign researchers in the field of environmental law, one of the main problems in addressing the issue of environmental damage compensation in the framework of classic tort law is the need for the environmental good, which is public in nature, to belong to an individual. Another equally significant problem in characterising liability for environmental damage more as public law is the methods for assessing the damage caused.[9] Calculating environmental damage may not be possible in certain cases from an economic standpoint, for example in the case of loss of fauna and flora that do not have a market value, and in the case of damage to ecosystems or landscapes where economic value cannot be estimated using traditional approaches to damage assessment.[10]

Russian scientists are developing a concept of the public-law nature of environmental damage and an independent form of legal liability – environmental legal liability for causing such damage.[11]

In some countries of the European Union, thanks to the supranational regulation of environmental issues, the institution of compensation for environmental damage has evolved from a private-law institution into public-law one.[12]

In accordance with Directive 2004/35/CE of the European Parliament and the Council of the European Union on environmental liability with regard to the prevention and remedying of environmental damage, environmental damage is compensated in kind and, if it is necessary to recover a monetary compensation from the responsible enterprise, the direct cost method is applied. The Directive mentions the prevention of environmental damage and the elimination of its consequences (environmental restoration) as the goals for environmental damage liability. Thus, compensation for damage includes potential (future) environmental damage in addition to current damage.

In accordance with Resolution of the Inter-Parliamentary Assembly of the States Parties to the Commonwealth of Independent States, No. 33-10,

---

8   *N.A. Robinson & L. Kurukulasuriya*, Training Manual on International Environmental Law: Pace Law Faculty Publications, 2006, p. 52.

9   *M. Hinteregger*, Environmental Liability and Ecological Damage in European Law, Cambridge University Press, 2008, p. 12.

10 *Supra*, note 9 at p. 54.

11 *M.M. Brinchuk*, Ecological and legal responsibility – an independent type of legal responsibility, Lex Russica, 2016 (6), p. 33.

12 *Hinteregger, supra*, note 9 at p. 10; *G. Winter, J.H. Jans, R. Macrory & L. Krümer*, Weighing up the EC Environmental Liability Directive, Journal of Environmental Law, 2008 (20/2), p. 164.

of 3 December 2009, CIS countries adopted a recommendatory legal act – the Model Law of the CIS on Environmental Liability in Prevention and Elimination of Harm Caused to the Environment. This legal act is in many respects an adaptation of the Directive for CIS countries, and it is recommended within the territory of the CIS for the purpose of harmonisation with the European legislation.

It should be noted that the model legislation of the CIS, following the European legislation, establishes the public-law regime of environmental liability, gives priority to in-kind compensation over monetary compensation of environmental damage, and establishes the determination of actual costs necessary for environmental restoration as the main method of economic assessment of environmental harm, replenishment of degraded natural resources and rehabilitation of living organisms through the most effective engineering, organisational, technical and technological measures.

In accordance with the 2017–2019 Model Legislation Drafting Programme, recommendations and other documents of the Inter-Parliamentary Assembly of the CIS, in 2017 the St. Petersburg Scientific Research Center for Ecological Safety at the Russian Academy of Sciences began to develop a draft Model Law on the Assessment of Environmental Damage.

This draft Model Law consists of the following main provisions:

(1) economic entities that caused environmental damage are obliged to compensate for the damage caused by them in accordance with the legislative acts of the state, including through the mechanisms of compulsory environmental insurance;

(2) economic assessment of damage to the environment is performed by officials in the field of environmental protection if violations of environmental legislation are detected during the state environmental control procedures;

(3) the officials of the competent authority shall consider, as a matter of priority, the possibility of restoring the environment in-kind by making the economic entity that caused such damage to the environment take measures to eliminate it;

(4) the monetary forms of damage compensation include using financial means to restore the protected site to the state it was in at the time of the damage, to take measures to restore natural resources, and to compensate the plaintiff for other damage, including lost profits;

(5) the amount of compensation for damage caused to protected sites is mainly determined in a priority form based on the actual costs of restoring the disturbed state of the protected sites, taking into account the loss of profits;

(6) the economic assessment of damage caused to protected sites is determined using direct or indirect methods in accordance with the legislation of the state;

(7) the direct method of economic assessment of environmental damage consists of determining the actual costs required to restore the environment, replenish degraded natural resources and rehabilitate living organisms using the most efficient engineering, organisational, technical and technological measures;

(8) the cost of specific measures to eliminate damage to the environment using direct methods is determined by their market value; when using the direct method of economic assessment of damage, officials of the competent authority may engage independent experts (auditors, project design specialists, engineers and scientific organisations);

(9) if, at the time of filing claims, it is not possible to exhaustively determine the costs of remedial measures, the amount of damages may be calculated indirectly using special rates and methods, subsequently conclusively revised after the completion of the entire range of restoration works.

As a general rule, the indirect method of economic assessment of damage is used for cases of pollution of atmospheric air and water resources, the disposal of production and consumption wastes, and excessive removal of natural resources.

The indirect method of economic assessment of damage is based on the difference between the actual impact on the environment and the established standard for all types of pollutants, as well as on the basis of the size of the monthly calculated indicator, the levels of environmental hazard and environmental risk.

The indirect method of economic assessment of environmental damage is determined by summing up the damage for each factor depending on the type of environmental impact.

4. CONCLUSION

In conclusion, the author would like to note that in order to implement the "polluter pays" principle, it is extremely important to identify specific mechanisms that determine the procedure for the economic assessment of environmental damage at the domestic level.

The main method of economic assessment of environmental damage should consist of determining the actual costs needed to restore the environment, replenish degraded natural resources and rehabilitate living organisms using the most efficient engineering, organisational, technical and technological measures. Indirect methods of economic assessment of environmental damage should only be applied in cases where the direct method of economic assessment of damage cannot be applied.

COMPENSATION OF LAWFUL ENVIRONMENTAL DAMAGE IN THE RUSSIAN LEGAL SYSTEM

Nikolay KICHIGIN

1. INTRODUCTION

Compensation for damage to the environment is one of the most important problems in environmental law. The problem of compensation for environmental damage is the subject of long-term research in Russian legal academia.[1] Unfortunately, numerous legal studies have not yet led to the development of a unified approach towards understanding the legal institution of compensation for damage to the environment. Much less attention in the legislation and legal practice is paid to damage to the environment as lawful environmental damage. Moreover, there is a point of view that lawful damage in the field of environmental protection does not exist, and any damage to the environment implies a violation of environmental requirements. At the same time, the need to formulate a legal structure for the "lawful damage to the environment" is raised not only by legal scientists but also by practitioners, in other branches of scientific knowledge. This article discusses the concept of lawful damage to the environment, as well as how it is different from damage caused to the environment by committing an environmental offence.

2. "DAMAGE TO THE ENVIRONMENT" AS A CATEGORY OF LEGAL LIABILITY FOR ENVIRONMENTAL OFFENCES

The category of "environmental damage" is traditionally defined in legal literature as a result of violations of legislation in the field of environmental protection.

---

[1]   G. *Misnik*, Compensation of environmental damage in the Russian law, Dissertation for the degree of Doctor of law, 2008; *N. Narysheva*, Compensation for damage caused by violation

In legal literature, compensation for environmental damage is traditionally recognised as a form of legal liability for an environmental offence, along with criminal, administrative and disciplinary liability. As a result, the elements of a civil offence include details inherent to any elements of an environmental offence: an unlawful act (act or omission); the fact of causing damage to the environment; the cause-and-effect connection between the act and causing damage; and the fault of the perpetrator.

At the same time, it can be concluded from the systematic analysis of the term "damage to the environment" in the Federal Law of 10 January 2002, No. 7-FZ, on Environmental Protection that in the federal legislation, the damage caused to the environment is not a consequence of solely committing an environmental offence.

Providing a systematic analysis of the terms used in the Federal Law on Environmental Protection ("negative impact", "environmental pollution", "facilities that have a negative impact on the environment"), Chapter XIV allows us to conclude that negative activities within the established standards cannot be qualified as an offence and cannot entail legal liability. However, any negative change in the environment is recognised as environmental damage. Are economic entities obliged to compensate for such environmental damage? And if so, to what extent?

In this regard, it is noted in the legal literature that environmental legislation allows for a negative impact on the environment within the established standards. Compliance with these standards is a sign of legitimate behaviour. According to environmental legislation, lawful actions do not entail the obligation of compensation for damage caused to the health and property of citizens.[2]

3. THE CONCEPT AND FEATURES OF LEGAL DAMAGE TO THE ENVIRONMENT, THE PROCEDURE OF ITS COMPENSATION

According to point 3 of Article 1064 of the Civil Code of the Russian Federation, damage caused by lawful actions is subject to compensation in the cases provided for by the law. According to point 2 of Article 77 of the Federal Law on Environmental Protection, damage to the environment inflicted by a legal entity or an individual entrepreneur, including activity covered by a positive

---

of legislation on environmental protection, Dissertation for the degree of Candidate of legal sciences, 1998; S. *Bogolyubov et al.*, Legal regulation of compensation for environmental damage: scientific-practical manual, N. Kichigin (ed.), INFRA-M, 2017.

[2]   M. *Androsov et al.*, Commentary to the Federal law of 10 January 2002 No. 7-FZ "on Environmental Protection", O. Dubovik (ed), 2016.

state ecological examination statement, as well as the activity on extraction of components of natural environment, is subject to compensation by the customer and/or legal entity or the individual entrepreneur.

This provision, in the author's opinion, applies to cases of compensation for lawful environmental damage, in contrast to point 1 of Article 77, which establishes the obligation of full compensation for environmental damage. However, we should note an unfortunate error on the part of the federal legislator, who put this provision in the chapter on liability for violation of environmental legislation and did not clearly express in the wording of the law the purpose of adopting this provision and the range of public relations it regulates.

Thus, the federal legislation does not contain a clear and unambiguous regulation of compensation for lawful damage to the environment, but it does not reject such a possibility. In the legal literature, lawful damage to the environment is included in the concept of environmental damage by certain academics. Prof. Zhavoronkova, for example, proposes including the following types of environmental damage in the complex concept of "environmental damage":

- damage caused to the environment as a result of its pollution;
- damage caused to individual components of the natural environment, compensated in accordance with the approved fees and methods of compensation;
- damage caused to the health and property of citizens as a result of a violation of legislation in the field of environmental protection;
- past (accumulated) environmental damage; and
- damage to the environment arising from lawful actions of the subject of economic activity (having a non-delictual character).[3]

In view of the above, the relationship between lawful environmental damage and environmental damage caused as a result of an offence presents a question. In that context, Velieva indicates that Article 77 of the Federal Law on Environmental Protection establishes the principle of full compensation for damage caused by environmental offences, which means that compensation for environmental damage is possible only in the system of liability for environmental offences and does not include a mechanism for compensation for damage caused by lawful activities, i.e. pollution within the limits provided by the standards.[4]

The present author cannot but agree with this conclusion, as, according to Article 42 of the Constitution of the Russian Federation, everyone is guaranteed

---

[3] N. *Zhavoronkova*, Compensation for environmental damage: the legislative innovations, Lex Russica 2016 (8), pp. 130–140.

[4] D. *Veliyeva*, System of constitutional environmental rights and obligations in the Russian Federation, V. Kabyshev (ed.), DMK Press, 2009.

the right to compensation for the damage caused to their health or property by an environmental offence.

It should be noted that lawful environmental damage, as a form of environmental damage taken as a whole, is identified in foreign legislation. Prof. Broslavsky notes that environmental damage can occur, first, as a result of non-compliance with or violation of legislative and other normative acts regulating production, economic and other activities, including regulatory and technical acts that reinforce requirements for the quality of objects (components) of the environment, and second, as a result of lawful actions of the economic entity and (or) the natural user.[5]

4. DIFFERENCES BETWEEN LAWFUL AND UNLAWFUL DAMAGE TO THE ENVIRONMENT

Let us now try to point out the similarities and differences between lawful environmental damage and environmental damage caused by an offence. What these types of environmental damage have in common is the actual result of lawful and unlawful activities: the fact of causing environmental damage and the need for its compensation as one of the basic principles of environmental protection in the Federal Law on Environmental Protection. The amount of lawful and unlawful environmental damage must be justified and determined.

Let us now turn to the characterisation of the differences between lawful and environmental damage resulting from an unlawful act. First of all, the difference lies in the legal qualification of the action (or inaction) that leads to environmental damage. Unlawful environmental damage is caused by committing an offence (crime or misdemeanour). Lawful environmental damage is a consequence of the implementation of planned or ongoing economic activities carried out in a normal manner, in compliance with established standards and environmental restrictions.

As a result, causing "undue" environmental damage entails the involvement of legal liability, while the fact of causing lawful environmental damage does not entail imposing legal liability on the company.

The state has approved special fees or methods for the assessment of most types of unlawful environmental damage, and even though they are imperfect, they allow for an approximate assessment of environmental damage. For the

---

5   L. *Broslavskiy*, Compensation for environmental damage in the USA, in S. Bogolyubov, N. Kamynina & M. Ponomarev (eds.), Legal problems of compensation of damage caused to the environment: Proceedings of the International Scientific-Practical Conference (Moscow State University of Geodesy and Cartography, Institute of Legislation and Comparative Law under the Government of the Russian Federation, 23 March 2017), 2017, p. 60.

assessment of lawful environmental damage, with a number of exceptions, the relevant methods have not yet been developed. Therefore, the calculation of the costs of compensation can only be carried out based on the actual costs of the restoration of the environment provided for by the project to restore the damaged objects (components) of the environment.

Environmental legislation is based on the principle of full compensation for unlawful environmental damage. According to point 1 of Article 77 of the Federal Law on Environmental Protection, the legal entities and physical persons which caused damage to the environment as a result of its pollution, exhaustion, damage, destruction, irrational use of natural resources, degradation and deterioration of natural ecological systems, natural landscapes and other violations of the legislation in the field of environmental protection are obliged to fully compensate for it in accordance with the law. In this case, actual damage caused and lost profits, as well as moral damage caused to citizens, are subject to compensation.[6]

The principle of full compensation for environmental damage has not been established with regard to lawful environmental damage. Moreover, as already mentioned above, compensation for damage caused to human life and health, in the case of lawful environmental damage, is not provided for by the current legislation. In connection with the above, when it comes to compensation for lawful damage to the environment, it can only be a question of compensation for environmental damage actually caused.

Environmental legislation establishes the offender's obligation to compensate for the unlawful damage to the environment in kind or in cash. The procedure for the compensation of such environmental damage still requires some improvement; however, it already allows for efforts to compensate such damage at the present time.

In the current legislation, the mechanism of compensation for lawful environmental damage, with a number of exceptions, is not regulated at all. In particular, there is no procedure for fixing the fact of causing such damage, since there are no grounds for carrying out measures for state environmental supervision in the absence of a violation of mandatory requirements.

The legal literature provides the following example of lawful environmental damage to be compensated: lawful damage caused by the military forces during exercises, manoeuvres and other activities of military formations in peacetime.[7] However, the legislation does not provide the procedure for fixing such damage

---

[6]   N. Vukolova, Problems of compensation for moral damage caused by environmental crimes, Advocate 2015 (7), pp. 49–54.

[7]   A. Anisimov (ed.), Scientific-practical commentary to the federal law "on Environmental Protection" (article by article), Business Yard, 2010, p. 125.

or for filing claims for its compensation. As in the given example, since the Ministry of Defence of the Russian Federation is not the violator of the current legislation, the procedures for compensation of environmental damage for committing an environmental offence established by the legislation are not applicable to it.

Another significant difference between lawful and unlawful environmental damage is the ratio of the fee to a negative impact on the environment. The previous wording of Article 16 of the Federal Law on Environmental Protection (point 4) revealed that the introduction of charges for negative impact does not exempt the subjects of economic and other activities from the implementation of measures for the protection of the environment and compensation of damage to the environment. However, the Federal Law of 29 December 2015, No. 404-FZ, on Amendments to the Federal Law on Environmental Protection and certain legislative acts of the Russian Federation excluded this legislative requirement.

In the author's opinion, this decision is controversial, since the infliction of unlawful environmental damage should not take into account the payments for the negative impact made by the nature user. Payment for the negative impact on the environment within the standard or temporarily agreed limit, as an element of the economic mechanism of environmental protection, is aimed at compensating for negative consequences of lawful economic activity and should not be correlated with the environmental damage caused as a result of an environmental offence.

In return, legal damage to the environment should take into account the amount of payment for the negative impact on the environment. In other words, the amount of compensation for the lawful damage to the environment shall exceed the amount of payment for the negative impact on the environment paid by the natural resource user. The question of the payment time frames, which also must be considered in the reimbursement of lawful damage to the environment, still remains debatable.

Environmental damage caused in the implementation of large-scale projects of economic activity is not only manifested in environmental pollution as a result of emissions, discharges and waste disposal, but is also translated into the death of animals and plants, into the reduction of natural areas and deterioration of the quality of habitats, deterioration of the food supply and other negative consequences. Unfortunately, it is impossible to completely eliminate the negative impact on fauna, especially in the implementation of large investment projects. Therefore, it is necessary to implement preventive and ongoing measures aimed at the preservation and restoration of populations of fauna and species diversity of flora at all stages of the project.

It should be recognised that in the environmental legislation the issue of compensation for damage to the fauna is regulated mainly from the point of view of eliminating the consequences of committed environmental offences.

Thus, Article 56 of the Federal Law of 24 April 1995, No. 52-FZ, on Fauna establishes the responsibility of legal entities and citizens for damage caused to the fauna and their habitats. Legal entities and citizens who have caused damage to the fauna and their habitats compensate for the damage voluntarily or by a court or arbitration court decision in accordance with the rates and methodologies of calculation of damage to the animal world, or, in their absence, in line with the actual cost of compensation for damage caused to the fauna and their habitats, taking into account the losses incurred, including lost profits.

According to Article 53 of the Federal Law 20 December 2004, No. 166-FZ, on Fishery and Preservation of Water Biological Resources, compensation for the damage caused to water bio-resources is performed on a voluntary basis or on the basis of a judgment, according to the rates approved in accordance with the established procedure and the methods of calculation of the size of the damage caused to water bio-resources, or, in the absence of those, based on the cost of water bio-resources restoration.

In the author's opinion, these norms, on the basis of their content, should not be applied to the relations in which in the course of authorised, legitimate economic activities – for example construction of a road – damage is caused to the environment, especially flora and fauna. Meanwhile, in practice, to assess the damage to the flora and fauna it is necessary to use rates and methodologies which assess the environmental damage caused by violations of the law. Thus, persons engaged in lawful activities are automatically treated as violators of the law.

The analysis of the legislation on flora and fauna allows us to conclude that it does not clearly distinguish between cases of damage caused by the implementation of legitimate activities and those resulting from violations of the current legislation. Almost all compensation methods and rates for damage to the flora and fauna provide for compensation for damage caused as a result of an offence.[8] As a result, any planned economic activity, from the point of view of the legislator, is considered illegal and entails imposing the appropriate type of legal liability.

First of all, the above problem is manifested in the implementation of the procedure for assessing the impact of planned economic and other activities on the environment in the Russian Federation (the OVOS procedure)[9] in

---

[8] Order of the Ministry of Natural Resources of the Russian Federation of 28 April 2008, No. 107 "on approval of the methodology for calculating the amount of damage caused to fauna listed in the Red List of the Russian Federation, as well as other fauna not related to hunting and fishing and their habitat"; Decree of the Government of the Russian Federation of 8 May 2007, No. 273 "on calculating the amount of damage caused to forests due to violation of forest legislation".

[9] In the US, EU, and other countries, this procedure is called an environmental impact assessment (EIA).

accordance with the order of the State Committee of Ecology of Russia of 16 May 2000, No. 372, in which the impact of the planned activities is provided, including the flora and fauna. In addition, similar difficulties arise in the preparation of project documentation for the construction and reconstruction of capital construction projects, since the Government decree of 16 February 2008, No. 87, on the Composition of Sections of Project Documentation and Requirements for their Contents provides, in section 7 on "environmental protection measures", for the preparation of a list and calculation of costs for the implementation of environmental protection measures and compensation payments.

However, the current legislation hardly provides for special fees and methods for calculating compensation payments. As a result, the cost of compensatory measures in the planning of lawful activities should be assessed on the basis of rates and methodologies provided for violators of the law. Thus, law-abiding users of natural resources are equated with violators of the law.

Therefore, the task of amending the environmental legislation and the legislation on flora and fauna in terms of differentiation of approaches to the definition of lawful and unlawful environmental damage seems appropriate. Doing so will distinguish the consequences of actions committed by a violator of the legislation from the lawful actions of economic entities. On the basis of these changes, it is advisable to develop special fees and methods for assessing the legal damage caused to flora and fauna by the implementation of legitimate activities.

In the context of aquatic bio-resources protection, it is noted in the legal literature that special legal regulation of compensation for lawful environmental damage is necessary.[10]

It seems that the priority in the compensation for damage to animals and plants should be given to in-kind forms of compensation over compensation in monetary terms. Unfortunately, the current legislation take the opposite approach: priority is given to the monetary form of compensation for environmental damage, calculated on the basis of rates and methodologies.

One of the reasons for this situation is that, in addition to the absence of appropriate rates and methodologies of compensation for lawful environmental

---

[10] A. Belousov & V. Voronkov, Some features of the assessment and redress of lawful environmental damage, in S. Bogolyubov et al. (eds.), Constitutional and legal bases of responsibility in the field of ecology: materials of the International Scientific-Practical Conference – "The constitutional principles of legal regulation of environmental relations: from ideas to implementation (the 25th anniversary of the Constitution of the Russian Federation)" (Moscow State University of Geodesy and Cartography, 20 December 2018) and "The relationship of types of legal liability in environmental sphere" (Moscow State University of Geodesy and Cartography, Institute of Legislation and Comparative Law under the Government of the Russian Federation, 14 March 2019), 2019, pp. 267–270.

damage, including damage from the planned economic activity, there is no regulation of the order of environmental protection measures designed to minimise damage or compensate it in kind at the stages of placement, design or construction of facilities. This problem is particularly relevant for the protection of fauna (with the exception of aquatic biological resources) and flora, including Red List species of flora or fauna of the Russian Federation.

For instance, in the case of Red List species of flora or fauna, there may be situations in which it is not possible to change design decisions, for example the route of a road or railway or the location of a factory, due to technical, economic and other reasons or natural conditions. At the same time, in the course of engineering and environmental surveys or studies in the framework of the OVOS procedure, it may become clear that the populations of Red List species of flora or fauna will be affected as a result of the implementation of project decisions. On one hand, environmental legislation prohibits the encroachment/ infringement upon Red List species of flora or fauna; on the other hand, if the decision is still taken to implement the planned economic and other activities, the project of the planned activities must ensure the highest possible level of minimisation of negative consequences and environmental damage.

This requires the preparation of a special programme of activities, including but not limited to the capture and transfer of organisms, the relocation of endangered plant species to other places, and the search for and arrangement of new undisturbed habitats. Meanwhile, in the legislation, any encroachment/ infringement upon Red List species of flora or fauna is considered a violation of the legislation, entailing criminal or administrative liability. Mechanisms of damage minimisation are almost absent.

In exceptional cases, environmental legislation provides for the possibility of obtaining permits for the extraction of Red List species of flora or fauna.[11] However, there are no methods or guidelines that describe the procedure or the sequence of such activities in detail, providing for the preparation of the necessary documentation and reporting, or for the participation of environmental authorities and the public in this procedure.

This gap in the legislation was particularly evident during the preparations for the Winter Olympic and Paralympic Games in Sochi in 2014. Perhaps in

---

[11]   In relation to the Red List of flora and fauna, the procedure is regulated by the Government of the Russian Federation from 6 January 1997, No. 13, "on approval of the rules of extraction of fauna belonging to the species listed in the Red List of the Russian Federation, except for aquatic biological resources" and the Order of the Ministry of Natural Resources of Russia of 18 February 2013, No. 60, "on approval of the administrative regulations of the federal service for supervision of natural resources of the provision of public services for the issuance of permits for the extraction of fauna and flora, listed in the Red List of the Russian Federation". In relation to the Red List water biological resources: Decree of the Government of the Russian Federation of 24 January 2008, No. 1017, "on the extraction (catch) of rare and endangered species of aquatic biological resources".

order to overcome the existing legal gap, upon the order of the Ministry of Natural Resources of Russia of 28 April 2010, No. 10-p, the methodology for rehabilitating resettled plants and animals exposed to the danger of direct negative impact in the mountainous and flat part of the territory of the Winter Games was approved.

The methodology defines the general principles and methods of such rehabilitation. The aim of the methodology is to provide scientific support for the resettlement of rare and endangered plant and animal species exposed to the danger of direct negative impact during the construction of Olympic facilities. The system of rehabilitation of resettled species, local populations (species) of plants and animals includes several blocks: scientific and practical. The scientific block (programme) includes:

- identification of protected species specified for the construction zone;
- identification of limiting factors of protected species; and
- development of methods and techniques for species conservation.

The practical block (programme) includes the following activities:

- inventory of plant and animal species exposed to the danger of direct negative impact of the Winter Games in Sochi on the mountainous and flat part of the territory;
- removal of species from habitats;
- collection of reproductive material;
- selection of sites for replanting and relocation of animals;
- transportation;
- reproduction of species outside their natural habitats (*ex situ*);
- repatriation, reintroduction and rehabilitation;
- comprehensive status monitoring of rehabilitated plant and animal species and disturbed habitats; and
- protection of planted plants and resettled animals, and of the habitats disturbed as a result of negative impact from the introduction of adventitious species of flora and fauna.

It is unfortunate that the programme was limited and only temporary. In addition, the results of its practical implementation are unclear. Given the importance of the problem under consideration, it is obvious that there is a need to develop and approve the regulatory and methodological framework that applies to any cases of transfer or resettlement of Red List species of flora and fauna at the federal level.

Examples of law enforcement practice were discussed above. Judicial practice, on the other hand, when it comes to the compensation of lawful damage to the environment, is quite sparse. However, a very interesting court decision should be cited that directly addresses the issue of compensation for lawful damage to the environment. The Supreme Court of the Russian Federation in its decision of 29 March 2018, No. AKPI18-3,[12] rejected an administrative claim of the joint-stock company the Ilim Group on several provisions of the methodology for calculating the amount of damage caused to hunting resources, approved by the order of the Ministry of Natural Resources and Ecology of 8 December 2011, No. 948.

The methodology is used to calculate the amount of damage caused to hunting resources, including damage that is a result of violation or destruction of the hunting resources' habitat, if due to such violation hunting resources have permanently (or temporarily) left the habitat, which led to their death, a reduction in the number in this territory, a decrease in productivity of their populations, as well as a reduction in the reproductive function of certain species.

The Ilim Group turned to the Supreme Court of the Russian Federation with the administrative claim on a several provisions of the methodology as they allow imposing property liabilities on persons performing lawful logging activity for the damage caused to hunting resources during such activity, and define rules of calculating the size of damage for this category of cases. The Ilim Group stated that the disputed provisions contradict Article 1064 of the Civil Code of the Russian Federation, Articles 77–78 of the Federal Law on Environmental Protection", Article 56 of the Federal Law of 24 April 1995, No. 52-FZ, on Fauna, and Articles 57–58 of the Federal Law of 24 July 2009, No. 209-FZ, on Hunting and Preservation of Hunting Resources and on Amendments to Certain Legal Acts of the Russian Federation, according to which the necessary condition for applying measures of civil liability is the illegality of the violator's actions.

In support of its claims, the administrative plaintiff pointed out that the Ilim Group is as a commercial organisation, engaged on a paid basis in logging activities on the territory of operational forests located in the Irkutsk region, including territories with public hunting grounds status. Forest plots were granted to the company on the basis of lease agreements for a period up to 31 December 2057 for the use and for the implementation of a priority investment project in forest development. The Ilim Group has been, due to judicial decisions, held civilly liable for the damage caused to the hunting resources as a result of lawful economic activities (the cutting of trees) on the base of the disputed provisions of the methodology.

The Supreme Court of the Russian Federation refused to satisfy the claim. The Court considered that the disputed provisions of the methodology do not establish the grounds and conditions of civil liability for the damage caused to

---

[12]   https://legalacts.ru/sud/reshenie-verkhovnogo-suda-rf-ot-29032018-n-akpi18-3.

hunting resources and their habitats and do not regulate the questions related to proving the fact of a violation of current legislation. In the matters in dispute there are no provisions that allow for establishing a causal relationship between the actions of the economic entity and the damage caused. The disputed provisions are suitable quantifying damage the infliction of which, as well as the presence of fault on the part of the violator in the application of the methodology, has already been proven.

Thus, this judgment of the Supreme Court of the Russian Federation allows the conclusion to be drawn that in judicial practice cases of compensation of damage to the environment as a result of committing an offence and as a result of lawful activity are not distinguished. In these cases, the same methodology of compensation for damage caused to hunting resources is used. It is difficult to agree with this approach in judicial practice.

5. FEATURES OF THE COMPENSATION OF LAWFUL DAMAGE TO AQUATIC BIOLOGICAL RESOURCES

It should be noted that the legislation on fisheries provides for mechanisms for the participation of nature users in the conservation and restoration of aquatic biological resources. In accordance with Article 50 of the Federal Law on Fisheries and Conservation of Aquatic Biological Resources, the Russian Government decree of 29 April 2013, No. 380, on Approval of the Regulations on Measures for the Conservation of Aquatic Biological Resources and their Habitat provides for measures for biological resources and conservation of their habitats. Among such measures are the elimination of consequences of a negative impact on the status of aquatic biological resources and their habitats through artificial reproduction and acclimatisation of aquatic biological resources or fishery melioration of water bodies, including the creation of new production facilities or the expansion or modernisation of existing facilities that ensure implementation of such measures.

These measures, including maintenance and operation of production facilities, are fully carried out by legal entities and individuals, including individual entrepreneurs, at their own expense or with the involvement of legal entities and individual entrepreneurs engaged in artificial reproduction, acclimatisation of aquatic biological resources or fishery melioration of water bodies on a contractual basis until such impact on biological resources and their habitats is terminated.

Despite the fact that a regulatory framework for the implementation of measures for the protection and restoration of aquatic biological resources intended to improve the efficiency of regulation of social relations already exists, forms of relevant agreements, methods and guidelines to determine the volume and cost of compensation measures must be approved.

Experts note that fisheries management organisations give preference to in-kind compensation over monetary compensation in the framework of contractual relations with economic entities in accordance with regional (basin) programmes for the conservation of aquatic biological resources.[13]

In order to optimise the existing mechanism for the conservation of aquatic biological resources and their habitats, as well as to improve the efficiency of its work, regional (basin) programmes for the conservation of aquatic biological resources are proposed to be used as the basis for the management of the compensation measures system.[14]

Thus, the federal legislation must distinguish between compensation of the damage caused to the environment and compensation of the planned ecological damage which is caused as a result of the implementation of the corresponding project. It is important that legislation provides for the obligation of initiators of economic and other activities to carry out periodic monitoring of the project and fix the environmental damage in the framework of industrial environmental control. The environmental user is obliged to inform the authorised executive bodies about the results of this monitoring.

It is obvious that compensation of lawful environmental damage requires special legal regulation. This aspect of social relations is hardly regulated in environmental and natural resource law, except for compensation for damage to aquatic biological resources. At the same time, legal environmental damage is also not a homogeneous legal category. When designing project documentation, the initiator of the activity should assess the future environmental damage that will be caused during the construction (reconstruction) of the facility. In this regard, there are two problems: first, the lack of methods for assessing such damage, so in practice, designers have to take the methodology for determining the amount of illegal environmental damage as a basis; and second, the law (with the exception of aquatic biological resources) does not provide for the procedure for compensation for damage caused in the process of planning of economic activities.

---

[13]   A. Belousov & V. Voronkov, On natural and monetary forms of compensation for damage caused to aquatic biological resources, in S. Bogolyubov, N. Kamynina & M. Ponomarev (eds.), Legal problems of compensation for damage caused to the environment: proceedings of the International Scientific-Practical Conference (Moscow State University of Geodesy and Cartography, Institute of Legislation and Comparative Law under the Government of the Russian Federation, 23 March 2017), 2017, p. 146.

[14]   V. Voronkov & A. Tortsev, On the regional (basin) programme for the conservation of aquatic biological resources as the basis for the planning of compensatory measures, in S. Bogolyubov, N. Kamynina & M. Ponomarev (eds.), Legal problems of compensation for damage caused to the environment: proceedings of the International Scientific-Practical Conference (Moscow State University of Geodesy and Cartography, Institute of Legislation and Comparative Law under the Government of the Russian Federation, 23 March 2017), 2017, pp. 152–155.

Such a procedure cannot be universal: it must be conditioned by the peculiarities of compensation for environmental damage to a particular natural resource. A similar situation occurs in cases of lawful environmental damage that may be caused in the course of operation of the corresponding facility.

6. DIRECTIVE 2004/35/CE AND RUSSIAN LEGISLATION: COMPARISON OF APPROACHES

It is interesting to analyse the approaches used in the Russian legislation and Directive 2004/35/CE of the European Parliament and of the Council on environmental liability (Environmental Liability Directive) in relation to the issues of compensation for damage to the environment in the context of the study of legal problems of compensation for lawful damage to the environment.

It should be noted that the approaches are different. The legislation of the Russian Federation hardly regulates the application of measures aimed at preventing damage to the environment. The Environmental Liability Directive, by contrast, aims at preventing environmental damage (Articles 5 and 8). This approach could be used to improve the legislation of the Russian Federation. Besides the EU level, compensation for damage caused to the environment is also regulated at the level of national legislation of the Member States of the European Union.

The concept of "environmental damage" is defined more widely in Article 2 of the Environmental Liability Directive than it is in the Russian legislation. Features of environmental damage in relation to the damage to protected species, habitats, water resources and lands are addressed separately. Moreover, in the Environmental Liability Directive, environmental damage is broadly defined as a professional activity, corresponding to established criteria (Article 3). It does not matter whether this activity is a violation of the law or a lawful activity. This approach seems to be fair for the purposes of prevention of damage compensation, but for the purposes of assessment and compensation of damage it is important to distinguish damage to the environment caused by an offence from lawful damage to the environment.

7. CONCLUSION

Lawful damage to the environment can be considered a negative change to the environment and its components as a result of planning or implementing lawful economic activities. The need to identify the category of "lawful damage to the environment" in legislation and law enforcement practice is vital due to the fact that such a need objectively exists in law enforcement practice, in particular in the field of protection of aquatic biological resources, and this need is also reflected in judicial practice.

The Federal Law on Environmental Protection needs to be improved in terms of its regulation of compensation for lawful damage to the environment. The title of Chapter XIV of the federal law must be corrected in such a manner that the requirements for compensation of lawful environmental damage would not enter into conflict with the title of the chapter, which is currently to do with establishing types of legal liability for violating environmental legislation. This Chapter should distinguish between cases of causing lawful and unlawful environmental damage and define the features of compensation for lawful damage to the environment.

Recovery of lawful environmental damage from the nature user caused in the course of economic activity is not regulated in the legislation; there are no methodological documents, fees or methods. The calculation of compensation for lawful damage to the environment should be carried out at the planning stage of activity, in the development of the project and other supporting documentation. This is due to the fact that often much of the negative impact on the environment is inflicted in the process of construction or reconstruction of the corresponding facility. As we know, it is easier to prevent or minimise any damage than to compensate for it later. Therefore, the problem of compensation for lawful environmental damage at the planning stage of an economic activity is very relevant and important.

For the purpose of optimal legal regulation, it is necessary to legally distinguish the procedures for compensating for future lawful environmental damage in the planning or design of facility from compensation for actual environmental damage that may be caused at the operation stage of the corresponding facilities.

When analysing the Russian environmental legislation and the European Environmental Liability Directive, it should be noted that the approaches used are different. The legislation of the Russian Federation hardly regulates the application of preventive measures aimed at preventing damage to the environment. The Environmental Liability Directive, by contrast, aims, among other things, at preventing damage to the environment (Articles 5 and 8). This approach could be used to improve the legislation of the Russian Federation.

ECOLOGICAL ENVIRONMENTAL DAMAGE LIABILITY RULES IN THE LIGHT OF THE PRIVATE LAW REGIME

Problems and Experience in China

Yu Cheng, Congwen Yao and Wenhong Ren[*]

1. INTRODUCTION

Ecological or ecological environmental damage liability[1] has become a fast-evolving theme both in international and national environmental law.[2] Many traditional questions have been reiterated and redeveloped in this field, including liability principles (fault or no-fault), causality, legal standing, damage calculation and so on. In theory, there are basically two types of ecological damage liability. First, there is liability for restoring the damaged ecological environment, i.e. to restore the damaged ecological environment to the state

---

[*]   The authors would like to extend their deep gratitude to Professor Luc Lavrysen at Ghent University for providing a lot of help and support during the process of writing this chapter.

[1]   In the Chinese legal research literature, the professional terms often used together are ecological damage, environmental damage and ecological environmental damage. Generally speaking, environmental damage includes damage to human beings and the environment itself, while ecological damage and ecological environmental damage refer specifically to the damage to the environment itself. Since the concept of ecological environmental damage is adopted by almost all Chinese policy and legal documents, this chapter also uses this concept in during discussion, but there is no substantial difference between the concept of ecological environmental damage and the concept of ecological damage.

[2]   On 2 February 2018 the International Court of Justice rendered its first decision on environmental damage and compensation in the case Certain Activities Carried Out by Nicaragua In the Border Area (Costa Rica v. Nicaragua) Compensation Owed by the Republic of Nicaragua to the Republic of Costa Rica, available at: https://www.iucn.org/fr/node/30026.

provided that has no damage,[3] or to a state that required by law. For some damage which cannot be restored, the liable parties can also be required by law to restore other places alternatively. Second, there is monetary compensation liability: when ecological damage cannot be restored (and there is no applicable alternative restoration), or the restoration is not cost-effective, then liable parties shall pay monetary compensation for the losses of ecological services. Restoration liability is the primary form of liability in modern environmental law. However, ecological damage liability does not specifically belong to private law or public law. In different countries, ecological damage liability rules may be stipulated either in private law or in public law, or in both.[4]

China has a tradition of protecting ecological public interest through public law and traditional tort law. However, the incomplete public liability rules for ecological damage[5] and weak environmental administrative enforcement[6] and judicial supervision[7] cause many problems in the enforcement of

---

[3]   Since the ecological environment will change naturally, it is necessary to refer to the state of the ecological environment when no damage is assumed to occur when restoring the damaged environment.

[4]   There are many jurisdictions applying public law to enforce liability rules for remedying ecological damage, such as the public or administrative approach of environmental liability in ELD and corresponding EU Member States' transposing Laws; However, some jurisdictions choose to apply private law (i.e. tort law) to enforce liability rules for ecological damage, such as Article 4 of French Law No. 2016-1087, which introduces liability rules for pure ecological damage into French Civil Code.

[5]   The liability rules under traditional public law in China do not authorise competent authorities to issue general administrative orders requiring liable parties to remedy ecological damage, except the reclamation duty under Article 42 Land Administration Law. However, the practical effect of Article 42 is weak because of several institutional defects. Firstly, Article 42 can only apply when the operation on land terminates. Secondly, Article 42 only focuses on a single environmental element (i.e. land), rather than the whole ecosystem. Thirdly, Article 42 establishes the reclamation standard from the perspective of human use. Theoretically, administrative orders used to eliminate adverse effects of environmental damage in traditional administrative law in China can be used to remedy ecological damage, such as a "restoration work notice" or notices on "demolition within a fixed time", "clean up within a fixed time" or "elimination of pollution". However, both the shackles in interpreting the above-mentioned orders in legal practice (e.g. "restoration work notice" cannot be used to restore ecological damage) and the preference of applying penalties other than administrative orders leave the above-mentioned orders unused. See *Jing Hu*, The System of Environmental Administrative Order, Journal of Huazhong University of Science and Technology (Social Science Edition) 2017 (6), p. 82, 89.

[6]   The weak enforcement of environment law can be attributed to the decentralisation of environmental law enforcement in China, which allows local government to have substantial power to resist environmental laws enacted by the central government. See *R.J. Ferris & Hongjun Zhang*, Reaching Out to the Rule of Law: China's Continuing Efforts to Develop an Effective Environmental Law Regime, William & Mary Bill of Rights Journal 2003 (11), p. 569, 595.

[7]   *Haisong Chen*, Origin and Meaning of State Obligation of Environmental Protection, Chinese Journal of Law 2014 (3), p. 62, 74 (stating that "weak enforcement of environmental administrative powers and inadequate oversight from judiciary are the reasons why China choose the method of judicial activism based on private law to improve the weak enforcement of environmental law").

environmental law.[8] Traditional private liability rules are designed to protect traditional private interests, which makes it less ideal for remedying ecological environmental damage, which embodies a public interest. Chinese judicial legislators[9] (namely the Supreme People's Court) have used the opportunity of the judicial activism reform in China to design a system of ecological damage litigation (EDL) to protect public ecological interests and achieve sustainability goals. The EDL system includes: (1) environmental private interest litigation with an ecological dimension (EPILwED); (2) environmental civil public interest litigation (ECPIL); and (3) ecological environmental damage compensation litigation (EDCL). Those instruments all have their basis in tort law, which emphasises the concept of environmental multi-governance and provides a legal framework engaging the participation of multiple stakeholders. In legal reality and practice, these legal instruments, especially ECPIL, are playing an important role in the enforcement of Chinese environmental law.[10]

However, EDL in China is still in its early stages. It needs to be enhanced with better-designed rules by drawing on experience from judicial practice. There are problems relating to conflicts of the right to sue among multiple qualified claimants and the narrow scope of the liable parties and related liability rules, and these problems obviously constrain the effectiveness of EDL. Based on the elements of claimants, liable parties, liability confirmation and claim procedure, this chapter analyses the four core elements of EDL rules in China with the intention of identifying problems and providing some possible legislative suggestions.

2. *LOCUS STANDI*: CONFLICTS OF THE RIGHT TO SUE AMONG MULTIPLE CLAIMANTS

In China, EDL claims are brought by persons or parties who have right to file EDL, mainly including: (1) environmental non-governmental organisations (ENGOs) for ECPIL; (2) governmental authorities (e.g. departments of marine environment protection) stipulated in the laws and People's Procuratorates; and (3) provincial or municipal government authorised by the State Council

---

8   *P. Goldman*, Public Interest Environmental Litigation in China: Lessons Learned from the U.S. Experience, Vermont Journal of Environmental Law 2007 (8), p. 251, 273.

9   In China, the Supreme People's Court is a specialised judicial body, but it can formulate various judicial interpretations, which can be used as the legal basis for the trial of cases. Therefore, some scholars believe that the Supreme People's Court of China has quasi-legislative powers.

10   *Mingde Cao & Fengyuan Wang*, Environmental Public Interest Litigation in China, Asia Pacific Law Review 2011 (19), p. 217, 221; *Richard Zhang & Benoit Mayer*, Public Interest Environmental Litigation in China, Chinese Journal of Environmental Law 2017 (1), p. 202, 228.

(normally, their designated agencies), or administrative branches managing natural resources authorised by the State Council. According to legal practice in recent years, these legal subjects have all brought civil cases on remedying ecological damage, but there is a structural imbalance.[11] Furthermore, because there is no specific stipulation concerning the order of priority of the legal subjects who have legal standing, there are conflicts among these legal subjects' right to sue.

2.1. LEGAL RULES AND JUDICIAL PRACTICE FOR ECOLOGICAL DAMAGE CLAIMANTS

Article 55 of the Civil Procedure Law (2012) and Article 58 of the Environmental Protection Law (2014) provide the legal basis for ECPIL practice.[12] According to these two articles, "an authority or relevant organisation prescribed by law" has the legal right to initiate a civil action on environmental pollution or ecological disruption that infringes a public interest. However, the legislation and related judicial interpretation do not provide a clear definition of the term "authority prescribed by law". Generally, only the State Oceanic Administrative Department (which has been incorporated into the Ministry of Natural Resources) is included.[13] As for ENGOs, they must meet two requirements: (1) they must have registered with the civil affairs departments of the local government at the city (divided into the district) or above level in accordance with the law; and (2) they must specially engages in environmental public interest protection activities for five or more years consecutively and have no legal violation records. The Supreme People's Court set out specific requirements for ENGOs in Articles 2–5 in its Interpretation on Several Issues concerning the Application

---

[11] According to statistics from the 2016–2017 White Paper on China's Environment & Resource Trials, there were 57 ECPIL cases (44 pending cases) litigated by ENGOs from July 2016 to June 2017. Meanwhile, there were 71 ECPIL cases (50 pending cases) litigated by People's Procuratorates. In terms of EDCL, there are three cases (two pending cases) from 2015 to June 2017. See SPC, 2016–2017 White Paper on China's Environment & Resource Trials, 13 July 2017, http://law.wkinfo.com.cn/news/detail/NDAxMDAxMDI2OTk%3D?q=.

[12] Article 55 Civil Procedure Law; Article 58 Environmental Protection Law.

[13] Article 89(2) Marine Environmental Protection Law. Essentially, the SPC stated that civil actions litigated by the State Oceanic Administrative Department in China under Article 89(2) are torts and public environmental interest litigations. Therefore, the SPC Interpretation on Several Questions Concerning Applicable Law in Adjudication of Environmental Tort Liability Dispute Cases and the SPC Interpretation on Several Issues Concerning the Application of Law in Environmental Civil Public Interest Litigation Cases are applicable in the field of marine environmental protection. In this sense, it can be said, the SPC Provisions on Several Issues Concerning the Trial of Cases Involving Damages for Harm to Marine Natural Resources, Ecology and Environment provide some special rules for the Marine Natural Resources Damage Litigation or Marine Eco-environmental Damage Compensation Litigation.

of Law in the Conduct of Environmental Civil Public Interest Litigation. The most important is the interpretation of the phrase "specially engages in environmental public interest protection activities", which means "an ENGO's major business scope is to maintain environmental public interest and engages in public environmental protection activities".[14] Soon afterwards, the newly amended Civil Procedure Law (2017) extended the right to sue to the People's Procuratorates.[15] Some environmental law scholars estimate that the number of claims pursued by the People's Procuratorates will increase and will exceed the number of claims pursued by ENGOs from the year 2016.[16] This prediction was correct. In 2018, the national courts accepted 65 environmental civil public interest litigations filed by ENGOs and concluded 16 cases; the national courts accepted 1737 environmental civil public interest litigations (including criminal affiliated civil proceedings) filed by People's Procuratorates and concluded 1252 cases. In 2019, the national courts accepted 179 environmental civil public interest lawsuits filed by ENGOs and concluded 58 cases; the national courts accepted 1954 environmental civil public interest litigations (including criminal affiliated civil proceedings) filed by People's Procuratorates and concluded 1618 cases.[17]

In 2015, China initiated a pilot programme for an ecological environment damage compensation system[18] and extended this programme to the national level in 2018.[19] According to the pilot programme, entities that have the right to sue in ecological damage cases are provincial and municipal governments authorised by the State's Council.[20] Specifically, these governmental authorities

---

[14] Supreme People's Court, China Biodiversity Conservation and Green Development Foundation v. Ningxia Ruitai Technological Company, Minshen No. 3377, 2015.

[15] Article 55(2) Civil Procedure Law; Article 13 SPC and SPP Interpretation on Several Questions Concerning Applicable Law in Environmental Civil Public Interest Litigation Cases litigated by People's Procuratorates.

[16] *Xuguang Wang & Zhanfei Wang*, New Progress in China's Environmental Public Interest Litigation, Journal of Law Application (Judicial Case), 2018 (2), p. 6, 9.

[17] The White Paper of China Environmental Resources Trial (2019); The White Paper of China Environmental Resources Trial (2017–2018).

[18] General Office of the State Council of the People's Republic of China, The Plan for the Pilot Reform of the Ecological Environment Damage Compensation System, effective on 3 December 2015.

[19] General Office of the State Council of the People's Republic of China, The Plan for the Pilot Reform of the Ecological Environment Damage Compensation System, effective on 1 January 2018.

[20] In the pilot areas of the National Natural Resources Asset Management System, the provincial governments entrusted by the public may designate a department to uniformly take on the duties of being responsible for specific work of compensation for ecological environmental damage; if the State Council directly exercises ownership of all natural resources assets for the public, departments entrusted to act on behalf of the State Council will be in charge of claiming compensation for eco-environmental damage. See Article 3.2 Plan for the Pilot Reform of the Ecological Environment Damage Compensation System, effective on 1 January 2018.

are responsible for negotiating with the liable parties and reaching an agreement on the liabilities to repair the damaged ecological environment or pay monetary compensation, and in the event that a consultation agreement cannot be reached beforehand, these authorities will bring a civil action.

Lastly, just like Article 16 of Germany's Environmental Liability Act, the environmental private liability mechanism in China also has a public interest protection function.[21] The victims in an environmental private interest litigation can sue the tortfeasor to restore the damaged private property to its original state in an environmental private interest litigation with an ecological dimension (EPILwED). Since private property is part of a wider ecosystem, the prerequisite for private property restoration is to restore a wider ecosystem. Therefore, when the court supports the plaintiff's claim, it means that the defendant should repair other elements of the ecological environment that are beyond the private property. The court can also order a polluter to assume restoration liability and determine the restoration cost if the polluter fails to carry out the restoration.[22] These claims in EPILwED are based on the interdependence and interconnection of environmental elements, which makes it difficult to clearly distinguish between ecological public interest and private interest. For example, in the case of soil contamination, restoring the damaged private land would naturally extend to the ecological public interest on this land.[23] In other words, when the court's final judgment is to restore damaged private land, implementation of the judgment would indirectly protect the ecological public interest to a certain indirect extent. From the experience of legal practice, there have already been some cases where individual victims have claimed for the restoration of particular environmental damage while claiming for compensation of individual damage.[24] However, the regime of remedying ecological damage based on environmental private interest litigation is indirect and incomplete. If private owner only chooses to claim private interest damage, rather than requiring the

---

[21] *Chao Liu*, Reviewing the Performance of Environmental Liability by the Request of Environmental Restoration: Analysis from Legal Provisions and Cases, Journal of China University of Geosciences (Social Sciences Edition) 2016 (2), p. 1, 8.

[22] Article 14 SPC Interpretation on Several Questions Concerning Applicable Law in Adjudication of Environmental Tort Liability Dispute Cases.

[23] Obviously, it is not limited to cases related to land property rights. In the case of a water pollution liability dispute determined by the Fangcheng'gang Intermediate People's Court of Guangxi Province in 2017, the Court clearly supported the plaintiff's claim that the liable parties shall bear the costs incurred for discharging bottom sludge and improving the water quality. See Fangcheng'gang Intermediate People's Court of Guangxi Province, Fangcheng'gang Guangyuanfa Aquaculture Co. Ltd v. Guangxi Luqiao Engineering Group Co. Ltd, Gui No. 6 Minzhong No. 137, 2017.

[24] Victims of traditional tort cases (i.e. EPILwED) may simultaneously claim both corresponding soil remediation costs and personal property losses. See Nantong Intermediate People's Court of Jiangsu Province, Jianjun Zhang v. Qingdao Haidelong Biotechnological Co., Ltd & Jun Zhang, Su No. 06 Minzhong No. 180, 2017.

liable parties to restore or compensate damage to an ecological public interest, ENGOs or People's Procuratorates, whether on the court's suggestion or not, can file an ECPIL case.[25]

2.2. POSITIVE CONFLICTS OF THE RIGHT TO SUE AMONG MULTIPLE CLAIMANTS

The establishment of multiple public interest representatives who can bring litigation on remedying ecological damage comes with one big theoretical and practical issue, that is the order of priority of these legal entities who have right to sue. Do all these parties have a right to sue at the same time? Is there any order of priority among these rightsholders? These important questions will not only affect the reasonable arrangement of judicial resources but also the cooperation among these parties.[26] As we know from existing legislation, governmental authorities prescribed by law, ENGOs, People's Procuratorates, and authorised provincial and municipal branches of government all have the right to bring an EDL against a polluter. Consequently, the situation might arise where all the qualified entities file civil actions regarding the same ecological damage, which may cause positive conflicts among all these rights to sue. From another perspective, it would give rise to a "tragedy of the commons" among these rights to sue, that is, these parties may "free ride" and tend to rely on other entities' right to sue in terms of protecting the ecological public interest.[27]

---

[25] Because the collective landowner did not claim for the remedy of ecological damage, the Jiang'yin Intermediate People's Court recommended that the Jiang'yin People's Procuratorate promptly intervene the criminal action procedure and file an incidental civil public interest litigation. Finally, the polluter shall not only be criminally liable for the damage, but also shall also bear civil liability for restoring the damaged land to its original state. See Jiang'yin Intermediate People's Court of Jiangsu Province, Jiang'yin People's Procuratorate of Jiangsu Province v. Mr Hongbing Wang, Chen Huan Xin Chu No. 1, 2014. In the following year, the Guangzhou Intermediate People's Court of Guangdong Province confirmed the litigious right of All-China Environmental Protection Foundation to require the liable parties to remedy fish pond damage caused by environmental pollution. See Guangzhou Intermediate People's Court of Guangdong Province, All-China Environmental Protection Foundation v. Mr Yaohong Tan & Mr Yunshuang Fang, Sui Zhong Fa Min Zi No. 3804, 2015.

[26] Many legal scholars have already paid attention to this issue and published several articles. See *Xiao Zhu*, Construction of the Main Mechanism for Claiming Ecological Damage, Law Science 2016 (3), pp. 3–12; *Hui Deng & Man'yang Zhang*, On the Conflicts and Resets of the Litigation Rights in Civil Environmental Public Interests Litigation in China, Journal of Jiangxi University of Finance and Economics 2018 (3), p. 124, 130. See also *Feng Zhang*, The Sequence Design of Environmental Public Litigation Subject, Legal Forum 2017 (2), p. 136, 142; *Zhaoxia Yang*, Study on the Basement of the Right and the Prosecute Sequence of Environmental Public Interest Litigation: Both on Theory points of real right to natural resources and environmental right, Legal Forum 2013 (3), p. 102, 112.

[27] Some scholars state that sequence rules on litigation rights for EDL cases can be helpful in terms of urging litigation right holders to file EDL. See *Feng Zhang*, supra note 26, p. 138.

Chinese judicial legislators have already realised this problem and have issued some judicial interpretations, trying to provide some defined rules on the order of priority among multiple parties' rights to sue. First of all, as to ECPIL cases, a People's Procuratorate is required to issue a public notice 30 days before initiating litigation. If no other authorities or ENGOs prescribed by law do so, the People's Procuratorate would be able to initiate litigation.[28] Second, as to the relationship between ECPIL and EDCL, the State's Council's Plan for the Pilot Reform of the Ecological Environment Damage Compensation System (Pilot Plan) stipulated that the Supreme Court should give a judicial interpretation.[29] On 5 June of 2019, after several provinces in China issued some guidance or opinions on the ecological environmental damage compensation trials,[30] the Supreme People's Court issued a judicial interpretation, entitled Some Provisions on Trial of Cases of Compensation for Eco-environmental Damage (Trial Implementation), seeking to clarify the relationship between EDCL filed by government authorities and ECPIL.[31] However, those existing legal rules are inadequate to solve the potential conflicts among all rights to sue.

First, there is no specific provision for orders of priority in ECPIL between the Marine Supervision and Management Department and the ENGOs prescribed

---

[28]　Article 13 of the SPC and SPP Interpretation on Several Questions Concerning Applicable Law in Environmental Civil Public Interest Litigation Cases litigated by People's Procuratorates.

[29]　Article 5(3) of the Plan for the Pilot Reform of the Ecological Environment Damage Compensation System.

[30]　Generally, different provinces have different regulations. In Shandong Province, an EDCL filed by the provincial government cannot stop ENGOs from filing an ECPIL relating to the same ecological damage. In this situation, courts may determine to combine the two kinds of cases and ensure consistency and coherence of judgments. See Article 7 of the Shandong High People's Court's Opinions on Eco-environmental Damage Compensation Cases (effective on 20 April 2017). While in Jiangsu Province, People's Courts shall not refuse to hear the ECPIL case litigated by ENGOs or People's Procuratorates when that provincial governments have already litigated an EDCL case about the same ecological environmental damage. However, the court trying the EDCL case shall suspend the ECPIL case. During the period of suspension, ENGOs or People's Procuratorates may withdraw the action, or the ECPIL case will be tried by the court once the trial of EDCL case is finished. See Articles 52 and 53 of the Jiangsu High People's Court's Trial Guidelines on Eco-environment Damage Compensation Litigation Cases (effective on 24 July 2018).

[31]　According to Articles 16 and 17, if an ECPIL is brought in the trial course of an EDCL, it shall be accepted by the court that accepts the EDCL and tried by the same judicial organisation. At this point, the court should suspend the hearing of the ECPIL, and wait for the completion of the EDCL, and make a judgment according to law on the ECPIL cases that do not cover the litigation requests. According to Article 18(1), if an ECPIL is brought after the judgment of the EDCL takes effect, the court shall accept the ECPIL once the environmental protection public interest organisation can prove the existence of the damage not found in the previous case. According to Article 18(2), if the litigation time of EDCL is after the judgment of ECPIL takes effect, the court shall accept the EDCL once the government agency can prove the existence of the damage not found in the previous trial.

by law. However, many courts do not recognise that ENGOs are qualified to file an ECPIL case related to marine ecological environmental damage. In 2015, Qingdao Maritime Court admitted a case, in which China's Biodiversity Conservation and Green Development Foundation sued ConocoPhillips and CNOOC for marine pollution damage liability disputes. It is likely that more ENGOs will file marine environmental public interest litigation.[32] Therefore, legislators or judiciary need to define the relationship between governmental authorities and ENGOs in the field of ECPIL, especially in marine ecological damage cases.

Secondly, as to the order of priority between People's Procuratorates and ENGOs, there are doubts as to the reasonability of Article 55(2) of the Civil Procedure Law and Article 13 of the Judicial Interpretation of People's Procuratorates' Public Interest Litigation. Some scholars argue that People's Procuratorates' right to sue should be ranked first.[33] Some argue that the order of priority between ENGOs and People's Procuratorates should be repealed to allow them to bring lawsuits independently.[34] Furthermore, the current rules on the order of priority of rights to sue do not consider the role of individual citizens. Individual citizens do not have right to independently file an ecological damage claim in China. It is argued that, in the long run, citizens should be given indirect rights.[35] In fact, even if legislation does not establish citizens' rights to sue, we should also consider the position of the citizens' environmental private interest litigation in EDL, because there will be overlaps between citizens' individual claims for the restoration of damaged property rights, such as land, and claims from other ecological damage claimants. The current rule that "ECPIL and EDCL do not affect environmental private interest litigation" is not enough to solve this overlap.

---

[32] Although some scholars state that "[t]he new Civil Procedure Law will authorise ENGOs to litigate an ECPIL case related to marine ecological environmental damage", many courts do not recognise the qualification of ENGOs in terms of filing an ECPIL case related to marine ecological environmental damage. See *Tao Bie*, A New Starting Point of the Legislation for Environmental Public Interest Litigation: Analysis of the Revision of the Civil Procedure Law and Suggestions for the Amendment of the Environmental Protection Law, Law Review 2013 (1), p. 101, 105. Currently, there is only one case, which is pending: Qingdao Maritime Court of the People's Republic of China, China Biodiversity Conservation and Green Development Foundation v. Conoco Phillips China Co., Ltd & China National Offshore Oil Co., Ltd.

[33] *Feng Zhang, supra*, note 26 at pp. 136–142.

[34] *Hui Deng & Manyang Zhang, supra*, note 26 at pp. 124–130.

[35] *Yun Liu*, The Construction of Plaintiff in Environmental Public Interest Litigation from the perspective of Concentric Circle Theory, Journal of Dalian University of Technology (Social Sciences), 2018 (39), p. 93, 100.

2.3. SOLUTIONS TO CONFLICTS OF RIGHTS TO SUE

In order to solve possible conflicts of rights to sue triggered by multiple qualified claimants, some Chinese environmental law scholars have proposed different or even opposing solutions based on different research perspectives and purposes.[36] First and foremost, the purpose of stipulating the order of priority of rights to sue is to overcome the waste of judicial resources and to avoid the situation where different claimants filed regarding the same damage. The order can also have the function of "encouraging litigation". Secondly, different claimants' abilities to represent the ecological public interest (subject matter, functional orientation,[37] etc.) determines the order of their respective claims. Moreover, the economic resources of different bodies (financial capacities, litigation specialisation, etc.) determines the order of their respective right to appeal. Fourth, the design of the order of priority should avoid unnecessary delays in litigation.

However, the present authors do not agree with current academic efforts to explore the order of priority of rights to sue in EDL cases. On the contrary, they argue that there is no need to stipulate an order of priority of different claimants' rights to sue regarding remedying ecological damage. Firstly, any effort to evaluate different claimants' ability to represent the public interest is incomplete and unfeasible, because different claimants may have problems with "representative failures".[38] Moreover, the criteria for evaluating the best or strongest public welfare representatives can be extremely vague and uncertain. Second, in the long term, differences in litigation capabilities of different claimants can be resolved as time progresses or with the improvement of

---

[36]   For instance, Feng Zhang (2017) argues that based on the Best Public Representative Standard and the Legal Economic Benefit Standard, People's Procuratorates should be the primary actor, ENGOs the secondary actor, and citizens the last resort actor. See *Feng Zhang, supra*, note 26 at pp. 136–142. Hui Deng (2018) suggests that in order to avoid unnecessary delays in litigation, the order of priority for litigation between ENGOs and People's Procuratorates should be eliminated to allow both to bring litigation independently. See *Hui Deng & Manyang Zhang, supra*, note 26 at pp. 124–130. On the basis of the theory of concentric circles, Yun Liu (2018) advocates that ENGOs should be the primary actor in the EDL, citizens and their primary collectives as secondary actor, People's Procuratorates as an indirect actor, and appropriate participation of administrative authorities (exhaustion of using administrative supervision and management power). See *Yun Liu, supra*, note 35, at pp. 93–100. Based on differentiation theory, Zhaoxia Yang (2013) proposes two schemes. Based on the ownership of natural resources, environmental protection authorities are the primary actor, People's Procuratorate the secondary actor, and citizens and ENGOs are a last resort. Whereas, based on environmental rights, citizens and ENGOs are the primary actors, environmental authorities the secondary actors, and People's Procuratorates the last actor. See *Zhaoxia Yang, supra*, note 26 at pp. 102–112.

[37]   Such as government and People's Procuratorates have different functions and responsibilities in China.

[38]   "Representative failures" means that no representative can totally and completely represent the public ecological interest.

litigation rules.[39] Furthermore, the waste of judicial resources arising from EDL cases mainly refers to the problem that one single ecological damage case is handled by the same or different courts with different trial procedures. The waste of filing resources for different plaintiffs in the same ecological damage case is actually not serious. Fourth, any orders of priority for different claimants' rights to sue will result in certain delays in litigation and prolong the waiting period for trials. The SPC and SPP Interpretation on Several Questions Concerning Applicable Law in Environmental Civil Public Interest Litigation Cases litigated by People's Procuratorates has removed the court's obligation to make an announcement after an ECPIL case is filed.[40] However, pre-trial announcement procedure and court delivery period of People's Procuratorates will still need 35 days before a court hearing the case. Fifth, to avoid the problem of different claimants being remiss in exercising their rights to sue, it is only necessary to stipulate one claimant as a last resort – that is, in the event that the other claimants do not sue, this specific claimant has the final right to sue. Obviously, this is actually a kind of litigation obligation.

In order to avoid delays in litigation and the general difficulty of selecting the best public interest representative, the authors propose abolishing the order of priority and allowing all claimants to sue independently. First, after the court admits claims from claimants, a certain announcement period should be preserved to ensure other eligible claimants' rights to sue. Meanwhile, the law should encourage different claimants to cooperate on their claims and litigation evidence through pre-litigation negotiations.

Second, after the announcement period, the court will face two situations, namely (1) the different litigants converge into a single claim, or (2) the different claimants still insist on their own demands. In both cases, the court may decide to conduct a combined trial of different ecological damage claims to ensure the coherence and consistency of judgments. In current judicial practice, the Jiangsu Provincial High Court has adopted a plan to separately admit ECPIL cases and governmental ECDL cases, but then suspend the trial of ECPIL cases.[41] This approach is not desirable because it essentially erodes the rights to sue of ENGOs and People's Procuratorates.

Third, during the trial of the case, the intervening right of other eligible claimants should be retained, but their rights shall be limited, for example no

---

[39] For example, the problem of insufficient litigation ability of ENGOs can be improved by establishing rules for exempting and reducing litigation expenses, and special aid funds for ecological damage identification and quantification.

[40] Article 17(2) of the SPC and SPP Interpretation on Several Questions Concerning Applicable Law in Environmental Civil Public Interest Litigation Cases litigated by People's Procuratorates.

[41] Article 53 of the Jiangsu High People's Court's Trial Guidelines on Eco-environment Damage Compensation Litigation Cases.

new claims can be filed. Fourth, government authorities should be set as the last resort. The reason why People's Procuratorates and ENGOs cannot be set as the last resort is that it is difficult to place a constraint on their laches in litigation through legal channels, because no other eligible claimants have the right to supervise People's Procuratorates and ENGOs if they do nothing. Government authorities are different, because once they decide not to sue, ENGOs and People's Procuratorates still enjoy the legal channel to urge them to sue through environmental administrative public interest litigation (EAPIL). This kind of system design that does not set an order of priority for different claimants' rights to sue in filing EDL cases and encourages all parties to participate in the litigation process through the court announcement procedure has a strong positive institutional benefit. It is in line with the principle of equality of procedural rights and guarantees the rights to sue for all eligible claimants. It is conducive to promoting litigation cooperation, encouraging different litigants to participate in the same case, and consulting with each other on evidence and different claims. The system design of governmental authorities as the last resort may also better conform to the new institution of EAPIL in the near future.

Last but not least, the new rules on the order of priority or no order of priority should also take into account the EPILwED filed by citizens. The authors argue that EPILwED and other EDL should not interfere with each other in principle, which has been confirmed by current legal rules.[42] However, two key issues should be noted. For one thing, legislation should allow public representatives to file EDL if private or collective entities do not sue to protect the public ecological interest. For another, as a result of the possible overlap between the judgments of EPILwED cases and that of other EDL cases, courts' consideration should be given to eliminating the corresponding legal liabilities already assumed under EPILwED cases, and to avoiding double relief for the same ecological damage.

3. LIABLE PARTIES: EXPANDED LIABLE PARTIES TO BE CONFIRMED BY LAW

Tort law and the judicial interpretations on ECPIL define liable parties as *polluters*, that is, persons who directly conduct emissions or discharges causing ecological damage, namely direct polluters. However, judicial practice continues to expand in the concept of "polluter" from *direct polluters* to various *indirect polluters*. The Pilot Plan for EDCL Cases formally allows pilot areas to expand the scope of liable parties. Some pilot areas have already enforced this kind

---

[42]   Article 29 of the SPC Interpretation on Several Issues Concerning the Application of Law in Environmental Civil Public Interest Litigation Cases; Article 3(2) of the Plan for the Pilot Reform of the Ecological Environment Damage Compensation System.

of power, such as Jiangsu Province. Due to the lack of uniform legal rules on expanding the scope of liable parties, and the flattening and unification of the elements of traditional legal liability, extended liable parties are not the same as the traditional direct polluter in terms of establishing liability, meaning that the rules on the liable parties in judicial practice are somewhat fragmented.

3.1. LEGAL RULES CONCERNING THE SCOPE OF PERSONS LIABLE FOR ECOLOGICAL ENVIRONMENTAL DAMAGE

As to ECPIL, the Interpretation of the Supreme People's Court on Several Issues concerning the Application of Law in the Conduct of Environmental Civil Public Interest Litigations did not clearly stipulate who shall be liable for ecological damage. However, since the applicable legal basis of ECPIL is tort law and judicial interpretation on environmental tort liability,[43] it can be inferred that the person liable for ecological damage in the ECPIL should be a "polluter".[44] However, unfortunately, there is no clear definition of the concept of "polluter" in Chinese environmental laws. Moreover, there are even differences in the terminology used by different secondary environmental protection laws for the concept of "polluter".[45] For EDCL, the Pilot Plan defines the liable party as "an enterprise or individual who violates law or regulations and cause damage

---

[43]   See Respondent of the Research Office of the Supreme People's Court on the SPC Interpretation on Several Questions Concerning Applicable Law in Adjudication of Environmental Tort Liability Dispute Cases – Unifying standard for judgment of environmental tort liability case, using a strict legal system to protect the ecological environment, People's Court Daily, 2 June 2015, http://rmfyb.chinacourt.org/paper/html/2015-06/02/content_98485.htm.

[44]   In addition, as to the common deceptions and fraud of environmental impact assessment agencies, environment monitoring authorities and some specific agencies (i.e. agencies engaged in the operation and maintenance of monitoring equipment and pollution prevention and control) in providing ecological environmental services, the Law also provided a kind of joint and several liability between the above-mentioned agencies or authorities and the polluters. Article 65 of the Environmental Protection Law; Article 16 of the SPC Interpretation on Several Questions Concerning Applicable Law in Adjudication of Environmental Tort Liability Dispute Cases.

[45]   For example, Article 64 of the Environmental Protection Law and Chapter 8 of the Tort Law stipulate "polluters"; Article 125 of the Air Pollution Prevention and Control Law (2015) and Article 96 of the Water Pollution Prevention and Control Law (2017) respectively referee to "enterprises and individuals that emit atmospheric pollutants causing damage" and "sewage dischargers"; Article 89 of the Marine Environmental Protection Law and Soil Pollution Prevention and Control Law (2018) provided as "liable parties" and "liable parties for soil pollution" (in fact, the general liability of soil pollution also includes land use rights holders in specific situations). And the Measures for Soil Environmental Management of Polluted Lands (Trial) stipulates "enterprises or individuals that cause soil pollution." Article 10 of Administrative Measures for the Soil Environment of the Contaminated Land Parcel (for Trial Implementation).

to the ecological environment". In addition, it authorises each pilot area to respectively expand the scope of the liable parties.[46] Taking the Guidelines for the Trial of Compensation for Ecological Environmental Damage in Jiangsu Province (Jiangsu Province Guidelines), issued by the High People's Court of Jiangsu Province, as an example, these guidelines expand the scope of liable parties for ecological environmental damage into four categories.[47] Among them, the first type of liable parties should be the primary liable parties, and the last three types should be liable jointly for remedying ecological damage together with the first type of liable parties.

It is worth noting that, according to formal legal rules, even though the scope of the liable parties within the framework of EDCL is broader than that of EPILwED and ECPIL, judicial practice of ECPIL shows that the scope of the liable parties is not limited to "direct polluters" in a general sense. Liable parties in ECPIL also include "indirect polluters" under specific circumstances, such as the original producer of pollutants,[48] the transporter of pollutants,[49] the owner of a contaminated site, the manager and contractor,[50] the lessor of a polluting

---

[46]　Article 4(2) of the Plan for the Pilot Reform of the Ecological Environment Damage Compensation System.

[47]　Namely: (1) citizens, legal persons and other organisations violating laws or regulations, resulting in environmental pollution and ecology destruction; (2) citizens, legal persons and other organisations that provide, sell and entrust the transportation of hazardous wastes or other pollutants in violation of laws and regulations; (3) environmental impact assessment agencies, environment monitoring agencies and other specific agencies engaged in the maintenance and operation of environmental monitoring equipment and pollution prevention facilities shall be liable for environmental pollution or ecological damage caused by their deception or fraud in performing environmental service activities; (4) citizens, legal persons and other organisations in violation of laws or regulations, knowing that others' behaviour can cause environmental pollution and ecological destruction, continue to lend (borrow) business premises, provide business qualifications, and sign false contracts, etc., to others. Articles 11–14 of the Jiangsu High People's Court's Trial Guidelines on Eco-environment Damage Compensation Litigation Cases.

[48]　Jiangsu High People's Court held that generator of pollutants shall be liable as result of his fault in discharging a pollutant. See Jiangsu High People's Court, Taizhou Environmental Protection Foundation v. Jiangsu Changlong Agrochemical Co. Ltd, Taixing Jinhui Chemical Industry Co. Ltd et al., Su Huan Gong Min Zhong No. 1, 2014. Shandong High People's Court held that Jiande Chemical Second Factory shall be liable for entrusting private persons who were not qualified to do so to discharge a phosphate mixture generated by their operation. See Shandong High People's Court, China Environmental Protection Foundation v. Zhejiang Xin'an Chemical Group Co., Ltd, Jiande Chemical Second Factory, Lu Min Zhong No. 1577, 2017.

[49]　Shandong High People's Court held that Hong'an Freight Co. Ltd shall be liable for overseeing transporting pollutants to a designated location. See Shandong High People's Court, China Environmental Protection Foundation v. Zhejiang Xin'an Chemical Group Co., Ltd, Jiande Chemical Second Factory, Lu Min Zhong No. 1577, 2017.

[50]　Chaozhou Intermediate People's Court of Guangdong Province held that Mr Guo shall be liable jointly and severally with his lessee, because Mr Guo knew that the purpose of renting his land was to engage in pollution activities. See Chaozhou Intermediate People's Court, Shantou Municipal People's Procuratorate of Guangdong Province v. Mr Guo et al., 2016.

facility, and the subcontractor of pollution control facilities.[51] The so-called "specific circumstances" here refers to the precondition for indirect polluters to bear ecological damage liabilities in judicial practice, that is, only indirect polluters with fault shall be liable. In other words, the liable party shall be the person who intentionally or knowingly allows direct polluters to discharge pollutants or carry out waste disposal.

3.2. CHALLENGES CAUSED BY EXPANDING THE SCOPE OF LIABLE PARTIES

The common practice for the court's extension of the scope of liable parties from direct polluters under tort law and related judicial interpretations on ECPIL to various indirect polluters can have some positive effects. For one thing, it will be helpful to pursue the idea of environmental justice and *"polluter pays" principle*, because some indirect polluters surely contribute to ecological damage. For another, this arrangement can improve liable parties' overall financial capacities to remedy ecological damage, because indirect polluters always shall be jointly or separately liable with direct polluters in judicial practice, which has already been inserted into the Jiangsu High People's Court's Trial Guidelines on Eco-environment Damage Compensation Litigation Cases.[52] However, without unifying extension principles in terms of the scope of liable parties, it can also bring a lot of issues.

Firstly, without an underlying principle to determine which indirect polluters shall be liable for remedying ecological damage, different courts in different areas may develop different scopes of liable parties. This might lead to some negative effects on market competition, that is, a "race to the pollution bottom" may encourage unfair market competition. In other words, the indirect polluters who would be liable for remedying ecological damage in some areas may move to other places where they would not be liable.[53] Furthermore, different rules

---

Guangzhou Intermediate People's Court of Guangdong Province held that Mr Fang shall be liable jointly and severally with his lessee, because Mr Fang knew that the lessee was going dump waste into the pond. See Guangzhou Intermediate People's Court of Guangdong Province, *All-China Environmental Protection Foundation v. Mr Yaohong Tan & Mr Yunshuang Fang*, Sui Zhong Fa Min Zi No. 3804, 2015.

[51] *Zhiping Li*, Mechanism Innovation and Its Reflection of Ecological Environment Restoration Justice, Journal of South China Normal University (Social Science Edition) 2018 (50), p. 152, 154.

[52] Articles 11–14 of the Jiangsu High People's Court's Trial Guidelines on Eco-environment Damage Compensation Litigation Cases.

[53] For a long time, many Chinese economic scholars have analysed the environmental regulation competition among different provincial or local governments, especially the research on race-to-the-bottom competition and its related negative impacts on ecological environment. *Ku Xun, Xiaolong Li & Guanghe Ran*, An Empirical Analysis on the Impact of Local

about the scope of liable parties in different places may also be negative for the development of the environmental insurance market in China, because environmental insurance companies may not be able to predict who will be liable for remedying ecological damage.[54]

Second, this "disorderly expansion" of the scope of liable parties has led to the departure from the principle of liability rules (namely the no-fault principle) in the application of tort law. In order to fully realise the legislative purpose of compensating the victims of environmental pollution and promoting social justice, China's tort law has established "the most stringent no-fault liability",[55] which not only cancels the "illegality requirements" for establishing environmental liability (namely a conviction for civil liability does not require the liable parties' behaviour to violate national laws and regulations), but also establishes the principle of no-fault liability for environmental torts as the only applicable principle (i.e. it does not distinguish the nature of the activity from the nature of the damaged rights, and applies the principle of no-fault liability in every case).[56] Since the Judicial Interpretation on Environmental Civil Public Interest Litigation does not specifically regulate this issue, ECPIL shall also pursue "no illegality requirements" and the "no-fault liability principle".[57]

Government Competition on Environmental Pollution in China, Journal of Beijing Institute of Technology (Social Sciences Edition), 2016 (4), p. 18, 23. Obviously, in addition to regulation strategies or regulation standards, different liabilities requirements for liable parties for ecological damage in different areas may also have negative impacts on competition.

54   China has already initiated the institution of compulsory environmental liability insurance in several fields of industry sectors that can have serious impacts on the ecological environment. Obviously, if there is no general principle about the scope of the liable parties, then the market of environmental liability insurance for ecological damage may not encounter several developing problems to be solved.

55   *Xinbao Zhang & Chao Zhuang*, Expansion and Strengthening: Comprehensive Application of Environmental Tort Liability, Social Sciences in China 2014(3), p. 125, 127.

56   Article 65 of the Tort Law.

57   There are theoretical arguments on the issue of whether the no-fault rule under traditional tort law should be applicable in the field of liability rules for ecological damage. Xin Yin states that the no-fault liability rule should be applicable. See *Xin Yin*, Discussion of the Remedy Mechanism for Ecological Damage with Tort Liability Law, Journal of Henan Normal University (Philosophy and Social Sciences) 2016 (5), p. 54, 56–57. However, Hai Jin states that it should be reasonable that we need to apply fault liability rules in remedying ecological damage. See *Hai Jin*, On Liability Principle of Ecological Damage Compensation, Journal of Hunan University of Science & Technology (Social Science Edition) 2017 (5), p. 89, 94–95. Based on the argument that there is a need to change the no-fault rule in the field of remedying traditional environmental damage, more and more scholars tend to stand by dualist approach. In other words, if ecological damage is caused by normal other than dangerous operation activities, the fault liability rules shall be applicable. See *Guangfa Tong*, The Doctrine of Liability Fixation of Environmental Tort, Oriental Law 2015 (3), pp. 36–38. However, this kind of discourse in the theoretical circle has not affected the "popularity" of monism (i.e. no-fault liability rules) in judicial practice. When the court determines the legal liability for remedying ecological damage, it will clearly point out the applicability of Article 65 of the Tort Law.

From the perspective of the Pilot Plan and the trial guidelines or opinions issued by local courts, only the "illegal requirements" are specified, but the "no-fault liability principle" is not involved. Therefore, it can be inferred that EDCL based on tort law shall also apply the general principle of tort law, that is the no-fault liability principle, which is also confirmed by the corresponding judicial practice.[58] For indirect polluters, once they can be covered under the concept of "polluter" under tort law and the related Supreme People's Court Interpretation of Environmental Tort Liability, it can be inferred that the principle of no-fault liability should also apply to them. However, ECPIL practice and EDCL rules are based on the principle of fault to determine whether polluters (including indirect polluters) shall assume liabilities. Moreover, the "illegality requirements" are clearly defined in the EDCL rules.[59] In other words, for the same ecological damage, if ENGOs or People's Procuratorates decide to file an ECPIL case, the illegality issue is not considered, and if the case is filed by government agencies, they must prove that relevant national laws or regulations have been violated. The disorderly expansion of the scope of liable parties will eventually lead to a fragmentation effect in the application of liability rules for ecological damage, that is, there may be a chaotic situation in which different liability principles and different illegality requirements are applied. From the perspective of the burden of proof, this kind of "faulty requirement" for indirect polluters will increase the plaintiff's burden of proof.[60]

Third, even though the scope of liable parties for ecological damage liability extends from direct polluters to indirect polluters and persons who have been confirmed by the ECPIL judicial practice and the ECDL rules, its scope is still limited. Many areas of liability that may or should be included are still outside the scope of legal rules in judicial practice, such as the liability of credit institutions,[61] the liability of insurance companies, the liability of polluters'

---

[58] See Chongqing First Intermediate People's Court, People's Government of Chongqing Municipality & Chongqing Liangjiang Voluntary Service Center v. Chongqing Cangjin'ge Property Management Co., Ltd & Chongqing Shouxu Environmental Protection Technology Co. Ltd, Yu No. 1 Min Chu No. 733, 2017.

[59] In general environmental tort law, "illegality requirements" had been cancelled by legislators, but these requirements are clearly defined in the EDCL rules.

[60] *Zhiping Li, supra*, note 51 at p. 154.

[61] Green Home of Fujian filed an ECPIL case against Yicheng Xiangda Agriculture and Livestock Co., Ltd for its water pollution of the Han River before Shiyan Intermediate People's Court of Hubei Province on 6 June 2018. One month later, Green Home of Fujian submitted an Additional Defendant Application, stating that both Agricultural Bank of China Co., Ltd Yicheng Sub-branch and Hubei Yicheng Rural Commercial Bank Co., Ltd would be the co-defendants in the case. The Shiyan Intermediate People's Court finally decided to make a ruling on whether to add the two banks as co-defendants at first. However, the Shiyan Intermediate People's Court has not yet ruled. See Two banks lending to illegal sewage company will be co-defendants with polluter, China Environmental News, No. 8, August 2018, http://news.cenews.com.cn/html/2018-08/15/ Content_75356.htm.

parent or grandparent companies or successors,[62] the liability of polluter companies' shareholders and senior management, and the government's liability.

3.3. LEGISLATIVE RECOMMENDATIONS

Although extending the scope of liable parties for remedying ecological damage has several positive effects, disorderly expansion may not be the best approach. In view of the practical problems arising from the expansion of the scope of liable parties for remedying ecological damage, the authors argue that adjustments should be made through the revision of legal rules.

First, since EDCL and ECPIL have the same function in terms of maintaining the ecological public interest, the authors argue that the determination of the scope of the liable parties and whether the liable parties shall assume liability according to the principle of non-fault or the requirements of illegality should have the same standards, rather than forming two different sets of liability rules.

If two different sets of liability rules are ultimately formed, it will inevitably produce a fragmented system, that is, for the same ecological damage incident, different potential parties are liable for different degrees of liability based on different requirements.[63] Secondly, with the goal of protecting the ecological environment, the scope of liable parties for remedying ecological damage should not be limited to "direct polluters", but should be extended to "indirect polluters" in different specific situations. It is still in question whether a different liability principle should be applied to different scenarios between direct polluters and indirect polluters. Finally, the expansion of the scope of liable parties should be carried out in an orderly manner. Because China has no case law tradition, it is not a long-term legal policy to rely on the expanded scope of liable parties originating from judicial practice. Because judicial precedents do not have legally binding force for other cases, different courts will have different judgments on the same or similar situations, which is not conducive to the standardisation of judicial decisions. Obviously, this can also have some negative impacts on market competition and increase unpredictability about liabilities for remedying ecological damage constraining the development of the environmental insurance market.

---

[62] It should be noted that Article 47 of New Soil Prevention and Pollution Control Law (2018) set a liability rule for polluters' successors. According to this article, polluters' successors shall be liable for performing risk control actions and remedy actions, or for costs incurred by these actions.

[63] *Zhiping Li, supra*, note 51 at p. 154.

From a long-term perspective, since ECPIL and EDCL aiming at implementing the liability rules for remedying ecological damage are based on tort law, it may be considered to amend the relevant provisions of the Tort Law or the Civil Code. The new Chapter VII (entitled "The Liability for Remedying Eco-environmental Damage") of the proposed Civil Code accepts the unified concept of "tortfeasor". Consideration should also be given to an important issue with the nature of legal policy, i.e. how to establish justified and reasonable principles for applying liability rules for remedying ecological damage, including the requirements for elements of liabilities such as "illegal requirements" and "faults". In this way, it is also possible to overcome the shortcomings of the current environmental tort legislation, which is too flat. The rules of specific liable parties' liabilities can also be stipulated in other relevant laws. For example, liabilities of parent companies and shareholders and senior management can be considered in the Company Law or other environmental, laws such as Article 47 of the Soil Pollution Prevention and Control Law (2018).

4. REMEDIES INCLUDING RESTORATION AND COMPENSATION FOR LOSSES

Civil remedies in Chinese civil law are not limited to restitution to the original state and monetary compensation, but also include other various specific remedies.[64] Based on this special legislative tradition and the nature of EDL in terms of protecting a public interest, judicial legislators established six types of remedies in Article 13 of the Judicial Interpretation of Environmental Tort Liability and article 18 of the Judicial Interpretation of Environmental Civil Public Interest Litigation. These remedies are: stop the infringement; remove the impediment; eliminate the danger; provide restitution, apologise; and compensate for losses. Article 19 of the Jiangsu Province Guidelines also stipulates these six forms of civil remedies. Among them, as forms of preventive liability, *stop the infringement, remove the impediment* and *eliminate the danger* are similar to injunctive relief in the Anglo-American system. It means that "the court forces the person who causes or may cause environmental damage to eliminate possible environmental hazards, or to stop activities that has caused environmental damage and to eliminate the continued environmental hazard."[65] Apology is normally applied to the illegal infringement of the right to personality, but as result of the extension of judicial practice, the claimant in EDL can also

---

[64]   Article 179 of the General Provisions of the Civil Law; Article 15 of the Tort Law.
[65]   *Hui Zhang*, Assumption of Responsibility in Environmental Public Interest Civil Litigation, Legal Forum 2014 (5), p. 58, 61.

claim an apology.[66] In the case of EDL, the two most common types of litigation claims are "restitution" and "compensation for losses".[67]

4.1. RULES ON "RESTORATION" AND "COMPENSATION FOR LOSSES" IN EDL

One of the most striking features of China's recent rapid development of environmental law is the establishment of some new rules of ecological restoration with a focus on restitution, which is not the same as the restitution in traditional private interest damage cases. In EPILwED cases, courts may decide that defendants to bear liabilities for restoring damaged environment (if complete restoration cannot be obtained, courts can alternatively order defendants to perform off-site restoration) and determine corresponding restoration costs that defendants should bear should they fail to perform the restoration.[68] In the same way, in ECPIL cases, the court may decide that the defendant should assume liabilities for ecological restoration (namely returning the damaged ecological environment to its state and function before the damage occurred),[69] and also ask defendants who do not restore damaged environment to bear corresponding restoration costs.[70] Courts may also directly hold that defendants shall be liable for bearing ecological restoration costs.[71] Generally, restoration costs include the costs of developing and implementing restoration plans, as well as related monitoring and supervision costs.[72] Restoration costs (namely ecological restoration) are generally determined by the appraisal opinions given by special agencies providing environmental services or experts in the field of assessing ecological damage. When restoration costs are difficult to define or the costs

---

[66] For example, Dezhou Intermediate People's Court of Shandong Province held that Dezhou Jinhua Group Zhenhua Co., Ltd must offer a public apology in the media that is provincial level or above. See Dezhou Intermediate People's Court, All-China Environmental Protection Foundation v. Dezhou Jinhua Group Zhenhua Co., Ltd, De Zhong Huan Gong Min Chu Zi No. 1, 2015.

[67] Among the 49 ECPIL cases which have already been judged, in 44.44 per cent of cases the courts allowed damages, and in 55.56 per cent the courts allowed restoration. *Zhongmin Zhang*, Limitations of the Defendant in Environmental Public Interest Litigation and Ways of Overcoming Them, Global Law Review 2016 (5), p. 42, 54.

[68] Article 14 of the SPC Interpretation on Several Issues Concerning the Application of Law in Environmental Civil Public Interest Litigation Cases.

[69] If complete restoration for ecological damage is impossible, then courts may allow complementary restoration. See Article 20(1) of the SPC Interpretation on Several Issues Concerning the Application of Law in Environmental Civil Public Interest Litigation Cases.

[70] Id., Article 20(1) and (2).

[71] Id., Article 20(2).

[72] Id., Article 20(3).

of identifying them are too high, courts may also set the restoration costs by exercising their discretionary judicial power.[73]

In addition to ecological restoration, there is another kind of remedy in terms of remedying ecological damage, namely "compensation for losses".[74] ECPIL clearly lists the types of compensated losses, including "loss of ecological service and/or function pending restoration",[75] as well as "inspection, appraisal costs, reasonable attorney fees and other reasonable expenses for litigation".[76] If the plaintiff claims expenses incurred by stopping the infringement, removing the impediments, eliminating the danger and taking reasonable prevention and disposal measures, it can be concluded that the above-mentioned losses should also be "compensated losses".[77] In order to ensure ecological restoration, the Judicial Interpretation on Environmental Civil Public Interest Litigation clearly provides a special rule, which is different from the traditional rule in private interest litigation (namely that the plaintiff in the latter can use the compensation for damages as they want), requiring the plaintiff to use the full compensation for ecological restoration.[78] Finally, in order to encourage the plaintiff to actively participate in ECPIL cases, judicial legislators amended the one-way principle for winning litigation costs, namely, court may, at its discretion, pay some of the defendants' compensation to the "losing plaintiff" to reimburse its necessary expenses for investigation and evidence collection, expert consultation and inspection.[79]

At present, there is no specific legislation for EDL at national level. Each pilot area can conduct "experimental legislation" according to local situations, and independently determine corresponding liability rules for remedying ecological

---

[73] If it is difficult to determine the restoration costs, or if the assessment cost is very high, then courts can directly determine the restoration cost, taking several factors into account. The factors include, but are not limited to, the scope and extent of the ecological damage, the scarcity of the ecological damage, the difficulty of restoring the ecological damage, the operating cost of preventing and controlling pollution equipment, the degree of the defendants' fault for and benefits received from the unlawful act, and opinions from experts or departments responsible for environmental protection supervision and management. See Article 23 of the SPC Interpretation on Several Issues Concerning the Application of Law in Environmental Civil Public Interest Litigation Cases.

[74] Although some legal scholars state that damages cannot be a kind of remedy in EDL cases, it has already been a kind of applicable remedy both in theory and in judicial practice. See *Hui Zhang, supra*, note 65 at pp. 61–62; *Xinyu Li*, Study on Damages in Environmental Public Civil Litigation, Political Science and Law 2016 (10), p. 19, 20.

[75] Id., Article 21 of The SPC Interpretation on Several Issues Concerning the Application of Law in Environmental Civil Public Interest Litigation Cases.

[76] Id., Article 22.

[77] Id., Article 19(2).

[78] Id., Article 24(1).

[79] Id., Article 24(2).

damage.[80] Taking the Jiangsu High People's Court as an example, a government claimant can directly request defendants to remedy the damaged environment (namely returning the damaged ecological environment to the state and function before the damage occurred).[81] Courts may make the following judgments: (1) that the defendants shall be liable for ecological restoration; the courts may also determine the restoration costs that the defendant shall bear when the defendant fails to perform;[82] (2) if defendants are unable to carry out ecological restoration, the courts may decide that the defendants shall entrust an independent third party to perform restoration, for which the defendants shall bear the costs;[83] or (3) the courts may decide that the defendants shall pay the restoration costs to the plaintiffs and latter carry out restoration actions once the costs have been paid to the plaintiffs' account.[84] The Jiangsu High People's Court also made detailed provisions on implementation of alternative restoration if there is "incomplete on-site restoration".[85] For how to carry out alternative restoration, courts may decide that defendants shall pay ecological restoration costs to a bank account held by an *ecological environmental restoration base* specifically for restoring damaged ecological environment according to judgments, and the base institution will be in charge of carrying out the ecological restoration, and plaintiffs will be responsible for supervision.[86] As for compensation for losses, the Jiangsu High People's Court considers that

---

[80]   Min Li states that the concept of experimental legislation, necessity, function, theoretical rules and the status of experimental legislation shape local governments in China. *Min Li*, Theoretical Construction and Empirical Analysis of Experimental Legislation: Taking Article 13 of China's Legislation Law as the Center, Political Science and Law 2017 (36), pp. 84–94.

[81]   Article 39(1) of the Jiangsu High People's Court's Trial Guidelines on Eco-environment Damage Compensation Litigation Cases.

[82]   Id., Article 36.

[83]   Id., Article 37.

[84]   Id., Article 38.

[85]   The Jiangsu High People's Court also made detailed provisions on the implementation of alternative restoration if there is "incomplete on-site restoration", namely where: (1) the damaged ecological environment cannot be restored as it was or cannot be completely restored to original state; (2) it is too difficult or costly to carry out a complete on-site restoration, or it is not necessary to restore the damaged ecological environment according to planning adjustments, etc.; (3) the choice of alternative off-site restoration is more economical and more conducive to maintaining the overall ecological environment of the region and the basin. Article 39(2) of the Jiangsu High People's Court's Trial Guidelines on Eco-environment Damage Compensation Litigation Cases.

[86]   Article 40 of the Jiangsu High People's Court's Trial Guidelines on Eco-environment Damage Compensation Litigation Cases. In China, Provincial and local governments have set up many ecological environmental restoration bases. In EDL cases, if the liable parties who have obligations of ecological environment restoration are unable to restore the damaged ecological environment or natural resources, they shall pay restoration costs to the ecological environmental restoration base, and the base will carry out some ecological environmental restoration works.

damages or losses to be compensated are: costs for emergency actions; ecological restoration costs; functional losses (including losses of ecological environmental services and/or functions pending restoration, permanent losses of ecological environmental services and/or functions, losses caused by environmental health damage); auxiliary costs; and other reasonable expenses.[87]

Courts may quantify and determine the restoration costs and compensable losses on a case-by-case basis using the following types of evidence: (1) appraisal opinions; (2) investigation, inspection, test and/or assessment reports or monitoring data provided by government agencies or agencies appointed by them; (3) experts' opinions; and (4) other evidence.[88] For ecological restoration costs, the Jiangsu Province Guidelines establish a rule similar to that of ECPIL, that is, without proper appraisal agencies, without qualification conditions, when it is impossible to identify or determine the specific amount or when the cost of identification is obviously too high, the court can make a reasonable discretion based on specific factors and reference to expert opinions.[89]

One issue worth mentioning is that the Ministry of Environmental Protection (succeeded by the Ministry of Ecology and Environment) has published some guidelines for assessing ecological environmental restoration costs and losses of ecological environmental services and/or functions pending restoration (namely the concept of ecological environmental damage under these guidelines),[90] but these guidelines are not legally binding, which means that appraisal and assessment agencies do not need to be consistent with the guidelines, and those conclusions inconsistent with these guidelines are not necessarily inadmissible.[91] For assessment techniques, the guidelines also dictate a hierarchy of assessment techniques, starting with alternative equivalency analysis methods and moving to environmental valuation methods where alternative equivalency analysis

---

[87]   Id., Article 20.

[88]   Id., Article 30.

[89]   If there is no qualified assessment agencies or the facts of the case make it difficult to assess the restoration cost, or the assessment cost is very high, then courts can determine the restoration cost themselves, taking several factors into account, including but not limited to: the scope and extent of the ecological damage, the scarcity of the ecological damage, the difficulty of restoring the ecological damage, the operating cost of preventing and controlling pollution equipment, the degree of the defendants' fault for and benefits received from unlawful act, and opinions from experts or departments responsible for environmental protection supervision and management. Article 35 of the Jiangsu High People's Court's Trial Guidelines on Eco-environment Damage Compensation Litigation Cases.

[90]   Article 8.1.1 of the Technical Guidelines for Identification and Assessment of Eco-environmental Damage: General Programme, 30 June 2016, http://www.mee.gov.cn/gkml/hbb/bgt/201607/t20160705_357139.htm.

[91]   See General Office of the Ministry of Environmental Protection, Technical Guidelines for Identification and Assessment of Eco-environmental Damage: General Programme, Damage Investigation, 30 June 2016, http://www.mee.gov.cn/gkml/hbb/bgt/201607/t20160705_357139.htm.

methods are unable to value ecological environmental damage.[92] In addition to impossible application, there are also several special situations where the use of environmental valuation methods may be recommended.[93]

In judicial practice, the most often used environmental evaluation method is the virtual governance cost method (VGCM), which is to multiply quantity of pollutants and unit governance cost by the corresponding sensitivity coefficient to arrive at the final "ecology remediation cost".[94] Although the Ministry of Environmental Protection issued its Opinions on the limited applicable range of VGCM, the nature of its vague applicable scope and the simplification of the identification process still make it a popular method in judicial practice.[95]

---

[92] For the alternative equivalency analysis method, there are four kinds of methods: resources equivalency analysis, service equivalency analysis, value-to-value, and value-to-cost. Generally, the value-to-value method is preferable to the value-to-cost method under the same conditions. If it is impossible to apply the alternative equivalency analysis method, then environmental valuation methods should be used, including the four main kinds of specific methods, namely: direct market value method, the revealed preference method, the stated preference method, and the benefit transfer method. It should be noted that there is also a hierarchy of environmental valuation methods: the Guidelines recommend applying the above-mentioned methods in turn. See Article 8.2 of the Technical Guidelines for Identification and Assessment of Eco-environmental Damage: General Programme, 30 June 2016, http://www.mee.gov.cn/gkml/hbb/bgt/201607/t20160705_357139.htm.

[93] The special situations include: (a) when assessing biological resources, if the concentration of pollutants in the organism or the incidence of the control area is selected as the baseline level evaluation index, it is recommended to use the environmental value assessment method because it is difficult to measure it during the ecological environment recovery process; (b) due to certain restrictions, the ecological environment cannot be fully restored through the project, and the environmental damage assessment method is used to assess the permanent damage of the ecological environment; and (c) if the cost of the eco-environmental restoration project is greater than the expected benefit, an environmental value assessment method is recommended. See Article 8.2.5 of Technical Guidelines for Identification and Assessment of Eco-environmental Damage: General Programme, 30 June 2016, http://www.mee.gov.cn/gkml/hbb/bgt/201607/t20160705_357139.htm.

[94] Chongqing First Intermediate People's Court, People's Government of Chongqing Municipality & Chongqing Liangjiang Voluntary Service Center v. Chongqing Cangjin'ge Property Management Co., Ltd & Chongqing Shouxu Environmental Protection Technology Co. Ltd, Yu No. 1 Min Chu No. 733; Jiangsu High People's Court, Taizhou Environmental Protection Foundation v. Jiangsu Changlong Agrochemical Co., Ltd, Taixing Jinhui Chemical Industry Co. Ltd et al., Su Huan Gong Min Zhong Zi No. 1, 2014.

[95] According to the Opinions, VGCM shall only be applied in the following three situations: (1) although the fact that emitting pollutants exists, ecological damage is not certain because observation or emergency monitoring is not timely, or the damaged ecological environment has been already restored by natural recovery; (2) ecological damage cannot be fully restored by restoration; (3) the cost of ecological restoration is grossly disproportionate to the benefits. Moreover, there are two situations in which VGCM should not be applied: (1) there are certain costs of emergency actions or costs of restoration actions that can be obtained through surveys and ecological damage assessment methods; (2) for the assessment of the direct economic loss of the ecological environmental damage caused by usual environmental events or pollution discharges. See Ministry of Environmental Protection, Policy Reply on the application of virtual governance cost method in terms of identifying and assessment for Eco-environmental damage, No. 1488, 2017.

Moreover, the VGCM has already become almost the only type of environmental valuation method applied in EDL cases, and it can also be used to assess ecological environmental damage even in situations where alternative equivalency analysis methods are appropriate.[96]

4.2. PROBLEMS WITH REMEDIES IN EDL CASES

It can be concluded that ecological restoration and compensation for losses (including losses of ecological environmental services and/or functions, and other related losses recognised by law) have been the main remedies in EDL cases, even though there is no special law on EDL (only Judicial Interpretations). For the relationship between those two types of remedies, courts prefer to regard the ecological environmental restoration as the primary remedy, and compensation as secondary. Obviously, if defendants do not take liability for restoration of the damaged ecological environment, then they will be liable to pay the restoration costs, and other appropriate third parties will carry out the restoration work. However, legal rules governing these two types of remedies are not very specific, which lead to a lot of problems in judicial practice.

Regarding the legal rules on ecological restoration, there are several problems. First, the goal of restoration is unclear and unreasonable. According to Article 20(1) of the Judicial Interpretation of Environmental Civil Public Interest Litigation and Article 39(1) of the Jiangsu Province Guidelines, the "original state" in restitution means "the state or function before the damage occurred". However, the Guidelines for the Assessment of Ecological Damage Assessment and Damage Investigation do not provide a definition of "state and function before the damage occurred". In addition, due to lack of information and data on the baseline conditions of the state and functioning of the ecosystem, the restoration goal is only a theoretical goal, which in fact cannot actually guide any practices. At the same time, the restoration goal requires returning to the state before the damage occurred, rather than the expected state had the damage not occurred, contrary to the principle of environmental fairness and justice.[97] Moreover, "complete restoration" of all damaged ecological environment in

---

[96]   The authors conducted an empirical research on 21 closed ECPIL cases. The results show that a total of 14 cases use the VGCM. All courts responsible for hearing water pollution cases and air pollution cases have approved the VGCM adopted by the appraisal and evaluation agencies. Some courts may adjust (i.e. appropriately increase or decrease) the sensitivity coefficient in the formula according to the facts of the case. In addition, there is also a case of soil pollution using the VGCM.

[97]   Since the ecological environment will change naturally, it is necessary to refer to the state of the ecological environment when no damage is assumed to occur when restoring the damaged environment.

every case may not be economically cost-effective. Second, there are conflicts in the application of liability rules for ecological environmental restoration. For example, when the damage cannot be "completely remedied", the court can decide to use alternative restoration, so the quantification of the ecological environmental damage should be measured by the cost of the alternative restoration measures, but the court may also allow the VGCM to be used to assess the ecological environmental damage, which means there is a conflict in the application. Moreover, the relatively simplified VGCM, as well as the ambiguity of the qualified standard while applying the VGCM, make judges prefer to apply VGCM rather than restoring damaged environment. Because the outcome obtained from the VGCM may be not applicable and fair, it may have a negative impact on the ecological environmental restoration.[98] Finally, ecological environmental restoration is a systematic project, and the preparation and selection of its programme necessarily involves multiple parties. Due to the lack of uniform guiding rules for the planning and implementation of restoration, there is a lack of clear legal requirements and judgment criteria for the parties to debate the rationality and feasibility of the restoration plan. In judicial practice, there are only few cases where courts allow public to participate in preparation for ecological environmental restoration.

As to the legal rules on compensating losses, there are also several flaws, especially in the quantification rules for compensating losses caused by ecological environmental damage. At present, the methods used in practice to identify or quantify ecological environmental damage claims mainly rely on the following schemes: judicial authentication for ecological environmental damage; reports or data issued by government agencies or their subsidiary bodies; and opinions of those with specialised knowledge. From a procedural point of view, China has already established some uniform rules on the admissible qualification and management of appraisal institutions, and the assessment and authentication procedures. However, the process of assessing the evidential effects of appraisal opinions is confusing, which is reflected in the following issues, namely: (1) qualifications of appraisal institutions and appraisers are complicated and sometimes overlap; (2) statement of appraisal items is unclear in the final opinion; (3) the basis and standards for identification are complex and diverse; (4) the standard that the court shall follow when accepting appraisal opinions

---

[98]   In fact, given that all of the environmental valuation methods may have their relative drawbacks and advantages, it is hard to say which one is the best method for certain cases. It is for this reason that the US court rejected the hierarchy of different environmental valuation techniques in Ohio v. DOI. In the judicial practice in China, the VGCM has been a domain method in assessing ecological environmental damage. However, the compensation for ecological environmental damage based on the VGCM may also fail to meet the costs of restoring the damaged ecological environment, and this method also fails to fully reflect the true value of the ecological environment, including various use values and non-use values.

does not exist; and (5) there has been a "hollowing out" of the authentication process.[99] Furthermore, there is still a lack of clear procedural rules for the participation of persons with specialised knowledge in court proceedings.

Finally, rules governing the probative value for the outcomes of different schemes are not perfect. First, appraisal opinions are regarded as a type of statutory evidence and should be subject to unified rules for process of cross-examination and identification. However, due to of the highly scientific and technical nature of environmental cases, the court's judgment is often taken over by judicial appraisal opinions, and the result is that courts either unhesitatingly adopt all appraisal opinions or refuse to adopt any appraisal opinion (namely an all-or-nothing approach).[100] Second, Article 122(2) of the Judicial Interpretation of Civil Procedure Law treats "the opinions of those with specialised knowledge" as "parties' statements", which is theoretically untenable and difficult to operate in practice.[101]

4.3. LEGISLATIVE SUGGESTIONS

In order to solve the above-mentioned problems with the rules about remedies in EDL, it is important to establish a set of new and complete liability rules for remedying ecological environmental damage. Because EDL in China is based on tort law, it should be noted that some liability rules for remedies in private law should be emphasised and others may need to be adjusted. First, the goal of restoration should be further defined. If the goal is "complete remediation", it is very important to establish databases on the basic conditions of certain ecosystems, which can be auxiliary instruments in realising the restoration goal. Relevant government agencies that are responsible for environmental protection and supervision should oversee the identifying and managing of the baseline conditions of different ecological environments. Moreover, it would be better to change the existing "complete restoration goal" (namely to the state and function before the damage occurred) to a "reasonable restoration goal"

---

[99] *Xin Cheng & Jin'gen Chen*, Study on Judicial Expertise Certification in Cases of Marine Environmental Pollution: In the perspective of judge's misuse of abstract belief in maritime procedure, Hebei Law Science 2018 (36), pp. 98–109.

[100] *Yu Cheng*, A Study on the Insurability of Ecological Damages and Viewpoints on Measures for Compulsory Liability Insurance for Environmental Pollution (for comment), Insurance Studies 2018 (38), pp. 106–109.

[101] Shuxia Dou stating that the rule if regarding opinions from experts as statement of parties can lead to several diplomas, including confusion between Testimonial Proof and Opinion Testimony, ignorance the professional ethics of expert assistants encouraging experts to sacrifice scientific values for benefits, weakening of evidentiary effect of expert opinions. See *Shuxia Dou*, Judge's Judgment on Expert Assistance and Path Analysis, Law Science Magazine 2018 (2), p. 108, 112.

(namely to the state and function that would be expected had the damage not occurred). In determining the "reasonable restoration goal", we should also consider the future use of specific ecological environment or natural resources determined by various governmental development plans.

Secondly, the designation of a unified restoration guidance can not only guide the appraisal agency to prepare the restoration plan, but also serve as the statutory guideline for judging whether the restoration plan has reasonable feasibility in the trial process. In order to avoid repeated assessment or identification problems after the event, courts should take the initiative to participate in the preparation and selection process of the restoration programme. The court is responsible for entrusting a qualified appraisal institution to prepare restoration programmes with the participation of all parties and stakeholders.

Thirdly, when the court decides on alternative restoration, the restoration cost should be used as a quantitative method for ecological damage, and the VGCM should not be directly applied. Finally, establishing more detailed guidelines for assessment of ecological environmental damage, and making more detailed regulations on the restoration of the ecological environment where the cost cannot be evaluated, can restrict the court's discretion to apply the simple VGCM.

In view of the quantitative rules on compensation losses, the following aspects should be emphasised. First, procedural rules on judicial appraisal should be further unified, and the basic appraisal rules that judicial appraisal agencies shall comply with should be clarified. At the same time, the procedural rules on people with specialised knowledge participating in trials and expressing opinions should be emphasised. Secondly, in line with the rules stipulated in the Jiangsu Province Guidelines, the applicable procedures for quantifying various types of losses caused by different ecological environmental damages should be established. The order of priority for applying judicial appraisal opinions to identify and quantify the ecological damage needs to be clarified. When parties have not used judicial appraisal opinions, or when judicial appraisal techniques are not applicable under certain circumstances, or when the appraisal cost is obviously too high, People's Courts may concur with various reports and data provided by government agencies or their appointed agencies, or opinions of persons with specialised knowledge. Finally, the probative value of conclusions or opinions of different ecological environmental damage quantification schemes should be further clarified. For one thing, it will be very important to determine more specific certification and cross-examination rules for appraisal opinions to avoid the excessive dependence of judges on appraisal opinions and possible repeated appraisals by both parties. For another, in relation to specialists' opinions, it is suggested to adopt the provisions of Articles 32 and 33 of the Jiangsu Guidelines. For those specialists appointed by the parties, opinions expressed may be considered as the "parties' statements"; but for specialists appointed by the courts, who are also referred to a "trial counselling experts", the opinions shall be a type of "opinion testimony" and not the "parties' statements".

5. IMPLEMENTATION PROCEDURE FOR EDL JUDGMENTS

As described above, the implementation regime of the legal liability rules for ecological environmental damage in China is a regime based on private law, namely tort law. Therefore, the claim procedure in EDL is a tort lawsuit relying on the traditional tort liability rules with some adjustments. Generally speaking, the claim procedure in EDL includes at least three sub-procedures, including the settlement procedure, the court trial procedure, and the enforcement of judgments. It is foreseeable that the court trial procedure is the most complicated, because it involves discovery of facts, cross-examination and certification of evidence, legal debate between the parties, etc. As space is limited, this chapter focuses on the settlement sub-procedure and enforcement of judgments.

5.1. RULES OF THE IMPLEMENTATION REGIME FOR EDL JUDGMENTS

5.1.1. Settlement or Mediation Procedures

In general, the claimants can voluntarily initiate a civil litigation. Therefore, before the commencement of the lawsuit, the claimants (namely the plaintiffs) and the liable parties (namely the defendants) may reach a settlement on their own to avoid litigation. In addition, in order to save judicial resources, some pre-trial mediation institutions for disputes on compensation losses under tort law have been established in some secondary environmental laws in China, for example Article 97 of the Water Pollution Prevention and Control Law and Article 96(3) the Law on Prevention and Control of Soil Pollution (2018).[102]

---

[102]   In fact, the newly revised Environmental Protection Law in 2014 deleted the original Article 41(2), that is, the relevant administrative body handled (i.e. via mediation) the civil damages disputes between equal subjects at the request of the parties. The reason for the change of the law is the Simplification of Legal Rules, because Article 64 of the New Environmental Protection Law provides that, "those who cause damages through environmental pollution and ecological destruction shall bear liabilities from infringement in accordance with the Tort Law of the People's Republic of China". The Article 5 of the Tort Law stipulates that "[i]f other laws have special provisions on tort liability, then it should be no doubt that special provisions shall be applicable." However, it is strange that the newly revised Air Pollution Prevention and Control Act of 2015 directly removed the pre-litigation mediation regulations.

Although the legal rules on ECPIL do not clearly provide for settlement or mediation procedures before a lawsuit, the general rules of tort law should apply in the absence of specific rules, so settlement or mediation before litigation are also allowed. For EDCL, the Pilot Plan has established a pre-settlement procedure for claimants (namely designated governmental authorities) before litigation.[103] Only when the settlements are not reached shall government claimants file a lawsuit within a reasonable time.[104] Once a case enters into the litigation procedure, in order to better resolve the case, the court or the parties may initiate a settlement or mediation procedure to suspend the proceedings. The rules on ECPIL clearly stipulate such a settlement or mediation procedure.[105] Although the Pilot Plan does not clearly provide this, based on the principle of litigation and the general rules of tort law, it should allow a settlement or mediation procedure during the litigation process, which is also the statutory rule recognised by Article 42 of the Jiangsu Province Guidelines.[106] Therefore, in EDL, settlement or mediation before or in the process of litigation should be allowed, and settlement before litigation in ECDL is a pre-procedure, that is, government claimants cannot directly claim for ecological environmental damage without having a consultation with the liable parties ahead of time.

---

[103]   The government claimants must consult with liable parties on several specific issues, including the facts and extent of the damage, the time and duration of the expected ecological environmental restoration, and the manner and duration of the compensation in EDCL cases.

[104]   Article 4(4) of the Plan for the Pilot Reform of the Ecological Environment Damage Compensation System.

[105]   In the course of litigation, if the parties reach a mediation agreement (chaired by the court) or reach a settlement agreement on their own, the People's Court shall make an announcement on the content of the agreement for a period of not less than 30 days. After the expiration of the announcement, the court should take the initiative to examine whether the content of the settlement agreement has an adverse impact on the public interest. If the answer is no, the court should issue a judicial mediation statement. Moreover, the judicial mediation statement shall be made public; the public statement must include several elements, including the complaint, the basic facts of the case, and the contents of the agreement. See Article 25 of the SPC Interpretation on Several Issues Concerning the Application of Law in Environmental Civil Public Interest Litigation Cases.

[106]   After reaching a mediation agreement or a settlement agreement between the parties to the ecological environmental damage compensation litigation, the People's Court shall announce the contents of the agreement for not less than 30 days. After the expiration of the announcement, People's Courts shall examine the mediation agreement or settlement agreement without prejudice to the national interests, public interests and the legitimate rights and interests of others and shall issue a judicial mediation statement. Moreover, the judicial mediation statement shall be made public; the public statement must include several elements, including the complaint, the basic facts of the case, and the contents of the agreement. Article 42 of the Jiangsu High People's Court's Trial Guidelines on Eco-environment Damage Compensation Litigation Cases.

5.1.2. Enforcement of Judgments

Due to the preventive characteristics of EDL and the continuous and repetitive nature of ecological environmental damage, enforcement of EDL judgments is more complicated than in traditional private interest litigation. It is necessary to change the traditional civil judgment enforcement regime. However, current judicial interpretations regulating ECPIL only stipulate that "if a legally effective judgment needs to take enforcement measures, it shall be transferred to the execution tribunal of the courts",[107] and provide no clear rule on the enforcement regime. Therefore, more and more local courts have taken advantage of the reform of the environmental judicial specialisation to carry out subjective judicial innovation in the enforcement of ECPIL judgments.

To begin with, for the enforcement of judgments associated with ecological environmental restoration, courts can take initiative to intervene in the enforcement procedure and transfer them to the execution tribunal of the courts under certain conditions.[108] In *Taizhou Environmental Protection Foundation v. Jiangsu Changlong Agrochemical Co., Ltd, Taixing Jinhui Chemical Industry Co. Ltd et al.*, the collegial panel of the Jiangsu High People's Court decided to transfer the enforcement of judgment to the executive judges of this court, because the collegial panel found that the liable parties did not fulfil their liabilities within the statutory time limit by conducting a follow-up investigation. The courts may entrust the claimants or independent third parties to supervise the enforcement of judgments, as for example in *Guiyang Public Environmental Education Center v. Qingzhen Bailong Ceramics Co., Ltd.*[109] The courts may also entrust related administrative agencies and the People's Procuratorate to supervise the enforcement of judgments to ensure liable parties shall perform their liabilities

---

[107] See Article 10 of the SPC Provisions on Several Issues Concerning the Trial of Cases Involving Damages for Harm to Marine Natural Resources, Ecology and Environment; Article 32 of the SPC Interpretation on Several Issues Concerning the Application of Law in Environmental Civil Public Interest Litigation Cases.

[108] In China Environmental Protection Foundation v. Wuxi Huihu Huishan Scenic Spots Management Committee, the liable parties performed their obligation to plant trees under the supervision of collegial panel and executive judges of Binhu District People's Court. Enforcement procedures ended after the judgments were all fulfilled, so there was no need to transfer the judgment to the executive tribunal of Binhu District People's Court. See Binhu District People's Court of Wuxi City, Jiangsu Province, All-China Environmental Protection Foundation v. Wuxi Huihu Huishan Scenic Spots Management Committee, Xi Bin Huan Min Chu ZI No. 2, 2012, No. 8 of Nine Model Trial Cases Involving Environmental Resources Published by the Supreme People's Court.

[109] The People's Court entrusted Guiyang City Public Environmental Education to supervise the performance of the liabilities imposed on the tortfeasors for damaging ecological environment. Subsequently, Guiyang City Public Environmental Education Centre, three ceramics factories (the defendants in the case) and Guiyang Ecological Civilization Foundation of Guizhou Province signed the Third Party Supervision Agreement on Environmental Protection.

for restoring damaged ecological environment in time, as in *Tongren People's Procuratorate of Guizhou Province v. Guizhou Yuping Xiangsheng Chemical Co. Ltd & Guangdong Shaoguan Woxin Trading Co. Ltd.*[110]

Second, for the enforcement of judgments related to compensation for losses, local courts generally require liable parties to pay compensation, including the costs of ecological environment restoration, to a special financial account designated by the government agencies or courts,[111] to the national treasury,[112] or to a specially established fund for public welfare.[113] Moreover, in judicial practice, the funds can be paid to a special account to be used exclusively for restoration of the local ecological environment.[114] In addition, some courts have also used various methods including "delayed payment" and "technical improvement compensation" (with an improvement in the level of compliance to offset some of the restoration costs that should be compensated) to encourage liable parties to actively rectify polluting facilities and improve environmental

---

[110] In one case, Zunyi Intermediate People's Court of Guizhou Province constructed a new compound governance path for the enforcement of judgment. Firstly, liable parties shall be liable for remedying ecological damage. Secondly, the local government shall supervise the remediation process. Thirdly, the People's Court shall enforce the judgment. Lastly, the People's Procuratorate will also play an important role in supervising the remediation process. This new path will not only promote soil remediation and restoration, but also make the agricultural production environment in the area safe. See Zunyi Intermediate People's Court of Guizhou Province, Tongren People's Procuratorate of Guizhou Province v. Guizhou Yuping Xiangsheng Chemical Co. Ltd & Guangdong Shaoguan Woxin Trading Co. Ltd, Case No. 1 of Ten Typical Cases about Environment and Natural Resources from Guizhou Province.

[111] Lian Yungang Intermediate People's Court of Jiangsu Province held that Mr Shenjie Wang shall pay 51,000 yuan to a financial account designated by the court to remedy the ecological damage. See Lian Yungang Intermediate People's Court of Jiangsu Province, Lianyungang Environmental Protection Association v. Mr Shenjie Wang, Lian Huan Gong Min Chu No. 1, 2014.

[112] Guangzhou People's Court of Guangdong Province held that Mr Yun Jiao shall pay about 420,000 yuan to the State Treasury to remedying the ecological damage. See Guangzhou People's Court of Guangdong Province, Guangdong Environmental Protection Foundation v. Mr Yun Jiao, Yue No. 1 Min Chu No. 51, 2016.

[113] Jiangsu High People's Court held that Xuzhou Hongshun Paper Co., Ltd shall pay 1.0582 million yuan for ecological damage restoration cost and ecological services damage pending restoration to Xuzhou City Environmental Protection Public Welfare Fund. See Jiangsu High People's Court, Xuzhou People's Procuratorates of Jiangsu Province v. Xuzhou Hongshun Paper Co., Ltd, Su Min Zhong No. 1357, 2016.

[114] See Jiangsu High People's Court, Taizhou Environmental Protection Foundation v. Jiangsu Changlong Agrochemical Co., Ltd, Taixing Jinhui Chemical Industry Co. Ltd et al., Su Huan Gong Min Zhong No. 1, 2014; Changzhou Intermediate People's Court, Environmental Welfare Association of Changzhou City v. Mr Chu Weiqing and Changzhou Bosch Material Recycling Co., Ltd, et al., Chang Huan Gong Min Chu Zi No. 2, 2014; Chongqing First Intermediate People's Court, People's Government of Chongqing Municipality & Chongqing Liangjiang Voluntary Service Center v. Chongqing Cangjin'ge Property Management Co., Ltd & Chongqing Shouxu Environmental Protection Technology Co. Ltd, Yu No. 1 Min Chu No. 733, 2017.

management.[115] Some courts have also established a system of return visits to supervise the enforcements of judgments, such as the Enhanced System on Enforcing Courts' Rulings, which was formulated by the Qingzhen Municipal People's Court of Guizhou Province.[116]

For EDCL filed by governmental claimants, the trial guidelines issued by the Jiangsu High People's Court have made a lot of detailed provisions on enforcement of judgments. Firstly, depending on the contents of the judgment, the ultimate liability for performing ecological environmental restoration may rest: (1) with the ecological environmental judicial restoration base institution (EJRBI), which will be in charge of carrying out the alternative restoration actions, and liable parties shall pay the restoration costs to EJRBI, while claimants are responsible for supervision;[117] (2) with the claimants, assume the liability for ecological environmental restoration, and liable parties pay claimants the restoration costs;[118] (3) if liable parties are unable to carry out the restoration actions, the court may decide that the liable parties shall entrust third parties to restore, and the liable parties pay the restoration costs to the third parties;[119] or (4) the court may decide the liable parties have to bear liabilities of restoring the damaged ecological environment, and they can be required at the same time to bear the restoration costs if the restoration liability is not fulfilled.[120] Secondly, for effective judgments that have not been performed, plaintiffs may apply to the court for mandatory enforcement of the effective judgments.[121] *Inter alia*, in respect of judgments related to liability for compensation of losses, the court shall enforce and exhaust relevant enforcement measures according to law.[122]

---

[115]   See Jiangsu High People's Court, Taizhou Environmental Protection Foundation v. Jiangsu Changlong Agrochemical Co., Ltd, Taixing Jinhui Chemical Industry Co. Ltd et al., Su Huan Gong Min Zhong No. 1, 2014; Changzhou Intermediate People's Court, Environmental Welfare Association of Changzhou City v. Mr Chu Weiqing and Changzhou Bosch Material Recycling Co., Ltd, et al., Chang Huan Gong Min Chu Zi No. 2, 2014; Chongqing First Intermediate People's Court, People's Government of Chongqing Municipality & Chongqing Liangjiang Voluntary Service Center v. Chongqing Cangjin'ge Property Management Co., Ltd & Chongqing Shouxu Environmental Protection Technology Co. Ltd, Yu No. 1 Min Chu No. 733, 2017.

[116]   Qinzhen Municipal People's Court of Guizhou Province issued some rules about the enforcement of courts' rulings, judgments or mediation statements: the Enhance System on Enforcing Courts' Rulings, Judgments or Mediation Statements of Environmental Case. The rules stipulate that, for environmental protection civil cases with a prestation-judgment, courts can have direct visits (judges' visits) or indirect visits (by telephone, via written investigation, or by inviting National People's Congress deputies and Chinese People's Political Consultative Conference members to visit, etc.), and track and monitor the enforcement of the judgment.

[117]   Article 40 of The Jiangsu High People's Court's Trial Guidelines on Eco-environment Damage Compensation Litigation Cases.

[118]   Id., Article 38.

[119]   Id., Article 37.

[120]   Id., Article 36.

[121]   Id., Article 54.

[122]   Id., Article 55.

For judgments relating to liability for ecological environmental restoration, the court may order the liable parties to continue to take their liabilities, and designate the claimants to be responsible for supervision.[123] Furthermore, in order to promote public participation, the court may make restoration plans within the corresponding region before giving the judgment, and announcement period for this shall be no less than 30 days. Although the legal rules on ECPIL do not clearly stipulate the sub-procedures for announcement of the restoration plans before refereeing, the courts have adopted this in judicial practice.[124] It is also possible to solicit opinions from the public in the area of pollution by organising seminars and other forums.[125]

5.2. PROBLEMS WITH THE CLAIM PROCEDURE FOR EDL CASES

5.2.1. Weak Public Participation in the Settlement/Consultation Procedure

There are several problems related to weak public participation in the settlement/conciliation procedure in EDL cases. First, public participation in EDL only exists at the announcement stage of the settlement agreement. Specifically, it stipulates that in ECPIL the public can only participate during the announcement period of the settlement agreement or mediation before the trial of the case; and in EDCL, the public can participate in the consultation agreement reached before the trial or the new settlement/mediation agreement reached during the trial. In the settlement procedure, the public does not have the right to request to participate. In this system, not only can the public not substantially participate in the pre-litigation settlement/consultation procedure, but also those whose rights or interests may be harmed cannot participate either. For example, in the case of illegal waste dumping in Dayingtian, Xiaozhaiba Town, Xifeng County,

---

[123] Id., Article 56.

[124] Changzhou Intermediate People's Court held that defendants shall be jointly or severally liable for paying 2.83 million yuan to a special account called the Eco-environmental Legal Protection Public Fund of Changzhou City. In the course of the trial, the court entrusted professional institutions by law to identify environmental damage and issued three sets of restoration plans for remedying soil damage. The judges of the collegial panel hearing this case went to the contaminated to let the local people vote on the various restoration plans. The Changzhou Intermediate People's Court finally determined the ecological environment restoration plan based on the public opinions and facts of the case. See Changzhou Intermediate People's Court, Environmental Welfare Association of Changzhou City v. Mr Chu Weiqing and Changzhou Bosch Material Recycling Co., Ltd, et al., Chang Huan Gong Min Chu Zi No. 2, 2014.

[125] Article 50 of The Jiangsu High People's Court's Trial Guidelines on Eco-environment Damage Compensation Litigation Cases.

the main parties to the consultation were the Guizhou Provincial Department of Ecological Environmental Protection, which represents the Guizhou Provincial Government, Guiyang Kaiyang Fertilizer Co., Ltd and Chengcheng Labor Services Co., Ltd (both are liable parties), as well as the third-party Guizhou Provincial Lawyers Association and some invited experts. As a result, the channel for other stakeholders and the public to participate in various types of settlement/mediation procedures in EDL is limited to post-announcement procedures.

Second, the post-announcement procedure is merely a formality. Because of the complexity of EDL and the highly scientific and technical restoration programmes, it is difficult for the public to have a substantial and complete understanding of the restoration procedure. Without the corresponding scientific understanding, the public will not be able to understand the settlement/ conciliation agreement, which makes it difficult for the public to provide valuable opinions.

Third, when other stakeholders (namely the public or ENGOs) disagree with the settlement agreement and its restoration plan, the public participation mechanism does not provide corresponding rules for this. Like the lack of institutional guarantees, this inadequacy of the public participation system also negatively affects the public participation in the final selection of the restoration plan.

5.2.2. Problem-Solving-Oriented Judicial Innovation Weakening Judicial Rationality

A problem-solving-oriented thinking pattern is a kind of "wilfulness" that makes judicial innovations through constant innovative enforcement methods of ecological environmental damage claims in the absence of a legal basis and without sufficient argumentation.[126] On the one hand, in the process of fulfilling an ecological restoration liability, there are no clear legal rules concerning the roles (rights and obligations) of different entities or stakeholders, which leads to different judicial practices in different places. The main subjects include the party implementing the restoration plans, the supervising party and the evaluating party, etc. However, no matter what kind of scheme is adopted, the unclear roles will constitute a reverse constraint on the performance of restoration liabilities. On the other hand, according to judicial practice, different local courts have adopted different procedures for fulfilling liabilities of compensating

---

[126] *Zhongmei Lv*, Judicial Rationality on Environmental Protection Should Not Be Overridden by the Pricey Compensation: An Analysis on Environmental Public Interest Lawsuit in Taizhou City, China Legal Science 2016, p. 244, 264.

monetary losses, especially regarding how compensation funds are managed. The direct consequence is that the compensation funds have been retained in financial accounts for a long time and cannot be used to restore the damaged ecological environment. In addition, some regions require liable parties to pay compensation to the national treasury, it means this money may not be used to restore the ecological environment. Finally, some judicial innovations are too dynamic, and their legitimacy remains questionable. For example, in the famous Taizhou's ECPIL case[127] with sky-high compensation, the liable parties can reduce the compensation they are required to pay by the original judgment by showing "technical improvement". Although this practice may encourage enterprises to invest in pollution control measures, it obviously does not comply with the "full compensation principle" and the "polluter pays principle".

5.2.3. Questionable Content of the Judgment Enforcement Rules

There is a lack of legal rules or guiding regulations on implementing judgments regarding three aspects: ecological environmental restoration, implementation measures and evaluation problems after the completion of the restoration measures. For instance, there are no provisions about who has the right to apply for or decide whether to change the restoration measures, or about the inspection procedure after the completion of the restoration (namely whether the restoration measures meet the restoration criteria or objectives). Article 57 of the Jiangsu High People's Court's Trial Guidelines provides that the court ultimately decides and terminates the judgments,[128] but the question of which procedure to use to carry out the inspection procedure is still unclear. For the implementation of judgments on compensation for losses, although it has become a judicial precedent to put compensation funds into special accounts and ensure that funds be used for ecological environmental restoration in specific areas, this precedent still lacks formal legal recognition. Moreover, there are still no specific rules on how to use these funds, such as who can apply for these funds, how to regulate their use, how the People's Procuratorate and the public participate in using them, etc. Finally, the most critical issue is how to improve the ability of the liable parties to assume liabilities. At present, although the environmental pollution liability insurance system in China is advancing, it is still restricted to specific industry areas and does not extend to all types of liable parties. Therefore, the aim of judicial action to solve this problem is to

---

[127] Jiangsu High People's Court, Taizhou Environmental Protection Foundation v. Jiangsu Changlong Agrochemical Co., Ltd, Taixing Jinhui Chemical Industry Co. Ltd et al., Su Huan Gong Min Zhong Zi No. 1, 2014.

[128] Article 57 of the Jiangsu High People's Court's Trial Guidelines on Eco-environment Damage Compensation Litigation Cases.

avoid the bankruptcy of the liable parties and actively encourage them to meet their additional liabilities for restoration and monetary compensation.

5.3. POSSIBLE SOLUTIONS TO THESE PROBLEMS

The most critical issue relating to the settlement/mediation procedure is how to ensure the substantive and effective participation of different stakeholders. From the participation stage, the current focus on the practice of announcement-based participation after the completion of the restoration plan is not enough. In cases involving ecological environmental restoration, early participation should be allowed. As to the forms of participation, the general public does not have professional scientific knowledge, so their participation is greatly restricted. It is worthwhile to learn from the practice of the High People's Court of Jiangsu Province, where, besides announcement, the court may also seek the opinions of the public in the polluted area by organising seminars and other forums.[129] The present authors believe that the public consultation methods that courts can take outside the announcement process should be detailed, including hearings, symposiums, expert consultations, etc. Moreover, for cases involving more complex ecological environmental restoration, it is better for courts to adopt a hearing that can be better protected by procedural justice. However, considering the cost of hearings is relatively high, symposiums and expert consultations should be used for cases with low complexity. In any case, detailed guidance is needed on how to select different ways to solicit opinions and how to put them into practice. Finally, some entities should be given the right to challenge the settlement agreement, and such rights can be reviewed by administrative or judicial procedures. Generally speaking, in accordance with legal practice, this right may be given to stakeholders who may be affected by the settlement agreement or ENGOs that meet certain conditions; for the corresponding objection review procedures, "administrative review" and "administrative litigation" may be adopted.

On the one hand, for the execution of the referee procedure, the most critical issue is the "wilfulness" of judicial innovation due to the ambiguity and inconsistency of the implementation rules. This "wilfulness" is derived from the particularity of ecological environmental damage claims and the change in the function of courts in such claims, namely from "negative middle referees [to] active programme managers and promoters".[130] The court in the EDCL

---

129   Id., Article 50.
130   *Housheng Duan*, Research on Basic Theories of Environmental Public Interest Civil Litigation, Peking University Law Journal 2016 (4), pp. 889–901.

case will be a quasi-administrative agency with "administrative management" authority.[131] However, judicial innovation without order may not only sacrifice the spirit of the rule of law, but also cause disorder in the judicial system. In order to realise the rule of law, legislators should clarify a set of uniform civil implementation rules for ecological environmental damage claims. There shall be no difference between the implementation measures for the compensation of ecological environmental loss and compensation in traditional civil law. However, in terms of how to ensure that the management, use and supervision of compensation can achieve the purpose of "applying to ecological environmental protection", legislators should still make efforts to establish clear and uniform rules. In addition, new ways of meeting the bar for liability to compensate for losses arising in judicial practice should be treated with greater caution. On the other hand, legislators should establish unified rules for implementing judgments regarding ecological environmental restoration, especially the issue of who has the right to change the repair measures according to the change of circumstances, and of identifying whether the restoration has met its goal. Finally, the most critical issue is the liable parties' ability to fully assume the liabilities for ecological restoration and whether the liability to compensate for the losses will affect the economic productivity of the enterprise. The financial guarantee mechanism used by China to ensure the ability of liable parties has been in its infancy and cannot support the goal of decentralising the risks of corporate environment liabilities. Therefore, legislators should further accelerate the development of a diversified financial security mechanism with environmental liability insurance as the main part in the future.

6. CONCLUSION

How to construct a scientific and rational implementation mechanism for legal liability rules on ecological damage has become a key environmental law issue that is of universal concern to all countries in the world. China has established a mechanism to implement legal liability for ecological environmental damage via private law, and it is mainly based on ecological environmental damage compensation litigation and environmental civil public interest litigation. Ecological environmental damage compensation litigation is the same as environmental civil public interest litigation. Both of them are a form of public interest litigation under private law rules to ensure that legal liability rules

---

[131]   *Hui Wang*, Specialization of Execution Procedure for Public Interest Litigation to Environmental Civil Cases, Journal of Gansu Political Science and Law Institute 2018 (1), p. 116, 118.

for remedying ecological environmental damage are implemented. However, Chinese legislators currently place too much emphasis on the differences between the two types of litigation, and are prepared to construct two completely different private law enforcement mechanisms for liability rules on ecological environmental damage. This practice not only deliberately ignores the fact that the two kinds of litigation are essentially the same, but also leads to the fragmentation of the rules on EDL, which is not conducive to the integration of judicial resources and litigation cooperation between the parties. The authors believe that both ecological environmental damage compensation litigation and environmental civil public interest litigation are forms of EDL, and the objective of the system is to maintain ecological public interests. Therefore, the analysis in this chapter centres on the basic components of ecological environmental damage claims, including the claimant, the liable party, remedies and the specific claims procedure. Combined with China's judicial practice and existing relevant legal rules, it can be seen that there are some institutional defects in the current EDL rules, and that corresponding institutional innovations and amendments are needed.

As far as claimants are concerned, considering the current complex and diversified qualified claimants, the authors believe that the order of priority of claimants should not be set, but that government agencies shall be regarded as the claimant of last resort in the event that no parties want or are able to initiate a litigation. If the government agency does not bring an action, then a People's Procuratorate or environmental protection organisation may file an environmental administrative public interest lawsuit against the government agency. In addition, in order to ensure the equality of appeals of all eligible claimants, the announcement process should be carried out after the case is filed, and claimants should be allowed to participate in the claim during the litigation process, but the claimants participating at different stages may have different restrictions on the right to appeal.

For the liable parties, the current judicial practice on the continuous expansion of the definition of "polluter" urgently needs to be confirmed by law, and the single no-fault principle for liability in traditional environmental tort law also needs to be amended.

As for remedies, it is necessary to promote the specific rules. Firstly, the goal of restoration should be changed, a special restoration guideline formulated, and the VGCM clearly applied to identify and quantify ecological environmental damage. Secondly, the evidentiary effects of the various appraisal opinions, the specialists' opinions, and the corresponding cross-examination and certification rules for different evidences should be quantified.

For the claim procedure, the authors believe that efforts should be made to improve the current settlement/conciliation procedures and the judgment enforcement procedures. *Inter alia*, the settlement/conciliation procedure should focus on improving the rules of public participation to ensure substantive and effective participation. Of course, this public participation mechanism can also be extended to the procedure of selecting the ecological environmental restoration plan in the litigation. The judgment enforcement should focus on constructing a set of systematic scientific execution rules, formulating regulations on the use of damages received from the liable parties, and promoting the procedural rules for the supervision and termination of judgments.

TRANSPLANTING CIVIL LAW MODELS IN CHINA

Compensation of Personal Damages Caused by Environmental Pollution

Nadia Coggiola

1. INTRODUCTION

China is today facing very high levels of pollution and its associated large human and economic costs, because of the burden placed by environmental pollution on both natural resources and on the population's well-being and health.

Although the problem of environmental pollution has traditionally been largely neglected in China, even when the Chinese environmental situation sharply deteriorated as the consequence of the fast industrial development of the country at the end of the last century, it must be highlighted that that enduring attitude has recently undergone a profound change. Indeed, probably as a consequence of the increased general awareness of the dangers of environmental pollution and of the huge economic development enjoyed by the county, the new century has brought with it a different political approach to the issue.

That different approach started in 2014 with the declaration of war on pollution by Li Kequiang[1] and was shortly after confirmed during the 19th National Congress of the Communist Party of China, in October 2017, when President Xi Jinping clearly reaffirmed China's commitment to sustainable development and a "beautiful China". On that occasion, in fact, President Xi Jinping affirmed that "[t]he modernization that we pursue is one characterized by harmonious coexistence between man and nature" and that "[i]n addition to creating more material and cultural wealth to meet people's ever-increasing

---

[1]   China to "declare war" on pollution, premier says, Reuters, 5 March 2004, https://www.reuters.com/article/us-china-parliament-pollution/china-to-declare-war-on-pollution-premier-says-idUSBREA2405W20140305.

needs for a better life, we need also to provide more quality ecological goods to meet people's ever-growing demands for a beautiful environment".[2]

The seriousness of the government's intentions was soon revealed by the efforts dedicated to the task, the successes already acquired[3] and the severe enforcement of administrative violations by central authorities.[4] In practice, the actions of the central government aimed at reducing environmental pollution are apparently reaching their goals.

Unfortunately, the goal of compensating the victims of the same pollution have apparently not yet been attained, although the same central government enacted rules aimed at that purpose. It is interesting to observe that those rules are shaped on civil law models, following traditional paths of negligence and strict liability. Those rules have features that have proved to work well, or at least to be sufficiently satisfying, in many civil law countries, where they are routinely applied to compensate damages caused by environmental pollution. But, in truth, those rules have not provided the same level of protection to the persons harmed in cases of environmental personal damages occurring in China. Therefore, many Chinese victims of environmental pollution are left uncompensated.

The aim of this chapter is therefore to highlight the problems that may arise in transplanting civil law models of environmental damages compensation in China, even though two caveats are needed. The first is that the investigation of issues such as that of the compensation of personal damages caused by environmental pollution in China not only entails the scrutiny of judicial acts and scholarly writings, but also requires social, political and cultural factors to be taken into consideration, The second is that this limited research will not be able to highlight general trends on transplanting legal rules from civil law countries to China, although it can certainly provide some useful hints on the general picture.

This investigation will apply a comparative methodology. In this regard, although the author is perfectly conscious that the distinction between common law and civil law is mostly outdated for systematic purposes, she has decided to maintain that very distinction, as in her opinion it still retains all its relevance in cases of private law, such as the tortious cases under examination.

---

2   The translation of the words of President Xi Jinping could be found in the Government website, at http://english.gov.cn/news/top_news/2017/10/18/content_281475912455778. htm.

3   *M. Greenstone*, Four Years After Declaring War on Pollution, China Is Winning, New York Times, 12 March 2018, https://www.nytimes.com/2018/03/12/upshot/china-pollution-environment-longer-lives.html.

4   China jails hundreds of officials for pollution violations, Reuters, 10 July 2018, https://www.reuters.com/article/us-china-pollution/china-jails-hundreds-of-officials-for-pollution-violations-idUSKBN1JZ2VP.

The first step will be a brief overview of the main theories on legal transplants. In the second step, the rules that were enacted in China to provide for the compensation of environmental personal damages will be illustrated, and it will be ascertained if they actually comply with their civil law model and the main features of civil liability, such as negligence, strict liability and burden of proof. The third step will be devoted to the ascertainment of the actual implementation of those rules by Chinese courts in cases of environmental personal damages compensation. Finally, we shall try to provide some conclusive remarks on the outcome of our findings. It must be emphasised that this investigation is aimed not only at understanding how the civil law rules are introduced in the Chinese system, enacting provisions and regulations under Chinese law, but also at how they are actually implemented in real cases by Chinese courts and, eventually, other social actors. As we shall see, in fact, the implementation of rules apparently inspired by civil law models may be hindered by many different obstacles, deeply rooted in Chinese culture and traditional political and social features.

2.   THE THEORETICAL CONTEXT

As we all know, the concept of "legal transplant" is used to denote the phenomenon of borrowing legal rules and institutions from one legal system and transferring them into another. The metaphor of "legal transplant", taken from the world of anatomy and surgery, successfully conveys the idea that law and legal institutions can sometimes be transferred outside of their natural habitat, if some conditions are fulfilled.

The starting point of every academic discussion on the concept of a "legal transplant" begins with the famous quotation by Montesquieu: "*Les lois politiques et civiles de chaque nation [...] doivent être tellement propres au peuple pour lequel elles sont faites, que c'est un grand hasard si celles d'une nation peuvent convenir d'une autre.*"[5] In Montesquieu's opinion, therefore, geographical, cultural, climatic and environmental differences among countries make legal transplants from one country to the other so difficult that it would be a huge coincidence if one of those transplants were to be successful. This sceptical approach earned him the label of founder of the culturist school.

The reference to Montesquieu was the starting point of Otto Kahn-Freund's theory on the subject, in which he proposed a context-sensitive approach to legal reform based on legal borrowings, which need to be very attentive when

---

[5]   *C.-Louis de Secondat Montesquieu*, De l'esprit des lois, livre I, ch. 3, Des lois positives, 1748. "The political and civil laws of each nation [...] should be adapted in such a manner to the people for whom they are framed, that it is a great chance if those of one nation suit another", tr. *Thomas Nugent,* The Spirit of the Laws, J. Nourse & P. Vaillant, London, 1766.

taking into consideration the various groups of "environmental criteria", that is to say geographical, sociological, economic, cultural and political elements. In his opinion, the relevance of these different criteria was deemed to change over time, with geographical, cultural, religious, economic and sociological factors losing their importance at different speeds because of changes in technology, ways of living and communications, and with political and ideological factors seeing an increase in their significance. Therefore, particular attention should be paid to the necessity to take into account the socio-political context of the "donor" country and of the "recipient" country.

Moreover, to ascertain which rules could actually be implemented, he ordered legal rules ranging from rules very close to "organic matter", as they are deeply rooted in the national context and therefore difficult to transplant, holding that in these cases it was actually appropriate to use the metaphor of "legal transplants", to rules close to "mechanical matter", in which case it was instead, in his opinion, generally possible to replace a "spare part" with another.[6] An example of the first category of rules are constitutional laws, which may require broad public acceptance in order to be replaced, while an example of the second type of rules are certain commercial provisions that only apply to few stakeholders and therefore may require the acquiescence of only those same few stakeholders to be implemented. He also stressed that while the success of the first type requires a deep knowledge of the donor country's legal and political system, the same is not true where "mechanical" transplants are involved.

Of a contrary opinion was Alan Watson, one of the main supporters and the initiator of the "transferist school", who, with the historical support of the wide influence of Roman law even on present-day civil law systems in Europe and elsewhere – the so-called "reception of Roman law" – affirmed the possibility of "transplanting" laws without knowing or even caring about the context of the transplanted legal rules in the donor country. In his opinion, legal transplants could be successful despite the socio-political differences between donor and recipient countries, because of the autonomy of legal rules and institutions, and the need for authority, which encourage the members of the legal profession to refer to the authority and prestige of the foreign system's legal solutions, rather than forge their own legal rules.[7]

It should be noted that Watson's legacy could be broken down into "strong Watson" and "weak Watson" writings. The former affirmed that law was an entirely freestanding and culturally independent phenomenon, while in the others he recognised that, although law was freestanding, it also had a cultural dimension. This latter position was the one generally adopted by other later

---

6   O. *Kahn-Freund*, On Uses and Misuses of Comparative Law, MLR 1974 (37), p. 1.

7   A. *Watson*, Legal Transplants, Scottish Academic Press; University Press of Virginia, 1974, pp. 88 et seq.

scholars, also because it is thought to be the more reasonable and analytically robust. It provides that the test to be used to ascertain the actual transplant of a certain law, concept or institution in a host country is to simply verify if it is socially useful in the recipient country.

These two different approaches to the question of legal transplants soon erupted into a heated debate, which mainly concentrated on the issue of the actual existence and spread of legal transplants, on their desirability, and on the assessment of their success.[8]

The existence of the concept of "legal transplants" was in fact denied by Pierre Legrand, who voiced their impossibility from a cultural perspective. In his opinion, it is impossible to transfer from one jurisdiction to another anything but "a meaningless form of words" and the support of legal transplants is that of "reducing law to rules and rules to bare propositional statements".[9] For a transplant to be deemed successful, the transplanted rules must function exactly in the same way in the host country and in the donor country.[10]

Scholars such as William Ewald supported Watson's theory on the at least partial autonomy of law and its ability to evolve independently of social contexts,[11] while others, such as legal sociologist Gunther Teubner, although in principle adhering to Watson's thesis, called for a more conceptual debate on the issue, suggesting the use of the less misleading "legal irritants" metaphor, in place of that of "legal transplants". He underlay that legal rules and institutions do not mirror society, but rather are linked to different discourses and fragments of society, with a different degree of proximity depending from the sector of law and the related social processes. Therefore, all the rules, even those that

---

[8]   See, among the others, *A. Watson*, The Evolution of Law, Johns Hopkins University Press, 1985; *A. Watson*, Legal Origins and Legal Change, Humbeldon, 1991; *A. Watson*, Law out of Context, University of Georgia Press, 2000; *W. Ewald*, Comparative Jurisprudence (II): The Logic of Legal Transplants, Am. J. Comp L. 1995 (43), p. 489; *E. Stein*, Uses, Misuses and Nonuses of Comparative Law, North U. Sch. L. 1977 (72/2), p. 198; *U. Mattei*, Efficiency in Legal Transplants: An Essay in Comparative Law and Economics, Int. Rev. Law & Ec. 1994 (14), p. 3; *G. Teubner*, Legal Irritants: Good Faith in British Law or How Unifying Law Ends Up in New Divergences, MLR 1998 (61/1), p. 11; *J. Gillespie*, Transplanting Commercial Law Reform, Ashgate, 2006; *K. Alter, L. Helfer & O. Salidis*, Transplanting the European Court of Justice: The Experience of the Andean Tribunal of Justice, Am. J. Comp. L. 2012 (60), p. 629; *D. Kennedy*, Three Globalizations of Law and Legal Thought, in D.M. Trubek & A. Santos (eds.), The New Law and Economic Development, Cambridge University Press, 2006, p. 19; *P.G. Monateri*, The "Weak Law": Contaminations and Legal Cultures (Borrowing of Legal and Political Forms), Transnat'l & Contemp. Probs. 2003 (13), p. 575; *D. Nelken*, Comparatists and Transferability, in P. Legrand & R. Munday (eds.), Comparative Legal Studies, Cambridge University Press, 2003, pp. 446, 457 et seq.; *R. Sacco*, Legal Formants: A Dynamic Approach to Comparative Law (pts. 1 & 2), Am. J. Comp. L. 1991 (39/1) p. 343.

[9]   *P. Legrand*, The Impossibility of Legal Transplants, Maastricht J. Eur. & Comp. L. 1997 (4), pp. 111–124.

[10]   Id. at pp. 115–117.

[11]   *Ewald, supra*, note 8.

Kahn-Freund classified as belonging to the category of "mechanical matter", may not remain unaffected by the new environment once they are transferred into a different national context. Moreover, those same transplanted rules will interact with the host legal system, sometimes triggering a change in some sectors, with effects different from, and sometimes even unpredictable compared to, those generated in the donor legal system.[12]

More recently, new developments based on anthropological and sociological studies, underlying the complexities of the features of society and culture and of their relationship with the legal system, empowered the idea that transplants always entail a degree of cultural integration and offered a more articulated description of legal transplants whose meanings are intensified by local cultural and social influences.[13]

It is also important to remember that the concept of "legal transplant" is not enclosed within the borders of legal theory, but was instead adopted by a number of development aid agencies and international organisations, such as the World Bank and the International Monetary Fund, to implement legal and institutional reforms especially in those countries that were under the Soviet Union sphere of influence before the collapse of communism in the late 1980s.

These reforms mainly concerned civil and commercial law, even if in some cases they also involved constitutional law, and consisted in an actual "exportation" of provisions and rules from developed countries to transitioning economies, with important effects even on other research fields, mainly economics.[14] The transplant of models from Western countries into Eastern former socialist countries was probably motivated by the fact that the collapse of the communist systems of Eastern countries was generally interpreted as the demonstration of "the end of history as such: that is, the end point of mankind's ideological evolution and the universalization of Western liberal democracy as the final form of human government".[15] But we should also not forget the urgency to undertake political and economic reforms in those countries, and therefore

---

[12] *Teubner, supra*, note 8 at pp. 11–32.

[13] See for example *D. Nelken & J. Fest*, Adapting Legal Cultures, Hart Publishing, 2001; *A. Riles*, Comparative Law and Socio-Legal Studies, in M. Reimann & R. Zimmermann (eds.), The Oxford Handbook of Comparative Law, Oxford University Press, 2007, p. 775; *M. Graziadei*, Comparative Law as the Study of Transplants and Receptions, in id. at p. 441; *R. Cotterrell*, Comparative Law and Legal Culture, in id. at p. 709.

[14] For a first approach to the issue, see *J. Braithwaite & P. Drahos*, Global Business Regulation, Cambridge University Press, 2000; *C.J. Milhaupt & K. Pistor*, Law and Capitalism: What Corporate Crises Reveal about Legal Systems and Economic Development Around The World, University of Chicago Press, 2008; *M. Likosky* (ed.), Transnational Legal Processes: Globalisation and Power Disparities, Cambridge University Press, 2002; *D.M. Trubek & A. Santos* (eds.), The New Law and Economic Development, Cambridge University Press, 2006; *A. Bakardjieva Engelbrekt*, Legal and Economic Discourses on Legal Transplants: Lost in Translation, Scandinavian Stud. L. 2015 (60), p. 111.

[15] *F. Fukuyama*, The End of History?, National Interest, 1989; this ideas were later detailed in *F. Fukuyama*, The End of History and the Last Man, Hamilton, 1992.

the need for efficient legal models, able to guarantee the functioning of the new market economy and at the same time the establishment of the rule of law and of democratic institutions.[16] The transplants were so swift, and involved all the possible economic, social and legal fields, that they were described as "repairing the ship at sea".[17] Certainly, as some scholars stressed, there was not time to develop original legislation, able to cover so many aspects of the law, especially when some of the issues concerned legal institutions completely unknown in the host countries.[18] Nonetheless, these rushed legal transplants did not please everyone and in fact some scholars pointed out the need for a greater awareness of local contexts and a wider involvement of local actors.[19]

3. THE TORT LAW REFORM IN CHINA AND COMPENSATION OF ENVIRONMENTAL DAMAGES

To fully understand the rules providing for compensation for the damages caused by environmental exposure in China, it is certainly advisable to start from a general overview of the Chinese legal provisions concerning the compensation of tortious damage in general, and thereafter investigate the rules explicitly devoted to the compensation of environmental damages.

The first Chinese Civil Code (CCC) was enacted, book by book, from 1929 to 1930, and is still effective in Taiwan, although with many amendments and modifications.[20] That code was largely inspired by the Swiss Civil Code,

---

[16]   On the issue G. *Ajani*, By Chance and Prestige: Legal Transplants in Russia and Eastern Europe, Am. J. Comp. L. 1995 (43), pp. 93–117, talking about "optimistic normativism" in the transition countries.

[17]   J. *Elster, C. Offe & U. Preuss*, Institutional Design in Post-Communist Europe. Repairing the Ship at Sea, Cambridge University Press, 1998.

[18]   T. *Waelde & J. Gundersson*, Legislative Reform in Transition Economies: Western Transplants – a Short-cut to Social Market Economy Status?, ICLQ 1994 (43), p. 347.

[19]   D. *Berkowitz, K. Pistor & J.-F. Richard*, The Transplant Effect, Am. J. Comp. L. 2003 (51), p. 163; K. *Pistor & C. Xu*, Incomplete Law, Intern. Law & Politics 2003 (35), p. 931; A. *Seidman & R. Seidman*, Drafting Legislation for Development: Lessons from a Chinese Project, Am. J. Comp. L. 1996 (44), p. 1.

[20]   For reasons of space, we cannot sketch here the outlines of civil law evolution in China. On that topic, readers are kindly referred to, among others, X. *Huai*, Chinese Legal History, China University for Political Science and Law Press, 1998, p. 9; A. *Tay*, The Struggle for Law in China, U. British Columbia L.R. 1987 (21), p. 563; J. *Zhang*, The Tradition and Modern Transition of Chinese Law, Law Press, 3rd ed., 2009, pp. 247–277; J. *Yu*, Law and Academia in Contemporary China, Beijing University Press, 2007, p. 155; K.W. *Norr*, The Problem of Legal Transplants and the Reception of Continental Law in China before 1930, in Festschrift für Zentaro Kitagawa, Duncker & Humblot, 1992, p. 231; Z. *Mei*, Key Points of Civil Law, China University of Political Science and Law Press, 1998, p. 19; R. *Pound*, The Chinese Civil Code in Action, Tul. L.R. 1955 (29), p. 289; Q. *He & X. Yin* (eds.), A History of Civil Law in the People's Republic of China, Fudan University Press, 1999; T.F. *Chen*, Transplant of civil code in Japan, Taiwan, and China: with the focus on legal evolution, Nat'l Taiwan Univ. L.R. 2011 (6), p. 389.

(Zivilgesetzbuch, ZGB)[21] and, similarly to the German Civil Code (Bürgerliches Gesetzbuch, BGB), only provided, in the three general clauses of Article 184, rules of tortious liability based on fault, without recognising strict liability as an independent ground of liability.[22] Other rules were subsequently adopted to deal with the development of industrialisation and urbanisation, which potentially conflicted with the civil liability rules in the CCC.

The People's Republic of China abolished, on political grounds, all the laws from republican times, including the CCC, enacting in their place rules modelled on the Soviet Union's examples, which were strongly influenced by the denial of the need to govern horizontal social relations by means of civil law and of market transactions and personal freedom principles.

Nonetheless, three attempts,[23] all of them unsuccessful, were made to draft a new Civil Code, until the promulgation of the General Principles of Civil Law (GPCL) in 1986. In the GPCL, non-contractual and contractual liability are integrated in a unified system of civil liability. Liability for fault is provided for by Article 106(2) GPCL, which was regarded as a copy of Article 1382 of the French Code Civil, and is the general liability rule, while strict liability is only provided for specific cases, such as liability for highly dangerous activities, traffic accidents and environmental liability.

Rules on tortious liability were also enacted in some economic laws, such as the Anti-Trust Law (2007) and the Unfair Competition Law (1993), and in administrative laws and regulations.[24] Moreover, we should not forget to mention that the Chinese Supreme People's Court (SPC) also issued some Juridical Interpretations (sifafieshi), which in the Chinese legal system are considered to be even more important than laws and regulations, and the aim of which is to fill existing gaps in laws and regulations and direct court decisions concerning issues of civil liability.[25]

---

[21] *Mei, supra,* note 20 at p. 19; *Pound, supra,* note 20.

[22] Art. 184 CCC: "(1) A person who, intentionally or negligently, has wrongfully damaged the rights of another is bound to compensate him for any injury arising therefrom. The same rule shall be applied when the injury is inflicted intentionally in a manner against the rules of morals. (2) A person who violates a statutory provision enacted for the protection of others and therefore prejudice to others is bound to compensate for the injury, unless no negligence in his act can be proved."

[23] Respectively, from 1954 to 1956, from 1962 to 1964 and from 1979 to 1982.

[24] Such as Environmental Protection Law of 1989, modified in 2008; Product Quality Law of 1993, modified in 2000; Consumer Protection Law of 1993, modified in 2013; Road Traffic Safety Law of 2004, last modified in 2008; Medical Malpractice Regulation of 2002; Workmen's Accident Insurance Act of 2003; Implementing Regulation of Road Traffic Safety Law of 2004; Regulation for Emergency Rescue, Investigation and Handling of Railway Accidents of 2007.

[25] SPC Opinions on the GPCL of 1988; Answer to Some Questions Concerning the Right of Reputation of 1993 and of 1998; Interpretation Concerning Personal Injury due to

Starting from 1993, the Chinese legislator attempted to enact a new Civil Code, equally inspired by civil law models. As it proved impossible to enact the Civil Code as a whole – in the opinion of some scholars due to the lack of theoretical preparation and of its political complexity – the path followed by the Chinese National People's Congress (NPC) was that of the adoption of a "step-by-step policy".[26] Therefore, after the enactment of the Contract Law in 1999 and a long series of drafts, the Tort Liability Law of the People's Republic of China (CTL)[27] was finally adopted at the 12th Session of the Standing Committee of the 11th National Congress of the Communist Party on 26 December 2009, and came into effect on 1 July 2010.

The CTL only governs tortious liability cases and is subdivided into 12 chapters: general provisions; bases of liability and remedies; circumstances excluding or mitigating liability; special provisions on subjects of liability; product liability; liability for motor vehicle traffic accidents; liability for damage due to medical malpractice; liability for environmental pollution; liability for highly dangerous activities; liability for harm caused by domestic animals; liability for harm caused by objects; and supplementary provisions.

As far as we are concerned, the following articles of the CTL should be taken into consideration. In Article 1, the CTL stresses that its purpose is to protect legal rights and interests, in line with European tendencies,[28] and points out its preventive function. However, it does not mention compensation among its purposes, which is conversely what is privileged in modern European legislation,[29] favouring instead the aim of punishment and the purpose of

---

High Tension Electricity of 2000; Interpretation Concerning Emotional Damage of 2001; Interpretation Concerning Misrepresentation in the Stock Market of 2003; Interpretation Concerning Personal Injury of 2003.

[26] For a more detailed illustration of the coming into existence of the Chinese Civil Code, see *H. Koziol & Y. Zhu*, Background and Key Contents of the New Chinese Tort Liability Law, JETL 2010 (1), p. 332. The two main model drafts could be found here *L. Wang* (ed.), The Model Draft of Chinese Civil Code with Comments – Tort Law, Law Press, 2005; *H. Liang* (ed.), The Model Draft of Chinese Civil Code with Comments – Part for Tort Law and Succession Law, Law Press, 2005. The Civil Code of the People's Republic of China was finally issued on 28 May 2020, and shall enter into force on 1 January 2021. The new Civil Code provisions shall obviously not be taken into consideration for the purposes of our investigation, as they are yet to take effect.

[27] Zhōnghuá Rénmín Gònghéguó Qīnquán Zérèn fǎ（中华人民共和国侵权责任法）[Tort Law of the People's Republic of China] (promulgated by the Standing Committee of the National People's Congress, 26 December 2009).

[28] See for example Art. 2:102 Principles of European Tort Law (PETL) and *H. Koziol*, General Conditions of Liability, in European Group on Tort Law, Principles of European Tort Law. Text and Commentary, 2005, p. 24.

[29] See Art. 10:101 PETL and *U. Magnus*, Comparative Report on the Law of Damages, in U. Magnus (ed.), Unification of Tort Law: Damages, Kluwer Law International, 2001, p. 185.

promoting "social harmony and stability". Article 2 provides that liability must be borne for any infringement of civil rights, and subsequently provides a list of examples of civil rights, that is to say personal and property rights and interests, which includes the right to live, the right to health and other personal and property rights and interests.

Article 5 CTL states that, if other laws provide special provisions on tort liability, those provisions should prevail. This rule leaves a wide scope for special provisions to come into action.

The general liability rule is provided for by Article 6 CTL, which states in its first section that a person shall bear liability for the infringement of other people's rights when that infringement was with fault. The second section allows the fault to be declared, if the law so provides, on the basis of presumption, where the liable person is not able to prove otherwise.[30] This double system of liability for fault, which distinguishes between cases where the fault must be proved and cases where it can instead be presumed, generally depending on the degree of dangerousness of the act of the tortfeasor, is not uncommon in European civil liability systems.[31]

Strict liability is instead provided for by Article 7 CTL, which states that liability may be established, when the law so provides, even when the tortfeasor is not at fault.

The Chinese system is therefore not different from most European civil codes, which consider fault the pre-eminent basis of liability, and other bases of liability as more or less secondary.[32] It is interesting to point out that the adoption of such a general rule on strict liability was backed by some Chinese scholars, on the basis of a comparative analysis[33] supporting the theory that strict liability is based on a general idea,[34] and that the provision of a strict liability rule covering only part of the whole area would have made the system inconsistent.

---

[30] It is unclear if this presumed fault should be considered as a variant of general fault liability, because of the reversal of the burden of proof – see X. Zhang, Tort Law, Renmin University Press, 2005, p. 33; M. Zhang, A Study of Fault Liability, China University of Political Science and Law Press, 2002, p. 689 – or if it should be considered as equidistant between general fault liability and strict liability – L. Wang, A Study of the Principles of Attribution in Tort Law, China University of Political Science and Law Press 1991, p. 30; L. Yang, Tort Law, People Court Press, 2nd ed., 2004, p. 129.

[31] For some examples, B.A. Koch, Liability Based on Fault, in European Group on Tort Law, Principles of European Tort Law. Text and Commentary, 2005, Art. 4:201 no. 8 et seq.

[32] See for a first introduction on the subject P. Widmer, Liability Based on Fault, in European Group on Tort Law, Principles of European Tort Law. Text and Commentary, 2005, Art. 4:101 no. 6.

[33] Y. Zhu, Gefahrdungshaftung (Strict Liability) and its Legislation by Means of a General Clause, Zhongguo Faxue [China Legal Science] 2009 (3), pp. 30–52.

[34] On the issue, read B.A. Koch & H. Koziol, Comparative Conclusions, in B.A. Koch & H. Koziol (eds.), Unification of Tort Law: Strict Liability, Kluwer Law International, 2002, pp. 407 et seq.

In any case, it should be observed that the special section of the law, devoted to different occasions of liability, does not distinguish between fault and non-fault liability, but rather mixes the provisions related to the two different kinds of liability.

Regarding causation, although the CTL does not provide a definition of it, nonetheless it details the rules to be applied to cases of alternative (Article 10) and concurrent (Article 11) causes, providing for the joint and several liability of all the actors.

Compensable forms of damage include, among other things: the costs and expenses of treatment and rehabilitation; lost wages; the costs of disability assistance and disability indemnity; death (Article 16); serious mental distress suffered by the victim; and damage to property rights (Articles 19, 20, and 22). If the victim dies, the tortfeasor shall pay the medical expenses, the funeral service fee and death compensation to close relatives.

As mentioned before, the CTL also provides special rules for individual sectors of liability, among them liability for environmental pollution, governed by Chapter VIII, entitled Environmental Pollution Liability, Articles 65 and 66 of which respectively provide that "[f]or damage caused by pollution of the environment, the polluter shall bear tort liability" and that "[f]or disputes arising from pollution of the environment, the polluter shall bear the burden of proving non-liability or diminished liability in accordance with the provisions of the law and the non-existence of a causal relationship between their actions and the damage".[35] In substance, the CTL provides for strict liability of the tortfeasors in cases of damage caused by environmental pollution, when this damage is to legal rights and interests of persons, that is to say in cases of bodily harm, death or damage to property rights.

These rules replaced the former Article 41 of the Environmental Protection Law of 1989,[36] which provided that the unit that caused environmental pollution damage was obliged to eliminate it and to compensate the unit or individual that

---

[35]   This English translation can be found at http://www.npc.gov.cn/englishnpc/Law/2011-02/16/ content_1620761.htm. For an interesting examination of the translation and interpretation issues concerning these rules, see M. *Timoteo*, Law and language: issues related to legal translation and interpretation of Chinese rules on tortious liability of environmental pollution, China-EU Law J. 2015 (4), p. 121. For an insightful study on the circulation of European models M. *Timoteo*, Legal Transplants and the Chinese Legal Process: The Case of Circulation of the Rules on Civil Liability for Environmental Harm from Europe to China, in M. Timoteo (ed.), Towards A Smart Development. A Legal and Economic Enquiry into the Perspectives of EU-China Cooperation, Bononia University Press, 2016, pp. 145–155.

[36]   Zhōnghuá Rénmín Gònghéguó Huánjìng Bǎohù Fǎ (中华人民共和国环境保护法) [Environmental Protection Law of the People's Republic of China] (promulgated by the Standing Committee of the National People's Congress, Dec. 26, 1989). That article was cancelled by the revised version of the Environmental Protection Law, which entered into force on 1 January 2015.

suffered direct losses as a consequence of the pollution. That rule also provided for strict liability of the tortfeasor, as the only chance for the polluter to exempt himself from liability was to prove that the environmental pollution losses were the consequence of natural disasters that could not be averted even after the prompt adoption of reasonable measures.

Liability for environmental pollution was in any case already provided for by other rules, such as Article 124 GPCL,[37] for damages caused to others in violation of state provisions for environmental protection and the prevention of pollution, and by some special laws, such as the 1984 Law of the People's Republic of China on the Prevention and Control of Water Pollution,[38] the 1995 Law on Prevention and Control of Environmental Pollution by Solid Waste,[39] and the 2000 Law on Prevention and Control of Atmospheric Pollution.[40]

Although all the rules mentioned above follow paths that are familiar to civil law scholars, it should be noted that nonetheless those paths sometimes significantly diverge on important issues, as in the case of Article 67 of the CTL, which states that "[i]f the environment is polluted by two or more persons, the degree of liability shall be determined by factors including, *inter alia*, the type of pollutants and the quantity emitted".[41] Therefore, the special rules on environmental damage of the CTL provide that where harm is caused by environmental pollution, if it is caused by multiple tortfeasors, each of them shall be severally liable for the damages caused, proportionally to their share of liability.

It is important to underline that this rule not only differs from the general joint and several liability of multiple tortfeasors provided for cases of damages by environmental pollution in civil law systems, but that it also contradicts the same Chinese general rules, as the provisions from Article 8 onwards of the CTL explicitly provide, in cases of multiple tortfeasors, for their joint and

---

[37] Zhōnghuá Rénmín Gònghéguó Mínfǎ Tōngzé (中华人民共和国民法通则) [General Principles of the Civil Law of the People's Republic of China] (promulgated by the National People's Congress, 12 April 1986, effective 27 August 2009).

[38] Zhōnghuá Rénmín Gònghéguó Shuǐ Wūrǎn Fángzhì Fǎ (2008 xiūdìng) (中华人民共和国水污染防治法(2008修订) [Water Pollution Prevention and Control Law of the People's Republic of China (2008 Revision)] (promulgated by the Standing Committee of the National People's Congress, 28 February 2008).

[39] Zhōnghuá Rénmín Gònghéguó Gùtǐ Fèiwù Wūrǎn Huánjìng Fángzhì Fǎ (2013 Xiūzhèng) (中华人民共和国固体废物污染环境防治法(2013修正) [Law of the People's Republic of China on the Prevention and Control of Environmental Pollution by Solid Wastes] (Promulgated by the Standing Committee of the National People's Congress, 29 June 2013).

[40] Zhōnghuá Rénmín Gònghéguó Dàqì Wūrǎn Fangzhì Fǎ (2000 xiūdìng) (中华人民共和国大气污染防治法(2000修订)) [Law of the People's Republic of China on the Prevention and Control of Atmospheric Pollution (2000 Revision)] (promulgated by the Standing Committee of the National People's Congress, 29 April 2000).

[41] On these rules, see *B. Pozzo & L. Wang*, Liability for environmental pollution within the framework of the new Chinese tort law, ERPL 2011 (19/1, p. 87; *B. Pozzo*, Tutela ambientale e modelli giuridici. Il caso cinese, Riv. Giur. Amb. 2010, pp. 877, 886.

several liability, and this rule already applied before by virtue of the general rule of Article 130 GPCL.[42]

This different, more favourable treatment of those multiple tortfeasors who engaged in polluting activities, who are only asked to pay for their share of damages, while all other multiple tortfeasors are obliged to pay for the whole of the damages, coupled with the less advantageous treatment of victims of environmental damages, who may be left uncompensated or undercompensated, when some of the polluters are unable to pay the compensation or no longer exist, may be interpreted as a signal of the actual intentions of the Chinese legislator.

On the other hand, it should also not be forgotten that the new version of the above-mentioned Environmental Protection Law, which came into force in 2015, not only strengthens companies' and individuals' liability for preventing and controlling pollution, provides for more severe punishments in cases of violation and gives more responsibilities to local governments in the control and enforcement of environmental protection rules, but also tries to empower the victims of environmental damages, providing, at Article 58, that registered groups engaged in environmental protection can qualify as plaintiffs in public interest litigation against polluting activities. That rule, at first sight, appears to be a duplicate of the provisions contained in Article 55 of the Code of Civil Procedure of 2012, which already set out the possibility of making use of public interest litigation, *inter alia*, in cases of environmental pollution.

The will of the Chinese government to make the best use of those procedural rules was reaffirmed with the enactment, on 6 January 2015, of the Supreme People's Court Interpretation on Several Issues Regarding the Application of Law in Public Interest Environmental Civil Litigation, which tries to facilitate access to public interest litigation in environmental civil cases, permitting certain NGOs to file a case in a court different from the local court where the pollution occurred; enabling injured private parties to take advantage of the NGO's action and reducing the costs of the litigation; providing that the damages paid by the polluters are to be put in a pool of money, which should be used to compensate all the injured parties; requiring the control of the settlements of the cases, to avoid that the settlement is the consequence of intimidation of the petitioners by the polluter or the local government; and, lastly, putting the onus on the polluter to prove all the information concerning the pollution and providing that the same courts can investigate the facts of the case and allow the hearing of experts.[43]

---

42   Zhōnghuá Rénmín Gònghéguó Mínfǎ Tōngzé (中华人民共和国民法通则) [General Principles of the Civil Law of the People's Republic of China] (promulgated by the National People's Congres, 12 April 1986, effective 27 August 2009).

43   For some preliminary information on the issue, see Y. Zhao, Innovative measures to improve environmental law enforcement in China, China-EU Law J. 2015 (4), p. 155.

Taking into account all this febrile legislative activity, we can certainly affirm that the Chinese legal system is endowed with every useful tool, as long as it concerns positive rules, inspired by civil law models and institutions, to provide satisfying compensation to the victims of the damages caused by environmental pollution. The issue is whether and how those rules are actually transplanted into Chinese legal system.

4. APPLICATION OF THE RULES ON THE COMPENSATION OF ENVIRONMENTAL DAMAGE

Although China's legal system possesses all the necessary laws, written following civil law models, on the compensation of damages caused by environmental pollution, the application of those rules to actual cases is unfortunately not so straightforward and successful as the Chinese legislator certainly would have wished. In truth, the compensation of damage caused by environmental pollution, which represents a major problem in the Chinese fight against pollution, may represent a good example that the road of legal transplants may be paved with many cultural and social obstacles.

First of all, it cannot be denied that, compared to the large volume of polluting activities in China, and therefore the very likely large number of cases of damages resulting from environmental pollution, the glittering legal rules are seldom put in action, although there has been some increase in the number of cases that have come before the courts.

The reason for this limited number of cases apparently has its roots in the Chinese society and the anthropocentric Confucian belief that man should exploit nature to his own advantage. This attitude has entailed a tradition of an antagonistic relationship between man and nature, which was more recently also adopted by Mao and still permeates Chinese society. For this reason, in China environmental damage is often probably not considered compensable damage.[44]

---

[44]   J. Shapiro, Mao's War Against Nature, Cambridge University Press, 2001; R. Muschkat, Contextualizing Environmental Human Rights, Pace Envtl. L. Rev. 2009 (29), pp. 119, 149. For a first general introduction to the transplant of western rules in China, please read C. Lei, Contextualizing Legal Transplant: China and Hong Kong, in P.G. Monateri (ed.) Methods of Comparative Law, Edward Elgar Pub, 2012, p. 192; L. Wang, Historic Characteristics of Modern Civil Code and its Codification Process, Tsinghua L. Rev. 2014 (8), p. 6; L. Huixing, The Reception of Foreign Civil Law in China, Shandong U. L. Rev. 2003 (1), p. 5; P.R. Luney Jr., Traditional and Foreign Influences: Systems of Law in China and Japan, Law & Contemp. Probs. 1989 (52), p. 129; X. Xu et al., The Similarities Between Civil Law Legal Family and Chinese Legal Family, J. Ocean U. of China 2005 (5), p. 48; S. Zhuang, Legal Transplantation in the People's Republic of China: A Response to Alan Watson, Eur. J.L. Reform 2005 (7), p. 215; S. Wen, The Ideals and Reality of a Legal Transplant – The Veil-Piercing Doctrine in China, Stan. J. Int'l L. 2014 (50), p. 319.

Moreover, Chinese people traditionally prefer to have recourse to non-judicial methods of resolution, rather than to judicial procedures. Therefore, positive legal rules are rarely applied to cases of damage caused by environmental pollution, because in these cases the compensation to the victims of the environmental pollution, if any, is generally acknowledged on the basis of extra-legal rules. The wide popularity of non-judicial methods of resolution in China is coupled with the array of different procedures, as we can distinguish between conciliation, mediation and *xìnfǎng* procedures.

Conciliation may occur between the litigants before or during administrative or judicial proceedings.[45] The first kind is considered extra-judicial, and therefore the agreement does not need to be approved by any authority, whereas an agreement reached during the administrative or judicial proceedings does need to be approved by the same administrative or judicial body.[46] Some scholars have underlined that the lack of external bindings on the outcome of the conciliation and the disparities in the bargaining powers of the parties are often the cause of the unfavourable results of conciliation procedures for the victims of environmental damages.[47]

Conciliation procedures are in any case very much surpassed in numerical terms by the widespread traditional system of mediation, which is led by mediators, whose task is to help the parties to freely achieve a reasonable settlement. As the mediation procedures are endowed with authority, the final settlement is enforceable on the parties. Three types of mediation can be distinguished – people's mediation, administrative mediation and judicial mediation – depending on the authority charged with the mediator role.

A large number of mediation procedures are so-called "people's mediations", led by persons without administrative or judicial functions, generally the People's Mediation Committees of the Residents' Committees in urban areas or of the Villager's Committees in rural areas. The outcome of these mediation procedures cannot be modified or repudiated, but can only be disputed in court, and performance can be enforced by the People's Courts.

Recourse to people's mediation is common in certain environmental damages compensation cases – such as nuisance caused by manufacturers, small or communal enterprises, solely owned workshops and stalls – and is mainly confined to poor and less educated people in the countryside and

---

45   Under Article 51 of the Civil Procedure Law: Zhōnghuá Rénmín Gònghéguó Mínshì Sùsòng Fǎ (Shìxíng) (中华人民共和国民事诉讼法(试行)) [Civil Procedure Law of the People's Republic of China (For Trial Implementation)] (promulgated by the Standing Committee of the National People's Congress, 8 March 1982).

46   Supreme People's Court interpretation of the Civil Procedure Law (1992), Article 191.

47   *Y. Zhao*, Environmental Dispute Resolution in China, J. Envtl. L. 2004 (16/2), pp. 157, 160–161.

small towns.[48] Although the mediators should in theory resolve civil disputes in accordance with the law,[49] that is not always the case, and in many cases the agreement may reflect the limited legal abilities of the mediator, the application of highly sensitive criteria, the existence of incentives to mediate the case instead of fighting it before a court[50] and sometimes even the personal power and social position of the litigants.[51] Notwithstanding their legal shortcomings, the Chinese government apparently strongly supports the use of people's mediations, because they may reinforce its power and control over the people and reduce litigation costs.[52]

Administrative mediation is instead performed by administrative bodies, and is generally very efficient and respectful of the legal reasons of the parties, because administrative bodies usually have good knowledge of and expertise in the subject of the dispute.[53]

Lastly, judicial mediation has a long tradition in China, as it has been practiced in Chinese civil courts since the late 1930s[54] and was finally formally institutionalised in 1982 in the Civil Procedure Law of the People's Republic of China.[55] Judicial mediation consists in the settlement of cases by voluntary agreements between the parties, before or during the trial; these agreements must comply with the law.

Today judicial mediation is often used by the parties in a dispute, also because the policies of the Chinese Supreme Court place great emphasis on its use, even evaluating judges on the basis of the percentage of mediations they conduct in comparison with their overall caseload. Moreover, apparently, the same judges believe that mediation is their primary duty before adjudication, encouraging

---

48   C. Wang, Preliminary Study of Environmental Dispute Resolution in China, in C. Wang (ed.), Theory and Practice of Environmental Dispute Resolution, China University of Political Science and Law Press, 2002, p. 12.

49   Civil Procedure Law: Zhōnghuá Rénmín Gònghéguó Mínshì Sùsòng Fǎ (Shìxíng) (中华人民共和国民事诉讼法(试行) [Civil Procedure Law of the People's Republic of China (For Trial Implementation)] (promulgated by the Standing Committee of the National People's Congress, 8 March 1982), Article 16.

50   Zhao, supra, note 47 at pp. 162–164.

51   A. Chan & G. Crothall, Is It Worth Going to Court?, J. Comp. L. 2010 (5), pp. 281, 307–309.

52   B.L. Read & E. Michelson, Mediating the Mediation Debate, J. Conflict Resol. 2008 (52/5), pp. 737, 755.

53   X. Ma & L. Ortolano, Environmental Regulation in China, Rowman & Littlefield, 2000; Zhao, supra, note 47 at pp. 164–170.

54   R. Cullen & F. Hualing, From Mediatory to Adjudicatory Justice: The Limits of Civil Justice Reform, in M.Y.K. Woo & M.E. Gallagher (eds.), Civil Dispute Resolution in Contemporary China, Cambridge University Press, 2011, p. 25; Z. Xianyi, Mediation in China – Past and Present, APLR 2009 (17), p. 1.

55   Civil Procedure Law: Zhōnghuá Rénmín Gònghéguó Mínshì Sùsòng Fǎ (Shìxíng) (中华人民共和国民事诉讼法(试行) [Civil Procedure Law of the People's Republic of China (For Trial Implementation)] (promulgated by the Standing Committee of the National People's Congress, 8 March 1982).

its use by the parties, when not actually imposing it.[56] Unfortunately, the superimposition of the role of mediator and judge in the same person is often troubling, as it may entail substantial injustices and be used by lay judges to avoid applying to difficult cases rules they do not know well enough, such as those on the damage caused by environmental exposure.[57]

The Chinese government is certainly conscious of these problems, as well as of the fact that the widespread recourse to judicial mediation may easily interfere with the application of positive laws on the compensation of environmental pollution. For that reason, the Chinese government, for a short period following the Court Reform Five-Year Plan commencing in 1999, successfully limited the number of judicial mediation cases, especially in large coastal cities and urban courts, promoting judicial efficiency and justice by improving judges' professionalism and carrying out procedural justice reform. Unfortunately, for reasons still debated by scholars,[58] soon afterwards the Chinese government promptly reversed this attitude, and since the early 2000s, the number of judicial mediation procedures has risen again, with the inevitable negative consequences. It cannot in fact be denied that judicial mediations may affect judges' decisions and their handling of cases, and therefore the implementation of positive rules, including those providing the compensation of environmental damages.[59]

Lastly, we should not forget to mention the extensive recourse to another procedure, namely *xìnfǎng*, equally widely used in China. *Xìnfǎng* is a traditional instrument of redress, consisting in a petition in front of petition-level bodies, called *xìnfǎng* bureaus, which exist outside formal legal institutions but at the same time are formally established. *Xìnfǎng* bureaus can be found in almost all Chinese government bodies, including courts, local government offices, and Party committees.[60] It is very important to underline that these bureaus are empowered by the Chinese Communist Party and its individual officials, and can take decisions even against court decisions, which are therefore delegitimised by the use of *xìnfǎng*. In some cases, judges are obliged, by provincial regulations to hear *xìnfǎng* petitions, overlapping their functions.[61]

---

[56]   *C. Minzner*, China's Turn Against Law, Am. J. Comp. L. 2011 (59/4), pp. 935, 959.

[57]   *Zhao, supra,* note 47 at pp. 170–175.

[58]   For the different opinions of the scholars on the issue, see *Minzner, supra,* note 56 at p. 397; *Cullen & Hualing, supra,* note 54 at pp. 39–40; *B. Liebman*, A Populist Threat to China's Courts?, in M.Y.K. Woo & M.E. Gallagher (eds.), Civil Dispute Resolution in Contemporary China, Cambridge University Press, 2011, pp. 269, 303–306.

[59]   *B. Van Rooij*, The People's Regulation: Citizens and Implementation of Law in China, Colum. J. Asian L. 2012 (59), pp. 116, 169–171.

[60]   *S. Lubman*, Bird in a Cage. Legal Reform in China After Mao, Stanford University Press, 1999, pp. 130–288; *Y. Cai*, Managed Participation in China, Pol. Sci. Q. 2004 (119), pp. 425, 431–432.

[61]   *C.F. Minzner*, Xinfang: An Alternative to Formal Chinese Legal Institutions, Stan. J. Int'l L. 2006 (42), pp. 103, 126–139.

The Chinese government makes extensive use of *xìnfǎng* as a multipurpose political governance tool, even in cases of environmental damage, because it is extremely sensitive to populist pressure as a consequence of the political concerns about social stability.[62] For their part, Chinese people equally very often make use of *xìnfǎng* petitions, either because they have no confidence in the independence and impartiality of the judicial system or because they want to influence it since, as we said above, *xìnfǎng* petitions can be filed even against court decisions. In truth, scholars have pointed out that courts may also be extremely sensitive to populist pressures because of the strain put on them by the government and the fears of social stability. Therefore, it is apparently not uncommon for the courts to agree to change their decisions, rehear the case, ignore the letter of the law or consider cases without any legal basis, because of the significant pressures put on judges.[63]

Moreover, it should not be forgotten that traditionally Chinese people are more accustomed to petitioning practices and *xìnfǎng* bureaus than to pleading before a court, even if today simultaneous recourse to both remedies is not uncommon. The inevitable consequence of this situation is the limitation of the number of cases, included those related to the compensation of environmental damage, that are brought before the courts.[64]

The second problem in the application of the rules provided for cases of environmental damages is equally linked to another cultural and social factor, related to the interpretation and application of the provisions of the law. In fact, contrary to civil law systems, where the provisions of the law generally have an immediate prescriptive meaning, in China laws are generally considered to be policy statements and declarations of intents that need to be implemented by other legal rules and regulations.[65] Furthermore, definitions of the legal terms can sometimes be not as clear as they should,[66] causing difficulties in the application of some legal terms. This situation is probably rooted in tradition, as the Chinese guidelines for legislative drafters, approved by Mao in the 1950s, dictate that primary legislation should be both "general" and "flexible", following the idea that general and flexible national legislation can best be implemented throughout the country and be adapted to local conditions.[67] In truth, it should

---

[62] Id. at p. 107; *Liebman, supra*, note 58 at p. 306.

[63] N. *Liu*, A Vulnerable Justice: Finality of Civil Judgment in China, Colum. J. Asian L. 1999 (13), p. 35; *Van Rooij, supra*, note 59 at pp. 169–217.

[64] Z. *Xie*, Petition and Judicial Integrity, J. Pol'y & L. 2009 (2/1), pp. 24, 25–27; *Minzner, supra*, note 61 at pp. 105–107.

[65] W.P. *Alford & Y. Shen*, Limits of the Law in Addressing China's Environmental Dilemma, Stan. Envtl. L.J. 1997 (16), pp. 125, 135.

[66] S. *Beyer*, Environmental Law and Policy in the People's Republic of China, Chinese J. Int'l L. 2006 (5/1), pp. 185, 205–206.

[67] P. *Keller*, Sources of Order in Chinese Law, Am. J. Comp. L. 1994 (42), pp. 711, 749–752.

also not be forgotten that general and flexible legislation also best enables political control, leaving a wide scope for policy in the hands of the Chinese Communist Party. In any case, the direct consequence of these characteristics of generality and flexibility is an actual lack of independence of the laws from political directives and Chinese bureaucracy.[68]

Good examples of these issues can be found in some cases of compensation of environmental pollution.[69]

A first example is that of the application of the rule of strict liability, clearly provided for, as mentioned above, by Article 41 of the former version of the Environmental Protection Law. Under that rule, polluters could be held liable for damages when (even lawfully) they discharged wastewater or emitted air pollutants or caused other environmental pollution, if it was proved that such (even lawful) acts caused any harm.[70] That rule, in fact, was not interpreted and applied as a strict liability rule by some courts and administrative bodies, which instead preferred to support the idea that the discharge of pollutants in compliance with the permit limits or state standards was not a basis for civil liability, even where environmental harm was caused.[71]

In the end, that same provisions of that rule were reaffirmed by several different legal acts[72] and lastly by Articles 65 and 66 of the new version of the CTL, over the course of 20 years. That proves to us the difficulties in implementing concepts such as strict liability for environmental damage.

In fact, it is still quite common for Chinese courts in environmental liability cases to require the petitioners to prove the liability of the defendants, with the inevitable and frequent consequence of the claimants' petition being dismissed because of the impossibility of proving the defendants' responsibility, either

---

[68]   Lubman, supra, note 60 at pp. 130–288; R. Peerenboom, China's long march toward rule of law, Cambridge University Press, 2002; M.S. Tanner, The Politics of Law-Making in China, Oxford University Press, 1999.

[69]   K. Fürst, Access to Justice in Environmental Disputes: Opportunities and Obstacles for Chinese Pollution Victims, unpublished thesis, University of Oslo, 2008; R.V. Percival, China's "Green Leap Forward" Toward Global Environmental Leadership, Vt. J. Envtl. L. 2010–2011 (12), pp. 633, 641; R.E. Stern, Environmental Litigation in China, Cambridge University Press, 2013.

[70]   See D. Han, Textbook on Environmental Protection Law, Wuhan University Press, 2003; K. Zhou, Ecological Environmental Law, Chinese Law Book Company, 2001.

[71]   On this issue, see C. Wang (ed.), Theory and Practice of Environmental Dispute Resolution, China University of Political Science and Law Press, 2002, p. 127.

[72]   Environmental Protection Agency, the Reply on Deciding the Compensation Liability for Environmental Pollution, 1991; Supreme People's Court's Opinion on Several Issues in Applying the Civil Procedure Law of the People's Republic of China 1992. In 2001, the Supreme People's Court issued the Several Provisions on the Evidence of Civil Litigation, on which Zhao, supra, note 47, and C. Wang (ed.), Theory and Practice of Environmental Dispute Resolution, China University of Political Science and Law Press, 2002.

under the negligence or the causal profile.[73] In these cases, to prove the liability of the defendants is therefore almost impossible, especially considering the difficulties in showing the existence of a causal link between the pollution and the damage, because of the costs of doing so and in some cases the practical impossibility.

Nevertheless, on some occasions the Chinese courts have applied the strict liability rule to cases of damages caused by environmental pollution. Apparently, in fact, the principle of strict liability of the defendants in cases of environmental damages is slowly creeping into Chinese courts, as we can see from the reports of some Chinese cases. Probably one of the first was *Sun Youli et al. v. Qianan Diyi Zaozhichang et al.*,[74] which concerned damages to 18 fish and shellfish farmers caused by the death of fish and shellfish as a consequence of the discharge of an excessive amount of wastewater from nine pulp factories and chemical plants. In that case, all the tortfeasors were held liable for the compensation of the damages, including the one that had complied with the legal limits on waste, although this latter was not held jointly and severally liable with the other defendants for the damage.

That brings us to the point of the joint and several liability of the tortfeasors in cases of environmental damages. The principle of joint and several liability is usually adopted by civil law systems in cases of damage caused by environmental pollution consequent to the illicit actions of multiple tortfeasors, because it clearly offers better protection to the victims, granting compensation for the damage suffered even when one or more of the tortfeasors no longer exist or cannot pay for their share of compensation. In my opinion, it is really interesting that the principle of joint and several liability of multiple tortfeasors was adopted by Chinese law as a general principle, with Article 130 GPCL, but not for cases of environmental damage, since Article 67 CTL explicitly provides for several liability of multiple defendants. Although that choice may have its rationale in the presumption that the polluters do not have a joint intent and that the pollution is caused by independent acts, certainly the choice does not favour the victims of environmental pollution. In any case, that same rule may certainly please Chinese judges who, before the enactment of the new Article 67 CTL, and therefore under the general rule of joint and several liability, have held, in cases of environmental damages, with different reasoning, multiple tortfeasors to be severally liable.[75]

---

[73]   See for example the cases Zhang Changjian et al. v. Pingnan Rongping Chemical Plant (Pingnan Interm. People's Court, April 2005); Zhang Changjian et al. v. Pingnan Rongping Chemical Plant (Fujian Provincial High People's Court, November 2005); on these decisions see A. Wang, The Role of Law in Environmental Protection in China: Recent Developments, Vt. J. Envtl. L. 2006–2007 (8), pp. 192, 214. On the issue *Wang, supra*, note 61 at p. 205; *Stern, supra*, note 69.

[74]   Sun Youli et al. v. Qianan Diyi Zaozhichang et al., Hebei Court, 2002 and 2003.

[75]   *Zhao, supra*, note 47 at pp. 179–185.

5.   FINAL REMARKS

The reason the author has chosen to use the word "remarks" instead of the word "conclusion" clearly lies in the fact that we do not think to have at our disposal enough sources – especially cases but also scholarly writing – to enable us to express a clear opinion on the actual impact of the transplant in China of civil law rules concerning the liability for the compensation of personal damages caused by environmental pollution.

Therefore, the author's observations are to be considered tentative, as they are only supported by a limited amount of research materials and only concern the narrow boundaries of the present field of research.

In the author's opinion it cannot be denied that the "mechanical" transplant into Chinese laws of provisions aimed at compensating the damages caused by environmental pollution that are modelled on civil law rules was successful. In fact, the existing Chinese laws provide all the necessary tools to compensate the victims of environmental damage, tools which have already proved to be generally suitable for their purpose in civil law countries.

By contrast, if we measure the success of the same transplants in terms of their capacity to shape the Chinese legal system according to civil law legal principles and therefore actually being able to compensate the victims of environmental damage, on the basis of the shortcomings that emerged from this research, the judgment cannot be very positive.

First of all, this is because the outcome of the effects of applying the rules providing for the legal compensation of environmental damages certainly suffers from the limited number of cases where these rules have actually been applied. In fact, the wide recourse to non-judicial remedies by Chinese victims largely hinders the efficacy of the legislative tools, reducing the number of legal decisions and therefore their capacity to affirm the legal principles and influence other cases. As long as judicial cases on the compensation of environmental damages are far and few between, their influence not only on the legal system, but also on the industrial system and society in general, will be hugely limited. Moreover, the authority of the courts will be restricted by their limited influence capacities. This is not to mention the fact that non-judicial decisions do not generally apply legal rules, and are easily influenced by the often significantly different bargaining powers of the parties.

Secondly, the uncertainties and reluctance in the application of the provisions of the laws on the compensation of environmental damages certainly undermine the authority of Chinese judges. In the author's opinion, in fact, only when the courts are able to independently pronounce and interpret – without any temptation to accommodate the words of the laws to the needs of one of the parties, generally the defendants, or to continue to pay deference to legal traditions that are contrary to the laws' aims – will the victims of environmental damages be able to trust them and will the courts be able to establish strong and uniform case law. Unfortunately, the attachment to traditional attitudes, which often entails a disregard for the victims of environmental damages in favour of the tortfeasors, also sometimes shapes the choices of the legislator.

From what has been presented above, it is easy to infer that the impairments in the transplantation of civil law models of compensation of environmental damages in China probably mostly depends on the attitude of the government toward those issues. This attitude may perhaps be better described as "swinging", as the Chinese government at the same time enacts strict rules on the compensation of environmental damages and does not give the courts all the powers they need to implement these rules, or affirms that it wants all the victims to be restored regarding the damage they suffered and then provides for the several liability of the multiple tortfeasors of environmental pollution.

Certainly, we should never forget that the Chinese government is constantly fighting against local governments and the fear of social unrest. The powerful local governments, which generally directly finance local courts and therefore easily influence their decisions, may in fact often be opposed to the policies of the central government, because they may be shareholders of the polluting industries, or those same polluting industries may be their principal taxpayers.[76] And the fear of social unrest may lead the central government to favour non-judicial systems of dispute resolution, because they are easier to accommodate to political needs than court decisions and the central government probably fears the possible outcomes of an independent judicial system in certain sensitive fields.[77]

On the other hand, the fight for a "beautiful China" undertaken by President Xi Jinping should not be undervalued. Indeed, we may consider that the enactment of the revised version of the Environmental Protection Law, which entered into force from 1 January 2015, was probably a first step towards a new approach by the government to Chinese environmental problems, environmental damages compensation among them. Apart from strengthening companies' and individuals' liabilities for preventing and controlling pollution

---

[76]   R. Peerenboom, Law Enforcement and the Legal Profession in China, in J. Chen, Y. Li, & J.M. Otto (eds.), Implementation of Law in the People's Republic of China, Kluwer Law International, 2002, pp. 125, 128–129; B. Van Rooij, Implementing Chinese Environmental Law Through Enforcement, in J. Chen, Y. Li & J.M. Otto (eds.), Implementation of Law in the People's Republic of China, Kluwer law International, 2002, p. 149; C. Wang, Chinese Environmental Law Enforcement: Current Deficiencies and Suggested Reforms, Vt. J. Envtl. L. 2007 (8), pp. 161, 172; Van Rooij, supra, note 59 at pp. 128–134, 162–163; Lubman, supra, note 60 at pp. 103–110, 130–288,. For a contrary opinion, see S. Zhu, The Party and the Courts, in R. Peerenbom (ed.), Judicial Independence in China, Cambridge University Press, 2010, p. 52.

[77]   V.R. Johnson, The Rule of Law and Enforcement of China Tort Law, T. Jefferson L. Rev. 2011 (34), pp. 43, 88–92.

and providing for more severe punishments in the case of violations, the new rules in fact give more responsibilities to local governments regarding the control and enforcement of environmental protection rules and empower the courts to establish a system of environmental public interest litigation.[78]

As mentioned above, the importance of this latter point was shortly afterwards emphasised by the issuing of the Interpretation on Several Issues Regarding the Application of Law in Public Interest Environmental Civil Litigation[79] by the Supreme People's Court on 6 January 2015. The facilitation of the access to court decisions in environmental damages compensation cases using the tool of public litigation could in fact provide a viable solution to some of the issues highlighted above, as the new rules allow NGOs to file cases in a court different from the local court where the pollution occurred, enable the victims of the pollution to take advantage of the NGO's actions without costs, clearly state that the polluter must provide all the required evidence, permit the courts to investigate the facts and hear experts, and require the control of the settlements of the cases, with the purpose of avoiding that the decisions of the courts being the consequence of the intimidation of the petitioners by the polluter or the local government.

The Chinese Supreme Court also published, on 3 July 2017, a document called "Ten Model Cases regarding Environmental Public Interest Litigation",[80] with the clear intent of showing the achievements of the public interest litigation tool in cases of environmental damage, while providing examples of successful cases and promoting its usage in other cases.

The aim pursued by the Chinese government is today, therefore, clear: there is certainly a strong political will to actually implement liability rules modelled on civil law for cases of damage caused by environmental pollution. As the efforts needed to successfully implement those rules mainly concern, in the author's opinion, cultural and political factors, considering the recent attempts of the Chinese government we will most probably soon be able to judge whether "beautiful China" will also be populated by "compensated victims".

---

[78] For a critical approach to the 2015 changes, see *T. Liu*, China's Revision to the Environmental Protection Law: Challenges to Public Interest Litigation and Solutions for Increasing Public Participation and Transparency, J. Energy & Environ. L., Spring 2015 (60).

[79] Supreme People's Court, of the Interpretation on Several Issues Regarding the Application of Law in Public Interest Environmental Civil Litigation, http://en.pkulaw.cn/display.aspx?cgid=f81c55e05ed7c7f6bdfb&lib=law. On the issue, see *M. He*, Sustainable Development through the Right to Access to Justice in Environmental Matters in China, Sustainability 2019 (11/3), p. 900; *R. Zhang & B. Mayer*, Public Interest Environmental Litigation in China, Chinese J. Env. L. 2017 (1/2), p. 202.

[80] Chinese Supreme Court, Ten Model Cases regarding Environmental Public Interest Litigation, http://en.pkulaw.cn/display.aspx?cgid=49ed69106365f7a4bdfb&lib=law.

PART V
STATE AND INTERNATIONAL
ENVIRONMENTAL LIABILITY

THE MYTH OF PLURALITY OF REGIMES IN THE LAW OF STATE RESPONSIBILITY

Khazar Masoumi*

1. INTRODUCTION

In international environmental law, as well as other branches of public international law, the state's responsibility for environmental harm[1] might be engaged when a breach of an international obligation is attributable to the state. This is reaffirmed[2] by the International Law Commission (ILC) – the United Nations' body in charge of codification and progressive development of international law – in the Draft Articles on the Responsibility of States for Internationally Wrongful Acts (2001), Article 2.

---

* The author would like to thank Megan Garrett-Jones and Taymaz Azimi for their precious help by reviewing this chapter.

[1] In this chapter, the term "harm" is used as a synonym for "prejudice" and differs from "damage", as harm refers to a legally protected interest, while damage is a factual injury suffered by the environment. See particularly *M. Lucas*, Étude juridique de la compensation écologique, LGDJ, 2015, p. 376. See in general *M.E. Roujou de Boubée*, Éssai sur la notion de réparation, LGDJ, 1974, p. 90. For this reason, "harm" is preferable while speaking of state responsibility for wrongful acts contrary to "damage", which seems more suitable for liability. As we will see afterwards, any wrongful act of a state – consisting of a breach of an international obligation attributable to it – gives rise to harm but not necessarily to damage. This is for example the case of the breach of the state's obligation to realise an environmental impact assessment.

[2] The foundation of state responsibility for wrongful acts is a part of the codification work of the ILC – and not its progressive development – since the international tribunals had already recognised the principle. In this respect see ILC, Draft Articles on the Responsibility of States for internationally wrongful acts, 2001, commentary on Article 1, para. 2. Yet a "relative originality" (*relative originalité*) – using the words of P.M. Dupuy – in the ILC's work must be recognised as it eliminates the damage from the engagement of responsibility by transferring it to the domain of the quantum of reparation. *P.M. Dupuy*, Responsabilité et Légalité, in La responsabilité dans le système international, A. Pedone, 1991, pp. 263–264. Also ILC, Draft Articles on the Responsibility of States for internationally wrongful acts, 2001, commentary on Article 2, para. 9 and Article 31(2).

However, the implementation of the regime of state responsibility for internationally wrongful acts (hereinafter referred to as "the common regime") in cases of international environmental law faces some significant obstacles.[3] The major obstacle is that of environmental damage arising while the state is complying entirely with its international obligations. In fact, the states are directly (as operators) or indirectly (because the activity occurs within their jurisdiction, in their territories or under their control) involved in a vast range of activities related to economic development. These activities involve, either by nature or accidentally, environmental risks. The main question then would be whether it is reasonable that victims – nature or human – have to bear their prejudicial consequences without at least a large participation of the state in the reparation.[4] Answering negatively to this question, the doctrine was taken to underline the necessity of a complementary and *sine delicto* responsibility regime where the only condition would be the causal link between the damage and the conduct of the state.[5]

Tempted by this idea, the ILC decided to undertake the codification of rules related to what was initially called "state responsibility for lawful acts".[6] Thus, between 1980 and 2006, the ILC had been working on "International liability for injurious consequences arising out of acts not prohibited by international law". Observing the final outcomes, one can say that the ILC had failed to establish a second regime in the law of state responsibility. Indeed,

---

3   For a detailed analysis of the normative insufficiencies in international environmental law preventing the effectiveness of the states' responsibility for wrongful acts see K. Masoumi, La responsabilité environnementale des États : Un régime juridique en émergence, PhD thesis, University of Strasbourg, 2017, pp. 37–84.

4   For P.M. Dupuy, the reason why the doctrine or even some states had chosen the public international law as their preferred framework is the state's sovereignty privileges. "Ces tentatives ont eu naturellement pour cadre privilégié l'ordre juridique dans lequel l'État est perçu fondamentalement à raison de ses privilèges de souveraineté, c'est à dire l'ordre juridique international public". *P.M. Dupuy*, L'État et la réparation des dommages catastrophiques, in F. Froncioni & T. Scovazzi (eds.), International Responsibility for Environmental Harm, Graham & Trotman/Martinus Nijhoff, 1991, p. 126.

5   *J.M. Arbour* et al., Droit international de l'environnement, Editions Yvon Blais, 3rd ed., 2016, p. 1228 and 1229–1235. *P.M. Dupuy*, Le rôle de l'État dans l'indemnisation des dommages catastrophiques internationaux, in La réparation des dommages catastrophiques. Les risques technologiques majeurs en droit international et en droit communautaires, Bruylant, 1990, pp. 219–220; *G. Hafner*, Le contexte particulier de la responsabilité dans le droit international de l'environnement, in Droit international 5, A. Pedone, 2000/2001, p. 42; *C.W. Jenks*, Liability for ultra-hazardous activities in international law, in Collected courses of The Hague Academy of International Law, 1966, vol. 117, pp. 173–175; *L. Cavaré*, Le droit international public positif, vol. 2, Les modalités des relations juridiques internationales, les compétences respectives des États, A. Pedone, 3rd ed., 1969, p. 409.

6   The expression was quite frequently used by the members of the Commission while determining the scope of the project on state responsibility for wrongful acts. Y. B. Int'l L. Comm'n, 1973, vol. 1, 1202nd meeting, paras. 12, 34, 41 and 44; 1203rd meeting, paras. 4, 16 and 32; 1204th meeting, paras. 3–5, etc.

---

both of the initial project's subdivisions, i.e. the Draft Articles on Prevention of Transboundary Harm from Hazardous Activities (2001) and the Draft Principles on the Allocation of Loss in the Case of Transboundary Harm Arising out of Hazardous Activities (2006) are far from being a parallel to the common regime. In fact, none of the texts make the states liable for the damage caused by hazardous activities despite licit conduct of the states.

To determine if such a parallel regime in the law of state responsibility may conceptually be possible, one must firstly analyse what the international liability of states is (section 2) and secondly examine its compatibility with the common regime (section 3).

2. THE INTERNATIONAL LIABILITY OF STATES: A CIVIL LAW MISUNDERSTANDING

First of all, it is necessary to distinguish two stages of failure of the ILC's work on international liability of states. One is real, whereas the other arises from a misunderstanding. The real failure of the ILC's work, as the author has already mentioned in the introduction and will cover in more detail below,[7] relies on the fact that it is not the state after all that may be liable for the environmental damage caused by the hazardous activities. The misunderstanding arises because the ILC's work on international liability of states did not establish a proper regime of *sine delicto* responsibility in public international law. This interpretation, which has a central importance in the context of the present chapter, results from the lack of a common comprehension between jurists from the common law and civil law traditions.

Undoubtedly, uncovering the reasons behind this misunderstanding would clarify the contours of the notion of international liability of states. There are two reasons, probably with equal weight, behind this misunderstanding. While the first source of misunderstanding is merely a linguistic problem (section 2.1), the second has its origin in the conception of "liability" in both civil law and common law traditions (section 2.2).

2.1. THE INEXISTENCE OF THE TERM: HOW DO YOU SAY LIABILITY?

The linguistic confusion around liability appeared very soon within the Commission. In the first draft report of the ILC on its 25th session in 1973,

---

[7] See *infra* section 2.2.2.

we can observe that the word "responsibility" was also used referring to what was called later the "international liability of states". While editing the text, the American member R.D. Kearney had "proposed that before the words 'for possible injurious consequences' ..., the word 'responsibility' should be replaced in the English text by the word 'liability'".[8] Yet, regarding the French text, R. Ago – the Italian Special Rapporteur – noted that the term "'*responsabilité*' appeared to be the only word available ... to express both notions".[9]

Indeed, in all of the Romance languages, there is only one word for both "responsibility" and "liability". It is *responsabilité* in French, *responsabilidad* in Spanish, *responsabilità* in Italian and so on. That is why in its French version the ILC's work on "International liability for injurious consequences arising out of acts not prohibited by international law" is called "*La responsabilité internationale pour les conséquences préjudiciables découlant d'activités qui ne sont pas interdites par le droit international*". In the same manner, the Spanish title of the same work is "*Responsabilidad internacional por las consecuencias prejudiciales de actos no prohibidos por el derecho internacional*". Subsequently, each time the words "*responsabilité internationale de l'État*" in French or their synonyms in the other Romance languages are used in a text, the reader must interpret from the context whether it is about the responsibility for wrongful acts or it concerns the international liability of states.

Furthermore, this linguistic obstacle is also supplemented by a conceptual misunderstanding of "liability".

2.2. THE INTERNATIONAL LIABILITY OF STATES: FROM THE DOMESTIC LAW'S OBJECTIVE RESPONSIBILITY TO THE ILC's STATES' (NON-)LIABILITY

The second source of confusion around the notion of international liability of states is related to the divergence of its definition (section 2.2.1). Regrettably, the ILC's work on the international liability of states did not provide a proper clarification of the notion among the civil law tradition jurists, as the Commission chose not to render the states liable (section 2.2.2).

2.2.1. An Equivalent for the Domestic Law's Objective Responsibility?

In fact, jurists from the common law and most jurists from the civil law traditions do not understand the international liability of states in the same way.

---

8   Y. B. Int'l L. Comm'n, 1973, vol. 1, 1243rd meeting, para. 37.
9   Id. at para. 38.

Moreover, even within the first group there is not a unique definition of the term "liability". Whereas for some authors liability is the "international obligation to compensate",[10] according to others it refers to "the consequences of a failure to perform [a] duty, or to fulfil the standards of performance required ... once responsibility and injury arising from [that failure] have been established".[11] In other words, while in the first definition the liability may have an independent existence from the wrongfulness of the state's act, in the second it is a consequence of a breach of an obligation.

Yet, with regard to the civil law tradition, the major confusion arises from the association of "liability" with the domestic law's "objective responsibility".[12] Also known as responsibility without fault, for risk or for damage, in domestic law, this legal regime stands in opposition to fault-based responsibility. Thus, in this conception, a person or an entity is – in the fullest sense of the word – responsible. Nonetheless, instead of fault, the responsibility is based on the damage caused by the person or entity itself, or on what is under its control. Transposing this notion to public international law would mean that the state must be – again in the strict sense – responsible for the damage caused by its activities, activities it has under its control or because they are occurring within the state's territory.

Being aware of this conceptual misunderstanding, the first Special Rapporteur on the ILC's project, the New Zealand member of the Commission, R.Q. Quentin-Baxter, begun his preliminary report with some considerations of the distinction between the two concepts of "responsibility" and "liability". According to him the term liability refers to "a negative asset, an obligation, in contra-distinction to a right. It is not used to mean only the consequences of an obligation, but rather to mean the obligation itself."[13] Underlining the triggering effect of loss or injury to liability, he pointed out one essential difference between the said concepts: "an obligation in respect of an act not prohibited arises only when a primary rule of international law so provides".[14]

---

[10] In Principles of International Law (Cambridge University Press, 3rd ed., 2012, p. 703, note 14) P. Sands & J. Peel quote P.M. Dupuy & H. Smets, Compensation for Damage Due to Transfrontier Pollution, in Compensation for Pollution Damage, OECD, 1981, p. 182.

[11] L.F.E. Goldie, Concepts of Strict and Absolute Liability and the Ranking of Liability in Terms of Relative Exposure to Risk, in Netherlands Y. B. Int'l L. 1985, p. 180.

[12] This is for instance the way that A. Kiss explains the state's liability for the damage caused by its space objects according to Article 2 of the 1972 Convention on International Liability for Damage Caused by Space Objects. A. Kiss & J.P. Beurier, Droit international de l'environnement, A. Pedone, 3rd ed., 2004, pp. 434–435. Also J.M. Arbour et al., supra, note 5 at p. 1240.

[13] Y. B. Int'l L. Comm'n, 1980, vol. 2 (1), p. 250, para. 12.

[14] Y. B. Int'l L. Comm'n, 1973, vol. 2 (1), p. 251, para. 13.

2.2.2. The Art of (Non-)Liability of the States in International Law

Later, the present author will come back to the notions of primary and secondary rules.[15] Nonetheless, considering the aforementioned words of the Special Rapporteur R.Q. Quentin-Baxter, it is not surprising that the final outcome was no longer about the international liability of states. In fact, if liability originates from the content of a primary rule of international law – either custom or convention – it would hardly be possible to codify rules applicable to all the domains of the states' activities that might cause damage to the environment. In other words, the ILC's task would have been to codify – if they already existed – or suggest – under its progressive development mission – rules determining when and how the state would be liable for the damage caused by any activity it is engaged in, despite its licit conduct.

It would be difficult not to agree with P.M. Dupuy, according to whom any attempt to create a general formulation of a rule applicable to the damages with diverse origins would face intractable problems in determining objective criteria for identifying situations in which the invocation of objective liability could be carried out.[16] In his view, which is fully endorsed by this chapter, the criterion is to be found in the practical improvement of the conditions of access of victims to the reparation.[17] Yet this would need to establish case by case a system of guarantees adapted to the particular nature of each activity and the type of risk it generates, which can only be done through convention.[18]

Additionally, state practice does not attest to indications that reparation might be available despite licit conduct. This implies that the existence of a customary obligation imposing on the states such reparation is – even now, years after the ILC's work in this area – seriously questioned. Moreover, concerning the conventional obligations, the one and only 1972 Convention on International Liability for Damage Caused by Space Objects does not provide enough "reason to conclude that such rules could be generalized".[19]

---

[15]   See *infra*, section 3.2.

[16]   "[T]oute tentative de formulation générale d'une règle applicable à des dommages d'origines diverses se heurte à des problèmes insolubles de détermination des critères objectifs permettant d'identifier les situations dans lesquelles l'invocation d'une responsabilité objective pourrait être effectuée". *P.M. Dupuy, supra*, note 4 at p. 132.

[17]   "Le critère n'est pas en effet à trouver dans la qualification, licite ou illicite, de l'activité à l'origine du dommage mais dans l'amélioration pratique des conditions d'accès des victimes à la réparation". *P.M. Dupuy, supra*, note 4 at p. 133.

[18]   "Ce qui est en cause, c'est l'établissement cas par cas d'un système de garantie adapté à la nature particulière de l'activité considérée et des types de risques qu'elle engendre. Ceci ne peut pas se faire que par voie de convention". *P.M. Dupuy, supra*, note 4 at p. 134.

[19]   Comments by A. Pellet, ILC member, Y. B. Int'l L. Comm'n, 1990, vol. 1, 2185th meeting, p. 263, para. 34.

Confronting these theoretical obstacles, the suggestion primarily advanced by ILC member A. Pellet[20] had spread throughout the Commission and finally led to the subdivision of the initial work into two separate parts.[21] The first part, i.e. prevention of transboundary harm from hazardous activities (2001), provides a series of obligations related to prevention, cooperation, assessment of risk, notification and provision of information, and consultation with reporting to the public. Taking into consideration the customary value of these obligations, any violation of them would trigger the state's responsibility for internationally wrongful acts. Yet, with regard to the second subdivision, relating to the allocation of loss in the case of transboundary harm[22] arising out of hazardous activities[23] (2006), the result is draft principles encouraging the states to develop liability regimes of private operators[24] of pollutant activities.[25]

In this way, according to the Principle 4.1, the states "should take all necessary measures to ensure that prompt and adequate compensation is available for victims of transboundary damage caused by hazardous activities located within [their territories] or otherwise under [their jurisdictions] or control". However, the same Principle determines in its paragraph 2 that the liability should be imposed "on the operator or, where appropriate, other person or entity" and without requiring "proof of fault".

Indeed, this "very modest"[26] outcome emerged from the nonexistence in positive international law of the general obligation of reparation despite

---

20 A. Pellet "suggested that the draft articles should be divided into two separate parts. The first part would contain a set of relatively detailed and stringent articles devoted exclusively to defining the obligation of States to be vigilant; it would include questions of both prevention and co-operation … The second part would be composed of 'model clauses' in respect of strict liability as such … Those clauses, which might be adjusted according to the types of activities envisaged, would serve as a reference for States during negotiations on specific activities". Comments by A. Pellet, ILC member, Y. B. Int'l L. Comm'n, 1990, vol. 1, 2185th meeting, p. 263, para. 37.

21 Y. B. Int'l L. Comm'n, 1997, vol. II (2), Report of the ILC on the work of its 49th session, A/52/10, p. 59, para. 168.

22 It seems that the terms "harm" and "damage" are used as synonyms in the Draft Principles. While "harm" appears in the title ("transboundary harm arising out of hazardous activities"), Principle 1 defines the scope of application as "transboundary damage caused by hazardous activities not prohibited by international law". According to Principle 2(a), "'damage' means significant damage caused to persons, property or the environment; and includes: (i) loss of life or personal injury; (ii) loss of, or damage to, property, including property which forms part of the cultural heritage; (iii) loss or damage by impairment of the environment; (iv) the costs of reasonable measures of reinstatement of the property, or environment, including natural resources; (v) the costs of reasonable response measures."

23 According to Principle 2(c), "'hazardous activity' means an activity which involves a risk of causing significant harm".

24 According to Principle 2(g), "'operator' means any person in command or control of the activity at the time the incident causing transboundary damage occurs".

25 Y. *Kerbrat*, Le droit international face au défi de la réparation des dommages à l'environnement, in Le droit international face aux enjeux environnementaux, A. Pedone, 2009, p. 126.

26 Id.

---

the state's licit conduct. Nevertheless, one must ask if the existence of a convention-based state liability – such as the Space Objects Convention – could be considered to be a second regime in the law of state responsibility and make the dream of an international "objective responsibility" come true. The response to this question must be sought in regards to the compatibility or incompatibility of such a regime with the one on state responsibility for internationally wrongful acts as imagined and founded by the ILC's Italian Special Rapporteur R. Ago.

3. THE COMMON REGIME: ROBERTO AGO'S SELF-SUFFICIENT FORTRESS

When in 1969 R. Ago presented his first report on the topic of international responsibility of states, the ILC had already spent 13 years on the codification of this specific issue. Analysed through the problem of diplomatic protection and injuries to the person and property of aliens, the codification had not advanced very far. In order to avoid a new cycle of confusion, R. Ago insisted from the beginning on two fundamental characteristics of the state responsibility regime. In fact, the common regime's self-sufficiency arises from objectivity (section 3.1) and H.L.A. Hart's distinction of rules (section 3.2).

3.1. THE OBJECTIVITY OF THE COMMON REGIME

As was briefly mentioned before,[27] in domestic civil law the objective responsibility refers to a regime with a basis other than fault. That is, for instance, the French law's *responsabilité du fait des choses*, according to which one is responsible not only for the damage caused by one's own acts, but also for those caused by the people one has to answer for, or the things one has under one's supervision.[28] Consequently, in the absence of fault, the responsibility is triggered under no more than two – simultaneous – conditions, i.e. damage and causal link, making the responsibility rest on objective elements, independent of the particular conduct of a person.

However, on the international plane using the adjective "objective" would not be particularly illustrative. On the contrary, "trying to distinguish liability

---

[27]   See *supra* section 2.2.1.
[28]   "On est responsable non seulement du dommage que l'on cause par son propre fait, mais encore de celui qui est causé par le fait des personnes dont on doit répondre, ou des choses que l'on a sous sa garde": French Civil Code, Article 1242.

for its 'objective' character may lead us into ambiguity".[29] Indeed, in the law of state responsibility, the term "fault" in the meaning of *culpa lato sensu* is known as the "subjective element". Likewise, when it comes to the "fault" in its second sense, i.e. the violation of an obligation, we are talking about the "objective element".[30]

Meanwhile, international law has distanced itself from the civil inspiration and ruled out fault – in its first meaning of *culpa* – among the required conditions to engage a state's responsibility. Instead, under the influence of the positivist voluntarist doctrine, the notion of "wrongful act" has been enshrined.[31] The main reason was to avoid the "twists and turns of psychological research of [the states'] intentions", since "the State and the international organizations, being legal entities, are an abstraction".[32] In fact, according to the ILC's 2001 Draft Articles on State Responsibility (Article 1), "every internationally wrongful act of a State entails the international responsibility of that State".[33] Therefore, if the basis of state responsibility is nothing more than an internationally wrongful act, this means that the subjective element has been left aside. Consequently, the regime of state responsibility for internationally wrongful acts can also by nature be characterised as "objective".

In other words, while the objectivity of the civil liability is founded on the disposal of fault – maintaining the damage and the causal link – as regards to the common regime in international law – damage being a matter of reparation and not the engagement of responsibility – the objectivity originates from the wrongful act of the state. Thus, if an international instrument like the 1972 Space Objects Convention establishes a state liability framework, objectivity would not be its distinctive feature as compared with the common regime.

This explains, moreover, the ILC's terminological choice to avoid objectivity and insisting, at least at the beginning, on the licit aspect of the activity concerned by the topic. For instance, for J. Barboza – the second Special Rapporteur of this work – the best expression to use for the purposes of the ILC's work was that of *sine delicto* liability. According to him, in the absence of "breach of obligation, there could be no fault either. That would exactly correspond to the title of the ILC topic: liability for the injurious consequences of acts not prohibited by international law".[34] Yet this suggestion has its flaws as,

---

[29] *J. Barboza*, International Liability for the Injurious Consequences of Acts not Prohibited by International Law and Protection of the Environment, in Collected Courses of The Hague Academy of International Law, Vol. 247, Brill/Nijhoff, 1994, p. 307.

[30] Id.

[31] *P.M. Dupuy & Y. Kerbrat*, Droit international public, Dalloz, 13th ed., 2016, pp. 508–509.

[32] "Selon cette conception aujourd'hui consacrée, point n'est besoin d'abord, puisque le fait illicite n'est pas une faute mais un simple manquement au droit, de s'engager dans les méandres de la recherche psychologique des intentions des auteurs de l'acte". Id. At p. 509.

[33] "Cette notion [i.e. fault] paraît en effet d'autant plus inappropriée que l'État et les organisations internationales, personnes morales, sont une abstraction". Id. at p. 509.

[34] *J. Barboza, supra*, note 29 at p. 309.

by using the term *delicto*, it refers to the notion of "fault", which is precisely and deliberately absent in the common regime's sphere. Nonetheless, to avoid those terminological considerations resulting in doctrinal confusions, finally the ILC has decided to underline the dangerousness of the activity in question instead of its conformity with the international obligations of the state or the objectivity of the regime, which was expected to be founded.

That being said, there still remains a second characteristic of the common regime which makes unimaginable – and additionally unnecessary – the emergence of any new regime in the law of state responsibility. To understand this fundamental characteristic, the regime of state responsibility for internationally wrongful acts must be appreciated in the light of H.L.A. Hart's theory of rules.

3.2. IT IS ABOUT THE SECONDARY OBLIGATIONS

In his distinguished book *The Concept of Law* – first published in 1961 – the British legal philosopher H.L.A. Hart "discriminate[s] between two different though related types"[35] of rules. The first category, which can be called "basic or primary", is composed of rules requiring doing or abstaining from certain actions.[36] However, the other category, namely "secondary rules", which may be considered "parasitic upon ... the first" type, are so called because they let the introduction of new primary rules extinguish or modify the old primary rules. It is important to mention that the second category is so called not because the rules it contains would be less important, but because they have no autonomous existence[37] without the primary rules. Nonetheless, each category of rules fulfils its function: while the primary rules "impose duties", the secondary rules "confer powers".[38]

This classification of rules had an undeniable role in the foundation of the ILC's work on the state responsibility as released in 2001. In fact, R. Ago succeeded in convincing the Commission of the importance of "maintaining a strict distinction between" its principal task, namely "the determination of the principles which govern the responsibility of States for internationally wrongful acts", and what must be avoided, which is "defining the rules that place obligations on States, the violation of which may generate responsibility".[39] Hence, through reference to H.L.A. Hart's classification of rules, the Special Rapporteur R. Ago

---

[35] *H.L.A. Hart*, The Concept of Law, Oxford University Press, 3rd ed., 2012, pp. 80–81.
[36] Id. at p. 81.
[37] "Elle est une conséquence directe de cette violation du droit, dont il incombera à la victime de rapporter la preuve; elle n'a pas, en d'autres termes, d'existence autonome". *P.M. Dupuy, supra*, note 4 at p. 129.
[38] *H.L.A. Hart, supra*, note 35 at p. 81.
[39] Y. B. Int'l L. Comm'n, 1970, vol. II, p. 178, para. 7.

drew attention to the fact that "it is one thing to define a rule and the content of the obligation it imposes and another to determine whether that obligation has been violated and what should be the consequences of the violation. Only the second aspect comes within the sphere of responsibility proper."[40]

Considering this theoretical observation, a new understanding of the international liability of states appears before us. Indeed, since the acts in question "are not prohibited, by definition [they] do not breach any obligation and therefore pertain to the primary rule".[41] In the words of J. Barboza – the ILC's Special Rapporteur on the topic of international liability of states – "international liability rules were primary rules, for they established an obligation and came into play not when the obligation had been violated, but when the condition that triggered that same obligation had arisen".[42] Evidently, the condition to which he refers stands for the damage caused by the act.

However, there is no evidence of a general rule – as has already been mentioned above[43] – in positive public international law requiring that any damage – no matter its origin – caused by the state's activity must be repaired by the state. As such it is up to the states themselves to determine, by way of a treaty, in which areas of economic activities and under what conditions they would assume liability. Within the framework of each specific treaty, there would be primary obligations imposing on the state compensation in the case of damage caused by that particular activity.

So far, nothing – except for the 1972 Space Objects Convention – demonstrates the states' desire to exert themselves in the domain of international liability. Quite the opposite: looking over the international treaties reveals the states' tendency to "canalise" liability exclusively to private persons and more particularly to operators.[44] For this reason, the Space Objects Convention will inevitably serve as an example to illustrate concretely the interaction between state responsibility for internationally wrongful acts and the international liability of states through the primary/secondary obligation classification.

According to the Space Objects Convention's Article 2, "[a] launching State shall be absolutely liable to pay compensation for damage caused by its space

---

40   Id.
41   *J. Barboza, supra*, note 29 at p. 311.
42   Y. B. Int'l L. Comm'n, 1987, vol. II (2), p. 43, para.146.
43   See *supra*, section 2.2.2.
44   By way of example, as regards the maritime accidental pollution, the 1992 Civil Liability Convention for Oil Pollution Damage aims to render the shipowners liable. It is the same regarding the International Convention on Civil Liability for Bunker Oil Pollution Damage of 2001. As concerned the 2003 Protocol on Civil Liability and Compensation for Damage Caused by the Transboundary Effects of Industrial Accidents on Transboundary Waters, the 1992 Convention on the Protection and Use of Transboundary Watercourses and International Lakes, and the 1992 Convention on the Transboundary Effects of Industrial Accidents, it is the operator who shall be liable.

object on the surface of the earth or to aircraft in flight".[45] Based on H.L.A. Hart's classification and R. Ago's explanation, this article contains a primary obligation imposing on the Member States compensation for the damage caused. This obligation may be triggered by mere damage, regardless of the state's conformity with international law, i.e. licit or illicit conduct prior to the damage. Furthermore, as the Convention mentions, it does not matter whether there is fault[46] in the conduct of the state or in that of persons for whom the state is responsible.[47] In other words, the compensation is not a consequence of the state's responsibility – triggered by the latter's wrongful act – but the consequence of a primary obligation to which the state had committed through a treaty.

So far, the Convention has only once been the subject of a claim for compensation. This is the Kosmos 954 case, which occurred between Canada and the Soviet Union. In 1978, a Soviet satellite containing enriched uranium, previously placed in orbit, re-entered the Earth's atmosphere. Disintegrating in Canada's airspace, its debris spread across Canadian territory. The latter justified compensation, *inter alia*, based on Article 2 of Space Objects Convention.[48]

Now, let us imagine the scenario in which a launching state whose space object had caused damage refuses to pay the due compensation. Would this not be a violation of an international obligation, or, in other words, a primary obligation? The response is definitely positive, and that is why the common regime would have the basis for an internationally wrongful act attributable to a state. Therefore, the state that had refused to compensate for the damage caused by its space object would find itself experiencing the consequences arising from its responsibility. According to the ILC's Draft Articles on State Responsibility (2001), the legal consequences of an internationally wrongful act are: the continued duty of performance (Article 29); cessation if the act is continuing and assurances and guarantees of non-repetition if circumstances so require (Article 30); and reparation (Articles 34–39) taking three forms, namely restitution, compensation and satisfaction.

What we can understand from this illustration is also discernible in R. Ago's explanation before his colleagues at the ILC in 1973. As we have already noted,

---

[45] It is not surprising that the term used for "liability" in the official French version is "responsabilité": "Un État de lancement a la responsabilité absolue de verser réparation pour le dommage causé par son objet spatial".

[46] It had already been mentioned that the notion of "fault" had in principle disappeared from the public international law. However, the Convention refers to it in its Article 3. See *infra*, note 47.

[47] It is appropriate to specify that according to the Article 3 of the same Convention, if the damage is caused elsewhere than on the surface of the Earth to a space object of one launching state or to persons or property on board such a space object, the presence of fault is necessary as to trigger the liability of the state.

[48] Claim Against the Union of Soviet Socialist Republics for Damage caused by Soviet Cosmos 954, Annex A, Statement of Claim, in International Legal Materials, 1979, vol. 18, p. 907.

for him, imposing on the state the obligation to make reparation for an injury caused by its lawful activity is "not, strictly speaking, a matter of responsibility, but of a guarantee".[49] Following this logic, similarly to the above-mentioned imaginary scenario, "[t]here could be a violation if the person causing the damage refused to make reparation, thus failing to fulfil an international obligation and committing an infringement which generated responsibility".[50]

4. CONCLUSIONS

The doctrine's concerns about the specificities of environmental harm are incontestable. To restrict the reparation to the existence of a violated international obligation at the origin of the harm leaves a considerable number of environmental harms unrepaired. Admittedly, there would still remain those particular civil liability conventions imposing compensation on private operators. Yet there is no reason to exclude the states – promoting activities likely to cause environmental harm and benefiting vastly from them – from among those who have the obligation to compensate. However, neither customary international law nor international treaties provide a general obligation requiring that the state must compensate damage caused by activities occurring in its territory, under its jurisdiction or somehow under its control. The lack of such an obligation is the essential reason behind the failure of the ILC to codify or even develop the domain of the international liability of states. Nonetheless, the eventual codification of the international liability of states would not make that framework a new regime in the law of state responsibility. Even if the absence of an equivalent term for "liability" among Romance languages had led the civil law tradition jurists to amalgamate "liability" with "responsibility", they belong to entirely different spheres. Each of them represents a category of rule according to H.L.A. Hart's classification. While "liability" arises from the content of a primary obligation – either customary or conventional – "responsibility" as a secondary obligation emerges only when a primary obligation has been violated. In fact, the fortress that R. Ago had founded on "legality", unobstructed by primary obligations, would lead the emergence of a new responsibility regime towards a theoretical impasse. Yet there is another path before the doctrine, and that is to advocate for more primary obligations imposing on the states the reparation of environmental harms caused by hazardous activities despite their licit conduct. This requires the determination of the states in order to develop new treaties. However, the current state of the international community does not express states' desire for solidarity around collective interests, including the protection of the environment.

---

49 Y. B. Int'l L. Comm'n, 1973, vol. I, p. 14, para. 4.
50 Id.

THE RIGHT TO A HEALTHY ENVIRONMENT AND ITS CONSEQUENCES FOR OTHER HUMAN RIGHTS

A Challenging Approach

Laura Stănilă and Sergiu Stănilă

1. INTRODUCTORY CONSIDERATIONS ON THE RIGHT TO A HEALTHY ENVIRONMENT

The environmental challenges of current times, especially those registered in recent decades, have had dramatic effects on people's health and affected the quality of their everyday life. These consequences have led to the shaping of a new human right that was not provided for in the European Convention on Human Rights (ECHR), but is becoming more and more important both at the national and international level. This is the right to a healthy environment, which "is intended to ensure that everyone has access to clean air, safe water, fertile soil and nutritious food, as well as the conservation of biological diversity an ecosystem functions".[1]

The first formal articulation of the right to a healthy environment occurred in 1972, with the adoption of the Stockholm Declaration,[2] which stated in its Principle 1: "Man has the fundamental right to freedom, equality and adequate conditions of life, in an environment of a quality that permits a life of dignity and well-being, and he bears a solemn responsibility to protect and improve the environment for present and future generations."

It is beyond doubt that at present times, the right to a healthy environment is a genuine human right because it meets the three general features of any other human right – it is universal, moral and essential:

(a) it is universal because it is held by all human beings;

---

[1]   *D.R. Boyd,* The right to a healthy environment. Revitalizing Canada's Constitution, UBC Press, 2012, p. 1, https://www.ubcpress.ca/asset/9095/1/9780774824125.pdf.

[2]   Declaration of the United Nations Conference on the Human Environment adopted by the United Nations Conference on the Human Environment, having met at Stockholm from 5 to 16 June 1972, http://www.un-documents.net/unchedec.htm.

(b) it is moral because it exists for certain, no matter whether a state, authority or legal system recognises it or not;

(c) it is essential because it ensures the dignity and quality of life of all human beings living on our planet.

As a matter of fact, the issue of declaring and recognising the right to a healthy environment as a fundamental human right is settled, since 92 per cent of the world's countries recognise it as so[3] through their fundamental laws, special legislation or case law, in addition to an important number of treaties and declarations adopted or ratified by them. Of course, these numbers do not suggest also that this important human right is also being adequately enforced.

Scholars[4] have proposed a possible triple approach to the right on the healthy environment, as follows:

(1) In a very narrow and, in the authors' opinion, unfair approach, it is argued that there is no distinct right to a healthy environment, at least not yet, since the common international documents providing for and guaranteeing human rights do not refer to it as such.[5]

(2) In another approach, the environment is viewed as a precondition for the enjoyment of human rights. Environmental factors may therefore influence or determine the level of rights fulfilment and environmental degradation can amount to a violation of those rights. In this line of thinking, it can be argued that the environment can also have an indirect impact on the enjoyment of human rights, because a poor environment may affect an individual's or a community's capacity to exercise their human rights generally, or impede a government's ability to protect the rights of its citizens.[6]

(3) Last, but not least, an analysis of the relationship between human rights and the environment provides that the right to a healthy environment is a distinct right, a right to which human beings are entitled, independent

---

3   *Boyd, supra,* note 1 at p. 2.

4   B. *Lewis,* Environmental Rights or a Right to the Environment? Exploring the Nexus Between Human Rights and Environmental Protection, Macquarie Journal of International and Comparative Environmental Law 2012 (8/1), pp. 37–38, https://www.researchgate. net/publication/265050937_Environmental_Rights_or_a_Right_to_the_Environment_ Exploring_the_Nexus_Between_Human_Rights_and_Environmental_Protection.

5   O.W. *Pedersen,* European Environmental Human Rights and Environmental Rights: A Long Time Coming?, Georgetown International Environmental Law Review 2008 (21/1), available at SSRN: https://ssrn.com/abstract=1122289.

6   Office of the High Commissioner for Human Rights, Meeting of Experts on Human Rights and the Environment, 2002, paras. 5, 12, cited by S. *Glazebrook,* Human Rights and the Environment, Victoria University of Wellington Law Review 2009 (40/1), p. 300, https:// papers.ssrn.com/sol3/papers.cfm?abstract_id=1556767.

from other human rights. This conclusion may be drawn from the United Nations' Draft Principles on Human Rights and the Environment, which state in Principle 5: "All persons have the right to a secure, healthy and ecologically sound environment. This right and other human rights, including civil, cultural, economic, political and social rights are universal, interdependent and indivisible."

2. INTERFERENCE OF THE RIGHT TO A HEALTHY ENVIRONMENT WITH OTHER HUMAN RIGHTS IN THE LIGHT OF ECtHR CASE LAW

In the authors' opinion, before coming down in favour or not of an independent right to a healthy environment, it is necessary to discuss the issue from a different perspective, trying to identify the relation between a healthy environment and the other fundamental human rights, especially the right to life, the right to respect for family life and home, the right to health and bodily integrity and the right not to be tortured or to be subject to inhuman or degrading treatment. Therefore, the research tends to be focused on the connections between these elements and not on the elements themselves.

Moreover, recent international discussions on environmental rights, sustain this view, as they have focused on the indivisibility of the right to a quality environment and fundamental human rights.[7]

Scholars have been also preoccupied by the connection between the right to a healthy environment and the other human rights, addressing the question whether human rights are the proper legal tools for dealing with the increasing degradation of the environment.[8] Two reasons have been given in order to explain why this issue has now become more timely than ever. According to Francioni, "first, contemporary developments at the level of treaty law have tended to fashion the entitlement of individuals, communities, and groups to take part in environmental decisions affecting their lives, and to access justice with respect

---

[7] The Hague Declaration on the Environment 1989 recognised a fundamental duty to preserve the ecosystem and also the right to live in dignity in a viable global environment, thus expressing a connection between the environment and human rights. Also, the United Nations General Assembly held in 1990 observed that environmental protection is indivisible from the achievement of full enjoyment of human rights by all, heralding the recognition of the right of all individuals to live in an environment adequate for their health and well-being. Four years later, the Special Rapporteur to the Sub-Commission on the Prevention of Discrimination and Protection of Minorities proposed a set of Draft Principles providing for a stand-alone environmental right, described as the right to a secure healthy and ecologically sound environment. *Apud Glazebrook, supra*, note 6 at p. 299.

[8] *F. Francioni*, International Human Rights in an Environmental Horizon, European Journal of International Law 2010 (21/1), p. 49.

to adverse impacts caused to their environment in terms of human rights".[9] This phenomenon was called the "proceduralisation of environmental rights". The second reason for revisiting the issue of the nature and scope of environmental rights was addressed as substantive: "recent practice shows that the protection of the natural environment in special socio-cultural contexts is a *sine qua non* for the enjoyment of human rights by members of the relevant group or community".[10]

As environmental concerns have become more important nationally and internationally since 1950, the case law of the Court has increasingly reflected the idea that human rights law and environmental law are mutually reinforcing.[11] As a consequence, even though no explicit right to a clean and quiet environment is included in the Convention or its protocols, the case law of the Court has shown a growing awareness of a link between the protection of the rights and freedoms of individuals and the environment. However, it is not primarily upon the ECtHR to determine which measures are necessary to protect the environment, but rather upon national authorities, according to the principle of subsidiarity.[12]

In the past 25 years, the Strasbourg Court has made a positive contribution to the construction of an environmental dimension of several rights enshrined in the Convention. The Strasbourg case law has contributed to the development of certain environmental obligations incumbent upon states parties by virtue of the Convention. These obligations are:[13]

(a) the obligation to regulate activities of an industrial or technological nature which might adversely affect the sphere of protected rights, such as the right to life (provided by Article 2 ECHR) and the right to private and family life (provided by Article 8 ECHR);

(b) the obligation effectively to enforce legal, administrative or judicial measures designed to prevent or remedy the unlawful interference with such rights; and

(c) the obligation to provide information and engage in consultation with affected individuals and people with regard to the actual risk and danger of the environmental impact in issue.

---

9   Id.
10   Id.
11   L.C.B. v. the United Kingdom [1998] ECHR 108, (1998) 27 EHRR 212, [1998] HRCD 628, 4 BHRC 447, judgment of 9 June 1998; Öneryıldız v. Turkey [GC], no. 48939/99 [2004] ECHR 657, (2005) 41 EHRR 20; Florea v. Romania, no. 37186/03, judgment of 14 September 2010; Elefteriadis v. Romania, no. 38427/05, judgment of 25 January 2011; Brânduşe v. Romania, no. 6586/03, of judgment 7 April 2009; López Ostra v. Spain, no. 16798/90, judgment of 9 December 1994; Tătar v. Romania, no. 67021/01, decision of 27 January 2009.
12   Council of Europe, Manual on Human Rights and the Environment, Council of Europe Publishing, 2012, pp. 33–35.
13   Id.

The European Convention for the Protection of Human Rights and Fundamental Freedoms, adopted in 1950, does not provide an explicit right to a healthy environment. However, the ECtHR has emphasised that the effective enjoyment of the rights which are encompassed in the Convention depends notably on a sound, quiet and healthy environment conducive to well-being.[14] The subject matter of the cases examined by the Court shows that a range of environmental factors may have an impact on individual Convention rights, such as noise levels from airports, industrial pollution or town planning.

Analysing the provisions of the ECHR from the perspective of the case law built around their interpretation may lead us to an undeniable conclusion in this matter.

2.1. THE RIGHT TO LIFE (ARTICLE 2 ECHR)

According to Article 2 ECHR, everyone's right to life shall be protected by law. This provision does not solely concern deaths resulting directly from the actions of the agents of a state, but also lays down a positive obligation on states to take appropriate steps to safeguard the lives of those within their jurisdiction.[15] The Court has found that the positive obligation on states may apply in the context of dangerous activities, such as nuclear tests, the operation of chemical factories with toxic emissions or waste-collection sites, whether carried out by public authorities themselves or by private companies.[16]

The case law of the Court is prolific in this matter. For example the Court found a violation of Article 2 in the case of *Öneryıldız v. Turkey* (2004). In this case, an explosion occurred on a municipal rubbish tip, killing 39 people who had illegally built their dwellings around it. Nine members of the applicant's family died in the accident. Although an expert report had drawn the attention of the municipal authorities to the danger of a methane explosion at the tip two years before the accident, the authorities had remained passive. The Court found that since the authorities knew – or ought to have known – that there was a real and immediate risk to the lives of people living near the rubbish tip, they had an obligation under Article 2 to take preventive measures to protect those people.

---

[14]   See *supra*, note 11.
[15]   L.C.B. v. the United Kingdom, [1998] ECHR 108, (1998) 27 EHRR 212, [1998] HRCD 628, 4 BHRC 447, judgment of 9 June 1998, para. 36.
[16]   Öneryıldız v. Turkey [GC], no. 48939/99 [2004] ECHR 657, (2005) 41 EHRR 20, para. 71.

2.2. PROHIBITION OF INHUMAN OR DEGRADING TREATMENT (ARTICLE 3 ECHR)

2.2.1. Florea v. Romania

In 2002 the applicant, who suffered from chronic hepatitis and arterial hypertension, was imprisoned. For approximately nine months he shared a cell with between 110 and 120 other prisoners, with only 35 beds. According to the applicant, 90 per cent of his cellmates were smokers. The applicant complained in particular of overcrowding and poor hygiene conditions, including having been detained together with smokers in his prison cell and in the prison hospital.[17]

The Court observed in particular that the applicant had spent in detention approximately three years living in very cramped conditions, with an area of personal space falling below the European standard. As to the fact that he had to share a cell and a hospital ward with prisoners who smoked, the Court noted that the applicant had never had an individual cell and had had to tolerate his fellow prisoners' smoking even in the prison infirmary and the prison hospital, against his doctor's advice. However, a law in force since June 2002 prohibited smoking in hospitals and the domestic courts had frequently ruled that smokers and non-smokers should be detained separately. It followed that the conditions of detention to which the applicant had been subjected had exceeded the threshold of severity required by Article 3 ECHR, in violation of this provision.

2.2.2. Elefteriadis v. Romania

The applicant, who suffered from chronic pulmonary disease, was serving a sentence of life imprisonment. Between February and November 2005 he was placed in a cell with two prisoners who smoked. In the waiting rooms of the courts where he had been summoned to appear on several occasions between 2005 and 2007, he was also held together with prisoners who smoked.[18]

The Court held that there had been a violation of Article 3 of the Convention, observing in particular that a state is required to take measures to protect a prisoner from the harmful effects of passive smoking where, as in the applicant's case, medical examinations and the advice of doctors indicated that this was necessary for health reasons.

---

[17] Florea v. Romania, no. 37186/03, judgment of 14 September 2010.
[18] Elefteriadis v. Romania, no. 38427/05, judgment of 25 January 2011.

2.3. THE RIGHT TO RESPECT FOR PRIVATE AND FAMILY LIFE AND THE HOME (ARTICLE 8 ECHR)

The right to respect for private and family life and the home is protected under Article 8 of the Convention and implies respect for the quality of private life as well as the enjoyment of the amenities of one's home or one's "living space".

In *Brânduşe v. Romania*,[19] the Court did not require an actual impact on the health of the applicant to find Article 8 applicable. In this case, the Court was required to determine firstly whether Article 8 of the Convention applied in the case of an applicant who considered the cell in which he was serving a prison sentence to be his "living space", and secondly whether the bad odours from a nearby rubbish tip breached the gravity threshold to fall within the scope of Article 8. The Court agreed with the applicant that Article 8 applied to his cell as the cell represented the only "living space" available to the prisoner for several years. Moreover, the Court clearly held that the applicant's quality of life and well-being had been affected in a manner that had impaired his private life

In *López Ostra v. Spain*,[20] the applicant complained that the fumes and noise from a waste treatment plant situated near her home made her family's living conditions unbearable. After having had to bear the nuisance caused by the plant for more than three years, the family moved elsewhere when it became clear that the nuisance could go on indefinitely and when her daughter's paediatrician recommended that they relocate. The national authorities, while recognising that the noise and smells had a negative effect on the applicant's quality of life, argued that they did not constitute a grave health risk and that they did not reach a level of severity breaching the applicant's fundamental rights. However, the Court found that severe environmental pollution may affect individuals' well-being and prevent them from enjoying their homes in such a way as to affect adversely their private and family life, even though it does not seriously endanger their health. In this case, the Court found a violation of Article 8.

Another example is *Fadeyeva v. Russia*.[21] In this case, the applicant lived in the vicinity of a steel plant. The Court observed that in order to fall under Article 8, complaints relating to environmental nuisances have to show, firstly, that there has been an actual interference with the individual's "private sphere", and, secondly, that these nuisances have reached a certain level of severity. In the case in question, the Court found that over a significant period of time the concentration of various toxic elements in the air near the applicant's house seriously exceeded safe levels and that the applicant's health had deteriorated as a result of the prolonged exposure to the industrial emissions from the steel plant.

---

[19]   Brânduşe v. Romania, no. 6586/03, judgment of 7 April 2009, para. 67.
[20]   López Ostra v. Spain, no. 16798/90, judgment of 9 December 1994.
[21]   Fadeyeva v. Russia, no. 55723/00, judgment of 9 June 2005.

Therefore, the Court accepted that the actual detriment to the applicant's health and well-being reached a level sufficient to bring it within the scope of Article 8 of the Convention. Here the Court concluded that there had been a violation of Article 8.

The case of *Tătar v. Romania*[22] is also notable. In this case, the applicants, who lived near a gold ore extraction plant, had lodged several complaints with the authorities about the risks to which they were being exposed because of the use by the company of a technical procedure involving sodium cyanide. In 2000, despite the fact that the authorities had reassured the applicants that sufficient safety mechanisms existed, a large quantity of polluted water spilled into various rivers, crossing several borders and affecting the environment of several countries. In this particular case, the Court was confronted with the problem that there was no internal decision or other official document stating explicitly how much of a threat the company's activities posed to human health and the environment.[23] The Court found that the applicants had failed to prove that there was a sufficient causal link between the pollution caused and the worsening of their symptoms. Nevertheless, on the basis of environmental impact studies of the spillage submitted by the respondent state, the Court concluded that a serious and substantial threat to the applicants' well-being existed. Consequently, the Court found that there had been a violation of Article 8 of the Convention, thus interpreting environmental issues and environmental principles into the Convention.[24]

Although the Court found that the applicants had failed to prove causality between the use of sodium cyanide and the asthma from which one of the applicants suffered, it found that the material risk which the operations posed to the applicants' health and well-being entailed a duty upon the state to assess such risks. Moreover, the Court found that the risks faced by the applicants gave rise to a series of positive obligations requiring the state to construct a legislative and administrative framework that regulates the licensing, start-up, operation and control of the hazardous activity carried out and that must include appropriate public surveys and studies allowing the public to assess the risks and effects associated with the relevant activities.

In *Băcilă v. Romania*,[25] the applicant complained of the emissions of a lead and zinc plant in the town of Copşa Mică. Analyses carried out by public and private bodies established that heavy metals could be found in the town's waterways, in the air, in the soil and in vegetation, at levels of up to 20 times

---

22 Tătar v. Romania, no. 67021/01, decision of 27 January 2009.
23 Id. at para. 93.
24 *O.W. Pedersen,* The Ties that Bind: The Environment, the European Convention on Human Rights and the Rule of Law, European Public Law 2010 (16/4), p. 571, available at SSRN: https://ssrn.com/abstract=1673125.
25 Băcilă v. Romania, no. 19234/04, judgment of 30 March 2010.

the maximum permitted. The rate of illness, particularly respiratory conditions, was seven times higher in Copşa Mică than in the rest of the country. The Court found that the authorities had failed to strike a fair balance between the public interest in maintaining the economic activity of the biggest employer in a town (the lead and zinc plant) and the applicant's effective enjoyment of the right to respect for her home and for her private and family life.

3. *BRÂNDUŞE v. ROMANIA* AND ITS SUBTILTIES

The case of *Brânduşe v. Romania* has already been referred to above in our analysis on the interconnection between the right to a healthy environment and the prohibition of torture and inhuman treatment. But this case deserves a more exhaustive discussion since the issues involved are many and in this case the Court took some important steps in its interpretation of the relationship between the rights of the applicant and the right to a healthy environment.

In this case the Court held unanimously that there had been:

- a violation of Article 3 ECHR (prohibition of inhuman or degrading treatment) on account of Mr Brânduşe's conditions of detention; and
- a violation of Article 8 ECHR (right to respect for private and family life) on account of the Romanian authorities' failure to take the necessary measures to deal with the problem of offensive smells coming from the tip.

The applicant was sentenced to 10 years' imprisonment for fraud. While in pre-trial detention, he was initially held in the Arad police headquarters. Following his conviction, he was transferred to prisons in Timişoara and Arad. The applicant brought judicial proceedings to complain of his conditions of detention and the fact that in Arad prison he had had to put up with stale air and the nauseous stench from a site, about 20 metres from the prison, that had formerly been used for the disposal of household waste. This former refuse tip, managed by company S., which was itself run by Arad City Council, was in use from 1998 to 2003. The applicant's applications were rejected by the domestic courts. Mr Brânduşe complained of the conditions in which he had been held in Arad police headquarters and Timişoara and Arad prisons, particularly in respect of prison overcrowding, the poor quality of the food and hygiene conditions. Although there was nothing in the present case to indicate that there had been a real intention to humiliate or degrade the applicant, the absence of such an objective could not rule out a finding that there had been a violation of Article 3 ECHR. The conditions of detention in issue, which the applicant had had to endure for several years, had subjected him to an ordeal of an intensity which went beyond the level of suffering inherent in detention. Therefore the Court had unanimously concluded there had been a violation of Article 3.

The Romanian authorities were found responsible for the offensive fumes and smells complained of by the applicant, as company S. was run by Arad City Council. In addition, responsibility had been transferred from the Council to S. only in February 2006, and even after that date the environmental authorities had made the City Council directly responsible for closing the refuse tip. Moreover, the file showed that the tip in question had been in operation effectively from 1998 to 2003, and that it had even continued to be used by private individuals thereafter, since the authorities had not taken measures to ensure effective closure of the site. However, throughout that period, the tip had had no proper authorisation either for its operation or for its closure. By failing to follow the required procedure, the local authorities had failed in several of their obligations. Although the relevant authorities were required to commission studies in advance to assess the effects of the polluting activity in question in order to ensure a fair balance between the various competing interests at stake, they had fulfilled that obligation only later. Studies had shown that the activity was incompatible with environmental requirements, that there was a high level of pollution exceeding the established norms and that persons living nearby had to put up with significant levels of nuisance caused by offensive smells.

Although it was incumbent on the authorities to carry out preliminary studies to measure the effects of pollution, it was only after the event, in 2003 and after a serious fire on the site in 2006, that they did so. The studies concluded that the activity was incompatible with environmental requirements, that there was a high level of pollution exceeding the standards established in 1987 and that persons living nearby had to put up with significant levels of nuisance caused by offensive smells. The competent authorities had explicitly penalised Arad City Council for the absence from the site of any means of informing the public about risks for the environment and the health of the population arising from the existence of the refuse tip. The Romanian government has not indicated what measures had been taken to ensure that the inmates of Arad prison, including in particular the applicant, could have effective access to the conclusions of the studies mentioned and to information whereby they could assess the risks to their health.

While noting that Mr Brânduşe's health had not deteriorated through proximity to the former refuse tip, the Court considered that, in the light of the conclusions of the environmental studies and the length of time for which the applicant had to suffer the nuisances concerned, the applicant's quality of life and well-being were affected to the detriment of his private life in a way which was not merely the consequence of his deprivation of liberty. Indeed, the applicant's complaint related to aspects which went beyond the context of his conditions of detention as such and which, moreover, concerned the only "living space" the applicant had had available to him for a number of years. It therefore considered that Article 8 was applicable in the case. The Court observed that the Romanian authorities were responsible for the offensive smells, as company S. was run by Arad City Council.

Although Mr. Brânduşe had not shown any effects on his health, the very fact that he had to endure the stench for seven years had affected his quality of life to such an extent that Article 8 became applicable. The Court noted that the prison cell was his living space during the period of his sentence and focused on procedural issues, such as the failure of the authorities to abide by their own rules and the lack of access to environmental information for the prisoner. The conclusion of the Court was that even detainees have certain rights concerning a reasonable environment.

4. CONCLUDING REMARKS

Human rights and environmental law occupy a very special place in the field of public international law. Both have developed as branches of the law where states undertake commitments to respect not another state's rights, but the objective value of human dignity and environmental quality.[26] As Francioni has stated, "progress has been made toward the integration of environmental considerations in the process of human rights adjudication. At the substantive level, progress has been achieved by an evolutionary interpretation of established human rights provisions – notably, the right to life, family and private life, and minority rights".[27]

In conclusion, the extended and creative interpretation of the human rights provided by ECHR inevitably and naturally leads to shaping of a consistent right to a healthy environment.

Cases like *Brânduşe v. Romania* show us all the importance of the connection between the "new" right to a healthy environment and the other "old" human rights, and the importance of the proactive action of state authorities in preserving a healthy environment with the purpose of ensuring the guarantees needed for fully exercising those rights by a human being. As a matter of fact, human rights may be seen, from an environmental perspective, as environmental rights – a notion used by Taylor in order to refer to the traditional rights approach of granting rights and creating duties and obligations towards the environment, at a level sufficient to ensure the continued survival of present and future generations of humanity.[28]

---

[26] *Francioni, supra*, note 8 at p. 55.
[27] Id.
[28] P.E. Taylor, From Environmental to Ecological Human Rights: A New Dynamic in International Law, Georgetown Environmental Law Review 1998 (10), p. 309.

PART VI
CLIMATE CHANGE LIABILITY

CLIMATE CHANGE LIABILITY

Some General Remarks in a Comparative Law Perspective

Valentina JACOMETTI

1. INTRODUCTION: SETTING THE SCENE

For several years now, climate change issues have been intensively debated within scientific and political contexts at both national and international level. Indeed, climate change is one of the most dramatic problems that current and future generations are called to address. Climate change is taking place at an unknown speed when compared with previous similar phenomena. Furthermore, it is caused mostly by human activities and, therefore, can be mitigated through regulatory and institutional solutions which affect human behaviour (mitigation strategy); and given that the increase in temperatures (global warming) inevitably results in changes to ecological cycles, changes in precipitation patterns, melting glaciers and rising sea levels, strategies to adapt to such results must be adopted (adaptation strategy).[1]

Climate change has been the object of a complex international regulatory process, starting with the United Nations Framework Convention on Climate Change (UNFCCC) in 1992 via the Kyoto Protocol of 2005 to the Paris Agreement of 2015. However, the international regulatory process has experienced its ups and downs in developing a global framework in order to identify the goals and the tools for addressing the challenge of climate change.[2]

In addition, whilst climate change is a global phenomenon that needs to be addressed at a global level through comprehensive strategies agreed to at supranational level, the legal rules that are used to implement the strategies of

---

[1]   IPCC 5th Report, Climate Change 2014, Synthesis Report, Summary for Policymakers, at http://www.ipcc.ch/report/ar5/syr/.
[2]   See among others: *D. Freestone & C. Streck*, Legal Aspects of Implementing the Kyoto Protocol Mechanisms: Making Kyoto Work, Oxford University Press, 2005; *D. Bodansky, J. Brunnée & L. Rajamani*, International Climate Change Law, Oxford University Press, 2017.

mitigation and adaptation are necessarily rooted in local legal systems, a point that is often underestimated. In actual fact, the effective implementation of legal rules is largely dependent on the structural characteristics of each legal system, i.e. the underlying *legal process*. In this "global/local" dialectic, the legal and regulatory framework that has emerged is multilevel and highly fragmented, resulting from a variety of legal instruments – national, but also transnational – that are uncoordinated or at least poorly coordinated and have different levels of binding force and different geographical scope.[3]

Indeed, although we have witnessed the development of an extensive international legal framework, there remain – among the different legal systems – different strategies for dealing with the risks posed by climate change.[4]

From a global and comparative perspective, two different models of institutional response can be identified: the regulatory model aimed at directly regulating the problem, i.e. the causes and consequences of climate change and the measures to tackle them; and the litigation model, where climate-change-related issues are addressed through a judicial process.[5]

2. THE EMERGENCE OF CLIMATE CHANGE LITIGATION

Climate change, being one of the most dramatic problems of our times, involves a variety of liability issues both with regard to the emission of greenhouse gases and the adaptation to climate change consequences. Indeed, faced with the insufficient public and private commitments to contrast climate change, there is

---

[3] See: *A. van Harro, F. Sindico & M. Mehling*, Global Climate Change and the Fragmentation of International Law, Law & Policy 2008 (30), pp. 423 et seq.; *D.A. Farber & M. Peeters* (eds.), Climate Change Law, Edward Elgar, 2016; *K.R. Gray, R. Tarasofsky & C. Cinnamon* (eds.), Oxford Handbook of International Climate Change Law, Oxford University Press, 2016; *A. Averchenkova, S. Fankhauser & M. Nachmany* (eds.), Trends in Climate Change Legislation, Edward Elgar, 2017.

[4] *C.P. Carlarne*, Climate Change Law and Policy: EU and US Approaches, Oxford University Press, 2010; *Averchenkova, Fankhauser & Nachmany, supra*, note 3.

[5] According to the most comprehensive definition, climate change litigation is "any piece of federal, state, tribal, or local administrative or judicial litigation in which the tribunal decisions directly and expressly raise an issue of fact or law regarding the substance or policy of climate change causes and impacts": *D. Markell & J.B. Ruhl*, An Empirical Assessment of Climate Change in the Courts: A New Jurisprudence or Business as Usual?, Fla. L. Rev. 2012 (64), pp. 15–86. Literature on climate change litigation is already quite extensive, see among others *W. Burns & H. Osofsky*, Adjudicating Climate Change: State, National and International Approaches, Cambridge University Press, 2009; *R. Lord, S. Goldberg et al.*, Climate Change Liability: Transnational Law and Practice, Cambridge University Press, 2011; *M. Faure & M. Peeters*, Climate Change Liability, Edward Elgar, 2011; *J. Lin*, Climate Change and the Courts, in Legal Studies 2012 (32), pp. 35–57; *J. Spier & U. Magnus* (eds.), Climate Change Remedies: Injunctive Relief and Criminal Law Responses, Eleven International

a growing number of judicial cases dealing with "climate liability" from various perspectives – international, administrative, private and even criminal – aiming to change governmental and business approaches to combating climate change.

Nowadays, climate change litigation covers a number of cases in several jurisdictions, involving different actors and a wide variety of claims, based on a plurality of grounds.[6]

Looking at the development of climate change litigation, one can observe that it first developed in the United States and Australia, also as response to the poor or inexistent climate change regulation, and then spread all over the world. Currently, these types of cases are continuing to multiply: lawsuits have been filed in all continents, from the Netherlands to Pakistan, Colombia, New Zealand, to mention just a few. Actions against corporations responsible for greenhouse gas emissions, public authorities or governments as a whole can be prompted, depending on the specific jurisdiction, by private individuals, but also by legal persons, such as public authorities and non-governmental organisations (NGOs).[7] All these actors put in place innovative strategies, drawing on civil and administrative liability, environmental law, human rights and also soft law documents in order to substantiate their claims. The judicial initiatives also appear to be facilitated where there are courts specialising in environmental matters, as in Australia, or where it is possible to resort to legal instruments developed for protecting public interests and collective goods (e.g. air and water) in other contexts, such as "public trust theory" in the United States and "public interest litigation" in India.[8]

However, the enormous increase in litigation is also to be viewed within the general expansion of climate change issues, which tend to absorb all other

---

Publishing, 2014; *J. Peel & H. Osofsky*, Climate Change Litigation: Regulatory Pathways to Cleaner Energy, Cambridge University Press, 2015; *M.B. Gerrard & M. Wilensky*, The role of the national courts in GHG emissions reductions, in D.A Farber, S. Sato & M. Peeters (eds.), Climate Change Law, Edward Elgar Publishing, 2016, pp. 359 et seq.; *M. Spitzer & B. Burtscher*, Liability for Climate Change: Cases, Challenges and Concepts, JETL 2017, pp. 137–176; *M. Burger & J. Grundlach*, The Status of Climate Change Litigation: A Global Review, UNEP, 2017, https://www.unenvironment.org/resources/publication/status-climate-change-litigation-global-review; *F. Sindico & M.M. Mbengue* (eds.), Comparative Climate Change Litigation: Beyond the Usual Suspects, Springer, 2020, forthcoming.

6   Useful information can be found in the Litigation database by the Sabin Centre for Climate Change Law (Columbia University), https://climate.law.columbia.edu/. For a comprehensive overview on climate change lawsuits see among others *V. Jacometti*, Climate Change Litigation: Global Trends and Critical Issues in the Light of the Urgenda 2018 Decision and the IPCC Special Report "Global Warming of 1.5 °C", Global Jurist 2019.

7   *M. Zemel*, The Rise of Rights-Based Climate Litigation and Germany's Susceptibility to Suit, Fordham Envtl. L. Rev. 2018 (29), pp. 484 et seq.

8   See *M.C. Wood & C.W. Woodward*, IV, Atmospheric Trust Litigation and the Constitutional Right to a Healthy Climate System: Judicial Recognition at Last, Wash. J. Envtl l. & Pol'y 2016 (6), pp. 633–683; *T. Hester*, Private Claims for a Global Climate: US and Indian Litigation Approaches to Climate Change and Environmental Harm, NGT International Journal on Environment 2014, pp. 1–16.

environmental problems: for almost all environmental issues it is possible to identify problems connected to climate change.[9] In fact, one can also observe that there is also a number of cases where climate change, although not being the central issue of the claim, is increasingly used as a supplementary argument.

3. POTENTIALS AND DIFFICULTIES OF CLIMATE CHANGE LITIGATION

Although many point out that litigation is not the most appropriate tool to deal with climate change issues,[10] the "socio-legal" function of climate change litigation cannot be neglected as a mechanism capable of promoting greater awareness and involvement of citizens and of directly or indirectly influencing the development of regulation.[11]

In fact, a large part of climate lawsuits is aimed not so much at seeking compensation for damage caused by climate change, but rather at forcing policy makers to take appropriate action to combat climate change, especially in those countries where government action has been rather limited or almost completely lacking, as in the United States. Indeed, according to some scholars the idea that courts have a unique role to play in shaping regulatory action may be construed as an American export that has circulated around the word.[12] In any case, as court decisions dealing with requests for more significant intervention actually address relevant regulatory issues,[13] it is possible to place this litigation trend with the more general "regulation through litigation movement".[14]

---

[9] See *C. Hilson*, It's all about climate change, stupid! Exploring the relationship between environmental law and climate law, Journal of Environmental Law 2013, pp. 359–370.

[10] *E. Fisher, E. Scotford & E. Barritt*, The legally disruptive nature of climate change, Modern Law Review 2017 (80), pp. 173–201; *L. Bergkamp & J.C. Hanekamp*, Climate Change Litigation against States: The Perils of Court-Made Climate Policies, EEELR 2015, pp. 102–114; *A. Huggins*, Is climate change litigation an effective strategy for promoting greater action to address climate change? What other legal mechanisms might be appropriate?, Local Government Law Journal 2008 (13), p. 184; *J. Hersh & W.K. Viscusi*, Allocating Responsibility for the Failure of Global Worming Policies, U. Pa. L. Rev 2007 (155), pp. 1657, 1663.

[11] See *Peel & Osofsky, supra*, note 5 at pp. 28 et seq.; *H.M. Osofsky*, Conclusion: Adjudicating Climate Change Across Scales, in W.C.G. Burns & H.M. Osofsky (eds.), Adjudicating Climate Change: State, National, and International Approaches, Cambridge University Press, 2009, p. 375.

[12] *S. Roy & E. Woerdman*, Situating Urgenda v. The Netherlands within comparative climate change litigation, Journal of Energy & Natural Resources Law 2016, pp. 165–189; *D. Hare*, Blue Jeans, Chewing Gum, and Climate Change Litigation: American Exports to Europe, Legislation and Policy Brief 2013, pp. 223–273.

[13] *M. Faure & M. Peeters*, Liability and climate change, in H. von Storch (ed.), Climate Science, Oxford University Press, 2019, pp. 1–30.

[14] *Hersh & Viscusi, supra*, note 10 at p. 1662; *J. Peel & H.M. Osofsky*, Litigation as a Climate Regulatory Tool, in C. Vogt (ed.), International Judicial Practice on the Environment. Questions of Legitimacy, Cambridge University Press, 2019, pp. 311–336.

Furthermore, the United States is at the centre of the climate change litigation phenomenon, at least from the quantitative point of view, given the enormous number of cases filed in this jurisdiction,[15] but also from the "qualitative" point of view, by often proposing innovative approaches that may be a source of inspiration for litigation in other legal systems. In fact, although the expansion of climate litigation in the United States is also the result of some factors particular to that legal system – from the lack of federal legislation on climate change, to the application of specific common law concepts like the public trust doctrine, to the greater readiness to resort to litigation, which is connected to the specific US *legal process*[16] – this developing climate litigation is also the source of the circulation of legal concepts, principles and standards among legal systems.

On one side, climate change is a global problem, probably the "most global" of all environmental problems, involving common issues that often lead to common responses. Therefore, even if the litigation that has developed in the various legal systems is shaped by the specific characteristics of each legal, political, economic, social, cultural and, not least, environmental context, it is possible to identify some trends that are spreading globally.[17] In fact, the most recent climate lawsuits tend to apply a model that could be defined as global: they are based on the same scientific, economic and social data on the causes and effects of climate change and use similar arguments to support similar claims by the applicants, namely the protection of the rights of individuals who suffer the effects of climate change. In addition, these lawsuits often face common difficulties. In particular, one of the main obstacles to the recognition of climate change liability is the difficulty in proving a direct and certain causal link between the various activities that have an impact on climate change and a certain harmful event, given the various – human and natural – causes that can have an influence on it. Other obstacles arise from the difficulties in clearly quantifying the damages that can be considered to be of anthropic origin compared to those of natural origin, in identifying the responsible parties

---

[15] See Litigation database by the Sabin Centre for Climate Change Law (Columbia University), https://climate.law.columbia.edu/.

[16] *Peel & Osofsky, supra*, note 5 at pp. 310 et seq.

[17] See *Jacometti, supra*, note 6; *J. Setzer & R. Byrnes*, Policy Brief. Global trends in climate change litigation: 2020 snapshots, Grantham Research Institute on Climate Change and the Environment, 2020, https://www.lse.ac.uk/granthaminstitute/wp-content/uploads/2020/07/Global-trends-in-climate-change-litigation_2020-snapshot.pdf; *M.L. Banda & S. Fulton*, Litigating Climate Change in National Courts: Recent Trends and Developments in Global Climate Law, Envtl. L. Rep. 2017 (47), pp. 10121 et seq.; *M. Nachmany, S. Fankhauser, J. Setzer & A. Averchenkova*, Global trends in climate change legislation and litigation, Grantham Research Institute on Climate Change and the Environment, 2017, http://www.lse.ac.uk/GranthamInstitute/publication/global-trends-in-climate-change-legislation-and-litigation-2017-update/; *D. Estrin*, Limiting Dangerous Climate Change: The Critical Role of Citizen Suits and Domestic Courts – Despite the Paris Agreement, CIGI Papers No. 101, May 2016, https://www.cigionline.org/publications/limiting-dangerous-climate-change-critical-role-citizen-suits-and-domestic-courts.

and in quantifying their liability. However, on the other side, even if the legal problems to be addressed are largely the same, they take different shapes across jurisdictions, according to the characteristics of each legal system.[18]

In view of all the above, adjudication of climate change has the potential to influence the evolution of norms in some field of law since courts are required to face new questions at the border between science and ethics – especially with regard to liability, harm and causation, but also in relation to many other issues – so that it could result in new legal rules.[19] Indeed, litigation already succeeded in the past in shaping the evolution of norms in several other contexts, from work and car accidents to tobacco and medical treatments, and this also may be the case with regard to climate change lawsuits.[20] In this respect, some legal scholars consider that private law has great underdeveloped potential in the definition of the climate change regime through the activity of the courts.[21] In fact, law is a dynamic phenomenon, and in particular civil liability rules have always been able to adapt over time, so it is quite possible that a new model will emerge in this field.[22] In particular, with regard to the proof of causation, where climate models are accepted as adequate evidence in certain circumstances, and faced with cases of cumulative causation, where the damage is caused by the cumulative effect of multiple actors, a contributory cause and partial causation could be deemed sufficient to establish causation.[23]

4. THE EVOLUTION OF THE JUDICIAL APPROACH TO CLIMATE CHANGE CLAIMS

Although climate change litigation is still developing and despites its shortcomings,[24] some cases have already been qualified as "strategic" cases as

---

[18] *M. Wilensky*, Climate change in the courts: an assessment of non-US climate litigation, Duke Envtl. L & Pol'y 2015 (26), pp. 131 et seq.

[19] See for example *D. Kysar*, What Climate Change Can Do about Tort Law, Environmental Law Review 2011 (41), pp. 1 et seq.

[20] For a comparison with tobacco litigation, see *M. Olszynsky, S. Mascher & M. Doell*, From Smokes to Smokestacks: Lessons from Tobacco for the Future of Climate Change Liability, Geo. Envtl. L. Rev., 2017 (30), pp. 1 et seq.

[21] See *C.V. Giabardo*, in this volume; *K. Bower*, The Unsexy Future of Climate Change Litigation, JEL 2018 (30), pp. 483 et seq.; *G.G. Geetanjali, J. Setzer & V. Heyvaert*, If at First You Don't Succeed: Suing Corporations for Climate Change, OJLS 2018 (38), pp. 841 et seq.; *D.A. Kysar*, The Public Life of Private Law: Tort Law as a Risk Regulation Mechanism, EJRR 2018 (9), pp. 48 et seq.

[22] *S. Porchy Simon*, Droit de la responsabilité civile et changements climatiques, in M. Hautereau-Boutonnet (ed.), Quel droit pour savuer le climat ?, [Rapport de recherche] Université Lyon 3 Jean Moulin, 2018, https://halshs.archives-ouvertes.fr/halshs-01684948.

[23] *Kysar, supra*, note 19. *M. Burger, J. Wentz & R. Horton*, The Law and Science of Climate Change Attribution, Columbia Journal of Environmental Law, 2020 (1), pp. 57 et seq.

[24] See above and most recently among others: *K. Bouwer and J. Setzer*, New Trends in Climate Litigation: What Works? Working paper presented at the New Trends in International Climate and Environmental Advocacy Workshop, hosted by Johns Hopkins University SAIS

they have succeeded in influencing governmental and business approaches to climate change mitigation and adaptation and may be a source of inspiration for pending and future cases. Even unsuccessful cases might well inspire litigation around the world.[25]

Strategic climate change lawsuits may be considered important legal precedents in legal systems that recognise this, but even where precedent is not legally recognised, they have the potential to influence courts and others.[26] In fact, some of these cases – such as *Urgenda* or *Leghari*[27] – are now considered "global" precedents, if obviously one goes beyond a jurisdictional understanding of the word "precedent".[28]

Moreover, most probably because of the eminently global nature of their object – climate change – these cases are clearly giving rise to a form of dialogue between courts belonging to different jurisdictions, thus leading to a certain convergence and to the development of common trends. In addition, this dialogue is not limited to courts, but also involves claimants, which more and more often establish connections between themselves and with the associative and academic world and share expertise and arguments that can be used before courts. This developing climate litigation is therefore leading to the circulation of legal concepts, principles and rules.

On the other hand, in many jurisdictions the attitude of courts towards climate-change-related issues seems to have changed in recent times. Thus, while in the past courts tended to refrain from intervening in this field, both because it was considered an area reserved to the discretionary choices of the executive or legislative branches and because of the difficulties linked to the evaluation of still uncertain scientific data, today several courts seem to have abandoned this tendency towards self-restraint. Certainly, a fundamental role is played in this change by the fact that climate change litigants and courts can today resort to a quantity of scientific research from the major world experts on the subject, first and foremost the Intergovernmental Panel on Climate Change (IPCC), which offer a solid scientific basis that in the past was often questioned.[29]

Europe and European University Institute, 15 May 2020, https://www.researchgate.net/publication/341802178_New_Trends_in_Climate_Litigation_What_Works.

25   *Geetanjali, Setzer & Heyvaert, supra,* note 21.

26   M. Dellinger, See You in Court: Around the World in Eight Climate Change Lawsuits, Wm. & Mary Envtl. L. & Pol'y Rev. 2018 (42), pp. 525 et seq.

27   The State of The Netherlands v Urgenda Foundation, 20.12.2019, The Hague Court of Appeal, Civil Law Division, decisions and translations available at http://climatecasechart.com/non-us-case/urgenda-foundation-v-kingdom-of-the-netherlands/; *Asghar Leghari v. Federation of Pakistan* [2015] W.P. No. 25501/2015, Lahore High Court Green Bench Pakistan.

28   S. Roy & E. Woerdman, Situating Urgenda v. The Netherlands within comparative climate change litigation, Journal of Energy & Natural Resources Law 2016 (34), pp. 165–189. E. Barritt & B. Sediti, The Symbolic Value of Leghari v Federation of Pakistan: Climate Change Adjudication in the Global South, King's Law Journal, 2019 (2), pp. 203 et seq.

29   M.B. Gerrard, Court Rulings Accept Climate Science, NYLJ, volume 250, No. 52, 12 September 2013; *Banda & Fulton, supra,* note 17.

Obviously the outcomes will not be the same in all jurisdictions, because even when the litigation strategies are analogous, the judicial outcomes depend essentially on variables that differ in the various jurisdictions. Following a comparative law approach, it appears clear that if environmental law rules tend towards an ever-greater uniformity on a global level, especially where global problems are at stake, such as climate change, their implementation is still local and depends profoundly on the *legal process* in which they are inserted.[30]

---

[30]   *B. Pozzo*, Climate Change Litigation in a Comparative Perspective, in F. Sindico, M. M. Mbengue (eds.), *supra*, note 5.

CLIMATE CHANGE LITIGATION, STATE RESPONSIBILITY AND THE ROLE OF COURTS IN THE GLOBAL REGIME

Towards a "Judicial Governance" of Climate Change?

Carlo Vittorio GIABARDO

1. INTRODUCTION: THE "SUBVERSIVE" NATURE OF CLIMATE CHANGE AND THE NEED FOR A NEW LEGAL GRAMMAR

Climate change has a *subversive* character. Its nature, characteristics, scale and intensity are so different from any other problem or menace humankind has faced so far that it requires a radical reconceptualisation of almost every field of human knowledge and its practices. The social, ethical, political and geopolitical, economic and legal dimensions are all inextricably entangled in this effort. The subversive or disruptive, so to speak, nature of climate change consists precisely in this, i.e. in the fact that – in all these domains – previous categories, institutions, procedures, ideas and, more generally, "modes of thought" need to be re-imagined and therefore redefined, if not completely and radically re-thought, to address the new global climate situation.

The legal domain is no exception. Let us briefly emphasise this point from a philosophical viewpoint, as it will be crucial for the arguments set out below. Climate change is such a pervasive and boundary-less phenomenon that classical and traditional legal doctrines are proving insufficient to provide efficient relief in relation to it. We must therefore operate according to what could be called a "methodological detour" in our mode of constructing legal theories and concepts. Why a methodological detour? Because in the history of legal thought we often see that categories have *first* been created and *then* the "outer" reality has been fitted into those categories. It is the outer reality that has been often adapted to the legal world, and not vice versa. By inventing our "legal universe" (a universe made up of doctrines, distinctions, interests, criteria, and so on), jurists have created a legal reality (their own reality); differently put, they have made it possible for things to be true or false from the standpoint of the law, or "in the eye of the law".[1] Now, the urgency and the immense severity of the environmental crisis, its unavoidable and *inescapable* presence, requires us to do the inverse. It is our categories of thought that must be re-considered in order first to face, and finally to provide a solution to, global warming.[2] In other words, we need to ask ourselves not whether, and to what extent, our (legal, or political, or economic) categories allow us to act according to the climate change reality, but rather how to modify these categories in order to avoid, and possibly not simply mitigate, its disastrous, imminent and soon irreversible effects.[3] Now, it is quite clear that all this is not only true for the legal domain, and those considerations might well be extended to economics or politics. Yet, the legal system and its practices occupy a central position in this discourse. As law provides the general normative framework and conditions for political, social, technological and, above all, economic action, it should be the first area to adapt to the new condition.[4] Both private law and public law are involved in this radical overturning – bearing in mind, for that matter, that "private" and "public" law are nothing but distinctions that tend to disappear when dealing with climate change issues.[5]

---

[1] This point is beautifully made, in a very general way, by the legal philosopher *J.M.* Balkin, The Proliferation of Legal Truth, HJLPP 2004, p. 101. To select a highly significant passage: "In fact, one of the most interesting features of law as a system of social conventions is its ability to make things true or, to put in another way, to create legal categories that permit characterizations of situations and practices that are true or false. My point, however, is not simply that propositions of law are true in virtue of legal conventions. It is rather that law creates truth – it makes things true as a matter of law"; and then later on (at 104): "But the proliferation of legal truth is also important because it helps shape what people believe and what they understand. Law has power over people's imaginations and how they think about what is happening in social life. Law in this sense is more than a set of sanctions. It is a form of cultural software that shapes the way we think about and apprehend the world. Law adds things to reality" (citing *J.M. Balkin*, Cultural Software: A Theory of Ideology, 1998, pp. 3–5).

[2] *E. Fisher, E. Scotford & E. Barritt*, The Legally Disruptive Nature of Climate Change, MLR 2017, p. 173; *J. Preston*, The Adequacy of the Law in Achieving Climate Justice – Some Preliminary Comments, JENRL 2016, p. 45; *J.B. Ruhl*, Climate Change Adaptation and the Structural Transformation of Environmental Law, EL 2010, p. 363; see also *J. Peel*, Climate Change Law: The Emergence of a New Discipline, MelbourneULR 2008, p. 922. For more general considerations, *L. Douglas et al.*, A Jurisprudence of Catastrophe: An Introduction, in A. Sarat & M.M. Umphrey (eds.), Law and Catastrophe, Stanford University Press 2007, p. 1.

[3] Significantly, Professor Douglas Kysar, from Yale Law School, in a well-known article (What Climate Change Can Do About Tort Law, EL 2011, p.1) reverses the classical question, that is "what tort law can do to climate change" (i.e. how we can use classical private law doctrines to solve the climate crisis) to "what climate change can do to tort law" (i.e. how the awareness of the present climate catastrophe must guide us in changing our previous mode of thought in private law).

[4] See the influential book by *R. Cox*, Revolution Justified. Why Only the Law Can Save Us, Planet Prosperity Foundation, 2012.

[5] As will be touched upon later, the boundaries between "private litigation" and "public regulation" is blurred at best in climate change law. This is just one example of how the private/public distinction might collapse in this context.

On the one hand, legal scholars have acknowledged that private law doctrines –
and especially those pertaining to tort law – do not function in climate change
cases in the same way as they do in ordinary litigation.[6] Traditional notions
such as individual responsibility, negligence, causation, damage and harm,
duty of care, reasonable behaviour, and the like, as well as procedural law
mechanisms and tools, such as the *locus standi* doctrine, burden of proof,
access to justice and class actions, as we understand them conventionally, all
show their limits and inefficiencies in deterring those harmful behaviours that
cause climate change.[7] Even the very foundational concept of "personal right",
which lies at the root of our legal thinking, also seems unsuitable in our so-called
"Anthropocene" age.[8]

On the other hand, long-held public law categories that have shaped our legal
worldview for centuries seem to collapse when confronted with the worldwide
problems posed by global warming. Concepts such as state sovereignty and
statehood,[9] human rights, and state institutions with all their powers and
authority (parliaments, governments and courts), as well as recognised values
such as the separation of powers doctrine and the rule of law, all need to be

---

[6] And this for the intrinsic characteristics of climate change; see *M.C. Blumm & M.C. Wood*,
"No Ordinary Lawsuit": Climate Change, Due Process and the Public Trust Doctrine, AULR
2017, p. 1, quoting, in the title, the words of the American judge Ann Aiken (a Federal Judge
of the District of Oregon) in the famous case Juliana, et al. v. United States of America (D Or,
6:15-cv-1517-TC, 8 April 2016), where 21 youths, along with prominent climate scientists
and non-profit organisations, filed a lawsuit against the US government for failing to protect
them from climate change. See also *D. Markell & J.B. Ruhl*, An Empirical Assessment of
Climate Change in the Courts: A New Jurisprudence or Business as Usual?, FLR 2012, p. 15.

[7] Basically, this is because tort law has been historically built on "paradigm of harm in which
A wrongfully, directly, and exclusively injures B" (*Kysar, supra*, note 3 at 3), which clearly
does not apply to climate harm. Therefore "trying to force climate change into traditional
[common law] categories calls into question basic features of tort law itself. At each stage
of the traditional tort analysis – duty, breach, causation, and harm – the climate change
plaintiff finds herself bumping up against doctrines that are premised on a classical liberal
worldview in which threats such as global climate change simply do not register. And just
as environmental economists are faced with a choice between reforming the underlying
architecture of their discipline or failing to adequately characterize the climate change
problem, courts will be forced to either radically alter existing features of tort law or deem
non-tortious activities that nevertheless threaten core interests tort law claims to protect"
(id. at pp. 9–10). Emblematically, the *locus standi* doctrine, too (that is, the legal requirements
that allow certain subjects to go to court) as it is designed, it is quite problematic when it
comes to climate change litigation. It is problematic because it is increasingly used by courts
to restrict access to justice, and in this sense it might represent a powerful device that allows
judges to dismiss highly sensitive cases on procedural grounds, and not on their merits (see
infra, section 4).

[8] *K.C. Sokol*, Rethinking Rights in the Age of the "Anthropocene", in G. Ziccardi Capaldo (ed.),
The Global Community Yearbook of International Law and Jurisprudence, Oxford University
Press 2017.

[9] From the point of view of political theory, see *J. Vogler*, International Relations Theory and
the Environment, in G. Kütting (ed.), Global Environmental Politics: Concepts, Theories and
Case Studies, Routledge 2011, p. 11.

reconfigured, at least in part, to permit the effective management of the new climate conditions on our planet and foster a radical change in decision-making processes – both a national and at a supranational level.[10] When dealing with the complexities and urgency of climate change, our entire legal constructions show their weaknesses, simply because they have been created to tackle social problems that are different in nature, extension and intensity. There is thus a real urgency for legal philosophers and legal scholars in every field and specialisation to create a "new legal grammar", capable of rethinking in new terms the multifaceted relationship between the states as a sovereign bodies, their legal structures, and the rightsholders, that is the people.

This need to construct a new "legal vocabulary", or a new "horizon of concepts", provided with imaginative frames, forms and rules, becomes especially evident in the topic here addressed, that is, the responsibility of the states in relation to climate change and the role of domestic courts in establishing this responsibility. To name just a few theoretical questions that, in the area here considered, are still "in search" of an answer: is a (constitutional, or human) right to a "stable climate" even conceivable? And if yes, how can we construct it?[11] To put it another way: do people have a justiciable right, in the current sense of the world, towards their governments to a "climate system capable of sustaining human life"?[12] And if so, to what extent, and at what costs, can we claim its protection? Does the state have a precise (constitutional) duty to protect its citizens against climate change, even beyond or regardless of the existence or the "compulsoriness" of supranational conventions? Could the state be held liable towards its citizens for its indirect contribution to climate change, that is, *not* for being a polluter itself, but for not making enough efforts to reduce greenhouse gas emissions of companies operating within its boundaries, for example, or even for failing to change its own legal system (e.g. being responsible simply for having democratically enacted legislation that still permits, or even subsides and supports, fossil fuel exploitation and production)?[13] And how should we evaluate and assess the contribution of a given state to climate change, provided that *no* state alone on earth is responsible, strictly speaking, of the global rise of temperatures? Should and could a single state be held directly accountable for the premature death of people caused

---

[10] P. Sands, Climate Change and the Rule of Law: Adjudicating the Future in International Law, JEL 2016, p. 19.

[11] J. Peel & H. Osofsky, A Rights Turn in Climate Change Litigation?, TEL 2018, p. 37; R. Bratspies, Do We Need a Human Right to a Healthy Environment?, SCJIL 2015, p. 42.

[12] For the analysis of this notion and the problems it poses, see Blumm & Wood, supra, note 6. See also B.J. Preston, The Evolving Role of Environmental Rights in Climate Change Litigation, CJEL 2018, p. 131.

[13] See B. Mayer, State Responsibility and Climate Change Governance: A Light through the Storm, Chinese Journal of International Law 2014, p. 549; M.G. Faure & A. Nollkaemper, International Liability as an Instrument to Prevent and Compensate for Climate Change, SELJ 2007, p. 123.

by high levels of pollution, and called to repay those losses? And if so, who is called to decide upon those issues? Could courts represent a suitable forum for debating state liability in this area?

The "juridical difficulty" that is common to all these questions lies almost entirely in the fact that the effects of climate change are worldwide, and so are their causes. On the contrary, the logical structure of legal liability requires, among other things, (a) that there exists and (b) that is possible to identify precisely both (i) a subject that causes the damage and (ii) someone who is affected by that same damage – two conditions that are almost impossible to meet when dealing with climate change.[14]

What role are courts expected to play in this landscape? As will be argued, courts nowadays represent a crucial part of the global governance of climate change, at all levels, and many scholars have emphasised their potential in providing those solutions that have long been expected from, and denied by, the political and democratic arenas. Specifically, over the past few years there has been a growing tendency to consider courts the proper venue to debate, establish and decide the legal responsibility of states in causing climate change, through their omissions. This chapter aims to highlight and assess the *ambivalence*, the *ambiguity* of climate change litigation as a mechanism for deciding the responsibility of the state. Failure or opportunity, vehicle for bottom-up initiatives through private law, or a boomerang that might rebound against initial hopes – these are just some of the different angles from which to look at the same phenomenon. After briefly looking at the place courts occupy in the current "post-Paris" regime, this chapter considers the pros and cons of judicial governance in climate change law, and finally assesses some pushback that seems to characterise the most recent context.

2. CLIMATE CHANGE LITIGATION AS A FAILURE AND AS AN OPPORTUNITY

It is commonly argued that climate change governance is multi-layered.[15] This means that different types and structures of governance coexist together and interact with each other in many complex ways: supranational bodies and international organisations, states, non-governmental organisations, lobbies, national parliaments and governments, companies and their inner

---

[14] For a description of how these conditions might represent an insuperable obstacle to an effective climate change litigation, see *infra*, section 4, final part.

[15] *J. Peel, G. Lee Godden & R.J. Keenan*, Climate Change Law in an Era of Multi-Level Governance, TEL 2012, p. 245; *D. Bodansky*, A Tale of Two Architectures: The Once and Future U.N. Climate Change Regime, Ariz. SLJ 2011, p. 697.

procedures (that is, best practices and corporate accountability processes), but also civil society and social movements, scientists and academics and so on, all contribute to designing the architecture in which the battle against climate change takes place.[16] It is also well known that courts and tribunals both at a national and at a supranational level play a central role in regulating the climate crisis.[17] Climate change litigation (in whatever sense we choose to understand this phenomenon) is indeed a worldwide movement that has long been investigated by environmental lawyers both for its enormous potential to challenge existing climate-harming policies and for its capacity to attract global attention.[18] This chapter is not concerned with detailing how this global practice has taken, and is taking, place.[19] Suffice it to note that, on the one hand, a series of so-called "strategic court cases" has proliferated in many jurisdictions around the world – where the words "strategic" here stands for the fact that those cases generally aim to have an impact beyond the parties and the dispute involved. In those claims, the judiciary is increasingly exposed to climate change arguments, whereas, until in recent times, the reasoning in favour of the protection of the environment would have been framed differently.[20] On the other hand, and more specifically for our purposes, courts around the world have been called upon to decide controversies (often of a private law nature and involving tort law) that have the objective of declaring the legal responsibility of national governments for failing to protect the environment against climate change as they should, this responsibility being caused by their inaction (or insufficient action). What is worth underlining is also that the role of courts in establishing state responsibility is expected to grow after the entry into

---

[16]   On global governance of environmental law, see *R.J. Lazarus*, Super Wicked Problems and Climate Change: Restraining the Present to Liberate the Future, CLR 2009, p. 1153.

[17]   *J. Peel & H. Osofsky*, The Role of Litigation in Multilevel Climate Governance: Possibilities for a Lower Carbon Future, EPLJ 2013, p. 303. See also *D. Bodansky*, The Role of the International Court of Justice in Addressing Climate Change: Some Preliminary Reflections, Ariz. SLJ 2017, p. 1.

[18]   *M. Wilensky*, Climate Change in the Courts: An Assessment of Non-U.S. Climate Litigation, DELPF 2015, p. 131; *E. Fisher*, Climate Change Litigation, Obsession and Expertise: Reflecting on the Scholarly Response to Massachusetts v. EPA, LP 2013, p. 236. The Sabin Center for Climate Change Law, run by the Columbia University School of Law, has a database that maps climate change litigation across the United States. See. http://climatecasechart.com/.

[19]   For a good and updated overview, see however *J. Setzer & L.C. Vanhala*, Climate Change Litigation: A Review of Research on Courts and Litigants in Climate Governance, WIREs Climate Change (Wiley Interdisciplinary Review: Climate Change) 2019, p. 1.

[20]   *J. Setzer & M. Bangalore*, Regulating Climate Change in the Courts, in A. Averchenkova, A. Fankhauser & S. Nachmany (eds.), Trends in Climate Change Legislation, Edward Elgar Publishing 2017, p. 175; *B.J. Preston*, The Contribution of the Courts in Tackling Climate Change, JEL 2016, p. 11. Recently, on this topic, *R.H. Weaver & D.A. Kysar*, Courting Disaster: Climate Change and the Adjudication of the Catastrophe, NDLR 2017, p. 295.

force of the Paris Agreement.[21] Indeed, among many different things, the Paris Agreement requires countries to implement their "nationally-determined contributions" (NDCs) and to raise their ambitions progressively over time, which is necessary to hold "the increase in the global average temperature to well below 2°C above 2 pre-industrial levels and pursuing efforts to limit the temperature increase to 1.5°C above pre-industrial levels", as stated in Article 2. This will require countries to do various things, such as to enact new laws and policies, or to revisit and strengthen existing laws and norms. In this scenario, the Paris Agreement potentially opens up new spaces and opportunities for climate change litigation, not in the sense that people will seek to enforce directly the Agreement before domestic courts, but in the sense that they will increasingly submit to judicial scrutiny the domestic policies and measure enacted to give legal effect to the commitments undertaken under the Agreement itself.

In sum, climate change litigation has therefore become so important that it would not be an exaggeration to describe the current and future climate change regime as characterised by "judicial governance", a concept strictly linked to judicial activism, understood as "the prominent phenomenon of courts assuming tasks which are, under the classic separation of powers doctrine, reserved to the executive and legislative power".[22]

Of course, the key question is inherently political and it deals whether it is right and/or legitimate for courts to overstep their functions and decide a matter that is best left to the political or executive branches, that is, in the case of state responsibility in climate change, if it is suitable for courts to force national governments to take more effective political action or to pay for the damage caused by their ineffective legislation. The well-known *Urgenda* case has posed this very problem with global resonance and many of the climate change litigation questions today are framed in

---

[21]   *S.I. Karlsson-Vinkhuyzen, M. Groff, P.A. Tamás, A.L. Dahl, M. Harder & G. Hassall,* Entry into Force and Then? The Paris Agreement and State Accountability, CP 2017, p. 593; *C. Streck, M. von Unger & P. Keenlyside,* The Paris Agreement: A New Beginning, JEEPL 2016, p. 3; *D. Bodansky,* The Legal Character of the Paris Agreement, RECInt'lLEL 2016 (25), p. 142.

[22]   This clear definition is taken from Professor Christoph Schmid, who employs it in the different context of the legal harmonisation within the European Union; see *C.U. Schmid,* Judicial Governance in the European Union: the ECJ as a Constitutional and a Private Law Court, in O. Eriksen, C. Joerges & F. Rödl (eds.), Law, Democracy and Solidarity in Europe's Postnational Union. The Unsettled Political Order of Europe, Routledge, 2008, p. 85. In the context of climate change regulation, see also *S. Varvaštian,* Climate Change Litigation, Liability and Global Climate Governance – Can Judicial Policymaking Become a Gamechanger? Berlin Conference "Transformative Global Climate Governance après Paris" 2016, available at https://refubium.fu-berlin.de/bitstream/handle/fub188/18585/Varvastianxclimatexchangexlitigation.pdf?sequence=1&isAllowed=y.

quite similar terms.[23] The focus of this chapter is not to discuss this milestone *arrêt* in the history of climate change litigation. What is worth underlying, however, is that the issue of the national sovereignty of the state, and thus its right to a large margin of appreciation in deciding which measures to take in addressing climate change, was at the centre of the appeal of the Netherlands government against the first instance ruling. It is interesting to note that the District Court seemed to have adopted, so to speak, a more nuanced notion of the separation of power doctrine, making the striking argument that "Dutch law does not have a full separation of state powers, in this case, between the executive and judiciary. The distribution of powers between these powers (and the legislature) is rather intended to establish a balance between these state powers" (para. 4.95[24]) but rather a sophisticated system of intertwined checks and balances that controls how each branch of the state performs its duties and functions.[25] This could be viewed as an attempt of the Court to "re-read" the doctrine of the separation of powers to adapt it to the peculiarities of the climate change situation, so as to legitimise its intervention. Keeping in mind the methodological commitment stated in the previous section, that is, the need to reason outside our long-held legal categories, what is to be considered is not the conformity of this solution with our legal system, but its *effectiveness*.

3. THE AMBIGUITY OF THE ROLE OF COURT IN ESTABLISHING STATE RESPONSIBILITY FOR CLIMATE CHANGE

The reality is that climate change litigation is an *ambiguous*, double-edged phenomenon. It can be seen both as a symptom of a problem or as a tremendous opportunity for the battle against global warming – but even in this second case, many risks persist in the way in which it could be used.

First of all, as highlighted by Professor Marleen van Rijswick in her keynote speech delivered at the 6th European Environmental Law Forum,[26] climate change litigation is indeed a failure – a failure of states and government to tackle climate

---

[23] R. Cox, A Climate Change Litigation Precedent: Urgenda Foundation v' The State of the Netherlands, JENRL 2016, p. 143; J. van Zeben, Establishing a Governmental Duty of Care for Climate Change Mitigation: Will Urgenda Turn the Tide?, TEL 2015, p. 339; J. Lambrecht & C. Ituarte-Lima, Legal Innovation in National Courts for Planetary Challenges: Urgenda v State of the Netherlands, ELR 2016, p. 1; R.H. Weaver & D. Kysar, supra, note 20. See also section 4 (discussing two recent cases).

[24] The full text of the sentence could be found at: https://uitspraken.rechtspraak.nl/inziendocument?id=ECLI:NL:RBDHA:2015:7196.

[25] J. de Graaf & J.H. Jans, The Urgenda Decision: Netherlands Liable for Role in Causing Dangerous Global Climate Change, JEL 2015, p. 517; S. Roy & E. Woerdman, Situating Urgenda v the Netherlands Within Comparative Climate Change Litigation, JENRL 2016, p. 165.

[26] Held at the University of Insubria, School of Law (Como, Italy), 12–14 September 2018.

change effectively with the necessary force, a sign of lack of either political ambition or capacity of action, and therefore ultimately a failure of the environmental law system, as built over the past decades, considered in its entirety.[27] But it is a failure that possesses per se great potential. On the one hand, it represents an opportunity for mobilisation. The absence of an adequate political response brings up new spaces for the social and legal community to become involved in the fight against climate change. Top-down political processes could then be increasingly replaced by bottom-up judicial actions.[28] On this view, every legal case *counts*. Every judicial initiative *matters*. Not only "big" lawsuits brought before courts by powerful advocacy and non-governmental organisations are important; small individual actions are crucial too.[29] In this bottom-up scenario, cases do not need to be brought only with an activist intent, but also simply in the pursuit of a private interest, that is, seeking compensation and damages from a greenhouse-gas-emitting defendant (a company) for causing "climate harm".[30] Scholars that endorse this view believe (rightly) that private law, a corpus of norms that aims to regulate private conduct, has a great under-explored potential in shaping public climate policies through the work of courts. Moreover, a multitude of private law initiatives might have a public law resonance. This kind of litigation could have a more indirect, "irradiating" effect, in the sense that it may have the function of raising gradual awareness in designing state policies, not only in civil society, but also among academics, legal scholars and ultimately lawmakers – and that even if the lawsuits are unsuccessful.[31] Private lawsuits, in sum, can perform a truly public law role, functioning as a (indirect) risk regulation mechanism.[32]

After all, the history of law teaches us that courts step in when political bodies fail to fulfil their tasks. The case of racial desegregation of schools in the United States shows us emblematically that courts have been proved to be

---

[27] The words of Professor van Rijswick are remembered also by *L. Squintani*, Tort-Law Based Environmental Litigation: A Victory or a Warning?, JEEPL, 2018, accessed online. This view is also shared by *E. Fisher, supra*, note 18.

[28] See *R. Cox, supra*, note 4.

[29] This is the core argument made by *K. Bouwer*, The Unsexy Future of Climate Change Litigation, JEL 2018, p. 483.

[30] *D. Grossman*, Warming Up to a Not-So-Radical Idea: Tort-Based Climate Change Litigation, CJEL 2003, p. 1; *D. Hunter & J. Salzman*, Negligence in the Air: The Duty of Care in Climate Change Litigation, UPLR 2007, p. 1741; *D. Kysar, supra*, note 3. In practice, see Massachusetts v. U.S. Envtl. Prot. Agency, 549 U.S. 497 (2007), in which the claimants framed greenhouse gas emissions as common law tort of nuisance. For an early discussion, *P. Cane*, Using Tort Law to Enforce Environmental Regulation, Washburn LJ 2002, p. 427.

[31] *K. Bouwer, supra*, note 28; *G.G. Geetanjali, J. Setzer & V. Heyvaert*, If at First You Don't Succeed: Suing Corporations for Climate Change, OJLS 2018, p. 841; *G. Nosek*, Climate Change Litigation and Narrative: How to Use Litigation to Tell Compelling Climate Stories, W&MELPol'yR 2018, p. 733.

[32] *D.A. Kysar*, The Public Life of Private Law: Tort Law as a Risk Regulation Mechanism, EJRR 2018, p. 48; see also *D. Gifford*, Climate Change and the Public Law Model of Torts: Reinvigorating Judicial Restraints Doctrines, SCLR 2011, p. 201.

effective vehicles of legal change in a progressive way when states were unwilling to act,[33] and the case of the tobacco-related litigation, also in the United States, testifies to the fact that tort law can be, under certain conditions, a mechanism of regulation of a particular sector.[34]

That being said, and on the other hand, it should also be noted that the reality is more complex. Judicial governance for state responsibility, although promising, seems to pose some problems. Two of them merit being stressed. First of all, as emphasised at the outset of this chapter, climate change law requires a re-writing of many legal categories, and this, in turn, is possible, in many jurisdictions, only if there is political willingness. What is really needed is a change in the "patterns of thinking" in law, and this is something that only imaginative legislation (and legal scholars too) can do. Moreover, litigation, by its very nature, is linked to a single, individual case at stake, and as such it is not the ideal place to set long-term goals.[35] Only rarely can the outcomes of legal cases be turned into general rules. This is not to say *a priori* that judges should not have an "environmental competence", in the sense that courts do not possess *at all* the scientific and technical expertise to assess and decide complex policy questions related to climate change – although this concern should be taken seriously.[36] This could be, and should be, overcome by providing the judge, over the course of the legal process, with all the technical means and knowledge they need to evaluate scientific evidence and decide accordingly. What should be stressed is that litigation and adjudication, as they are currently designed, have limits that are linked not to their structural characteristics, but rather to their classical and normal functions – that is, to decide "looking backward" a specific controversy between two or more parties applying the existing law, i.e., addressing a wrong that has occurred in the past, and not to manage, govern or plan situations for the future that affect an indeterminate range of subjects

---

[33] The reference goes obviously to Brown v. Board of Education of Topeka (1954); see, on this phenomenon, the two classical studies of O. Fiss, The Civil Rights Injunction, Indiana University Press, 1978, and A. Chayes, The Role of Judge in Public Law Litigation, HLR 1976, p. 1281.

[34] See E.A. Posner, Tobacco Regulation or Litigation?, UCLR 2003, p. 1141, at 1151 ("Tort law is a form of regulation, and always has been. ... Judicial decisions ex post will often have the effect of creating regulation-like commands ... There is nothing new about regulation by litigation"). Anyway, for a critical appraisal by Professor Posner that a human rights-driven litigation in climate change would lead to a desirable outcome, see E.A. Posner, Climate Change and International Human Rights Litigation: A Critical Appraisal, UPaLR 2006–2007, p. 1935. For a parallelism between the two areas, M. Olszynski, S. Mascher & M. Doelle, From Smokes to Smokestacks: Lessons from Tobacco for the Future of Climate Change Liability, GInt'lELR 2017, p. 1.

[35] L. Bergkamp & J.C. Hanekamp, Climate Change Litigation Against States: The Perils of Court-made Climate Policies, EEELR 2015, p. 102, where the authors also add that judgments in climate change litigation are likely to affect the interest of third parties not represented.

[36] Id.

(which is the task of politics).[37] As such, legal judgments and decisions are, at best, nothing but a form of temporary redress for a planetary-scale problem that requires long-term vision.

The second problem is more subtle and, so to speak, *psychological*. Attributing the task of assessing state responsibility entirely to courts could have a side effect, a "boomerang" effect that might turn against itself. The more courts take action, the less states feel obliged to act. In the long run, states, before deciding by themselves to revise targets and implement new climate policies, might "wait" for a judge to order them to do so. And, more dangerously, if a court, in a particular case, refuses to rule against the state, for whatever reason (for example, because it does not perceive itself as having legitimacy to command the state to do a certain thing, or because it has a particularly conservative view on the matter, and this could happen frequently, due to the uncertainties of the state of affairs), the state might see this as an implicit statement of the rightness of its governmental action, and use the judgment as a justification to avoid reforming its laws. Differently put, the risk of a "juridification of politics", especially in the environmental law context, is that it may simply endorse and reinforce political inaction.[38]

4. SOME PUSHBACK (AND SOME REASONS FOR BEING PESSIMISTIC): TWO CASE STUDIES

If we look at the global landscape, what we see is that, despite the promising decision in the *Urgenda* case, recently upheld by the Dutch Court of Appeal, there is an ongoing general reluctance from judicial bodies to challenge governmental inaction (or inaction of supranational institutions) that may aggravate climate change, or to declare state responsibility in implementing stronger and more stringent laws. The "precedential value" of *Urgenda* seems less strong than thought.[39] To put it briefly, it seems that wins in courts by climate change activists are less likely to occur in future. Two recent legal cases show this tendency.

---

[37] From a very general perspective, for a critique of this trajectory of the functions of the civil judge, from "deciding" cases to "planning" future events, see S. La China, Dal giudice giudicante al giudice pianificante (variazioni minime su un tema scabroso), RDP 2007, p. 847.

[38] On the global tendency of the "juridification" of politics, in a general fashion, see the classical study of R. Hirschl, Towards Juristocracy. The Origins and Consequences of the New Constitutionalism, Harvard University Press 2007. For an earlier account, C. Tate & T. Vallinder, The Global Expansion of Judicial Power, New York University Press 1995.

[39] C. Roddy, The Precedential Value of Urgenda v. The Netherlands, MJIL 2019, http://www. mjilonline.org/the-precedential-value-of-urgenda-v-the-netherlands/ (discussing also the second case here presented in the text that follows).

The first is the case brought in court by Plan B Earth – a UK charity, funded by crowdsourcing – joined in the lawsuit by 11 citizens, against the UK government, in the person of the Secretary of State for Business, Energy, and Industrial Strategy. Plan B claimed in court that the UK government's refusal to amend its 2050 climate targets was in breach of its international obligations under the Paris Agreement. Plan B, thus, did not seek to enforce directly the Paris Agreement in domestic law, but rather it argued that this international treaty, as well as general scientific development, represents the criterion through which to assess domestic policies. Legally speaking, the objective of the lawsuit was therefore to obtain (a) declaratory relief that the Secretary of State acted unlawfully in violation of his responsibilities under the Climate Change 2008 Act and (b) a mandatory order that the Secretary of State revise the 2050 targets in accordance with the UK's international law obligations and that they conform to the precautionary principle.[40] Even though the case was run by a former government barrister, Tim Crosland, and had the support of Professor Sir David King, the government's former chief scientific adviser, its legal path has been quite unfortunate. At its first stage, in February 2018, the initial request for judicial review was denied on all the grounds, on the basis that the existing carbon targets set by the UK Committee on Climate Change are compatible with the Paris Agreement.[41] The claimants then renewed their application for review, but on 20 July 2018 the High Court denied permission for the case to proceed, considering it as "not arguable". On 25 January 2019, the Court of Appeal rejected Plan B's appeal against the High Court's refusal to hear the case in full hearing, marking the end of the process.[42]

Just like in *Urgenda*, the core of the claimants' argument was the inadequacy of legislative targets for greenhouse gas emissions reductions, and the fact that governments enjoy a very limited degree of discretion in it. In particular Plan B argued that the Secretary of State's statutory discretion to amend the target has been *exercised unlawfully*, because his refusal to improve the (allegedly insufficient) targets frustrates the legislative purpose of the Climate Change Act.

---

[40] See, for all these arguments, the text of the renewed permission to apply for judicial review, then refused (Supperstone J), https://planb.earth/wp-content/uploads/2018/07/Plan-B-v-BEIS-judgement-permission.pdf. For a balanced and updated assessment of the UK Climate Change Act, see S. Fankhauser, A. Averchenkova & J. Finnegan, 10 years of the UK Climate Change Act, Grantham Research Institute on Climate Change and the Environment 2018, http://www.lse.ac.uk/GranthamInstitute/publication/10-years-climate-change-act/.

[41] The permission for judicial review was asked on the grounds that the Secretary of State's failure to revise the 2050 target because (1) it is *ultra vires*, since it frustrates the legislative purpose of the 2008 Act; (2) it is based on an error of law regarding the objective of the Paris Agreement; (3) it is irrational, because it fails to take into account and/or inappropriately weighs considerations including the risks of global climate change and predictions of future technical innovation; (4) it violates the Human Rights Act 1998; and (5) it breaches the public sector equality duty set out in section 149 of the Equality Act 2010.

[42] No. C1/2019/1750 (Ct. App. (Civ. Div.), 22 January 2019.

Yet the judge (Supperstone J) stated that "the Secretary of State was plainly entitled ... to refuse to change the 2050 target at the present time" since "there is not now a single 'correct' 2050 target to which the UK should commit itself" – a statement even the claimants agreed with.[43]

The second case worth recalling here – *Carvalho and Others v. Parliament and Council,* commonly known as "the People's Climate Case" – was brought against the Council of the European Union and European Parliament before the General Court of the Court of Justice of the European Union (CJEU) by a group of 10 families living in and outside of Europe (in particular coming from Portugal, Germany, France, Italy, Romania, Kenya, Fiji and Sweden), whose livelihood and future have been allegedly impacted by the effects of climate change.[44] As reported, the claimants suffered different and apparently unrelated damage, such as the loss of a tree plantation, due to Hurricane Ophelia that struck Portugal in 2017, or a decrease in honey production due to the altered changes between seasons. According to the families, what links all these events together is, however, climate change.[45] The claimants therefore decided to sue the EU institutions, contesting the present European regulation of climate change, on the basis of the incorporation in Article 11 TFEU of the objective of "sustainable development". More specifically, what the claimants contested was the adequacy, and thus the legality, of the Greenhouse Emissions Acts which compel EU Member States to reduce greenhouse gas emissions by only 60 per cent compared to 1990 levels by 2030, and by 80 per cent compared to such levels by 2050. These thresholds are considered insufficient to avoid dangerous climate change and therefore they permanently threaten the claimants' fundamental rights of life, health, education, occupation and equal treatment. From a strictly legal viewpoint, the objective of this lawsuit was twofold. On the one hand, on the procedural basis of Article 263 TFEU, the claimants sought to obtain the nullification (that is, a declaration of invalidity) of three EU legal acts, that is, (a) Directive 2003/87/EC governing emissions from large power generation installations (ETS); (a) Regulation (EU) No. 2018/842 on emissions from industry, transport, buildings, agriculture ("Effort Sharing Regulation", ESR); and (c) Regulation

---

[43]   https://planb.earth/wp-content/uploads/2018/07/Plan-B-v-BEIS-judgement-permission.pdf (para. 41).

[44]   Case T-330/18, Carvalho and Others v. Parliament and Council, ECLI:EU:T:2019:324. The full text of the case is available on official website of the European Union Court of Justice, at http://curia.europa.eu/juris/document/document.jsf?text=&docid=204870&pageI ndex=0&doclang=EN&mode=lst&dir=&occ=first&part=1&cid=397496. All the information here reported is available also on the official website of the case, https://peoplesclimatecase. caneurope.org/. In the legal scholarship, see *L. Krämer*, Climate Change, Human Rights and Access to Justice, JEEPL 2019, p. 21.

[45]   For a general discussion that takes into account the scientific dimension, see *S. Marjanac & L. Patton*, Extreme Weather Event Attribution Science and Climate Change Litigation: An Essential Step in the Casual Chain?, JENRL 2018, p. 265.

(EU) No. 2018/841 on greenhouse gases emissions and removals from land use, land use change, and forestry ("Land Use, Land Use Change and Forestry", LULUCF).[46] On the other hand, they asked for the declaration of the non-contractual (i.e. tortious) liability of the EU, on the procedural basis of Article 340 TFEU, which provides a mechanism for injunctive relief. In this second part of the lawsuit, the aim of the claimants was not to seek damages, but to obtain an injunction forcing the European Commission and European Parliament to adopt higher targets that reduce emissions "to the full extent of its technical and economic capability".

However, on 22 May 2018, the EU General Court ruled against the claimants, dismissing the action as inadmissible on the procedural ground of "lack of individual concern" – as asked both by the EU Parliament and Council.[47] As a general matter, the CJEU has always been clear in saying that, under the fourth paragraph of Article 263 TFEU, individuals who want to bring an action for annulment before the Court must prove "individual concern", that is that a certain legislative act affects the claimants "by reason of certain attributes peculiar to them, or by reason of a factual situation which differentiates them from all other persons and distinguishes them individually in the same way as the addressee".[48] This means that the Court did not dismiss the case on the merits, but on the procedural fact that the claimants in this case do not possess the requirements that would entitle them to go to court to challenge the EU's climate policy since "they are not sufficiently and directly affected by these policies". Now, it is self-evident that such a standard is almost impossible to meet when it comes to evaluating the effects of climate policies on certain subjects. Indeed, it is in the very nature of climate change that it affects every individual on earth (although to different degrees), in a very pervasive and indistinct way, causing different types of harm in different contexts that impact a whole range of different life situations, and whose effects, even when determinable, are often only evident in the long run. The use by the Court of this procedural notion reveals the insufficiency of our legal categories (as stated at the outset of this chapter) and their entire inability to prompt effective action, in this case at a judicial level.

---

[46]   To avoid a legal vacuum, the Court was also asked to order that all these normative documents stay in force until a stronger version of them is enacted.

[47]   This judgment is available at https://peoplesclimatecase.caneurope.org/wp-content/uploads/2019/05/european-general-courts-order-_15.05.2019.pdf.

[48]   See e.g. Joined Cases C-408/15 P and C-409/15, Ackerman Saatzuch and Others v. Parliament and Council, ECLI:EU:C:2016:893.

LIABILITY OF STATES IN CLIMATE CHANGE MIGRATION AND COMPENSATION FOR ENVIRONMENTAL MIGRANTS

Francesco MARTINES

1. INTRODUCTION

This chapter studies the effects of climate change on migration from a legal perspective. In fact, climate change as a cause of migration is a phenomenon that has not been studied very much so far and as yet there are no agreed-upon objectives.

An interesting study was published by the World Bank on 19 March 2018 about the most important social consequences of climate change.[1] According to the data reported in the World Bank's dossier, by 2050 the number of people who will be forced to leave their homeland due to severe phenomena of climate change could reach 143 million. The areas mainly affected by this migration will be Sub-Saharan Africa (86 million), Southern Asia (40 million) and Latin America (17 million).

One of the first questions that should be answered concerns the final destination of these migratory flows:

- could the climate migrations from the above-mentioned macro-areas be cross-border, involving other states or continents?
- could this phenomenon significantly involve Europe?
- if there is no massive influx into Europe, could it be said that the issue of environmental migration is not a priority interest for European policies?

The World Bank's report presents data concerning the main causes of the migration out of developing countries (in particular Ethiopia, Bangladesh and Mexico),

---

[1]   *World Bank*, Groundswell: Preparing for Internal Climate Migration, 2018, https://openknowledge.worldbank.org/handle/10986/29461.

which are: (a) temperature increase (global warming); (b) changing amounts of rainfall, either less or more; and (c) rising sea levels.

There are many scientific studies on migration in recent literature,[2] but they generally focus on the cross-border migration of refugees (who leave their country of origin to escape wars and persecution, looking for survival conditions in other states or continents).

Climate migration that is mainly domestic has not been studied extensively. The main reason for this lack of interest, in the author's opinion, is connected to the low interest in the issue from the government institutions and the other actors (NGOs, multinational corporations, etc.) who, in an international scenario, can manage the problem. A lack of interest at the institutional level, demonstrated by the absence of formal and legal acts, inevitably leads to a low scientific research interest.

Scientific studies on climate migration can foster greater attention from state and non-state actors. John Roome, Senior Director of the Study Group of the World Bank, stated that migration induced by climate change does not necessarily need to be a crisis, "provided that we act promptly and courageously". In particular, there are three actions (at national and global level) that the report suggests:

- an acceleration in greenhouse gas emission reduction policies;
- inclusion of climate migration in the national development planning of the various countries; and
- investing in data gathering and analysis to improve understanding of climate migration trends.[3]

Finally, one last aspect should be considered: even if climate migration has a naturally domestic nature, the possibility cannot be excluded that it may progressively take on a cross-border nature, since migrant populations could decide to make a courageous choice by trying to reach the most developed geographic areas of the world to start a new life.

---

[2]   *J. McAdam* (ed.), Climate Change and Displacement. Multidisciplinary Perspectives, Hart Publishing, 2010; *G. Kibreab*, Climate Change and Human Migration: a Tenuous Relationship? Fordham Environ. Law Rev. 2009 (2), p. 357; *R. Black et al.*, The Effect of Environmental Change on Human Migration, Glob. Environ. Change 2011 (2), p. S3; *R. Black et al.*, Climate Change. Migration as Adaptation, Nature 2011 (478), pp. 447 et seq.; *N. Myers*, Environmental Refugees: a Growing Phenomenon of the 21st Century, Philos. Trans. R. Soc. Lond., B, Biol. Sci. 2002 (357), pp. 609 et seq.; *C. Cattaneo*, Cambiamento climatico e migrazione, Equilibri 2016 (1), pp. 101 et seq.; *E. Piguet*, Linking Climate Change, Environmental Migration: a Methodological Overview, Climate Change 2010 (4), pp. 517 et seq.; *F. Perrini*, Circular Migration and International and European Protection of Environmental Migrants, www.federalismi.it /2017 (1).

[3]   See https://blogs.worldbank.org/climatechange/climate-change-negotiations-action.

2. THE RIGHT TO MIGRATE (*IUS MIGRANDI*)

Looking at the issue of climate migration from a strictly juridical point of view, it should be noted that the *ius migrandi* is not a human right; it is not regulated as such in any international charter and is not entirely recognised in any of the 194 existing constitutions around the world. Thus, although migration is a human phenomenon that has always characterised the human species,[4] it does not find legal recognition in the catalogue of human rights.

In the global world, commodities circulate more easily than people, whose mobility is subordinated to state sovereignty: the displacement of each of us on the planet is therefore conditioned by the discretionary authorisation of the state to which we go. There is a real paradox: the freedom to emigrate (leave one's country of origin) is recognised in many constitutional papers (in Italy, Article 35 of the Constitution), but it is not specifically assisted by a freedom of movement and mobility to other states. Therefore, the freedom to emigrate is an unattainable freedom if the person who wishes to emigrate cannot get an access permit from the destination state where he/she would like to live.

With respect to this situation, the legal system provides an important exception for those who leave their country to escape situations of danger exhaustively listed under international law and which can be integrated at the discretion of the domestic law of individual states: these are the cases in which the right to asylum is recognised. In Italy this is regulated by Article 10 of the Constitution, while at the international level it is articulated by the 1951 Geneva Convention.[5]

Entering a state without authorisation puts the migrant in a position of unlawfulness, which can be classified by the states as a criminal or administrative offence and entitles the state to repatriate the offender.

3. THE DIFFERENT CATEGORIES OF MIGRATION

Legal systems in general distinguish different types of migration by linking them with a different regime. The traditional distinction is between economic migration and migration due to conditions of vulnerability. Currently a third category is being added, although not yet clearly regulated: migration due to environmental causes, in which the sub-category of migrations for causes related to climate change is distinguished.

---

[4] *V. Calzolaio & T. Pievani*, Libertà di migrare. Perché ci spostiamo da sempre ed è bene così, Einaudi, 2016.

[5] *P. Benvenuti*, La Convenzione di Ginevra sullo status dei rifugiati, in L. Pineschi (ed.), La tutela internazionale dei diritti umani, Giuffrè, 2006; *F. Cherubini*, L'asilo dalla Convenzione di Ginevra al diritto dell'Unione Europea, Cacucci, 2012.

3.1. ECONOMIC MIGRATION

Economic migrations are those related to the need to improve one's personal living conditions. These flows involve different types of migrants: from those who leave their country of origin to avoid situations of extreme poverty to those who move to find better and more fulfilling job opportunities (so-called "brain drain" or "scientific migrants"), or to those who – for the particular type of work they do – are forced to go outside their country of origin (e.g. to Silicon Valley in California, USA, which has become a magnet for computer scientists and mathematicians coming from all over the world).

The legal regime of economic migrants is entirely subordinated to the migration policies of the individual states; international law, in fact, does not recognise economic migrants as holders of *ius migrandi*.

3.2. MIGRATION DUE TO VULNERABILITY

Migrations due to vulnerability are typified by the Geneva Convention on the basis of an exhaustive list of reasons that may justify recognition of refugee status (persecution for reasons of race, religion, political opinions, belonging to a particular social group). In all these cases, since migration is a necessity determined by the objective impossibility of continuing to live in one's own country, international law and many national constitutions recognise the right to asylum as a remedy which, in accordance with what has previously been observed, converts migration from a behaviour that should be authorised by the state of destination into a real *ius migrandi*.

3.3. ENVIRONMENTAL MIGRATION

Migration due to environmental causes describes the cases in which the environment contributes to causing migration; as mentioned, environmental migration is divided into two sub-categories: migration connected to calamitous events (tsunamis, earthquakes, natural explosions, etc.) occurring in the country of origin; and climate migration, determined by the climate change caused by man.

The most common forms of climate change connected to migration flows are droughts, floods, rising seas, rising temperatures, and the disappearance of islands or parts of coastline (but also wars linked to changes caused by the Anthropocene age, such as "water wars"[6]).

---

[6]   *P. Crutzen & T.E. Graedel*, Atmospheric Change: An Earth System Perspective, Int. J. Climatol. 1995 (5) p. 585; *C. Hamilton, F. Gemenne & C. Bonneuil* (eds.), The Anthropocene and the Global Environmental Crisis: Rethinking Modernity in a New Epoch, Routledge, 2015.

What is the legal treatment of environmental and climate migrants? So far, legal systems tend to combine the category of environmental and climate migrants with that of economic migrants, without thereby recognising any *ius migrandi*. For example, the Article 20 of the Italian Immigration Act (Legge no. 40/1998) has given relevance to environmental migration by establishing that "temporary protection measures to be adopted may be established, also by way of derogation from the provisions of this text, for significant humanitarian needs, in case of conflicts, natural disasters or other particularly serious events in countries not belonging to the European Union". The formula "natural disasters" is very broad and generic and should be interpreted in the sense of including natural events *stricto sensu* and events caused by man (such as climate change). However, the use of the term "disasters" leaves us thinking of sudden and contingent phenomena, leaving out events or changes due to gradual and long-term climatic conditions.

4. CLIMATE CHANGE AS A CAUSE OF MIGRATION

Climate change acts in a complex way on migration choices. Sometimes it directly makes life in a certain place impossible; more frequently it indirectly influences migration flows, adding to other existing factors (e.g. poor technological skills, political instability).

The possibility of giving legal significance to the climatic and environmental factor as a constitutive element of an *ius migrandi* is currently much debated. On the one hand, there are those who insist on recognising climate and environmental migrants as refugees on the assumption that environmental factors would pose a situation of vulnerability analogous to the cases of persecution listed by the Geneva Convention.[7]

In particular, first, according to one theory (theory of responsibility), the foundation of the extension of asylum rights to climate migrants would be connected to the liability that industrialised countries have in causing (or contributing to) climate change in many areas of the planet. According to this responsibility, people of these areas forced to migrate due to the effects of climate change would be compensated by the destination industrialised countries, who should grant them the protection provided by international rules for refugees (Article 1/A of the Geneva Convention).[8] In opposition to this theory, it has been observed that climate change results from historical and collective responsibilities;[9] for this reason it is not obvious that the present generations

---

[7]   *F. Gemenne*, Géopolitique du Climat, Armand Colin, 2015.
[8]   *J. Carens*, The Ethics of Immigration, Oxford University Press, 2013; *M.J. Lister*, Climate Change Refugees, CRISPP 2014 (17), pp. 618–634.
[9]   *M. Banks*, Individual Responsibility for Climate Change, South. J. Philos. 2013 (51), pp. 42 et seq.

must pay for the illegal behaviour of those who preceded them. Moreover, even if we succeed in asserting the collective responsibility of industrialised states for climate change in the at-risk areas of the planet, none of their individual citizens is causally responsible for climate change; it is not easy to assert that individual citizens who now live in industrialised states should give compensation to climate migrants.

According to another theory (benefit theory), the protection linked to the recognition of refugee status to climate migrants arises from the consideration that industrialised countries have drawn economic benefits and continue to do so from the exploitation of the areas where the effects caused by climate change are felt: thus the obligation results in compensating the populations fleeing from these areas (through the right of asylum).[10] This solution, however, does not appear convincing for two fundamental reasons: firstly, because the benefits connected to exploitation are temporally very distant from the effects of climate change, so, it is very difficult to assert a direct link between cause and effect; and secondly, because it is possible that causal behaviours imputable to industrialised countries are unproductive of benefits remaining unjustly excluded from the attribution of a compensatory obligation.

Finally, there are those who promote the idea of the extension of refugee status to climate migrants based on the humanitarian theory: people who abandon their lands because of climate change are victims of inefficient governments and unable to face and reduce climate change effects; for this reason, climate migrants must be recipients of humanitarian and welfare interventions by efficient and more organised states that can accept them as refugees.[11] Although the humanitarian theory is appreciable, it meets with objective difficulties linked to the various systems of the individual states in terms of humanitarian protection, which do not allow the state to affirm general protection of climate migrants.

Lastly, a recent doctrinal position should be pointed out that affirms the right of asylum for climate migrants, given the protection that must be accorded to the right of residence in their country of these populations, which, due to climate change, is irretrievably compromised (theory of the right of residence). The only remedy to compensate for the infringement of the right of residence is to recognise that these forced fugitives have the right to settle in more hospitable areas of the planet.[12]

On the opposite side, many researchers exclude the autonomous importance of climate change as a source of *ius migrandi* because climate can, at most, be

---

[10]   C. *Baatz*, Reply to my Critics: Justifying the Fair Share Argument, Ethics, Policy & Environment 2016 (19), pp. 1–9.

[11]   M.J. *Gibney*, The Ethics and Politics of Asylum. Liberal Democracy and the Response to Refugees, Cambridge University Press, 2004, pp. 48–57.

[12]   G. *Pellegrino*, I diritti dei rifugiati climatici, Equilibri 2017 (1), pp. 29 et seq.

a contributing factor to a migratory flow, together with economic, political, social reasons.[13] According to the supporters of this orientation, identifying an autonomous cause of migration due only to climate change would paradoxically imply the irresponsibility of the political and administrative institutions who must guarantee the improvement of the living conditions of the local community: there is no emigration from a country because of climate change if the administrative and political authorities are able and active to reduce the negative effects of climate change.

At a political level, the recent xenophobic tendencies across industrialised countries in general (especially EU countries) are well known, which predictably will oppose any broader interpretation of international standards of the international protection for migrants.

The above considerations may lead one to be very perplexed about any possible extensive interpretation of the current refugee rules in favour of climate migrants. Nevertheless, the current debate, together with the latest data reported in the 2018 World Bank Dossier and the scientific studies that are taking place, may constitute a useful basis for the formalisation of new specific rules for this particular category of migrants.

5. EUROPEAN PROTECTION LAW

As EU citizens, we must ask ourselves whether climate migration is taken into account by EU law. Similar to what happens at the level of international law, in EU law too climate migration is not the object of specific regulation, although the theme of climate change is at the centre of attention of EU policies: the fight against climate change is included among the EU's environmental goals (Article 191 TFEU). Among the concrete measures for achieving these goals are:

-   the exception to the rules about economic competition in the case of state aid to companies investing in the mitigation of the effects harmful to the environment (Article 191(2)(b) TFEU);
-   the mutual assistance between Member States in the event of natural or man-made disasters (Article 21(2)(g) TFEU); and
-   the EU's commitment to providing humanitarian support to non-European populations affected by natural or man-made disasters (Article 214(1) TFEU).

Although the EU is demonstrating an interest in the dangers of climate change, this is not associated with climate migration; as is known, EU law on asylum and

---

13   J. McAdam, Climate Change, Forced Migration, and International Law, Oxford University Press, 2012, pp. 196 et seq.

protection towards migrants has been the subject of recent regulatory actions: the Qualifications Directive 2011/94/EU; the Eurodac Regulation 603/2013; the Dublin III Regulation 604/2013; the Procedures Directive 2013/32/EU; and the Reception Directive 2013/33/EU.

In all these acts, no relevance to the category of environmental and/or climate migrants is recognised, maintaining the close link between the migrant's international protection and the risk of persecution or other serious damage for the migrant.

This regulatory gap is not destined to be filled in the near future because the current debate on the reforms of the Dublin III Regulation does not involve the protection of climate migrants. For example, the Communication of the EU Commission of 6 April 2016 entitled "Towards a reform of the common European Asylum system and enhancing legal avenues to Europe"[14] suggests a downsizing and coordination of the different categories of migrants and related protection instruments, but does not consider the category of climate migrants.

Rebus sic stantibus, also in the field of EU law, the solution of the extensive and widening interpretation of the rules concerning analogous cases could be the right approach.

In this direction, a toehold should be gained from the Directive 2001/55/EU, which covers the temporary protection of displaced people in the case of a massive influx (mentioned by the article 78 TFEU). The Directive defines temporary protection as "the exceptional procedure, which guarantees immediate and temporary protection, in cases of massive influxes of displaced persons from extra EU countries who cannot return to their country of origin" (Article 2(a)). Displaced persons are "extra-EU or stateless persons who have had to leave their country of origin and whose repatriation is not possible because of the situation in their own country" and in particular "a) people who have escaped from conflict zones armed or endemic violence; b) persons who are subject to a serious risk of systematic violations of human rights". Finally, a massive influx means the arrival "of a considerable number of displaced persons coming from a specific geographical area, whether they arrive spontaneously or are facilitated through an evacuation program" into EU territory.

Temporary protection needs to be activated by a decision of the European Council adopted by a qualified majority on the proposal of the EU Commission. The application of the rules on temporary protection (Directive 2001/55) to the category of climate migrants encounters some difficulties related to:

- the wording of the provisions, which are very specific, and, for this reason, extensive interpretations are not easily available;

---

[14]   COM(2016) 197.

- the fact that, when Directive 2001/55 was approved, the Economic and Social Committee (an EU Commission Advisory Body) had suggested the opportunity to include environmental migrants among the beneficiaries of temporary protection,[15] but the Commission did not accept the suggestion;
- as yet, the institute of temporary protection has never yet been concretely applied.

Another instrument that could be adapted to recognise protection to climate or environmental migrants is circular migration. Circular migration, according to the definition accepted by the International Organization for Migration (since 2016 constituted as an agency connected to the UN with 165 Member States), is the "fluid movement of people between countries tending to temporary or non-permanent needs determined by economic and labor market needs of the countries of origin and destination". Traditionally, it involves all the occupational mobility cases connected, on the one hand, to the need for the professional advancement of citizens in developing countries and, on the other hand, to the need of industrialised countries to acquire a new labour force.

According to a Communication of the EU Commission of 16 May 2007,[16] circular migration must be based on a close partnership between the incoming and outgoing countries involved in order to ensure legality and effective circularity. In this way, circular migration becomes a development opportunity for the countries who are involved.

Although the Communication does not consider climate migrants, they have two features in common with circular migrants: (a) their temporary establishment in the destination state; and (b) the tendency of displaced persons to return to their own countries.

These features should convince public institutions to adapt their protection for circular migration to climate migrants as regulated by the EU Commission Communication. However, this is a solution that – at present – seems politically unattainable.

6. CONCLUSIONS

In conclusion, it is necessary to present some considerations that could enrich the debate, especially at the EU and Italian levels.

The author believes that the focus of the issue is not so much the identification of the specific protection measure applicable to the category of environmental/climate

---

[15]   Opinion No. 2001/C155/06.
[16]   COM(2007) 248.

migrants (the aspect that so far has most interested the academic literature) but rather the need to recognise:

- whether protection is due;
- what the assumption that climate migrants have rights to be protected is founded on; and
- the margins within which, in practice, the legal system (in particular the Italian legal system) grants protection to climate migrants.

Climate change is an anthropic factor that is attributable to land changes, mainly connected to the need to exploit natural resources for economic, social and technological progress. The same goes for the effects of global warming connected to the emissions of greenhouse gases because of human activities. Changes in the global climate are a direct consequence of technological progress; therefore, they could have been avoided by renouncing the scientific, social and economic progress of the human species.

There has been a rich debate about sustainable development: the results of this debate are very important and are contained in regulatory acts (mainly international agreements) that engage future generations (e.g. the Kyoto Protocol of 1997 and the Paris Climate Agreement of 2015).[17]

6.1. HUMANITARIAN PROTECTION FOR CLIMATE MIGRANTS

Apart from the commitments for the future, it is necessary to resolve the questions about the measures which can be taken by the international community against the effects of climate change that have already been produced and about what responsibilities can be recognised by industrialised states for the damage resulting from the aggressive exploitation of large areas of the planet. These areas are mostly located in underdeveloped countries, represented by institutions that are often complicit or otherwise unable to protect the human rights of the populations living there.[18]

The populations forced to leave their homeland for reasons connected to climate change are certainly victims of intolerable conduct put in place by the richest countries. As has been observed, "the 20 nations most affected by climate change are responsible for 1% of global emissions; developing countries support 98% of those affected, 99% of all deaths and more than 90% of economic losses

---

[17]   M. Montini, Riflessioni critiche sull'accordo di Parigi sui cambiamenti climatici, Riv. dir. intern. 2017 (3), pp. 719 et seq.; S. Nespor, La lunga marcia per un accordo globale sul clima dal protocollo di Kyoto all'accordo di Parigi, Riv. trim. dir. pubbl. 2016 (1), pp. 81 et seq.

[18]   A.E. Shacknove, Who is a Refugee?, Ethics 1985 (2), p. 274.

related to climate change".[19] The only way to protect against the injuries suffered by these populations is to recognise the general responsibility of the international community and the industrialised states towards those who are forced to leave their own land because of the effects of climate change. The responsibility for the aggressive exploitation of resources, the increase in the temperature of the planet and other anthropic factors closely linked to progress, industrialisation, globalisation of the economy and the rule of the markets must be accepted.[20]

6.2. ITALIAN RULES ABOUT CLIMATE MIGRATION

From this perspective, looking at the Italian system of migrant acceptance, the most suitable form of protection for climate migrants seems to be that of humanitarian protection regulated by Article 5(6) of Legislative Decree 286/1998 (Immigration Act). It functions as a residual measure of protection for cases where the conditions for issuing the access permit according to the general rules are absent but there are "serious humanitarian reasons or came from international or domestic obligations to grant the stay".

Humanitarian protection is a domestic measure to manage the acceptance of migrants; it is flanked by the two forms of protection recognised, however, at the international level (refugee status, provided for by the 1951 Geneva Convention, and subsidiary protection, recognised to anyone who risks serious harm in the event that he/she returns to his/her country).[21] The European Court of Justice (ECJ) has stated that these forms of protection (introduced by Member States) must be compatible with the measures laid down by EU law and must respond to a different *ratio* in respect to them.[22]

Among the "serious humanitarian reasons" that can justify humanitarian protection, there may be several cases related to serious danger to life or safety of the applicant in the case of repatriation, including – in the author's opinion – those related to the effects of climate change. In these cases, the government has a wide discretion in assessing the individual and concrete situation of the applicant.

In 2015, the Italian Minister of the Interior released a Communication (Circular 3716/2015) to the Domestic Commissions (*Fra le fattispecie di riconoscimento della protezione umanitaria rientrano le gravi calamità naturali o*

---

[19]   I. *Caruso & B. Venditto*, I flussi migratori Le migrazioni di transito nel Mediterraneo, in P. Malanima (ed.), Rapporto sulle economie del Mediterraneo, Il Mulino, 2008, pp. 43–66.

[20]   R. *Huseby*, Should the Beneficiaries Pay?, Politics Philos. Econ. 2013 (2), p. 21.

[21]   N. *Zorzella*, La protezione umanitaria nel sistema giuridico italiano, Dir. imm. citt. 2018 (1) fasc. no. 3/2018, pp. 28 et seq.; F. *Perrini*, Cambiamenti climatici e migrazioni forzate. Verso una tutela internazionale dei migranti ambientali, Editoriale Scientifica, 2018, pp. 161 et seq.

[22]   ECJ, Case C-57/09, Germany v. B, ECLI:EU:C:2010:661.

altri gravi fattori locali ostativi ad un rimpatrio in dignità e sicurezza) regarding granting the right to asylum, setting out the humanitarian reasons that may justify issuing residence permits; among these reasons the Minister included "serious natural disasters". This interpretation from the Minister induced the Domestic Commissions to grant the right to asylum and the courts to guarantee humanitarian protection also in some cases of environmental migrations.

In this context, three relatively recent judgments deserve to be mentioned. Firstly, in its judgment of 16 September 2015, the Tribunal of Milan held that: "Article 5(6) of the Immigration Act is susceptible to wide interpretation and allows consideration of objective situations, that are related to the country of origin, such as famines, natural or environmental disasters and similar situations".

Secondly, the Appeal Court of Bologna, in its judgment of 29 March 2016, no. 524, held that among the reasons justifying humanitarian protection are "situations of instability that, in the event of repatriation, integrate a condition of extreme vulnerability that jeopardize the exercise of fundamental rights" (in this case it was a subject who escaped from a serious flood event in the country of origin).

Finally, a recent judgment of the Italian Supreme Court of Justice (23 February 2018, no. 4455) established that humanitarian protection must be guaranteed whenever the applicant would not be able to meet his/her basic needs in his country, including those strictly connected to his/her livelihood, deriving from economic or environmental factors (drought, famine, absolute poverty).[23] The Court emphasised the need for an examination as concrete and individualised as possible of the personal situation and vulnerability profiles of the applicant.

However, even though Italian courts have seemed inclined towards recognising climate change as a cause of possible humanitarian protection (making Italy one of the most advanced countries in the perspective of protection of environmental migrants), the new strategy of the Italian Government does not support this interpretive evolution. On 5 July 2018, the Minister of the Interior released strict new rules (Circular 8819/2018) about humanitarian protection, inviting the Commissions handling the right to asylum to be very prudent and rigorous in assessing whether the personal situation of the migrant justifies protection. Furthermore, on 4 October 2018, the Government approved a recent Legislative Decree (113/2018, approved by Parliament in the Act of 1 December 2018, no. 132) that cancelled humanitarian protection by introducing special forms of access permits designated for people who leave their own country for exceptional reasons. Among these reasons it was established that a special

---

[23]   The judgment is published *in extenso* in Foro It., 2018, pp. 1657 et seq.

permit should be authorised/released to the migrant who escapes from a land where there is a "temporary and exceptional calamitous situation"[24] (Article 1, paragraph 1, of Legislative Decree 113/2018, which added Article 20bis to the text of the Immigration Act 286/1998).

The consequence of these new rules is that general humanitarian protection can no longer be granted to environmental migrants and that hereafter, in Italy, the only way to give protection to climate migrants should be the new measure introduced by Article 20bis of the Immigration Act (permit for calamitous reasons).

Although, on the one hand, the new Italian rules have the merit of recognising (for the first time at domestic law level) natural disasters as an autonomous cause of protection, on the other hand it should be considered that the conditions set out in Article 20bis of the Immigration Act are particularly strict, establishing that the situation of calamity must be "exceptional" and "temporary". It seems that all those cases in which the conditions of climatic adversity are not a direct consequence of an environmental disaster (earthquake, flood, etc.), but rather a consequence of an anthropic factor (such as over-exploitation of natural resources for which industrialised countries are responsible in the lands of developing countries), should be excluded from this category.

Consider that in the Congo there are entire communities that have been forced to change their living conditions due to large industrial groups interested in the production of electronic devices (*in primis*, smartphones); that area is rich in coltan, a mineral mixture used for the construction of these devices. The extraction of coltan from the subsoil causes exploitation of poor Congolese people who work in the mines. Their land is being transformed and the resulting climate change is a direct effect of the low-cost extraction of the precious mineral. These areas are rapidly and irreversibly changing: an age-old balance has been interrupted between the populations settled in those villages and the territory, which will rapidly induce the younger generations to flee because it will no longer be able to do anything else other the extraction of coltan from the subsoil. With regard to these populations, victims of the effects of climate change caused by progress, we are all responsible and cannot accept the idea that this is a problem that does not involve us, including from a legal perspective.

An optimistic approach to the subject leads the present author to believe that Article 20bis of the Italian Immigration Act could still represent a very important step in the process of recognition of protection for climate migrants, even if at this specific historical moment the Italian Government seems to be

---

[24]   The special permit will have a duration of six months (extendable for another six months if the conditions of exceptional calamity remain) and cannot be converted into a residence permit for work.

inspired only to greatly reduce the flows of migrants from countries south of the Mediterranean.

Governments and politicians will change, but the written rules remain and must be interpreted and applied in the future. Therefore, in the author's opinion, any definitive consideration of these rules needs to wait until concrete results have been achieved by the public administration, judges and academics who will take care to interpret and apply the norms.

REUSING OFFSHORE HYDROCARBON INFRASTRUCTURE FOR THE PERMANENT STORAGE OF CARBON DIOXIDE

Joris GAZENDAM

1. INTRODUCTION

Carbon capture and storage (CCS) is one of the instruments that can be used to mitigate global climate change.[1] CCS is not a single technology, but rather a combination of technologies that are applied in the three stages of the CCS chain, which consists of capture of carbon of dioxide from industrial installations, transport to a storage location, and the permanent geological storage of carbon dioxide in the subsoil.

CCS is regulated by international, European and national law covering the both the "environmental" and the "CCS-chain" aspects of the capture, transport and storage activities. The environmental aspects are mostly related to the capture activities at industrial installations and non-pipeline transport of carbon dioxide, whereas the CCS-chain aspects deal with the transport through pipelines and the permanent storage in subsoil storage locations.

The European Union introduced the Emission Trading Scheme (EU-ETS) in order to incentivise low carbon technologies such as CCS. The EU-ETS aims to put a price on emissions of carbon dioxide through a cap-and-trade regime.[2] However, the price of emission allowances has never risen to the necessary level to incentivise CCS.[3] Another obstacle for CCS is the high cost associated with it. This is partially caused by the potential high liability risks for carbon dioxide storage operators. Finally, the perceived risks of CCS are currently so substantial that onshore CCS development is unlikely in various EU Member

---

[1]   *Intergovernmental Panel on Climate Change*, IPCC Special Report on Carbon Dioxide Capture and Storage, Prepared by Working Group III of the Intergovernmental Panel on Climate Change, Cambridge University Press, 2005, p. 54.

[2]   *M.M. Roggenkamp, C. Redgwell & A. Rønne et al.*, Energy Law in Europe, Oxford University Press, 3rd ed., 2016, p. 337.

[3]   €21.35/tonne CO2 (31 May 2020). It is thought that a minimum price level of €100/tonne would be required to incentivise CCS, but this may vary due to specific circumstances.

States.[4] The alternative is to develop offshore CCS and the North Sea region offers opportunities for CCS. There are several industrial centres where carbon dioxide can be captured, and the North Sea has for decades been an important region for hydrocarbon[5] activities, resulting in a significant number of pipelines, platforms, wells and subsoil reservoirs that can be reused for CCS.[6]

In the coming decades, the offshore oil and gas industry in the North Sea region will reach the end of its lifespan and operators of offshore oil/gas platforms are obliged to decommission (i.e. remove) these platforms and close off the wells before abandoning them. Once decommissioned and sealed off, the reservoirs cannot be reused for CCS, or would require significant effort to be made available again for CCS. This problem is made worse be the existence of a temporal gap between the decommissioning of hydrocarbon infrastructure due to the cessation of production in the near future and the start of CCS activities in the distant future. A possible solution to deal with the temporal gap could be to keep the offshore platform and well "in use" until these can be transferred to a carbon dioxide storage operator. This can be done by extending the existing hydrocarbon production licences or appointing a temporary operator who would be responsible for the infrastructure during the temporal gap.

The goal of this chapter is to elaborate on the relevant liability risks that have to be considered when reusing existing hydrocarbon infrastructure. It will start by presenting an overview of the CCS technology and the legal regime for CCS in the EU. Next, reuse options for offshore hydrocarbon infrastructure are explored, as well as the decommissioning requirements under international, European and national law, whereby the decommissioning regimes of the Netherlands, Norway and the UK are scrutinised to find reuse possibilities. The last part of the chapter will focus on the legal barriers for reuse and particular attention will be paid to those barriers that are caused by liability risks.

2. CCS TECHNOLOGY AND ASSOCIATED LIABILITY RISKS

2.1. TECHNICAL BASICS OF CCS TECHNOLOGY

The CCS chain consists of three parts: capture, transport and storage. In each part of the CCS chain, different entities are active (capture, transport and

---

[4]   *R.M. Kraus, S.R. Carley, D.C. Warren, J.A. Rupp & J.D. Graham,* "Not in (or Under) My Backyard": Geographic Proximity and Public Acceptance of Carbon Capture and Storage Facilities, Risk Analysis 2014 (34), pp. 536–538.

[5]   Hydrocarbons are more commonly known as oil and natural gas.

[6]   *IEAGHG,* Case studies of CO2 storage in depleted oil and gas fields, 2018; IEAGHG Technical Report 2017-01, IEA Greenhouse Gas R&D programme, pp. 133–134.

storage operators).[7] The capture of carbon dioxide takes place at industrial installations. There the carbon dioxide is separated from industrial emission streams. There are various technologies to capture carbon dioxide from emission streams and these can be divided into pre-combustion capture technologies and post-combustion capture technologies.[8] The application of pre-combustion capture technologies entails that the carbon dioxide is separated from the fuel before it is burned. Post-combustion capture technologies separate the carbon dioxide from the emission stream after the fuel has been burned. In addition to these existing technologies, there is a new technology, oxy-fuel combustion process, whereby nitrogen is removed from the flue gas by combusting a hydrocarbon fuel in pure oxygen (instead of air) and this creates a far more pure carbon dioxide stream compared to the other capture technologies.[9] The capture phase in the CCS chain is important because it is during this phase that the level of impurities in the carbon dioxide stream is determined. These impurities, such as water or other chemical substances, can cause problems further on in the CCS chain during transport and storage. Water can cause corrosion to the pipelines during transport[10] and impurities in the carbon dioxide might influence the behaviour of the carbon dioxide in the storage location.[11]

Carbon dioxide can be transported by pipelines, transport ships, trains, trucks or in small compressed gas cylinders. Pipelines and ships are generally considered the most economically viable modes for transporting large quantities of carbon dioxide, as bulk transport is more efficient compared to transporting small batches. Additionally, it is also more efficient for large carbon dioxide emitters such as power plants to dispatch carbon dioxide in large quantities, as the carbon dioxide is captured in large amounts.[12]

Carbon dioxide is permanently stored by injecting the carbon dioxide into a suitable storage location. Such storage locations are deep, stable rock formations in which there are countless tiny pores that trap the carbon dioxide.[13] Oil fields, depleted gas fields, deep coal seams and aquifers (sediment or rock body containing brackish water or brine) are all possible storage locations.[14] When

---

[7] Hypothetically, it is possible for one undertaking to perform all activities in the CCS chain. It is found that it is country-dependent whether the CCS chain is operated by an integrated undertaking or whether different entities are responsible for the separate parts of the chain.

[8] R. Surampalli, S. Brar & B. Gurjar, Carbon Capture and Storage: Physical, Chemical, and Biological Methods, American Society of Civil Engineers, 2015, p. 219.

[9] Id. at p. 224.

[10] E. de Vissera, C. Hendriks & M. Barrio et al., Dynamic CO2 quality recommendations, International Journal of Greenhouse Gas Control 2008 (2), p. 481.

[11] J.C. de Diose, M.A. Delgadoa & J.A. Marína et al., Short-term effects of impurities in the CO2 stream injected into fractured carbonates, International Journal of Greenhouse Gas Control 2016 (54), p. 735.

[12] https://www.globalccsinstitute.com/why-ccs/what-is-ccs/transport/.

[13] Intergovernmental Panel on Climate Change, supra, note 1 at p. 199.

[14] Id.

assessing the suitability of a storage location, there are various aspects that have to be taken into consideration. The primary prerequisite is that the injected carbon dioxide remains within the appointed storage location, so both horizontally and vertically a sealing body of rock, also known as a caprock, is required. Once a possible location is found, the potential carbon dioxide storage operator will look at four aspects: (1) containment, (2) injectivity, (3) connectivity, and (4) capacity.[15] These four aspects can be summarised into two criteria: the total amount of carbon dioxide that can be stored in the reservoir, and the speed at which the carbon dioxide can be injected into the reservoir. Based on these two criteria, the two most likely types of storage locations are depleted hydrocarbon reservoirs and aquifers.[16] Aquifers possess a large storage potential, but at the expense of high uncertainty because of the very poor characterisation of their storage properties, especially their sealing capacity.[17] Depleted hydrocarbon reservoirs offer reduced risk because of better reservoir knowledge and proven sealing capacity,[18] but the storage capacity is smaller compared to aquifers.[19] In recent years, much research has been conducted into reuse options for existing offshore hydrocarbon reservoirs.[20] The North Sea region in particular has attracted a significant amount of attention and it is therefore important to understand the EU legal framework for CCS.

2.2. THE EU REGULATORY FRAMEWORK FOR CCS

The European legal framework for the permanent storage of carbon dioxide is codified in the CCS Directive (Directive 2009/31/EC).[21] The CCS Directive mainly focuses on the transport and storage parts of the CCS chain. The CCS Directive applies to the geological storage of carbon dioxide in the territory of the Member States, their exclusive economic zones[22] and their continental shelves[23] (Art. 2 Directive 2009/31/EC). The CCS Directive was enacted in 2009, and since then only a limited number of CCS projects have been licensed under this Directive. In 2015, the CCS Directive was evaluated by the European

---

[15] *IEA Greenhouse Gas R&D Programme*, Re-use of Oil & Gas facilities for CO2 transport and storage, IEA Greenhouse Gas R&D Programme, 2018, p. 28.

[16] *Intergovernmental Panel on Climate Change, supra*, note 1 at p. 199.

[17] Id. at p. 221.

[18] *IEA Greenhouse Gas R&D Programme, supra*, note 16 at p. 15.

[19] Id.

[20] See for example: *IEA Greenhouse Gas R&D Programme, supra*, note 16 at pp. 84–85.

[21] European Parliament and Council Directive 2009/31/EC of 23 April 2009 on the geological storage of carbon dioxide and amending Council Directive 85/337/EC, European Parliament and Council Directives 2000/60/EC, 2001/80/EC, 2004/35/EC, 2006/12/EC, 2008/1/EC and Regulation (EC) No 1013/2006, OJ 2009 L 140/114.

[22] Art. 55 UNCLOS.

[23] Art. 76 UNCLOS.

Commission. It was found that the Directive provided developers of CCS with sufficient legal certainty and that the non-application of the Directive was caused by external factors such as the low carbon dioxide emission allowance prices.[24]

Despite the significant potential of CCS for combating climate change, CCS is not a mandatory technology that the Member States have to apply.[25] First, the Member States have to decide which areas of their territory, onshore and offshore, are available for CCS development (Art. 4(1) Directive 2009/31/EC). Second, it must be assessed whether a potential storage location meets the criteria that are set out in Annex I of Directive 2009/31/EC. The crucial benchmark that a storage location must meet is that carbon dioxide can be stored in a manner whereby there is no significant risk of leakage and no significant environmental or health risks (Art. 4(4) Directive 2009/31/EC).

The permitting process for CCS activities is similar to the European hydrocarbon licensing framework that is codified in Directive 94/22/EC (Hydrocarbon Licensing Directive).[26] Permits are exclusive, granting the holder the sole right to perform the exploration or storage activities, and are awarded through competitive procedures based on objective, published and transparent criteria.

When a potential location has been identified for carbon storage, exploratory drilling and injection tests have to be performed. These activities require an exclusive exploration permit (Art. 5 Directive 2009/31/EC). The exploration permit is awarded on the basis of objective, published and non-discriminatory criteria. The permanent storage of carbon dioxide is performed under a storage permit (Art. 6 Directive 2009/31/EC). This storage permit can be awarded once the exploration activities have been completed, but the exploration can sometimes also be skipped when the storage is to take place in a depleted oil or natural gas reservoir. Sufficient knowledge was gathered during the exploitation and/or exploration phase by the hydrocarbon operator on the storage capacity of the hydrocarbon reservoir.[27] The storage permit is to be granted based on objective, published and transparent criteria (Art. 6(1) Directive 2009/31/EC). In order to stimulate exploration activities, exploration permit holders have priority in the storage permit granting procedure.

---

[24] *European Commission*, Report on the review of Directive 2009/31/EC on the geological storage of carbon dioxide – Accompanying the document Report from the Commission to the European Parliament and the Council, COM(2015) 576 final.

[25] The CCS explicitly mentions that Member States are entitled not to allow CCS in their territory (Recital 19 Directive 2009/31/EC).

[26] European Parliament and Council Directive 94/22/EC of 30 May 1994 on the conditions for granting and using authorisations for the prospection, exploration, and production of hydrocarbons, OJ 1994 L 164. See also: *M.M. Roggenkamp, K.J. de Graaf & J.M. Holwerda*, Afvang, Transport en Opslag van CO2: De Implementatie van Richtlijn 2009/31/EG in Nederland, M&R 2010, p. 553.

[27] *IEA Greenhouse Gas R&D Programme, supra*, note 16 at p. 16.

During the injection phase, the storage operator must implement a monitoring plan that aims to ensure that no irregularities, such as leakages of carbon dioxide, occur (Art. 13 Directive 2009/31/EC).[28] Monitoring has two aims. Firstly, the monitoring plan aims to compare the actual and the modelled behaviour of the carbon dioxide and the storage site. Secondly, it aims to prevent irregularities, the release of carbon dioxide into the atmosphere and adverse effects to the surrounding environment.[29]

The closure of the storage location marks the end of the injection phase, but the carbon dioxide storage operator remains responsible for the site after the closure and this will mean that the operator has to monitor the site in order to ensure that no leakages occur. After 20 years, the storage location, together with the responsibilities attached to it, can be transferred to the state (Art. 18 Directive 2009/31/EC). After the transfer, the carbon dioxide storage operator is finally relieved of any liabilities attached to the carbon dioxide in the storage location.

2.3. LIABILITY RISKS FOR CCS

Liabilities for CCS activities are caused by various operational risks associated with CCS activities. These operational risks are:[30]

- Carbon dioxide leakage: there is the risk that the carbon dioxide migrates from the reservoir to another subsoil formation. This migration can cause the release of carbon dioxide to the atmosphere or cause damage to hydrocarbons/water reserves in other subsoil formations.
- Methane leakage: when carbon dioxide is injected into nearly depleted natural gas reservoirs, it is possible for a leakage to cause not only the carbon dioxide to escape but also methane.
- Seismicity: the injection of carbon dioxide can cause earth tremors.
- Ground movement: carbon dioxide injection can cause pressure changes in the subsoil that can lead to subsidence or uplift of the earth surface.
- Brine leakage: when carbon dioxide is injected into aquifers, this can cause the displacement of highly salted brine into other formations, including freshwater formations.

---

[28] The EU Member States have to organise a system of routine and non-routine inspections in order to ensure that irregularities do not occur (Art. 15 Directive 2009/31/EC). Routine inspections have to be carried out every year until three years after concluding the injection and closure of the reservoir, and every five years until the transfer of the responsibility of the reservoir to the competent authority.

[29] An explicit reference is made to preventing adverse effects to drinking water, for human populations, or to users of the surrounding biosphere (Art. 13(1)(e) Directive 2009/31/EC).

[30] K. Damen, A. Faay & W. Turkenburg, Health safety and environmental risks of underground CO2 storage – overview of mechanisms and current knowledge, Climate Change 2006 (74), p. 292.

The relevant operational risks for a given CCS project are determined by the specific circumstances of that storage operation. When aquifers are used as storage locations, the risk of brine leakage is relevant, and when nearly depleted gas reservoirs are used, the risk of methane leakage is relevant. The risk of carbon dioxide leakages, seismicity and ground movements are relevant for all CCS projects. However, the location of the project determines which risks are more relevant. In an onshore setting where a storage reservoir is located beneath a residential area, the risks of seismicity and tremors are of far more importance compared to an offshore storage location where there are no nearby residents. Given the perceived risks of CCS by the public, it has been very hard to realise onshore carbon storage.[31] Offshore CCS is a good alternative if acceptance of onshore CCS projects cannot be achieved.[32]

The carbon dioxide storage operator faces civil, environmental and climate liability risks. The civil liabilities for CCS activities are governed by national law (Recital 34 Directive 2009/31/EC). However, when storing carbon dioxide in the seabed under the continental shelf, the chance of other individuals suffering damage from leaked carbon dioxide is low. Therefore, the most relevant types of liability risks are environmental and climate liability risks.

The release of large quantities of carbon dioxide can have detrimental effects for the direct environment.[33] Exposure by humans or animals to high levels of carbon dioxide in the atmosphere can lead to headaches, dizziness and even suffocation. Because of the potential danger to protected species, natural habitats, water and land, the European legislator made CCS activities subject to environmental liability under Directive 2004/35/EC[34] (Art. 34 Directive 2009/31/EC). This means that preventive (Art. 5 Directive 2004/35/EC) and remedial action (Art. 6 Directive 2004/35/EC) can be taken when CCS activities lead to environmental damage.[35] The risk of environmental damage will be most likely when carbon dioxide is released from the platform or pipeline due to an accident. It should however be remembered that carbon dioxide dissipates quickly in the atmosphere, which reduces the chances of fatalities.

---

[31] See the cancelled Barendrecht project in the Netherlands as an example of how public perception can effectively terminate a CCS project.

[32] *European Commission*, Communication from the Commission to the European Parliament, the Council, the European Economic and Social Committee and the Committee of the Regions on the Future of Carbon Capture and Storage in Europe, COM(2013) 180 final, p. 18.

[33] *M.M. Roggenkamp & E. Woerdman* (eds.), Legal design of carbon capture and storage, Intersentia, 2009, p. 234.

[34] Directive 2004/35/CE of the European Parliament and of the Council of 21 April 2004 on environmental liability with regard to the prevention and remedying of environmental damage, OJ 2004 L 143/56.

[35] For more information on the interaction between the CCS Directive and the Environmental Liability Directive: *M. Bergsten*, Environmental Liability Regarding Carbon Capture and Storage (CCS) Operations in the EU, EEELW June 2011, pp. 108–115.

In practice, the most relevant type of risk is climate liability. Each of the parties in the CCS chain (capture, transport and storage) bears climate liability, i.e. liability for the emission of carbon dioxide into the atmosphere.[36] Storage operators in particular face long-term climate liability, as they remain responsible for the storage location for 20 years. The problem with long-term climate liability is the difficulty of quantifying the potential size of the liability.[37] If carbon dioxide leaks from a storage reservoir, the storage operator will have to surrender the equivalent number of EU-ETS emission allowances to the national emission authority. Should the operator not have these allowances at its disposal, it will have to buy them on the ETS market at prevailing market prices. Current market prices for emission allowances are relatively low, but there is no guarantee that the price will remain unchanged over the next 20 years.

What is more, storage operators will have to wait for at least 20 years before they can transfer responsibility for the site to the state. Making an accurate estimation of the potential liability for possible leakages in the distant future with varying emission prices is impossible.

3. REUSE POTENTIAL OF EXISTING HYDROCARBON INFRASTRUCTURE

3.1. REUSE POTENTIAL OF HYDROCARBON INFRASTRUCTURE AND RESERVOIRS

In the context of offshore CCS, the concept of reusing hydrocarbon infrastructure for CCS activities has attracted a significant amount of attention and is well documented.[38] The main drivers for reuse are to bring down the cost of CCS and to reduce decommissioning cost. In the North Sea region, it is estimated that there are 500 platforms and 10,000 kilometres of pipeline that have to be decommissioned in the coming decades. The estimated cost for this clean-up of hydrocarbon infrastructure is €80–100 billion.[39] It is therefore no surprise that the offshore hydrocarbon operators are interested into investigating reuse possibilities. Consider for example the *Nexstep* initiative in the Netherlands,[40]

---

[36] All three activities have been added to Annex I to the EU-ETS Directive and an ETS licence is required for all parties in the CCS chain.

[37] In this regard, see also *CO2 Capture Project*, Regulatory Challenges and Key Lessons Learned from Real World Development of CCS Projects, 2012, p. 21.

[38] See for example: *Gasunie Engineering B.V.*, Existing infrastructure for the transport of CO2, CO2Europipe WP2.1 report, 2011; *IEA Greenhouse Gas R&D Programme*, *supra*, note 16; *World Energy Council*, The North Sea Opportunity, report, 2017.

[39] *World Energy Council*, supra, note 41 at pp. 18–19.

[40] https://nexstep.nl/.

which is a joint initiative by EBN[41] and NOGEPA[42] that aims to make a selection of potential reuse options before initiating decommissioning. Although it is important to highlight that the costs of reusing a platform or pipeline for carbon dioxide injection differ on a case-by-case basis, particular CCS projects could benefit from reuse when the costs of reusing old infrastructure are lower than the costs of constructing new pipelines or platforms.

In the context of reuse, the concept of enhanced recovery has to be mentioned. Enhanced recovery is a technique whereby carbon dioxide, or other substances such as water or nitrogen, are injected into a hydrocarbon reservoir in order to increase pressure within the reservoir and increase the amount of recoverable hydrocarbons.[43] Enhanced recovery has a long history,[44] and historically most carbon dioxide has been stored in the context of enhanced recovery.[45] However, Recital 20 of the Preamble to the CCS Directive states that enhanced recovery is not covered by Directive 2009/31/EC. Nevertheless, as a backdoor, it is provided that where enhanced hydrocarbon recovery is combined with the permanent geological storage of carbon dioxide, the provisions of the CCS Directive should apply. Article 3(1) of the Directive defines the "geological storage of carbon dioxide" as "injection accompanied by storage of carbon dioxide streams in underground geological formations". Because of the definition in Article 3(1), the question is whether the distinction made in Recital 20 between enhanced hydrocarbon recovery and geological carbon dioxide storage is tenable. This discussion is highly important when considering the reuse of hydrocarbon infrastructure. Combining continued hydrocarbon production with the permanent storage of carbon dioxide is an effective and efficient method of reuse.

A particular issue with reusing platforms is that hydrocarbon production requires different equipment compared to carbon dioxide storage. This means that redundant equipment has to be removed or that new equipment has to be installed.[46] A similar problem exists for pipelines. Since pipelines are usually connected to various wells, they can only be reused when hydrocarbon production is ceased at all connected wells. This in practice seriously will hamper the availability of offshore pipelines for reuse in the coming decades.[47]

---

[41] The national authority that participates in hydrocarbon projects on behalf of the state (https://www.ebn.nl/en/).

[42] The representative body of the Dutch oil and gas industry (https://www.nogepa.nl/?lang=en).

[43] *IEA Greenhouse Gas R&D Programme, supra*, note 16 at p. 24.

[44] *IEA*, 20 years of Carbon Capture and Storage, 2016, p. 20.

[45] *Global CCS Institute*, The Global Status of CCS, 2019, p. 30, https://www.globalccsinstitute.com/resources/global-status-report/.

[46] *Gasunie Engineering B.V., supra*, note 38 at pp. 7–14.

[47] Id. at p. 20.

3.2. DECOMMISSIONING OBLIGATIONS FOR HYDROCARBON INFRASTRUCTURE

Although there are numerous options for reuse of existing hydrocarbon infrastructure, there remains the issue of decommissioning. Under the international law of the sea, a balance is struck between the interest of coastal states who want to exploit the natural resources in the offshore area under their jurisdiction and other users of the sea. The United Nations Convention on the Law of the Sea (UNCLOS) provides the treaty framework for the decommissioning of offshore installations. Article 60 UNCLOS covers the decommissioning obligation and refers to international accepted standards that were developed by the International Maritime Organization (IMO). In 1988, during its 55th session, the Maritime Safety Committee as part of the IMO adopted guidelines and standards for the removal of offshore installations and structures on the continental shelf and the exclusive economic zone. The IMO guidelines and standards on the removal of offshore installations are divided into three subsections: general removal requirements, guidelines and standards.

The general removal requirements reiterate the text of Article 60 UNCLOS by stating that abandoned or disused offshore installations or structures on the continental shelf or in the exclusive economic zone are required to be removed, except where non-removal or partial removal is consistent with the guidelines and standards (1.1 IMO removal guidelines). Coastal states are allowed to leave parts of the installations in place, but this requires a justification and the IMO has to be informed (1.2 and 1.3 IMO removal guidelines).

The guidelines provide a framework to assess whether installations can remain *in situ*. The decision to allow an offshore installation, structure or parts thereof to remain on the seabed should be based, in particular, on a case-by-case evaluation, by the coastal state with jurisdiction over the installation or structure, of the following matters:

(1) any potential effect on the safety of surface or subsurface navigation, or of other uses of the sea;
(2) the rate of deterioration of the material and its present and possible future effect on the marine environment;
(3) the potential effect on the marine environment, including living resources;
(4) the risk that the material will shift from its position at some future time;
(5) the costs, technical feasibility and risks of injury to personnel associated with removal of the installation or structure; and
(6) the determination of a new use or other reasonable justification for allowing the installation or structure or parts thereof to remain on the seabed.

It is clear that the general rule is that installations have to be completely removed unless there are good reasons to leave part of the installations in place for future reuse. It is also good to bear in mind that the IMO standards and guidelines apply to installations; the obligation to remove disused pipelines is not addressed by the IMO. Pipelines that are part of an installation are covered by the IMO standards;[48] other pipelines are covered by the Convention for the Protection of the Marine Environment of the North-East Atlantic (OSPAR) that regulates dumping at sea. Finally, as there is no harmonised EU legal framework for offshore decommissioning, it is left to EU Member States to incorporate the international standards into national law. Because of this, the national regimes on decommissioning are different in each North Sea coastal state.

The Netherlands is a signatory to UNCLOS and OSPAR, and the international rules for the abandonment of offshore hydrocarbon installations are implemented through the Mining Act in Dutch law, which prescribes the complete removal of unused installations (Art. 44 Mining Act).[49] The Dutch continental shelf is relatively shallow, with a maximum depth of 55 meters, and therefore the only option is complete removal in compliance with the IMO standards. The question whether reuse of hydrocarbon installations and pipelines is allowed under Dutch law is somewhat ambiguous. The main criterion for the Minister of Economic Affairs and Climate to approve or reject a decommissioning plan is safety. The Minister has no explicit discretionary powers to decide that an installation has to be reused.[50]

The United Kingdom is also a contracting party to UNCLOS and OSPAR, and the international regime on decommissioning of hydrocarbon installations is implemented in the Petroleum Act 1998.[51] The main instrument in the decommissioning procedure is the Notice Procedure (section 29(1) Petroleum Act 1998). Under this procedure, the Secretary of State may require the operator to submit an abandonment programme. The programme is to be drafted in cooperation with the relevant stakeholders. The Secretary of State may approve this programme (conditionally or unconditionally) or reject it. The programme is to be executed according to the conditions set by Secretary of State (section 36 Petroleum Act 1998). In UK legislation, the waste hierarchy is implemented and, as a result, the abandonment programme must consider reuse before removal options are explored.

Norway is a signatory to UNCLOS and OSPAR. The Norwegian regime on abandonment and decommissioning of offshore hydrocarbon installations is codified in the Petroleum Act 1996.[52] The licence-holder of a production

---

[48] This becomes different when national law considers the connected pipelines as part of the installation; then the decommissioning rules also apply to the pipelines connected to the installation.

[49] *Roggenkamp, Redgwell & Rønne et al., supra,* note 3 at pp. 746–747.

[50] A bill for amending the Mining Act was presented in May 2020. The aim of the proposal is not only allow but also to stimulate reuse. *Kamerstukken II* 2019/20, 35 462, no. 2.

[51] *M.M. Roggenkamp, C. Redgwell & A. Rønne et al,* Energy Law in Europe, 2016, p. 1070–1072.

[52] Id. at pp. 847–849.

or a pipeline licence is under the obligation to prepare an abandonment plan (section 5-1 Petroleum Act 1996). The abandonment plan must describe the alternative actions that can be taken for the removal of pipelines and installations, as well as the environmental impact that these actions will have. There are a number of alternatives for the operator ranging from complete removal, to keeping the installations/infrastructure *in situ* for other purposes. The operator is under the obligation to elaborate on all the different alternatives and has to recommend one of them to the Ministry. The Ministry of Petroleum and Energy does not approve the abandonment, but the Ministry will select one of the presented alternatives, not necessarily the recommended option, which has to be executed.

4. LIABILITY RISKS ASSOCIATED WITH REUSING HYDROCARBON INFRASTRUCTURE

The reuse of existing hydrocarbon infrastructure presents the carbon dioxide storage operator with a number of potential liability risks. These risks are related to the storage location and the infrastructure consisting of the platforms and pipelines.

With regard to the storage location, it must be remembered that the storage location is going to be a nearly depleted oil or gas field. During the production phase of hydrocarbon production, the pressure within the subsoil reserve has decreased as the hydrocarbons are extracted. The benefit of this lower pressure is that less energy is needed to inject carbon dioxide into the reservoir. However, this decreased pressure is also detrimental for the integrity of the caprock, as the caprock may bend because of the pressure from the layers on top of it.[53] This means that the caprock decreases in strength, i.e. it may not be able to contain as much carbon dioxide in the reservoir as would be possible, or may even collapse due to the decreased pressure in the reservoir. A collapse of the caprock might cause the carbon dioxide to migrate and even reach the surface. The carbon dioxide storage operator has to present emission allowances for the carbon dioxide that is emitted into the sea and the atmosphere. It must however be remembered that a release of carbon dioxide from the storage reservoir does not mean that this carbon dioxide is emitted into the atmosphere straightaway. There might well be secondary trapping mechanisms above the storage reservoir, in the form of a secondary smaller caprock, that prevent the carbon dioxide from reaching the surface.[54]

---

[53]   *IEA Greenhouse Gas R&D Programme, supra*, note 16 at p. 30.
[54]   *W. Kuckshinrichs & J.-F. Hake* (eds.), Carbon capture, storage and use: technical, economic, environmental and societal perspectives, Springer, 2015, p. 130.

With regard to the reuse of platforms, is has to be noted that every platform is designed for a particular number of service years. This number of years is usually equal to the number of years that were considered necessary to recover the hydrocarbons located in a particular reservoir. Reusing the platform will in practice mean that the platform will remain in service longer than was foreseen in its design. Additional analysis will be necessary on whether the platform can safely stay in place for a longer period. Moreover, platforms have often been designed with a particular purpose in mind. This in practice means that the existing equipment, such as compressors and pumps, may not necessarily be suitable for the injection of carbon dioxide. When the equipment needs to be upgraded or replaced, the original design of the platform may result in spatial or weight constraints, as the placement of larger or heavier equipment has not been foreseen in the design stage.[55] This can lead to problems with the integrity of the platform and the safety of the people working on the platform.

The same liability issues more or less apply to pipelines. Pipelines have also been constructed with particular time horizons in mind. An assessment of corrosion levels and the fatigue of the pipeline materials is therefore necessary to assess the remaining lifetime of a pipeline.[56] Concerning design, it is important to note that the transport of natural gas usually takes place at lower pressure levels than the transport of carbon dioxide. For carbon dioxide in the dense phase, a pressure of 85 bar is seen as the minimum pressure needed for safe transport. Although the current offshore pipelines in the North Sea are designed for transport at pressure levels between 80 and 180 bar, this still puts them at a significant disadvantage in terms of capacity when compared to newly constructed pipelines for carbon dioxide transport with potential capacities between 200 and 300 bar.[57] Transporting carbon dioxide through a pipeline that is unable to handle high pressure due to its design or as a result of wear and tear might cause the pipeline to fracture. A leak from a pipeline causes the direct release of carbon dioxide in large quantities into the atmosphere or sea water. This entails not only climate liability risks, but also environmental liability, as a high concentration of carbon dioxide in the atmosphere or water will have an adverse effect on the direct surroundings.

The predominant types of risks are potential failing infrastructure and unsuitable storage locations. Civil liability in an offshore setting is less relevant, but the carbon dioxide storage operator still bears the environmental and climate liability. Due to the presence of secondary trapping mechanisms surrounding

---

[55]   *Gasunie Engineering B.V.*, *supra*, note 38 at pp. 7–14.
[56]   *Energy Institute*, Hazard analysis for offshore carbon capture platforms and offshore pipelines, 2013, p. 75.
[57]   *Element Energy, Pöyry Energy and British Geological Survey*, Development of a CO2 Transport and Storage Network in the North Sea, Report to the North Sea Basin Task Force, 2007, pp. 22–23.

the storage location, the escape of carbon dioxide from the storage location into the atmosphere is not a certainty. However, there is a lack of real life experience with CCS in Europe and it is therefore not possible to predict how secondary trapping mechanisms will function. The leakage of carbon dioxide from reused pipelines or valves on the reused platforms is assumed to be a bigger risk. A small leakage will primarily be relevant for climate liability and a large leakage will additionally bring environmental liability into the picture.

5. CONCLUSION

It has been shown that there are reuse possibilities for existing hydrocarbon infrastructure for CCS activities. However, there is a temporal mismatch as hydrocarbon activities, especially in the North Sea region, are declining and the associated infrastructure is being decommissioned and/or abandoned. Knowing that CCS activities will not be starting in the near future, The infrastructure has to be kept in place by either extending the existing licences or introducing a temporary operator.

Regardless of the legal solution to preserve the infrastructure, the carbon dioxide storage operator acquires the assets in the future and faces increased environmental, civil and climate liability risks. It therefore remains to be seen whether the reuse of hydrocarbon infrastructure will not create substantial liability risks for the storage operator, resulting in actually increasing the cost of CCS.

PART VII
LIABILITY, CLIMATE CHANGE AND NATURAL HAZARDS

The Role of Insurance

INSURANCE INSTRUMENTS FOR ADAPTING TO CLIMATE CHANGE

A Comparative Perspective

Stefano FANETTI

1. INTRODUCTION: PROBLEMS AND WEAKNESSES OF *EX POST* COMPENSATION MECHANISMS FOR NATURAL DISASTERS

Despite efforts to reduce greenhouse gas emissions, the climate is changing and will continue to change globally and in Europe.[1] As is well known, climate change produces an increasing number of natural disasters[2] leading to ever more victims and ever greater economic damage.[3] Much of this damage concerns houses, whose vulnerability to extreme events depends above all on their location in dangerous areas and the use of poor-quality materials in their construction.[4]

---

[1] *European Environment Agency*, Climate change, impacts and vulnerability in Europe 2016. An indicator-based report, EEA Report No. 1/2017, p. 14.

[2] In this light, the European Environment Agency underlines that "[t]he number of climate extremes ... increased between 1980 and 2013, from around 80 per year in the 1980s to 120 in the 1990s and almost 140 in the 2000s. The contrast between the increasing incidence of climate extremes and the apparently constant number of reported geophysical events has been previously used to dismiss the possibility of reporting bias" (*European Environment Agency, supra*, note 1 at p. 192).

[3] *European Commission*, Green Paper on the insurance of natural and man-made disasters, Strasbourg, 16 April 2013, COM(2013) 213 final, p. 2. According to the European Environment Agency: "climate extremes accounted for 82% of the total reported losses in the EEA member countries over the period 1980–2013, whereas geophysical events such as earthquakes and volcano eruptions are responsible for the remaining 18%"; "[t]he total reported economic losses caused by climate-related extreme events in the EEA member countries over the period 1980–2013 were almost EUR 400 billion ... The average damage has varied between EUR 7.6 billion per year in the 1980s and EUR 13.7 billion in the 2000s" (*European Environment Agency, supra*, note 1 at p. 195).

[4] On this issue e.g. *A. Revi et al.*, Urban areas, in C.B. Field et al. (eds.), Climate Change 2014: Impacts, Adaptation, and Vulnerability. Part A: Global and Sectoral Aspects. Contribution of Working Group II to the Fifth Assessment Report of the Intergovernmental Panel on Climate, Cambridge University Press, 2014, p. 535, 562.

Faced with these increasing risks, governments often do not take *ex ante* mitigation measures,[5] focusing on costly *ex post* interventions after every natural disaster.[6] This short-sighted approach reflects, however, accurate political calculus: from a short-term perspective, precautionary expenditures produce immediate costs and pass mostly unnoticed. On the contrary, *ex post* intervention offers a great opportunity for political visibility and can be used as "a stage for political campaigns";[7] thus, as Michael Faure points out, politicians "have the tendency to play Santa Claus", providing remarkable amounts of compensation for disaster-affected people.[8]

This *ex post* compensation (and particularly *ad hoc* compensation) reveals several problems. First of all, it discourages people from adopting preventive measures to mitigate the risks,[9] since they rely on government intervention.[10] Secondly, *ex post* compensation could "exacerbate governments' budget difficulties"[11] and be no longer financially sustainable. Moreover, the so-called *ex post* Santa Claus payment reveals a high degree of inefficiency (in quantification and timing) and inequity (since it is usually funded from general taxation and therefore also paid for by non-owners of real estate).[12] A related problem is the possible rise of negative distributional effects "since some victims (who probably purchased houses at low prices in flood prone areas) may free ride on other individuals (the general tax payers) who finance the *ex post* relief".[13]

---

[5]   Several preventive measures can be taken at different levels of government: keeping people away from risk-prone areas through spatial planning and development control, building flood walls, elevating dikes against sea level rise, etc. See *European Commission*, Green Paper from the Commission to the Council, the European Parliament, the European Economic and Social Committee and the Committee of the Regions – Adapting to climate change in Europe – options for EU action, Brussels, 29 June 2007, COM(2007) 354 final, p. 3; *C. Suykens et al.*, Dealing with flood damages: will prevention, mitigation, and ex post compensation provide for a resilient triangle?, Ecol. Soc. 2016 (21), http://dx.doi.org/10.5751/ ES-08592-210401.

[6]   *G. Dari-Mattiacci & M.G. Faure*, The Economics of Disaster Relief, Law & Pol'y 2015 (37), p. 180, 180.

[7]   Id. at p. 181.

[8]   *M. Faure*, The government should promote insurability of natural disasters, not play Santa Claus!, 13 December 2016, https://www.maastrichtuniversity.nl/blog/2016/12/government- should-promote-insurability-natural-disasters-not-play-santa-claus.

[9]   For example, not building in flood prone areas or "avoiding to put valuables in the basement" (*Faure, supra*, note 8).

[10]   E.g. *V. Bruggeman & M. Faure*, The Compensation for Victims of Disasters in Belgium, France, Germany and the Netherlands, Loy. Consumer L. Rev. 2019 (31), p. 259, 262.

[11]   COM(2013) 213 final, p. 12.

[12]   See the response of the insurance company UNIPOL to the public consultation promoted for the drafting of the Italian Climate Change Adaptation Strategy, https://www.minambiente.it/ sites/default/files/archivio/allegati/clima/snacc_UNIPOL.pdf.

[13]   *V. Bruggeman, M.G. Faure & K. Fiore*, The Government as Reinsurer of Catastrophe Risks?, Geneva Papers on Risk and Ins. 2010 (35), p. 369, 373.

2. ROLE OF DISASTER INSURANCE AND OBSTACLES TO ITS SPREAD

There are obviously alternatives to this *ex post* compensation mechanism. First and foremost, governments should, as already mentioned, invest more in preventive measures (even if the opportunism of politicians hinders an effective preventive approach) and, in addition, encourage the development of insurance instruments in the field of natural disasters.[14]

Indeed, on several counts, insurance is an essential "form of adaptive capacity for the impacts of climate change".[15] First, insurance allows "risk pooling within a portfolio of insurance policies" and "risk spreading through reinsurance, cat bonds or other alternative risk transfer mechanisms".[16] A disaster risk insurance mechanism may also be helpful in all phases of the risk management cycle: from identification and modelling of the risks to risk transfer and, lastly, recovery.[17] Furthermore, insurers can offer market incentives for preventive actions: if the premium is calculated in consideration of the level of risk, people would be encouraged to take measures to limit those same risks (e.g. not building new houses in risk-prone areas).[18]

However, even today, insurance markets show uneven developments across countries[19] and, including in several EU Member States, coverage for natural disasters has extremely limited penetration.[20] In this regard, the European Environment Agency (EEA) reports that only around 33 per cent of the total reported economic losses from climate extremes in the EEA member countries over the period 1980–2013 were insured.[21]

Admittedly, the improvement of a functioning disaster insurance system is anything but easy. One of the most significant problems is the underestimation of the real risk of a disaster.[22] Due to limited awareness, many individuals misjudge

---

[14] COM(2013) 213 final, p. 12. The discussion on the role of insurance in natural disaster management has been going on for many years. See e.g. *H. Kunreuther*, The Case for Comprehensive Disaster Insurance, J.L. & Econ. 1968 (11), pp. 133–163; *D.G. Friedman*, Insurance and the natural hazards, ASTIN Bull. 1972 (7), pp. 4–58.

[15] *E. Mills*, Insurance in a Climate of Change, Science 2005 (309), p. 1040, 1043.

[16] *P. Picard*, Natural Disaster Insurance and the Equity-Efficiency Trade-Off, J. Risk Ins. 2008 (75), p. 17, 18.

[17] COM(2013) 213 final, p. 6.

[18] See *Picard, supra*, note 16 at p. 18; COM(2013) 213 final, pp. 12 et seq.

[19] *M.D. Gavriletea*, Catastrophe risk management in Romania and Transylvania' specifics. Issues for national and local administrations, Econ. Res.-Ekon. Istraz. 2017 (30), p. 761, 762.

[20] COM(2013) 213 final, p. 6.

[21] *European Environment Agency, supra*, note 1 at p. 195.

[22] *H. Kunreuther*, Mitigating Disaster Losses through Insurance, J. Risk Uncertain. 1996 (12), p. 171, 175.

the likelihood of a disaster, taking an "it will not happen to me" attitude;[23] thus, they do not understand the need to invest in protective measures such as making their houses more resilient or taking out an insurance policy.[24]

Secondly, because of this underestimation of risk, people generally prefer the uncertain damage of a natural disaster to the certain damage caused by the payment of insurance premiums.[25] This may lead to so-called adverse selection, which, according to the EU Commission, can be defined as: "the phenomenon in insurance whereby groups of people who feel that they are at a higher risk will purchase insurance to a large extent, whereas those who do not perceive such a high degree of risk will not feel it is necessary to purchase insurance".[26] This phenomenon is particularly problematic in the area of disaster insurance: if only the exposed people buy insurance, the cost of the insurance will be too high and "the pool will be too small to cope with disasters, since there is no buffer from unaffected members of the pool".[27]

Thirdly, as mentioned above, *ex post* government compensation can hinder the spread of disaster insurance.

3. POSSIBLE SOLUTION TO THE LOW PENETRATION OF DISASTER INSURANCE: COMPULSORY OR SEMI-COMPULSORY SCHEMES

A practical and obvious solution to the lack of demand for disaster insurance could be the introduction of compulsory first-party insurance offering protection against natural disasters.[28] Since it is mandatory, this type of insurance is supposed to result in high penetration with a large pool of insured people.[29] In this regard, an interesting example is represented by the Romanian compulsory insurance for dwellings that was introduced in 2008.[30] Other countries (such as France) instead opted for a mandatory catastrophe extension of voluntary

---

[23]   See H. *Kunreuther*, Disaster Mitigation and Insurance: Learning from Katrina, Annals Am. Acad. Pol. & Soc. Sci. 2006 (604), p. 208, 209; M. *Faure*, In the Aftermath of the Disaster: Liability and Compensation Mechanisms as Tools to Reduce Disaster Risks, Stan. J. Int'l L. 2016 (52), p. 95, 162.

[24]   *Kunreuther, supra*, note 23 at p. 209.

[25]   *Faure, supra*, note 23 at p. 162.

[26]   COM(2013) 213 final, p. 8.

[27]   Id.

[28]   See *Faure, supra*, note 23 at p. 163.

[29]   COM(2013) 213 final, p. 8. See also: R. *Van den Bergh & M. Faure*, Compulsory Insurance of Loss to Property caused by Natural Disasters: Competition or Solidarity?, World Compet. 2006 (29), p. 25, 27.

[30]   *Gavriletea, supra*, note 19 at p. 763.

first-party insurance for property damages[31] (hence the use of the term "semi-compulsory" to define these systems[32]).

Therefore, it is worthwhile to consider the systems just mentioned to try to reveal their strengths and weaknesses.

4. AN EXAMPLE OF COMPULSORY INSURANCE: THE ROMANIAN CATASTROPHE INSURANCE SCHEME

Romania is very exposed to natural perils[33] and homeowners have been generally the most affected by the several disasters that have occurred.[34] For this reason, on 4 November 2008, the Romanian Parliament passed Law no. 260[35] that introduced mandatory insurance for dwellings, covering three basic risks arising from landslides, floods and earthquakes.[36]

In accordance with the provisions of this law, Pool Against Natural Catastrophes (PAID) was set up as an insurance-reinsurance undertaking[37] in order to manage the compulsory home insurance system.[38] More specifically, PAID is intended, as the official website clearly states: to offer a simple insurance product that is accessible to any homeowner; to ensure prompt payment of the indemnity in case of damage due to a catastrophic event; to build a strong financial reserve to financially protect Romania in the face of extreme natural phenomena; to reduce the budgetary impact of natural catastrophes on the Government of Romania, so that public resources can be devoted to the reconstruction of hospitals, schools and public infrastructures; and to support the development of the financial education of the population and the promotion of home insurance as a fundamental means of protection.[39]

---

[31]   See *O. Moréteau*, Policing the Compensation of Victims of Catastrophes: Combining Solidarity and Self Responsibility, Loy. L. Rev. 2008 (54), p. 65, 85 et seq.

[32]   *G. Turchetti, S. Cannizzo & L. Trieste*, Natural and Man-Made Disasters: Challenges and International Perspectives for Insurance, in A. de Guttry, M. Gestri & G. Venturini (eds.), International Disaster Response Law, T.M.C. Asser Press/Springer, 2012, p. 685, 700. See also: *R. Jongejan & P. Barrieu*, Insuring Large-Scale Floods in the Netherlands, Geneva Papers on Risk and Ins. 2008 (33), p. 250, 261.

[33]   *European Commission*, Insurance of weather and climate-related disaster risk: Inventory and analysis of mechanisms to support damage prevention in the EU, Final Report, August 2017, p. 135.

[34]   *Gavriletea, supra*, note 19 at p. 763.

[35]   Legea nr. 260/2008 privind asigurarea obligatorie a locuinţelor împotriva cutremurelor, alunecărilor de teren şi inundaţiilor (Law no. 260/2008 on compulsory home insurance against earthquakes, landslides and floods).

[36]   *I.M. Dragotă, A. Semenescu & A. Gherasim*, Compulsory insurance for dwellings in Romania between mitigating the impacts of natural disasters and giving rise to social inequities, Afr. J. Bus. Manage. 2012 (6), p. 177, 182.

[37]   PAID was formed by the association of 12 insurance companies and uses private capital.

[38]   See https://www.paidromania.ro/despre-noi.

[39]   Id.

So, according to the law, homeowners are obliged to purchase an insurance policy against natural disasters (PAD). Depending on the quality of the building, houses are divided into two categories (class A and class B[40]), with different premiums and insured amounts.[41] The maximum amount of coverage is €20,000 for class A houses and €10,000 for class B houses, while the annual premium to be paid is €20 for class A houses and €10 for class B houses.

Therefore, the premium and the insured sum are exclusively based on the type of dwelling, not taking into account the hazard probability and the exposure, which significantly vary from region to region.[42] Several scholars object to the fact that the premium and the insured amount do not reflect the level of risk since this aspect does not encourage risk prevention.[43]

Another important issue is that the insured sum does not consider the real value of the houses. For example, the owner of a high-value house in Bucharest can receive a maximum of €20,000, which, in the event of total loss or considerable damage, could cover only a part of the damage; instead, in the case of a rural class B dwelling, the insured amount could exceed the real value of the property.[44]

In addition to these inequities, the Romanian mandatory insurance shows a (quite unbelievable) problem of low penetration:[45] according to official data provided by PAID, the penetration rate at 30 April 2020 was less than 20 per cent,[46] with higher rates in urban areas than in rural ones.[47] These data seem even more absurd if we consider that if the natural or legal persons do not insure their dwellings, they will not receive any compensation from the state or local budget for damage caused by one of the types of natural disaster considered by Law no. 260/2008.[48]

---

[40] "A type means the construction whose frame structure is of reinforced concrete, metal or wood, or whose exterior walls are of stone, baked brick, wood or of any other materials resulting from a heat and/or chemical treatment; B type means the construction whose exterior walls are of un-baked brick or of any other material that has not been exposed to a heat and/or chemical treatment" (Article 2, let. c, of Law no. 260/2008, as amended by Law no. 191/2015. Translation from https://asfromania.ro/files/ENGLEZA/legislation/insurance/Legea%20260_2008%20ENFinal.pdf).

[41] *Gavriletea, supra*, note 19 at p. 763.

[42] See *Dragotă, Semenescu & Gherasim, supra*, note 36 at p. 191; S. *Hanger et al.*, Insurance, Public Assistance, and Household Flood Risk Reduction: A Comparative Study of Austria, England, and Romania, Risk Anal. 2018 (38), p. 680, 683.

[43] E.g. *Dragotă, Semenescu & Gherasim, supra*, note 36 at p. 191.

[44] Id. at p. 183.

[45] See *Gavriletea, supra*, note 19 at pp. 763 et seq.; *Hanger et al., supra*, note 42 at p. 683; *European Commission, supra*, note 33 at p. 135.

[46] The exact percentage is 19.27 per cent. See https://paidromania.ro/harta-pad.

[47] *Hanger et al., supra*, note 42 at p. 683.

[48] See https://paidromania.ro/produse-si-servicii.

These low results may be caused by several factors. First, until 2015, PAD was mandatory unless homeowners had facultative insurance.[49] In 2015, an amendment to Law no. 260/2008 was passed to overcome this problem: according to the new paragraph 9 of Article 3, "[i]nsurance-reinsurance undertakings authorised to cover catastrophe risks may not conclude voluntary insurance for a dwelling for which no PAD compulsory insurance has been previously concluded".[50]

A further problem could be related to the fact that people in rural areas often cannot prove ownership of their home, which is a prerequisite for obtaining insurance coverage.[51]

Other compelling reasons for the low performance may be the lack of clear information on the policy (and especially on how to buy it) and the lack of trust in insurers.[52]

Finally, yet importantly, a role in this failure is certainly played by the ambiguous and passive behaviour of local public administrations.[53] In this regard, Law no. 260/2008 provides that non-compliance with the obligation to insure property shall be sanctioned with a fine of 100–500 lei (approx. €20–100) and entrusts the control to mayors (or their representatives). Unfortunately, public authorities do not carry out these tasks for many reasons, such as the lack of personnel to handle the fines and the concern of local politicians of losing electoral consensus.[54]

5. A WELL-KNOWN SEMI-COMPULSORY SCHEME: THE FRENCH CatNat SYSTEM

Another significant model in the field of natural disaster insurance is the French one (the so-called French CatNat system), which is well-known and internationally appreciated.[55]

---

[49]   *European Commission, supra*, note 33 at p. 135.
For more details see also *D.C. Dănuleţiu & A.E. Dănuleţiu*, Natural disasters effects' financing through insurance in Romania (2010–2015), Ann. Univ. Petroşani Econ. 2016 (16), p. 83, 88; *European Commission*, Study on consumers' decision making in insurance services: a behavioural economics perspective, Final Report – Country fiches, May 2017, p. 191.

[50]   This provision is part of the wider revision of the law carried out in 2015. See Legea nr. 191/2015 pentru modificarea şi completarea Legii nr. 260/2008 privind asigurarea obligatorie a locuinţelor împotriva cutremurelor, alunecărilor de teren şi inundaţiilor (Law no. 191/2015 for the amendment and completion of Law no. 260/2008 on compulsory home insurance against earthquakes, landslides and floods).

[51]   *Hanger et al., supra*, note 42 at pp. 683 et seq.

[52]   *I. Armas, R. Ionescu & C. Nenciu Posner*, Flood risk perception along the Lower Danube river, Romania, Nat Hazards 2015 (79), p. 1913, 1922.

[53]   *Gavriletea, supra*, note 19 at p. 770.

[54]   Id. at pp. 770 et seq.

[55]   *Bruggeman & Faure, supra*, note 10 at p. 299. As further proof of the fact that the French scheme is praised, Belgium has quite recently (2005) followed this model, adopting a

In France, the natural catastrophes coverage system was introduced several years ago by Act no. 82-600 of 13 July 1982.[56] From a historical point of view, this act followed the dramatic events related to the devastating floods that occurred in 1981 in the Saone and Rhone valleys:[57] these events showed the inadequacy of the *ex post* case-by-case compensation used at the time.[58]

In more detail, the first feature of the current French system is the provision of a mandatory extension of the voluntary first-party insurance policies that cover damage against property[59] (or motorised land vehicles) to include coverage of the consequences of natural disasters. Thus, catastrophe insurance has to be bundled with ordinary house or car insurance.[60]

In other words, there is no generalised obligation to insure disaster risks, but if voluntary insurance against damage to property has been taken out, it is obligatory to extend it to cover natural catastrophes.[61]

However, even though the property insurance is not mandatory, it is widespread, reaching a penetration rate of around 100 per cent and, consequently, all households have a right to compensation for the damages due to natural disasters.[62]

Act no. 82-600 does not offer a definition of the term "natural catastrophes", but the current version of the Law (as codified in the Insurance Code) states that the effects of natural catastrophes are defined as:[63] "[n]on-insurable direct material damage the determining cause of which was the abnormal intensity of

---

      mandatory extension system that, however, presents some peculiarities compared to the French model. See, for example, *Faure, supra*, note 23 at p. 164.

[56]   Loi no. 82-600 du 13 juillet 1982 relative à l'indemnisation des victimes de catastrophes naturelles. This act is presently codified at: Code des assurances, Articles L125-1 et seq.

[57]   *Consorcio de Compensación de Seguros*, Natural Catastrophes Insurance Cover. A Diversity of Systems, 2008, p. 61, https://www.consorseguros.es/web/documents/10184/48069/CCS_ Natural_Catastrophes_Insurance_Cover.pdf/d7cf67cc-9591-476b-87d9-728e6a57ca60.

[58]   *Suykens et al., supra*, note 5.

[59]   As Faure explains, "typical example of such a policy is the so-called *multi-risque habitation*, covering most risks with respect to real estate and movables within the house" (e.g. fire, theft, etc.). See *Faure, supra*, note 23 at p. 164.

[60]   *V. Bruggeman, M. Faure & T. Heldt*, Insurance Against Catastrophe: Government Stimulation of Insurance Markets for Catastrophic Events, Duke Envtl. L. & Pol'y F. 2012 (23), p. 185, 194.

[61]   *Bruggeman & Faure, supra*, note 10 at p. 299; *Moréteau, supra*, note 31 at p. 85.

[62]   *European Commission, supra*, note 33 at p. 56. These data refer only to metropolitan France (the mainland and Corsica) and not to France's overseas *départements*. In this regard, Calvet and Grislain-Letrémy note that: "France's overseas *départements* (DOMs) are more exposed to natural hazards than metropolitan France (mainland + Corsica). Yet only 52% of DOM households have taken out insurance for their main residence – which includes mandatory coverage of natural disasters – compared with 99% of households in metropolitan France". See *L. Calvet & C. Grislain-Letrémy*, Home insurance in overseas départements: a low proportion of households insured, English article abstract, https://insee.fr/en/ statistiques/1377347?sommaire=1377358&q=household+insurance (original article: *L. Calvet & C. Grislain-Letrémy*, L'assurance habitation dans les départements d'Outre-mer : une faible souscription, Écon. Stat. 2011 (447), pp. 57–70).

[63]   *V. Bruggeman*, Compensating Catastrophe Victims. A Comparative Law and Economics Approach, Wolters Kluwer, 2010, p. 304.

a natural agent, when normal measures taken to avoid such damage have been unable to prevent the occurrence thereof or could not be taken".[64]

Thus, in order to be considered a natural catastrophe, the phenomenon must not be caused by human activity, should be abnormal (that is, unusual due to the exceptional intensity or duration of the event) and should be "irresistible" in the sense that the consequences cannot be avoided with normal care.[65]

A controversial aspect of the definition is that the damage has to be "uninsurable": the use of this paradoxical word has been criticised since the risk must be mandatorily insured.[66] However, according to Bruggeman and Faure:

> [t]he paradox ... disappears if one realizes that compulsory insurance allows for a sufficient spreading of risks and functions as a remedy to adverse selection, which may make natural disasters uninsurable. By imposing a duty to insure, the law transforms an uninsurable risk into an insurable one. Compulsory insurance may enable the private insurance market to cover damage caused by natural disasters in geographically limited areas.[67]

Nevertheless, there is not an exhaustive list of perils[68] covered by the mandatory extension. This absence and the open notion of "uninsurable damages due to abnormal intensity of natural hazards" could leave too much room for a subjective interpretation.[69]

The coverage for catastrophic loss is funded by an additional premium surcharge that is fixed by state decree and is currently equal to 12 per cent[70] of the property insurance premium.[71] The application of the same additional-premium

---

[64] Code des assurances, Article L125-1. Translation from https://www.legifrance.gouv.fr/ content/location/1744. As Bruggeman underlines: "Act No. 92-665 of 16 Jul. 1992 Adapting the Insurance and Credit Legislation to the Single European Market ... introduced the idea of 'uninsurable damage', which had been implicit up until then, in order to prevent the Cat.Nat. scheme from being forced to cover risks which are insurable in the normal way". See *Bruggeman, supra*, note 63 at p. 304.

[65] M. Cannarsa, F. Lafay & O. Moréteau, France, in M. Faure & T. Hartlief (eds.), *Financial Compensation for Victims of Catastrophes. A Comparative Legal Approach*, Springer, 2006, p. 81, 86.

[66] Id.

[67] *Bruggeman & Faure, supra*, note 10 at pp. 299 et seq.

[68] To give some examples: floods, mudslides, landslides, earthquakes, etc. See *Cannarsa, Lafay & Moréteau, supra*, note 65 at pp. 86 et seq.

[69] *European Commission, supra*, note 33 at p. 56. In fact, however, "there is likely to be a tendency to err on the side of generosity rather than caution". See id. at pp. 56 et seq.

[70] For motorised land vehicles the additional premium is equal to "6% of premiums for fire and theft insurance (or, failing this, 0.50% of the property insurance premium)". See *Caisse Centrale de Réassurance*, Natural disasters compensation scheme, 3 February 2015, https:// www.ccr.fr/en/-/indemnisation-des-catastrophes-naturelles-en-france.

[71] The average addition for the catastrophe coverage is approximately equal to €25–30 (*European Commission, supra*, note 33 at p. 56).

insurance rates to all reflects the constitutional principle of national solidarity in the face of disasters.[72] However, this flat premium does not take into account the level of exposure to natural disasters and the level of loss prevention and could exacerbate moral hazard.[73]

In addition to the principle of solidarity, the French CatNat system is inspired by the principle of responsibility, which should be ensured by the provision of deductibles and risk prevention plans.[74] The deductibles are mandatory, non-redeemable – they cannot be "bought back" – and set by a state decree.[75] Nevertheless, since 2001, a sliding scale has been established to adjust deductibles (except for land motor vehicles) in communes without a risk prevention plan. The scale is a sort of multiplicative coefficient (from 1 to 4) that is applied to the deductibles, taking into consideration the number of government declarations of disaster concerning the same type of peril.[76] This is, of course, a way to incentivise municipalities to introduce risk prevention plans and, in a broader sense, to strengthen the relationship between financial compensation and risk prevention.[77] However, this link seems quite weak precisely because the

---

[72] This principle was set in the Preamble of the French Constitution of 1946 (which remains part of the current constitutional framework): "The Nation proclaims the solidarity and equality of all French people in bearing the burden resulting from national calamities". See *Consorcio de Compensación de Seguros, supra*, note 57 at p. 61; *Caisse Centrale de Réassurance, supra*, note 70; *Moréteau, supra*, note 31 at p. 81.

[73] *European Commission, supra*, note 33 at p. 57. According to the EU Commission moral hazard "corresponds to a behavioural change of the individual who, once insured, has fewer incentives to prevent a loss from occurring and, therefore, the negative impacts of the insured event may be more likely to arise". See COM(2013) 213 final, p. 15.

[74] *Caisse Centrale de Réassurance, supra*, note 70.

[75] Id. The deductibles are currently fixed as follows: "a) For land motor vehicles, property not for professional use, and property for domestic use, the deductible is €380, irrespective of the terms in this respect in the base contract. If the damage is the result of subsidence, the deductible reaches €1,520, and in the case of vehicles for professional use, the rate to be applied is the one that is stipulated in the base policy if this is higher than the legal deductible. b) In the case of property for professional, commercial, farm or craft use, or properties owned by local communities, 10% of direct damage, per establishment and event, with a minimum of €1,140. If the damage was the result of subsidence, the deductible will reach €3,050, or the amount provided for in the base policy if higher. c) For business interruption, the deductible is 3 days worked, with a minimum of €1,140, with application of that stipulated in the base contract if the amount of this deductible is more" (*Consorcio de Compensación de Seguros, supra*, note 57 at p. 65).

[76] See *Caisse Centrale de Réassurance, supra*, note 70; *Bruggeman, supra*, note 63 at pp. 307 et seq. The sliding scale is formulated as follows: 1–2 declarations of disaster: basic deductible; 3 declarations of disaster: basic deductible multiplied by 2; 4 declarations of disaster: basic deductible multiplied by 3; 5 declarations of disaster: basic deductible multiplied by 4. It is important to note that only the government declarations issued during the five years that precedes the "new" declaration of natural catastrophe must be taken into account (*Bruggeman, supra*, note 63 at p. 307). This fact could limit their potential effectiveness (*European Commission, supra*, note 33 at p. 57).

[77] *Bruggeman & Faure, supra*, note 10 at p. 300.

deductibles are adjusted depending on the risk only if there is no risk prevention plan in the municipality.[78]

Another fundamental keystone of the French regime is the presence of a state reinsurance company, the Caisse Centrale de Réassurance (CCR).[79] It's important to say that CCR does not have a monopoly on the catastrophe reinsurance market[80] and insurers have the choice to contract with private reinsurance companies.[81] Nevertheless, the preferred option is to contract with CCR because the reinsurance premiums are low and there is unlimited coverage that is guaranteed by the French government in the event that CCR's resources are exhausted.[82] The contract between insurer and CCR is basically a quota-share contract: insurers generally cede half of the premium (levied to provide coverage of natural disasters) to CCR, which consequently covers half of the damage insured and pays for it.[83] So far, the system has worked well and has proven to be capable of absorbing the losses caused by natural disasters: as evidence of this, the governmental guarantee has had to be called upon only once since 1982.[84]

Lastly, it is worth mentioning that there are two conditions that must be satisfied in order to trigger the compensation scheme. The first obvious condition (which could be defined as being "of a private nature") is that the damaged property has to be covered by a property insurance policy.[85] In addition, there is a condition "of a public nature": the government must first declare (by an inter-ministerial decree published in the Official Journal) that a certain incident is a natural disaster before the insurer is bound to compensate for damage.[86] As a result, whenever a disaster occurs, the government is put under pressure by the victims and local authorities.[87] Thus, "Ministers, and even the President of the Republic, will promptly appear on the scene and promise an immediate declaration, so that the victims may be quickly compensated".[88]

---

[78] *Suykens et al., supra,* note 5.
[79] *Bruggeman, supra,* note 63 at p. 309.
[80] *Caisse Centrale de Réassurance, supra,* note 70.
[81] J. McAneney et al., Government-sponsored natural disaster insurance pools: A view from down-under, Int. J. Disast. Risk Re. 2016 (15), p. 1, 4.
[82] *Bruggeman, supra,* note 63 at p. 309.
[83] *Moréteau, supra,* note 31 at p. 89; *McAneney et al., supra,* note 81 at p. 4. Insurers can also conclude a stop-loss contracts in which "the reinsurance company covers all claims that exceed an agreed multiple of annual premium income". However, this type of contract is reserved to "those insurance companies who also buy quota-share contracts from the CCR with a minimum participation of 40%" (*Bruggeman, supra,* note 63 at pp. 309 et seq.).
[84] European Commission, *supra,* note 33 at p. 57. For further details, see C. Quinto, Insurance Systems in Times of Climate Change. Insurance of Buildings Against Natural Hazards, Springer, 2012, pp. 39 et seq.; *Bruggeman, Faure & Fiore, supra,* note 13 at pp. 380 et seq.
[85] *Caisse Centrale de Réassurance, supra,* note 70.
[86] See *Caisse Centrale de Réassurance, supra,* note 70; *Faure, supra,* note 23 at p. 164. Of course, a causal link must exist between the declared natural disaster and the sustained damage.
[87] *Moréteau, supra,* note 31 at p. 86.
[88] Id.

What emerges from the analysis just carried out is that the French CatNat system has worked well overall, revealing a satisfactory level of stability.[89] In this regard, it must be acknowledged that the legislative amendments that have occurred over the years cannot be considered real reforms, having simply made useful adjustments to the original structure of the Act, without however calling it into question or overturning it.[90]

However, in recent years there have been some attempts to introduce deeper changes. First of all, there is the bill deposited by the Government in the Senate on 3 April 2012.[91] This proposal, which has not been implemented, should have, *inter alia*, intervened on two aforementioned critical aspects of the legislation: the absence of a list of phenomena eligible for the compensation scheme (which can, in fact, give rise to application uncertainties and unfairly differentiated treatments) and the weakness of the preventive aspect of the system (partly due to the fact that the additional-premium insurance rate, using the logic of national solidarity, is uniform throughout the country, without taking into account the level of exposure to natural disasters or the efforts made by the policyholders to reduce their vulnerability).[92] On this last aspect, the bill proposed introducing a controlled modulation of the additional premium for natural disaster coverage, reserving, however, this modulation to subjects that, according to the government, have the tools to strengthen prevention: specifically, local communities and businesses of a certain size.[93]

The failure of this initiative did not, however, stop the discussion on the revision of the CatNat system.[94] In this regard, the President of the Republic, Emmanuel Macron, announced on 30 September 2018 (during a visit to Saint-Martin in the French Antilles a year after the devastation of Hurricane Irma) a reform of the CatNat system, though without providing precise guidelines, with the aim of ensuring a more incentivising system, "quicker indemnity payments and more generous insurance cover for overseas territories".[95]

---

[89] D. Cerini, Green Insurance e cambiamenti climatici, in D. Cerini (ed.), Assicurazioni e appalti: etica, legalità, responsabilità, Giappichelli, 2016, p. 159, 177.

[90] Id. at p. 171.

[91] Projet de loi portant réforme du régime d'indemnisation des catastrophes naturelles (enregistré à la Présidence du Sénat le 3 avril 2012).

[92] Cerini, supra, note 89 at p. 178.

[93] In this light, the Impact Assessment accompanying the bill underlines that, for these subjects, the modulation could have had a real effect on the implementation of adequate prevention measures: the reduction of the premium would have made it possible to offset the cost of the preventive measures to be implemented. See Projet de loi portant réforme du régime d'indemnisation des catastrophes naturelles, Étude d'Impact, March 2012, p. 33.

[94] See, in this regard: Livre blanc "Pour une meilleure prévention et protection contre les aléas naturels" (White Paper "For better prevention and protection against natural hazards"), presented in 2015 by the Fédération Française de l'Assurance.

[95] See Global Insurance Law Connect, Risk Radar report: July 2019, p. 13, https://www.globalinsurancelaw.com/wp-content/uploads/2019/06/GILC-Risk-Radar-2019-Digital.pdf.

This project, in Macron's words, was expected to be unveiled by summer 2019. This, however, did not happen.[96] In the meantime, Nicole Bonnefoy and other members of the French Senate submitted a bill on the reform of the natural disaster regime,[97] which was unanimously adopted in the Senate on 15 January 2020.[98] The amendments introduced by the bill are aimed at ensuring a fairer treatment of insured persons – reinforcing their right and the amount of compensation to which they are entitled – and offering incentives for taking preventive measures.[99] More specifically, among the major changes, the bill amends the scheme "in order to improve the operation and transparency of the procedure for recognising a state of natural disaster" and includes "a tax credit allowing private owners of property to deduct from their income 50% of the costs of reinforcing their property against natural disasters".[100] The bill, sent to the National Assembly, is however far from being definitively approved.[101]

6. ITALY: LOW PENETRATION OF DISASTER INSURANCE AND OPPOSITION TO MANDATORY INSURANCE

Among OECD countries, Italy, along with Japan and the United States, has been "most affected by large-scale disruptive events over the past 40 years".[102] These events – not only earthquakes, but also climate-related extreme events such as floods – are responsible for annual losses approximately equal to 0.2 per cent of the national gross domestic product.[103]

These premises should certainly invite a serious reflection at the political level about the introduction of an insurance scheme in line with those just analysed. Unfortunately, the discussion only takes place when tragic catastrophes occur.[104]

---

[96] Id.

[97] Proposition de loi visant à réformer le régime des catastrophes naturelles (enregistré à la Présidence du Sénat le 27 novembre 2019).

[98] The legislative dossier is available at the following link http://www.senat.fr/dossier-legislatif/ppl19-154.html.

[99] *Global Insurance Law Connect*, Risk Radar report: April 2020, p. 17, https://www.globalinsurancelaw.com/wp-content/uploads/2020/04/GILC-Risk-Radar-2020-Digital-Final.pdf.

[100] Id.

[101] See https://www.catnat.net/gestion-des-risques/reglementation/veille-reglementaire/27253-la-reforme-du-regime-d-indemnisation-des-catastrophes-naturelles-avance.

[102] *OECD*, Boosting Resilience through Innovative Risk Governance, OECD Publishing, 2014, p. 29.

[103] *OECD*, Disaster Risk Assessment and Risk Financing. A G20/OECD methodological framework, 2012, p. 13, at https://www.oecd.org/gov/risk/G20disasterriskmanagement.pdf.

[104] *D. Porrini*, L'assicurazione sui disastri naturali: motivi della scarsa diffusione e soluzioni di politica economica, Politica Economica 2010 (26), p. 123, 123.

As a matter of fact, starting from the 1990s, timid attempts to introduce compulsory (or semi-compulsory) insurance systems have taken place, but these proposals have never become law.[105] Indeed, it is a slippery slope for politicians: whenever the topic is discussed, opponents define compulsory disaster insurance as a "tax"[106] or even "an abdication by the State of its duty to protect its territory and citizens".[107]

This negative attitude towards the introduction of compulsory disaster insurance could be due to the fact that the citizens have very low awareness of the problem and rely on the intervention of the public authorities.

Almost certainly, these issues also explain the low penetration of voluntary disaster insurance among households. In this light, the data provided by ANIA (the Italian National Association of Insurance Companies) highlight that 91.5 per cent of voluntary fire insurance policies do not extend to natural catastrophes.[108] These data also show that there are only around 1 million residential units with catastrophe risk coverage (3.2 per cent of the total number of dwellings).[109]

Nonetheless, if we compare this value with that of 2009, we can observe a 30-fold increase in coverage, which could indicate a growing awareness of the importance of insuring against these risks.[110] This positive trend is probably influenced by the recent introduction of two forms of tax relief:[111] a tax deduction equal to 19 per cent of the insurance premium for coverage against calamitous events taken out on residential properties and the exemption of these policies from the insurance tax (equal to 22.25 per cent).[112]

However, it should be noted that the distribution of catastrophe extensions is very uneven in Italy: thus, in some cities in northern Italy (Trento, Mantua and Brescia) the percentage of dwellings insured against catastrophes exceeds 7 per cent, while in southern Italy the percentage is approximately 1 per cent.[113]

Despite these quite encouraging data, recent surveys commissioned by ANIA show that there is still much to do in relation to risk awareness: about 83 per cent of Italian families do not believe or do not know that they are exposed

---

[105] See *F.T. Gizzi, M.R. Potenza & C. Zotta*, The Insurance Market of Natural Hazards for Residential Properties in Italy, Open J. Earthquake Res. 2016 (5), p. 35, 36; *Porrini, supra*, note 104 at pp. 126 et seq.; *Cerini, supra*, note 89 at pp. 184 et seq.

[106] See e.g. https://quifinanza.it/soldi/rc-casa-polizza-obbligatoria-contro-calamita-naturali-costi-polemiche/2052/.

[107] *S. Settis*, Una ferita per la nostra storia, La Repubblica, 5 May 2012, p. 1, 11.

[108] This extension can concern floods, earthquakes or both risks. See *ANIA*, Assicurazione Italiana 2018–2019, 2019, p. 242, https://www.ania.it/documents/35135/126701/LAssicurazione-Italiana-2018-2019.pdf/6975f9f6-77a4-985b-bcda-8fe835c55eee?t=1575543865117.

[109] The data are updated to 31 March 2019. See *ANIA, supra*, note 108 at p. 243.

[110] Id.

[111] Id.

[112] See Legge 27 dicembre 2017, no. 205 "Bilancio di previsione dello Stato per l'anno finanziario 2018 e bilancio pluriennale per il triennio 2018–2020", Art. 1 (768–770).

[113] See *ANIA, supra*, note 108 at p. 244.

to catastrophe risk.[114] In this light, Salvati et al. conducted a specific analysis of the perception of landslide and flood risk in Italy.[115] Not surprisingly, the surveys show that Italian people feel themselves more exposed to technological risks (e.g. environmental pollution) than to natural risks.[116] More significantly, among the natural risks, people consider that their exposure to earthquakes is higher than their exposure to floods and landslides.[117] The poor awareness of disaster risk is therefore even greater with reference to climate extremes.

Another previously mentioned problem is the widespread dependency culture: when a natural disaster occurs, Italians generally expect state intervention and aid.[118] This behaviour has very deep historical roots.[119] As Monti and Chiaves candidly explain:

> [t]he traditional Italian idea of State, which developed in the last three centuries and especially after World War II (State based on the principle of solidarity, fully recognized in art. 2 of the Italian Constitution), brings people to unconsciously rely upon the State for any unexpected, unaffordable, unbearable matters, which implies that persons expect Government intervention as a right and demand full restoration of damages whenever a disaster occurs.[120]

This mentality is also persistent because many people think that the state has a sort of obligation to intervene to repay (totally or partially) the damage to private houses due to a natural disaster.[121] Yet in Italy there is no law that imposes on the state a general obligation to compensate these damages.[122]

However, this widespread misunderstanding can be explained by looking at the usual reaction of the state after a disaster, which is, of course, *ex post*

---

[114] ANIA, Assicurazione Italiana 2017–2018, 2018, p. 245, https://www.ania.it/documents/35135/126701/LASSICURAZIONE-ITALIANA-2017-2018.pdf/5b2219b5-ce05-076e-6bfa-ba700ce3561a?t=1575543855675. The analysis even shows that in some cases people who think they are insured are not insured. This is probably due to the fact that insurance contracts are often signed by the building managers and the residents in an apartment block do not know precisely the contractual clauses (id. at p. 244).

[115] P. Salvati et al., Perception of flood and landslide risk in Italy: a preliminary analysis, Nat. Haz. Earth Syst. Sci. 2014 (14), pp. 2589–2603.

[116] Id. at p. 2601.

[117] Id.

[118] A. Monti & F.A. Chiaves, Italy, in M. Faure & T. Hartlief (eds.), Financial Compensation for Victims of Catastrophes. A Comparative Legal Approach, Springer, 2006, p. 145, 146.

[119] Gizzi, Potenza & Zotta, supra, note 105 at p. 45.

[120] Monti & Chiaves, supra, note 118 at p. 146. According to Gizzi, Potenza and Zotta, this mentality has also religious reasons. In particular, the principle of solidarity has been well developed since the end of the 19th century in the Social Doctrine of the Church (Gizzi, Potenza & Zotta, supra, note 105 at p. 45).

[121] See ANIA, supra, note 114 at p. 244. In particular, the ANIA's analysis show that 46 per cent of Italian citizens think that the state has this duty. This percentage rises to 54 per cent if we consider people who believe they live in areas of high catastrophe risk.

[122] Porrini, supra, note 104 at p. 123.

compensation provided through an *ad hoc* measure.[123] This practice has rarely been questioned by the entire political class, worried about losing popularity, and has instead been exploited to obtain significant political recognition. This is especially true in southern Italy, which has always been plagued by significant economic and social problems and by a strong economic disparity with the north of the country.[124] As Gizzi, Potenza and Zotta put it, "[i]n this context, any of these *ex-post* aids can be viewed by people as being 'the right chance' to solve the atavist question and politicians could benefit from such community's hope".[125]

Therefore, these elements, on the one hand, explain the persistently low demand for insurance against catastrophe risk and, on the other hand, shape the debate on this issue, complicating the possible identification of an insurance scheme to be applied on a national scale.[126] Despite this, scholars, economists and experts in the field continue to insist on the need for structural choices on the subject, especially considering that the economic sustainability of *ex post* interventions will be increasingly challenged by the need to contain public spending;[127] moreover, they underline that this type of intervention has shown serious inefficiencies and inequities, often turning into indiscriminate all-round distribution under the Italian traditional "clientelistic approach" and very long timescales.[128]

So, what can be done? Certainly, the forms of tax relief introduced for those who take out insurance against calamitous events represent a significant first step, even if they will not definitely lead to the attainment of a high penetration of insurance against natural disasters.

If we look at the two schemes analysed above, the Romanian system appears hard to replicate in Italy: beyond the problems of effectiveness (which occur in Romania), it seems particularly difficult to oblige Italian citizens to purchase specific insurance for the coverage of natural disaster risks. Past experiences seem to suggest that such a proposal could turn into a political firestorm, with strong protests against the introduction of a new "unfair tax".

Probably a "softer" approach would be preferable.[129] Indeed, the solution proposed by many would be to follow the French model, providing a mandatory extension of fire insurance, a similar reinsurance system and, in any case,

---

[123] S. *Paleari*, Disaster risk insurance: A comparison of national schemes in the EU-28, Int. J. Disast. Risk Re. 2019 (35), Article 101059 at p. 7.

[124] *Gizzi, Potenza & Zotta, supra*, note 105 at p. 47.

[125] Id.

[126] Id.

[127] E.g. *L. Buzzacchi & M. Pagnini*, Terremoti: intervento pubblico e/o assicurazione privata, Cons. dir. merc. 2012 (3), p. 74, 74.

[128] In this regard, see, for example, https://www.intermediachannel.it/2017/10/13/konsumer-italia-per-le-catastrofi-naturali-agire-subito-su-prevenzione-e-coperture-assicurative/.

[129] In this light, see *Cerini, supra*, note 89 at pp. 181 et seq.

state backing.[130] The latter is a key element: the adoption of the French model would involve, in any circumstance, the state acting as guarantor in the event of exceptional events;[131] as illustrated above, "this is of course routine in Italy in case of disasters, hence it should be easily achieved as a form of continuity with the past".[132]

However, even this option would not result in a level of disaster coverage comparable to France since in Italy only 46 per cent of housing units have an insurance policy against fire risk.[133] In addition, the data show a significant difference in penetration rates among the various Italian regions (with much higher percentages in northern Italy[134]) and, for obvious reasons, do not take into account the illegally constructed buildings that are widespread in some regions (especially in southern Italy).

Regardless of regional differences, the low penetration of this property insurance can be explained only partially by the financial difficulties that afflict many Italian families and individuals. Indeed, a crucial factor concerns the limited insurance culture (with poor knowledge of insurance, which is considered to be more an investment – or rather an expense – than an instrument providing protection against possible eventualities).[135]

7. CONCLUDING REMARKS

The increase in the number of catastrophes due to climate change requires a policy change that goes beyond the inefficient and unsustainable *ex post* compensation system to focus on the adoption of *ex ante* mitigation measures and, above all, on the control of development in risk-prone areas.[136] This obviously does not mean that the government should not act after a disaster and, in this sense, the literature that criticises *ex post* intervention does not object "to the government providing shelter and immediate help in the aftermath of a disaster".[137]

---

[130] *Monti & Chiaves, supra*, note 118 at p. 184.
[131] Id. See also: *Gizzi, Potenza & Zotta, supra*, note 105 at p. 56.
[132] *Monti & Chiaves, supra*, note 118 at p. 184.
[133] See *ANIA, supra*, note 108 at p. 242. These data taking into account not only single-risk policies (fire), but also other typology of insurance such as multi-risk policies (that bundle several risks such as fire, theft and civil liability) and the so-called "*polizza globale fabbricati*" (related to apartment buildings).
[134] For example, Biella, Genoa, Milan and Trieste (northern Italy) exceed 80 per cent of residential units covered against fire risk, while Agrigento and Crotone (southern Italy) are still less than 8 per cent (*ANIA, supra*, note 108 at p. 244).
[135] G. Ursino, La sicurezza resta un optional, Il Sole 24 ore, 11 February 2012, https://st.ilsole24ore.com/art/finanza-e-mercati/2012-02-16/sicurezza-resta-optional-190729.shtml?uuid=AaZjxzsE.
[136] COM(2013) 213 final, p. 12.
[137] *Dari-Mattiacci & Faure, supra*, note 6 at p. 202.

However, it is necessary to distinguish between immediate relief in the aftermath of natural disasters and post-disaster recovery.[138]

This last aspect should not be addressed with the obsolete *ex post* compensation methods that have revealed inefficiencies and inequities, as well as discouraging people from taking preventive actions to limit the risks to which they are exposed. Rather, the taking out of insurance against natural disasters should be promoted, perhaps with the introduction of compulsory or semi-compulsory insurance schemes, with the state as the guarantor of last resort. In this sense, the success of the French model for the management of natural disasters shows that it is possible to develop a similar solution that is able to face the challenges of most, if not all, natural disasters.[139]

However, as demonstrated by the unsuccessful attempts to introduce mandatory insurance for natural disasters in Italy and in other countries,[140] these efficient solutions are not often adopted since politicians do not want to lose the consensus, exposing "households to the payment of premiums in a time of financial crisis",[141] and, above all, they do not want to give up the formidable electoral mechanism of *ex post* compensation.[142] This is also the reason why many governments underinvest in *ex ante* disaster prevention, since, unlike *ex post* compensation, preventive policies do not contribute to increasing electoral consensus.[143]

It would take a radical change of mindset to overcome this dependency culture that characterises different countries, including Italy. Nevertheless, this operation requires public administrations and insurance companies to actively invest in financial and insurance education to shift the attention of citizens from the price to the value of insurance as a fundamental tool for managing and mitigating risks, including those related to natural disasters.

Without an adequate insurance culture, attempts to promote compulsory insurance will always be opposed by the population; without knowledge and trust in the insurance instrument, even the introduction of a compulsory insurance scheme could lead to a substantial failure, as the case of Romania shows.

---

[138] Id.
[139] *Bruggeman & Faure, supra,* note 10 at p. 369.
[140] Id. at pp. 368 et seq.
[141] Id.
[142] *Faure, supra,* note 8.
[143] Id.

MULTI-COUNTRY POOLING SCHEMES FOR THE FINANCING AND TRANSFER OF CLIMATE-RELATED DISASTER RISK

A Comparative Overview

Alberto Monti

1. INTRODUCTION

The impacts of climate change and the increasing loss and damage resulting from weather-related extreme events continue to pose critical challenges to governments across the world.[1]

At sovereign level and from a risk governance perspective, dealing with climate change not only requires a proper scientific understanding and an accurate knowledge of the complex phenomena that are occurring, but it also requires the careful design and implementation of a sophisticated financial management strategy to cope with the potentially overwhelming damaging effects of changing climate patterns.[2]

The economic and financial dimensions of climate-related risks are indeed crucial, as the financial capacity to absorb and recover from losses is now recognised as a key component of disaster resilience and a pre-condition for development and growth.[3]

In this field, the peculiar features of the risk do not allow for a simple and straightforward application of standard risk-transfer and risk-financing tools, such as traditional insurance, and require new and innovative approaches, especially for the most vulnerable economies.

---

[1] *R. Mechler, L.M. Bouwer, T. Schinko, S. Surminski & J. Linnerooth-Bayer* (eds.), Loss and Damage from Climate Change: Concepts, Methods and Policy Options, Springer, 2019.

[2] *OECD/G20*, Methodological Framework on Disaster Risk Assessment and Financing, 2012.

[3] "All countries – especially developing countries, where the mortality and economic losses from disasters are disproportionately higher – are faced with increasing levels of possible hidden costs and challenges in order to meet financial and other obligations": Sendai Framework for

With a view to addressing these issues, some countries – with the support of international aid – have decided to join forces to develop risk-sharing platforms that allow for more effective access to global risk transfer markets, taking advantage of the positive effects of risk pooling.

Risk pooling means the aggregation of individual risks to manage the consequences of independent risks. Risk pooling is based on the law of large numbers. In insurance terms, the law of large numbers demonstrates that pooling large numbers of roughly homogenous, independent exposure units can yield a mean average consistent with actual outcomes with a smaller standard deviation. Thus, pooling risks allows an accurate prediction of future losses and helps determine insurance premium rates.

This chapter presents and discusses from a comparative viewpoint and from a legal and public policy perspective three multi-country disaster risk transfer and financing schemes, namely:

- the African Risk Capacity (ARC);
- the Caribbean Catastrophe Risk Insurance Facility (CCRIF); and
- the Pacific Catastrophe Risk Insurance Company (PCRIC).

The multi-country schemes presented in this chapter use parametric risk transfer tools. These instruments make payments based not on an assessment of the individual loss, but rather on measures of a parametric index that is assumed to proxy actual losses. Basing payouts on such an objective index allows for timely payments, without relying on potentially lengthy and subjective loss assessments or evidence of incurred costs. Parametric approaches can be used with all risk transfer instruments and contingency financing approaches.

2. FINANCIAL VULNERABILITY AND FINANCIAL RESILIENCE TO CLIMATE CHANGE

One of the main critical implications of climate change has been identified as its impact on the frequency and severity of extreme weather-related events, such as floods, storms, hurricanes, cyclones, heatwaves and droughts.[4]

As loss and damage resulting from such phenomena are also continuing to increase due to the growing concentration of people and assets in exposed locations, such as coastal areas, natural hazards linked to climate and weather

---

Disaster Risk Reduction 2015–2030, adopted at the Third UN World Conference in Sendai, Japan, on 18 March 2015.

[4]   *IPCC*, Climate Change 2014: Impacts, Adaptation, and Vulnerability, 2014.

pose serious challenges to those countries whose economic systems are structurally vulnerable to climate-related disaster risks.[5]

Extreme disaster events can have severe financial and economic implications for governments, businesses and households through the direct damage they cause to buildings, equipment and infrastructure, as well as through indirect consequences such as business interruption, loss of employment and output, and decreased fiscal revenues. These impacts are particularly severe for emerging economies, and especially for the poorest households within those countries, due to their more limited capacity to manage climate risks.

Developing countries, in fact, are generally viewed as the most vulnerable to climate change due to their lower levels of physical and financial resilience, lower financial coverage through private insurance markets and more limited fiscal flexibility.

Improving resilience, or the capacity to absorb and recover from losses, requires the careful design and implementation of targeted disaster risk financing and transfer strategies to ensure that the financial consequences of disasters can be managed efficiently by the affected populations and economic sectors. From this perspective, the scale and distribution of risks across the territory and major segments of the economy – namely, households, the corporate sector, the financial sector and the government – and the financial capacities to absorb these risks need to be evaluated with a view to identifying possible financial vulnerabilities or financing gaps.[6]

Risk financing involves the retention of risks combined with the adoption of an explicit financing strategy to ensure that adequate funds are available to meet financial needs should a disaster occur. Such financing can be established internally through the accumulation of funds set aside for future use or obtained externally through pre-arranged credit facilities. The banking sector, capital markets and international lending institutions are sources of risk financing.

Risk transfer involves the shifting of risks to others who, in exchange for a premium, provide compensation when a disaster occurs, ensuring that any financing gap that might emerge is partially or fully bridged. Risk transfer may be obtained through insurance policies or capital market instruments such as catastrophe bonds. The insurance and reinsurance sectors are the main sources of risk transfer, although capital markets provide an alternative source.

The payouts of risk transfer instruments may be quantified on the basis of actual losses sustained by the protection buyer (indemnity based), or the value of the payment may be agreed upon by the parties irrespective of actual losses and triggered by a physical parameter measuring the intensity of the hazard at

---

[5] A. *Monti*, Public-private initiatives to cover extreme events, in Extreme events and insurance: 2011 annus horribilis, The Geneva Reports. Risk and Insurance Research 2012 (5), pp. 27–38.

[6] *OECD/G20, supra*, note 2.

given locations (parametric) or by an index comprising multiple measurements of such parameters for each event (parametric index).

In addition to providing the resources necessary to fund post-disaster needs, risk financing and transfer markets can convey signals regarding disaster risks and incentivise cost-effective disaster risk reduction measures.[7]

Where competitive markets exist, pricing may provide important signals regarding existing and emerging risks and their costs, which can help governments in identifying critical risk reduction measures, evaluating their costs and benefits and measuring the extent to which disaster costs are reduced over time, thus promoting effective implementation of disaster risk management. These signals may be complemented by loss-sharing arrangements (e.g. deductibles, co-insurance in insurance policies) that, by ensuring some retention of risk at the individual or group level, may further incentivise feasible risk reduction actions.

3. POLICY OPTIONS IN DISASTER RISK FINANCING

At present there is significant international experience in the design and implementation of policy measures to encourage the development of disaster risk financing instruments and to support coverage of climate-related risks by private insurance and reinsurance markets.[8]

Policy makers bear the responsibility of carefully assessing the potential role of disaster risk financing and risk transfer instruments in their fiscal management strategy;[9] this assessment should be made within a disciplined framework that is based on a sound risk assessment process and risk financing approach that seeks to identify any financing gaps.

From a theoretical viewpoint, governments have the option of financing climate-related disaster losses *ex post* through budget cuts and reallocations, post-event debt financing and taxation, thereby spreading disaster costs across present and future generations.

Many countries, however, have complemented their investment in physical risk reduction with *ex ante* disaster risk financing tools. These instruments can

---

[7] A. *Monti*, Climate Change and Weather-related Disasters: What Role for Insurance, Reinsurance and Financial Sectors?, Hastings Int'l & Comp. L. Rev. and West Northwest J. of Env. Law & Policy, Combined Issue, 2009 (15), pp. 151–172.

[8] A. *Monti*, Policy Approaches to the Financial Management of Large-Scale Disasters, in *OECD*, Financial Management of Large-Scale Catastrophes, Policy Issues in Insurance no. 12, OECD, 2008, pp. 9–142 (also available in French).

[9] S. *Moratti*, The Role of Taxation in Climate-Related Disaster Risk Management Policies: Focus on a More Efficient Reallocation of Risk, Rivista di diritto finanziario e scienza delle finanze 2018 (3), pp. 354–363.

address short-term (emergency response), mid-term (recovery) or long-term (reconstruction) financial needs, and can be used in combination to cover different risk layers, based on the relative frequency and severity of the expected events. Policy options in this field include:[10]

- *government reserves*, such as dedicated contingency reserves for disasters (with allocated funds lapsing at year end), or multi-year disaster reserve funds (with allocated funds building up over time);
- *insurance*, which enables the transfer of risks and indemnifies against damage (e.g. to cover damage to government assets such as buildings and infrastructure);
- *contingent credit arrangements* with a financial institution or international organisation; and
- *catastrophe bonds* or other types of catastrophe-linked securities or derivatives, which provide an alternative means for risk transfer.

In the next sections of this chapter attention will be focused on a number of *ex ante* policy measures that combine risk financing and risk management, taking advantage of the diversification that can be achieve by sharing risks across a region.

4. INNOVATIONS IN RISK TRANSFER MARKETS

In those economies in which private disaster risk financing markets and infrastructures are underdeveloped, and government resources are severely constrained, or the paying capacity of the most vulnerable levels of the population is extremely low, the promotion of risk financing and transfer tools requires the introduction of innovative products, instruments and solutions.

Several innovative insurance and micro-insurance solutions, including weather-index-based products and portfolio protection tools aimed at strengthening the resilience of rural banks, credit cooperatives, microfinance lenders and other financial institutions against disaster risk, have been the subject of experimentation and testing in various countries, with the support of the international donor community.[11]

Other innovative tools promote investment in the mitigation of disaster risks by introducing special features into the structure of the risk transfer product,

---

[10] A. *Monti*, Il Danno Catastrofale. Strumenti Giuridici e Modelli Istituzionali per la Gestione dei Rischi Estremi, Iuss Press, 2012.

[11] A. *Monti* (lead author), Disaster Risk Financing: A global survey of practices and challenges, OECD Publishing, 2015.

such as the requirements (i) to have previously adopted a risk and emergency management plan and (ii) to use the payouts to implement such plan.[12]

With a view to reducing transaction costs, non-traditional products using parametric or index-based structures have also been developed, for instance in the areas of crop insurance and weather insurance.

Parametric risk transfer tools make payments based not on an assessment of the individual loss, but rather on measures of a parametric index that is assumed to proxy actual losses. Basing payouts on such an objective index allows for timely payments, without relying on potentially lengthy and subjective loss assessments or evidence of incurred costs.

In this way, parametric insurance is different from traditional insurance, which requires an assessment of individual losses on the ground for settlement. Parametric insurance assesses losses via a predefined formula based on variables that are exogenous to both the individual policyholder and the insurer – that is, the physical parameters of the event – but that are strongly correlated to losses.

Parametric structures, therefore, require reliable data and technology to monitor hazard levels, which may be costly to acquire, manage and maintain, presenting significant implementation challenges.

5. A COMPARATIVE OVERVIEW OF MULTI-COUNTRY POOLING SCHEMES

5.1. AFRICAN RISK CAPACITY

The African Risk Capacity (ARC) was established as a Specialized Agency of the African Union (AU) to help Member States improve their capacities to better plan, prepare and respond to extreme weather events and natural disasters, therefore protecting the food security of their vulnerable populations. The ARC is a sovereign index-based weather insurance scheme and continental risk pool aimed at providing immediate, short-term liquidity to participating countries after a severe drought has occurred.

AU Member States that sign the ARC Establishment Agreement become ARC Member States and are eligible to participate in and benefit from ARC's disaster risk management facilities, as well as contribute to the governance of ARC through the Conference of Parties. Currently, there are 33 ARC Member States: Benin, Burkina Faso, Burundi, Central African Republic, Chad, Comoros, Cote d'Ivoire, Djibouti, Gabon, Ghana, Guinea, Guinea Bissau, Kenya, Liberia, Libya,

---

12   *OECD/APEC*, Disaster Risk Financing in APEC Economies: Practices and Challenges, 2013.

Madagascar, Malawi, Mali, Mauritania, Mozambique, Niger, Nigeria, Republic of Congo, Rwanda, Sahwari Arab Democratic Republic, Sao Tome and Principe, Senegal, Sierra Leone, Sudan, the Gambia, Togo, Zambia and Zimbabwe.

The ARC interacts with its Member States through a country engagement process that spans from introducing disaster risk financing concepts to insuring a country's climate risks.

The three declared objectives of the ARC are the following:

– African governments gain access to a set of tools that provide a summary of risks as well as a quantification of costs and impacts of drought at district, national and regional levels;
– African governments, through the risk pool, establish and manage a dedicated quick-disbursing contingent funding mechanism that strengthens the continent's ability to respond and improve disaster planning; and
– African governments join in solidarity to pool risks across the continent, thereby reducing the cost of insurance coverage for severe and catastrophic events.

The ARC is composed of two entities: the Specialized Agency and a financial affiliate, the ARC Insurance Company Limited (ARC Ltd).

The ARC Agency is a cooperative mechanism that:

– provides general oversight and supervising development of ARC capacity and services;
– provides capacity building to individual countries; and
– approves contingency plans and monitors their implementation.

ARC Ltd is the financial affiliate, incorporated as mutual insurance company in Bermuda, which carries out commercial insurance functions of risk pooling and risk transfer in accordance with national regulations for parametric weather insurance.

Pooling risk across the African continent allows the ARC to significantly reduce the cost to countries of emergency contingency funds, while decreasing reliance on external aid. The pool reinsures itself and benefits from investment income, so that it builds and protects the capital available for coverage to member governments.

From an operational viewpoint, participating countries pay a premium to ARC Ltd based on customised risk transfer parameters, and receive an immediate payout in the event of rainfall shortfall during the agricultural season, as calculated by predetermined settings in Africa RiskView, an advanced weather surveillance software developed by the UN World Food Programme which translates satellite-based rainfall information into near real-time response cost estimates.

In order to participate in the ARC, countries must complete several processes, including customising the Africa RiskView software, signing pre-participation agreements, defining a contingency plan for ARC payouts, and determining risk transfer parameters (deductible/attachment point, limit and ceding percentage). After the participation requirements have been met, a country may join ARC Ltd by paying a premium calculated on the basis of an actuarial analysis. Countries choose the level at which they wish to participate by selecting the amount of risk they wish to retain and the financing they would want from the ARC for droughts of varying severity.

Through its capacity building and risk pooling, the ARC's objective is to strengthen the continent's disaster risk management systems through innovation and solidarity. By capitalising on local expertise and the natural diversification of weather risk across Africa, the ARC allows countries to manage their risk as a group in a financially efficient manner in order to respond to probable but uncertain risks.

It is important to note that, under the applicable terms of the scheme, the payout must be used by participating countries to scale up social safety nets and other response programmes as indicated in each country's pre-approved operations plan, which seeks to optimise the use of early funds. To be effective, the ARC needs to be linked to defined contingency plans within a national risk management framework.

Solvency and sustainability objectives are pursued using a variety of different financing approaches and instruments, which include the coordinated use of risk retention, risk transfer and contingent financing to create a layered financing structure:

- *Retention by country participants:* members retain a portion of the risk, using existing resources to manage the impact of less severe, localised or frequent events.
- *Risk pool reserves (ARC retention):* the reserves layer of the pool is based on contributions of the participating countries in the form of annual premiums, in addition to initial donor capitalisation.
- *Risk pool contingent financing (ARC risk transfer):* the ARC risk pool transfers extreme drought risk that it believes it would be inefficient to hold as reserves within the pool to international carriers via reinsurance, derivative contracts and/or catastrophe-linked securities.

5.2. CARIBBEAN CATASTROPHE RISK INSURANCE FACILITY

The Caribbean Catastrophe Risk Insurance Facility (CCRIF) was the first multi-country risk pool in the world, and was the first insurance instrument to successfully develop parametric policies backed by both traditional and capital markets.

The CCRIF's mission is to assist Caribbean and Central American governments and their communities in understanding and reducing the socio-economic and environmental impacts of natural catastrophes.

The CCRIF was originally designed to limit the financial impact of catastrophic hurricanes and earthquakes on participating countries by quickly providing short-term liquidity through a range of affordable insurance products, developing innovative and dynamic tools and services, and operating in a way that is financially sustainable and responsive to the needs of the region.

In 2014, the facility was restructured into a segregated portfolio company (SPC) to facilitate expansion into new products and geographic areas and is now named CCRIF SPC. The new structure, in which products are offered through a number of segregated portfolios, allows for total segregation of risk.

CCRIF SPC is owned, operated and registered in the Cayman Islands as a virtual organisation, supported by a network of service providers covering the areas of risk management, risk modelling, captive management, reinsurance, reinsurance brokerage, asset management, technical assistance, corporate communications and information technology.

The facility aims to limit the financial impacts of catastrophic hurricanes, earthquakes and excess rainfall events to participating governments by quickly providing short-term liquidity when a parametric insurance policy is triggered, thereby allowing public facilities to continue their operations. Payments from the pool go directly into the general budget of the affected country and are not earmarked or monitored thereafter.

Nineteen Caribbean governments and three Central American governments are currently members of the facility:

- *Caribbean*: Anguilla, Antigua and Barbuda, Bahamas, Barbados, Belize, Bermuda, British Virgin Islands, Cayman Islands, Dominica, Grenada, Haiti, Jamaica, Montserrat, St. Kitts and Nevis, Saint Lucia, Sint Maarten, St. Vincent and the Grenadines, Trinidad and Tobago, and Turks and Caicos Islands.
- *Central America*: Nicaragua, Panama and Guatemala.

Each participating country determines the level of aggregate coverage and attachment points, which are then used to determine their individual premiums. Claims are based on model-derived estimates of government losses generated using a pre-defined and escrowed catastrophe loss model and input data regarding the nature of each physical hazard event, as set out in the Claims Procedures Manual and not with reference to actual losses incurred by the respective participating countries.

The CCRIF cedes layers of its risk exposure to commercial reinsurers and the International Bank for Reconstruction and Development (the World Bank).

The regional pooling of risks makes the overall risk more stable and therefore more attractive to the reinsurance market, thereby reducing the cost of risk transfer.

In this way, CCRIF becomes a cost-effective way to pre-finance short-term liquidity to begin recovery efforts for an individual government after a catastrophic event, thereby filling the gap between immediate response aid and long-term redevelopment. As a result, members benefit from:

- the ability to transfer a portion of their climate-related risk to the CCRIF at a price lower than what they would pay if they were able to obtain coverage individually in international insurance markets or the cost of the capital they would need in order to self-insure; and
- the financial protection of prompt cash payout, within two weeks or less, following a covered event.

5.3. PACIFIC CATASTROPHE RISK INSURANCE COMPANY

Pacific island governments face critical challenges for financial resilience to disasters, being constrained by their size, borrowing capacity, and limited access to international insurance markets.

The Pacific Catastrophe Risk Insurance Company (PCRIC), a captive insurance company incorporated in the Cook Islands, was established in June 2016 after the completion of a pilot insurance programme from 2013 to 2015, via the Pacific Catastrophe Risk Assessment and Financing Initiative (PCRAFI).

The PCRAFI is a joint initiative of the SPC Geoscience Division, the World Bank, and the Asian Development Bank, with the financial support of the Government of Japan, the Global Facility for Disaster Reduction and Recovery (GFDRR) and the ACP-EU Natural Disaster Risk Reduction Programme, and technical support from AIR Worldwide, New Zealand GNS Science, Geoscience Australia, the Pacific Disaster Center (PDC), OpenGeo and GFDRR Labs. The PCRAFI aims to provide the Pacific Island Countries (PICs) with disaster risk modelling and assessment tools.

During the pilot programme period, the risk-sharing facility was structured in the form of a pool of country-specific derivative contracts aimed at transferring catastrophic risks to the international reinsurance market. Acting as an intermediary, the World Bank – through the International Development Agency (IDA) – entered into catastrophe swap contracts with participating countries on one side and a group of reinsurance companies on the other. Through this intermediation, the country-specific individual catastrophe risk swap contracts stipulated with the World Bank were placed on the international reinsurance market as a single, diversified portfolio.

At present, the PCRIC is designed to increase the financial resilience of PICs to natural disasters and to improve their capacity to meet post-disaster funding needs by means of parametric insurance contracts that allow access to immediate funds for swift post-disaster emergency response actions in the aftermath of a disaster. The PCRIC also aims to engage in a dialogue with the PICs on integrated financial solutions for the reduction of their financial vulnerability to natural disasters and to climate change. The initiative is part of the broader agenda on disaster risk management and climate change adaptation in the Pacific region.

At present, only five countries participate in the PCRIC: Cook Islands, Republic of the Marshall Islands, Samoa, Tonga, and Vanuatu.

6. CONCLUSIONS

Improving financial resilience to losses and damage caused by climate-change-related risks is one of the top priorities for governments in developed and emerging economies.[13]

The Sendai Framework for Disaster Risk Reduction 2015–2030[14] recognised the role of risk financing and risk transfer tools in supporting adaptation to climate impacts as a key component of an effective sovereign disaster risk management strategy.[15] To meet these needs, some countries have joined forces in the design and implementation of risk-sharing platforms that allow for more effective access to global risk transfer markets, taking advantage of the positive effects of risk pooling.

The examples offered by the ARC, CCRIF and PCRIC, presented in this chapter, show how non-traditional risk transfer mechanisms, such as parametric insurance, coupled with technological innovation and risk pooling, can be used to simplify the operation of the scheme and to save transaction costs.

These regional risk-sharing initiatives have similar but not identical objectives, insofar as:

- The ARC aims to assist AU Member States in planning, preparing and responding to extreme weather events and in particular drought, with a view to protecting the food security of vulnerable populations.
- The CCRIF's purpose is to limit the financial impact of catastrophic hurricanes and earthquakes on Caribbean governments by quickly providing contingent funds allowing public facilities to continue their operations.
- The PCRIC is designed to help participating countries improve their budget flexibility and strengthen their early response capabilities by ensuring rapid access to funds for post-disaster costs.

---

[13] *UNISDR*, The Human Cost of Weather-Related Disaster, 1995–2015.
[14] Adopted at the Third UN World Conference in Sendai, Japan, on 18 March 2015.
[15] See also *OECD*, Recommendation on Disaster Risk Financing Strategies, 2017.

In terms of their legal structure:

- The ARC is a treaty-based organisation composed of two entities:
  - the ARC Agency; and
  - ARC Insurance Company Limited, established as a mutual insurance company under the laws of Bermuda.
- The CCRIF was a captive insurance company incorporated and licensed under the laws of the Cayman Islands. In 2014, it was restructured into a segregated portfolio company (SPC). The company's sole shareholder is the CCRIF Star Trust.
- The PCRIC is a captive insurance company owned by the PCRAFI Foundation, both established in the Cook Islands in 2016. The Foundation is governed by a Council of Members that own the captive insurer PCRIC.

From a comparative viewpoint, it is interesting to observe that while the ARC scheme requires that the payouts of the risk transfer tool are used by participating governments to implement a pre-approved risk and emergency management plan, both the CCRIF and the PCRIC leave the beneficiaries free to determine how to use the proceeds.

While it is still early to assess the effectiveness of these institutional arrangements, they constitute notable examples of innovative combinations of risk reduction, risk financing and risk transfer tools designed to meet the compelling need to improve financial resilience to climate-related risks.

ENVIRONMENTAL LIABILITY, CATASTROPHIC RISK MITIGATION AND SUSTAINABILITY

The Role of Insurers Beyond the Insurance Coverage

Anna Teresa MEMOLA

1. RISK ASSESSMENT: THE MAIN RISK FACTORS DERIVING FROM NATURAL CATASTROPHES IN THE GLOBAL CONTEXT

It has been outlined during the 6th EELF annual conference that, according to the World Economic Forum's global risk perception,[1] environmental risks are growing in prominence year by year and are commonly classified into several different categories.

In relation to this topic, climate change – i.e. an increased volatility of extreme weather events in many parts of the world – is a reality that a growing number of people have to face at a global level. This is shown by the available data, which indicate that total economic losses from disasters across the world were an estimated USD 165 billion in 2018, with around USD 155 billion resulting from natural catastrophes and the remainder from man-made events, and that almost 13,500 people died or were missing.[2]

Among the most significant environmental challenges are: extreme weather events (e.g. hurricanes, extreme rainfall, storms and other weather-related hazards – especially in connection with their consequences in terms of displacement); rising temperatures and more frequent heatwaves, which may have consequences in terms of disruption of agricultural systems (causing famine and hardship, by reason of interconnectedness); accelerating biodiversity loss; pollution of air, soil and water; and failures of climate-change mitigation

---

[1]   *World Economic Forum*, The Global Risk Report, 2020.
[2]   *Swiss Re*, Sigma Report n. 2/2019, Natural catastrophes and man-made disasters in 2018: "secondary" perils on the frontline.

and adaptation, as well as transition risks, as we move to a low-carbon future.

Moreover, under a traditional categorisation adopted for insurability purposes, extreme natural events have been related to their catastrophic consequences and included by insurers and reinsurers within the definition of "natural catastrophes", in contrast to the other kind of events that we would call "man-made disasters". Regarding the former, the term "natural catastrophe" refers to an event caused by natural forces, generally resulting in a large number of individual losses, depending both on natural forces and on man-made factors, and also being the subject of many insurance policies. As to the latter, the category of man-made or technical disasters usually encompasses explosions, aviation and space disasters, shipping disasters, rail disasters, mining accidents, the collapse of buildings/bridges, and other similar events (including terrorism).[3]

It has to be observed that the consequences of climate change, natural catastrophes and man-made disasters are nowadays considered a priority both by the insurance sector, from a private angle, but also by governments, from a public angle.

The scale of the phenomenon also has to be considered taking into account the "insurance coverage gap", since according to Lloyd's of London and the available reports of the main players on the reinsurance market, weather-related losses have significantly grown over the last 10 years, as for instance in 2017 total economic losses were US$337 billion, making an all-peril global catastrophe protection gap of US$193 billion.[4]

In 2013, the importance of a reaction to the growing factors of climate risks and related losses in the European Union was already outlined by the European Commission in the "*Green Paper on the insurance of natural and man-made disasters*",[5] which included an analysis of the main insurance schemes and contractual solutions to the issue, together with the positive effects and the attitude of the European states. The Green Paper made reference to the intervention of insurance and reinsurance companies in order to obtain an

---

3   *The Geneva Association*, Managing Physical Climate Risk: Leveraging Innovations in Catastrophe Risk Modelling, The Geneva Association – International Association for the Study of Insurance Economics, November 2018.

4   *Swiss Re*, Sigma Report 1/2018: an extract of the most significant data and figures relating to losses caused by extreme weather events and catastrophic factors in 2017. As highlighted, total insured losses from natural catastrophes and large man-made disasters were US$144 billion in 2017. An active hurricane season in the North Atlantic, and a series of wildfire, thunderstorm and severe precipitation events across different regions pushed global catastrophe claims to their highest level ever recorded in a single year. Globally, more than 11,000 people lost their lives or went missing in disasters, while millions were left homeless.

5   COM(2013) 213 final, The Green Paper can be found at https://eur-lex.europa.eu/legal-content/EN/TXT/PDF/?uri=CELEX:52013DC0213.

expansion of the knowledge base, helping to promote insurance as a tool of disaster management and thus contributing to a shift towards a general culture of disaster risk prevention and mitigation, as well as bringing in further data and information.

Since then, natural disasters and climate change shifted from being only an issue of scientific, environmental and social responsibility impact, to being one of the priorities of socio-economic development and risk management.[6]

As a matter of fact, 2015 was a defining year, showing the strong interconnection between climate change, disaster risk reduction and sustainable development, as well as the public interest in these issues, through the adoption of several governmental and political agreements at an international level.

A public commitment on these issues was the object of the Sendai Framework for Disaster Risk Reduction (2015–2030), adopted at the Third UN World Conference in Sendai, Japan, on 18 March 2015, after the Hyogo Framework for Action (HFA) 2005–2015, where states also reiterated their commitment to addressing disaster risk reduction and the building of resilience to disasters through the appropriate policies, plans, programmes and budgets at all levels, with a renewed sense of urgency within the context of sustainable development and poverty eradication.[7]

In addition, the Paris Agreement adopted in 2015 among the strategies of climate-related risk reduction, must be considered a milestone in the transition to a low-carbon economy, as it requires large-scale investments oriented towards sustainable development goals, involving 189 national climate plans covering some 98 per cent of all emissions, leading to becoming climate change a truly global effort. The Paris Agreement set out a global action plan to contrast dangerous climate change, by supporting countries in their efforts to achieve a global peaking of greenhouse gas emissions as soon as possible as well as climate neutrality in the second half of this century. Among its key features, the Agreement set out a long-term goal to put the world on track to limit global warming (to well below 2°C above pre-industrial levels – and pursue efforts to limit the temperature increase to 1.5°C), sending a clear signal to all the relevant market players that resources have to shift away from fossil fuels.[8]

In legal terms, what is important is that the parties to the Paris Agreement have a legally binding obligation to pursue domestic mitigation measures, with

---

[6] *The Geneva Association*, Climate Change and the insurance industry: taking action as risk managers and investors, The Geneva Association – International Association for the Study of Insurance Economics, January 2018.

[7] Id.

[8] *European Commission*, Communication from the Commission to the European Parliament and the Council – The Road from Paris: assessing the implications of the Paris Agreement and accompanying the proposal for a Council decision on the signing, on behalf of the European Union, of the Paris agreement adopted under the United Nations Framework Convention on Climate Change, COM(2016) 110.

the aim of achieving the objectives of their contributions and encouraging greater cooperation among themselves to share scientific knowledge on adaptation, as well as information on practices and policies at an international level.

It must be noticed that the direct obligation of governments in reducing the consequences of climate change is due to the growing impact of the costs associated with the effects of climate change, as well as those of natural catastrophes, leading to a more active approach of the States and to a more integrated risk management.

In this context, besides the governmental and public efforts to reduce the impact of climate change, insurers can also play a role by cooperating in relation to climate-related risks.

As better explained later in this chapter, insurers are increasingly considering climate change and environmental risks as a core business issue, in relation to which they can act both as underwriters of the risks (for so-called physical risks) and as investors (with regard to so-called transition risks).

2. THE ROLE OF INSURERS BEYOND THE INSURANCE COVERAGE: RISK AWARENESS, RISK PREVENTION

As already observed, the global impact of climate change is a crucial issue both for public and government institutions and for the private sector.[9] According to the World Economic Forum,[10] extreme weather events, natural disasters and the failure of climate change mitigation should be considered among the most important emerging risks in 2019. In this context, insurers and insurance solutions can make society more resilient to the impacts deriving from extreme events in several ways, such as providing compensation or assessing, managing and signalling the main threats and risks.[11]

It is thus important, before analysing the role of the main players of the insurance market in front of the threats, to identify the main categories of climate-related risks to which insurers are exposed and committed in different ways: respectively as underwriters or as investors.

The first category is represented by physical risks deriving from the impact in terms of damage and losses due to climate trends (e.g. rising sea levels, changing

---

9   OECD, Global Insurance Market Trends 2018, OECD Insurance and Private Pensions Committee, 2019.

10   World Economic Forum, supra, note 1.

11   H. Kunreuther, Mitigating Disaster Losses through Insurance, Journal of Risk and Uncertainty 1996, (12), pp. 171–187; D. Cerini, Assicurazioni contro i rischi di catastrofi naturali: profilature italiane dopo il Green Paper UE, DFA – Diritto e Fiscalità dell'Assicurazione 2013 (4), pp. 460–467.

weather patterns), extreme weather events (e.g. storms, hail and flooding) and other natural catastrophes (e.g. earthquakes).[12]

This kind of risk mainly involves non-life insurers and reinsurers[13] as underwriters and, although the insurance protection gap in this field is still very high, insurers may prevent the effects of these factors and adjust the cost of coverage through periodic re-pricing, even though they may be exposed to a non-linear growth of claims in relation to single events.[14]

It has been observed that uninsured losses from physical risks may have a disruptive impact at the macro-economic level, considering the possible negative effects on resource availability, economic productivity across sectors and profitability of firms and individual assets, as well as the possible cascading impacts across the financial system.

The reaction of insurance companies to this kind of risk, according to EIOPA,[15] may result in a limitation of their exposures by not renewing policies at all or by stopping underwriting the risks, especially in areas where natural disasters may be more likely to happen. This attitude on the one hand reduces the exposure of insurers, but since the insurance protection gap remains very high, it may on the other hand create a supply crisis and have a strong impact on public finances.

Thus, instead of limiting their own exposure by not renewing or not writing coverage, underwriters should be encouraged, including through forms of public–private partnerships or risk-sharing models, to change their policies and commitments in several ways.

As a matter of fact, they can take advantage of their high level of technical skills and experience, for example by raising public awareness of and giving advice on climate-related risks on issues like prevention and mitigation strategies. In terms of lines of coverage, insurers may also develop new solutions to meet the growing demand (e.g. mitigating the consequences of business disruption and interruption), as well as explore the "opportunities" offered by climate change through scenario analyses and stress-testing for risk management, creating new products or making ongoing efforts to reduce greenhouse gas emissions.

The second category of climate-related risks consists of transition risks, which are more relevant for life insurers, arising from disruptions and shifts linked to the transition to a lower-carbon economy and result in a financial impact on the value of assets or the costs of doing business.[16]

---

[12]   OECD, Financial Management of Earthquake Risk, 2018.
[13]   OECD, The Contribution of Reinsurance Markets to Managing Catastrophe Risk, 2018, www.oecd.org/finance/the-contribution-of-reinsurance-markets-to-managing-catastrophe-risk.pdf.
[14]   The Geneva Association, supra, note 3.
[15]   EIOPA, Financial Stability Report: Climate risk and sustainable insurance, June 2018, p. 14.
[16]   The Geneva Association, supra, note 3.

To give some examples, transition risks may be connected to policy changes, regulatory reforms affecting carbon-intensive sectors (e.g. energy, industry and transport), market dynamics, technological innovation, and reputational factors. This category of risk is thus consistent for life insurers, with large investment exposures, in the form of loans or equity holdings in carbon-intensive industries, but also of commercial and real-estate investments, affected by tightened sustainability requirements.

As a reaction, it has been observed that the current trend for many insurers is an "active green" approach, involving investing in clean energy, mitigating their carbon footprints, increasing the proportion of green bonds in their portfolio, and ceasing to provide coverage for companies that receive a considerable share of their revenues from non-clean energy sources.

In addition, and from the public angle, as already outlined in the first part of this chapter, after the adoption of the Paris Agreement the approach of many governments has been oriented towards reducing greenhouse gas emissions, including increasing investments in biomass, wind farms, energy-efficiency measures, and hydrogen technology and carbon emission markets.[17]

Governments are in fact often involved *ex post* in the compensation of the victims of natural disasters, and their policies and incentives for prevention are not always effective.[18] Besides their impact on the investment side, transition factors may also result in a change of the coverage demanded by firms due to the disruption of the industrial organisation in the face of the need for new technologies, products and services. A typical case is that of the cost of energy, which is getting cheaper for some types of renewable energy technologies (such as solar power), and is already cheaper than conventional technologies in certain markets, which has an impact on insured assets.[19]

Besides physical and transition risks, insurers may also be exposed to risks arising from climate-related litigation, including over action – or inaction – relating to climate mitigation and adaptation efforts, especially in light of the significant increase in major lawsuits being filed with respect to climate change. These risks are classified as liability risks and the category also includes the risk of climate-related claims under liability policies, under Directors' and Officers' liability policies ("D&O"), professional indemnity insurance ("PI"),

---

[17] *OECD*, Financing Climate Futures – Rethinking infrastructure, 2018.

[18] This is the case of four major countries (France, Netherlands, Belgium, Germany), among many others. *V. Bruggeman and M. Faure*, Compensation for victims of disasters in Belgium, France, Germany and the Netherlands, The Netherlands Scientific Council for Government Policy, 2018, p. 75.

[19] *A. Monti*, Policy approaches to the financial management of large-scale disasters, Financial Management of Large-scale disasters, OECD, 2008.

and third-party environmental liability policies, as well as direct claims against insurers for failing to manage climate risks.[20]

Liability risks could also arise from management and boards of insurers not fully considering or responding to the impacts of climate change, or appropriate disclosure of current and future risks (including through damages and tort litigation).

The above analysis of the most relevant categories of climate-related risks involving insurers, both as underwriters and as investors, allows us to understand why insurance may be considered a tool for building resilience to extreme weather events in a dual manner: by providing financial compensation for losses as well as incentives to reduce, mitigate and prevent risk.[21]

As a matter of fact, while on the one hand insurance companies are increasingly considering climate risks as a core business issue, by linking them to their governance, strategy and risk management, on the other hand governments are recognising the role and benefits deriving from the private sector, since a market-based insurance industry can efficiently bear and transfer climate-related risks. Indeed, evidence has been found that countries with widespread market-based insurance coverage recover faster from the impacts of extreme-weather events and that the uninsured part of the losses is what drives the majority of the macro-economic costs.[22]

The insurance industry thus plays a fundamental role in building socio-economic resilience and boosting the achievement of climate change goals and targets, mainly through its expertise in pricing, by providing risk information and innovative risk transfer products and services, by improving the distribution channels and compensation mechanisms, and also by shifting its underwriting business and investment strategies in a green direction and reducing its carbon emissions.

Concerning the issuance of extreme weather coverage and the related compensation, insurers must be able to understand the monetary terms of the risks – the so-called actuarial insurability criteria – as well as to find a balanced price that results in a market equilibrium of demand and supply – the so-called economic conditions of the coverage. These requirements may significantly vary depending on the different sources and extreme weather events, generating a different claim ratio, for example, between widespread events such as windstorms and more localised events such as fluvial floods.

---

[20]   *J. Brunnee, S. Goldberg, R. Lord QC & L. Rajamani*, Overview of legal issues relevant to climate change, Climate Change Liability – Transnational law and practice, Cambridge University Press, 2012.

[21]   *European Commission, Directorate-General for Climate Action*, Insurance of weather and climate-related disaster risk: Inventory and analysis of mechanisms to support damage prevention in the EU, August 2017.

[22]   *The Geneva Association, supra*, note 3.

According to the findings of the Directorate-General for Climate Action of the European Commission,[23] in terms of the main objectives and benefits of insurance instruments in the risk management of extreme weather events, insurance has been appointed by stakeholders as an instrument that may increase risk awareness and provide incentives for risk reduction, as well as promoting preparedness for disaster events and limiting cascading effects. In addition, coverage for climate-related events should be generally affordable and widely available by creating a wide pool of policyholders and reflecting nonetheless the risk, working in a way that keeps claims and losses within acceptable limits and covering all aspects of an event's consequences through affordable premiums and compensating for losses quickly, efficiently, fairly and reliably.

It has to be observed in a comparative perspective that countries have developed different approaches, evaluated through five key indicators identified to find best practices. In this sense, the features of the insurance market, as well the as legislative and governmental context, may vary significantly within a single state, as highlighted by the study and results summarised below.

For example, concerning private property insurance, the situation across Europe is multifaceted, taking into consideration the cases of voluntary coverage (Germany, Austria, Italy and Bulgaria), semi-voluntary coverage (Denmark, Sweden, Poland, Hungary and the UK) and mandatory coverage (France, Spain and Romania).[24]

In this sense, the best practices adopted in the individual systems use the benchmark of private property insurance, commercial coverage or agriculture rate, using the parameters of:

(i) insurance penetration rates (coverage gaps), defined as the rate of policyholders with an insurance policy;
(ii) risk signalling, representing the ability to increase policyholders' awareness and understanding of the potential threats, as well as risk reduction incentives that could promote the active management of the risks by policyholders;
(iii) the affordability and availability of insurance, considering the economic cost of the premium compared to individuals' disposable income;
(iv) the speed of payments, which corresponds to the speed at which compensation is paid to those affected by an extreme weather event,

---

[23] *European Commission, supra*, note 21. See also *The Geneva Association, supra*, note 3.
[24] *European Commission, Directorate-General for Climate Action*, Overview of insurance market performance and cost-effectiveness of insurance market approaches, in "Insurance of weather and climate-related disaster risk: Inventory and analysis of mechanisms to support damage prevention in the EU, August 2017, pp. 30–52. See also *Cerini, supra*, note 11 at p. 4; *Bruggeman and Faure, supra*, note 18; *Monti, supra*, note 19.

including the time for claim processing and eventually matching the indemnity to the policyholder; and

(v) the ability of insurers to absorb large losses, since the separate lines of business cannot be considered independently of one another, including under the criteria set out by the Solvency II Directive.[25]

Notwithstanding the positive effect of the conditions described above, which are more related to the attitude of insurers, according to the same study the insurance market is often affected by an asymmetry of information between the demand and supply sides. Thus, the parameters set out above must also be associated with at least three typical effects deriving from the behaviour of the potential policyholder. The first is moral hazard, which occurs when people decrease their use of risk-reduction mechanisms after purchasing the coverage. The second is adverse selection, described as the situation of individuals being unlikely to subscribe to insurance coverage because of its cost, which is higher where the risk is higher, leading to the paradox that the insurance gap is more evident in areas where extreme events are more frequent. The third effect is charity hazard, which comes about where individuals prefer not to insure themselves because they rely instead on economic help from third parties such as the government, their family or state emergency programs.[26]

3. APPROACH OF INSURERS AND REINSURERS: SOLUTIONS AND IMPACTS ON THE LINES OF INSURANCE

Considering the double role of insurers, which can act both as underwriters of the risks or as investors, climate change does have an impact on several lines of insurance, specifically on property insurance (e.g. agriculture, buildings, transport and marine, tourism, business interruption), liability insurance (e.g. directors and officers, professional liability, litigation connected to climate change) and personal insurance (e.g. life insurance, health insurance). As a consequence, climate change and extreme weather events offer several opportunities in terms of business, with new products that could be issued and distributed on the market, as well as in terms of an adaptation of existing products.[27]

---

25   Directive 2009/138/EC of the European Parliament and of the Council of 25 November 2009 on the taking-up and pursuit of the business of Insurance and Reinsurance, OJ 2009 L 335/1.

26   *European Commission, Directorate-General for Climate Action, supra*, note 24.

27   *C. Ross, E. Mills & S.B. Hecht*, Limiting liability in the greenhouse: insurance risk-management strategies in the context of global climate change, Stanford Environmental Law

Then, taking into account the single aspects of insurance contracts concerned by climate-related events, the predominant impact on the insurance sector is in terms of coverage of natural catastrophes, but considering the multifaceted and variable effects of climate change, other lines of property insurance are also involved.[28] In addition, as already highlighted, climate change may cause new types of liability, involving private and public professionals in several ways, both in terms of insurance coverage on the one side, and as a result of a growing litigation trend on the other side, despite the difficulty of proving causality and actual links between professional liability and climate change.

As a matter of fact, some members of professional categories may be held liable for the consequences of their activities in terms of climate, for instance, to architects, contractors, manufacturers or even bankers, who may be liable for having agreed to finance projects likely to have negative environmental implications. Public authorities may also be responsible for the failure to take preventive measures or in giving proper information to citizens in relation to extreme weather events.[29]

Moreover, personal insurance may also be increasingly affected by climate change, since it may cause some diseases and afflictions to develop (e.g. allergies, malnutrition due to drought, illnesses due to water contamination or excessive heat) and consequently have an impact on health insurance, which in some countries is the most important means of coverage.

As a consequence of the significant impact of natural extreme events and climate-related risks, insurance companies are called to adopt some defensive measures in order to improve prevention and management of the risks, both by modifying the drafting of contractual schemes and clauses and by adjusting their policies.

These aspects were well highlighted by the specialist group from the International Insurance Law Association (AIDA Association) during the World Congress held in Paris in 2010. The results of these studies are brought together and reformulated below to identify the main trends in insurers' actions, j in the broader context of the market.[30]

First of all, the so-called extra-legal defensive measures include regularly re-evaluating statistics in areas that are sensitive to extreme natural events, carrying out specific studies, and engaging in public or private information

---

Journal and the Stanford Journal of International Law, Symposium on Climate Change Risk 2007 (26A/43A), pp. 251–344.

[28] *The Geneva Association, supra*, note 3.

[29] Id.

[30] The main papers and references presented on the subject at the AIDA Congress held in Paris in 2010 are collected in Climate Change, Environmental Catastrophic Events and Insurance, Fondazione Cesifin Alberto Predieri. The authors include Marcel Fontaine, Marco Frigessi di Rattalma, Sara Landini, Roberto Manzato and Paolo Rainelli.

campaigns to promote prevention, which are all initiatives that indicate the importance of improving knowledge, information and risk awareness of insurers in relation to climate change and its monitoring. In addition, good practices of green conduct – such as saving energy, both in real estate investments and in day-to-day business, saving paper, and investing in sustainable development projects – can all be defined as behavioural measures to prevent the effects of climate change.

The insurance industry is actually moving towards risk prevention and awareness not only by sharing its expertise in risk modelling and pricing, but also with a wide range of research initiatives conducted by larger companies in-house or outsourced, as well as by creating new incubators to develop new ideas and solutions to the underinsurance of risks.[31]

Moreover, for the same objectives, insurers may adopt some legal defensive measures, as contractual solutions that are integrated into the drafting of the contractual clauses of the coverage in order to mitigate and reduce the impact of climate change, through the commitment of insurers but also with the involvement of the policyholders.

With regard to the drafting of the contracts, first of all insurers may graduate the indemnity depending on the damages occurred, via a forfeiture clause or by a reduction of the amount in cases where the policyholder has not adopted additional prevention measures required by the contract.

In addition, considering the strong economic impact of climate change for insurers, one of the most important things to pay attention to in the drafting of contracts is the extent of coverage regarding climate change. There are several measures that can be used, such as the definition of the maximum amount of coverage as well as variable and not fixed deductibles, which can be adjusted depending on whether the insured party implements risk-reduction mechanisms.[32]

Furthermore, policyholders can be encouraged to carry out more active risk management[33] through a reduction of the premium or even the negotiation of favourable terms and conditions upon the adoption of specific mitigation measures by the insured party, through the introduction of *bonus-malus* mechanisms, through a strictly risk-based premium strongly linked to the expected annual loss in relation to the insured events, or even by the insurer's withdrawal in the face of an excessive increase in the risk.

It should be added that besides the measures proposed by the private sector, public insurance schemes have been developed in several systems,

---

[31] *European Commission, supra*, note 24; *The Geneva Association, supra*, note 3.
[32] *M. Fontaine*, Climate Change and Insurance Law, General Report submitted to the AIDA World Congress held in Paris (May 2010), Fondazione Cesifin Alberto Predieri, 2012, pp. 107–142.
[33] *European Commission, supra*, note 24.

with different options varying from cases of public–private partnerships, as in France, to cases like Spain where part of the overall policyholders' premium is transferred to a public reinsurance entity, or like in Argentina where every entity prone to cause environmental harm must conclude an insurance policy in the form of a caution where the insured party is the state.[34]

In any case, it has been pointed out that all these mechanisms of risk reduction provided by the private sector should always be combined with government policies and strategies, since the interaction of private and public sector produces more efficient results.

Beyond the role of insurers in increasing risk awareness and incentivising customers to mitigate the effects of climate-related risks, as already highlighted, undertakings also have the opportunity (i) to develop new products and services in order to reduce the effects of climate change, or (ii) to adapt their existing ones by transforming them into green policies, as instruments to reduce greenhouse gases.[35]

The new products and services included in the first category are mainly composed of traditional or alternative risk transfer products for weather-related events (e.g. parametric insurance), crop insurance against climate risks, micro-insurance and other products available for low-income countries, specialised insurance products for renewable energy, and services supporting the issuance of catastrophe bonds, such as for infrastructure-related businesses and manufacturers with large production bases.

The second category of insurance policies acting as solutions for greenhouse gas reduction includes: coverage for energy-saving buildings ("green buildings' insurance"), which offers a reduction in the premium upon the adoption of energy-saving requirements by the insured good (the building); motor insurance policies[36] with a "pay-as-you-drive" formula or offering a premium reduction for installing a "black box" or if the car is a hybrid or low-emission model; and special policies binding the insurer to invest the premiums in projects relating to the reduction of greenhouse gas emissions or sustainable development.

In addition, existing products like third-party liability policies – including environmental liability policies, policies covering specific professional risks, especially involved in the construction sector, D&O policies, and business interruption policies – can also be adapted to include specific clauses to cover liabilities linked to climate change or to assess the impacts of a catastrophic event on a certain customer or industry.

---

[34]   *Fontaine, supra*, note 32.
[35]   *The Geneva Association, supra*, note 3.
[36]   S. *Landini*, Eco driving and motor insurance in the perspective of the European environmental principles, in Climate Change, Environmental Catastrophic Events and Insurance, Fondazione Cesifin Alberto Predieri, 2012, p. 59.

Beyond the solutions offered to private policyholders, the insurance industry is also issuing specialised products and services in order to protect public finances, such as regional pools (e.g. the Caribbean Catastrophe Risk Insurance Facilities or the Pacific Catastrophe Risk Assessment and Financing Initiative), as well as disaster expense insurance for local governments, aiming at compensating the costs of expenses needed to cope with the consequences of natural catastrophes, such as evacuation.[37]

4. CONCLUSION

To conclude, as for insurance companies, reinsurers are also considering climate change as a priority, both through extra-legal measures in the research and risk-prevention fields, via lobbying activities, and through contractual drafting and modelling in compliance with the coverages and insurance solutions they offer on the market.[38]

Moreover, climate change and catastrophic events have traditionally been the object of derivatives and alternative risk transfer solutions. Among these instruments, commonly referred to as weather derivatives[39] and sold by both bankers and insurers, the products related to climate change include: put options, offering protection if a certain variable index goes under a predetermined level and entitling the purchaser to receive compensation if the index turns out to be below the predetermined level; caps, conversely offering protection if the variable goes above the agreed level; and swaps, which are a combination of the other two and offer the payment of a compensation sum if the variable goes either under or above the predetermined level. Besides weather derivatives, another form of risk transfer is securitisation, which transfers the risk to the capital market, and is mostly issued for catastrophe risks and hence is called catastrophe bonds. In these cases, bonds are issued to investors at an agreed interest rate for the amount which is covered by the contract.[40]

---

[37]   *Monti, supra*, note 19.

[38]   *OECD, supra*, note 9.

[39]   P. *Rainelli*, Weather Derivatives' Regulation and Designation, in Climate Change, Environmental Catastrophic Events and Insurance, Fondazione Cesifin Alberto Predieri, 2012, p. 95.

[40]   The presentation "The Role of Insurers between Environmental Liability, Catastrophic Risk Mitigation and Sustainability" was given during the EELF Conference on Environmental Loss & Damage: Attribution, Liability, Compensation and Restoration held in Como, September 2018.

PART VIII

REAL COMPENSATION AND OFFSET REGIMES

The Strategy of "No Net Loss"

NO NET LOSS IN RECOVERY

The Overall End-of-Waste Impact Assessment

Topi TURUNEN*

1. INTRODUCTION

1.1. CIRCULAR ECONOMY AND END-OF-WASTE STATUS

The circular economy action plan[1] promotes more efficient utilisation of material resources. In order to pursue the objectives of the circular economy, the use of waste-based substances and objects should be promoted by creating a level playing field between them and virgin raw materials.[2] However, due to the lack of legal certainty in the commodification of waste materials, many operators prefer virgin raw materials over waste-based ones. Nonetheless using waste-based materials often provides environmentally better outcomes when one takes into account the whole lifecycle of the product.

Due to the scope of application of the waste legislation, the question of whether a substance or object is considered to be waste is crucial. Essentially, waste legislation applies to "waste", whereas product legislation applies to "non-waste". Article 3(1) of Directive 2008/98/EC (Waste Framework Directive, WFD) defines waste as any substance or object which the holder discards or intends or is required to discard.[3] However Article 6 of the WFD provides

---

* The author would like to thank Veera Salokannel (University of Lapland) for the excellent commentary she provided on this chapter.

1 *European Commission*, Communication from the Commission to the European Parliament, the Council, the European Economic and Social Committee and the Committee of the Regions: Closing the loop – An EU action plan for the Circular Economy, COM(2015) 614 final.

2 See e.g. Growth within: A circular economy vision for a competitive Europe, Ellen MacArthur Foundation, 2015, p. 22.

3 The applicability of the term "discard" is not limited to disposal operations in respect of waste, since substances or objects that are destined for recovery are also initially discarded and are usually considered waste. See e.g. Joined Cases C-418/97 and C-419/97, ARCO Chemie Nederland and Others, ECLI:EU:C:2000:318, para. 51; Case C-9/00, Palin Granit and Vehmassalon kansaterveystyön kuntayhtymän hallitus, ECLI:EU:C:2002:232, para. 27.

a set of criteria to determine whether the material has ceased to be waste (end-of-waste, EoW):

> Member States shall take appropriate measures to ensure that waste which has undergone a recycling or other recovery operation is considered to have ceased to be waste if it complies with the following conditions:
>
> a) the substance or object is to be used for specific purposes;
> b) a market or demand exists for such a substance or object;
> c) the substance or object fulfils the technical requirements for the specific purposes and meets the existing legislation and standards applicable to products; and
> d) the use of the substance or object will not lead to overall adverse environmental or human health impacts.

These criteria introduce a clear distinction between waste and non-waste: they separate safe recovered materials from those that still require the governance of waste legislation in order to control the risks involved in their utilisation. Therefore, the EoW criteria and their interpretation play a key role in the systemisation of circular economy.

The legislation that applies to similar non-waste products applies, instead of waste legislation, to materials after they cease to be waste. Usually this legislation regulates both the suitability of the material for the use to which it is being put and, through various kinds of product standards and limit values, the risks related to such use. Generally speaking, it would seem that after the EoW stage the use of the material is less restricted than under waste legislation. The reason for this is that waste legislation aims to control all kinds of risks from all kinds of wastes, while product regulation can focus on the specific risks posed by certain kind of products.

1.2. RESEARCH QUESTION

The criterion set out in point (d) of Article 6(1) of the WFD (hereinafter referred to as the "fourth criterion") provides that no overall adverse environmental or human health impacts shall be caused by the material ceasing to be waste. The fourth criterion refers to "overall" impacts. This means that while there can be both negative and positive impacts when material ceases to be waste, these impacts should overall be either be neutral or positive. If they are negative, the waste must remain as waste. However, the formulation of Article 6 leaves open the nature of the impact assessment as to EoW status.

It is usually possible to argue that using waste-based materials instead of virgin raw materials reduces environmental impacts at both ends of the lifecycle: it reduces the need to extract new raw materials and the need for waste disposal because, instead of being disposed of, the waste is used as a substitute for virgin raw materials. However, the use of waste-based materials may entail risks that are not present when using virgin raw materials for the same purpose. Because of this, the assessment of overall impacts should demonstrate that the material ceasing to be waste does not lead to overall adverse environmental or human health impacts.

Since the EoW criteria are part of the EU's waste legislation, a uniform interpretative model on the assessment of the fourth criterion seems necessary. However, none exists. This chapter examines the framework for the overall assessment of impacts involved in the EoW context and assesses its viability and potential problems. It also discusses the meaning of no net loss in the context of EoW status and the most typical impacts of ceasing to be waste.

2. ENVIRONMENTAL ACCEPTABILITY AT THE END-OF-WASTE STAGE

2.1. INTERPRETING THE FOURTH CRITERION

2.1.1. Basic Aspects

The first three EoW criteria set out in Article 6(1) of the WFD aim to ensure the use (and lawfulness of the use) of the substance or object.[4] The fourth criterion pursues the objective of environmental and human health protection. It is often referred to as the criterion of environmental acceptability. The initial assumption is that materials that are considered "waste" cause negative impacts. The fourth criterion stipulates that the use of the substance or object as non-waste should not cause any adverse environmental or human health impacts. In other words, material that ceases to be waste should have neutral or positive overall environmental and human health impacts.[5] This either means that the material was safe to use outside the scope of waste legislation all along or that the regulatory framework laid down for similar non-waste products is sufficient to control the use of the material in such a way that no overall adverse impacts are produced.[6] Additional control mechanisms can also be included in the framework of the decision granting EoW status.

---

[4]   T. Turunen, The Concepts of Waste and Non-waste in the Circular Economy, University of Eastern Finland, 2018, pp. 101–105.

[5]   See Monitoring impacts from Council Regulation (EU) No. 333/2011: End-of-waste criteria for Al/Fe scrap, JRC Scientific and Technical Reports, 2014, pp. 107–113, for the point that it would seem that regulation of EoW status in relation to iron, steel and aluminium has lived up to this standard. Environmental problems in connection with this regulation are caused by situations of non-compliance.

[6]   C-358/11, Lapin luonnonsuojelupiiri, ECLI:EU:C:2013:142, especially paras. 62–63. The CJEU argued that environmental acceptability could be achieved through a special regulatory

Naturally the fact that the material ceases to be waste does not have any impacts per se, since the definition of "waste" is an institutional concept: the impacts that arise from the regulatory framework governing the material change from that of waste legislation to that of the applicable product legislation.[7] This shift changes the nature of the legal framework governing the use of the material as it involves a move away from general precautionary regulation to specific product standards that deal with the typical impacts of these kinds of materials. Therefore, product regulation is often considered less stringent than that governing waste.

Assessing the fulfilment of the fourth criterion requires an in-depth examination of the substance or object and the impacts of its lifecycle. The criterion aims to ensure that the use of the substance or object does not cause impacts that would require it to be controlled under the framework of waste legislation.[8] The assessment of the environmental acceptability is bound up with purpose of use: different usages have different impacts.[9] The quantity, quality and the type of the emissions depend on whether the waste material is prepared for reuse, recycled or recovered for energy.[10]

All impacts have to be taken into account in the assessment, as it aims to achieve a complete understanding of the environmental and human health impacts and risks involved in using the material as non-waste instead of waste. The impact assessment should be based on comparative environmental studies[11] and should also be geographically wide and comprehensive. The direct and indirect impacts of the lifecycle of the product have to be considered, including the positive impacts alongside the negative effects. In addition to the

---

framework such as Regulation (EC) No. 1907/2006 of the European Parliament and of the Council of 18 December 2006 concerning the Registration, Evaluation, Authorisation and Restriction of Chemicals (REACH), establishing a European Chemicals Agency, amending Directive 1999/45/EC and repealing Council Regulation (EEC) No. 793/93 and Commission Regulation (EC) No. 1488/94 as well as Council Directive 76/769/EEC and Commission Directives 91/155/EEC, 93/67/EEC, 93/105/EC and 2000/21/EC, OJ 2006 L 396/1).

[7] The nature of the regulative frameworks is further described in T. Turunen, Deconstructing the Bottlenecks Caused by Waste Legislation: End-of-Waste Regulation, Journal for European Environmental & Planning Law 2017 (2), pp. 186–207.

[8] End of Waste Criteria: Final Report, JRC Scientific and Technical Reports, 2009, pp. 6, 9, 20.

[9] See Environment Agency, End-of-Waste and by-product hazard and risk assessment, November 2014, pp. 16–18, for the point that a new assessment has to be made for other end uses of the material. Naturally different purposes of use tend to have different kinds of impacts and on different environments. See O. Hjelmar et al., End-of-Waste criteria for waste-derived aggregates, WASCON Conference proceedings, 2012, p. 5, for the point that "if no restrictions or conditions are placed on the use of waste-derived aggregates with EoW status, then the source term must account for the 'worst case' release that may potentially take place".

[10] Study on the selection of waste streams for End of Waste assessment: Final report, JRC Scientific and Technical Reports, 2009, pp. 44–53.

[11] Id. at p. 30.

environmental impacts of the material ceasing to be waste, the impacts of the changes in the production processes have to be assessed. In many cases the same (or lighter) production processes used in relation to virgin raw materials can be used for waste-based materials. The assessment also takes into account the positive impacts of the EoW procedure.

The Joint Research Centre of the European Commission (JRC) guides interpretation of the fourth criterion in the following way:

> Assessing the impacts of introducing the end of waste criteria can best be achieved by comparing an "end of waste criteria scenario" with a "no action scenario".[12]

The JRC further elaborates that the assessment of the fulfilment of the criterion should cover all environmental and health impacts (through all environmental media, in particular soil, water and air) that are expected to be different as between the two scenarios, covering the full lifecycle of the product. In addition to the impacts that are caused by the normal operation of the recovery and use processes, the assessment should take into account the risks of impacts in the event of accidents or the possible misuse of the material. The JRC adds that, as far as possible, state-of-the-art lifecycle impact assessment methods should be used at the so-called mid-point or end-point impact levels.[13]

The JRC highlights that it is common practice for each impact category to be chosen and for the characterisation model to be applied to convert the relevant inventory results into a common unit. The JRC also argues that there is reasonable similarity between the impact categories included among the different existing impacts assessment methods and that the differences between the methods lie rather in the models applied to characterise each impact category and in the extent to which the mid-point results are modelled further in the impact chain towards a single end-point.[14] Nevertheless, the JRC does not provide any harmonised guidance on the balancing of different impact categories. On top of that, there is always a certain level of uncertainty as to the impacts of EoW status, as the comparison made is between the situation that existed before the material ceasing to be waste and a hypothetical assumption as to how the material ceasing to be waste may impact upon the environment and upon human health.[15]

---

[12] JRC, *supra*, note 8 at p. 35; JRC, *supra*, note 10 at p. 15.
[13] JRC, *supra*, note 8 at pp. 35–37. Reviews of lifecycle impact assessment can be found in H.A. *Udo de Haes et al.*, Life-Cycle Impact Assessment: Striving Towards Best Practice, Society of Environmental Toxicology and Chemistry, Pensacola, 2002; O. *Jolliet et al.*, The LCIA midpoint-damage framework of the UNEP/SETAC life cycle initiative, The International Journal of Life Cycle Assessment 2004 (6), pp. 394–404.
[14] See JRC, *supra*, note 8 at pp. 35–36, for the point that typical impact categories include acidification, global warming, mineral extraction and human toxicity.
[15] JRC, *supra*, note 8 at pp. 6, 9, 20. See JRC, *supra*, note 5 at pp. 107–113.

In the English EoW system, the assessment of environmental acceptability is guided in the following way: the applicant for EoW status needs to provide information on the environmental and human health impacts from the material. The applicant has to show that its material has no properties, including trace components or contaminants, which will lead to an unacceptable risk. If there is a non-waste comparator for the same end use, the operator can compare this with the material for which EoW status is being applied. The applicant needs to include any characteristics of the material that are different from the non-waste comparator. The applicant also needs to provide the analysis of the material, clearly demonstrating its composition and that it will cause no worse environmental impact than the relevant non-waste comparator. Alternatively the applicant can carry out a generic or site-specific risk assessment. For more practical details on the assessment, authorities have published a guidance document for EoW status and by-product hazard and risk assessment.[16]

2.1.2. Using a Comparator

EoW assessment in England is often based on a comparable virgin material or product. The guidance set out on the webpage of the IsItWaste tool states that if there is a non-waste comparator for the same end use, the operator can compare this with the material for which EoW status is sought. In the information provided, the applicant needs to include details of any characteristics of the material that are different from the non-waste comparator. The applicant also needs to upload analysis of the material, clearly demonstrating its composition and that it will cause no worse environmental impact than the relevant non-waste comparator.[17]

The guidance document provided by the Environment Agency further specifies the guidelines. Comparators refer to substances or objects that are the virgin counterparts of the EoW material. Supporting the logic of a level playing field between waste-based and virgin raw materials and the ideals of the internal market, it makes sense that where the impacts of waste-based material are no worse than those of a marketable non-waste product, such material should not be considered waste. The Environment Agency has collated and generated physicochemical data on different potential comparators, including non-waste wood, inorganic fertilisers and soil improver.[18] The comparator reports give an

---

[16]   IsItWaste tool user guidance – Step 6: environmental and impact assessment, updated on 26 June 2018, available at https://www.gov.uk/government/publications/isitwaste-tool-for-advice-on-the-by-products-and-end-of-waste-tests/isitwaste-tool-user-guide; *Environment Agency, supra*, note 9.

[17]   IsItWaste tool user guidance, *supra*, note 16.

[18]   For further information, see https://www.gov.uk/government/publications/defining-product-comparators-to-use-when-applying-waste-derived-materials-to-land.

indication of what this material is a comparator for, how data on a comparator might be collected and analysed and what summary statistics could be used in the comparison.[19]

The idea of comparators is based on the assumption that waste-based materials substitute for virgin materials. In many cases that is true and comparison between the waste-based and the virgin raw material can give a good indication of whether the fourth criterion has been met. However, data on the comparators might not be available or might not exist. In addition, the waste-based material can have different kinds of impacts from the virgin raw material due to being waste-based or being used in purposes of use where it does not directly substitute for virgin raw materials.[20] This should not prevent the materials from ceasing to be waste. Therefore, the assessment cannot always be done through comparator materials.

2.2. THE IDEOLOGY OF NO NET LOSS IN RECOVERY

In the situation where the waste-based material cannot be directly compared with a comparator material, the impacts should be compared against the no-action scenario in which the material would still be considered waste. The assessment procedure should not be confused with normal environmental impact assessment, even though these also require a "no-action alternative" to function as a means of comparing the impacts of different alternatives. The problem with environmental impact assessment methodology is that it focuses on the impacts of a certain operation, which will quite naturally be limited to a certain area, whereas in relation to EoW status the process could best be described as a form of product approval that allows the marketing of the waste-based material within the EU or its Member States.

The impact assessment in relation to the EoW stage has to produce a neutral or positive outcome. Therefore, a theoretically suitable model for the assessment could follow the logic of ecological compensation mechanisms, the *no-net-loss ideology* in particular. Compensation actions can have three kinds of outcomes: (1) full compensation where the overall state of the environment has not been weakened (no net loss); (2) over-compensation where the environment is left in a better condition than it was before the initial activity (net-positive impacts); and (3) partial compensation where the loss of environmental values is limited (limited loss).[21] A "normal environmental impact assessment" usually

---

19 *Environment Agency, supra*, note 9 at pp. 43–44.
20 See JRC, *supra*, note 8 at pp. 93–95.
21 For more information on (1) and (2) see *IUCN*, No Net Loss and Net Positive Impact Approaches for Biodiversity – Exploring the potential application of these approaches in the commercial agriculture and forestry sectors, 2015.

concludes in a limited loss outcome. As the fourth criterion states that there should be no "overall adverse environmental or human health impacts" from ceasing to be waste, the alternative of limited loss has to be ruled out and the EoW stage should achieve either no-net-loss or net-positive impacts.[22]

The requirements for achieving a no-net-loss outcome[23] are left undefined. The impact assessment in the WFD concerning EoW status focuses on impacts such as energy consumption and industrial emissions, whereas ecological compensation (from which the terminology of no net loss is borrowed) is based on prevailing trends in biodiversity conditions.[24] In biodiversity protection, the no-net-loss policy is usually divided into a four-step mitigation hierarchy that should be used in the evaluation of activities that are potentially harmful for the environment.[25] First, if the activity is likely to have negative impacts, these should be prevented. Second, if prevention is not possible, the negative impacts should be reduced or alleviated. Third, the negative impacts should be cured or mitigated *in situ*. The fourth step in the hierarchy is compensation for the environmental loss outside the area of the activity.[26]

This hierarchy does not completely fit in with EoW status because it is based on balancing a harmful action against an offset. In the EoW context, potential negative and positive impacts alike are dependent on the waste material in question, the regulations that apply to similar non-waste products and the conditions laid down in the EoW framework. Achieving a no-net-loss outcome depends on striking an overall balance between negative and positive impacts. The negative impacts of EoW status have to be considered as damage, while the positive impacts have to be considered as offsets. Nevertheless, it has to be taken into account that, unlike the offset measures that apply in respect of biodiversity protection, the positive impacts involved in the EoW context usually do not require separate action but are direct or indirect impacts of the increased use of waste-based materials. The no-net-loss outcome is not pursued between two different actions (the damaging action and the offset) but between different impacts of the same action (the EoW ruling).

---

[22] This is also the initial point of departure in respect of compensation measures in biodiversity protection. See Business, Biodiversity, Offsets and BBOP: An Overview, 2009, p. 4, available at https://www.forest-trends.org/publications/bbop-overview-2009/.

[23] Discussion of the objective of a no net loss from this point on also refers to net-positive impacts.

[24] See *J.W. Bull et al.*, Biodiversity offsets in theory and practice, Oryx, Fauna & Flora International, 2013, pp. 3–4.

[25] Assessment of plans and projects significantly affecting Natura 2000 sites: Methodological guidance on the provision of Article 6(3) and (4) of the Habitats Directive 92/43/EEC, European Communities, 2002. See also BBOP, Mitigation Hierarchy, available at https://www.forest-trends.org/bbop/bbop-key-concepts/mitigation-hierarchy/.

[26] *B.A. MacKenney & J.M. Kiesecker*, Policy Development for Biodiversity Offsets: A Review of Offset Frameworks, Environmental Management 2010 (45), p. 167.

3. NO NET LOSS IN THE IMPACT ASSESSMENT

3.1. NO NET LOSS AND LIFECYCLE ASSESSMENT

Despite the different natures of impacts, assessments of no net loss in biodiversity protection and in EoW rulings have similar features: there can be negative impacts as long as they are balanced or outweighed by the positive impacts.[27] However, there is no fixed methodology in use for EoW impact assessments. In order to examine the overall impacts of ceasing to be waste, the assessment has to take into account the impacts of all stages of the lifecycle of the material.[28] Therefore, lifecycle assessment can offer a suitable methodology for the assessment of the fourth criterion and its no-net-loss outcome.[29] The lifecycle of a product can be divided into five parts: (1) extraction of the raw materials; (2) production of the product; (3) packaging and distribution of the product; (4) use and maintenance of the product; and (5) disposal or recovery of the product. The input and output of all the stages determine the overall impacts.[30] This lifecycle assessment helps to provide a comprehensive understanding of all the impacts of the material ceasing to be waste and to ensure that the EoW stage has a no-net-loss outcome compared to the no-action scenario.[31]

The term "lifecycle assessment" refers to an approach where the assets and liabilities upstream and downstream of the product are assessed.[32] No EU-wide standard for lifecycle assessment has been laid down and therefore

---

[27] A similar idea as to acknowledging net benefits in the evaluation of lifecycle assessment has been recognised in the impact assessment of wastewater treatment. See *D. Godin, C. Bouchard & P.A. Vanrolleghem*, Net environmental benefit: introducing a new LCA approach on wastewater treatment systems, Water Science & Technology 2012 (9), pp. 1624–1631.

[28] JRC, *supra*, note 8 at p. 35.

[29] See *J. Schmidt et al.*, Life cycle assessment of the waste hierarchy – A Danish case study on waste paper, Waste Management 2007 (11), p. 1523.

[30] See *C. Hendrickson* et al., Economic Input-Output Models for Environmental Life-Cycle Assessment, Environmental Science & Technology 1998(7), p. 184.

[31] *E.M. Ekern*, Towards an integrated product regulatory framework based on life-cycle thinking, in B. Sjåfjell & A. Wiesbrock (eds.), The Greening of European Business under EU Law: Taking Article 11 TFEU Seriously, Routledge 2015, pp. 149–150. See e.g. International Reference Life Cycle Data System: Framework and Requirements for Life Cycle Impact Assessment Models and Indicators, JRC, European Commission, 2010; International Reference Life Cycle Data System. Analysis of Existing Environmental Impact Assessment Methodologies for use in Life Cycle Assessment, JRC, European Commission, 2010. The JRC has carried out a vast amount of research on the lifecycles of different products and production methods, which might significantly benefit assessments of departures.

[32] See *European Commission*, Guidance on the interpretation of key provisions of Directive 2008/98/EC on waste, p. 51.

there is no exact methodology to be referred to in a legal sense.[33] The ISO 14040:2006 standard divides lifecycle assessments into four phases: (1) goal and scope definition; (2) inventory analysis; (3) impact assessment; and (4) interpretation. The first phase aims to identify different aspects to take into account in this particular lifecycle assessment as the depth and the breadth of the assessment can vary considerably depending on its goal and subject. The second phase entails a lifecycle inventory analysis, comprising an inventory of input/output data in relation to the subject of the assessment. The third phase is the impact assessment, which provides information to help assess the results of the previous phase in order to better understand their environmental significance. The interpretation phase summarises the results of the study to draw conclusions on the impacts of different options in the product's lifecycle. In relation to EoW status, the interpretative phase should conclude in a no-net-loss outcome as compared to the no-action scenario where material remains waste.[34]

However, there are problems relating to the assessment. Firstly, the different kinds of environmental or human health impacts are not commensurate. This means that in the event that using certain waste reduces the amount of energy consumed in the production process, no rules are in place to objectively balance the positive environmental impacts of this against, for example, increased emissions in the purification process. As the pricing of environmental and human health impacts has long been the subject of scientific debate,[35] it is understandably impossible to lay down a single set of criteria in the impact assessment. Therefore, there can be no absolute objective standards for a no-net-loss outcome either. The existing methodologies for this kind of comparison are not mandatory. Furthermore, they are not based on objective scientific data but on value judgments that can always be contested on a national level or on a case-by-case basis.[36]

---

[33]   See *C. Dahlhammar*, The application of "life cycle thinking" in European environmental law: theory and practice, Journal for European Environmental & Planning Law 2015 (2), pp. 115–116, for discussion on the methodology of the assessment. See also *H. Kalimo*, E-Cycling: Linking Trade and Environmental Law in the EC and the U.S., Transnational Publishing, 2006, pp. 628–629; *Ekern, supra,* note 31 at p. 158.

[34]   ISO 14040:2006 Environmental management – Life cycle assessment – Principles and framework.

[35]   See e.g. *L.B. Burlington*, Valuing Natural Resource Damages: A Transatlantic Lesson, in G. Betlem & E. Brans (eds.), Environmental Liability in the EU: The 2004 Directive Compared with US and Member State Law, Cameron May 2006; *A. Enetjärn et al.*, Environmental Compensation: Key Conditions for Increased and Cost Effective Application, Nordic Council of Ministers, 2015, p. 17, for the point that the negative impacts on the environment are often undervalued; *N.D. Hanley & J. Wright*, Valuing the Environment: Recent UK Experience and an Application to Greenbelt Land, Journal of Environmental Planning and Management 1992 (2), pp. 145–160; *J.-P. Barde*, Valuing the Environment: Six Case Studies, Earthscan Publications Ltd, 1991.

[36]   See *K. Rogers et al.*, Multicriteria Decision Analysis and Life Cycle Assessment, in I. Linkov, E. Ferguson & S. Magar (eds.), Real-Time and Deliberative Decision Making: Application to

In addition, lifecycle assessment studies are very often affected by uncertainties relating to a lack of specific data and as to the validity of the model being used.[37] This emphasises the problem of assessing the no-net-loss outcome at the EoW stage: the final balancing between the negative and positive impacts often becomes ambiguous. The problem is also recognised in assessing the no-net-loss outcome in relation to ecological compensation.[38]

Of course, despite the JRC's suggestion, the formulation of the fourth criterion does not specifically require a lifecycle assessment. A lifecycle assessment is merely a way to ensure and show the no-net-loss outcome of the EoW ruling. The task of introducing clear objective criteria by which environmental acceptability at the EoW stage can be assessed seems rather complicated due to the lack of uniform methodologies for the conduct of such an assessment. There is a need for policy change at both EU and national level, together with awareness-raising, guidance and monitoring in order to address the problems and complexities involved in bringing about a no-net-loss situation.[39] The scope of the impacts that have to be taken into account in the assessment ultimately depends on the material involved and the potential impacts of its recovery and use.

3.2. IMPACTS OF CEASING TO BE WASTE

3.2.1. Negative Impacts of Ceasing to be Waste

The rationale behind the strict provisions of the waste legislation is that many waste streams potentially have negative impacts on the environment and on

---

Emerging Stressors, NATO Science for Peace and Security Series C: Environmental Security 2007, pp. 307–308, for the point that this problem could be addressed in the interpretative phase of the lifecycle assessment but the normalisation and weighing of different impact categories requires a common methodology. In addition, the normalisation and weighing are left optional in the ISO 14040 standard because they are not considered an objective standard but more of a value judgement.

[37] See e.g. *R. Heijungs & M.A. Huijbregts*, A Review of Approaches to Treat Uncertainty in LCA, in Proceedings of the Second Biennial Meeting of the International Environmental Modelling and Software Society, iEMSS, 2004, Complexity and Integrated Resources Management, 14–17 June 2004, Osnabrück, Germany, 2004, pp. 332–339; *M. Guo & R.J. Murphy*, LCA data quality: sensitivity and uncertainty analysis, Science of the Total Environment 2012, pp. 230–243, 435–436; *T. Mattila et al.*, Uncertainty in environmentally conscious decision making: beer or wine?, The International Journal of Life Cycle Assessment 2012 (6), pp. 696–705; *S. Koskela et al.*, Reusable plastic crate or recyclable cardboard box? A comparison of two delivery systems, Journal of Cleaner Production 2014 (69), pp. 83–90.

[38] *Bull, supra*, note 24 at pp. 371–376.

[39] *G. Tucker et al.*, Policy Options for an EU No Net Loss Initiative, Report to the European Commission, Institute for European Environmental Policy, 2013, pp. 14–15.

human health if they are used outside the legal framework for waste.[40] After the EoW stage, there is a risk of unregulated negative impacts if the framework for EoW is not carefully formulated as the nature of the regulatory framework goes from precautionary (waste) to precise (products). The JRC argues that there is a theoretical possibility that applying a strict quality standard to a non-waste product may actually have a greater negative impact on the environment due to the increased processing impact (caused, for example, by an increased need for energy) than that represented by the original risk itself.[41] However, this is not very likely since the processes carried out before the step where the material ceases to be waste remain within the ambit of waste law and require the necessary permits.[42]

The impact assessment should take into the account the risks related to the quality, properties, impurity or possible heterogeneity of the waste-based materials. Furthermore, it is often overlooked that even if wastes are disposed of by burning or landfilling, they still have negative impacts on the environment and on human health.[43] In addition, their potential for being recovered is lost.

It is important to acknowledge that after the EoW stage the material does not fall into a legal vacuum, even though the provisions of waste legislation no longer apply to it. The legislation on similar non-waste products applies to EoW materials and introduces new kinds of criteria that influence product quality.[44] Therefore, the negative impacts, as well as the quality and properties of the material, are subject to a strict legislative framework and product standards. These restrictions and rules have to be taken into account in the assessment in order to provide accurate information on the impacts of ceasing to be waste.

This perspective was highlighted with regard to hazardous wastes ceasing to be waste in the *Lapin luonnonsuojelupiiri* case.[45] For example, after waste

---

[40] See O. Hjelmar et al., End-of-Waste Criteria for Construction & Demolition Waste, TemaNord, 2016, pp. 44–64, for a detailed overview of the possible negative impacts of EoW status of construction and demolition wastes.

[41] The impacts of the materials and their processing are really case-specific and although these kinds of impacts were not detected in any pilot cases, the possibility has to be taken into account in case-by-case assessments of impacts at the EoW stage.

[42] JRC, *supra*, note 8 at pp. 33–34, 37.

[43] See *Tucker*, *supra* note 39 at p. 96. For example, waste disposal has negative impacts such as losses in land use, soil and water storage as well as reducing the aesthetic values of the natural environment.

[44] JRC, *supra*, note 8 at p. 30.

[45] Case C-358/11, Lapin luonnonsuojelupiiri, ECLI:EU:C:2013:142. See *J. Alaranta & T. Turunen*, Drawing a Line between European Waste Regulation and European Chemicals Regulation, RECIEL 2017 (2), pp. 169–170. The *Lapin luonnonsuojelupiiri* case clarified that the regulatory framework post-waste can have a substantial influence on the impacts assessment applicable to EoW status if it restricts the use of the material or lays down standards concerning its use or properties.

ceases to be waste, the authorisation system of Regulation (EC) No. 1907/2006 (REACH Regulation) can apply to the chemical content of the waste-based material. The authorisation process restricts the use of waste-based materials if they contain certain chemicals in order to protect the environment and human from the negative impacts of these chemicals.[46] In some situations, the negative impacts of the EoW stage could materialise due to potential loopholes in the EU product legislation. This is the case where the use of waste-based material involves certain risks that are not addressed in this legislation because virgin raw materials do not pose these risks.[47] If the total impacts of the EoW stage would be negative (i.e. they would result in a worse outcome than the no-action scenario), the fourth criterion cannot be fulfilled and EoW status is not available.

3.2.2. Positive Impacts of Ceasing to be Waste

When waste-based material ceases to be waste, the regulatory burden for its use is usually reduced. This usually increases its use. When waste-based materials are substituted for virgin raw materials, the demand for the virgin raw material is reduced, the production process is often altered to a lighter version of the previous processes and the lifecycle of the waste material is prolonged, thus reducing the need for landfilling.[48] The popularity of waste-based substitutes typically derives from a reduction in the cost of acquiring raw materials: for example, it is usually cheaper to organise a recycling loop for scrap metals than mining the minerals.

The production process often does not change significantly when waste-based materials are substituted for virgin raw materials. However, unlike virgin raw materials, waste-based materials have often been processed to a high standard in their previous lifecycle while virgin raw materials may require extensive processing before their initial use in a product. Consequently, it is often possible

---

[46] See *J. Alaranta*, Kemikaalit ja kiertotalous – Tutkimus huolta aiheuttavien aineiden ja materiaalikierron sääntelystä REACH-asetuksen mukaan, University of Eastern Finland, 2018, pp. 58–60.

[47] See *K. Talus & T. Turunen*, Regulating Emerging Technologies: Regulation and Innovation in WtE, in H.H.G. Post (ed.), From Waste to Energy: Technology, the Environment and the Implications under EU Law, Eleven International Publishing 2018, pp. 184–186, for the point that it is extremely difficult to compare waste-based gas with natural gas due to the fact that the waste-based gas contains substances that are not regulated under the EU limit values for natural gas because natural gas does not usually contain them.

[48] See End-of-Waste Criteria for Glass Cullet: Technical Proposals, JRC Scientific and Technical Reports, European Union, 2011, p. 60, for the point that prolonging a product's lifecycle and avoiding its disposal are important factors in increasing the material efficiency of all waste materials. Nonetheless, these benefits are even more significant for waste streams such as glass cullet that can in principle retain all their physical features after infinite recycling loops.

Figure 1. Balancing positive and negative impacts of EoW

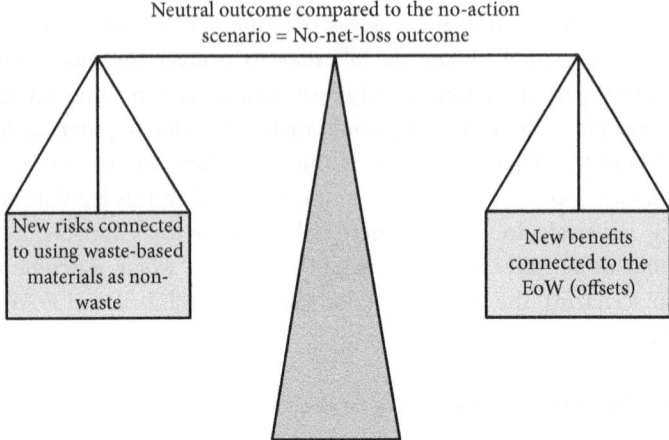

Source: Created by the author.

to bypass certain production stages when using waste-based materials. This can reduce the environmental impacts and emissions involved in the production, resulting in substantial savings during the process. Multiple EU EoW pilot projects have acknowledged that using waste-based materials can give rise to substantial energy savings. For instance, manufacturing copper products from scrap copper requires 35–85 per cent of the energy consumed when using virgin copper.[49]

In addition, the waste is naturally no longer destined for disposal if it has been recovered. It is usually obvious that prolonging a material's lifecycle has positive impacts,[50] particularly in terms of reduced emissions in disposal operations and in the processes of waste management and transportation. Where feasible, the recovery of waste is an environmentally preferable option to disposal, which involves losing the material potential and energy capacity of the waste. In addition, by creating new product standards and enforcement

---

[49]   End-of-Waste Criteria for Copper and Copper Alloy Scrap: Technical Proposals, JRC Scientific and Technical Reports, European Union, 2011, p. 41. See End-of-Waste Criteria for Aluminum and Aluminum Alloy Scrap: Technical Proposals, JRC Scientific and Technical Reports, European Union, 2010, p. 20, for the point that for aluminium products this figure is only 7 per cent and as for waste paper it is between 20 per cent and 60 per cent. See also End-of-Waste Criteria for Waste Paper: Technical Proposals, JRC Scientific and Technical Reports, European Union, 2011, p. 44.

[50]   However, this is not necessarily the case in relation to hazardous materials, as their disposal may be mandatory, e.g. products containing high concentrations of persistent organic pollutants (POPs).

mechanisms, EoW criteria can reinforce the application of regulatory controls and reduce the environmental impacts and risks posed by non-compliant materials.[51]

The JRC has indicated that the existing risks and negative impacts of the EoW stage can be deemed acceptable if they are balanced against the overall benefits (offsets) and if there are proportionate measures to address them.[52] In other words, when a no-net-loss outcome is reached in the impacts of the whole lifecycle between EoW and a no-action-scenario, the negative impacts can be accepted. Table 1 below illustrates the lowest acceptable net impacts of the EoW stage: the no-net-loss outcome (net-positive impacts are preferred).

4. SHORTCOMINGS IN THE ASSESSMENT OF THE FOURTH CRITERION

The fourth EoW criterion is not flexible.[53] The fact that no common practices apply to its interpretation can cause difficulties in regulating on EoW status: it can result in the use of inconsistent and unequal interpretative practices that result in obtaining EoW status being either too easy or too hard. Moulding a circular economy entails ensuring that EoW status guarantees that materials are recovered back into the production processes in a safe manner, with consideration for the environment and for human health. Certain common standards and/or guidance are necessary in order to create rules for the assessment of the fourth criterion that are more concrete.

The assessment of the fourth criterion is carried out taking into account the overall impacts of the lifecycle of the product by comparing the current situation (no-action-scenario) to the hypothetical scenario after the EoW ruling.[54] This task is dogged by some key problems. First, no criteria or standards have been laid down for how to carry out the assessment in the EoW procedure. Second, the negative and the positive environmental and human health impacts are not commensurate. There are no rules for evaluating the balance between the negative and positive (offsets) impacts of a material ceasing to be waste. Even though extensive studies on the impacts have been carried out, the evaluation is likely to remain sketchy and ambiguous if there is no objective framework for it. Uncertainty as to the exact impacts is also a typical issue because the assessment

---

51 JRC, *supra*, note 8 at p. 34.
52 Id. at p. 37.
53 T. Turunen, Jäteluokittelusta poistumisen kriteerit ja niiden tulkinta, Ympäristöjuridiikka 2014 (2), pp. 54–55.
54 JRC, *supra*, note 8 at pp. 6, 9, 20. See JRC, *supra*, note 5 at pp. 107–113.

is based on a comparison between the present situation and a hypothetical situation after the EoW ruling.[55]

These problems can hamper the development of new recovery routes for waste-based materials. The wording of Article 6 of the WFD would seem to allow the use of some sort of offsets scheme in order to achieve a no-net-loss outcome in recovery but does not provide an interpretative platform for it. Nonetheless, the issue was not addressed in Directive 2018/851/EU,[56] which amended the WFD, even though the first EoW criterion was amended. In order to promote the use of waste-based materials in the EU, a harmonised assessment framework would seem necessary.

---

[55] Similar problems have been recognised in respect of ecological compensation. See *Bull*, *supra*, note 24 at pp. 371–376.

[56] Directive 2018/851/EU of the European Parliament and of the Council of 30 May 2018 amending Directive 2008/98/EC on waste, OJ 2018 L 150/109.

NO NET LOSS AND FOREST OFFSETS IN THE FLEMISH REGION

A Cautionary Tale of How Not to Reconcile Science-Based Conservation Policies with Economic Interests and Vested Rights?

Hendrik Schoukens and Geert Van Hoorick

1. INTRODUCTION

Notwithstanding the widespread conservation efforts throughout recent decades, the world is currently witnessing an unprecedented decline of the remaining biodiversity, which some authors now equate to a "sixth extinction wave".[1] In spite of its progressive environmental legislation, such as the EU Habitats Directive (92/43/EEC)[2] and Birds Directive (2009/147/EC)[3] (the "Nature Directives"), the EU is no exception to the general rule of continuing biodiversity decline, with a major share of the EU's protected species and habitats currently under an unfavourable conservation status.[4] Even common or "ordinary" biodiversity is not faring better in many Member States,[5] whilst

---

[1] A. Barnosky et al., Has the Earth's sixth mass extinction already arrived?, Nature 2011 (473), pp. 51–57; G. Ceballos et al., Accelerated modern human-induced species losses: entering the sixth mass extinction, Science Advances 2015 (1), e1400253, DOI: 10.1126/sciadv.1400253.

[2] Council Directive 92/43/EEC on the conservation of natural habitats and of wild fauna and flora, OJ 1992 L 206/7 (hereinafter referred to as the Habitats Directive).

[3] Council Directive 79/409/EEC on the conservation of wild birds, OJ 1979 L 103/1 (hereinafter referred to as the Birds Directive). The initial Birds Directive was codified in European Parliament and Council Directive 2009/147/EC on the conservation of wild birds, OJ 2010 L 20/7.

[4] European Environment Agency, State of nature in the EU. Results from reporting under the nature directives 2007–2012, EEA Technical Report, No. 2/2015, 2015.

[5] S.O. Petrovan & B.R. Schmidt, Volunteer Conservation Action Data Reveals Large-Scale and Long-Term Negative Population Trends of a Widespread Amphibian, the Common Toad (Bufo bufo), PLoS ONE 2016 (11/10), e0161943, DOI: 10.1371/journal.pone.0161943.

landscape fragmentation is continuing to unabatedly affect a large share of the EU's territory.[6] In 2010, the EU established the overarching objective of halting the loss of biodiversity and the degradation of ecosystem services by 2020, and of restoring 15 per cent of the degraded ecosystems wherever feasible.[7] In order to limit further loss and to achieve its progressive restoration pledges,[8] there is a broad consensus that further biodiversity loss needs to be avoided or, at the very minimum, compensated. The same year, the European Commission made a commitment to propose an initiative to ensure that there is no net loss (NNL) of ecosystems and their services (e.g. through compensation or offsetting schemes).[9] To that end, the Environment Council of Ministers explicitly stated in its conclusions of 21 June 2011 that "a common approach is needed for the implementation in the EU of the 'no net loss' principle", inviting the Commission to draw on the experience and specificities of each Member State.[10] It was further clarified that within this context, the NNL principle entails "that conservation/biodiversity losses in one geographically or otherwise defined area are balanced by a gain elsewhere, provided that this principle does not entail any impairment of existing biodiversity as protected by EU nature legislation."[11]

Although the European Commission has presented several studies on the further operationalisation of NNL[12] in recent years, no explicit set of binding EU rules currently exists to comprehensively address NNL outside the specific context of biodiversity, which is already explicitly protected under the EU Nature Directives, or, to a certain extent, the water bodies covered by the Water Framework Directive (2000/60/EC).[13] Nor has any other policy instrument been adopted to lay down a more comprehensive approach to NNL.

---

[6]   *European Environment Agency*, Landscape fragmentation in the EU, 2011, Joint EEA FOEN Report, EEA Report, No. 2/2011, 2011.

[7]   *European Commission*, Communication from the Commission to the European Parliament, the Council, the Economic and Social Committee and the Committee of the Regions, Our life insurance, our natural capital: an EU biodiversity strategy to 2020, COM(2011) 244 final (hereinafter further referred to as the EU Biodiversity Strategy).

[8]   More extensively on this ecological restoration objective, see: *A Cliquet, K. Decleer & H. Schoukens*, Restoring nature in the EU: The only way is up?, in C.H. Born et al. (eds.), The Habitats Directive in its EU Environmental Law Context: European Nature's Best Hope?, Routledge, 2015, pp. 265–284.

[9]   For more information on the European Commission's policy towards no net loss (NNL), see: http://ec.europa.eu/environment/nature/biodiversity/nnl/index_en.htm.

[10]   Council Conclusions, No. 11249/11, 21 June 2011, http://data.consilium.europa.eu/doc/document/ST-11249-2011-INIT/en/pdf.

[11]   Council Conclusions, No. 18374/11, 19 December 2011, footnote 12, http://data.consilium.europa.eu/doc/document/ST-18374-2011-INIT/en/pdf.

[12]   See for instance: *Institute for European Environmental Policy (IEEP), in collaboration with VU, IVM, Eftec and GHK*, Policy Options for an EU No Net Loss Initiative, 2014.

[13]   Directive 2000/60/EC of the European Parliament and of the Council of 23 October 2000 establishing a framework for Community action in the field of water policy, OJ 2000 L 371/1 (further referred to as the Water Framework Directive).

So far, the closest the EU has come to introducing a more robust mitigation and offsetting scheme aimed at addressing general biodiversity loss was the 2014 revision of the Environmental Impact Assessment (EIA) Directive (2011/92/EU),[14] which as of 2017, explicitly requires authorities to consider measures to avoid, prevent, reduce and, if possible, offset significant effects on the environment when authorising projects are subject to a prior EIA.[15] Yet, while the revised EIA Directive explicitly referred to the EU's NNL commitments under the Convention on Biological Diversity as a source of inspiration,[16] it remains dubious at best to read into the new provisions a substantive duty to fully offset the damage to nature.[17]

The absence of a detailed regulatory framework at the EU level requiring compensation for the loss of "ordinary" biodiversity notwithstanding, the notion of biodiversity offsets for future damage to nature has generated much appeal in the business, government, finance and conservation sectors in recent decades.[18] Over the past two decades, achieving NNL through biodiversity offsetting has gradually turned into one of the overarching objectives of many conservation policies, at both the international and the domestic levels. Whereas biodiversity compensation actions have garnered a lot of attention in the specific context of protected areas, such as the Natura 2000 Network,[19] a shift in focus is noticeable, with many stakeholders expressing a wish that biodiversity offsets be directed towards the mitigation and compensation of habitat loss and other impacts on "normal" landscapes or "ordinary" biodiversity.[20] Member States like Germany, which introduced an Impact Mitigation Regulation back in 1976 under the Federal Conservation Act,

---

[14]   Directive 2011/92/EU of the European Parliament and of the Council of 13 December 2011 on the assessment of the effects of certain public and private projects on the environment, OJ 2011 L 26/1 (hereinafter referred to as the EIA Directive).

[15]   Directive 2014/52/EU of the European Parliament and of the Council of 16 April 2014 amending Directive 2011/92/EU on the assessment of the effects of certain public and private projects on the environment, OJ 2014 L 124/1.

[16]   See for instance Recital 10 of the preamble to Directive 2014/52/EU.

[17]   See also: *H.T. Anker*, Simplifying EU environmental legislation – Reviewing the EIA Directive?, Journal for European Environmental & Planning Law 2014, pp. 338–339.

[18]   *R. Lapeyre et al.*, Biodiversity Offsets as Market-Based Instruments for Ecosystem Services? From Discourse to Practices, Ecosystem Services 2015, pp. 125–133.

[19]   Article 6(4) of the Habitats Directive stipulates that planning authorities need to require additional compensation measures when granting permits for large-scale projects which are eligible to qualify as "Imperative Reasons of Overriding Public Interest" (IROPI). See more extensively: *D. McGillivray*, Compensating Biodiversity Loss: The EU Commission's Approach to Compensation under Art 6 of the Habitats Directive, Journal of Environmental Law 2012, pp. 417–450.

[20]   *W. Wende et al.*, Introduction of a European Strategy on No Net Loss of Biodiversity, in W. Wende et al. (eds.), Biodiversity Offsets. European Perspectives on No Net Loss of Biodiversity and Ecosystem Services, Springer, 2017, pp. 5–6.

have extensive experience when it comes to mitigating and compensating for general biodiversity losses.[21]

The Business and Biodiversity Programme (BBOP) currently defines the concept of "biodiversity offset" as "measurable conservation outcomes resulting from actions designed to compensate for significant residual adverse biodiversity impacts arising from project development after appropriate prevention and mitigation measures have been taken."[22] While no fixed legal definition of the latter notion exists, conventional wisdom has accepted that biodiversity offsetting is to be applied in the context of the so-called mitigation hierarchy.[23] The overall goal of biodiversity offsetting is to achieve NNL or preferably a net gain of biodiversity in the field.[24] These gains are primarily to be achieved through the creation of new habitats or the restoration of damaged habitats.[25]

In recent years, however, more market-based approaches to biodiversity mitigation and offsetting have gained traction among politicians and business people.[26] Sophisticated economic regimes of biodiversity offsetting – such as habitat banking, bio-banking and wetland mitigation banking – have been implemented in countries such as the USA, Germany and Australia.[27] These banking approaches assume the creation of a regulated market in which credits from actions with beneficial biodiversity outcomes can be purchased to offset the debit from environmental damage.[28] When compared with *ad hoc*

---

[21] For an analysis of the German offsetting scheme, see: *M. Reese*, Habitat offset and banking – will it save our nature?, in C.H. Born et al. (eds.), The Habitats Directive in its EU Environmental Law Context: European Nature's Best Hope?, Routledge, 2015, pp. 483–498.

[22] *BBOP (Business and Biodiversity Offsets Programme)*, Standards on Biodiversity Offsets, Washington DC, 2012.

[23] *K. ten Kate & M. Crowe*, Biodiversity Offsets: Policy Options for Governments. An Input Paper for the IUCN Technical Study Group on Biodiversity Offsets, Switzerland, 2014, p. 7.

[24] *K. ten Kate et al.*, Biodiversity Offsets: Views, Experience, and the Business Case, IUCN, Insight Investment, 2014, p. 13.

[25] Although contested by some, even the improved protection of existing habitats against future degradation, better known as "compensated or averted loss", is sometimes brought under the umbrella of NNL. See for instance the definition of "biodiversity offsets" used by Maron et al. in *M. Maron et al.*, Faustian bargains? Restoration realities in the context of biodiversity offset policies, Biological Conservation 2012, p. 142. Very critical in this respect is: *J.W. Bull et al.*, Biodiversity offsets in theory and practice, Oryx, 2013, pp. 369–380.

[26] The European Commission has also issued several studies on the topic of "habitat banking". These studies can be consulted at the: http://ec.europa.eu/environment/enveco/taxation/index.htm#hab_bank.

[27] For an overview of the distinct types of biodiversity banks, see: *G. Froger et al.*, Towards a Comparative and Critical Analysis of Biodiversity Banks, Ecosystem Services 2015, pp. 152–161.

[28] For an overview, see: *M. Caroll et al.* (eds.), Conservation & Biodiversity Banking. A Guide to Setting Up and Running Biodiversity Credit Systems, 2008.

compensation implemented by permittees, market-based approaches to offsetting are believed to lead to more cost-effective nature conservation strategies, capable of offering both additional flexibility and less administrative burdens for project developers whilst generating more robust biodiversity gains.

It needs little consideration to understand that the concrete implementation of biodiversity offsets requires planning authorities to perform complex balancing exercises, in which vested property rights and land-use plans need to be aligned and balanced with emerging, science-based recovery policies. The region of Flanders represents an interesting case study to analyse the multitude of obstacles that need to be addressed in order to operationalise a performant compensation scheme.[29] The reasons therefore are twofold. Firstly, the need for proactive biodiversity compensation schemes in the Flemish region is beyond dispute. Flanders is one of the most densely populated regions of Europe, with around 470 inhabitants per square kilometre.[30] Nearly a quarter of the Flemish region is urbanised and about half of its surface is occupied by agriculture. By the same token, Flanders is often tagged as "one big city",[31] with growing residential areas and a patchwork of open space fragments in between.[32] In spite of recent policy efforts to halt further fragmentation, six hectares of "open space" in Flanders are still lost every day.[33]

Secondly, the environmental track record of the Flemish region is far from satisfactory, with the area managed in view of biodiversity targets confined to a mere 6 per cent of the total surface area, and the majority of the habitats and species listed in the EU Habitats Directive under an unfavourable conservation status.[34] A recent area of concern is the limited forest cover.

---

[29] See also: *V. Dupont et al.*, Belgium, in W. Wende et al. (eds.), Biodiversity Offsets. European Perspectives on No Net Loss of Biodiversity and Ecosystem Services, Springer, 2017, pp. 55–89.

[30] *European Environment Agency*, Urban sprawl in Europe: the ignored challenge, 2006.

[31] *V. Van Eetvelde & M. Antrop*, The significance of landscape relic zones in relation to soil conditions, settlement pattern and territories in Flanders, Landscape and Urban Planning 2005 (70), pp. 614–622.

[32] *T. Verbeek & B. Tempels*, Measuring fragmentation of open space in urbanised Flanders: an evaluation of four methods, Revue belge de géographie 2016 (2), https://belgeo.revues.org/17164.

[33] Elke dag verdwijnt 6 hectare open ruimte, DeRedactie.be, 28 July 2014.

[34] For more information, see: https://www.inbo.be/nl/natuurindicator/de-staat-van-instandhouding-van-de-habitattypen-van-de-habitatrichtlijn. For more background and analysis with respect to the policy causes behind this limited forest cover, see: *P. Van Gossum et al.*, Implementation failure of the forest expansion policy in Flanders (Northern Belgium) and the policy leaning potential, Forest Policy and Economics 2008, pp. 515–522; *P. Van Gossum et al.*, New environmental policy instruments to realise forest expansion in Flanders (northern Belgium): A base for smart regulation?, Land Use Policy 2009 (26), pp. 935–946.

In comparison with other EU Member States, only a relatively modest area of Flanders is covered by forests. Around 160,000 hectares are covered in trees, which represents 11 per cent of the total surface area. Most of these forests (70 per cent) are held in private hands. A significant portion of these forests (approximately 40 per cent) are moreover situated in areas that have not been allocated a green designation on the applicable land-use plans. In addition, while there exists a legal prohibition – called a "moratorium" – on deforestation since 1996, in combination with a compensation duty, the forest cover continues to decline at an average rate of 200 hectares every year.[35]

The recent Flemish experiences with biodiversity offsets for deforestation are indicative of the many critical analyses that have recently been published in the scientific literature.[36] Even so, recent attempts to overcome and remedy the many inherent flaws in the forest compensation rules – such as the adoption of a Forest Protection Map aimed at the protection of woodlands situated in housing zones and industrial estates – have not led to any substantial improvements, while the existing compensation mechanisms are not working effectively enough to outdo the ongoing impairments. Based upon a thorough analysis of the past Flemish experiences with the applicable forest compensation schemes over the past two decades, as well as new draft proposals for new legislation and recent case law developments, this chapter tries to draw some overarching conclusions as to the operationalisation of offsetting mechanisms targeting 'ordinary' biodiversity, which is not strictly protected under EU law. It is posited that the Flemish lessons can also be instructive for the operationalisation of offsetting schemes in other EU Member States.

2. THE GENESIS OF THE LEGAL FRAMEWORK ON FOREST OFFSETTING AND NATURE PROTECTION

In this preliminary section, a brief overview of the Flemish protection schemes and their recent evolutions is presented. The focus is on forest protection and offsetting. However, given the blatant lack of coherency when it comes to regulations aimed at nature protection, several mutually overlapping legal regimes apply to forests in the Flemish region and therefore need to be addressed in order to obtain a comprehensive overview of the applicable protection level for forests and woodlands in the Flemish region.

---

[35] For an overview, see: *H. Schoukens et al.*, Handboek natuurbehoudsrecht, Kluwer, 2011, pp. 470–500.

[36] See for instance: *M. Moreno-Mateos et al.*, The true loss caused by biodiversity offsets, Biological Conservation 2015, pp. 552–559; *M. Curran et al.*, Is there any empirical support for biodiversity offset policy?, Ecological Applications 2014, pp. 628–630.

2.1. THE STEEP ROAD TOWARDS A MORATORIUM ON DEFORESTATION

It would be unfair to state that forests were unprotected before the entry into force of the so-called Forest Decree (*Bosdecreet*) in 1990.[37] Indeed, from as early as 1946 onwards, activities leading to deforestation were made subject to a prior planning permit. However, given the lack of substantive criteria to be taken into account when considering such planning applications and the fact that in most instances the local municipalities were the competent planning authorities, limited protection resulted from these planning permit schemes. This was all about to change in 1990, when the Flemish Parliament decided to update the old rules on forest management and codified them in the Forest Decree.[38] In essence, this new piece of legislation aimed to protect forests, regardless of their location and/or ownership status.[39] The former element was important, given that from the 1970s onwards detailed land-use plans had been adopted – the so-called *gewestplannen*. Even when these land-use plans were located the majority of the most pristine forests in areas with a green designation – which meant that no other damaging activities were permissible, with the exception of forest and nature management – the remaining 40 per cent were still located in areas intended for industrial development, agricultural activities or housing zones pursuant to the applicable land-use plans.[40]

Against this bleak backdrop, the relevance of the newly passed forest protection rules became evident. Whereas the presence of forests on agricultural lands leaves limited options for logging and deforestation, this was obviously not the case for trees that are located on sites which have been assigned an industrial or housing development designation in the applicable zoning plans.[41] In time, the trees present on these lands might disappear in view of other economic considerations. Future building plans inevitably led to the shrinking of the forest cover in these areas.

That said, the definition of the notion of "forest" did not explicitly refer to the applicable land-use plans. The absence of such a reference to zoning plans is not without importance, seeing that it offers a general level of protection to all forests, irrespective of the applicable land-use destination. The mere presence of trees – alongside shrubs – was deemed sufficient to fall within

---

[37] Flemish Forest Decree of 13 June 1990, Belgian Official Gazette, 28 September 1990 (hereinafter referred to as the Flemish Forest Decree).
[38] *Schoukens et al., supra,* note 35 at pp. 476–488.
[39] See Article 3 of the Forest Decree.
[40] See: https://www.natuurpunt.be/pagina/beleidsdossier-zonevreemde-bossen.
[41] The applicable land-use plans are used as binding yardsticks when individual planning permits are granted. In principle, no activities are permissible in green zones in the applicable zoning plans which compromise the green character of the site.

the scope of application of the Forest Decree.[42] The relatively open definition connotes a progressive application of the newly established protection schemes for endangered forests. Since no explicit threshold is applicable, meaning that even a collection of three trees alongside some shrubs can qualify as a forest, the protection offered by the Forest Decree appears even more impressive at first glance. It seemed to prioritise ecological considerations over applicable land-use and zoning plans, even when this might clash with the underlying economic interests. The substantive underpinnings of the Forest Decree allowed the competent planning authorities to apply more scrutiny, even when considering planning applications for relatively limited areas of forest cover. However, back in 1990, no explicit moratorium on deforestation was put forward in law, severely limiting the practical effect of the newly adopted protection schemes. The latter only happened in 1996, with the adoption of a new decree modifying the Forest Decree. In essence, the moratorium on deforestation entailed that as a general rule deforestation is to be considered a prohibited activity, with the exception of public utility works.[43]

Even though poorly applied on the ground during the first years, this scheme of protection rules stood out as one of the early examples of a clear-cut NNL instrument within the Flemish region. Judged by many as too stringent, however, in 1997 the Forest Decree was subsequently relaxed to authorise deforestation in restrictive circumstances and under strict conditions, requiring compensatory measures in order to maintain the forest cover in the Flemish region.[44] The permitting scheme, which was still founded on a general prohibition on deforestation, is now basically two-tiered.[45] If a purported case of deforestation takes place in industrial or urban zones (as defined by the relevant land-use plans), is linked to projects of general interest or is part of a nature management plan, the moratorium can be lifted through the issuance of a general planning permit. In other words, such actions are exempted from the application of the strict forest protection rules. In all other instances, deforestation is subject to a prior derogation by the Agency for Nature and Forests. Only after having obtained this prior exemption can an application for a general planning permit for deforestation be considered by the competent planning authority. Accordingly, woodlands that are "out-zoned", i.e. located outside the green zones designated on the relevant land-use plans, enjoy less protection than woodlands that are located inside designated green zones. This is another illustration of how nature protection rules are rendered subordinate to the applicable zoning plans, thereby avoiding potential conflicts

---

[42]   For more guidance in this regard, see the guidelines published on the site of the Agency for Nature and Forests: https://www.natuurenbos.be/definitiebos.
[43]   *Schoukens et al., supra*, note 35 at p. 11.
[44]   Id. at pp. 476–479.
[45]   Flemish Forest Decree, Article 90bis(1).

between ecological assessments and future development scenarios. While the modified Forest Decree promulgated additional substantive criteria and prior consultation procedures to be taken into account when considering applications for planning permits, it still failed to get rid of the dichotomy between forest located in or outside "green zones" on the applicable land-use plans.

Turning to the question of forest compensation, the following set of rules applies. If deforestation is allowed in accordance with the above-mentioned regulations, it must in principle be compensated for by the owner of the permit.[46] Compensation may take place *in kind*, by paying an amount of money to a compensation fund, or by a combination of both.[47] Since 2014, the deforestation of areas larger than three hectares must be fully compensated *in kind*. Only in limited circumstances – such as the deforestation needed for the implementation of site-specific objectives for Natura 2000 sites or in a context of spontaneous reforestation – is no compensation required.

The Forest Decree lays down a set of specific rules regarding the determination of adequate offsets. Likewise, additional regulation promulgates specific rules with regard to the exact implementation of the forest offsets. Interestingly, it establishes standardised offset ratios based on the ecological value of the woodland that will be destroyed through the project development.[48] The decree itself sets minimum ratios starting at 1:1, i.e. an area at least equivalent to the deforested area.[49] This ratio increases to 1:3 if the clearing approval involves a forest that contributes to the conservation objectives of a special area of conservation under the EU Habitats Directive.[50] The Regulations include a table listing the different ratios applicable to each forest type. The total area in square metres that must be reforested/afforested is then multiplied by a certain figure in order to obtain the full price.[51] Currently, this figure is €3.56 per square metre and it increases to €10.68 if the clearing approval involves a forest that contributes to the conservation objectives of a special area of conservation (SAC) under the EU Habitats Directive.

The forest compensation, whether in the form of on-the-ground offsets or monetary payments into the fund, must involve the reforestation/afforestation of unforested land (except in rare circumstances) in certain green and public areas within applicable zoning plans. In principle, the payment of monetary

---

46 Flemish Forest Decree, Article 90bis(2).
47 Flemish Forest Decree, Article 90bis(4).
48 *Belgian Court of Auditors (Rekenhof)*, Ontbossing en compensatie. Ultvoering van de compensatieplicht bij ontbossing en werking van het Bossencompensatirfonds, Verslag van het Rekenhof aan het Vlaams Parlement, 2016, p. 38.
49 Flemish Forest Decree, Article 90bis(4), subpara. 2.
50 Flemish Forest Decree, Article 90bis(1), subpara. 3.
51 Flemish Regulation of 16 February 2001 relating to forest compensation and deforestation derogation, Belgian Official Gazette, 23 March 2001 (hereinafter referred to as the Flemish Forest Regulation), Article 5.

forest compensation has to be made within four months of the issuance of the permit.

2.2. A NEW, GREENER HORIZON WITH THE ADOPTION OF THE *RUIMTELIJK STRUCTUURPLAN VLAANDEREN* BACK IN ... 1997

As previously mentioned, the poor articulation between the general rules on planning law and forest protection gave way to inadequate protection on the ground. During the 1990s, a case was made for the better integration of nature and forest protection into the applicable planning instruments, both at the strategic (*structuurplannen*) as well as the executive (*ruimtelijk uitvoeringsplannen*) level. The adoption of the so-called Flemish Spatial Structure Plan (*Ruimtelijk Structuurplan Vlaanderen*) in 1997 was a milestone in terms of spatial planning management. It laid down the leading principles for spatial planning in Flanders based on a projection of the desired spatial structure of the Flemish region.[52] In terms of biodiversity protection, it set some ambitious policy targets, including the creation of a Flemish Ecological Network (*Vlaams Ecologisch Netwerk*) of 125,000 hectares, which is to constitute a coherent, interconnected ecological network of large nature areas in which nature conservation and/or restoration is to be the primary management objective. Many forests were included in this ecological network, which, however, was never fully designated, and ultimately ended up protecting only approximately 92,000 hectares.[53] This network of core areas, which was subsequently codified in the Flemish Nature Conservation Decree of 21 October 1997,[54] was to be supported by 150,000 hectares of nature areas with mixed functions (*natuurverwevingsgebieden*) and an undefined number of interconnecting corridor areas (*natuurverbindingsgebieden*) as well. These pledges were never really translated into extensive protection areas on the ground.

In order to reverse the landscape fragmentation, the Flemish government pledged through the Flemish Spatial Structure Plan to designate 38,000 hectares of additional "green" zones and 10,000 hectares of additional forest areas on the land-use plans by 2007. However, as will be established in the subsequent part of this chapter, turning these commitments into concrete action and results on the ground proved to be more troublesome than initially expected.

---

52 Decision of the Flemish Government of 23 September 1997, Official Gazette, 21 March 1998. The Flemish Spatial Structure Plan has been revised on several occasions. See more at: https://rsv.ruimtevlaanderen.be/RSV/Informatie/Over-het-RSV/Downloads.
53 https://www.inbo.be/nl/natuurindicator/oppervlakte-afgebakend-ven.
54 Flemish Nature Conservation Decree of 21 October 1997, Belgian Official Gazette, 10 January 1998 (hereinafter referred to as the Flemish Nature Conservation Decree).

2.3. OTHER PROTECTION REGIMES RELEVANT FOR FORESTS AND WOODLANDS

In addition to the general protection rules linked to woodlands, several types of biotope enjoy additional protection in the Flemish region. In a similar fashion to the Forest Decree, the 1998 Flemish Biotope Regulation now differentiates between two sets of protection schemes. Its Article 7 assigns strict protection to certain types of threatened biotopes in the Flemish region, such as swamps, semi-natural grasslands and dune habitats.[55] In limited cases, a derogation from this ban, which applies to the entire territory of the Flemish region and thus is in principle not subject to the applicable zoning plans, can be issued by the Agency for Nature and Forests. To a certain extent, forests may also benefit from these specific rules on biotope protection, for instance in the case of forest swamps. Even when located in future housing zones, such woodlands enjoy the protection offered by the 1998 Biotope Regulation.

Along similar lines, the Flemish Nature Conservation Decree also includes a set of so-called "horizontal protection instruments", loosely inspired by the German *Eingriffsregelung*.[56] The instruments aim to avoid or mitigate net losses in the context of "ordinary biodiversity" without overly impeding spatial developments. In many instances, these general protection instruments are also applicable in the context of forests. First, there is the generic due diligence obligation contained in Article 14 of the Nature Conservation Decree (*natuurzorgplicht*), which sets forth a duty of care towards nature that has to be observed by everyone who carries out certain activities liable to damage biodiversity. It is not explicitly linked to planning permitting schemes and is permanently applicable, implying that it is also of use whenever small-scale interventions in forests are conducted without there being any consideration for valuable nature. Whereas the duty of care is to be cumulatively applied with tailor-made protection schemes for specific biotopes, their added value is most prominent in cases of potential destruction of "ordinary nature", which does not harbour habitats or species that are explicitly listed on the annexes to the Flemish nature conservation regulations.

Alongside the general duty of care, a more comprehensive mitigation clause, to be applied in the context of planning permitting schemes, was established by Article 16 of the Nature Conservation Decree. To be more

---

[55] Regulation of the Flemish Government of 23 July 1998 laying down detailed rules for the implementation of the Decree of 21 October 1997 concerning nature conservation and the natural environment, Belgian Official Gazette, 10 September 1998 (hereinafter referred to as the 1998 Biotope Regulation).

[56] Articles 13–18 of the German Federal Nature Protection Act. See more extensively: *P. Fischer-Hüftle*, 35 Jahre Eingriffsregelung – eine Bilanz, Natur und Recht 2011, pp. 753–758.

precise, the latter provision imposes the obligation on permit-issuing agencies to guarantee that the activities they authorise cause no 'avoidable damage' to biodiversity (*natuurtoets*). Yet the concept of "avoidable damage" is not restrictively defined, which implies that the clause can in principle be used to avoid or mitigate encroachments upon biodiversity both in the context of strictly protected biodiversity, such as Natura 2000 sites, and in the context of so-called "ordinary" biodiversity.[57] Accordingly, forests are also included in its scope. Recent case law developments have exposed the importance of this provision for the protection of forests located in sites which have been assigned for industrial development.[58] It is important to highlight that, in theory, no *de minimis* threshold applies, which again underlines the broad scope of Article 16.[59] Moreover, various decisions of the Belgian administrative courts have revealed that the mitigation rule also applies when the specific rules on forest compensation have been applied.[60]

2.4. THE INCREASING RELEVANCE OF NATURA 2000 FOR FORESTS

The well-known "first pillar" of the EU Habitats Directive requires the EU Member States to conserve and protect the Natura 2000 sites that have been designated on their respective territories. A significant number of forest habitats are listed in Annex I to the Habitats Directive, implying that the Member States are required to designate a sufficient number of Natura 2000 sites in this regard. Many of the most ecologically valuable forests in Flanders are included in the Natura 2000 Network. When adequately enforced, Article 6(3) and (4) of the Habitats Directive evidently play an essential role in averting further net losses in the context of the national sites that have been included in the Natura 2000 Network. Although these specific conservation duties do not necessarily put a general ban on inherent harmful interventions in nature, such as deforestation,[61] their exclusive ecological focus considerably affects the leeway for planning authorities when issuing permits for potential harmful development in the context of a Natura 2000 site.[62] Evidently, such beneficial effects should therefore also materialise within the Flemish context. Yet the

---

[57] More extensively, see: *H. Schoukens*, Natuurbescherming buiten de lijntjes. De natuurtoets als imperfect antwoord op de biodiversiteitscrisis binnen Vlaanderen, Tijdschrift voor Omgevingsrecht en Omgevingsbeleid 2014, pp. 355–357.

[58] Belgian Council of State, case no. 189.901, 27 January 2009.

[59] *Schoukens, supra*, note 57 at pp. 355–356.

[60] Id. at pp. 357 et seq.

[61] CJEU, Case C-2/10, Azienda Agro-Zootecnica Franchini Sarl, ECLI:EU:C:2011:502, para. 46.

[62] See also: *P. Scott*, Appropriate Assessment: A Paper Tiger?, in G. Jones QC (ed.), The Habitats Directive – A Developer's Obstacle Course, Hart, 2012, p. 103.

long-lasting absence of strict assessment rules in the 1997 Flemish Nature Conservation Decree[63] effectively turned the ecological network into a "paper tiger" for more than a decade, which also left many valuable forests virtually unprotected.[64]

Apart from general regulations on nature-friendly forestry and agriculture, no specific provisions aimed at avoiding significant effects in the context of Natura 2000 were effectively enforced throughout the 1990s.[65] This loophole has severely undermined the effectiveness of the forest protection regime in the specific context of Natura 2000 sites in the Flemish Region for years. The 2002 landmark decision of the Belgian Council of State in a case concerning the construction of a new tidal dock (*Deurganckdock*) in the Antwerp port area served as a turning point.[66] Pressured by pending infringement proceedings, the Flemish Parliament decided to modify the Flemish Nature Conservation Decree in 2002[67] by including a strict assessment duty for plans and projects liable to damage Natura 2000 sites, among other things.

According to Article 36-ter, §4 of the Flemish Nature Conservation Decree, which now closely resembles Article 6(3) of the Habitats Directive, the competent authorities must not agree to any plan or project which, according to the appropriate assessment, is likely to have a significant effect on a Natura 2000 site.[68] By virtue of Article 36-ter, §5 of the Flemish Nature Conservation Decree, which serves as the counterpart of Article 6(4) of the Habitats Directive, plans or projects can still go ahead in spite of a negative assessment, provided that there is no alternative solution, that they are necessary for imperative reasons of overriding public interest (IROPI) and that all compensatory measures necessary to ensure the overall coherence of the Natura 2000 Network are taken. In recent case law, the application of these protection clauses has proven to be a valuable fall-back instrument for forests located in Natura 2000 sites.[69]

It should come as no surprise that the restoration of forest habitats – for instance through the additional afforestation of sites – is often mentioned as

---

63   Belgian Official Gazette, 10 October 1998.
64   *H. Schoukens et al.*, The Implementation of the Habitats Directive in Belgium (Flanders): back to the Origin of Species?, Journal for European and Environmental Planning Law 2007, pp. 127–128.
65   Id. at pp. 129–131.
66   Belgian Council of State, case no. 109.563, 30 July 2002.
67   Belgian Official Gazette, 31 August 2002.
68   More extensively on Article 6(4) of the Habitats Directive, see: *R. Clutten & I. Tafur*, Are Imperative Reasons Imperilling the Habitats Directive? An Assessment of Article 6(4) and the IROPI Exception, in: Jones QC (ed.), The Habitats Directive – A Developer's Obstacle Course, Hart, 2012, pp. 167 et seq.
69   See for instance this recent ruling related to a zone inside a Natura 2000 site, to be dedicated to future recovery actions: Belgian Council of State, case no. 242.577, 9 October 2018.

an explicit conservation action in the draft versions of the site-specific Natura 2000 management plans that are promulgated by the competent authorities. In some instances, however, the restoration of certain habitat types, such as heather or grasslands, might necessitate the conversion of less ecologically valuable coniferous forests into more desirable target habitats. Since 2014, the Flemish region has stepped up its efforts to operationalise its management actions in view of the established site-specific conservation objectives. This also helps to explain why a Flemish conservation organisation such as Natuurpunt vzw can be identified tagged as the largest deforester in the Flemish region.[70] However, in sharp contrast with other cases of deforestation, such actions do not lead to a net loss in terms of naturally managed areas if they are replaced by more valuable habitats.[71] As a result, such actions are to be treated differently when compared to deforestation aimed at the construction of buildings.

3. ANALYSIS OF THE CONTINUED NET LOSS: WHY IS THE FLEMISH REGION STILL LOSING FOREST COVER?

Even though the above-mentioned legislation is far from perfect, it could still serve as a useful instrument to contain forest loss. However, precisely the contrary has happened. In spite of the current moratorium on deforestation, Flanders is still losing more forests on average. Although in 2006 the forest cover in Flanders increased on average by 200 hectares, the Flemish Region is nevertheless losing 230 hectares of forest cover on a net basis every year. These numbers are based on the so-called *Bosmonitor*, published by the NGO BOS+ in 2015.[72] The same figures indicate that the area that is being afforested amounts to 130 hectares per year, whereas the yearly loss of forest cover amounts to 200–300 hectares every year. Even though these numbers remain contested and challengeable, due to an apparent lack of sound and scientifically validated data, among other reasons,[73] they still display a manifest gap between the ambitious policy pledges with respect to reforestation and the reality on the ground.[74]

---

[70] For a nuanced analysis of this statement, see: https://www.bondbeterleefmilieu.be/artikel/factcheck-natuurpunt-de-grootste-ontbosser-van-het-land.

[71] See: Elke dag een voetbalveld aan bos gekapt in Vlaanderen, VRTNWS, 11 April 2019.

[72] See: https://www.bosplus.be/l/library/download/urn:uuid:5af61876-c8f6-49f3-a736-127075396f31/bosbarometer+2015_bos%2B_def.pdf?format=&ext=.pdf.

[73] See the Forest Monitor (*Boswijzer*) accessible at the website of the Agency for Nature and Forests: https://www.natuurenbos.be/beleid-wetgeving/natuurbeheer/wat-de-boswijzer.

[74] For more background on the mismatch between the numbers used by environmental NGOs and the competent agencies, see: https://hseworld.wolterskluwer.be/nl/nieuws/milieu/bosbarometer-versus-boswijzer/.

As recently as spring 2019, both the competent Minister for the Environment and a political opposition party released new figures on deforestation. Both parties agreed that during the past five years, 1,200 hectares of forest had been destroyed, of which 536 hectares had been directly compensated by private developers and property owners. Depending on whether consideration is given to the multiplier to be taken into account when carrying out offsets, or alternatively the actual surface area of the woodland destroyed, the compensation ratio is 72 per cent or 82 per cent.[75] Yet these numbers do not reflect the effectiveness of the restoration actions on the ground, since they often take years to fully materialise, as well as the cases in which no compensation duty applies (see *infra*, section 3.5).

When set against surrounding regions and countries of a comparable size, the Flemish region continues to stand out as a well-developed region that nevertheless continues to falter in the operationalisation of an effective forest protection and recovery policy.[76] This was further highlighted in 2016, when the draft Forest Map (*Boskaart*) failed to be adopted. This map designated all of the ecologically valuable forests located outside the nature and forest zones as included in the applicable zoning plans. It took into account certain criteria, such as the ecological value of each site and the surface it covers. Deforestation was to become exceptional in these areas, only justifiable when necessary for reasons of public interest. The owners of such lands were still entitled to partial financial compensation, up to 80 per cent of the economic value of their private lands. However, after major protests on the part of the affected property owners and project developers, the Flemish Minister-President quickly decided to withdraw the map in September 2017. This was done in the midst of a public consultation on the context of the Forest Map, since it was assumed that the map had been drawn up in an inaccurate and careless manner. Among other problems, the provisional version of the Forest Map included several parcels of land where in fact no woodlands were present.[77] Restricting property rights for the preservation of a couple of trees was the framing that prevailed in the media, which explains the limited political support it enjoyed at the end of the day.[78] Since then, no follow-up for the zoning map has been adopted. The threat of future restrictions led to a rush of planning permits for "out-zoned" forests, thereby ironically speeding up the loss of forests.[79]

Below, the authors present the principal causes for the continued net loss and try to analyse why the Flemish region is still to be regarded as a

---

[75] See *supra*, note 71.
[76] *Dupont et al.*, *supra*, note 20 at pp. 74–78.
[77] More extensively, see: Ban lifted on building in newly protected woodlands, FlandersToday, 22 May 2017.
[78] See: Bouwgrond afgepakt voor paar bomen, Het Laatste Nieuws, 17 May 2017.
[79] Vrees voor massale aanvraag tot kappen, De Morgen, 22 May 2017.

net deforester. Due to the limited space available for this analysis, the discussion focuses only on the primary issues to be addressed, leaving other valuable elements open for future research.

3.1. THE POOR ARTICULATION BETWEEN FOREST PROTECTION AND URBAN AND SPATIAL PLANNING LAW

A first element of concern is related to the lack of proper integration between the Forest Decree and the rules on land-use planning. As has been demonstrated above, the concrete application of the deforestation moratorium is contingent on the precise location of the forests. Trees growing on a site which has not been accorded a green designation on the applicable land-use plans are *de facto* outlawed. This glaring mismatch between spatial planning and nature protection has been the subject of continued criticism in the literature, especially since the quality of the applicable land-use plans often leaves a lot to be desired.[80] Many of the applicable land-use plans date from the 1980s and were not subject to a prior strategic environmental assessment. In other words, economic interests often prevailed when designating housing and industrial zones, which was the primary reason behind the "out-zoning" of many forests. Therefore, no precedence was given to the ecological characteristics of the sites concerned, at least not when this information appeared to be at odds with the prevailing economic views on certain location. For instance, an isolated forest located at the edge of an industrial estate was very likely to be included in an industrial expansion zone on the applicable zoning plans. Seeing that at the time the societal impact of environmental NGOs was rather limited and access to justice in environmental cases in these years remained rather exceptional for NGOs, not many "guardians" were available to stand up for the provision of additional protection for forests, even when located close to housing zones or industrial estates. As a result, the out-zoning of the forests almost happened overnight, without much opposition.

This "chilling effect" was exacerbated by the inclusion of so-called "spatial exemption" clauses in the Nature Conservation Decree, further aimed at limiting the property restrictions tied to conservation schemes. Pursuant to these clauses, nature protection schemes need to be interpreted so as to not stand in the way of project developments that are in line with the established land-use plans.[81] This is yet another reassertion of the prioritisation of the often – from an environmental point of view – flawed zoning plans over ecological considerations.

---

[80] G. *Van Hoorick*, Juridische aspecten van het natuurbehoud en de landschapszorg, Intersentia, 2000, pp. 281–345.

[81] *Schoukens, supra*, note 57.

Of course, the subordination of forest protection to planning law is partly mitigated by the wording of the Forest Decree itself, as well as the application of other instruments, such as the above-mentioned Article 16 of the Nature Conservation Decree. For instance, in a 2009 landmark ruling, the Belgian Council of State had to consider development options in the context of a site which had been designated as an "industrial estate" on the applicable land-use plans, yet harboured a valuable patch of forest habitat. According to the developer, Article 16 could not be interpreted so as to limit his future development options, especially since he had complied with the specific rules on forest offsetting. However, the Council of State reasserted the applicability of Article 16 of the Flemish Nature Conservation Decree to biodiversity located in industrial zones.[82] By doing so, the Council of State effectively underlined the importance of assessing the impact of project developments on ordinary biodiversity, even when located outside protected areas.[83] Possibly, it opted for an outcome which was not in line with the original intentions of the drafters of the Nature Conservation Decree.

Even so, the practical effect of this progressive case law remains limited at best. Article 16 of the Nature Conservation Decree cannot be cited as an effective mitigation rule for the protection of forests that are out-zoned pursuant to old land-use plans. It is too vaguely and loosely formulated to halt further losses. For instance, it does not map out the substantive criteria to be taken into account when considering whether nature can be destroyed or not. It even does not contain an explicit balancing clause. To give but one example of its inherent shortcomings, pursuant to other case law developments, Article 16 of the Nature Conservation Decree is not applicable to "unavoidable damage" to nature. According to the Council of State, the notion of "avoidable damage" cannot be interpreted in such a way that a permit is refused with reference to the unavoidable impacts on the environment caused by the project.[84] Add to that the limited enforcement of such protection tools by local municipalities and it becomes clear that forests located outside protected sites are *de facto* "outlawed". Neither the relatively inadequate forest compensation mechanisms, nor the imperfect mitigation rules included in the Nature Conservation Decree were able to effectively prevent further net losses.

This being the case, the increased importance of the Natura 2000 Network is capable of partly mitigating the flawed articulation between forest protection and planning law. Pursuant to the case law of the Court of Justice of the European Union (CJEU), economic consideration cannot prevail over ecological criteria when assessing the suitability of a site in terms

---

[82]   Belgian Council of State, case no. 189.901, 27 January 2009.
[83]   Belgian Council of State, case no. 227.106, 14 April 2014; Belgian Council of State, case no. 204.673, 3 June 2010.
[84]   Belgian Council of State, case no. 165.664, 7 December 2006.

of Natura 2000 designation purposes.[85] This has led to the inclusion of some "out-zoned" forests in Natura 2000 sites, adding to their further legal protection.[86] However, given that Member States are not required to designate all patches of listed habitats on their land, yet are allowed to prioritise the most endangered and/or valuable ones, economic considerations can implicitly play a role.

Thus, by referring to the limited ecological potential of certain forests, which might be linked to past degradation, Member States can still indirectly exclude forests from Natura 2000 protection.[87] This has also materialised in the Flemish region, leaving many valuable forest habitats undesignated in terms of Natura 2000 protection. This, in turn, explains the recent surge in the number of contested cases in which "out-zoned" forests are destroyed in view of economic developments. Placing all hope on the "greening" of the existing land-use plans (i.e. issuing new zoning plans which assign a green destination to the forest habitats) might be futile, seeing that the revision of such plans takes years and might lead to additional compensation claims (*planschade*) from landowners who see their property drop in economic value. For now, it simply does not represent a top political priority. In many instances, the local municipalities will be the competent planning authorities. At present, the latter lack sufficient financial backing to carry out such a major policy shift. Local governments are financed in view of the population numbers and not in light of the ecological importance of the sites they harbour. Only when additional financial support is offered by the Flemish government for forest restoration will local authorities be proved willing to further green the applicable land-use plans, which might further bolster the protection of "out-zoned" forests and unprotected forest habitats that possibly qualify for Natura 2000 protection.

3.2. THE MITIGATION HIERARCHY IN THEORY AND IN PRACTICE: THE COMPLEXITY OF SAYING NO

The so-called mitigation hierarchy is frequently cited as the self-evident backbone of every effective NNL policy.[88] The mitigation sequence basically

---

[85] See for instance: CJEU, Case C-371/98, The Queen v. Secretary of State for the Environment, Transport and the Regions', ex parte First Corporate Shipping Ltd, ECLI:EU:C:2000:600, para. 24.

[86] For more information on the natural habitats present in the Flemish Natura 2000 sites: https://www.natura2000.vlaanderen.be/.

[87] See in this regard: *H. Schoukens & H. Woldendorp*, Site selection and designation under the Habitats and Birds Directive: a Sisyphean task?, in C.H. Born et al. (eds.), The Habitats Directive in its EU Environmental Law Context: European Nature's Best Hope?, Routledge, 2015, pp. 42–44.

[88] *K. ten Kate & J. Pilgrim*, Biodiversity Offsets technical study paper, IUCN Technical Study Group on Biodiversity Offsets, 2014, p. 11.

boils down to a sequence of different steps when assessing the damage incurred to biodiversity through project developments. Project developers should therefore first focus on measures capable of avoiding negative impacts on protected biodiversity from the outset, such as careful spatial or temporal placement of infrastructure or disturbances. The next step requires the project developer to inquire whether measures can be adopted aimed at reducing or minimising the expected negative impact of a plan or project. The third tier then involves so-called rehabilitation measures, which should remedy unavoidable residual damage or loss, if possible through the on-site restoration of habitats. If, after having taken all the above-mentioned measures, some residual damage still has to be addressed, offset measures or compensatory measures come into play.[89] To put it bluntly, offsets are only to be used as a so-called "last resort", if all other steps of the mitigation hierarchy have been observed.[90]

As could already have been inferred from the analysis above, the current legal regimes in the Flemish region for forest and nature protection do not comprehensively reflect this mitigation hierarchy. By providing a relatively strict moratorium on deforestation in forests located in green zones in the applicable land-use plans, the prevention principle is at least partially acknowledged. However, generally speaking, the above-discussed rules do not explicitly mandate the competent agency authorities to blatantly refuse authorisations for unsustainable projects that might lead to massive environmental degradation. Substantive criteria are not detailed in the legislation, opening the door for continued discretion and deference. Admittedly, an overly rigid application of the mitigation hierarchy might ultimately compromise the legitimacy of nature legislation itself, as if every single step of the mitigation hierarchy is to be taken to its ultimate extent, this might imply that no projects are to be carried out at all. Not every single plantation or intensively managed forest is worth rescuing; the focus should be placed on those forests that are important from an ecological point of view. Putting extensive efforts into saving plantation forests appears to be futile, if other cases of deforestation are not properly addressed. Moreover, a stringent application of the mitigation hierarchy also clashes with the paradigm of continued economic growth. Simply accepting a no-development scenario as a realistic alternative would urge authorities to reconsider their traditional view on economic growth. In itself that might represent an interesting side-effect of the latter provision. However, it should come as no surprise that such an outcome would require a paradigm shift in the heads of the permit issuing agencies. As of today, such systemic movement towards a

---

[89]   For a clear overview of the mitigation hierarchy, as currently understood: http://www. thebiodiversityconsultancy.com/mitigation-hierarchy/.

[90]   *Ten Kate & Pilgrim, supra*, note 88 at p. 11.

complete standstill of deforestation actions would require substantive political backing, which is still lacking.

With this being said, the available case law illustrates that even within the confines of Article 16, limited room remains available for advocating for a strict application of the mitigation hierarchy. This is irrespective of whether more scrutiny might be justified by the presence of ecologically valuable forest habitats on the ground. To give but one poignant illustration, in a 2010 ruling on the construction of a road cutting through a site which harboured several patches of ecologically valuable grasslands, the Council of State further clarified that Article 16 of the Flemish Nature Conservation Decree does not include a prohibition on declining permit applications for projects that inherently cause further damage to biodiversity. In the latter case, though, the project developer had included a compensation scheme in its permit application, which might perhaps help to explain the more liberal interpretation by the Council of State.[91] Yet at the same time, most of the compensation actions involved in the latter case consisted of qualitative restoration actions in the remaining grassland area, whereas a substantial part of the quantitative loss of grassland was not compensated at all.[92] It is hard not to see in this ruling a further weakening of the legal teeth of Article 16 of the Nature Conservation Decree.

In addition, the numbers related to the concrete application of forest compensation illustrate that limited attention is paid to prevention. In fact, a 2016 report of the Belgian Court of Auditors (*Rekenhof*) revealed that in the preceding years, more than 80 per cent of all applications for a derogation with a view to deforestation were granted.[93]

The latter findings should come as no major surprise, given the relatively poorly developed substantive framework when it comes to assessing application for nature destruction. Furthermore, in the Flemish region, agencies and permitting authorities typically use the existing compensation schemes to say "yes" to destructive logging proposals.[94] In other words, permitting forest loss remains the default option, which is further justified by the presence of the forest offset scheme. The glaring lack of substantive criteria to be taken into account when balancing the preservation of forests against other interests certainly leads to a further death by discretion.

However, seeing that the application of the existing offsetting schemes is far from perfect, as is demonstrated below (*infra*, section 3.4), the refusal to give precedence to prevention additionally compromises the future of forests in Flanders. This is because many planning authorities are adamant when it

---

[91]   Belgian Council of State, case no. 209.868, 20 December 2010.
[92]   *Schoukens, supra*, note 57 at pp. 358–360.
[93]   *Rekenhof, supra*, note 48 at pp. 20 and 32.
[94]   More generally speaking, see: *M.C. Wood*, Nature's Trust. Environmental Law for a New Ecological Age, Cambridge University Press, 2014, p. 60.

comes to prioritising economic developments over conservation considerations. If anything, offsetting should never be the departure point when old-growth forests are threatened by project developments. The literature holds that while biodiversity loss might be acceptable in some cases, especially when it relates to non-endangered habitats or species, using offset schemes as a tool to encroach upon old-growth and vulnerable habitats only leads to further losses.[95] The political farce surrounding the adoption of a Forest Map (*Boskaart*) aimed at protecting additional forests, underscores the limited political will to reinforce the preventative approach, even for valuable old-growth forests, which are relatively difficult to restore.

Again, countless examples can be given to further underpin the latter statements. The simple fact that in recent years a Flemish transport company, Essers, has received two permits for the deforestation of two forests – one old-growth forest located in an industrial zone and one ecologically valuable forest located inside a Natura 2000 site – poignantly illustrates the continued deference when it comes to reasserting the mitigation hierarchy against the backdrop of endangered forests. In both instances, reference was made to future forest compensation actions, alongside the urgent economic necessity to build on the site, as the principal argument to authorise the interventions. As is demonstrated further below, the Belgian Council of State ultimately quashed the permit for the deforestation located in a Natura 2000 site. However, as to the first application, the deforestation still went ahead. Ironically, the site itself is currently being used as a parking lot, which sheds a different light on the motivation that was added to the permit application.[96] Of course, these cases are to be treated as mere anecdotal evidence. Yet, seeing that in both instances there was massive public outcry and protest, they also indicate the persistent refusal to fully apply the preventative approach in the context of a valuable old-growth forest.

As such, such interim finds should not come as a major surprise. What is more, outside the context of forests, there exists a clear tendency to use offsets as a principal precursor of economic development, even in the context of protected areas, such as Natura 2000 sites. Recently, though, both the CJEU and the Belgian Council of State have consistently rejected such more liberal approaches to offsetting.[97] The most notorious example was offered by the *Orleans* decision of the CJEU, which rejected an approach whereby nature restoration actions could be used as a means to avoid the application of the

---

[95] See for instance: *Wende, supra,* note 20 at p. 6; *M. Curran et al.,* Is there any empirical support for biodiversity offset policy?, Ecological Applications 2014, pp. 628630.

[96] *B. De Somviele,* Essers maakt parking van waardevol bos, Apache.be, 2 January 2019.

[97] See for a more extensive analysis: *H. Schoukens,* Proactive habitat restoration and the avoidance of adverse effects on protected areas: Development project review in Europe after Orleans, Journal of International Wildlife Law & Policy 2017, pp. 125–154.

derogation schemes in the context of harbour expansion plans in Natura 2000 sites.[98] A similar rationale urged the Belgian Council of State to reject forest compensatory measures to be used as mitigation within the context of an appropriate assessment needed for a road construction project in the province of Limburg with an impact on forests located in Natura 2000 sites.[99] Instead of presenting forest offsets as a "licence to trash", recent case law developments – at least in the context of protected forests – seem to correct this flawed compensation narrative.

However, unfortunately this approach has not led to a conclusive and meaningful shift in the general permitting policies. In this context, compensation is often still treated as the easy route for permit approval, with only a limited number of applications being rejected. In late 2019, it was revealed that nearly all applications for deforestation that were filed during 2018 were granted, which once again underlines the difficulty of saying "no" and applying the mitigation hierarchy in a more rigid manner.[100] It also underlines that the permitting schemes – aimed at legalising biodiversity losses – are still seen as the primary objective of the application of environmental rules. At a very minimum, a delicate balancing exercise is to be carried out when logging ecologically valuable losses, and future offsetting measures – even when an application is made with very progressive compensation actions – should never be treated as a general facilitator for unsustainable project development, especially taking into account the many flaws inherent in the current Flemish compensation schemes that are identified below (*see infra*, section 3.4).

3.3. THE LIMITED MATERIAL SCOPE OF THE COMPENSATION SCHEME: NOT ALL LOSSES ARE COMPENSATED

When relying upon a compensation scheme, it evidently remains crucial to ensure that its scope is sufficiently wide. However, as was already partly highlighted above, the material scope of the Flemish compensation schemes for forest loss does not fully encompass all actions liable to destroy forest habitats. This explains why 23 per cent of the losses of forest cover are not compensated. Over a period of five years (2014–2019), an area of 268 hectares of deforestation did not require additional compensation. Not all exemptions are detrimental against the backdrop of conservation interests, though. As explained above, the exemption for deforestation in the context of ecological restoration action is certainly sensible, provided that the decisions are always

---

98   CJEU, Case C-387/15, Orleans, ECLI:EU:C:2016:583, paras. 36–38. See also: CJEU, Case C-521/12, Briels, ECLI:EU:C:2014:330, paras. 28–35.

99   Belgian Council of State, case no. 223.083, 29 March 2013.

100   See more extensively: Schoukens, *supra*, note 97.

based upon sound science. It can safely be assumed that this is mostly the case, since the exemption is confined to instances in which the deforestation is mandatory in view of the applicable conservation targets for Natura 2000 sites.

However, the other exemption clauses are subject to greater criticism. For instance, it remains contested whether the deforestation of spontaneously afforested woodlands that are less than 22 years old should not give rise to compensation duties. Along similar lines, one might also contest the exemption for social considerations, which explains why no offsets are required in habitation or housing zones whenever the purported deforestation does not surpass the threshold of 0.5 hectares. While one might submit that private property owners often might lack the necessary time and skills to opt for compensation in nature, this is not necessarily the case for the financial or in lieu payments that equally remain eligible in such instances. As long as the scope of the compensation duty does not encompass these cases of deforestation, the risk of enduring or accumulated net losses remains a very likely option. Accordingly, additional scrutiny appears to be warranted when crafting exemptions to a general compensation duty.

3.4. FINANCIAL COMPENSATION AS THE DEFAULT OPTION: THE "POLLUTER PAYS" PRINCIPLE?

In general, three approaches to biodiversity offsetting are currently present within the framework of conservation policies, namely permittee-led or *ad hoc* payments to a compensation fund[101] ("in lieu fees") and compensation through habitat banking.[102] None of these three approaches to biodiversity offsetting is flawless. For one, permittee-led compensations are often case specific and thus allow for a more precise (like-for-like) offsetting of biodiversity losses. Yet since they are third-party-led, they are often characterised by a relatively high number of failures, due to the lack of expertise and the absence of long-term protection commitments, among other factors.[103] At the other end of the spectrum, it has been stated that conservation banks might lead to more comprehensive and effective nature biodiversity offsets. At the same time, such an approach is associated with a clear risk of the further commodification of biodiversity.[104] In addition, the existence of conservation banking requires sufficient regulatory

---

[101]   *Froger et al., supra*, note 27 at p. 153.
[102]   *Ten Kate & Pilgrim, supra*, note 88 at p. 25.
[103]   Id.
[104]   C. *Bonneuil*, Tell me where you come from, I will tell you who you are: A genealogy of biodiversity offsetting mechanisms in a historical context, Biodiversity Conservation 2015 (192), pp. 488–489.

capacity, which might be particularly difficult to achieve in times of budgetary restraint.[105]

As could already be deduced from the analysis above, biodiversity offsets have primarily been implemented within the Flemish region through so-called permittee-led offsetting schemes until the beginning of the 21st Century. Even so, within the context of the Forest Decree, a specific forest compensation fund (*boscompensatiefonds*) has been operational since 2002. As stated above, project developers are permitted to comply with their offsetting obligations by transferring payments to a fund. Until 2014, in 78 per cent of all cases deforesters opted for compensation through payments to the compensation fund. In 2014, the Decree was modified so that payments to the forest compensation fund are now only permissible if the deforestation does not concern more than three hectares. The money in the compensation fund is to be used to create easily accessible forests near cities, for urban nature and to achieve the conservation objectives of Natura 2000.[106]

Be that as it may, the performance of the Flemish compensation fund is rather poor. As stated above, the Flemish region is still to be regarded as a "net deforester", which is partly caused by the many delays and obstacles that are encountered when attempting to make use of the money in the fund.[107] Other studies also revealed that funds have been "piled up" by the Agency for Nature and Forests but have not been used to purchase new lands in order to compensate for the deforested zones in a timely manner.[108] In 2016, this finding caused a major stir in the public debate, with the competent Minister being forced to explain why less money is spent than is reimbursed on a yearly basis in the fund. Moreover, it was disclosed that between the creation of the fund and 2014, approximately 637 hectares of land had been purchased in order to be afforested over time. Since in total 2,340 hectares needed to be offset, the fund has therefore only been able to realise 27 per cent of the required offsets.[109] The 2016 Report issued by the Belgian Court of Auditors concluded that as more than half of the available funds have already been used to purchase lands, the compensation fund is not likely to achieve its NNL objectives, let alone achieve future gains.[110]

The reasons for this manifest underperformance of the compensation fund are manifold. For a considerable time, ensuring the timely implementation of the money that was collected through the fund did not appear to be a political top priority. Moreover, the monetary payments to the compensation fund were

---

105   *Ten Kate & Pilgrim, supra,* note 88 at p. 25.
106   *Rekenhof, supra,* note 48 at p. 46.
107   Id. at pp. 45–58.
108   D. Anseeuw, Compensatieplicht: de mol in het Vlaamse natuur-, milieu- en landbouwbeleid, Oikos 2016, p. 17.
109   *Rekenhof, supra,* note 48 at pp. 47–48.
110   Id.

not framed as a "last resort option" but rather the starting position, relieving the project developers from their primary responsibility of avoiding deforestation in the first place. Factors such as the elevated price of land, the relatively high pressure on open space within the Flemish region and the additional budgetary checks that are included in the compensation fund scheme help to explain the current implementation failures.[111] There is also an important imbalance between the price that had to be paid by a deforester to destroy one hectare of forest – approximately €20,000 – and the financial means required to purchase one hectare of land to serve as an offset zone – on average €60,000. The current underpinnings of the forest compensation fund thus seem to underestimate the sums required to create effective biodiversity offsets for the authorised deforestations.[112] These observations prompted the Flemish government in 2017 to increase the compensation fee, which is now set at €3.56 per hectare. Yet this represents only a modest step forward in view of the important challenges ahead. Even after the recent revision, it can be stated that the true cost of biodiversity offsetting is not fully reflected in the applicable compensation fees, which raises the question whether this is in line with the "polluter pays" principle, which is still to be regarded as a core principle of EU environmental law. Needless to say, the latter findings make a strong case for a stricter application of the preventative approach regarding forest offsets in the Flemish Region, which no longer presupposes that a substantive majority of all applications for deforestation are authorised.[113]

3.5. ADDITIONALITY, TIME GAPS AND INTERIM LOSSES: HOW CAN DEGRADING BASELINES BE AVOIDED?

If one is aiming to achieve NNL or, in some instances, even net gains[114] through the use of biodiversity offsetting, the key question is against which counterfactual baselines these losses or gains are to be measured.[115] Only biodiversity benefits that are additional to a baseline scenario count as valid offsets.[116] In this respect, to what extent the proposed biodiversity offsets are additional when measured against the existing nature conservation policies and competing sources of funding will need to be assessed.[117]

---

[111]   Id. at pp. 50–51.

[112]   *Anseeuw, supra*, note 108 at p. 17.

[113]   Id. at p. 19.

[114]   See on this topic: *J.W. Bull & S. Brownlie*, The transition from No Net Loss to a Net Gain of biodiversity is far from trivial, Oryx, 2017, pp. 53–59.

[115]   *Ten Kate & Pilgrim, supra*, note 88 at pp. 19–20.

[116]   *M. Maron et al.*, Conservation: stop misuse of biodiversity offsets, Nature 2015 (523), p. 401.

[117]   *F. Quétier, B. Regnery & H. Levrel*, No net loss of biodiversity or paper offsets? A critical review of the French no net loss policy, Environmental Science & Policy 2014 (38), p. 126.

Ensuring additionality is evidently also crucial in the context of forest compensation. In this regard, four additional observations are in order when it comes to the Flemish practice of forest offsetting.

First, it needs to be noted that no general baseline exists in the Flemish region against which the so-called additionality of forest offsets can be measured. Indeed, whereas a multitude of commitments and pledges exist when it comes to forest recovery, no operational baseline scenario is used in order to ensure that the compensation measures and actions go beyond the existing commitments and thus avoid so-called "double dipping". From a practical point of view, one might submit that every compensated forest is to be applauded. However, if the goal is to avoid degrading baselines or, alternatively, net gains, a more comprehensive approach is needed in this regard. As of today, however, the only context in which measurable baselines are present is Natura 2000. In this respect, another striking example of the importance of ambitious recovery baselines and targets was offered by a recent ruling of the Belgian Council of State. The case revolved around the ecological impact of a road bypass (*Noordzuidverbinding*). When assessing the planning permit, the Council of State posited that if progressive restoration objectives are applicable to a Natura 2000 site, the loss of even 0.17 hectares of actual woodland habitats or, as the case may be, of potential habitats for bird species, is to be regarded as significant in terms of Article 6(3) of the Habitats Directive.[118] Accordingly, Flemish judges are increasingly inclined to use the applicable conservation objectives as baseline when assessing the significance of interventions in forests habitats that are designated as Natura 2000 site. Outside the context of the stringent Natura 2000 legislation, such a rigid stance would probably have been very unlikely. Admittedly, the recent jurisprudential shift could easily be dismissed as an example of regulatory creep. Yet such a stance would miss the very point about degrading baselines. The jurisprudence that has recently emerged does give proper weight to the restoration baseline that is to be implemented in the context of woodlands located inside Natura 2000 sites. It moreover appears pivotal to avoid further reference loss. Yet, once again, the importance of this case law is not to be overstated, seeing as many local municipalities do not bother to consult such jurisprudence. Even more so, these cases, in the context of which the Agency for Nature and Forests has often also consented to the destruction of woodlands, further underlines the current negligence at the level of the competent agencies when scrutinising the drafted environmental reports. At best, they check whether no manifest errors are made. Regardless of the motivations underlying this refusal, recent administrative practices still highlight that many competent agencies grapple to understand the importance of avoiding baseline losses. This manifest mismatch needs to be addressed in the context of future legislative proposals,

---

118 Belgian Council of State, case no. 238.181, 12 September 2017.

with an additional focus on peer-reviewed data on the available forest cover in the Flemish region. The lack of such data remains an important obstacle for performing an offsetting approach.

A second observation relates to the use of compensation ratios in the context of forest offsets, which is certainly to be welcomed against the backdrop of reference losses. As illustrated above, explicit compensation ratios apply in the context of forest offsets in the Flemish region. They start from 1:1 at a minimum for mixed forests, comprised of 20–80 per cent native deciduous trees. This ratio increases to 1:3 if a woodland is removed that is important for achieving the conservation objectives in a Natura 2000 site.[119] While these progressive ratios appear impressive at first sight, the available data underscore that they do not succeed in stemming ongoing losses, let alone achieve net gains in biodiversity. Taking into account the progressive compensation ratios that are sometimes used within the context of Article 6(4) of the Habitats Directive, derogations in other countries (up to 1:7)[120] and the time lags to be faced when implementing woodland compensation zones, a reconsideration of these ratios should still be envisaged.

The so-called risk of "death by a thousand cuts" should be singled out as a penultimate remark in the context of forest offsetting. A recurring element when discussing and analysing the effectiveness of biodiversity offsets is the extent to which they are able to encompass diffuse losses accumulated over time. In recent years, the "death by a thousand cuts" syndrome has gained popularity in environmental discourse, especially when pointing to the accumulation of smaller, insignificant and diffuse impacts, which is believed to be one of the greatest concerns for our remaining biodiversity. Indeed, the most damaging environmental effects often result not from the direct effects of a discrete action, but from the combination and accumulation of the individually minor effects of multiple actions over time (cumulative effects).[121] It is obvious that in highly urbanised and fragmented regions, such as the Flemish region, a particular focus on cumulative effects is instrumental to reversing the ongoing levels of fragmentation. Furthermore, EU environmental law places particular emphasis on the avoidance of cumulative effects, especially when caused by harmful project developments which are subject to a prior appropriate assessment and/or strategic environmental assessment (SEA) or EIA.[122]

---

[119]   Flemish Forest Decree, Article 90bis(4).

[120]   See for instance: *European Commission*, Opinion delivered at the request of Germany pursuant to Art. 6(4) subpara. 2 of the Habitats Directive, concerning the deepening and widening of the ship fairway of the river Main at the sections Wipfeld, Garstadt and Swcheinfurt (Bavaria, Germany), C(2013) 1871 final, p. 4.

[121]   J.T. *Dale*, Death by a Thousand Cuts: Incorporating Cumulative Effects in Australia's Environment Protection and Biodiversity Conservation Act, Pacific Rim Law and Policy 2011, pp. 150 et seq.

[122]   For instance, pursuant to Annex IV(4)(e) of the EIA Directive, an EIA needs to assess "the accumulation of effects with other existing and/or approved projects, taking into account any

The recent reports regarding forest protection in Flanders have showcased cases of creeping deforestation, in which the accumulation of a sequence of small-scale intervention ultimately leads to significant effects in the remaining woodlands. The case of the Forest of Kluisbergen (*Kluisbergen bos*) is revelatory. Once this woodland was a robust complex of forest habitats. After decades of fragmentation, the forest now harbours dozens of villas and can no longer be qualified as a resilient woodland.[123]

Another important observation relates to the location of the purported offset zones. In order to guarantee the additionality of the offsets in terms of ecological benefits, they are to be located in sites which are closely connected with other core nature areas. In recent times, the majority of in lieu payments that were collected in the compensation fund have been used to create large-scale woodlands and forests close to medium-sized cities. However, additional rules are instrumental to ensure that the implementation of offsets is further aligned with global recovery strategies. An additional caution is warranted in view of the continued loss of open space – at a pace of six hectares every year – in a highly urbanised area such as Flanders. As noted above, the offset actions need to be carried out in certain green and public areas in the applicable zoning plans. As such, this appears to make sense. However, in order to effectively augment the amount of biodiversity, priority should be given to afforestation in "grey areas" instead of focusing on the few remaining open spaces in the Flemish region.[124] Even so, following this line of argument, agricultural areas would remain bereft of additional biodiversity. Taking into account the limited ecological performance of current agricultural practices, which primarily focus on short-term profits, creating room for additional woodlands in agricultural lands should not be completely ruled out as a sensible future policy direction. That said, in order to afforest agricultural land other pieces of legislation also need to be observed, which – at present – effectively function as additional obstacles for swift compensation. For instance, pursuant to Article 35bis(5) of the Federal Field Code, afforesting agricultural lands has been made subject to prior authorisation by local municipalities, which opens up room for local politicians to hinder afforestation. Moreover, consistent efforts to review the Tenure Law, so as to explicitly authorise the termination of tenure by the landowner for reasons of afforestation, have been consistently rejected by the political majority in the federal parliament.[125]

---

existing environmental problems relating to areas of particular environmental importance likely to be affected or the use of natural resources".

[123] See on this topic: https://www.knack.be/nieuws/belgie/komen-er-huizen-in-kluisbos-of-niet/video-iwatch-768675.html.

[124] *Anseeuw, supra*, note 108 at p. 17.

[125] *Van Gossum et al., supra*, note 34 at pp. 518 and 519.

3.6. FALTERING ENFORCEMENT: WHO IS CONTROLLING THE ENFORCER AND AVOIDS FURTHER ABUSES?

An final element to be considered is the lack of the proper enforcement of offset actions. This is a well-known deficiency of many biodiversity offsets.[126] Against the backdrop of the persistent doubts concerning the effectiveness of offsets, especially in the context of old-growth habitats[127] and the recurring implementation deficits, strict monitoring and enforcement are key features of any effective NNL policy. In theory, strict monitoring requirements in the context of biodiversity offsets should already have been operational within the Flemish region, given the existing obligations imposed by the Habitats Directive on the one hand and the recently amended EIA Directive on the other hand.[128] However, it is not surprising to note that an important enforcement gap exists, as was also noted in the 2016 Report of the Belgian Court of Auditors.[129]

It is important to note that the current legislation puts forward certain requirements in respect of the further implementation of the offset actions, as was detailed above. The forest compensation *in natura* has to be carried out within two years. This can either be realised on land owned by the project developer or that of some third party. If the offsets are not implemented in a timely manner, the permit holder will be liable for criminal sanctions. Non-compliance with permit conditions is to be treated as an environmental criminal offence. Last but not least, the offset site must be maintained as forest for a minimum of 25 years.[130] In other words, there is no explicit requirement as such to conserve and manage the newly created forests until maturity.

In addition, there is also a large gap between theory and practice. Of course, the failure to effectively enforce nature conservation legislation is a well-known fact of life even when certain actions might constitute a criminal offence. Nature inspection has been granted a limited budget, which entails that on-site inspections are the exception rather than the rule. This finding also perfectly ties in with outcomes of the 2016 REFIT fitness check of the EU Nature Directives.[131] The fact that poor enforcement was also prone to affect strictly protected woodlands that were included in Natura 2000 sites still represented a

---

[126]   *Ten Kate & Pilgrim, supra*, note 88, at p. 25.
[127]   On offsets for old-growth habitats more extensively, see: *M. Moreno-Mateos et al.*, Structural and functional loss in restored wetlands ecoystems, PLOS Biol. 2012 (10), e1001247.
[128]   With the recent revision of the EIA Directive in 2014, this directive now also contains a clear-cut monitoring obligation. See *inter alia* Article 8bis(1)(b) of the recently revised EIA Directive.
[129]   *Rekenhof, supra*, note 48.
[130]   Flemish Forest Regulation, Article 4(3).
[131]   *European Commission*, Commission Staff Working Document – Fitness Check of the EU Nature Legislation (Birds and Habitats Directive), SWD(2016) 4725 final, 2016, available at: http://ec.europa.eu/environment/nature/legislation/fitness_check/index_en.htm.

major wake-up call in the Flemish context. Yet this is precisely what happened in what is to be regarded as one of the most mediatised nature conservation cases in the Flemish region of recent decades. Indeed, one of the most noteworthy illustrations of the poor enforcement of biodiversity offsets within the Flemish region was offered by the recent controversy surrounding the second expansion of a transport company (Essers) in a designated Natura 2000 site. In 2009, the Belgian company had been authorised to conduct a first extension of an industrial estate within an adjacent Natura 2000 site, which would lead to the destruction of 1.7 hectares of woodland habitats. Yet this was permitted on the condition that an adjacent zone of 10 hectares bordering the extended industrial site was to be developed as a more resilient and ecologically valuable woodland and heather restoration zone. In addition, the planning permit stipulated that this expansion had to be the final one, since the adjacent Natura 2000 site was already subject to an unfavourable conservation status and further fragmentation would compromise the already degraded baseline.[132] Nevertheless, the bulk of the restoration measures, which, moreover, were not framed as compensation within the context of Article 6(4) of the Habitats Directive, were not properly implemented. No trees were planted, nor was the heather restoration plan ever initiated.[133] In spite of the manifest non-observance of the compensation duties included in the permit conditions, the competent authorities declined to institute criminal proceedings against the permit holder. Most remarkably, the implementation deficit was subsequently used as an implicit argument to authorise a second expansion of the undertaking by another 10 hectares, precisely in the area (the "compensation zone") which ought to have been restored to a birch and oak woodland pursuant to the previous planning permit.

When finally authorising the second expansion in 2016, the Flemish government maintained that the expansion zone contained no actual habitat features and in view of the conservation objectives that had been adopted in the meantime, its further restoration was no longer deemed relevant.[134] However, no explicit attention has been paid to the cumulative effects arising from the new degradation and the non-compliance with the previous offset commitments. EU environmental law contains a clear-cut duty to remedy infringements of EU law.[135] Member States are moreover in principle barred from deriving

---

[132] All these conditions have also been translated into the regional spatial execution plan of 2009. See: *Flemish Government*, Regional Spatial Execution Plan for the Transport Company H. Essers, 2009.

[133] This was even explicitly recognised by the minister competent for nature conservation as a response to a parliamentary question. See: *H. Schoukens*, Wie doet Essers wat?, De Standaard, 19 January 2016.

[134] *Flemish Government*, Regional Spatial Execution Plan for the Expansion of the Transport Company H. Essers, 2016.

[135] CJEU, Case C-348/15, Stadt Wiener Neustadt, ECLI:EU:C:2016:882, paras. 48–47; CJEU, Case C-201/02, Wells [2004] ECR I-723, para. 68.

advantages from their own non-compliance with their protection duties under Article 6(2) and (3) of the Habitats Directive.[136] At a very minimum, the second expansion of the industrial site should have been subject to the application of the derogation procedure given the cumulative amount of habitat loss – which amounted to no less than 15 hectares in total over a 10-year period – that was validated through the successive authorisation procedures.[137]

It is obvious that this one case cannot be deemed indicative of the apparent deficiencies of the entire enforcement policy with respect to biodiversity offsets. Even so, the case clearly resonated in wider Flemish society, even before the final decision had been taken on the second expansion.[138] Against the backdrop of the ensuing public debate and the recent case law developments before the CJEU regarding Article 6(2) of the Habitats Directive, which is to be regarded as a generally applicable and enforceable non-regression clause,[139] one might at least have expected the Flemish region to act in a more reluctant manner and explicitly reassess the previous non-compliance elements. However, instead of reinforcing the earlier compensation commitments – which had a binding nature – the Flemish government showed remarkable leniency towards the project developer. Time and money were spent to argue that new offsets were to replace the forest to be destroyed, whereas no further attention was paid to the existing commitments. Accordingly, the case can rightly be quoted as yet another illustration of the lack of proper enforcement of mitigation and compensation duties.

Ultimately the Belgian Council of State decided to quash the planning decisions and permits for their failure to abide the conservation duties set out by Article 6(3) of the Habitats Directive in two decisions, one in 2017 and another one in 2018.[140] Yet, rather ironically, the transport company recently reached a deal with one of the NGOs that had initiated legal proceedings (Natuurpunt vzw) on the development of another site. Despite the new location of the expansion no longer being situated in Natura 2000 sites, it will still lead to the deforestation of an "out-zoned" forest.[141] This is simply another illustration of how nature is always on the losing side, even after having won in courtroom. Similarly it also exposes the ambivalent position in which environmental NGOs find themselves.

---

[136] CJEU, Case C-301/12, Cascina Tre Pini s.s., ECLI:EU:C:2014:214, para. 50.

[137] See more extensively: *H. Schoukens*, Schauvliege en de truc voor ontbossing, DeRedactie.be, 18 September 2015.

[138] See for instance: Deprez geeft niet toe aan Schauvliege: "Verwijder anders de gemaakte beloftes met tipp-ex", De Morgen, 23 September 2015.

[139] See more extensively: *H. Schoukens*, Non-Regression Clauses in Times of Ecological Restoration Law: Article 6(2) of the EU Habitats Directive as an usual ally to restore Natura 2000?, Utrecht Law Review 2017, pp. 124–155.

[140] See for the final annulment decision: Belgian Council of State, case no. 241.048, 20 March 2018.

[141] We hebben onze lessen getrokken uit het Essers-bos, De Tijd, 19 March 2019.

Understandably, these groups do not want to be perceived as "zealots" as Wood puts it,[142] which explains their willingness to broker deals even when – in this case less valuable – nature will be destroyed.

Be that as it may, the outcome of the latter case is exceptional to the extent that it saw an environmental NGO successfully enforcing earlier compensation commitments. Yet it merely represents the proverbial tip of the iceberg. The 2016 Report of the Belgian Court of Auditors revealed that a positive outcome of the compensation actions is only realised in 68 per cent of the cases in which project-led compensation is applied.[143] Additional manpower will be needed in order to enable the proper monitoring of all the existing compensation pledges.

4. DISCUSSION AND OUTLOOK

If this analysis of the Flemish approach to NNL has made one thing clear, it is that biodiversity offsets are not to be presented as a panacea for all ills. Although biodiversity offsetting is often repeated ad nauseam among entrepreneurs and policy makers, a wide-spread application of biodiversity offsetting tools is certainly not innocent, especially given the poor outcome of restoration measures in the context of NNL approaches so far. It should therefore not be used as a recurrent replacement for stricter preservation efforts, especially since it is prone to be misused by permit issuing authorities with a pro-development bias. Against this backdrop, biodiversity offsetting is increasingly to be identified as both the cause and symptom of the current failures of the existing nature conservation laws.[144] This is no different in the Flemish region. Of course, one might submit that the plight of the woodlands in Flanders should not be overstated, seeing that the largest deforestation takes place in the interests of nature recovery, namely in view of the implementation and realisation of the site-specific conservation objectives. In comparison with the forest losses elsewhere in the world, especially in the Amazon and Congo basins, the continued net loss of forest cover in the Flemish region might seem trivial. In addition, in other surrounding countries, forest cover has also been shrinking in recent years. More importantly, though, the reasons explaining the continued failure to reverse the negative trend in terms of forest cover in the Flemish region are universal. Ultimately, the loss of forest cover is but one indication

---

[142] *Wood, supra,* note 94 at p. 115.
[143] *Rekenhof, supra,* note 48.
[144] *Moreno-Mateos et al., supra,* note 36 at pp. 557–558.

of a wider trend, i.e. the ongoing decline of natural elements within the Flemish region.

This legal analysis of the Flemish forest offsetting regime serves as a cautionary tale for the many legal, policy-related and societal hurdles to be overcome when implementing compensation policies at the national level. Although the patchwork of different protection and offsetting schemes in the Flemish legislation appears impressive at first glance, its concrete application and enforcement fall short in view of the level of ambition set by the EU biodiversity strategy to 2020. At best, some compelling cases have recently emerged in which proactive offsetting strategies have been tested. Even so, the failure to take into account the social implications of these actions, combined with a blatant disregard for the mitigation hierarchy, ultimately led to their eventual demise after legal courtroom action.

In order to stop continued degradation and forest loss and, if possible, to achieve net gains of biodiversity, a shift towards a stricter authorisation policy will be inevitable, even if this would clash with the prevailing attitude towards green growth (which assumes that ecological restoration can be reconciled with continued economic development). Moreover, agencies and authorities will need to move beyond deference and discretion and take up their role as genuine trustees of common goods, such as woodlands.[145] This might sound simplistic, yet it should certainly not be treated as a truism. The legislation needs to clearly stipulate the substantive yardsticks to be taken into account when considering biodiversity offsets, with a clear observance of the mitigation hierarchy. Only if applied in such a strict context, with the provision of additional monitoring, biodiversity offsets might eventually stall the ongoing loss and create net gains. The usage of conservation banking, especially when applied within the context of the loss of "ordinary" biodiversity, might lead to less interim losses seeing that the available credits represent additional nature or woodlands that have already materialised on the ground.

However, given that there has also been a recent effort to strengthen the authorisation scheme for ecologically valuable woodlands that are located outside the designated green areas on the applicable zoning plans that failed to get adopted, little hope exists that we might soon witness a shift towards more coherent and cohesive biodiversity offsetting in Flanders.[146] Ironically, one of the main reasons the new draft proposal for the enhanced protection of

---

[145]   See in this regard: *Wood, supra*, note 94 at pp. 188–207.

[146]   For a concise analysis of the latest proposals, see: Vlaamse Regering heft nieuwe regeling klaar voor bescherming kwetsbare bossen, Knack, 14 December 2018, https://www.knack.be/nieuws/belgie/vlaamse-regering-heeft-nieuwe-regeling-klaar-voor-bescherming-kwetsbare-bossen/article-belga-1406807.html.

out-zoned forest was not adopted in 2019 was linked to the fact that it might need a prior SEA in order to get the go-ahead. While this could easily be framed as yet another example of administrative overkill, it might still help the authorities to set the scientific data straight before moving forward with new protection schemes. Such a scenario is to be preferred over rushing the adoption of another imperfect map of "out-zoned" forest, paving the way for additional legal challenges.

Beyond the specific Flemish context, this analysis puts forward the following general lessons in this regard.

First, there exists a clear need for a proactive integration of biodiversity conservation interests in the existing land-use planning schemes. The lack of the timely integration of offsetting policies in strategic planning frameworks explains the significant time lags that occur when implementing forest compensations. A more strategic approach to offsetting might eventually lead to robust nature core areas, where the recovery targets are more easily met and their implementation is faced with less delay. Instead of being *ad hoc* and reactive, a more timely integration allows offsets to be proactive and resilient.

Second, the so-called mitigation hierarchy should be properly reflected within the existing regulatory framework regarding biodiversity offsets, while sufficient attention needs to be paid to the topic of cumulative effects. The absence of this might lead to a situation in which exemptions are too easily granted by local municipalities and regional agencies, as has been the case in Flanders during recent decades. While one might provide additional leverage for biodiversity offsetting in the context of "ordinary" nature, it should never be treated as the default option.

Third, offsetting policies need to be based upon comprehensive ecological science, which requires a government to hold that some valuable woodlands are irreplaceable and thus non-offsetable. Sound monitoring programmes should ensure that offsets do not exacerbate ongoing losses. In order to facilitate the introduction of stricter protection regimes, sufficient attention should be paid to sound scientific underpinnings.

Fourth, the compensation ratios used need to be sufficiently ambitious to attain the applicable NNL (or even net-gains) rationale. The topic of collateral losses ("death by a thousand cuts") needs to be taken into consideration in this regard. While payments to a compensation fund and/or conservation banks might be recommended in some instances, one at least needs to ensure that such fees reflect the true cost of afforesting new lands. If not, offsetting policies will merely lead to more biodiversity losses, as was illustrated by the Flemish case study.

Fifth, the impact of future forest protection rules on vested property rights is to be fully acknowledged. Financial compensation schemes need to be put into place for the affected landowners, which will eventually also diminish the societal resistance to a more stringent protection of forests, even when located in previously designated housing zones. It is crucial that such financial compensation schemes are easily accessible and provide a short-term solution to the property value loss resulting from tighter protection rules.

ABOUT THE EDITORS

BARBARA POZZO is Professor of Private Comparative Law at the University of Insubria, Italy. She coordinates the interdisciplinary PhD program in Law and Human Sciences at the university. She is also Director of the Summer School Program in Comparative Environmental Law.

VALENTINA JACOMETTI is Associate Professor of Private Comparative Law at the University of Insubria, Italy. She is also a member of the Board of Directors of "Rivista giuridica dell'Ambiente".